Managing Legal Compliance in the Health Care Industry

George B. Moseley III, MBA, JD
Lecturer in Health Law and Management
Department of Health Policy and Management
Harvard School of Public Health
Boston, Massachusetts

JONES & BARTLETT
LEARNING

World Headquarters
Jones & Bartlett Learning
5 Wall Street
Burlington, MA 01803
978-443-5000
info@jblearning.com
www.jblearning.com

Jones & Bartlett Learning books and products are available through most bookstores and online booksellers. To contact Jones & Bartlett Learning directly, call 800-832-0034, fax 978-443-8000, or visit our website, www.jblearning.com.

Substantial discounts on bulk quantities of Jones & Bartlett Learning publications are available to corporations, professional associations, and other qualified organizations. For details and specific discount information, contact the special sales department at Jones & Bartlett Learning via the above contact information or send an email to specialsales@jblearning.com.

Production Credits
Executive Publisher: William Brottmiller
Publisher: Michael Brown
Editorial Assistant: Chloe Falivene
Production Manager: Tracey McCrea
Senior Marketing Manager: Sophie Fleck Teague
Manufacturing and Inventory Control Supervisor: Amy Bacus
Composition: diacriTech
Cover Design: Scott Moden
Cover Image: © jokerpro/Shutterstock, Inc.
Printing and Binding: Edwards Brothers Malloy
Cover Printing: Edwards Brothers Malloy

To order this product, use ISBN: 978-1-284-03371-7

Library of Congress Cataloging-in-Publication Data
Moseley, George B.
Managing legal compliance in the health care industry / George B. Moseley III.
pages; cm.
Includes bibliographical references and index.
ISBN 978-1-4496-3964-8 (casebound)
1. Medical care—Law and legislation—United States. 2. Health facilities—Law and legislation—United States. 3. Health services administration—Law and legislation—United States. I. Title.
KF3825.M67 2014
344.7303'21—dc23
2013012429

6048

Printed in the United States of America
17 16 15 14 13 10 9 8 7 6 5 4 3 2 1

Dedication

Dedicated to the education and empowerment of the students and faculty at the Oglala Lakota College in South Dakota and the Islamic University of Gaza in Palestine.

Contents

Preface

Every organization in the country, in every industry, must obey a long list of laws. Normally, it is not enough to simply be aware of the laws and assume that every employee will follow them. Some employees will make innocent mistakes in their work procedures, resulting in a technical violation of the law. Others may not fully understand the recommended way of performing the procedures and inadvertently carry them out in an illegal manner. A few people may approach their jobs with a casual, inattentive, even reckless attitude. It is not surprising then, when violations of the law occur. In the worst-case situation, an employee deliberately commits an illegal act, for monetary gain or under pressure to meet a performance goal. Regardless of the culpability of the employee or the organization, if the responsible government agency learns of the violation, there will be consequences.

The consequences may be trivial or extremely serious. The employee may receive a verbal warning and retraining in how to perform a particular task; the organization may be required to reimburse the government agency for an overpayment that was made. At the other extreme, the employee may be dismissed, while his or her employer negotiates a multimillion dollar settlement and is excluded from participating in federal programs for a period of years. It is far preferable to prevent the mistakes and subsequent violations in the first place.

The accepted method of doing this is to establish and maintain a compliance program. Over the last two decades in the United States, a template for such programs has evolved. It is now used by thousands of organizations in nearly every sector of the economy.

The healthcare industry has a special need for compliance programs and people who can manage them. It has been the subject of a never-ending stream of new laws and regulations unlike that faced by any other industry. The government agencies responsible for the laws are constantly ramping up their enforcement efforts. This is not surprising for an economic sector that accounts for nearly one-fifth of the U.S. gross national product.

These are just a few of the headlines for healthcare fraud cases during 3 months in early 2013.

- New Jersey Doctor Sentenced to Five Months in Prison for Taking Cash Kickbacks for Medicare and Medicaid Patient Referrals
- Former Registered Nurse Sentenced in Miami to 111 Months in Prison in Connection with $63 Million Mental Healthcare Fraud Scheme
- Florida Physician to Pay $26.1 Million to Resolve False Claims Allegations
- Maryland's St. Joseph's Medical Center Agrees to pay $4.9 Million for Medically Unnecessary Hospital Admissions
- Healthcare Practitioner Sentenced to Six Months in Prison, Six Months Home Detention, for Accepting Cash Kickbacks for Patient Referrals
- Major New Jersey Hospital Pays $12.5 Million to Resolve Kickback Allegations
- EMH Regional Medical Center and North Ohio Heart Center to Pay $4.4 Million to Resolve False Claims Act Allegations
- Florida-Based American Sleep Medicine to Pay $15.3 Million for Improperly Billing Medicare and Other Federal Healthcare Programs
- Amgen Inc. Pleads Guilty to Federal Charge in Brooklyn and Pays $762 Million to Resolve Criminal Liability and Civil Fraud Allegations
- Sanofi U.S. Agrees to Pay $109 Million to Resolve False Claims Act Allegations of Free Product Kickbacks to Physicians
- Doctor and Owner of Medical Supply Company Plead Guilty in Million-Dollar Power Wheelchair Scam

The agency of the Department of Health and Human Services, responsible for enforcing laws against fraud abuse, maintains a list of its 10 Most Wanted Fugitives: https://oig.hhs.gov/fraud/fugitives/index.asp. In the fiscal year 2012, the US Department of Justice recovered over $3 billion in cases of healthcare fraud.

Because of persistent dissatisfaction with the performance of the healthcare system, public and private payors, government enforcement authorities, accreditation agencies, industry and professional associations, and healthcare organizations themselves regularly launch new programs and initiatives. Accountable care organizations, balanced scorecards, evidence-based medicine, pay-for-performance, patient-centered medical homes, and bundled payments are some of the current examples.

Each imposes new laws, regulations, and program requirements that demand compliance.

The only effective way for healthcare organizations to keep up is to develop more and more sophisticated compliance programs. They must write policies and procedures to guide employee work behaviors, and back them up with education and training. They must apply disciplinary action against employees who do not follow their instructions. When misconduct occurs, the organizations must be prepared promptly to launch investigations and take corrective actions. They must appoint high-level people to manage this complex compliance infrastructure full time. As the laws change, compliance programs must be updated and expanded.

It always has been a wise business decision to adopt an effective compliance program. High-performing healthcare organizations have had them for at least 20 years. They have received strong encouragement to do so from the federal government, especially in the form of Compliance Program Guidances tailored to the unique features of different types of organizations. At the beginning, the Guidances made clear that they were voluntary. That has changed.

The healthcare reform law enacted in 2010, known officially as the Patient Protection and Affordable Care Act, has made compliance programs mandatory for healthcare organizations participating in Medicare, Medicaid, and the Children's Health Insurance Program. Because many organizations survive on the reimbursements from these programs, it is imperative that they operate compliance programs that meet the government's criteria.

Those that try to get by with inadequate compliance activities can expect to come under closer regulatory and enforcement scrutiny. There is a greater likelihood that they will be held liable for fraud, abuse, and waste. Organizations that embrace compliance will experience fewer investigations and prosecutions. If violations occur, the penalties will be less severe.

For most healthcare organizations, no time deadline has yet been set for implementation of compliance programs. The Department of Health and Human Services, with its Office of the Inspector General (OIG), has the responsibility for defining the "core elements" of the mandated compliance programs. It has not yet begun to issue the necessary regulations. The OIG rolled out the original Compliance Program Guidances over a period of years. The requirements for the new mandatory programs also are likely to come out one at a time for each type of healthcare organization, starting with the most troublesome. Some segments of the healthcare system have not yet voluntarily implemented even modest compliance programs.

Savvy organizations will not wait until firm, binding compliance guidelines have been published. When they do, they are not likely to differ substantially from the requirements in the existing Compliance Program Guidances. In those Guidances and other sources, there is an ample foundation for designing a compliance program that, with a few tweaks, will satisfy government regulators. Every healthcare organization should be developing its first compliance program or updating an existing program—now.

By themselves, healthcare organizations do not have the expertise to develop and maintain compliance programs. The initial designers and leaders of compliance programs were self-taught. Lawyers and consultants began to offer advice. Over time, a burgeoning industry has emerged to help organizations manage their compliance activities. There are compliance-oriented consulting firms, professional associations, journals and periodicals, webinars and conferences, and websites.

Several colleges and universities offer individual courses on compliance issues. At a few, it is possible to earn a graduate certificate in healthcare compliance. It is just a matter of time until associate degrees in compliance will be available. Extensive education in compliance matters is appropriate for people who one day, as chief compliance officers, will report directly to the CEO and the governing board of large organizations.

Helping healthcare organizations stay on the right side of the law has become a legitimate career path. This text is targeted at people pursuing such careers. It serves also as a comprehensive introduction to the compliance landscape for anyone who works, as a manager or employee, in healthcare organizations.

The structure of the text follows a learning progression. The starting point is to understand exactly what requirements must be complied with. Section I explains the primary laws that healthcare organizations must obey. Many of them are unique to the healthcare field. The organizations manage their compliance through complex, multifaceted compliance programs. Section II describes each of the components in the program recommended by the federal government. The specific terms of a compliance program will differ slightly for each type of healthcare organization. Section III covers all of the organization types that are the subject of a federal Compliance Program Guidance. Together, they encompass most of the U.S. healthcare system.

I wish the professionals and students who read this text, with the coaching of their instructors and mentors, great success in their careers as compliance officers and managers in the healthcare industry.

Section I

Laws and Requirements for Compliance

The chapters in this section explore the most significant laws on which healthcare compliance programs are focused. These are the laws with which they are expected to "comply."

These are not the only laws that apply to healthcare organizations, but they are the ones that have the most unique impact on healthcare operations.

The following are leading examples of other laws that concern entities in the healthcare sector:

State institutional (hospital, pharmacy) licensure

Clinical laboratory licensure and regulation

Accreditation by the Joint Commission

State-level determination or certification of need

Union rules and collective bargaining agreements

Employment laws

Fair Labor Standards Act (FLSA)

Family Medical Leave Act (FMLA)

Occupational Safety and Health Administration (OSHA) regulation

Workplace safety

Medicare certification and conditions of participation

Emergency Medical Treatment & Labor Act (EMTALA)

Controlled substance registration and management

Building, safety, food service, and fire codes

Waste disposal

Hazardous materials

Securities regulation (for-profit entities)

Sarbanes-Oxley Act (for-profit entities)

Intellectual property (patents, trademarks, copyrights, proprietary information)

Conflicts of interest in nonresearch positions

Chapter 1

False Claims Act

LEARNING OBJECTIVES

After completing class sessions based on this chapter, a student will:

- Understand the history and current application of the False Claims Act (FCA).
- Recognize the four primary types of actions that violate the FCA.
- Be alert to the high potential of qui tam lawsuits.
- Learn about the possibility of criminal convictions for FCA violations.
- Know the highest risk areas for FCA liability by different healthcare entities.
- Discover the best ways of reducing the risk of FCA violations and liability.
- Be familiar with the FCA enforcement trends in healthcare claims submissions.
- Hear about some typical cases of FCA violations and court decisions.

INTRODUCTION

The False Claims Act[1] (FCA) is the most powerful, oft-used tool of the federal government for fighting fraud, abuse, and waste in federal healthcare programs like Medicare and Medicaid.

The FCA was enacted by Congress in 1863 at the height of the American Civil War. In prosecuting that war, the federal government used a large number of private contractors, some of whom took advantage of the crisis situation to make false claims for payment. The FCA was designed to address those abuses.

After the war, the Act was largely unused until significant amendments in 1986 lowered the barriers and raised incentives for enforcement. More recently, the Act has been further expanded in the Fraud Enforcement and Recovery Act (FERA) of 2009 and the Patient Protection and Affordable

[1] 31 U.S.C. §§ 3729 - 3733 (2006)

Care Act (PPACA) that became law in 2010. The PPACA is the broad scope health reform act that Congress passed in that year.

Although the FCA continues to function as a broad-based statute intended to fight false claims made through all kinds of government contracts in the last two decades, it has developed into a weapon primarily against healthcare fraud. In fiscal year (FY) 2007, the U.S. government used the FCA to recover $2 billion in settlements and judgments in fraud cases, of which $1.54 billion came from healthcare cases.

WHAT THE FCA PROHIBITS AND HOW IT WORKS

The FCA prohibits the knowing submission of false claims for payment, the knowing use of false records or statements to support such claims, the knowing and improper retention of money owed or belonging to the federal government, or conspiring with others to commit any of those acts. These are the four most common sources of liability under the FCA. The specific language of each prohibition is important.

Direct Submission of False Claims

"Any person who knowingly presents, or causes to be presented, a false or fraudulent claim for payment or approval . . . is liable to the United States Government."[2]

Like most statutory laws, the precise interpretation of the language in the FCA depends on the meaning of key words. A quick reading of this phrase suggests that the terms "person," "presents," "claim," "false or fraudulent," and "knowing" are critical in understanding whether it applies to a

HEALTHCARE EXAMPLE OF THIS SOURCE OF FCA LIABILITY

This is the classic form of fraud and abuse in the healthcare industry. When a provider submits a claim for Medicare or Medicaid reimbursement, it is asserting that it provided specific services to a particular patient for which it is entitled to payment by the federal or state government. It asserts that the services were medically necessary, that they were actually provided, that they are covered by the Medicare/Medicaid programs, and that the patient is a qualified Medicare/Medicaid beneficiary. If any of these prerequisites is not true, the claim may be considered to be "false."

[2] §3729(a)(1)(A) of the FCA

particular healthcare organization. The FCA includes a section that defines key terms like these. For instance, "person" includes individuals and corporate entities, for-profit and not-for-profit organizations and partnerships, as well as independent contractors and vendors.

Making False Records or Statements in Support of a False Claim

"Any person who knowingly makes, uses, or causes to be made or used, as false record or statement material to a false or fraudulent claim . . . is liable to the United States Government."[3]

This prohibition is a companion to the first one. It can occur only when a false claim has been submitted. Furthermore, false claims are almost always accompanied by some form of documentation to back them up.

HEALTHCARE EXAMPLE OF THIS SOURCE OF FCA LIABILITY

Quite often, for a claim to be believable to the Medicare/Medicaid programs, it must be backed up by various forms of documentation, such as medical records, appointment records, and test results. If the claim is false, it may be supported by false "records or statements." A medical record may be altered to show a medical necessity that did not exist, to show that a service was performed when no service was performed, to show that a different service was performed than the one actually performed, or to show that the service was performed on a different patient. Certification may be offered to show that the patient was a Medicare beneficiary when he or she was not. This basis for FCA liability cannot exist unless a false claim has been submitted that the false records support.

Making False Records or Statements to Avoid Paying the Government

"Any person who knowingly makes, uses or causes to be made or used, a false record or statement material to an obligation to pay or transmit money or property to the Government, or knowingly conceals or knowingly and improperly avoids or decreases an obligation to pay or transmit money or property to the Government . . . is liable to the United States Government."[4]

---

[3] §3729(a)(1)(B) of the FCA
[4] §3729(a)(1)(G) of the FCA

This basis for FCA liability is commonly referred to as a "reverse false claim." Rather than filing a false claim that seeks money from the government, the person or organization improperly attempts to avoid paying money that it owes to the government. This may be accomplished by an affirmative action of preparing and using a false statement, or by hiding or avoiding an obligation owed to the federal government.

HEALTHCARE EXAMPLE OF THIS SOURCE OF FCA LIABILITY

Under the Medicare and Medicaid programs, the federal government distributes funds to healthcare providers periodically throughout the fiscal year. At the end of the year, the Centers for Medicare and Medicaid (CMS) performs a reconciliation of the amounts paid to a provider with the amounts actually owed to the provider. If the CMS has underpaid, it makes up the difference. If it has overpaid, the provider must pay back to the CMS the amount of the overpayment. False claim liability arises when the provider tries to conceal or avoid its obligation to repay the CMS or creates a false record to show that it was not overpaid.

Conspiring with Others to Violate Any of the Previous Three Provisions

"Any person who knowingly conspires to commit a violation of subparagraph (A), (B), (D), (E), (F), or (G) . . . is liable to the United States Government."[5]

Those subparagraphs refer to the several possible bases for liability under the FCA, including the three explained previously. Those violations are committed by individual persons acting alone. Under this section of the FCA, there must be at least one other person involved. The conspirators must agree with each other to do something that would violate any of the

HEALTHCARE EXAMPLE OF THIS SOURCE OF FCA LIABILITY

There are numerous healthcare scenarios in which it may be easier to file a false claim if two or more persons work together. A physician and a diagnostics lab might agree to submit claims for tests that were not necessary or never performed. A hospital and a physician might agree to provide medically unnecessary services to a hospitalized patient.

[5] §3729(a)(1)(C) of the FCA

specified subparagraphs, they must take action to carry out the agreement, and they must do it with the intent to defraud the government.

KEY TERMS AFFECTING THE MEANING OF FCA PROVISIONS

The application of FCA statutory language to specific provider situations often turns on the interpretation of a few individual words. These are some of the more important ones.

Persons. The "persons" subject to the FCA include virtually all individuals and organizations. Not only the direct contractors with the federal government, but their vendors, suppliers, and subcontractors are also covered by the FCA. It is not necessary that there be a direct contractual link between the person and the federal government. For instance, many physician practices contract with third parties to prepare and submit their claims for reimbursement to payers. If a subcontractor submits a false claim or false information to a primary contractor that passes it on to the federal government, with or without the primary contractor's knowledge, the subcontractor will be liable.

The FCA covers healthcare persons like physician practices (solo practices, partnerships, professional corporations, limited liability corporations), hospitals (not-for-profit, for-profit, freestanding, chains), healthcare systems, hospital systems or chains, integrated delivery systems, long-term care facilities, nursing homes (especially chains), academic medical centers, academic faculty practices, diagnostic laboratories (including chains), pharmaceutical companies, pharmacies, medical device manufacturers, medical supply companies, and managed care organizations.

Some healthcare entities are run by government agencies. Although there are some uncertainties in the law, as a general matter, federal and state agencies are not subject to the FCA, although local government agencies are.

False. Whether a claim is "false" or not often depends on the application of statute, regulation, and contract terms to the facts in specific cases. However, there are a few general principles. Minor, technical violations of federal laws and regulations do not result in a false claim, unless the violations are "material" (highly relevant) to the payment decision. Claims that are based on legitimate scientific or medical disputes will not be deemed false. The same is true of reasonable, well-founded estimates. Healthcare persons will not be held liable for reasonable interpretations of relevant laws, regulations, and contracts.

Knowingly. The term "knowingly" attempts to define the necessary state of mind of the person submitting the claim. The person either must have "actual knowledge" that the claim or the information behind it is false, or must act in "deliberate ignorance" or "reckless disregard" of the fact that it is false. It is not necessary to prove a "specific intent to defraud" in order to find a violation of the law. One indication that a person was deliberately ignorant or exercising reckless disregard is the inadequacy of his or her compliance, accounting, and other procedures that might have detected the problem and corrected it.

"QUI TAM" COMPLAINTS UNDER THE FCA

The primary responsibility for enforcing the FCA lies with the U.S. Department of Justice (DOJ). In addition, the FCA specifically provides that a private citizen may bring a lawsuit on behalf of the United States when he or she has information that an individual or organization has knowingly submitted or caused to be submitted a false claim. The term "qui tam" is Latin for "who as well." Such citizens are frequently called "whistle-blowers"; the FCA refers to them as "relators." They are frequently employees of the organization being sued and may have intimate knowledge of its inner workings. It is not necessary that the relator personally have suffered harm as a result of the violation.

The relator must be represented by an attorney and the legal complaint must be filed "under seal" (not open to the public). Copies of the complaint are given only to the DOJ. After studying it for as long as several months, the DOJ makes one of several decisions. It intervenes in all or part of the lawsuit, taking over most of the litigation responsibilities, or it does not intervene but allows the relator to continue prosecuting the action on his or her own. It also can attempt to settle the matter with the defendant without actually intervening or ask the court to dismiss the relator's complaint because it feels that it is not warranted.

In the course of reaching its decision, the DOJ prepares a memorandum summarizing the facts and the law of the case. The memorandum frequently looks at the advice the DOJ has given to the defendant about the complaint against it, the defendant's response to the advice, and any settlement efforts prior to a decision to intervene.

Armed with sufficient evidence of wrongdoing, a relator has a powerful incentive to bring a qui tam action. He or she may have complained to management about the problems that were discovered and been ignored. The relator also may be awarded up to 25% of the money recovered when the government intervenes, including the treble damages awarded and the penalties assessed, plus the fees and costs of the relator's attorney. The amounts involved can be very large. A single case may involve thousands of false claims filed over many years. The damages for each claim might be $50, which multiplies out to several hundreds of thousands of dollars in damages. When the penalties of $5,500 to $11,000 per claim are added in, the total recovery may run into tens of millions of dollars. Twenty-five percent of that amount is a powerful inducement.

DAMAGES AND PENALTIES

The consequences for violation of the FCA are several and serious.

The defendant person or organization may be temporarily *suspended* or permanently *disbarred* from participation in federal health programs (Medicare, Medicaid). For individuals and organizations that primarily serve Medicare patients or rely predominantly on federal reimbursements, this punishment could put them out of business.

A person found liable under the FCA will be required to pay the *damages* he or she has caused to the federal government. The damages are the difference between what the government paid to the person and what it would have paid without the FCA violation. In addition, the amount of the actual damages is trebled. For instance, if a physician practice filed 1,000 improperly upcoded claims for an average gain of $50, the damages he or she owes the government would be 1,000 × $50 × 3 = $150,000. It is possible for an individual or organization to be held liable under the FCA even if no damages have resulted from the violation.

The court also may assess a *penalty* of $5,500 to $11,000 for EACH false claim. Generally, the penalties are mandatory once liability has been established. Using the earlier very modest example of 1,000 false claims, a convicted person or individual would be subject to 1,000 × $5,500 = $5,500,000 in penalties.

The damages and penalties are the same whether the FCA legal action was initiated by the government or a qui tam relator. When the relator is successful with his or her FCA lawsuit, he or she is entitled to an award of reasonable attorneys' fees and costs.

CRIMINAL ENFORCEMENT

The FCA is a civil statute with a lower standard of proof (preponderance of the evidence) and a potential for civil remedies (damages, penalties, and program debarment). There also are federal criminal laws that cover many of the same activities but that require a higher standard of proof (beyond a reasonable doubt) and can result in more serious outcomes. Certain false statements involving federal healthcare programs constitute felonies, punishable by up to 5 years imprisonment and $25,000 in fines.

These are some of the actions for which criminal prosecution and conviction is possible.

> *False statements or representations.* Whoever "knowingly and willfully makes or causes to be made any false statement or representation of a material fact in any application for any benefit or payment under a federal healthcare program" is guilty of a felony.[6]
>
> *False statements relating to qualifications for participation.* It is a felony to knowingly and willingly make a false statement or representation of a material fact about the conditions or operation (e.g., adequately trained personnel, appropriate facilities, necessary equipment, proper physician/professional oversight) of a facility or entity in order to qualify the facility or entity under a federal or state healthcare program.[7]
>
> *Criminal healthcare fraud.* Whoever knowingly and willfully executes, or attempts to execute, a scheme or artifice
>
> - to defraud any healthcare benefit program or
> - to obtain, by means of false or fraudulent pretenses, representations, or promises, any of the money or property owned by, or under the custody or control of, any healthcare benefit program
>
> in connection with the delivery or payment for healthcare benefits, items, or services shall be fined under this title or imprisoned for not more than 10 years, or both.[8]
>
> *Obstructing statements to a criminal investigator.* Whoever willfully prevents, obstructs, misleads, delays, or attempts to prevent, obstruct, mislead, or delay the communication of information or records relating to a violation of a federal healthcare offense to a criminal investigator shall be fined under this title or imprisoned for not more than 5 years, or both.[9]

In FY 2010, there were just over 700 criminal convictions for healthcare fraud, up from a little more than 500 in FY 2005.

---

[6] 42 U.S.C. § 1320a-7b(a)(1)
[7] 42 U.S.C. § 1320a-7b(c)
[8] 18 U.S.C. § 1347
[9] 18 U.S.C. § 1518

RISK AREAS FOR HEALTHCARE PROVIDERS

It is possible and helpful to identify the areas of highest risk for FCA violations by healthcare entities. These are the leading types of fraudulent behavior by healthcare providers targeted by FCA enforcement officials.

Services not delivered. Filing a claim for healthcare services, treatments, diagnostic tests, medical devices, or drugs that were never delivered.

Nonexistent patients. Filing a claim for healthcare services, treatments, diagnostic tests, medical devices, or drugs delivered to a patient who does not exist or who never received the service or item claimed.

Anti-kickback violations. It has been accepted that violations of the federal Anti-Kickback Statute may simultaneously be violations of the FCA. The Anti-Kickback Law prohibits an offer, payment, solicitation, or receipt of money, property, or remuneration to induce or reward the referral of patients or healthcare services payable by a government health care program (Medicare, Medicaid).

Upcoding of service claims. Claims for reimbursement of healthcare services provided to patients use codes to designate specific services. The most common code systems are Current Procedural Terminology (CPT) codes, Evaluation and Management (E&M) codes, Healthcare Common Procedure Coding System (HCPCS), and International Classification of Disease (ICD-9) codes. A provider may submit a claim code for a service that was more serious, complicated, time consuming, and expensive than the one actually provided to the patient.

Unbundling related services. Government healthcare programs pay special rates for packages or bundles of related services that are usually provided at the same time to one patient. A provider may attempt to collect a higher total reimbursement by billing for the services individually. That is prohibited.

Medically "unnecessary." In order to be reimbursed, healthcare providers must be able to show that the patient services they delivered were "medically necessary." Seeking reimbursement for claims that were not necessary is a violation of the FCA.

Inappropriate physician investments or compensation arrangements.[10] The federal Stark Law prohibits physicians from referring patients to or ordering goods or services from entities with which they have

[10] 42 U.S.C. § 1395nn and § 1396b

investment or compensation relationships. A violation of the Stark Law is often considered an automatic violation of the FCA.

Falsified hospital cost reports. Hospitals participating in the Medicare program are required to file periodic reports on their costs, charges, other revenues, and profits. On the basis of these figures, Medicare determines how much it will reimburse the hospitals. A hospital may falsely report higher costs to gain higher reimbursements. This is an FCA violation.

Red-lining. Under the fixed-amount reimbursement schemes used by Medicare, Medicaid, and private sources of supplemental Medicare insurance, hospitals and insurance companies can increase their profits by enrolling only the healthiest people. This practice is called "red-lining" and violates several federal and state laws, including the FCA.

These are the leading types of fraudulent behavior by pharmaceutical manufacturers targeted by FCA enforcement officials.

Off-label marketing. A new drug product cannot be sold without the approval of the Food and Drug Administration (FDA). Before giving that approval, the FDA determines that the product is safe and effective for the particular uses for which it was tested. After it has been approved, however, a physician may prescribe it for another, "off-label" use. The FDA prohibits drug manufacturers from marketing or promoting a drug for a use that the FDA has not approved. To do so would be a violation of the FCA because drug companies that promote their products off-label can reasonably foresee that the physicians will submit claims for reimbursement to the Medicare and Medicaid programs, and that those claims for improperly used drugs will be false or fraudulent. The manufacturers cause providers to submit false claims.

Illegal kickbacks. Federal healthcare programs pay for medications that are medically necessary and clinically efficacious. A prescription drug marketing tactic that distorts a physician's clinical decision-making will be considered a prohibited kickback, and a claim submitted for an unnecessary medication will be considered false. Over the years, drug companies have used a variety of practices to persuade physicians to prescribe drugs that they otherwise would not prescribe. These are some examples:

- Excessive fees for speaking engagements, consulting services, training sessions, and advisory boards
- Excessive payment for research and data collection related to the physician practice
- Fees for participating in postmarket studies or participation in a registry

- Providing services to physicians at prices below cost or fair market value
- Educational grants and honoraria
- Expensive trips and dinners
- Free samples of drugs, which physicians then sell to patients
- Bonus payments to high-drug-volume physicians and hospitals
- Phony or sham drug trials

Inflating drug prices. Federal healthcare programs set their payment rates for drugs on the basis of average wholesale prices (AWP) or average sales prices (ASP) reported by the drug companies themselves to First DataBank (FDB), a publisher of drug prices that is used by most state Medicaid programs to set payment rates for pharmaceuticals. On several occasions, companies have reported inflated prices or markup percentages. This leads FDB to publish inflated AWPs, which, in turn, results in higher payments to the drug companies.

Medicaid "best price" fraud. In order to be able to sell drugs to the Medicaid program, manufacturers must agree to participate in the Medicaid Drug Rebate Program. Under this program, the drug companies pay a rebate on their drugs each time they are dispensed to Medicaid patients. The amount of the rebate is based upon the "average manufacturer's price" (AMP) and the "best price" (i.e., lowest price) of each drug for a given quarter—as reported by the drug companies. The companies have an incentive to inflate those prices and conceal discounts they offer; several have done exactly that. The result is claims for drug reimbursements that are higher than they should be—in violation of the False Claims Act.

Pharmaceutical benefits manager (PBM) fraud. PBM firms help insurance companies manage their claims for prescription drugs and administer prescription drug plans. They also offer to reduce costs for insurance companies by negotiating discounts and rebates with pharmaceutical companies, purchasing drugs in bulk, and through cost-controlling drug formularies. The for-profit PBMs earn hundreds of millions of dollars from contracts with government healthcare insurance programs. They also have been the target of numerous federal false claims cases for conduct ranging from illegal rebate and discount agreements with pharmaceutical manufacturers and offering kickbacks to insurance companies to violating contractual responsibilities by shorting prescriptions, switching medications, and canceling prescriptions to conceal failures to meet contractually mandated deadlines for filling prescriptions.

DOJ ENFORCEMENT TRENDS

In choosing which cases to prosecute, the DOJ gives high priority to those that present a genuine risk of patient harm. After that, the agency looks at the prospective impact of each case, measured in terms of the potential dollar recovery, the scope of the violative conduct, the relief that may be possible, the likelihood that other similarly situated persons will be affected (multiple defendants, chains of organizations), and the deterrent effect on other persons. It also takes into account the strength of the allegations against the person or organization and how easily it will be able to present evidence to show liability. Without the threat of patient harm, the DOJ will not expend its limited resources on smaller cases.

In FY 2010, the DOJ recovered $2.39 billion in settlements and judgments under the FCA. A total of $1.99 billion, or 83%, of this came from violations in the healthcare sector; $1.60 billion was the result of settlements or judgments against pharmaceutical and medical device companies. The total amount of recoveries represents a 20% increase over FY 2009.

Also in FY 2010, 573 new qui tam cases were filed, a 30% increase over FY 2009. Two-thirds of those were in the healthcare sector. These were added to the 1,246 such cases already pending.

For FY 2011, the Executive Branch proposed an increase of 5.4% to $29.2 billion in the total budget for the DOJ. This will support 2,880 additional positions including hundreds of agents and attorneys.

For at least a decade, the FCA has been the most commonly used tool in federal health care and life sciences litigation. There are numerous reasons why the FCA's popularity for enforcement will continue to grow. National healthcare spending keeps soaring, almost uncontrollably, with a large portion attributed to fraud and abuse. The amendments to the FCA, through the FERA and PPACA, have expanded the power and usefulness of the FCA significantly. There have been steady, substantial increases in the federal budget for enforcement under the FCA and other fraud laws. The dollar amount of government recoveries under the FCA is increasing dramatically year after year. The government sees great potential in attacking fraud through this legal mechanism. It recoups at least a share of the money lost to false claims, successful cases may serve as a deterrent, and it is relatively inexpensive to implement.

There is a large volume of ongoing government investigations and pending qui tam actions, and courts issue hundreds of decisions interpreting the FCA each year.

DOJ SOURCES OF HEALTHCARE FRAUD CASES

The DOJ learns about cases of alleged healthcare fraud from a variety of sources.

The overwhelming majority of FCA lawsuits originate with qui tam relators and the law firms that represent them. In FY 2010, approximately 80% of the $3 billion in FCA settlements and judgments was based on cases initiated by whistle-blowers. Because of the qui tam dominance in FCA lawsuits and recoveries, the relators and their lawyers are setting the trends in the types of violations that are targeted by FCA investigations and lawsuits. Once there is a multimillion dollar recovery in one area of claims submission, other qui tam lawsuits quickly appear in that same area.

In its own efforts to rein in the healthcare spending lost to fraud and abuse, the federal government has created national initiatives and task forces aimed at a specific industry or problem. One example is the Health Care Fraud Prevention and Enforcement Action Team (HEAT). This is a senior-level joint task force combining the resources of the DOJ and the Department of Health and Human Services (DHHS) to pursue all forms of healthcare fraud. Another collaboration between the DOJ and DHHS is the Medicare Fraud Strike Force. This group of federal, state, and local investigators attacks Medicare fraud through the use of data analysis techniques (including "data mining") and "community policing" initiatives. The latter involve the cooperation of healthcare professionals (doctors, nurses) managers and executives, nonprofessional employees, and patients.

The DOJ receives referrals of possible fraud cases from federal agencies like DHHS, the Federal Bureau of Investigation (FBI), and the National Institutes of Health (NIH), from state agencies, through data mining, and on the basis of media reports.

EXAMPLE CASES OF FCA VIOLATIONS AND CONVICTIONS[11]

In April 2012, a managed care organization, *WellCare Health Plans, Inc.*, agreed to pay $137.5 million to settle four FCA cases brought by qui tam whistle-blowers alleging that, among other things, WellCare inflated the amount it claimed to spend on medical care, knowingly retained Medicare and Medicaid overpayments, and "cherry-picked" healthy patients to avoid the costs of treating sick patients.

[11] The following case synopses are based on a Quarterly Review of Health Care Enforcement Trends by the law firm, Mintz Levin.

In another qui tam case, *14 hospitals* in several states agreed in February 2012 to pay $12 million to resolve allegations under the FCA that the hospitals submitted false claims to Medicare by performing kyphoplasty procedures (used to treat certain spinal fractures) on an inpatient basis when these procedures could have been performed safely, and at less cost, as an outpatient procedure. Including this settlement, DOJ reports that it has settled FCA claims relating to kyphoplasty procedures with more than 40 hospitals for a total of more than $39 million.

In yet another FCA case, *AmMed Direct, LLC*, a supplier of diabetes testing supplies, recently agreed to pay $18 million to settle a whistle-blower suit based on an illegal marketing scheme in which AmMed offered free cookbooks to induce Medicare beneficiaries to contact AmMed. When they did, AmMed tried to sell them diabetic supplies and then billed Medicare for those supplies. After the beneficiaries returned the supplies, AmMed failed to refund the Medicaid program for the funds it had received for delivering them.

In another settlement, an ambulatory cardiac telemetry (ACT) company, *LifeWatch Services, Inc.* (LifeWatch), agreed to pay the United States $18.5 million to resolve allegations brought in two qui tam lawsuits that LifeWatch billed Medicare for ACT monitoring services for patients who were not eligible for these services. In addition to the monetary settlement, LifeWatch entered into a 5-year Corporate Integrity Agreement (CIA) with DHHS's Office of Inspector General (OIG).

On March 28, 2012, *Dr. Joseph J. Kubacki*, the Chair of the Ophthalmology Department of the Temple University School of Medicine, was sentenced to 87 months in prison and ordered to pay restitution in the amount of $1,014,605.87 after being convicted by a federal jury on August 22, 2011, of 150 counts of healthcare fraud, wire fraud, and making false statements in healthcare matters. Dr. Kubacki submitted fraudulent claims and caused more than $1.8 million to be paid by Medicare and 31 other health insurers for services rendered to patients whom Dr. Kubacki did not personally see or evaluate.

MINIMIZING EXPOSURE TO FCA RISK

Every honorable, well-managed healthcare person or organization wishes to avoid violation of the FCA. The best way to accomplish that is to institute a system of procedures, programs, and practices that work together to ensure that the organization and its people are in compliance with all applicable laws and regulations. The purpose of this text is to describe such a system. These are the basic principles of organizational compliance, as set out in the Federal Sentencing Guidelines for Organizations.[12]

- Develop and distribute written standards of conduct, including policies and procedures concerning specific areas of possible fraud.
- Designate a compliance officer and appropriate bodies.
- Develop and implement appropriate education and training programs.
- Implement a process for identifying and reporting violations.
- Develop a protocol for handling allegations of improper actions, followed by appropriate discipline.
- Develop a mechanism for auditing and monitoring the system.
- Investigate and correct system problems that emerge.
- Develop policies for dealing with employees who commit prohibited acts.
- Identify and implement current industry best practices and DHHS standards for the compliance function.

The following are recommendations for addressing the particular risks associated with the FCA.

- Regularly assess the effect of the FCA law and regulations, including changes like the FERA and the PPACA, on the organization's operations and contractual relationships.
- Frequently assess revisions to the organization's billing and compliance procedure.
- Implement mechanisms to prevent, detect, and track overpayments.
- Add FERA and PPACA implications to education and training programs.
- Aggressively audit and monitor organization operations; use a third party if possible.
- Review personnel policies to protect against possible retaliation involving whistle-blowing employees, independent contractors, vendors, and contractors.
- Establish a meaningful employee grievance and complaint policy.
- Rigorously investigate any reports or suspicions of fraudulent activities.

---

[12] Effective Compliance and Ethics Program, §8B2.1, Sentencing of Organizations, Chapter Eight, 2010 Federal Sentencing Guidelines Manual.

STUDY QUESTIONS

1. Why do you think that the FCA has become such a popular and powerful tool for combating fraud in the healthcare industry?
2. What are the necessary ingredients of a "conspiracy" to violate the FCA?
3. Describe the differences between a "false claim" and a "reverse false claim."
4. What are the different states of mind that distinguish "actual knowledge," "deliberate ignorance," and "reckless disregard?"
5. What is the difference between "damages" and "penalties," how are they calculated, and what purposes do they serve?
6. Do you think that it is possible for an organization to completely prevent the filing of false claims?

Learning Exercises

1. On the Internet, look up the full meaning of the term "qui tam." To one of your friends or roommates, explain how the qui tam option in the FCA works.
2. Go to the following DHHS webpage to view the annual Health Care Fraud and Abuse Control Program Reports for the last 12 years prepared by DHHS and DOJ. Download the PDF report for the most recent year: https://www.oig.hhs.gov/reports-and-publications/hcfac/index.asp.

   Review the numerous brief summaries of the civil and criminal fraud cases in the previous year. They make for interesting reading. Get a sense of the types of individuals and organizations, the types of fraudulent action they engaged in, and the nature and amount of the remedies obtained from them by the government.

   Download this PDF from the Crowell & Moring website. Concentrate on the third and fourth pages concerning DHHS: www.crowell.com/pdf/FalseClaimStat.pdf.

   It is a summary of fraud enforcement statistics for the years 1978 to 2010, prepared by the Civil Division of the U.S. DOJ. Note the trends over the years, particularly in the breakdown between qui tam and non–qui tam actions, the total dollar value of the settlements and judgments for different types of cases, and the dollar value of the relators' awards. For a few years, calculate the average percentage of the relators' awards compared to the total qui tam awards.

References

1. LA Baumann, Editor-in-Chief, "Health Care Fraud and Abuse: Practical Perspectives, Second Edition, With 2010 Cumulative Supplement," ABA Health Law Section, BNA Books, 2007.
2. MK Loucks and CC Lam, "Prosecuting and Defending Health Care Fraud Cases, Second Edition," BNA Books, 2010.
3. C Valiant and DE Matyas, "Legal Issues in Healthcare Fraud and Abuse, Third Edition with 2009 Supplement," American Health Lawyers Association, 2006.

Chapter 2

Fraud and Abuse

Stark/Physician Self-Referral and Anti-Kickback

Learning Objectives

After completing class sessions based on this chapter, a student will:

- Have a solid understanding of the Physician Self-Referral Law (Stark Law) and the Anti-Kickback Statute (AKS).
- Know to which services, individuals, organizations, and transactions these laws apply.
- Comprehend the exact behaviors that are prohibited.
- Become familiar with the exceptions and Safe Harbors through which healthcare providers and organizations can escape liability.
- Be aware of some hints and clues that noncompliant activities and transactions are occurring.
- Learn the basic steps for anticipating and preventing Stark and AKS violations.
- Hear about some typical cases of fraud and abuse violations and court decisions.

INTRODUCTION

When government authorities and industry officials talk about prohibitions of "fraud and abuse" in health care, they often are referring to the two major statutes focused on the healthcare industry: the Physician Self-Referral Law[1] and the AKS.[2] Between them, they apply to many essential practices and procedures in healthcare organizations—practices and procedures that can be manipulated to produce undeserved financial benefit

[1] 42 U.S.C. §1395nn
[2] 42 U.S.C. '1320a-7b(b)

for the organizations or associated individuals. The laws aim to prevent or punish such manipulation and benefit. The purpose of a compliance program is to prevent and detect violations of these laws.

There is overlap between the coverage of the laws. Their provisions easily can be confused. It is useful to examine them at the same time, and then compare their features.

PHYSICIAN SELF-REFERRAL (STARK) LAW

The first Physician Self-Referral Law was the Ethics in Patient Referral Act enacted in 1989 (Stark I). It was championed by Congressman Pete Stark and came to be known as the Stark Law. It applied only to clinical laboratory services. The Omnibus Budget Reconciliation Act of 1993 (Stark II) expanded the law to include an additional 10 types of clinical services. The comprehensive health reform legislation, the Patient Protection and Affordable Care Act of 2010 (PPACA) added restrictions on physician-owned specialty hospitals and required the Centers for Medicare and Medicaid Services (CMS) to publish a self-referral disclosure protocol (SRDP).

What the Law Prohibits

The key language of the Stark Law states that:

> . . . If a <u>physician</u> (or an <u>immediate family member</u> of such physician) has a <u>financial relationship</u> with an entity . . ., then the physician may not make a referral to the entity for the furnishing of <u>designated health services</u> for which payment otherwise may be made [under Medicare or Medicaid]. . .
>
> The entity may not present . . . a claim . . . or bill to any individual, third party payor, or other entity for designated health services furnished pursuant to a referral prohibited [under this law] [underlining added].

What the Key Statutory Terms Mean

The application of even simple statutory language like this depends on the interpretation of key terms.

Physician. The person making the referral may be an MD, osteopath, dentist, podiatrist, optometrist, or chiropractor.

Immediate family member. Besides the referring physician himself, the person with the problematic financial relationship may be a spouse;

parent, child, or sibling (by birth or adoption); step-parent, stepchild, stepbrother, or stepsister; father-in-law, mother-in-law, son-in-law, daughter-in-law, brother-in-law, or sister-in-law; grandparent or grandchild; or spouse of a grandparent or grandchild.

Entity. The entity with which there is a financial relationship must be one that bills CMS for designated health services (DHS) or that furnishes all or most of the components of the DHS. This includes the person or entity that actually performs the DHS, or presents a claim for DHS services to the Medicare program. As a result, physicians may not have an ownership interest in an entity that provides services “under an arrangement” with a hospital that bills for the services. An example of this is a group that contracts with a hospital to provide radiology services.

Financial relationship. A prohibited financial relationship may take two forms. One is direct or indirect ownership of an entity. This includes equity stock, interest in a limited liability company (LLC), holding debt in the entity, and making loans to the entity. It does not include an interest in the physician's employer entity that arises from a pension plan. On the other hand, it will include an indirect interest in a DHS entity owned by the pension plan.

The other form is direct or indirect compensation from an entity. The most common example is the compensation a physician receives when employed by the entity. Other problematic relationships are leases between healthcare facilities and physicians/physician groups, medical director agreements, and independent contracts (not employment) with physicians. The factor to be concerned about is any flow of remuneration to a physician.

Designated health services (DHS). These are the services whose referral by a physician are considered most susceptible to abuse as a result of a prohibited financial relationship. They encompass nearly all the clinical services that a physician is likely to refer to another entity, including:

- Clinical laboratory services
- Physical therapy services
- Occupational therapy services
- Outpatient speech-language pathology services
- Radiology and certain other imaging services
- Radiation therapy services and supplies
- Durable medical equipment and supplies
- Parenteral and enteral nutrients, equipment, and supplies
- Prosthetics, orthotics, and prosthetic devices and supplies

- Home health services
- Outpatient prescription drugs
- Inpatient and outpatient hospital services

Penalties for Violation of the Stark Law

The Stark Law imposes strict liability, so that unless the physician has met an exception defined under the law, he or she will be considered to have committed a violation. It is irrelevant that he or she may have acted unintentionally, without knowledge that he or she was disobeying the law.

The penalties for violation of the Stark Law are civil (not criminal) in nature.

- The amount of the payment or overpayment made by Medicare or Medicaid for DHS delivered in response to a prohibited referral must be returned.
- Penalties up to $15,000 for each noncompliant service may be assessed under the Civil Monetary Penalties Law.
- The healthcare entities or providers involved in the prohibited self-referral may be excluded from participation in the Medicare or Medicaid programs. (For facilities or practices that rely extensively on Medicare/Medicaid reimbursements, exclusion for even a few years can put them out of business.)
- There may be a further civil assessment against the parties of up to three times the amount of reimbursement sought for the noncompliant services.
- Violation of the Stark Law may simultaneously incur liability under the False Claims Act.

Exceptions to the Law's Prohibitions

The basic Stark prohibitions are quite comprehensive and would prevent many forms of physician referral that are considered beneficial and desirable. The law and its underlying regulations have defined numerous exceptions to the prohibitions. It is mandatory that a questionable physician referral arrangement be configured to fit within one of the exceptions in order to avoid being subject to the Stark Law. If it does not fit, it is prohibited.

The Stark Law contains approximately 35 exceptions that describe acceptable financial relationships that allow a physician to refer to an entity for the provision of DHS. They fall into two broad categories: "ownership or investment interests" and "compensation arrangements."

There are several common requirements that apply to all the Stark exceptions dealing with compensation.

- The arrangement must be in writing, signed by the parties, and specify the services, space, or equipment covered. (This writing requirement does not apply to the bona fide employment exception.)
- The compensation must be set in advance and be consistent with fair market value (FMV).
- The compensation is not determined in a manner that takes into account the volume or value of referrals or other business generated between the parties.
- The arrangement must be commercially reasonable, even if no referrals were made between the parties.
- The arrangement must serve a legitimate business purpose.

These are the most significant or commonly used exceptions.

Ownership in publicly traded securities and mutual funds. If the stock of the entity in which the physician has an ownership interest is publicly traded or part of the portfolio of a publicly traded mutual fund, the Stark prohibition does not apply. The logic is that the physician's referral decisions are so small compared to the total business of the entity that he or she could not influence its sales or profits.

In-office ancillary services. Without this exception and the physician services exception, physicians would be prohibited from making referrals to their own practices which they owned and by which they were compensated. These are DHS offered within the practice but ancillary to the physician's primary professional services. Examples are physical therapy and diagnostic testing. The referring physician or another physician in the same "group practice" must personally furnish the services or directly supervise another person performing the tests.

Rental of office space or equipment. Payments for the use of office space or equipment made by a lessee (i.e., physician practice) to a lessor (i.e., hospital owning the space or equipment) are not prohibited financial relationships, if the lease or rental agreement satisfies the common requirements listed previously and these additional requirements:

- The agreement is for at least 1 year.
- The space or equipment rented or leased must be used exclusively by the lessee; it cannot be shared with or used by the lessor.
- The rental charges over the term of the agreement cannot be based on a percentage of revenue attributed to the services performed in

the space or through the use of the equipment, or reflect services provided to patients referred by the lessor to the lessee.

Personal service arrangements. Remuneration from an entity to a physician or to a group practice is not considered a prohibited financial relationship if the common requirements listed previously and the following additional requirements are satisfied:

- The arrangement covers all services furnished by the physician.
- If there are multiple agreements, the agreements incorporate each other by reference or cross-reference to a master list that is maintained, updated centrally, and available for review upon request.
- The term of the arrangement is for at least 1 year.
- If terminated during the term, the parties cannot enter into a new agreement during the first 12 months of the original agreement.

Bona fide employment relationship. Compensation paid by an employer to a physician who has a "bona fide" employment relationship with the employer is not considered a prohibited financial relationship if the following requirements are satisfied:

- The employment is for identifiable services.
- The compensation is consistent with the FMV of the services, and does not take into account the volume or value of referrals.
- The compensation is under an agreement that is commercially reasonable, even if no referrals were made to the employer.
- Productivity bonuses are not prohibited based on services personally performed by the physician.
- The employment agreement exception does not have to be in writing.

Payments by a physician. Payments made by a physician are not considered a prohibited financial relationship, if the following requirements are satisfied:

- The payments are to a laboratory in exchange for the provision of clinical laboratory services.
- The payments are to an entity as compensation for any other items or services that are furnished at FMV and that do not fall under any other Stark exception.

Certain arrangements with hospitals. Payments made by a hospital to a physician are not prohibited if they do not relate, directly or indirectly, to the furnishing of DHS. To qualify for this exception, the payment must be wholly unrelated to the furnishing of DHS and must not in any way take into account the volume or value of a physician's referrals.

Physician recruitment. In certain circumstances, an entity, like a hospital, may make payments to induce a physician to relocate to the hospital's geographic area in order to join its medical staff. To fit within the exception:

- The recruitment arrangement must be in writing and signed by the parties.
- It must not be conditioned on the physician's referral of patients to the hospital.
- The payment to the physician cannot be based, directly or indirectly, on the volume or value of referrals made by the physician to the hospital.
- The physician may not be prohibited from also establishing staff privileges at another hospital.
- The physician must move his or her practice at least 25 miles from the previous site of the practice, or at least 75% of the physician's revenues must come from new patients.

In addition to recruiting new physicians for its own employment, the hospital may assist a local physician group practice in recruiting a new physician to the hospital's service area. In such cases, the payment must pass through directly to the physician being recruited. In addition, the group practice may not impose additional practice restrictions (e.g., a noncompete agreement) on the recruited physician, but may impose conditions related to quality of care.

There also are exceptions applying to the following topics:

- Remuneration unrelated to the provision of DHS
- Nonmonetary compensation up to $355
- FMV compensation
- Medical staff incidental benefits
- Temporary noncompliance
- Professional courtesy
- Obstetric malpractice subsidies
- Community health information systems
- Isolated transactions
- Certain group practice arrangements with a hospital
- Payments by a physician for items or services
- Charitable donations by a physician
- Risk-sharing arrangements
- Compliance training
- Indirect compensation arrangements

- Retention payment in underserved areas
- Electronic health record (EHR) and e-prescribing items and services

Clues That Prohibited Physician Compensation Has Occurred

Aside from the reports coming from the comprehensive compliance programs every healthcare organization should have in place, there are a few common sense signs that something suspicious is happening with physician compensation.

- Some physicians have received windfall payments.
- Physician compensation figures appear inflated or distorted.
- Compensation seems to vary according the volume of physician referrals.
- Deal terms are not commercially plausible.
- Payments are designated as a reward for referrals.
- Deals or transactions exist for which there is no useful documentation.
- Deals do not match the supporting paperwork.

When these signs are observed, an immediate investigation should begin.

Reducing the Risks of Stark Violations

Begin with the premise that a healthcare organization should not make any payments or give anything of economic value to a physician or his or her family member. If it chooses to do so, it will not be able to bill Medicare for services ordered by that physician. The organization can override that premise by fitting the transaction into one of the exceptions defined by the Stark Law. If there is no suitable exception, a legal transaction is not possible. The actual intent of the parties is irrelevant.

Remember that the Stark Law reaches nearly every physician transaction. Both ownership and compensation relationships are defined in the broadest terms. Stark reaches virtually every physician family member as well. Almost every conceivable familial relationship is covered.

Watch out for forms of nonmonetary compensation. This includes apparently innocuous items like social dinners, entry fees for golf or other participatory events, tickets for sporting, theatrical, musical, or social events, gifts during a medical illness or in recognition of a key life event, and simple gifts like pens or wine. The maximum dollar value of such compensation from one source, such as a hospital, is set each year by the CMS. It was $359 in 2011 and $373 in 2012.

Aggressive reduction in the risks of Stark violations starts with the commitment of top leadership (governing board members, senior executives) to strict compliance in all physician transactions. This should lead to the development of a structure and processes that establish effective internal controls. These could take the form of legal and financial reviews of existing physician agreements, centralized physician contract approval, and a formal accounts payable check before physician payments are made. On a regular basis, physician contracts should be evaluated for compliance with Stark and other laws.

Several kinds of physician agreements should be scrutinized.

- All physician employment and independent contractor arrangements
- All economic relationships between physicians and the hospitals to which they make DHS referrals, including loan agreements, hospital guaranties of physician obligations, physician recruitment arrangements, independent contractor arrangements, and employment agreements
- Medical director positions
- Medical staff leadership roles
- Preceptor for residents
- Other physician services
- Call coverage responsibilities
- Membership on hospital committees (e.g., EHR, institutional review boards)
- Space and equipment leasing to/from physicians
- Office sharing agreements and time-share arrangements
- Income guarantees to physicians
- Honoraria for talks and presentations
- Practice acquisitions

The organizational and operational features of group practices are subject to examination. Qualifying as a "group practice" under Stark enables physicians to take advantage of certain exceptions, including the physician services exception and the in-office ancillary services exception. Group practices that provide DHS should review Stark's group practice requirements to make sure they qualify under the definition, in order to protect their referrals through the in-office ancillary services exception.

All group practice compensation arrangements, including all employment and independent contractor arrangements entered into by group practices with physicians are also subject to review. The methodologies used by group practices for distributing profits from the provision of DHS and for paying productivity bonuses to physicians should be particularly scrutinized for compliance with the regulations.

The services, compensation, and space allocations involving physicians should be monitored. When changes occur, agreements with the physicians should be updated. Procedures should be in place to identify, report, and reclaim overpayments in connection with noncompliant physician transactions.

A good review process will include the following steps.

- Accounts payable activity is watched for payments to physicians.
- Accounts receivable activity is watched for payments from physicians.
- The payroll account is monitored for compensation payments to physicians.
- All physician payments are compared to their contracts and the supporting documentation.
- Periodically, the contracts and leases involving physicians are checked to make sure they are up-to-date and the payments specified are correct.

The most advanced organizations use forms and checklists that must be completed before significant physician transactions may proceed. For example, these questions must be answered affirmatively before a payment for physician services is made.

- Is the applicable contract signed and in effect?
- Does the check request include appropriate supporting documentation for the payment amount?
- Does the payment amount agree with the related contract?
- Does the amount and purpose of this payment appear reasonable?
- Are there any contractual reconciliations or rate adjustments (e.g., consumer price index [CPI] inflation) that need to be made to the payment?

The appropriate manager then certifies the answers with his or her signature.

Recent Cases and Settlements Involving the Stark Law

March 2011. The Bradford Regional Medical Center adopted an economic credentialing policy permitting termination of medical staff privileges in the event a medical staff member financially competed with the Center. To avoid losing their privileges, the physicians in this case, Singh et al., subleased their nuclear camera to the Center. Under the sublease, the Center made a fixed monthly payment for the use of the equipment, and an additional flat monthly fee for a noncompetition agreement from the physicians. The noncompete fee was calculated by an independent accountant, who determined the Center's expected revenue with and without the sublease in place. The court held that the arrangement violated the Stark Law, finding that the compensation was not FMV—despite the fact that compensation was set at a flat fee, and despite the FMV analysis the Center obtained. The case was set for trial on the factual issues of whether the parties knowingly violated the Stark Law, and whether the AKS was also violated (see later discussion).

December 2008. Condell Medical Center in Illinois paid $36 million as part of a voluntary disclosure related to arrangements with referring physicians that did not always comply with a Stark exception. Some of the questionable arrangements allegedly related to recruitment deals, below FMV rent on office space, and failure to have written agreements.

July 2008. Lester Cox Medical Centers in Missouri paid $60 million to resolve allegations that it violated the False Claims Act, the Stark Law, and the AKS by entering into financial arrangements with one physician group that included medical director agreements not in writing, paying the physicians more than FMV, and paying them based on the volume of referrals.

May 2008. Baptist Health South Florida settled for $7.8 million for violating the Stark Law related to alleged excessive compensation to a community oncology group for physics and dosimetry services. The hospital believed that the arrangement was excepted under Stark, but a few years after the agreement was executed, Baptist conducted an internal compliance review and determined that compensation was excessive for a 2-year period. Baptist did a voluntary disclosure to the government.

ANTI-KICKBACK STATUTE

The AKS was originally enacted as part of the Social Security Amendments of 1972 to protect patients and federal healthcare programs from fraud and abuse. In 1977, Congress enacted the Medicare-Medicaid Anti-Fraud and Abuse Amendments, which increased the severity of penalties from a misdemeanor to a felony, and added an expansive list of proscribed payments. Through the Medicare and Medicaid Patient and Program Protection Act of 1987, the Office of the Inspector General (OIG) was given the authority to levy civil as well as criminal penalties, and to promulgate regulations defining practices that would be permissible under the statute. These are referred to as Safe Harbors.

There are a few reasons for the government's strong opposition to kickbacks. They encourage referrals based primarily on monetary reward to the referral source rather than the medical need of the patient. They lead to the overutilization of resources. This subjects patients to unnecessary procedures and interventions that may pose clinical risks of their own. Both public and private payors then bear the increased cost of the unnecessary services.

Be aware that some states have their own anti-kickback laws that apply to all payors in contrast with the federal law's restriction to federal government healthcare programs.

What the Law Prohibits

The AKS prohibits anyone from offering a kickback, paying a kickback, or receiving a kickback in return for the delivery of healthcare services.

> Whoever knowingly and willfully solicits or receives any remuneration (including any kickback, bribe, or rebate) directly or indirectly, overtly or covertly, in cash or in kind in return for . . .
>
> - referring an individual to a person for the furnishing or arranging for the furnishing of any item or service for which payment may be made in whole or in part under a *federal healthcare program*, or
> - purchasing, leasing, ordering or arranging for or recommending purchasing, leasing, or ordering any good, facility, service, or item for which payment may be made in whole or in part under a federal healthcare program.[3][italic added]
>
> Whoever knowingly and willfully offers or pays any remuneration (including any kickback, bribe, or rebate) directly or indirectly, overtly or covertly, in cash or in kind to any person to induce such person . . .
>
> - to refer an individual to a person for the furnishing or arranging for the furnishing of any item or service for which payment may be made in whole or in part under a federal healthcare program; or
> - to purchase, lease, order or arrange for or recommend purchasing, leasing, or ordering any good, facility, service, or item for which payment may be made in whole or in part under a federal healthcare program.[4]

What the Key Statutory Terms Mean

There are a few terms in this statutory language that are essential to an accurate interpretation.

[3] 42 U.S.C. Section 1320a-7b(b)(1)
[4] 42 U.S.C. Section 1320a-7b(b)(2)

Knowingly and willfully. One acts "willfully" when one acts with a bad purpose, with knowledge that his conduct is unlawful. But, must he know that he is violating the AKS specifically and intend to do so? That question was answered by the PPACA, the health reform law passed in 2010. It states that actual knowledge of an AKS violation or a specific intent to violate the AKS is not necessary for a conviction under the statute. The government must still prove that a defendant intended to violate some law, but no longer has to prove that it intended to violate the AKS itself. These amendments made by the PPACA make it easier for the government to prove an AKS violation.

It is conceivable that a healthcare entity might make payments to a healthcare provider for more than one reason, some legitimate and some not. For instance, a diagnostic testing facility may contract with a physician to read and interpret test results, while the physician also may be a source of referrals for testing to the facility. The payments by the facility to the physician will appear to have two purposes—to compensate him for the test interpretations and for his referrals to the facility. The courts hold that payment of any amount for referrals is illegal. Even though only part of the payments were "intended to induce" the patient to refer patients for testing, the statute is violated. A payment for referrals does not have to be the primary purpose of the payments received; it only has to be one purpose of the business arrangement.

Remuneration. The payment to the physician for a referral may take almost any form, including a kickback, a bribe, or a rebate. The language used to describe the payment is irrelevant. The payment may be in cash or in kind; anything of value will constitute a violation.

Federal healthcare programs. The statute is violated only if the kickback is intended to encourage a referral for services or products that will be reimbursed through a federal healthcare program. The technical definition of such programs is a "plan or program that provides health benefits, whether directly, through insurance, or otherwise, which is funded directly, in whole or in part, by the United States Government; or any State health care program." The primary examples are Medicare and Medicaid, but the term includes TRICARE (for active military), Veterans Administration (for military veterans), Indian Health Service, Public Health Service, and State Children's Health Insurance Programs (CHIPs). The statute excludes the Federal Employee Health Benefits (FEHB) Program from its application.

Penalties for Violation of the AKS

Unlike the Stark Law, the AKS does not impose strict liability. There must be some showing that the parties intended to take the actions prohibited by the law. The nature of that intention is covered by the term "knowingly and willfully," explained earlier. When the requisite intention is found, the penalties can be even more severe than under Stark.

The civil penalties are similar: potential civil monetary penalties of up to $50,000 per violation, civil assessments of up to three times the amount of the kickback, provider exclusion from federal healthcare program participation, and False Claims Act liability. On top of that are criminal penalties of fines up to $25,000 per violation and a maximum 5-year prison term per violation.

Exceptions to the Prohibitions of the AKS—Safe Harbors

Because of the broad scope of the AKS prohibitions, Congress created several statutory exceptions to protect legitimate business arrangements like these:

- Properly disclosed discounts or other reductions in price
- Payments to bona fide employees
- Certain payments to group purchasing organizations
- Waivers of coinsurance for Medicare services for certain individuals
- Certain risk-sharing arrangements with managed care organizations

In addition, the OIG has issued regulations under the AKS that define a further list of Safe Harbors. If the provider payment arrangement meets the requirements of one of the defined Safe Harbors, it will be free from liability under the statute. If it does not fit within a Safe Harbor, it does not automatically violate the statute. However, the government is more likely to scrutinize the arrangement for possible violations.

The following Safe Harbors have been established by regulation under the AKS:

- Investment interests
- Space rental
- Equipment rental
- Sale of practice
- Referral services
- Warranties
- Discounts
- Employees
- Group purchasing organizations

- Waiver of beneficiary coinsurance and deductible amounts
- Increased coverage, reduced cost-sharing amounts, or reduced premium amounts offered by health plans
- Price reductions offered to health plans
- Practitioner recruitment
- Obstetrical malpractice insurance subsidies
- Investments in group practices
- Cooperative hospital service organizations
- Ambulatory surgical centers
- Referral arrangements for specialty services
- Price reductions offered to eligible managed care organizations
- Price reductions offered by contractors with substantial financial risk to managed care organizations
- Ambulance replenishing
- Health centers
- E-prescribing items and services
- EHR items and services

A common characteristic of these Safe Harbors is commercially reasonable goods or services being exchanged for a "FMV" price. The FMV term is defined in some detail in the regulations on the space rental and equipment rental Safe Harbors. In addition, many of the Safe Harbors require that total compensation be set in advance and documented in a 1-year written agreement signed by the parties.

Reducing the Risks of AKS Violations

In the normal course of business, healthcare organizations enter into numerous arrangements that could violate the AKS. These risks can be anticipated and avoided. Start by asking these questions.

Is remuneration being exchanged and, if so, which party is giving it and which is receiving it? Does the arrangement involve referrals that will be paid for by a federal healthcare program? If so, who is making the referrals and who is benefitting from them? This establishes the outline of a potential kickback situation.

What is the intent of the parties regarding the remuneration and the referrals? How might the government perceive the intent of the parties in this arrangement? Is the actual or the perceived intent of the parties to induce any of these actions: Referrals for patients covered by federal healthcare programs, ordering/purchasing goods or services to be paid for by a federal healthcare program, or the recommending or arranging for the ordering of such items? If that type of intent can be proven, there is a potential problem.

The only way to avoid that problem is to identify a suitable Safe Harbor. Is there an applicable statutory exception or regulatory Safe Harbor? What are the characteristics and terms of the arrangement? If it does not fit exactly within a Safe Harbor, can it be modified enough so that it does?

The OIG has issued a list of compliance risk factors that may indicate an existing or proposed arrangement is in violation of the AKS.

- Overutilization of resources
- Increased program costs
- Adverse effects of care quality
- Reduced freedom of patient choice
- Compromising medical decision-making
- Unfair competition

If these conditions are present, the arrangement should be reexamined. At the least, an effort should be made to restructure it or to implement compliance safeguards to ease the risk of violations. The safeguards could include measures like these.

- Systematic recording and tracking of contracts, particularly when they are executed, amended, terminated, or expired. The contracts must be written. Services exchanged between payors and referral sources without an up-to-date supporting contract will attract the attention of enforcement authorities.
- There should be rigorous documentation of the FMV of the payments made through the arrangement. Official opinions of accountants with valuation expertise can be helpful.
- The need for the particular arrangement should be justified and well documented. For instance, many hospitals employ medical directors. The question is whether a hospital actually needs a physician to fill this medical director position.
- It must be possible to show, through careful monitoring, that the services being reimbursed were actually provided.

It would be a perfect example of noncompliance to verbally contract with a physician to pay too much money for unnecessary services that were never delivered.

The OIG often negotiates Corporate Integrity Agreements (CIAs) with healthcare providers and other entities as part of the settlement of federal healthcare program investigations arising under a variety of civil false claims statutes. The providers or entities agree to the obligations, and in exchange, the OIG agrees not to seek their exclusion from participation in Medicare, Medicaid, or other federal healthcare programs. The CIA typically requires the affected organizations to do what they should have been doing anyway. They are a good guide to compliance steps for avoiding AKS liability, such as AKS-specific policies, procedures, and training; a central system for tracking arrangements, payments, and services; a contract review and approval process (e.g., legal review, business rationale, FMV justification); and signed written contracts.

Fraud and Abuse Enforcement Activities

It is worth studying specific examples of the enforcement of fraud and abuse laws for lessons on the kinds of individual and organizational behavior that lead to civil or criminal liability.

> *July 2012.* A Rhode Island physician's assistant was sentenced to 1 year incarceration (6 months in prison, 6 months home confinement), to be followed by 2 years of supervised release and a $3,000 fine. Michael Cobb pleaded guilty to taking kickbacks from Orthofix, Inc., a medical device company, for ordering its bone growth stimulators. Cobb worked for a neurosurgeon who prescribed bone growth stimulators for patients who underwent spinal fusion surgery. The surgeon had no preference about which company's bone growth stimulator was used, believing that there were no clinical differences among the stimulators on the market. The surgeon left this decision to Cobb, who was in a position to direct the stimulator business to whichever medical device company he chose. Between 2004 and 2011, Orthofix paid Cobb for each bone growth stimulator that was ordered by the surgeon in payments ranging from $50 to $300. Cobb never disclosed to the surgeon that he was taking these payments, and the surgeon would not have authorized the arrangement. Cobb was paid approximately $120,000 between 2004 and 2011 for bone growth stimulator orders. In return, Cobb steered more than a $1 million of reimbursement from insurance carriers to Orthofix, including approximately $350,000 in payments from federal insurance carriers.

> *December 2011.* A New Jersey doctor, William Lagrada, pleaded guilty to accepting cash kickback payments from Orange Community MRI ("Orange MRI"), a diagnostic facility, in exchange for patient referrals. Twelve other New Jersey doctors and a nurse practitioner were arrested and charged in separate complaints with accepting similar cash kickback payments from Orange MRI. Each of the defendants was recorded taking envelopes of cash in exchange for their patient referrals. An Orange MRI executive also was arrested and charged in connection with his participation in the scheme. Starting as early

as 2010, Orange MRI began making monthly cash kickback payments in exchange for patient referrals to Orange MRI for diagnostic tests. At the end of each calendar month, individuals at Orange MRI printed Orange MRI patient reports that detailed how many magnetic resonance imagings, ultrasounds, echocardiograms, computed axial tomographies, and dual-emission X-ray absorptiometries were referred. These patient reports were used to calculate the kickback payments.

September 2011. The U.S. District Court in Miami sentenced the owner of a mental healthcare company, American Therapeutic Corporation (ATC), to 50 years in prison for orchestrating a $205 million Medicare fraud scheme involving fictitious mental health services. The court also sentenced a co-owner to 35 years in prison and a third codefendant to 91 months in prison following guilty pleas for their roles in the scheme. The defendants paid kickbacks to assisted living facilities and halfway houses in exchange for patients being brought to ATC facilities so they could bill Medicare for intensive mental health treatments that were medically unnecessary or never provided.

March 2011. Medline Industries, Inc. and The Medline Foundation paid the United States $85 million to resolve allegations that they improperly paid kickbacks (in the form of rebates, trips, gifts, and charitable donations) to healthcare providers in violation of the False Claims Act and the AKS. In particular, the settlement resolved allegations that Medline offered or paid unlawful remuneration to induce healthcare providers to purchase, lease, or order medical goods and supplies from Medline.

December 2010. Detroit Medical Center, a nonprofit company that owns and operates hospitals and outpatient facilities in Detroit, paid the United States $30 million after it reported to the government improper financial relationships with referring physicians. The Physician Self-Referral Law (Stark Law) and the AKS restrict the financial relationships that hospitals may have with doctors who refer patients to them. Most of the relationships at issue in this matter involved office lease agreements and independent contractor relationships that were either inconsistent with FMV or not memorialized in writing.

October 2010. Christ Hospital of Cincinnati, OH, and its parent system, the Health Alliance of Greater Cincinnati, agreed to pay $108 million and enter into a CIA with OIG to settle accusations that they violated the AKS and the FCA. The two entities were accused of illegally paying physicians in exchange for referring cardiac patients to the hospital. The OIG also notified Christ Hospital that it was considering excluding it from Medicare participation on the grounds that it improperly rewarded cardiologists for referring patients to the hospital in violation of the AKS.

STUDY QUESTIONS

1. What is the difference between the Stark Law and the AKS? Compare how the two deal with these issues: the referral sources covered, the types of services (or goods) referred, who can be held liable, criminal vs. civil violations, necessary intent to violate the law, types of exceptions, and penalties for violations.
2. Describe the types of financial relationships that can lead to problems under the Stark Law.
3. Do a little research on the "program exclusion" penalty, starting with this section of the OIG website: https://oig.hhs.gov/exclusions/index.asp. What types of exclusions are possible, how long do they last, and what is the effect on the healthcare provider?
4. Choose two or three of the Stark exceptions or the AKS Safe Harbors that were not explained previously and gather information on their requirements. Start with these websites, for Stark exceptions, http://www.starkcompliance.com/index.aspx?id=1046, and for AKS Safe Harbors, http://edocket.access.gpo.gov/cfr_2010/octqtr/pdf/42cfr1001.952.pdf. The AKS link is to the federal regulations defining the Safe Harbors. It is a good idea to become familiar with the Code of Federal Regulations, where to find them, and how to interpret them. They are usually designated with a citation number like the one here, 42 CFR 1001.952.
5. If the administrator of a five-physician medical practice asked you for recommendations of five steps she should take to reduce the risks of an anti-kickback violation, what would you tell her?
6. Have you ever committed an act "willfully?" Does that mean that you were breaking the law?

Learning Exercises

1. With the guidance of your instructor, set up and carry out the following role play. One person plays the role of the medical director of a 45-bed hospital in a semi-rural community. A second person plays the role of an

oncologist physician whom the hospital wishes to recruit to its medical staff. The third person acts as a business/legal advisor to the hospital and the doctor on the possible terms of an arrangement between them.

The hospital is concerned that primary care physicians in the area have been referring their cancer patients to the specialists in another hospital 30 miles away. As a result, the patients increasingly are choosing to obtain other inpatient services from that hospital as well. The first hospital has seen a slow, steady decline in admissions and revenues over the last 2 years. It wishes to hire the oncologist in the hope that he will bring most of the cancer patients back to its facility and refer them there for other services.

The hospital can afford to recruit and hire the oncologist only if he increases admissions to the hospital by a certain amount. The oncologist is willing to move to this relatively remote location only if he can be assured of a certain minimum income. The goal of the advisor is to help them to achieve their mutual aims in a way that does not violate fraud and abuse laws.

2. Arrange a brief visit with a local physician, perhaps your own primary care doctor. Tell her that you are doing some modest research for a course that you are taking. When you meet, ask if she receives small gifts from businesses in the healthcare field—like pharmaceutical manufacturers, durable medical equipment manufacturers, testing laboratories, or other entities whose goods or services she might use. Ask how she ensures that the gifts do not influence her decisions about using or prescribing those goods or services.

References

1. *A Roadmap for New Physicians: Avoiding Medicare and Medicaid Fraud and Abuse*, a booklet prepared by the OIG for physician self-study. Available at https://oig.hhs.gov/compliance/physician-education/roadmap_web_version.pdf
2. Audio narration of an OIG presentation summarizing the content of the above publication. Available at https://oig.hhs.gov/compliance/physician-education/index.asp
3. *The Department of Health and Human Services and The Department of Justice Health Care Fraud and Abuse Control Program Annual Report for Fiscal Year 2011*. Detailed annual report of government efforts to fight fraud and abuse in health care. Available at https://zig.hhs.gov/reports-and-publications/hcfac/index.asp
4. *Health Care Fraud and Abuse: Practical Perspectives, Second Edition*, with 2009 Cumulative Supplement, Linda A. Bauman, BNA Books; second edition, 2007. Detailed technical guidance on fraud and abuse issues for lawyers representing healthcare organizations.

Chapter 3

Antitrust

Learning Objectives

After completing class sessions based on this chapter, a student will:

- Be familiar with the basic provisions of the primary federal antitrust laws.
- Know the difference between a *per se* violation and one determined by a Rule of Reason analysis.
- Realize why the Clayton Act presents special legal risks for consolidation plans among healthcare entities.
- Be able to identify the legal defenses and enforcement exceptions to liability under the antitrust laws.
- Recognize what actions to avoid in order to minimize the risk of antitrust violations.
- Be aware of the process for seeking advisory opinions from antitrust enforcement agencies.
- Learn the basic elements of a compliance program focused on potential antitrust risks.
- Understand the first step to take when an enforcement agency launches an antitrust investigation.

INTRODUCTION

Healthcare organizations must be especially sensitive to the risk of antitrust violations in the current market climate for healthcare products and services. The consolidation among competitors that is natural to maturing industries is taking place right now in health care, presenting opportunities for illegal combinations of businesses. The strong incentives and pressures for the formation of accountable care organizations (ACOs) require otherwise competing providers to collaborate in treating patients. It is well established that clinical integration of physicians and hospitals improves the quality of care that they deliver.

Health plans, managed care organizations, and other large payors have overwhelming power when bargaining with small physician practices and single freestanding hospitals. The understandable reaction of those providers is to band together in order to carry greater weight in the negotiations. In the last decade or two, profit-driven executives have discovered the healthcare industry. As a result, competition in the healthcare industry has become much more intense, leading some individuals and organizations to take great risks in an effort to survive.

The sole purpose of the several antitrust laws, in any industry, is to protect competition. It is believed that independent individuals and entities fighting with each other for customers will result in the greatest benefits for those customers in terms of the price, quality, and other characteristics of the goods and services being offered. It is also believed that vigorous competition will produce the optimal allocation of the limited resources available to individual businesses and to the nation as a whole.

It is not the intent of the laws to protect a particular business or individual from the consequences of normal market forces, from aggressive competition by other businesses, from competitors that operate more efficiently, and even from unfair or arbitrary conduct that does not hinder competition in the overall market. In fact, it would not be unusual, in a vigorously competitive marketplace, for an inefficient competitor to fail and go out of business. That usually is what has happened when a company declares bankruptcy.

A person or organization can violate one of the several antitrust laws in two fundamental ways: through its own independent actions or through a conspiracy with another competitor in the same market. If a co-conspirator is required and none is present, there has been no violation.

SHERMAN ACT, SECTIONS 1 AND 2

Section 1 of the Sherman Antitrust Act prohibits "every contract, combination in the form of trust or otherwise, or conspiracy in restraint of trade or commerce among the several states." Two or more persons or entities must act together to violate this law. A single person or entity acting alone cannot violate Section 1.

The conspiracy need not be based on an express verbal or written agreement among the parties. It may be inferred from their deeds, perhaps the result of a tacit understanding and reflected in a long pattern of actions. The evidence often is circumstantial.

The meaning of the term "entity" is important in the context of the healthcare industry. If two or more individuals or organizations share common, unified economic interests, they can be considered a single entity. They can accomplish this by integrating their operations—clinically, financially, or legally—and otherwise removing any economic incentives for them to compete with each other.

A good example is an independent practice association (IPA), an association of independent physicians, or other organization that contracts with independent physicians and provides services to managed care organizations on a negotiated per capita or fee-for-service basis. Participating physicians join an IPA in order to gain the benefits of collective contracting with health plans without giving up their practice autonomy. The contracting process must be carefully managed to avoid the sharing of prices or other competitive information among the independent competing practices. Alternatively, the group of physicians can negotiate together with payors if they are willing to share substantial financial risk or clinically integrate their practices. In that case, the many separate physician practices would be considered a single entity for antitrust purposes and there would be no violation. Another example is when a hospital and its medical staff engage in peer review; in this case they are treated as a single entity.

"*Per se*" Violations

Under Section 1, certain restraints of trade are so serious and potentially damaging that they are deemed to be *per se* violations of the law. If the behavior takes place, no further analysis of the market or the action's affect on competition is conducted. The action is automatically a violation. These are the primary forms of *per se* antitrust violations.

Price fixing. This is the worst antitrust sin. Price fixing is an agreement among competitors to set the particular prices they will charge to customers or to establish a system that influences in any way the way prices are determined. Arrangements in danger of *per se* liability are IPA or physician-hospital organization agreements to follow common fee schedules. Any nonintegrated groups of physicians or hospitals that turn over management of their payor contracting to a single individual will also be challenged.

Horizontal market-allocation agreements. Under these agreements, two or more current or prospective competitors determine which geographic areas they will or will not serve, which customers they will or will not serve, and which goods or services they will or will not sell. For instance, there are two hospitals in a medium-size city. They agree that one will primarily admit patients from the east side of town, the other from the west side of town. Or, one hospital agrees to serve lower-income Medicaid patients while the other focuses on a more middle class patient population. Or, one hospital closes its maternity ward and enhances its cancer treatment unit; the other hospital does the opposite. All three are *per se* violations.

Group boycotts. A classic example of this type of violation is a group of physicians (or hospitals) in a particular market area agreeing that none of them will sign participation agreements with a new health plan that has just entered the area. One prerequisite is that the boycott participants have significant market power. A group boycott issue also may arise as the result of decisions by hospital medical staff to deny admitting privileges to particular physicians.

Tying arrangement. When an entity requires that a customer purchase a second product or service in order to be able to purchase a first product or service, a tying arrangement has been proposed. And it is *per se* illegal. This situation might arise when group purchasing organizations (e.g., a group of hospitals leverage their collective buying power to obtain discounts from vendors) compel their members to buy one set of products/services in order to buy the products/services they really want.

Rule of Reason Cases

The majority of cases brought under Section 1 do not involve *per se* violations. Instead, they are more equivocal cases that are subjected to the Rule of Reason. The courts use this test to balance the pro-competition and anti-competition effects of an arrangement in order to determine the net impact on competition in the affected market. To prove such a case, the prosecution must define the relevant market, show that the defendant has significant market power in that market, describe the anticompetitive effects of the defendants' actions, and demonstrate that they are not offset by any pro-competitive effects.

An arrangement usually analyzed under the Rule of Reason is the exclusive contract that many hospitals have with their radiologists, pathologists, and anesthesiologists. Such contracts are more likely to survive a legal challenge if they are for a shorter term (1 to 2 years), are regularly opened to competitive bidding, and are intended for valid objectives. Accepted objectives are improved hospital operating efficiency, consistency of procedures, round-the-clock coverage, and enhanced quality management.

Section 2 of the Sherman Act states that "every person who shall monopolize or attempt to monopolize, or combine or conspire with any other person or persons to monopolize any part of the trade or commerce among the several states or with foreign nations shall be deemed guilty of a felony." Despite the reference to felony guilt, most Section 2 cases are prosecuted under civil complaints.

The first thing to note is that Section 2 may be violated by the actions of a single person or organization. Conspiracies are not necessary, though they will be punished as well.

An entity has carried out monopolization if it has monopoly power in a relevant market, and has either acquired/maintained that power by exclusionary/noncompetitive means or used the power for exclusionary/noncompetitive purposes. "Monopoly power" is the ability to control prices in the defined market or to exclude competitors from that market. Those abilities usually require a dominant share of the market. The actual percentage necessary depends on the characteristics of the market, but a 70% share establishes prima facie evidence of a monopoly.

A crucial factor in deciding whether an entity has a monopoly is the way that the relevant market is defined. For instance, a hospital may dominate the market for maternity services in the medium-size city where it is located, but play a much smaller role in the immediate region where there are other larger cities with several hospitals. The market definition may be different for each of the services offered by a hospital (or other entity).

Part of the basis of a monopolization claim is that the entity is engaged in "predatory conduct." One does not gain a monopoly position by accident. Conduct will be considered predatory when it conspicuously excludes competitors from the market and there is no good business reason for it. However, a legitimate business rationale will allow an organization to drive its competitors to the brink of elimination.

CLAYTON ACT, SECTION 7

The Sherman Act is the broadest of the antitrust laws, covering a wide range of competitive behavior. Section 7 of the Clayton Act focuses on mergers, joint ventures, and other arrangements among two or more entities. This law has special relevance for the healthcare industry as it continues to transform itself. In response to both competitive and regulatory pressures, physician groups, hospitals, nursing homes, and other entities are consolidating through merger and acquisition. Where that is not happening, strategic partnerships and joint ventures are being formed.

Section 7 prohibits an organization from acquiring all or part of the stock or assets of another organization if the result will be to substantially lessen competition or tend to create a monopoly in a defined market. The acquisition of assets may encompass the sale of subscriber, member, or customer lists, entering into exclusive marketing agreements, and negotiating licenses to distribute a product. The Clayton Act is enforced by the Department of Justice (DOJ) and the Federal Trade Commission (FTC). Their interpretation of the Act's language is explained in the Horizontal Merger Guidelines of 2010.

ROBINSON–PATMAN ACT

This law makes it illegal to discriminate in price between different purchasers of products or services of similar grade and quality. A violation will occur when an organization, perhaps a vendor of hospital supplies, sells the same product to two different hospitals at different prices and the price difference affects competition. A buyer may also be held liable under the act for knowingly encouraging or accepting goods at a price different from that offered to its competitors.

The Non-Profit Institutions Act provides an exception to the restriction of the Robinson–Patman Act. It permits hospitals (and other nonprofit entities) to purchase supplies "for their own use" at discriminatory prices. This typically applies to a hospital's resale of preferentially priced drugs to its inpatients, emergency room patients, outpatients for use at the hospital, medical staff, employees, and students.

FEDERAL TRADE COMMISSION (FTC) ACT

The FTC Act incorporates elements of the Sherman and Clayton Acts into a broad prohibition of "unfair methods of competition." Its one distinctive feature is that it applies only to a "company . . . which is organized to carry on business for its own profit or that of its members."

PENALTIES FOR VIOLATION OF THE ANTITRUST LAWS

Lawsuits under the antitrust laws may be initiated by the DOJ, the FTC, the Attorneys General in any of the 50 states, and by private parties (individuals and corporations) affected by the violations. The defendants in the lawsuits are the organizations carrying out the illegal transactions or practices and, increasingly, their employees who made the relevant decisions.

When the lawsuits succeed, the penalties can be severe. In the most serious cases, such as *per se* price-fixing violations, criminal convictions are possible. These can lead to prison sentences of up to 10 years, and fines of up to $1 million per person and $100 million for the entire organization. If civil liability is found, there may be an award to the injured party of three times the damages it has suffered plus its attorneys fees. The court also has the option of issuing injunctions to cease any unlawful conduct, dissolve an unlawful arrangement or entity, or get rid of an unlawfully acquired entity.

Government-initiated antitrust actions tend to focus on mergers, joint ventures, collective provider negotiating and contracting with payors, and other competitor agreements on prices and terms of service. The most common legal actions by private parties deal with hospital medical staff decisions connected with peer review and exclusive contracts.

DEFENSES TO CHARGES OF ANTITRUST BEHAVIOR

One of the more important legal defenses in analyzing many healthcare antitrust cases is the *state-action doctrine*.[1] An entity may engage in acts that would normally violate antitrust laws if they are performed under a "clearly articulated and affirmatively expressed state policy" and the state "actively supervises" the acts. This exemption is likely to be raised in cases concerning state boards of medicine and state certificate of need programs.

Competitors may collaborate in attempts to influence government policy, even if the desired policy would reduce competition—according to the U.S. Supreme Court in three decisions 50 years ago. In what is known as the *Noerr–Pennington exception*, it said that "no violation of the [Sherman] Act can be predicated upon mere attempts to influence the passage or enforcement of laws," and that "joint efforts to influence public officials do not violate the antitrust laws even though intended to eliminate competition." This exception would protect groups of providers collectively attempting to change laws on their reimbursement, or an association of pharmaceutical manufacturers wishing to amend the patent laws affecting their drug discoveries.

Historically, physicians occasionally have challenged on antitrust grounds decisions made against them by the peer review committees of hospitals where they have staff privileges. Sometimes, the result of those decisions is that a physician will no longer be permitted to admit patients to the hospital. The physicians who participate in those peer review activities

[1] The exemption was created in a U.S. Supreme Court decision, *Parker v. Brown*, 317 U.S. 341 (1943), holding that federal antitrust laws do not apply to economic regulation by the states. It affects any field of economic endeavor, not just health care.

will not be held liable under any federal or state law for their actions. This protection comes from the Health Care Quality Improvement Act. To qualify, the physicians must act in the reasonable belief that they are enhancing the quality of care, after they have made a reasonable effort to gather all the facts, using adequate notice and due process hearing procedures, and in the reasonable belief that the action was necessary.

Federal courts below the Supreme Court level have held that because the antitrust laws are based on the federal government's authority to regulate "trade or commerce," and because *noncommercial activities* do not constitute trade or commerce, the business of most nonprofit entities is not subject to those laws. The problem is that many nonprofits do engage in some commercial activities and the court decisions have not yet clearly delineated the difference between commercial and noncommercial. A leading case held that the antitrust laws did not apply to medical residency matching programs.

ANTITRUST LIABILITY PROTECTION FOR COMMON HEALTHCARE ACTIVITIES

In recognition of the unique contexts that health care provides for antitrust law, the DOJ and FTC issued a set of standards that they will use in enforcing the laws—the *Statements of Antitrust Enforcement Policy in Health Care*. They describe particular healthcare arrangements that do not have to fear antitrust prosecution. A healthcare organization planning a project or venture that seems to fall within one of the following categories would be wise to make every effort to ensure that they do qualify.

Mergers among hospitals. There will be no antitrust challenge of any merger between two general acute-care hospitals where one of the hospitals (1) has an average of fewer than 100 licensed beds over the three most recent years and (2) has an average daily inpatient census of fewer than 40 patients over the three most recent years.

Hospital joint ventures involving high technology or other expensive healthcare equipment. There will be no antitrust challenge of any joint venture among hospitals to purchase or share the ownership cost of, operate, and market the related services of high-technology or other expensive healthcare equipment (e.g., MRI scanner), as long as the joint venture includes only the number of hospitals whose participation is needed to support the equipment.

Hospital joint ventures involving specialized clinical or other expensive health services. Most hospital joint ventures to provide specialized clinical or other expensive healthcare services do not create antitrust problems.

Although there is no safety zone protecting such arrangements, neither the DOJ nor the FTC have ever challenged them.

Providers' collective provision of non-fee-related information to purchasers of healthcare services. The collective provision of non-fee-related information by competing healthcare providers to a purchaser in an effort to influence the terms upon which the purchaser deals with the providers does not necessarily raise antitrust concerns. Generally, the provision of such information to a purchaser is likely either to raise little risk of anticompetitive effects or to provide pro-competitive benefits. There will be no enforcement action against providers who collectively supply medical data that may improve purchasers' handling of issues relating to the method, quality, or efficiency of treatment.

Providers' collective provision of fee-related information to purchasers of healthcare services. Price data are particularly sensitive as they may be the basis of price fixing, a prima facie antitrust violation. The collective provision by competing healthcare providers (e.g., hospitals, physicians) to purchasers of healthcare services (e.g., health plans) of factual information concerning the fees charged currently or in the past for the providers' services, and other factual information concerning the amounts, levels, or methods of fees or reimbursement, does not necessarily raise antitrust concerns. There will be no challenge to these arrangements as long as the collection of the information is managed by a third party (e.g., a purchaser, government agency, healthcare consultant, academic institution, or trade association), any fee-related information that is shared with other competing providers furnishing the data is more than 3 months old, there are at least five providers reporting data upon which each disseminated statistic is based, no individual provider's data represents more than 25% on a weighted basis of that statistic, and any information disseminated is sufficiently aggregated such that it would not allow recipients to identify the prices charged by any individual provider.

Provider participation in exchanges of price and cost information. There will be no antitrust challenge of provider participation in written surveys of (a) prices for healthcare services, or (b) wages, salaries, or benefits of healthcare personnel, if the following conditions are satisfied: the survey is managed by a third party (e.g., a purchaser, government agency, healthcare consultant, academic institution, or trade association), the information provided by survey participants is based on data more than 3 months old, and there are at least five providers reporting data upon which each disseminated statistic is based; no individual provider's data represent more than 25% on a weighted basis of that statistic; and any information disseminated is sufficiently aggregated such that it would not allow recipients to identify the prices charged or compensation paid by any particular provider.

Joint purchasing arrangements among healthcare providers. There will be no antitrust challenge of any joint purchasing arrangement among healthcare providers where two conditions are present: (1) the purchases account for less than 35% of the total sales of the purchased product or service in the relevant market, and (2) the cost of the products and services purchased jointly accounts for less than 20% of the total revenues from all products or services sold by each competing participant in the joint purchasing arrangement.

Physician network joint ventures. There will be no antitrust challenge of an exclusive physician network joint venture whose physician participants share substantial financial risk and constitute 20% or less of the physicians in each physician specialty with active hospital staff privileges who practice in the relevant geographic market. Similar protection is available to a nonexclusive physician network when the participants make up 30% or less of the same area physicians.

Multiprovider networks. There is no safety zone defined for multiprovider networks because of the many different forms that they may take. They can vary according to the number and type of providers they include, the contractual relationships among the providers in the network, the competitive conditions in the local market, and the operating efficiencies that the network may realize. The antitrust impact of these networks will be analyzed under the Rule of Reason.

CURRENT DOJ/FTC ANTITRUST ENFORCEMENT STRATEGIES

The DOJ and the FTC collaborate closely in the enforcement of the antitrust laws and are quite candid about the enforcement strategies they follow. As a general rule, the FTC exercises jurisdiction over mergers that involve only hospitals, while the DOJ enforces the antitrust laws against mergers between hospitals and health plans. Moving forward, enforcement activity will look most closely at "pay-for-delay" patent litigation settlements that delay the availability of generic drugs, physician price fixing, hospital mergers, health plan mergers, and health plan contracting practices.

The enforcement authorities have made clear that the healthcare reform laws passed in the last few years do not create an antitrust exemption for providers acting in response to those laws. The DOJ/FTC have issued a statement, entitled *Statement of Antitrust Enforcement Policy Regarding Accountable Care Organizations Participating in the Medicare Shared Savings Program*. It is intended to provide guidance on antitrust compliance for providers wishing to form pro-competitive ACOs that will operate in both the Medicare and commercial markets. (ACOs are viewed as a major innovation in integrated, provider-responsible, patient-centric healthcare delivery.) The policy statement describes (1) the ACOs to which the policy statement will apply, (2) when the agencies will apply Rule of Reason treatment to those ACOs, (3) an antitrust safety zone, and (4) additional antitrust guidance for ACOs that are outside the safety zone, including a voluntary expedited antitrust review process for newly formed ACOs.

MINIMIZING THE RISK OF ANTITRUST VIOLATIONS

Enforcement authorities have powerful investigatory tools for determining whether an entity should be charged with antitrust violations: voluntary requests for information, civil and criminal subpoena powers, and civil demands for document production and depositions. Responding to investigations is expensive, time consuming, and damaging to workforce morale. It gets much worse if the authorities decide to take formal legal action. If the action succeeds, the organization faces the burden of monetary damages, treble damages to private plaintiffs, and the unwinding of operational or strategic plans. It is best to avoid attracting the attention of government authorities in the first place. There are several preventive measures available.

- Never talk with competitors about the prices charged for the organization's services or the prices it pays for services from other organizations, costs, profit levels, allocation of customers or territories, or refusal to deal with certain suppliers or customers.
- Do not look for, ask for, or accept privileged information about the practices of competitors.
- Do not agree with competitors to divide up customer/patient markets or geographic territories.
- Do not attend meetings or trade conferences where there is likely to be talk among competitors about prices, sharing markets, or other forbidden practices.
- Do not make sales or purchases conditional on reciprocal sales or purchases.
- Do not accept discounts, rebates, price adjustments, or discriminatory terms or conditions of sale from a vendor supplier until assured of their legality.

When planning a merger with, a joint venture with, or an acquisition of another entity, it is a good idea to anticipate the reaction it will produce in the market. When studying such transactions for potential antitrust problems, the FTC frequently interviews area payors, employers, and other stakeholders to gauge the competitive effects. There is nothing to prevent the parties to the transaction from defining the pro-competitive and community benefits of their proposed arrangement and communicating them to those stakeholders. It is possible to shape their opinions of the deal before other forces influence them.

REQUESTING ANTITRUST ENFORCEMENT AGENCY ADVISORY OPINIONS

Sometimes an organization is unsure whether an arrangement it is planning may violate the antitrust laws. In those cases, it may ask either the DOJ or the FTC for its opinion on the matter. After describing the proposed action and the surrounding facts, the organization can obtain a formal statement indicating whether the agency would challenge the conduct. The FTC issues staff Advisory Opinions,[2] while the DOJ version is called a Business Review Letter.[3] Technically, the opinions apply only to the parties requesting them. However, they are a good indication of how the agencies will respond to other similar arrangements. This resembles the Advisory Opinion process available through the U.S. Department of Health and Human Services Office of the Inspector General (OIG).

The receipt of a favorable opinion from one of these agencies is not an absolute defense or an exemption from the antitrust law. They both retain the right to initiate a legal action if they later learn new information about the arrangement.

IMPLEMENTING AN ANTITRUST COMPLIANCE PROGRAM

For many healthcare organizations, there is not the same urgency for a compliance program to address antitrust issues as there is for a fraud and abuse compliance program. There is a persistent potential for fraud liability in the day-to-day operations of every provider and supplier in the healthcare

[2] Previously issued Advisory Opinions can be found here: www.ftc.gov/bc/healthcare/industryguide/advisory.htm

[3] Previously issued Business Review Letters can be accessed here: www.usdoj.gov/atr/public/busreview/index.htm

industry. The sorts of events that might trigger antitrust liability (mergers, acquisitions, joint ventures) occur much less frequently and do not require constant scrutiny. Nonetheless, there is a place in every healthcare entity for at least a basic antitrust compliance program, composed of the following elements:

- Formal written policy committing the organization to compliance with antitrust laws
- Written mandate for compliant behavior by all employees and agents
- Formal education of employees and agents on the principles of antitrust law
- Written mandate for all employees to report suspected antitrust misconduct
- Established procedure for responding to reports of possible antitrust violations
- Periodic legal review by an antitrust expert of high-risk operating areas

A good compliance program can entirely prevent most antitrust problems. Furthermore, if a violation does occur, the DOJ has a corporate leniency policy and a leniency policy for individuals that reduce the penalties when the violations are detected early and self-reported.

RESPONDING TO AN ANTITRUST ENFORCEMENT INVESTIGATION

There are several ways that the DOJ or FTC can first hear about a possible antitrust violation. A provider, payor, competitor, consumer, or other government agency may pass on information it has learned. There may be indications in the news media or trade publications. Suspicions may be raised as a result of the DOJ/FTC review of a proposed arrangement reported under the premerger notification requirements in the Clayton Act. Another federal or state agency may already have begun legal action on a related matter.

The first step taken by the DOJ or FTC in addressing a suspected antitrust violation is to begin an investigation of the concerned organization. When an organization becomes aware that an investigation has been launched, it has several things to do—promptly.

- Contact an attorney experienced in healthcare antitrust law.
- Designate a single employee to work under the attorney in managing the organization's interaction with the investigation and the government agency.

- As appropriate, work with the attorney to maintain maximum attorney-client protection for all internal communications about the matter.
- Instruct employees about their rights and options if contacted directly by investigators.
- Ensure that all possibly relevant documents are vouchsafed against alteration or destruction.

From that point on, the organization will be working actively with its legal counsel to resolve the matter with the investigating agency. It will determine whether the initial agency inquiry is formal or informal. It must obtain basic contact information about the agency. It should learn the nature of the inquiry, the organization's connection to the inquiry, and whether the organization is suspected of misconduct or is merely a source of information. If the organization is served with a subpoena or civil investigative demand, it will have to decide whether to comply, negotiate, or resist. Throughout the entire process, it is important to maintain good relations with agency personnel. Keep communication channels open and organization credibility high.

SOME RECENT FTC ANTITRUST CASES

This is a representative sample of antitrust cases brought by the FTC in the last few years.[4]

The FTC challenged *ProMedica Health System, Inc.*'s acquisition of rival St. Luke's Hospital in Lucas County, Ohio, on the grounds that it would reduce competition and allow ProMedica to raise prices for general acute-care and inpatient obstetrical services, significantly harming patients and local employers and employees. An administrative law judge ordered ProMedica to divest St. Luke's Hospital within 180 days to a FTC-approved buyer.

Hikma Pharmaceuticals proposed to acquire for $112 million the entire generic injectable pharmaceutical business from Baxter International. The FTC alleged that the market for two of the products in that business was already highly concentrated, with only three competitors–Hikma, Baxter, and Hospira, Inc. The acquisition would reduce that number to two. The FTC ordered Hikma to divest those two products in order to retain the other business from Baxter.

[4]Access to antitrust cases initiated by the FTC has been available since 1996. Includes initial complaint, subsequent court decisions, settlement agreements, and other materials. http://www.ftc.gov/bc/healthcare/antitrust/litigation.htm

DaVita, the second largest provider of outpatient dialysis services in the United States proposed to acquire DSI Renal, the fifth largest provider, for $689 million. In order to preserve competition in 22 geographic markets, the FTC required DaVita to sell 29 of the 106 dialysis centers that DSI was operating.

The FTC complaint charged that competing hospitals (22), physicians (114), and pharmacies (70) in rural southwestern Minnesota agreed to fix prices and collectively negotiate contracts–including price terms–with third party payors in Minnesota through the *Minnesota Rural Health Cooperative* (MRHC), and that MRHC has undertaken no efficiency-enhancing integration that could justify this conduct. The collective negotiated prices and other competitively significant terms with payors in Minnesota on behalf of MRHC physician and hospital members. The MRHC and its members refused to negotiate individually with payors. The MRHC also threatened to terminate contracts with payors to pressure them to increase reimbursement rates for MRHC physicians and hospitals. The complaint charged that, through its collective negotiations and coercive tactics, MRHC extracted higher payments and other favorable price-related terms from payors. The FTC imposed a consent order that prohibits MRHC from entering into or facilitating agreements between or among physicians, hospitals, or pharmacies (1) to refuse, or threaten to refuse, to deal with any payor regarding the terms upon they will provide their services, or (2) to not deal individually with any payor, or to not deal with any payor through any arrangement other than one involving MRHC.

Warner Chilcott Corporation agreed to pay Barr Pharmaceuticals $20 million in exchange for Barr's delaying entry of its generic version of Chilcott's highly profitable oral contraceptive for 5 years. In response to an FTC complaint and a court order, Warner Chilcottal reached a settlement not to enter into any supply agreements with generic manufacturers in which the generic agrees not to compete with Warner Chilcott. The settlement also prohibits Warner Chilcott from agreeing to provide a generic manufacturer with anything of value, if the manufacturer refrains from research development, manufacturing, marketing, distribution, or sale of a generic version, and there is an adverse affect on competition.

The FTC charged that *Gerald Friedman*, a physician who owned and operated dialysis services in Upland and Pomona, California, engaged in an illegal tying arrangement, requiring physicians who used his outpatient dialysis facilities to use his inpatient dialysis services when their patients were hospitalized. Friedman accepted a consent order under which he will not require any physician to use his inpatient dialysis service for the physician's patients as a condition for using Dr. Friedman's outpatient dialysis facilities, not bar physicians who want to treat their patients at Dr. Friedman's outpatient dialysis facilities from owning or operating a competing inpatient dialysis service, and not deny or otherwise impair a physician's staff privileges at one of Friedman's outpatient dialysis facilities because that physician has used or operated an inpatient dialysis service other than Dr. Friedman's.

The FTC held that the *Massachusetts Board of Registration in Optometry* (a state government agency) illegally conspired to restrain competition among optometrists, by promulgating and enforcing regulations that prohibited optometrists from truthfully advertising price discounts, that prohibited optical and other commercial establishments from advertising the names of optometrists or the availability of their services, and that prohibited the use of testimonial or sensational advertisements. The Commission found that the regulations were not protected by the state-action doctrine because state law did not embody a clearly articulated policy to prohibit optometrists from truthfully advertising discounts, fees, or other information. Under a consent order, the Board is prohibited from restraining truthful advertising but may adopt and enforce reasonable rules to restrict fraudulent, false, deceptive, or misleading advertising within the meaning of state law.

The complaint charged that members of the medical staff of the *Good Samaritan Regional Medical Center*, in Phoenix, Arizona, consisting of more than 500 physicians, conspired to prevent the hospital from opening a multispecialty clinic that would have competed with the physicians, by threatening to stop admitting patients to the hospital if it proceeded with plans to open the clinic. The order prohibits members of the medical staff from agreeing, or attempting to enter into an agreement, to prevent or restrict the services offered by Good Samaritan, the clinic, or any other healthcare provider. The order also prohibits the physicians from conspiring to use coercive tactics to prevent competition from other physicians or healthcare providers.

STUDY QUESTIONS

1. Is it possible for an organization to monopolize a market legally and without violating the antitrust laws?
2. In what ways might individuals or organizations "conspire" to restrain competition in violation of the antitrust laws? Exactly what actions would they take? What communications pass between them? What agreements or understandings do they reach?

3. What are some examples of commercial activities carried out by nonprofit hospitals that could be subject to the antitrust laws?
4. What are some examples of non-fee-related information that physicians could provide to health plans purchasing their services that might facilitate improvement in the efficiency or quality of those services?
5. For a physician network joint venture to be free of a threat of antitrust liability, its members must "share substantial financial risk." In what ways can physicians share financial risk with each other?
6. You have just received a call from a FTC representative who wishes to meet with you to discuss an "antitrust matter." List five steps that you will take immediately in response to the call and in anticipation of the meeting.

Learning Exercises

1. Do a little bit of Internet research on the ACO concept. Learn what individuals and organizations are likely to participate, and the means by which they will have to cooperate if the ACO is to succeed. Then, speculate on the interactions among the ACO participants that might raise antitrust concerns. Remember, some of the ACO participants may otherwise be in competition with each other.
2. A group of physicians would like to set up a formal network of area doctors with the intention of sharing the costs of investing in new technology, qualifying for formation of an ACO, streamlining the process of care delivery to their patients, and presenting a united front in dealing with health plans. What steps would you recommend the doctors take to minimize the chances of antitrust violations? Think in terms of structuring the new entity, the number and specialties of the physicians, favorably influencing other stakeholders in the local healthcare market, and the DOJ/FTC safe havens as described in the Statements of Antitrust Enforcement Policy in Health Care.

References

1. "Statements of Antitrust Enforcement Policy in Health Care," Issued by the U.S. Department of Justice and the Federal Trade Commission, August 1996.
2. "Statement of Antitrust Enforcement Policy Regarding Accountable Care Organizations Participating in the Medicare Shared Savings Program," Antitrust Division of the U.S. Department of Justice and Federal Trade Commission, October 20, 2011.

3. "Overview of FTC Antitrust Actions in Health Care Services and Products," Health Care Division, Bureau of Competition, Federal Trade Commission, June 2012.
4. "Horizontal Merger Guidelines," U.S. Department of Justice and the Federal Trade Commission, August 19, 2010.
5. "Antitrust Guidelines for Collaborations Among Competitors," Issued by the Federal Trade Commission and the U.S. Department of Justice, April 2000.
6. "Antitrust and Healthcare," Christine Varney, Assistant Attorney General, Antitrust Division, U.S. Department of Justice, May 24, 2010.
7. "Antitrust Division Manual," Fourth Edition, Antitrust Division, U.S. Department of Justice, December 2008.

Chapter 4

Federal Income Tax

Learning Objectives

After completing class sessions based on this chapter, a student will:

- Be familiar with the benefits of obtaining and maintaining tax-exempt status.
- Be sensitive to the legal risks that may lead to loss of tax-exempt status.
- Learn about the increased Internal Revenue Service (IRS) and state tax enforcement pressure on tax-exempt hospitals.
- Comprehend all the key prerequisites for maintaining tax-exempt status.
- Understand the different ways that a hospital can provide benefit to its community.
- Recognize the new requirements imposed on tax-exempt hospitals by the health reform law.
- Appreciate the problems with excess benefit transactions (EBTs) and how to avoid them.
- Know how to configure a legally safe physician recruitment incentive package.
- Understand the ways to safeguard tax-exempt status when entering a joint venture.
- Be able to design a basic tax-exempt status compliance program.

INTRODUCTION

All individuals and organizations that generate revenues must be concerned about their legal obligations to pay income taxes to the IRS. The rules and regulations governing the income taxes owed by for-profit entities are well established. There are minor questions about the duty of employers to withhold and pay income taxes for their employees and the classification of workers as employers and independent contractors. However, the greatest controversy is over the tax-exempt status of certain nonprofit organizations and what they must do to maintain that status. This has become a hot issue, legally and politically. Tax exemption for healthcare entities is available under section 501(c)(3) of the Internal Revenue Code.

The largest segment of the healthcare industry composed of nonprofit entities are hospitals. (Nongovernmental nonprofits represent 58% of all community hospitals.) As a result, most of the attention paid to tax issues has been focused on them. Some other types of healthcare entities have sought and qualified for federal tax-exempt status: home health agencies, assisted living centers, fitness centers, physician practice plans, integrated delivery systems, health maintenance organizations, and medical research organizations.

BENEFITS OF TAX-EXEMPT STATUS

There are several good reasons that organizations seek tax-exempt status.

- Once qualified for that status, they need not pay federal income taxes.
- They generally are exempted from paying state income taxes, state and local sales taxes, use taxes on the purchase of goods and services, and local property taxes.
- Individuals and other entities, like charitable foundations, may deduct the amount of their donations to nonprofit hospitals and similar organizations from their own income tax payments.
- They can apply directly for grants from foundations and government agencies.
- In certain areas, they are able to utilize tax-exempt bond financing.
- They are exempt from federal, but not state, unemployment taxes.
- They qualify for preferential postal rates.
- As nonprofit entities, hospitals are free from the pressures and controls of shareholders.

While enjoying those benefits, tax-exempt hospitals began to face competition from large, profit-driven hospital systems. In response, to survive, the hospitals began to adopt some of the same hardnosed management principles. To make more money, they invested in new, more expensive service lines, implemented aggressive revenue cycle management, and turned patient debts over to merciless collection agencies. To some observers, regulators, and politicians, the hospitals seemed to stray from their charitable purposes.

The IRS revised the 990 form that all tax-exempt organizations use to report their income. It added a new Schedule H that required exempt hospitals to report the total amounts of charity care and community benefits they provide to their service areas. The scrutiny of tax-exempt hospitals was increased dramatically by the Patient Protection and Affordable Care Act.

That law, enacted in 2010, mandates the conduct every 3 years of a community needs assessment and formulation of an implementation strategy. Fines may be imposed for failure to do so.

It is in state courts that some of the most serious legal challenges to the tax-exempt status of hospitals have occurred. In a precedent-setting 2011 case, the Illinois State Supreme Court revoked the property tax exemption of the Provena Covenant Medical Center in Urbana, Illinois. The court pointed out that "a mere 302 of its [Provena's] 110,000 admissions received reductions in their bills based on charitable considerations." Other states are raising similar questions and considering legislation that would set stricter limits for the charity care that exempt hospitals must provide.

In a variety of cases, courts have found the following indications that a hospital does not deserve its tax-exempt status.

- Only a very small number of patients are provided free or discounted care.
- The dollar value of free care that is provided is minimal.
- Unpaid bills are immediately referred to collections.
- Uninsured patients are charged the healthcare entity's full rates.
- The healthcare entity fails to publicize its Medicare and Medicaid services and indigent patient policies.
- The healthcare entity fails to provide apparent benefits to the immediate community it serves.
- The healthcare entity does not allocate surplus revenue to research, education, and medical training.
- The healthcare entity does not promote health for the benefit of its community.

BASIC REQUIREMENTS FOR HOSPITAL TAX-EXEMPT STATUS

Through regulations, private rulings, and court decisions, the IRS has enunciated a series of well-established requirements that hospitals must satisfy in order to retain their tax-exempt status.

Community Benefit

The preeminent prerequisite for tax-exempt status of a hospital, or other healthcare organization, is that it serve a charitable purpose. The IRS and the courts have recognized that the promotion of health and the diagnosis and treatment of disease constitute a charitable purpose. However, over many years, the IRS also has expanded the charitable purpose requirement to encompass a so-called "community benefit standard." It is not enough for a hospital to deliver high-quality, cost-effective medical care. The surrounding community must benefit in some way from its operations.

The scope of the community benefit standard has evolved over the years. As the IRS and state tax agencies have increasingly used the standard as a litmus test for tax-exempt status, they have given it clear definition. These are the activities that the IRS looks for in determining whether a nonprofit organization has met its community benefit standard.

> *Community-oriented governing board.* The board of directors or trustees of the organization should be representative of the community that it serves. A majority of the directors ought to be independent leading members of the community—from major political, social, community, and business organizations. Hospital employees (high-level executives, medical staff physicians, unit managers) may serve on the board, but their numbers should not dominate. When properly constituted, the governing board should be subject to conflict of interest guidelines to prevent the possibility of private inurement, private benefit, or any other excess benefit.
>
> *Open staff privileges.* Any physician in the community should be permitted to join the hospital's medical staff in order to practice and admit patients there. Staff privileges may be limited by reasonable clinical requirements such as medical education, licensure, accreditation, care standards (professional, regulatory, specialty board), and hospital capacity. Physicians may not be excluded for competitive reasons or to protect the practice interests of other doctors.
>
> *Emergency medical care.* The hospital must maintain a full-time emergency department (ED) that offers care to all patients regardless of their ability to pay. This means that no one ever is denied care in the ED for any reason related to his or her wealth, income, or insurance coverage. The IRS also likes to see hospital arrangements with local fire, police, and ambulance services for emergency patient transportation. Section 501(r) of the health reform law requires that a hospital organization establish a written policy that requires it to provide, without discrimination, care for emergency medical conditions to individuals regardless of their eligibility under the hospital's financial assistance rules.
>
> *Nonemergency medical care.* The hospital needs to provide its normal, nonemergency medical services to anyone in the community who

needs them and is able to pay for them, whether out-of-pocket, or through public or private insurance. In fact, the IRS places great value on a hospital's participation in the Medicare and Medicaid programs as a sign of its commitment to community benefit.

Use of surplus funds. When a hospital takes in more revenues than the costs it incurs, the amount left over is not called profit, but "surplus funds." In the interests of community benefit, those funds should be spent to improve the quality of care, expand the hospital's facilities, develop medical education and training programs, or enhance medical research activities.

Charity care. A hospital can provide substantial benefit to the community it serves by offering charity care—free or income-adjusted care to those who qualify for it. Section 501(r) of the health reform law requires hospital organizations to establish a written financial assistance policy that includes eligibility criteria for financial assistance and whether such assistance includes free or discounted care, the basis for calculating amounts charged to patients, the method for applying for financial assistance, and measures to widely publicize the policy.

Health promotion. The hospital can enhance its community benefit profile by going beyond treatment of disease and offering a variety of other programs to evaluate and promote health. Some examples are medical education programs (cardiac information, pregnancy counseling), self-help seminars (fitness, nutrition, smoking cessation), health fairs (blood pressure and cholesterol testing), wellness programs, health screenings, and health risk assessments.

A hospital need not perform all these activities, but must do enough to show that it is acting consistently with its charitable purpose. After enactment of the 2010 health reform law, hospitals can no longer wait for the IRS to request evidence of the benefits it provides to its community. Now, they must conduct their own community health needs assessment (CHNA) no less than once every 3 years. The assessment must take into account input from persons who represent the broad interests of the community served by the hospital and must be made widely available to the public. The hospital must also develop and publicize an implementation strategy for meeting the community health needs identified in the assessment. The strategy might include participation in an area-wide, multiple-institution community benefit initiative, budget allocations for services to meet the needs identified, and prioritization of the health needs of the community.

Excess Benefit Transactions

One of the most obvious ways that a hospital can compromise its tax-exempt status is to engage in an excess benefit transaction (EBT). It does this by providing an economic benefit to a "disqualified person" without receiving something of equivalent fair market value in return. Such arrangements are prohibited because they distribute to private individuals funds that were intended for a charitable purpose. A common example is a nonprofit, tax-exempt healthcare organization paying compensation to its president that exceeds the value of his services to the organization, as well as the compensation paid to presidents of other comparable organizations. Other instances that have occurred are excessive payments for vendor contracts, providing discounted office space, and providing free or discounted billing services.

A critical factor in these transactions is the participation of a disqualified person. This term definitely includes a voting director of the tax-exempt organization; its president, CEO, COO, or CFO; major donors; family members of those individuals; plus anyone with more than a 35% ownership interest in an entity sponsored by the exempt organization. Under the right circumstances, others with substantial influence over the organization may be considered disqualified persons: department or facility managers, major sources of revenue (high-referring doctors), those with the authority to hire and fire staff, supervisors of employees, and physicians with exclusive hospital contracts.

When there is evidence of an EBT, the disqualified person who receives the benefit may have to pay an excise tax. The initial tax is equal to 25% of the excess benefit. If the EBT is not corrected within the current tax period–that is, if the excess amount has not been repaid with interest, an additional tax of 200% of the excess benefit amount is levied. Organization managers who knowingly approved of the transaction are jointly and severally liable for a tax of 10% of the excess amount.

The prohibition of EBTs might seem to prevent any compensation plan that offers incentives tied to a percentage of the organization's net earnings. In fact, the IRS does allow such arrangements as long as the person receiving the incentive is not a disqualified party, the total compensation does not exceed the fair market value (FMV) of the person's work, and the compensation package is fully and properly reported.

Unrelated Business Income

There is a temptation for some tax-exempt entities, who frequently are financially stressed, to pursue certain activities that are only remotely related to their charitable purpose yet generate a steady cash flow that supports that purpose. Think of the parking garages and gift shops operated by many hospitals. The IRS places tight restrictions on such activities. Any trade or business that is "regularly carried on" and is not substantially related to the performance of the entity's charitable purpose is deemed an "unrelated trade or business" and the income that it produces will be taxed at normal corporate rates.

New Transparency Requirements for Tax-Exempt Hospitals under PPACA

The Patient Protection and Affordable Care Act (PPACA), the 2010 health reform law, imposed substantial new requirements for transparency and accountability on tax-exempt hospitals. In order to maintain their tax-exempt status, the hospitals must perform these tasks.

- After consulting with the community it serves, each hospital facility must conduct a CHNA at least once every 3 years, and adopt a strategy to implement its findings. Hospitals that fail to conduct the assessment and report the strategy on Form 990 will be subject to an excise tax totaling $50,000. Schedule H of Form 990 describes other items that the hospital must now report to the IRS, including audited financial statements and evidence of the community benefit that it is providing.
- Each hospital must create a written *financial assistance policy* and a written *emergency care policy*. The financial assistance policy must list the eligibility criteria for financial assistance at the hospital, including whether that assistance includes free or discounted care. The policy must also explain the way patient charges are calculated, the application process for financial assistance, measures for publicizing the financial assistance policy to the community, and how the hospital deals with nonpaying patients. The emergency care policy—designed to prevent discrimination against patients ineligible for financial or government assistance—must require the hospital to provide care for emergency medical conditions without discrimination.
- Collection actions may not be initiated until the hospital has made reasonable efforts to determine whether the patient is eligible for financial assistance. Even then, it must avoid certain abusive billing and collection practices.
- Hospital charges for emergency or other medically necessary care for patients eligible for financial assistance are limited to the amounts

usually billed to insured patients. The charges may be either the best or an average of the three best negotiated commercial rates, or the rate the hospital receives from Medicare.

- Every 3 years, the hospital must subject itself to an IRS review of its "community benefit activities."

Each facility that fails to comply with these requirements is in danger of having its 501(c)(3) status revoked.

Physician Recruitment and Retention

A hospital must keep its charitable purpose uppermost when planning incentives for recruiting and retaining physicians. Physicians may be recruited either to join the hospital's medical staff or to fill gaps in the community's need for medical services in particular specialties. Examples of incentives offered to attract new physicians include: signing bonus, malpractice insurance for a limited period, office space for a limited number of years at below market rent, mortgage guarantee on the physician's home, financial practice start-up assistance, private-practice income guarantee for a limited number of years, and reimbursement of moving expenses. The IRS has explained what hospitals must do to offer physician recruitment incentives that do not threaten their tax-exempt status.

- Conduct a community needs assessment, and document the results. There must be a demonstrated community need for the new physician.
- Alternatively, rely on a designation by the Public Health Service of a local health professional shortage area (HPSA).
- Prepare a formal written physician recruitment policy.
- Negotiate each recruitment package at arm's length.
- Ensure that the financial incentives in the package are reasonable—that is, within appropriate salary ranges revealed in market surveys.
- Each recruitment package is approved by the hospital board of directors, or by a board-appointed individual using board guidelines.
- The recruitment incentives are incorporated into a written agreement and no other terms are offered outside the agreement.
- Ensure that the recruitment arrangements do not violate the Anti-Kickback Statute.

The acceptability of physician retention practices often turns on the flow of physicians in and out of the local market. Retention is more important when a lot of physicians are leaving the area.

Mergers and Acquisitions

A variety of market and legal forces compel many healthcare organizations, particularly hospitals, to consider new relationships with other similar or complementary organizations. The general pressures of increased market competition, the need to amass sufficient capital to deploy new systems and technologies, the Health Reform Act's emphasis on the creation of multiprovider accountable care organizations, and the clinical and cost benefits of integrating provider operations are leading to mergers, acquisitions, strategic partnerships, joint ventures, and clinical affiliations involving hospitals, health systems, academic medical centers, and physician group practices. Pursuing these options presents challenges for tax-exempt entities.

The most common problem is ensuring that these transactions are conducted at FMV. The IRS does not look favorably on a tax-exempt organization that has been receiving tax-deductible donations paying more than the market demands for another entity, facility, or property. Such a distortion is more likely to occur when the seller has influence over the buyer and the deal is not negotiated at arm's length. Imagine a powerful medical staff physician, who admits many patients to a hospital, selling his practice to the hospital and becoming its employee. The physician wants to receive the highest price for the practice; the hospital wants to retain the loyalty of the physician. The result is an artificially high sale price.

These merger and acquisition FMV problems can take several forms. A hospital may pay an inflated purchase price for physician practice assets. Another hospital may sell some of its major assets for substantially less than their FMV. The transaction may be based on outdated valuations. The parties may fail to include all relevant assets in the valuation.

Not only do such transactions threaten a hospital's tax-exempt status, they increase the risks of Anti-Kickback Statute and Stark Law liability. It is imperative that the hospital be able to demonstrate the FMV of the exchange.

This is easier when the transaction involves hard assets. There are statistics on current market prices for comparable transactions readily available. The valuation of intangible assets is more difficult. Experts can disagree on the true worth of a business's good will, intellectual property, or specialized knowhow. Nonetheless, a properly conducted professional valuation by an independent third party is the best evidence of FMV.

Over the last several years, a growing number of corporate acquisitions have involved a for-profit entity buying up a nonprofit entity, usually requiring the conversion of the acquired organization from nonprofit to for-profit status. Blue Cross plans have been a common subject of such transactions. State attorneys general often intervene in these transactions to ensure that the nonprofit's original charitable purposes are respected. The amount for which the nonprofit entity is sold must be FMV or higher, whether the entire business or just its assets are involved. The proceeds of the sale must be dedicated to a comparable charitable purpose. This usually takes the form of a donation to a foundation doing similar benevolent work, the creation and funding of an equivalent organization, or a direct transfer into the state treasury. It also is important that the executives who negotiate the sale and conversion do not receive excessive severance pay.

Joint Ventures

In addition to mergers and acquisitions, another strategic response to the rapidly evolving healthcare marketplace is the participation by a tax-exempt hospital in a joint venture with a non-tax-exempt entity (e.g., physician group, health plan, another hospital). Such ventures are possible as long as the hospital's charitable principles are protected. The IRS uses a two-part test to evaluate such joint ventures. The first part asks whether the venture serves the hospital's charitable purpose. The second part demands that the hospital not surrender control over a substantial portion of its own activities to its non-tax-exempt venture partner. The best way to demonstrate control is through the hospital's majority voting control of the governing body of the joint venture entity. The argument is even more convincing if the venture agreement mandates some other protective measures.

The income tax form completed by all tax-exempt organizations, Form 990, specifically asks each entity to follow a written policy that requires it to negotiate, in its transactions and arrangements with other venture participants, terms and safeguards designed to protect its tax-exempt status. The form's instructions offer the following four examples of safeguards:

1. Control over the venture sufficient to ensure that it furthers the exempt purpose of the organization.
2. Requirements that the venture gives priority to exempt purposes over maximizing profits for the other participants.
3. The venture does not engage in activities that would jeopardize the organization's exemption (such as political intervention or substantial lobbying for a section 501(c)(3) organization).
4. All contracts entered into with the organization are on terms that are at arm's length or more favorable to the organization.

Tax-Exempt Bond Financing

In many states, tax-exempt hospitals are able either to issue tax-exempt bonds themselves or participate in special financing structures that are authorized to issue the bonds. The attraction of such bonds is that the hospital can pay a lower interest rate (typically 2% lower) on them because the bondholders do not pay income tax when they receive the interest.

To qualify to issue these bonds, a hospital must maintain its tax-exempt status by paying attention to the several issues discussed previously. Beyond that, its primary concern is the use to which it puts the funds raised through the sale of the bonds. Those funds must be spent to advance the charitable purpose that earned it a tax-exempt status. They must be put to a "qualified use" and not a "private use." For a hospital, a private use problem can arise in several ways. Facilities or equipment financed by the bonds may be owned by or leased to an individual or entity that is not a qualified user, but is instead a private business. It is not a qualified use to offer a hospital's laboratory services or pharmacy products to the general public. There is a similar problem with parking lots and gift shops marketed to persons unaffiliated with the hospital.

Management and service contracts are a particular source of legal risk. A hospital agreement with a for-profit physician group to provide professional medical services with property financed with tax-exempt bonds constitutes a private use. The same is true when bond-financed facilities or equipment are utilized by a hospital's non-tax-exempt subsidiary clinic, an ambulatory surgery center or imaging center run by a physician–hospital joint venture, or under a contract with any private provider entity.

The IRS has defined six Safe Harbors for hospital management and service contracts related to bond-financed spaces. The primary criteria for all six Safe Harbors are similar. Contract compensation must be reasonable and not based on a share of net profits from operation of the facility. The relationship between the parties must not inhibit the qualified user's ability to exercise its termination rights under the contract. Depending on the compensation methodology, the contracts have maximum term limits.

There also are two Safe Harbors for avoiding private use in connection with research conducted in a hospital's bond-financed facilities.

Employment Taxes

If a worker is considered an "employee" of an organization, that organization must annually report compensation it has paid to the worker on Form W-2 and withhold several different taxes (income, social security, unemployment) from the worker's compensation. This obligation applies equally to for-profit taxable and nonprofit tax-exempt entities. However, there are some aspects of the employee distinction that are unique to hospitals.

A frequent issue is whether physicians working in a hospital setting are employees for the purpose of employment taxes. Typical examples are medical directors and clinic physicians. The IRS states that an employer–employee relationship exists when an entity "has the right to control and direct the individual who performs the services, not only as to the result to be accomplished by the work, but also as to the details and means by which that result is accomplished." It further provides a list of 20 factors that it uses to determine a worker's classification as an employee or not. The factor that is given the most weight is the division of work control between the employer organization and the individual.

In the case of physicians, this determination is complicated by the ethics of the medical profession and other legal constraints on where and how physicians can perform their services. The guidelines that the IRS gives to its auditors of hospitals describe eight factors that are unique to physicians:

1. Physician has no private practice.
2. Compensation is a fixed salary.
3. Hospital provides supplies and professional support staff.
4. Hospital submits the claims for the physician's services.
5. Physician's fees are divided with the hospital on a percentage basis.
6. Hospital regulates or controls the physician's activities.
7. Physician is on duty at the hospital during specified hours.
8. Hospital's name/logo is on physician's uniform

In other official documents, the IRS has emphasized the extent of the physician's integration with the hospital's operations, the regularity and continuity of the physician's work for the hospital, the hospital's authority to require compliance with its general policies (not clinical matters), and physician access to same rights and privileges as employees.

In a 2010 decision, the U.S. Supreme Court supported the IRS in its determination that medical residents are employees.

COMPLIANCE ACTIVITIES TO PROTECT TAX-EXEMPT STATUS

The law and underlying regulations are clear about what a hospital needs to do in order to maintain its tax-exempt status. There are two approaches that a hospital may take to ensure its compliance with those prerequisites. One is to fold its tax compliance activities into the overall program addressing fraud and abuse risks. This is one example from the Children's Hospital in New Orleans, LA: http://www.chnola.org/PageDisplay.asp?p1=6899. As a compliance plan, it is very broad but not very deep. Protection of tax-exempt status is thrown in with a diverse group of other compliance issues.

A second approach is to deal with exempt status compliance in a separate program. This might be justified by the fact that transactions involving tax issues do not arise as regularly as the fraud dangers inherent in the routine filing of claims for reimbursement. In some tax areas such as compensation for high-level employees, unrelated business activities, and joint ventures involving decision events that do not occur often, the following steps can be taken: identify high-risk areas, focus attention on them, use checklists to ensure that transactions and arrangements are within IRS-recommended legal parameters, and conduct annual compliance audits of existing arrangements.

Certain areas are more legally sensitive and demand a more rigorous compliance effort. A critical topic is the use of tax-exempt bond financing. Once issued, the bonds can lose their tax-exempt status if the hospital issuer does not make sure that the proceeds are spent, and the bond-financed facilities are used, in compliance with IRS requirements. The IRS has stated that hospitals can provide this assurance by doing several things.

- Designate officials to monitor and review compliance.
- Describe the training it gives those officials.
- State how often compliance reviews will be conducted (at least annually).
- Explain the compliance measures that it is taking.
- Explain its procedures for identifying and resolving suspected violations.
- Explain its policies and procedures for retention of records demonstrating its ongoing compliance.

A program like this needs to be in place before the bonds are issued.

STUDY QUESTIONS

1. The chapter lays out the benefits of qualifying for tax-exempt status. In your mind, how do those benefits compare with the advantages of being a for-profit organization? Think about sources of financing and types of government regulation. If you were creating an ambulatory surgery clinic, which organizational form would you choose?
2. Of the several requirements for hospital tax-exempt status, which one do you think would be the easiest to implement? Which would be most difficult?
3. What are some examples of "unrelated business" that a tax-exempt hospital might engage in to earn income for its healthcare operations?

4. What sorts of incentives might a hospital offer a physician to recruit him or her to its medical staff?
5. In what way should a tax-exempt hospital carry out the acquisition of another hospital to assure the IRS that it has paid FMV?
6. In what ways might a hospital jeopardize its tax-exempt status when it pays for a new capital project with tax-exempt bond financing?
7. Are physician members of a hospital medical staff also employees of the hospital?
8. List a minimum of five components of a compliance program designed to protect a hospital's tax-exempt status. (Not just its tax-exempt bond financing.)

Learning Exercises

1. Conduct some research on the community benefits offered by a local tax-exempt hospital. Review its website to see how it describes its community activities. Visit the hospital and talk with a representative, perhaps in the community relations office, about other ways that it is serving the community. Are you satisfied that it has met the IRS community benefit standard?
2. Do a little Internet research on the Provena Covenant Medical Center case in Illinois. Search on that name and "tax-exempt," and read the listings that come up. Look for more detail about the reasons that Provena lost its tax-exempt status. If you were the CEO of Provena and had a chance to make corrections before the status was revoked, exactly what steps would you take?
3. To avoid engaging in an EBT by paying an employee more than FMV for her services, where would an employer look to find the FMV for a particular job in its geographic area? Try to find such information for a hypothetical job at a hospital in your area.
4. In a couple paragraphs, describe what practical steps a hospital could take to perform the CHNA required by the health reform law.

References

1. Return of Organization Exempt From Income Tax, Form 990, IRS, 2011.
2. Instructions for Form 990 Return of Organization Exempt From Income Tax, IRS, 2011.

3. "Health Care Provider Reference Guide," Gitterman and Friedlander, Continuing Professional Education Technical Instruction Program, IRS, 2004.
4. "Primer On Tax Exemption and Tax Issues," Johnson and Moroney, from Tax Issues for Healthcare Organizations, AHLA, October 2–4, 2011.
5. "IRS Warning to Tax-Exempt Issuers and Borrowers: Implement Compliance Procedures Now," Client Alert, Hunton & Williams (law firm), November 2011.
6. "Section 501(r)—Some Guidance Is Now Available for Charitable Hospitals," Speizman, Moore and Mitchell, KPMG, 2011.
7. "Commercial Activity and Tax-Exempt Status for Healthcare Organizations," King and Blais, Tax Issues For Healthcare Organizations, AHLA, October 12–13, 2009.

Chapter 5

HIPAA and HITECH

Learning Objectives

After completing class sessions based on this chapter, a student will:

- Understand the detailed requirements of the Privacy and Security Rules under the Health Insurance Portability and Accountability Act of 1996 (HIPAA), and the differences between the two rules.
- Know what a covered entity and a business associate are and how they relate to each other.
- Recognize what types of use and disclosure of protected health information (PHI) are permitted and prohibited by HIPAA.
- Be familiar with individuals' rights to their own PHI.
- Learn about the Breach Notification Rule and how it applies to healthcare organizations.
- Be acquainted with the safeguards, standards, and specifications of the Security Rule and how they relate to each other.
- Discover the civil and criminal penalties that may result from HIPAA violations.

INTRODUCTION

It is a national strategic goal to promote the adoption and use of electronic medical records (EMRs) throughout the healthcare system. The Centers for Medicare and Medicaid Services (CMS) has embarked upon a multiyear program of financial incentives to encourage the "meaningful use" of EMRs by hospitals and physicians. The United States is slowly moving toward the universal deployment of EMRs, computerized physician order entry (CPOE), health information exchanges (HIEs), and other forms of health information technology already achieved in other developed countries.

New technologies are constantly emerging. The healthcare industry is relying more and more on electronic information systems to pay claims, answer eligibility questions, provide health information, and conduct a host of other administrative and clinically based functions. This means that healthcare workers can be more mobile and efficient, while patients can be better informed and more involved in their own health care. This widespread dispersal of sensitive, personal healthcare information among multiple organizations, facilities, and personnel presents serious risks to security and privacy.

The HIPAA of 1996 was enacted to protect against these threats. The scope of HIPAA was modestly expanded by provisions of the Health Information Technology for Economic and Clinical Health (HITECH) Act, passed into law in 2009.

Under HIPAA's authority, the Department of Health and Human Services (DHHS) issued regulations that established national Standards for Privacy of Individually Identifiable Health Information (the Privacy Rule) and Security Standards for the Protection of Electronic Protected Health Information (the Security Rule).

WHO IS COVERED BY HIPAA

The Privacy and Security Rules apply to what are called "covered entities" and to the "business associates" of those entities. Covered entities encompass three categories of organizations and individuals.

Healthcare Providers

Every healthcare provider, regardless of size, that electronically transmits health information in connection with certain transactions, is a covered entity. These transactions include claims, benefit eligibility inquiries, referral authorization requests, or other transactions for which DHHS has established standards under the HIPAA Transactions Rule. Using electronic technology, such as email, does not mean a healthcare provider is a covered entity; the transmission must be in connection with a standard transaction.

The Privacy Rule covers a healthcare provider whether it electronically transmits these transactions directly or uses a billing service or other third party to do so on its behalf. Healthcare providers include all "providers of services" (e.g., institutional providers such as hospitals) and "providers of medical or health services" (e.g., noninstitutional providers such as physicians, dentists, and other practitioners) as defined by Medicare, and any other person or organization that furnishes, bills, or is paid for health care.

Health Plans

Individual and group plans that provide or pay the cost of medical care are covered entities. This includes health, dental, vision, and prescription drug insurers; health maintenance organizations (HMOs); Medicare, Medicaid, and Medicare Advantage and Medicare supplement insurers; and long-term care insurers. Health plans also include employer-sponsored group health plans, government and church-sponsored health plans, and multi-employer health plans.

Healthcare Clearinghouses

The healthcare system relies on organizations that process health information received from a client in a nonstandard format into a standard format, or from a standard format into a nonstandard format. The entities that perform these services are billing services, repricing companies, community health management information systems, and value-added networks and switches. Their clients typically are health plans and healthcare providers.

All these entities must comply with the Rules to protect the privacy and security of health information and provide individuals with certain rights with respect to their health information. If an entity is not a covered entity, it does not have to comply with the Privacy Rule or the Security Rule.

The term "business associate" applies to a person or organization (other than a covered entity's own employees) who does work or provides services for a covered entity that involves the use or disclosure of individually identifiable health information. Examples of business associate services are claims processing, data analysis, utilization review, and billing. Persons or organizations are not considered business associates if their functions or services do not involve the use or disclosure of PHI, and where any access to PHI by such persons would be incidental, if at all.

When a covered entity uses an independent contractor or other non-employee to perform "business associate" services or activities, the Rules require that the entity enter into a formal contract with the associate that includes specific information safeguards. The contract may not authorize the business associate to make any use or disclosure of PHI that would violate the Rules.

A covered entity violates the Security Rule if it knows of a pattern of activity or practice of its business associate that constitutes a material breach or violation of the business associate's obligations under the business associate contract, unless the covered entity takes reasonable steps to cure the breach or end the violation. If such steps are unsuccessful, the covered entity must terminate the contract.

The HIPAA Privacy and Security rules, as well as the civil monetary and criminal penalties, apply directly to business associates. These obligations and risks make it essential that covered entities and their business associates enter into a close dialogue with each other about their compliance efforts. It would be very easy for the inadvertent actions of one to create serious legal liabilities for the other.

HIPAA PRIVACY RULE

The purpose of the Privacy Rule is to ensure that the personal health information of individuals, referred to as PHI, is properly protected, while still allowing the flow of health information that is vital to the delivery of quality health care and the protection of the public's well-being. The Rule aims to strike a balance between the essential systemic uses of that information and the privacy of the people served by the healthcare system.

The Privacy Rule standards address the use and disclosure of PHI by covered entities, as well as the rights of patients to understand and control how their health information is used. Within the DHHS, the responsibility for implementing and enforcing the Privacy Rule has been delegated to the Office for Civil Rights (OCR).

WHAT INFORMATION IS PROTECTED BY THE PRIVACY RULE

The Privacy Rule protects all "individually identifiable health information" held or transmitted by a covered entity or its business associate, in any form or media, whether electronic, paper, or oral. The Privacy Rule calls this information PHI. This is information that concerns an individual's past, present, or future physical or mental health or condition; the provision of healthcare services to the individual; and the past, present, or future payment for those services—and that identifies the individual. Typical identification data points are name, address, birth date, and Social Security number.

There are no restrictions on the use or disclosure of de-identified information—information that neither identifies nor provides a reasonable basis for identifying an individual.

WHAT THE PRIVACY RULE PROHIBITS

The fundamental purpose of the Privacy Rule is to define and limit the circumstances in which an individual's PHI may be used or disclosed by a covered entity or its business associates. A covered entity may use or disclose PHI only when the Privacy Rule requires or permits it, or when the affected individual has given his or her written authorization.

REQUIRED DISCLOSURE OF PHI

There are only two situations in which a covered entity must disclose PHI. The first is when the affected individual specifically requests access to or disclosure of his or her PHI. The second is when the DHHS seeks access in the course of a compliance investigation or review, or an enforcement action.

PERMITTED DISCLOSURE OF PHI

There are six situations in which a covered entity may, but is not required to, use or disclose PHI without the affected individual's authorization.

1. When it discloses PHI to the individual who is the subject of the information.
2. For use in the entity's own treatment, payment, and healthcare operations activities.

    Treatment is the provision, coordination, or management of health care and related services for an individual by one or more healthcare providers, including consultation between providers regarding a patient and referral of a patient by one provider to another.

    Payment encompasses activities of a health plan to obtain premiums, determine or fulfill responsibilities for coverage and provision of benefits, and furnish or obtain reimbursement for healthcare delivered to an individual as well as activities of a healthcare provider to obtain payment or be reimbursed for the provision of health care to an individual.

    Healthcare operations are any of the following activities: (a) quality assessment and improvement activities, including case management and care coordination; (b) competency assurance activities, including provider or health plan performance evaluation, credentialing, and accreditation; (c) conducting or arranging for medical reviews, audits, or legal services, including fraud and abuse detection and compliance programs; (d) specified insurance functions, such as underwriting, risk rating, and reinsuring risk; (e) business planning, development, management, and administration; and (f) business management and general administrative activities of the entity, including but not limited to, de-identifying PHI, creating a limited data set, and certain fundraising for the benefit of the covered entity.

3. When the affected individual has the opportunity to agree with or object to the disclosure.

   Informal permission may be obtained by asking the individual outright, or by circumstances that clearly give the individual the opportunity to agree, acquiesce, or object. Where the individual is incapacitated, in an emergency situation, or not available, covered entities generally may make such uses and disclosures if, in the exercise of their professional judgment, the use or disclosure is determined to be in the best interests of the individual.

4. When the use or disclosure is incidental to an otherwise permitted use or disclosure, the entity has reasonable privacy safeguards in place, and the disclosed information is the "minimum necessary."
5. When the use or disclosure is on the list of "national priority purposes." These include legally required (by statute, regulation, or court order) public health activities; situations involving victims of abuse, neglect, or domestic violence; health oversight activities (audits and investigations); judicial and administrative proceedings; certain law enforcement purposes; decedents; organ donations; research; serious threats to individual or public health and safety; essential government functions; and workers' compensation.
6. When it is in the form of a "limited data set" from which specified direct identifiers of individuals and their relatives, household members, and employers have been removed.

AUTHORIZATION ALLOWING USE OR DISCLOSURE

If the Privacy Rule does not require or permit use or disclosure of PHI, the authorization of the affected individual must be obtained. An authorization must be written in plain language, and contain specific information regarding the PHI to be disclosed or used, the persons who will disclose or use the PHI, the expiration date of the authorization, and the individual's right to revoke it in writing, among other terms. The authorization may extend to the covered entity or one of its agents. Typically, an authorization would be necessary for disclosures to a life insurer for coverage purposes, disclosures to an employer of the results of a pre-employment physical or lab test, or disclosures to a pharmaceutical firm for their own marketing purposes.

BASIC "MINIMUM NECESSARY" PRINCIPLE OF THE PRIVACY RULE

The Privacy Rule applies a single basic principle to the use and disclosure of PHI, whether it is required, permitted, or authorized: the covered entity must make reasonable efforts to use, disclose, and request only the minimum amount of PHI needed to accomplish its intended purpose. The entity must develop and implement policies and procedures to reasonably limit the uses and disclosures to the *minimum necessary*. These are some examples.

- Access and usage should be limited on the basis of the specific roles of each employee. Policies and procedures should identify the persons, or classes of persons, in the workforce who need access to PHI to perform their duties, the categories of PHI to which access is needed, and any conditions under which that access should be allowed.
- There should be formal limits on access allowed through routine, recurring disclosures, or requests for disclosures. In these circumstances, individual review of each disclosure would not be necessary.
- A covered entity may assume that a PHI request is for the "minimum necessary" when it comes from another covered entity, a public official, a professional (lawyer, accountant) who is a business associate of the covered entity, or an authenticated researcher.

NOTICE OF PRIVACY PRACTICES

Each covered entity, with certain exceptions, must provide a notice of its privacy practices. The notice must contain several elements: a description of the ways in which the entity may use or disclose the PHI, the entity's duties to protect privacy, the privacy rights of individuals, and a contact for seeking more information and making complaints. The Privacy Rule specifies how a covered entity must distribute this notice to direct treatment providers, other healthcare providers, and health plans. This is a sample Notice of Privacy Practices offered by the American Medical Association: http://www.ama-assn.org/resources/doc/hipaa/privacy-practices.doc.

INDIVIDUALS' RIGHTS TO THEIR PHI

Individuals have rights with regard to their PHI.

With a few exceptions, individuals have the right to review and obtain a copy of their PHI. They have the right to request that a covered entity amend their PHI when they believe it to be inaccurate or incomplete. If the request is denied, covered entities must put the denial in writing and allow the individual to submit a statement of disagreement for inclusion in the record. Individuals have a right to an accounting of the disclosures of their PHI by a covered entity or its business associates.

Individuals have the right to request that a covered entity restrict its use or disclosure of PHI to the following: for treatment, payment, or healthcare operations; to persons involved in the individual's health care or payment for health care; or to family members or others entitled to information about the individual's general condition, location, or death. A covered entity is under no obligation to agree to requests for restrictions.

Individuals have the right to request that they receive communications of PHI by different means than those normally used by the covered entity. For instance, an individual may request that a provider communicate with the individual at a designated address or phone number.

COVERED ENTITIES' IMPLEMENTATION OF THE PRIVACY RULE

Every covered entity must take concrete measures to satisfy the requirements of the Privacy Rule. The scope and detail of those measures will vary according to the nature of the entity's business and its size and resources. The most fundamental step is the development and implementation of appropriate privacy policies and procedures. The covered entity must designate a privacy official to be responsible for overseeing the policies and procedures, for disseminating privacy information, and for receiving complaints.

A covered entity must train all its employees on the privacy policies and procedures that bear on the performance of their job functions. It also must institute and apply appropriate sanctions against employees who violate its privacy policies and procedures or the Privacy Rule.

A covered entity must mitigate, to the extent practicable, the harmful effects that may have been caused by the use or disclosure of PHI by its employees or business associates in violation of its privacy policies and procedures or the Privacy Rule.

A covered entity must maintain reasonable and appropriate administrative, technical, and physical safeguards to prevent intentional or unintentional use or disclosure of PHI in violation of the Privacy Rule. The Security Rule provides greater detail about these safeguards.

A covered entity must have in place procedures for individuals to complain about its compliance with its privacy policies and procedures and with the Privacy Rule. It must explain those procedures in its privacy practices notice, and identify the person to whom individuals can submit their complaints.

A covered entity may not retaliate against a person for exercising rights provided by the Privacy Rule, or for opposing an act or practice that the person believes in good faith violates the Privacy Rule.

A covered entity must maintain, for 6 years after the date of their creation or their last effective date, whichever is later, its privacy policies and procedures, its privacy practices notices, the disposition of complaints, and other actions, activities, and designations that the Privacy Rule requires to be documented.

BREACH NOTIFICATION

In 2009, the HITECH Act added what is called the Breach Notification Rule. This rule requires that covered entities and their business associates provide notification following a breach of unsecured PHI. Similar breach notification provisions are implemented and enforced by the Federal Trade Commission against vendors of personal health records and their third-party service providers.

A breach is defined as an impermissible use or disclosure under the Privacy Rule that compromises the security or privacy of the PHI to the extent that it poses a significant risk of financial, reputational, or other harm to the affected individual. There are three exceptions to the definition of "breach."

1. The unintentional acquisition, access, or use of PHI by an employee of a covered entity or business associate.
2. The inadvertent disclosure of PHI from a person authorized to access PHI at a covered entity or business associate to another person authorized to access PHI at the covered entity or business associate.
3. A covered entity or business associate has a good faith belief that the unauthorized individual, to whom the impermissible disclosure was made, would not have been able to retain the information.

Covered entities and business associates need only provide notification if the breach involved unsecured PHI. Unsecured PHI is health information that has not been rendered unusable, unreadable, or indecipherable to unauthorized individuals through the use of a technology or methodology such as encryption or destruction.

Following a breach of unsecured PHI, covered entities must provide notification of the breach to affected individuals, the DHHS, and, in certain circumstances, to the media. In addition, business associates must notify covered entities when a breach has occurred.

> *Individual notice.* Covered entities must notify affected individuals within 60 days following the discovery of a breach of unsecured PHI. Covered entities must provide this individual notice in written form by first-class mail, or alternatively, by email if the affected individual has agreed to receive such notices electronically. If the covered entity has insufficient or out-of-date contact information for 10 or more individuals, the covered entity must provide substitute individual notice by either posting the notice on the home page of its website or by providing the notice in major print or broadcast media where the affected individuals likely reside.
>
> *Media notice.* Covered entities that experience a breach affecting more than 500 residents of a single state are, in addition to notifying the affected individuals, required to provide notice to prominent media outlets serving the state.
>
> *DHHS notice.* In addition to notifying affected individuals and the media, covered entities must notify the DHHS of breaches of unsecured PHI. They will do this by visiting the DHHS website and electronically submitting a breach report form. To see how this can be done, visit this location: http://ocrnotifications.hhs.gov/.

To review the steps in deciding whether a breach notification is necessary as the following questions:

1. Was the incident a breach?
2. Did the incident fit one of the three exceptions to the definition of a breach?
3. Does the breach require notification?
4. Was the breach unauthorized?
5. Was the PHI that was accessed or disclosed unsecure?
6. Has the breach resulted in financial, reputational, or other harm to the affected individual?

Then, the affected individual must be notified.

These are examples of breaches that would require notification:

- Fax with unsecure PHI sent to the wrong number
- Lost laptop with unsecure PHI
- Lost flash drive with unsecure PHI

- Email with unsecure PHI sent to wrong address
- Intentional access to more PHI than permitted under HIPAA exception
- Access to personal medical record without good reason
- Sharing PHI with persons outside the organization who have no need to see it
- Sending PHI to an outside entity with no business associate agreement

HIPAA SECURITY RULE

The Security Rule is the other half of HIPAA. It applies to the same organizations as the Privacy Rule: covered entities, business associates, and subcontractors. However, this rule deals only with the security of electronic protected health information (E-PHI). This is in contrast with the Privacy Rule, which applies to all forms of PHI—electronic, written, or oral. The Security Rule does not apply to PHI transmitted orally or in writing.

Most healthcare organizations manage and transmit large volumes of electronic information other than E-PHI (e.g., financial, personnel, nonclinical operations). They are not required to implement the provisions of the Security Rule with regard to those kinds of information. However, many organizations find it easier to put the Rule into practice throughout their electronic systems, covering all forms of electronic information.

The requirements of the Security Rule are rationally organized. There are three broad categories of "safeguards"—administrative, physical, and technical. Within each category, there are "standards" that must be followed. For most of the standards, there are one or more "specifications" that offer more detail on how to implement the standard. Where there is no specification, the standard itself is deemed to provide enough guidance on implementation. Most of the specifications are "required"; a few are designated "addressable." The addressable specifications may be implemented as written or through closely restricted alternative means.

Due to the nature of computer systems, both hardware and software, security can be achieved through a variety of means. It is impossible to prescribe a single universal approach that all healthcare organizations could use. Accordingly, the HIPAA regulations allow some flexibility to those organizations in carrying out the Security Rule requirements. In deciding how much leeway they have, the organizations may take into account:

- The size, complexity, and capabilities of the organization
- Its technical infrastructure, hardware, and software security capabilities

- The costs to the organization of possible security measures
- The probability and criticality of potential risks to E-PHI

In addition, when they are making decisions about exactly how they will implement security measures, covered entities should keep in mind the end goals of the Security Rule.

- Ensure the confidentiality, integrity, and availability of all E-PHI that the covered entity creates, receives, maintains, or transmits.
- Protect against any reasonably anticipated threats or hazards to the security or integrity of the entity's E-PHI.
- Protect against any reasonably anticipated uses or disclosures of such information that are not permitted or required under the Privacy Rule.
- Ensure compliance with the Security Rule by the covered entity's employees.

SAFEGUARDS, STANDARDS, AND SPECIFICATIONS

The DHHS recommends that covered entities carry out a risk analysis to determine which security measures are reasonable and appropriate for their particular organization. In addition, they should conduct ongoing reviews to track access to E-PHI, recognize security incidents, evaluate the effectiveness of existing security measures, and reassess potential risks to E-PHI security. A good risk analysis procedure includes:

- Identifying the areas of highest risk to E-PHI security.
- Evaluating the likelihood and impact of those risks.
- Implementing appropriate security measures to address the risks identified.
- Documenting the chosen security measures and the rationale for adopting them.

With a better understanding of where its greatest security risks lie, a covered entity can proceed to develop and implement standards and specifications designed to address them.

In the modern world of healthcare delivery and financing, the protection of information privacy and security inevitably involves highly sophisticated technology systems. To be able to competently implement the following standards, it is important to have a good understanding of how those systems function. A Compliance Officer responsible for ensuring an organization's conformity with a wide variety of federal and state laws, as well as payor program requirements, may not have the time to acquire that understanding. He or she will rely on technology specialists, perhaps the organization's IT staff or outside experts. The section that follows is an overview of the individual security measures mandated by HIPAA.

ADMINISTRATIVE SAFEGUARDS

The administrative safeguards are concerned with the institutional structures that ensure the security and integrity of E-PHI.

Security Management Process Standard. A covered entity must identify and analyze potential risks to E-PHI, and implement security measures that reduce risks and vulnerabilities to a reasonable and appropriate level. It accomplishes this through these four specifications.

The required *Risk Analysis* and *Risk Management* specifications were described earlier in the chapter. Risk management is the program that a covered entity follows to minimize the risks identified by the risk analysis. The entity must institute a *Sanction Policy* that applies appropriate sanctions against workforce members who fail to comply with its security policies and procedures. Under the *Information System Activity Review* specification, a covered entity is required to implement procedures to regularly review records of information system activity, such as audit logs, access reports, and security incident tracking reports.

Assigned Security Responsibility Standard. A covered entity must designate a security official who is responsible for developing and implementing its security policies and procedures. Beyond this statement, there is no implementation specification.

Workforce Security Standard. Covered entities must ensure that all their employees have appropriate access to E-PHI and that employees who lack access authorization are not able to gain access to E-PHI. They can do this by implementing three specifications.

The entities must implement *Authorization and Supervision* of employees who work with E-PHI. They also must institute a *Workforce Clearance Procedure* that ensures that employees working with E-PHI have appropriate access. Finally, there must be a *Termination Procedure* that cuts off E-PHI access when an employee leaves the organization.

Information Access Management Standard. Consistent with the Privacy Rule limit on uses and disclosures of PHI to the "minimum necessary," the Security Rule requires a covered entity to implement policies and procedures for authorizing access to E-PHI only when it is appropriate to the user's job duties. This is accomplished through three specifications.

> If the covered entity is a healthcare clearinghouse that is part of a larger organization, it must install policies and procedures to *Isolate the E-PHI of the Clearinghouse* from the rest of the organization. The entity should implement policies and procedures for *Authorizing Access* to E-PHI. This should be complemented by *Access Establishment and Modification* policies and procedures that establish, document, review, and modify a user's right of access.

Security Awareness and Training Standard. This standard requires that covered entities implement a security and awareness training program for all its employees, including management. There are four implementation specifications.

> A covered entity should regularly issue *Security Reminders* of its security policies and procedures. It should implement measures that provide *Protection from Malicious Software*. There should be procedures in effect for *Monitoring Log-In Attempts* and reporting discrepancies. The entity also should maintain procedures for *Password Management*, creating, changing, and safeguarding them.

Security Incident Procedures Standard. This crucial standard asks covered entities to implement policies and procedures to address "security incidents," which are defined as "the attempted or successful unauthorized access, use, disclosure, modification, or destruction of information or interference with system operations in an information system." The single implementation specification under this standard requires that the entities *Identify and Respond* to the incidents, take action to mitigate their harmful effects, and document the final outcomes.

Contingency Plan Standard. Here, covered entities must establish policies and procedures for dealing with an emergency or other occurrence (fire, vandalism, system failure, or natural disaster) that could damage systems that contain E-PHI. There are five implementation specifications that contribute to this goal.

A covered entity must implement procedures to:

1. Create and maintain retrievable exact copies of E-PHI (*Data Backup Plan*).
2. Restore any loss of data (*Disaster Recovery Plan*).
3. Enable continuation of critical business processes for protecting E-PHI security during an emergency (*Emergency Mode Operation Plan*).

4. Periodically test and revise contingency plans (*Testing and Revision Procedure*).
5. Assess the relative criticality of specific applications and data in support of the other contingency plan elements (*Applications and Data Criticality Analysis*).

Evaluation Standard. This standard calls upon covered entities to perform a periodic assessment of how well their security policies and procedures meet the requirements of the Security Rule.

PHYSICAL SAFEGUARDS

Facility Access Controls Standard. A covered entity must limit physical access to its electronic information systems and the facilities where they are located, while also ensuring that authorized access is allowed. It will accomplish this by means of four specifications.

In conjunction with the *Contingency Plan Standard* (administrative safeguards), covered entities must develop a procedure to allow *Facility Access* in support of restoration of lost data under the disaster recovery plan and emergency mode operations plan in the event of an emergency. They also must create a *Facility Security Plan* that safeguards the facility and the equipment inside from unauthorized physical access, tampering, or theft. The law requires that covered entities implement *Access Control and Validation Procedures* that manage employee access to facilities based on their work responsibilities. This includes access to software programs and control of visitors to the premises. The entities have an obligation to document repairs and modifications to the security-related components of their facilities (*Maintenance Records*).

Workstation Use Standard. This standard deals with the functions to be performed at E-PHI accessible workstations, the manner in which the functions will be performed, and the physical surroundings of each type of workstation. There is no implementation specification for this standard.

Workstation Security Standard. Under this standard, covered entities must implement physical safeguards for all E-PHI accessible workstations to restrict access to authorized users. There is no further specification for this standard.

Device and Media Controls Standard. Each covered entity must put into place policies and procedures that govern the movement of hardware and electronic media containing E-PHI into and out of a facility, and within the facility. There are four implementation specifications to guide this effort.

The entity must create policies and procedures that address:

1. The final disposition of E-PHI and the media on which it is stored (*Disposal*).
2. The removal of E-PHI from electronic media before they are reused (*Media Reuse*).
3. The maintenance of a record of the movements of hardware and electronic media (*Accountability*).
4. The creation of a retrievable, exact copy of E-PHI before equipment is moved (*Data Backup and Storage*).

TECHNICAL SAFEGUARDS

Access Control Standard. The purpose of this standard is to allow access to E-PHI systems only to those persons or computer applications that have been granted access rights under the *Information Access Management Standard.* Four specifications have been defined for accomplishing this.

First, the covered entity must assign a unique name or number for identifying and tracking user identity. Second, it must establish procedures for obtaining needed E-PHI during an emergency. Third, it must set up procedures that terminate a computer session after a specified period of inactivity. Fourth, the entity must implement a mechanism to encrypt and decrypt E-PHI.

Audit Controls Standard. This standard requires that covered entities implement hardware, software, or procedural mechanisms that record and examine activity in computer systems that contain E-PHI. No implementation specification is provided.

Integrity Controls Standard. The goal of this standard is to protect E-PHI from improper alteration or destruction. Each covered entity is asked to implement *Electronic Mechanisms to Confirm* that no E-PHI has been altered or destroyed in an unauthorized manner.

Person or Entity Authentication Standard. Covered entities must institute measures to verify that a person or entity seeking access to their E-PHI are who they claim to be. There is no implementation specification here.

Transmission Security Standard. The function of this standard is to guard against unauthorized access to E-PHI that is being transmitted over an electronic network. There are two specifications.

One requires *Integrity Controls* to ensure that the E-PHI is not improperly modified without detection before it is discarded. The other calls for *Encryption* of E-PHI whenever it is appropriate.

ENFORCEMENT OF THE PRIVACY RULE

The HIPAA states that the DHHS will seek the cooperation of covered entities in complying voluntarily with the Privacy Rule. Failing that, the OCR within DHHS will enforce the Rule through civil monetary and criminal penalties. All these penalties can also be imposed on business associates.

Civil monetary penalties. The DHHS may impose civil monetary penalties (CMP) on a covered entity of at least $100 per failure to comply with a HIPAA requirement. There are four tiers of penalties reflecting increasing levels of culpability. They work like this.

1. Violations that the covered entity did not know about and could not have known about with "reasonable diligence." Each violation: $100-$50,000
2. Violations for which there was "reasonable cause" but no "willful neglect." Each violation: $1,000-$50,000
3. Violations caused by willful neglect that are corrected within 30 days. Each violation: $10,000-$50,000
4. Violations caused by willful neglect that are not corrected within 30 days. Each violation: $50,000-$50,000

At all four levels, the maximum total penalties imposed for identical violations during a single calendar year is $1,500,000.

Reasonable diligence is defined as "the business care and prudence expected from a person seeking to satisfy a legal requirement under similar circumstances." *Reasonable cause* is defined as "circumstances that make it unreasonable for the covered entity, despite the exercise of ordinary business care and prudence, to comply with the administrative simplification provision violated." *Willful neglect* is defined as the "conscious, intentional failure or reckless indifference to the obligation to comply with the administrative simplification provision violated."

The new CMPs are in addition to and not in lieu of any fines and penalties that a state might impose. State Attorneys General are also empowered to bring civil actions under HIPAA.

Criminal penalties. A person who knowingly obtains or discloses individually identifiable health information in violation of HIPAA faces a fine of $50,000 and up to 1 year of imprisonment. The criminal penalties increase to $100,000 and up to 5 years imprisonment if the wrongful conduct involves false pretenses, and to $250,000 and up to 10 years imprisonment if the wrongful conduct involves the intent to sell, transfer, or use individually identifiable health information for commercial advantage, personal gain, or malicious harm.

The HITECH Act requires DHHS to carry out periodic audits to ensure covered entities and business associates are complying with the HIPAA Privacy and Security Rules and Breach Notification standards. Beginning in November 2011 and concluding in December 2012, the OCR conducted a pilot program that performed 115 audits of covered entities to assess their privacy and security compliance.

CASE EXAMPLES OF HIPAA ENFORCEMENT

In September 2012, the *Massachusetts Eye and Ear Infirmary* agreed to pay the DHHS $1.5 million to settle potential violations of the HIPAA Privacy and Security Rules. The Infirmary has also agreed to take corrective action to improve policies and procedures to safeguard the privacy and security of their patients' PHI and retain an independent monitor to report on its compliance efforts. The OCR conducted an investigation following a breach report submitted by the Infirmary, as required by the HIPAA Breach Notification Rule, reporting the theft of an unencrypted personal laptop containing the E-PHI of patients and research subjects. The information included patient prescriptions and clinical information. The investigation showed that while management was aware of the Security Rule, the Infirmary failed to take necessary steps to comply with the Rule's requirements, such as conducting a thorough analysis of the risk to the confidentiality of E-PHI maintained on portable devices; implementing security measures sufficient to ensure the confidentiality of E-PHI that was created, maintained, and transmitted using portable devices; adopting and implementing policies and procedures to restrict access to E-PHI to authorized users of portable devices; and adopting and implementing policies and procedures to address security incident identification, reporting, and response.

In April 2012, *Phoenix Cardiac Surgery* agreed to pay DHHS a $100,000 settlement amount and implement a corrective action plan that includes a review of recently developed policies and other actions taken to come into full compliance with the Privacy and Security Rules. OCR's investigation found that the physician practice was posting clinical and surgical appointments for their patients on an Internet-based calendar that was publicly accessible. In addition, Phoenix Cardiac Surgery had implemented few policies and procedures to comply with the HIPAA Privacy and Security Rules, and had limited safeguards in place to protect patients' E-PHI.

INCORPORATING HIPAA/HITECH COMPLIANCE INTO THE OVERALL ORGANIZATIONAL COMPLIANCE PROGRAM

Compliance with HIPAA and HITECH requirements is a different matter than complying with laws like the False Claims Act and the Anti-Kickback Statute. HIPAA violations rarely are intentional or lead to overpayments and distortions in the healthcare system. Computer systems and electronic data transmission are pervasive features throughout healthcare delivery and financing. Their role will only grow in the future. Nonetheless, there are serious legal implications for ignoring HIPAA.

There are two general ways to approach HIPAA compliance. Because of its technological complexity, some organizations, usually larger entities with more resources, may prefer to create HIPAA compliance programs separate from the traditional fraud and abuse compliance activities they already conduct. On the other hand, it may make more sense for smaller, less well-endowed organizations, like physician practices or billing companies, to combine the two. In that second case, it will be necessary to hire or contract with someone with the necessary computer expertise.

The HIPAA and HITECH laws and regulations provide far more detail about how covered entities must manage their electronic data systems and the PHI that they use and transmit. Some of the standards and specifications overlap each other. The DHHS has shown flexibility in what it will accept as satisfactory compliance by healthcare organizations. In one form or another, every covered entity must carry out these steps.

- Designate a HIPAA compliance or patient privacy official.
- Write and put into practice the numerous policies and procedures called for in the standards and specifications.
- Train all members of the workforce on the HIPAA privacy requirements.
- Develop and apply sanctions to employees for violations of the privacy policies and procedures.
- Communicate with patients about their privacy rights and how to complain about privacy violations.
- Maintain a record of all actions, activities, and assessments that are required to be documented by the Security Rule.

There is a multipage explanation of an excellent HIPAA compliance program at the website of the University of Texas at San Antonio: http://www.uthscsa.edu/hipaa/.

STUDY QUESTIONS

1. What is the difference between the Privacy Rule and the Security Rule? How does each support and interact with the other?
2. Why is the HIPAA Security Rule needed and what is the purpose of the security standards?
3. Why is the HIPAA Privacy Rule needed?
4. When can a healthcare organization use or disclose a patient's PHI without the patient's permission?
5. Explain the "minimum necessary" rule of PHI use and disclosure.
6. When you are a patient in a hospital, what are your rights regarding the information that the hospital collects about you?
7. Explain in detail the "breach" to which the Breach Notification Rule applies.
8. After you have read through the Security Rule standards in all three safeguard categories, which of them do you understand well enough to implement (through policies and procedures) on your own? For which of them would you need some expert assistance?
9. List 10 types of organizations that are considered to be "covered entities" by HIPAA. What is a "healthcare clearinghouse"?

Learning Exercises

1. Choose one of these three standards (Security Incident Procedures, Workforce Security, Facility Access Controls) and prepare a 1-page written procedure that implements it.
2. Watch news reports closely and notice the next time that a breach of PHI is announced. They happen with surprising frequency. Read all you can about the incident and the organization where it happened. Get an idea of what led to the breach. What appears to have gone wrong? How could the incident have been prevented?
3. Describe five steps that a physician practice should take after it discovers that one of its staff has accessed the PHI of a local celebrity being treated by the practice and shared it with some of his or her friends.

4. Draw up a form that patients would be required to sign authorizing a covered entity to share their PHI with a research project being conducted within the entity.
5. In the course of enforcing HIPAA, the OCR has answered many questions raised by covered entities, business associates, patients, and others affected by the law. You can go to this webpage and, by entering a few keywords, gain access to the answers provided to questions about most aspects of the HIPAA law and regulations: http://www.hhs.gov/ocr/privacy/hipaa/faq/index.html.

References

1. Summary of the HIPAA Security Rule, DHHS, http://www.hhs.gov/ocr/privacy/hipaa/understanding/srsummary.html
2. Summary of the HIPAA Privacy Rule, DHHS, http://www.hhs.gov/ocr/privacy/hipaa/understanding/summary/index.html
3. Summary of the HIPAA Privacy Rule, OCR Privacy Brief, Department of Health and Human Services, Office for Civil Rights, May 2003.
4. HIPAA Administrative Simplification Statute and Rules, OCR, http://www.hhs.gov/ocr/privacy/hipaa/administrative/index.html
5. HIPAA Administrative Simplification: Enforcement, Federal Register, Vol. 74, No. 209, October 30, 2009.
6. Covered Entity, Business Associate, and Organizational Options, OCR PowerPoint presentation, Feb/Mar 2003, http://www.hhs.gov/ocr/privacy/hipaa/understanding/training/coveredentities.pdf
7. Protected Health Information, Uses and Disclosures, and Minimum Necessary, OCR PowerPoint presentation, Feb/Mar 2003, http://www.hhs.gov/ocr/privacy/hipaa/understanding/training/udmn.pdf
8. Administrative Requirements, OCR PowerPoint presentation, Feb/Mar 2003, http://www.hhs.gov/ocr/privacy/hipaa/understanding/training/adminreq.pdf
9. Compliance and Enforcement, OCR PowerPoint presentation, Feb/Mar 2003, http://www.hhs.gov/ocr/privacy/hipaa/understanding/training/compli.pdf

Chapter 6

Safe Harbors, Advisory Opinions, and Special Fraud Alerts

Learning Objectives

After completing class sessions based on this chapter, a student will:

- Know the differences between a Safe Harbor, a Special Fraud Alert, and an Advisory Opinion.
- Understand the practical legal effect of a Safe Harbor for a healthcare individual or organization.
- Become familiar with basic protections of each of the 24 current Safe Harbors.
- Know the typical terms of a Safe Harbor.
- Learn the purpose of the Office of the Inspector General (OIG) in issuing Special Fraud Alerts.
- Be aware of the typical language of a Special Fraud Alert.
- Know how to submit a recommendation to the OIG for developing a new Safe Harbor or Special Fraud Alert.
- Be aware of the narrow purpose and application of an OIG Advisory Opinion.
- Hear about the process for requesting an Advisory Opinion from the OIG.
- Recognize the types of issues that may and may not be the subject of an Advisory Opinion.

INTRODUCTION

In order to comply with a law, it is necessary to understand it. The meaning and practical effect of the fraud and abuse laws can be found in several places. The highest authority is the language of the statute as enacted by the Congress. Those words cannot anticipate and cover all the factual situations that may arise under the statute. The agency primarily responsible for enforcing these laws, the OIG in the Department of Health and Human Services (DHHS), is anxious to help individuals and organizations to understand and obey the laws. It has published numerous regulations and other documents that provide insight into how it interprets and applies the laws. The most prominent of these are Safe Harbors, Advisory Opinions, and Special Fraud Alerts.

SAFE HARBORS

The federal Anti-Kickback Statute (AKS) is a criminal statute that prohibits the solicitation, offer, payment, or acceptance of any *remuneration* (kickback, bribe, rebate) in any form (gifts, discounts, cross-referrals) for the purpose of inducing or rewarding another party to refer, purchase, lease, or order any goods or services reimbursable under a federal healthcare program. The OIG webpage dealing with Safe Harbors, including links to their actual language, can be found here: https://oig.hhs.gov/compliance/safe-harbor-regulations/index.asp.

The AKS could be applied to a wide range of healthcare business transactions that have legitimate purposes. The Congress included in the law five statutory exceptions from its application, covering these topics:

1. Properly disclosed discounts or other reductions in price
2. Payments to bona fide employees
3. Certain risk-sharing and other arrangements with managed care organizations
4. Certain payments to group purchasing organizations (GPOs)
5. Waivers of coinsurance for Medicare services for individuals who qualify for certain Public Health Service programs

In addition, the OIG has periodically issued regulations called "safe harbors." They are transactions that are not prohibited by the statute and will not be prosecuted by the OIG, even though technically they might come within the law's language. The Safe Harbors specify certain elements of a transaction that must be present to earn their protection. The transaction or arrangement must be structured and carried out exactly according to the Safe Harbor's terms. Congress also instructed the OIG to define additional Safe Harbors through regulations. This is what the OIG had produced as of the end of the year 2012.

Investment interests. Protects returns on investments in large publicly traded entities ($50 million or more in net assets) if certain criteria are met, and in small entities if (a) no more than 40% of all investment interests are held by investors in a position to generate business to the entity and (b) no more than 40% of the venture's gross revenues are generated by the investors.

Rental of space and equipment. The parties must sign a written agreement that describes the premises or equipment, is for a term of at least 1 year, with the aggregate payment set in advance. All payments and services must be reasonable and based upon fair market value (FMV). All arrangements between the lessor and lessee must be captured in one contract. The arrangement must serve a commercially reasonable business purpose.

Personal services and management contracts. The parties must sign a written agreement for a term of at least 1 year that specifies the aggregate payment in advance. It must set the exact services to be performed. Compensation must be reasonable, at FMV, and determined through arm's length negotiations. It must not take into account the volume or value of referrals. All arrangements must be captured in one contract. The arrangement must serve a commercially reasonable business purpose.

Sale of practice. The time from the date of the sale agreement to the completion of the sale is not more than 1 year. The seller must not be in a position to make referrals to the purchaser after 1 year from the date of the sale agreement. The sale price must be reasonable, at FMV, the result of arm's length negotiations, and not based upon the number or value of referrals by the seller.

Referral services. The referral service cannot exclude any individual or entity that is qualified to participate in Medicare or Medicaid. Payments to the referral service must be based only on the cost of operating the service and not on the volume or value generated by either party. The referral service may not impose requirements on the manner in which services are provided to a referred person. People seeking referrals must be told how the service selects its physician participants, whether they pay a fee to the service, and any restrictions imposed on the physicians.

Warranties. This Safe Harbor applies to remuneration made under a warranty provided by a manufacturer or supplier of an item to the buyer (such as a healthcare provider or beneficiary) of the item. To qualify, the buyer must report such warranty payments on its cost reports or payment claims to the federal government and supply full warranty information to the DHHS upon request. The seller must report the warranty item on its invoice and the cost to it of the warranty replacement.

Discounts. These are discounts on items or services for which payment may be made under a federal healthcare program. A discount will be protected only if it is a reduction in price for the original good or service. The buyer must earn the discount in a single fiscal year, claim the discount in the year earned or the following year, and report the discount on its cost report to the federal government. The seller must report the existence and amount of the discount on its invoice. The discount may not take the form of a cash payment, a price reduction not applicable to the Medicare or Medicaid programs, or the furnishing of a good or service at a reduced charge to induce the purchase of a different good or service.

Employees. Payments made by an employer to an employee under a bona fide employment relationship with the employer for employment in furnishing of any item or service for which payment may be made under federal healthcare programs are excepted from the statute's prohibitions. The employee's compensation must be reasonable, at FMV, the result of arm's length negotiations, and not based on the volume or value of referrals.

Group purchasing organization s (GPO). These are entities that are created to leverage the collective buying power of a group of individuals or entities (e.g., physician practices, hospitals) to obtain discounts from vendors. The potential legal problem lies in the administrative fees paid by the vendors to finance the services that the GPOs offer to their member healthcare providers. The problem is avoided if the GPO has a written agreement with each member stating that vendors will not pay a fee higher than 3% of the purchase price of the goods or services they sell through the GPO. The GPO also must annually inform each member entity of the amount received from each vendor with respect to purchases made by the entity.

Waiver of beneficiary coinsurance and deductible amounts. If a hospital wishes to waive the coinsurance or deductible amounts that a patient owes for inpatient hospital services that Medicare pays for under the prospective payment system, it must satisfy three standards. The hospital must not later claim the amount reduced or waived as a bad debt for payment purposes under Medicare. The waiver offer must be made without regard to the reason for admission to the hospital, the length of stay, or the diagnosis-related group for which the claim for Medicare reimbursement is filed. The waiver offer also must not be made as part of a price reduction agreement between a hospital and a third-party payer.

Increased coverage, reduced cost-sharing amounts, or reduced premium amounts offered by health plans. This Safe Harbor protects incentives sometimes offered by health plans to their enrollees. Examples are additional coverage offered by a plan to an enrollee, or the reduction of the enrollee's obligation to pay the plan or a provider for cost-sharing amounts (coinsurance, deductibles, or copayments) or for premium amounts attributable to items or services covered by the health plan or a federal healthcare program. The health plan must offer the same incentives to all enrollees. It also may not claim the costs of the increased coverage or the reduced cost-sharing or premium amounts as a bad debt for Medicare or Medicaid reimbursement purposes.

Price reductions offered to health plans. This Safe Harbor applies to reductions in price offered by a contracted healthcare provider to a health plan in accord with a written agreement between them. The language describes four types of health plans and the standards that they and the healthcare provider must follow in order to be safe. Although there are minor differences among the four types, generally the agreement must be for at least 1 year, and must specify the services and items the provider will deliver, as well as the method of computing their price. Neither the plan nor the provider may request payment from a federal healthcare program or a plan enrollee for the items furnished under the agreement. The fee schedule for the items or services must remain in effect for the term of the agreement.

Practitioner recruitment. Payments and benefits offered by hospitals to recruit physicians are protected if a number of prerequisites are satisfied. The hospital and the physicians must sign an agreement that specifies the benefits offered by the hospital, the terms under which they are offered, and the full obligations of both parties. The hospital may provide benefits for no more than 3 years and the terms of the agreement with the physician may not be renegotiated during that time. The amount or value of the benefits provided by the hospital may not vary on the basis of the volume or value of any expected referrals from the physician for which payment may be made under a federal healthcare program.

The agreement may not require that the physician make referrals to, be in a position to make or influence referrals to, or otherwise generate business for the hospital as a condition for receiving the benefits. The hospital may impose a condition that the physician maintain privileges on its medical staff. However, the physician cannot be restricted from establishing staff privileges at, referring patients to, or generating business for another hospital.

If the physician is leaving an established practice, at least 75% of the revenues of his/her new practice must be generated from new patients not previously seen by the practitioner at his/her former practice. At least 75% of the revenues of the new practice must be generated from patients residing in a health professional shortage area (HPSA) or a medically underserved area (MUA) or who are part of a medically underserved population (MUP). The physician agrees to treat Medicare or Medicaid patients in a nondiscriminatory manner.

Obstetrical malpractice insurance subsidies. This Safe Harbor protects payments made by a hospital or other entity to a malpractice insurer to cover the malpractice insurance premiums for a practitioner (including a certified nurse-midwife) who engages in obstetrical practice as a routine part of his or her medical practice in a primary care HPSA. At least 75% of the practitioner's obstetrical patients treated under the coverage of the malpractice insurance must reside in a HPSA. The practitioner may not be required to make referrals to, or otherwise generate business for, the entity as a condition for receiving the benefits. The amount of payment may not vary based on the volume or value of expected referrals to, or business otherwise generated for, the hospital by the practitioner.

Investments in group practices. There is no AKS liability for a payment that is a return on investment interest (e.g., dividend or interest income) made to a solo or group practice physician investing in his or her own practice or group practice as long as the equity interests in the practice or group are held by licensed healthcare professionals who work in the practice or group.

Cooperative hospital service organizations. Cooperative hospital service organizations (CHSOs) are owned and operated by their member-hospitals to provide services to those hospitals. The hospitals pool their resources to form the cooperative and pay the cooperative a fee designed to cover the cooperative's costs. To qualify for Safe Harbor protection, payments by the patron-hospitals to the CHSO must be for its bona fide operating expenses. Payments from the CHSO to its patron-hospitals must be for the purpose of distributing its net earnings.

Ambulatory surgical centers. There are four types of ambulatory surgical centers (ASCs) based on their ownership: surgeon owned, single-specialty physician owned, multispecialty physician owned, and hospital/physician owned. The Safe Harbor conditions are similar for all of them.

- All investors must be physicians who are in a position to refer patients directly to the ASC and perform procedures on those patients.
- The investment terms must not be related to the previous or expected volume of referrals to be generated from the investor to the entity.
- At least one-third of physician investors' medical practice income from all sources must be derived from the performance of procedures.
- At least one-third of the procedures performed by each physician must be performed at the ASC.
- The entity must not loan or guarantee funds to an investor to be used to acquire his or her investment interest.
- The return on investment paid to an investor must be directly proportional to the amount of his or her capital investment.
- All ancillary services performed at the ASC must be directly and integrally related to the primary procedures performed at the ASC.
- The entity and all physician investors must treat Medicare/Medicaid patients in a nondiscriminatory manner.

Referral arrangements for specialty services. Where one physician (typically in primary care) agrees to refer a patient to the another physician for the provision of a specialty service payable in full or in part under Medicare, Medicaid, or any other federal healthcare programs in return for an agreement by the other physician to refer that patient back to the first physician, the arrangement is protected if four criteria are satisfied. The time and circumstances for referring the patient back to the originating physician must be clinically appropriate. The service for which the referral is made is not within the medical expertise of the referring physician, but is within the special expertise of the physician receiving the referral. The two physicians receive no payment for the referral and do not split a global fee in connection with the referred patient. The only compensation received by the physicians is for services actually provided to the patient.

Price reductions offered to eligible managed care organizations. This Safe Harbor protects financial arrangements between managed care entities that receive a fixed or capitated amount from federal healthcare programs and providers with whom the entities contract for the provision of healthcare items or services. To receive the protection, there must be a signed, written, minimum 1-year agreement between the plan and the provider that prohibits the provider from claiming payment directly from a federal healthcare program unless the provider is one of several types of health maintenance organization or health center. In addition, neither party may give or receive remuneration to induce provision of any business other than that covered by the agreement. Neither party may shift its financial burden in a way that increases payments claimed under a federal healthcare program.

Price reductions offered by contractors with substantial financial risk to managed care organizations. This Safe Harbor covers financial arrangements between managed care plans (including employer-sponsored group health plans) and providers with whom they contract for healthcare items and services with respect to services reimbursed on a fee-for-service basis by a federal healthcare program—as long as the providers are placed at substantial financial risk for the cost or utilization of items or services furnished to federal healthcare program beneficiaries. To qualify, there must be a signed, written, minimum 1-year agreement between the plan and the provider that requires the provider's participation in a quality assurance program and specifies a payment methodology that is commercially reasonable and consistent with FMV established in an arms-length transaction. The provider's "substantial financial risk" must be manifested through one of four payment methodologies: periodic fixed amount per patient, percentage of premium, inpatient diagnosis-related groups (DRGs), or bonuses and withholds.

Ambulance replenishing. This Safe Harbor protects a gift or transfer of drugs or medical supplies by a hospital to an ambulance provider for the purpose of replenishing comparable drugs or medical supplies used by the ambulance provider (or a first responder) in connection with the transport of a patient by ambulance to the hospital. To qualify, either the hospital or the ambulance provider may bill for the replenished drugs, but not both simultaneously. The hospital or ambulance provider must maintain records of the replenished drugs and medical supplies and the patient transport for which they were used, and provide a copy of the records to the other party within a reasonable time. The replenishing arrangement must not take into account the volume or the value of any referrals or business otherwise generated between the parties.

Health centers. This Safe Harbor allows the transfer of goods, services, donations, or loans to a federally qualified health center if several criteria are satisfied.

- The transfer is made pursuant to a contract, lease, grant, loan, or similar agreement.
- The goods, items, services, donations, or loans are medical or clinical in nature or relate directly to services provided by the health center.
- The health center expects the arrangement to help it maintain the availability or enhance the quality of services provided to a MUP.
- At least annually, the health center must evaluate the effectiveness of the arrangement.
- The entity making the transfers does not require the health center to refer patients to a particular individual or facility.
- The agreement must not restrict the health center's ability to enter into agreements with other providers or suppliers of comparable goods, or services, or with other lenders or donors.
- The health center must provide effective notification to patients of their freedom to choose any willing provider or supplier.

Electronic prescribing items and services. This Safe Harbor is designed to allow a hospital to give non-monetary items (hardware, software, or information technology and training services) to a member of its medical staff to allow him or her to receive and transmit electronic prescription information. It also encompasses similar transactions between group practices and their member physicians, and between prescription drug plan sponsors and pharmacists and prescribing physicians. The prerequisites are:

- The items given are part of, or are used to access, an electronic prescription drug program.
- The donor does not restrict the use or compatibility of the items or services with other electronic prescribing or electronic health records systems.
- The recipient does not make the receipt of items or services a condition of doing business with the donor.

- Neither the eligibility of a recipient for the items or services, nor the amount or nature of the items or services, takes into account the volume or value of referrals, or other business generated between the parties.
- The arrangement is set forth in a signed written agreement.

Electronic health records items and services. This is similar to the previous Safe Harbor, but applies to electronic health records. To enjoy its protection, a health plan or other individual or entity that bills federal healthcare programs may give non-monetary items (software or information technology and training services) used predominantly to create, maintain, transmit, or receive electronic health records to a healthcare individual or entity if it meets several conditions. The software is certified as interoperable. The items given may not be limited in their use or compatibility with other electronic prescribing or health records systems. The recipient does not make the receipt of the items a condition of doing business with the donor. Neither the eligibility of a recipient for the items or services, nor the amount or nature of the items or services, is determined by the volume or value of referrals or other business generated between the parties.

The items and services do not include staffing of the recipient's office and are not used primarily to conduct personal business or business unrelated to the recipient's clinical practice or clinical operations. The electronic health records software contains electronic prescribing capability. Before receipt of the items and services, the recipient must pay 15% of the donor's cost for the items and services. The transfer of the items must take place before December 31, 2013.

TYPICAL TERMS OF A SAFE HARBOR

The full text of the regulations defining each of the Safe Harbors can be found here: http://www.complianceland.com/aks/index.html. They are written in legal language that is technical but comprehensible to a well-educated person. A good example is one of the first Safe Harbors, dealing with space rentals. The kickback threat lies in a scenario like the following.

A hospital is interested in attracting more patient admissions. It constructs a medical office building adjacent to the hospital facility and rents space within it to physicians who are likely to admit patients to the hospital or at least refer patients to the hospital's own physicians. The proximity of the hospital facilitates such referrals, and there is nothing wrong with that. However, the rental charge for the space is significantly less than the physician would have to pay elsewhere. It includes dedicated parking space and slots in the schedules for the hospital's diagnostic laboratory and imaging unit, for which there is no additional charge. If the hospital is particularly aggressive, it may offer to scale the rental charge in inverse proportion to the number of patients the physician sends to the hospital. More patients, lower rent.

"Space Rental" Safe Harbor Under the Anti-Kickback Statute[1]

Space rental. As used in Section 1128B of the Act, "remuneration" does not include any payment made by a lessee to a lessor for the use of premises, as long as all of the following six standards are met:

1. The lease agreement is set out in writing and signed by the parties.
2. The lease covers all of the premises leased between the parties for the term of the lease and specifies the premises covered by the lease.
3. If the lease is intended to provide the lessee with access to the premises for periodic intervals of time, rather than on a full-time basis for the term of the lease, the lease specifies exactly the schedule of such intervals, their precise length, and the exact rent for such intervals.
4. The term of the lease is for not less than 1 year.
5. The aggregate rental charge is set in advance, is consistent with fair market value in arms-length transactions, and is not determined in a manner that takes into account the volume or value of any referrals or business otherwise generated between the parties for which payment may be made in whole or in part under Medicare, Medicaid, or other Federal healthcare programs.
6. The aggregate space rented does not exceed that which is reasonably necessary to accomplish the commercially reasonable business purpose of the rental. Note that for purposes of paragraph (b) of this section, the term fair market value means the value of the rental property for general commercial purposes, but shall not be adjusted to reflect the additional value that one party (either the prospective lessee or lessor) would attribute to the property as a result of its proximity or convenience to sources of referrals or business otherwise generated for which payment may be made in whole or in part under Medicare, Medicaid, and all other Federal healthcare programs.

[1] 42 CFR §1001.952 (b)

The Safe Harbor attempts to address these potential problems in this way. All the terms of the lease arrangement between the hospital and the physician must be expressed in writing and signed by the hospital and the physician. No secret verbal side agreements are permitted. The lease must describe fully the premises that the physician is leasing from the hospital. If a space is not included in the description (e.g., parking, laboratory), the hospital is letting the physician use it for free, and that would not be acceptable. The lease term must be at least 1 year. This provision prevents the parties from frequently adjusting the rent rates to reflect the volume of admissions or referrals from the physician to the hospital.

Such attempts to modify the rent during the term of the lease are further prevented by the requirement that it be set in advance—before there is any indication of how many patients the physician will admit. It is a typical condition of Safe Harbors that any financial transactions—the payment of rent in this case—be at "fair market value in arms-length transactions." In other words, this is the dollar amount that would result if two parties conducted robust adversarial negotiations in the open market. The space rental charge should be such a value. It definitely cannot take into account "the volume or value of any referrals or business otherwise generated between the parties."

If the hospital and the physician can adapt their space rental arrangement to the terms of this Safe Harbor, they will indeed be legally safe.

SPECIAL FRAUD ALERTS

As the OIG gathers information about the nature of fraud and abuse practices in the healthcare industry, it occasionally issues Special Fraud Alerts about areas of activity that are causing it heightened concern. In the words of the OIG, "These Special Fraud Alerts provide the OIG with a means of notifying the industry that we have become aware of certain abusive practices which we plan to pursue and prosecute, or bring civil and administrative action, as appropriate. The alerts also serve as a powerful tool to encourage industry compliance by giving providers an opportunity to examine their own practices." Fraud alerts both inform providers about conduct that may be questionable and encourage the public to report to the OIG arrangements that may be "suspect" under the AKS.

Since 1994, the OIG has issued 12 Special Fraud Alerts on the following topics:

1. Joint venture relationships
2. Routine waiver of copayments or deductibles under Medicare Part B
3. Hospital incentives to referring physicians

4. Prescription drug marketing schemes
5. Arrangements for the provision of clinical laboratory services
6. Home health fraud
7. Fraud and abuse in the provision of medical services in nursing facilities
8. Fraud and abuse in nursing home arrangements with hospices
9. Fraud and abuse in the provision of services in nursing facilities
10. Physician liability in certification of medical equipment and supplies and home health services
11. Rental of office space in physicians' offices
12. Telemarketing by durable medical equipment suppliers

In addition, the OIG provides ongoing guidance on its interpretation and enforcement of the AKS through Special Advisory Bulletins and additional guidance on various topics, both available on its website.

TYPICAL TERMS OF A SPECIAL FRAUD ALERT

It is worthwhile to become familiar with the typical language of a Special Fraud Alert. Copies of all the issued fraud alerts can be found on the OIG website here: https://oig.hhs.gov/compliance/alerts/index.asp. The alert on Rental of Space in Physician Offices by Persons or Entities to Which Physicians Refer came out in February 2000 and is available here: https://oig.hhs.gov/fraud/docs/alertsandbulletins/office%20space.htm. It begins by briefly explaining the potential problems that the OIG sees in rental arrangements for space in physician offices. This is followed by a more detailed description of the features of these arrangements that are legally suspect. Space rentals are problematic when the rental amounts exceed those paid for comparable property rented in arms-length transactions, are subject to modification more often than annually, vary with the number of patients or referrals, and are for space that is unnecessary or not used.

To protect legitimate space rental arrangements, the OIG strongly recommends that the parties make every effort to comply with the space rental Safe Harbor to the AKS. The final section of every fraud alert contains a section entitled What to Do If You Have Information About Fraud and Abuse Against Medicare or Medicaid Programs. It provides the phone numbers for each of the 10 OIG field offices.

EXAMPLE TEXT OF A SPECIAL FRAUD ALERT

The following is the actual text of another special fraud alert.

Telemarketing By Durable Medical Equipment Suppliers

March 2003

Section 1834(a)(17) of the Social Security Act prohibits suppliers of durable medical equipment (DME) from making unsolicited telephone calls to Medicare beneficiaries regarding the furnishing of a covered item, except in three specific situations: (i) the beneficiary has given written permission to the supplier to make contact by telephone; (ii) the contact is regarding a covered item the supplier has already furnished the beneficiary; or (iii) the supplier has furnished at least one covered item to the beneficiary during the preceding fifteen months. Section 1834(a)(17)(B) also specifically prohibits payment to a supplier who knowingly submits a claim generated pursuant to a prohibited telephone solicitation. Accordingly, such claims for payment are false and violators are potentially subject to criminal, civil, and administrative penalties, including exclusion from federal healthcare programs.

Notwithstanding the clear statutory prohibition, the Office of Inspector General has received credible information that some DME suppliers continue to use independent marketing firms to make unsolicited telephone calls to Medicare beneficiaries to market DME. Suppliers cannot do indirectly that which they are prohibited from doing directly. Except in the three specific circumstances described in the statute, section 1834(a)(17) prohibits unsolicited telemarketing by a DME supplier to Medicare beneficiaries, whether contact with a beneficiary is made by the supplier directly or by another party on the DME supplier's behalf. Moreover, a DME supplier is responsible for verifying that marketing activities performed by third parties with whom the supplier contracts or otherwise does business do not involve prohibited activity and that information purchased from such third parties was neither obtained, nor derived, from prohibited activity. If a claim for payment is submitted for items or services generated by a prohibited solicitation, both the DME supplier and the telemarketer are potentially liable for criminal, civil, and administrative penalties for causing the filing of a false claim.

WHAT TO DO IF YOU HAVE INFORMATION ABOUT FRAUD AND ABUSE AGAINST MEDICARE OR MEDICAID PROGRAMS:

If you have information about DME suppliers or telemarketers engaging in any of the activities described above, contact any of the regional offices of the Office of Inspector General, US DHHS, at the following locations

Regional Offices	States Served	Telephone
Boston	MA, VT, NH, ME, RI, CT	617-565-2664
New York	NY, NJ, PR, VI	212-264-1691
Philadelphia	PA, MD, DE, WV, VA, DC	215-861-4576
Atlanta	GA, KY, NC, SC, FL, TN, AL	404-562-7603
Chicago	IL, MN, WI, MI, IN, OH	312-353-2740
Dallas	TX, NM, OK, AR, LA, MS	214-767-8406
Kansas City	CO, UT, WY, MT, ND, SD, NE, KS, MO, IA	816-426-4000
Los Angeles	AZ, NV, So. CA, HI,	714-246-8302
San Francisco	No. CA, AK, OR, ID, WA, AK	415-437-7961

Telemarketing By Durable Medical Equipment Suppliers, Special Fraud Alert, Office of the Inspector General, Department of Health and Human Services, March 2003.

PUBLIC SOLICITATION FOR RECOMMENDATIONS ON NEW SAFE HARBORS AND SPECIAL FRAUD ALERTS

On December 29, 2011, the OIG published its annual notice soliciting recommendations and proposals for developing new and modifying existing Safe Harbors under the AKS and developing new OIG Special Fraud Alerts.[2] Proposals had to be submitted to the OIG by February 27, 2012. The Health Insurance Portability and Accountability Act of 1996 (HIPAA) requires the OIG to solicit proposals for new OIG Special Fraud Alerts annually. This requirement is designed to ensure that the industry will have a recurring opportunity to seek clarification regarding what constitutes fraudulent behavior.

The solicitation also seeks proposals for developing new OIG Special Fraud Alerts. The OIG has issued such alerts periodically over time for the benefit of the healthcare community in order to identify certain practices that the OIG considers to be potentially fraudulent or abusive. Providers utilize these alerts to assist with structuring arrangements, and federal healthcare program administrators also use these alerts to gauge whether provider practices are compliant and appropriate. The OIG will evaluate submissions by considering the extent to which a practice identified in a new potential OIG Special Fraud Alert might impact any of the factors described earlier.

[2] https://www.federalregister.gov/articles/2011/12/29/2011-33345/solicitation-of-new-safe-harbors-and-special-fraud-alerts.

ADVISORY OPINIONS

The Safe Harbors are available to any healthcare organizations that choose to take advantage of them. The Special Fraud Alerts apply to any and all healthcare organizations that engage in the activities that they describe. The organizations have no choice. Both the Safe Harbors and the Special Fraud Alerts cover a lot of the arrangements and practices that healthcare organizations are likely to encounter. Sometimes, however, they plan ventures or projects that seem legally risky but are not covered by any of the OIG's special publications. In those cases, there is an option to request an Advisory Opinion from the OIG.

An OIG Advisory Opinion is a legal opinion issued by OIG to a requesting party about the application of the OIG's fraud and abuse authorities to the party's existing or proposed business arrangement. The opinion is legally binding on the DHHS and the requesting party. It is not binding on any other governmental department or agency. A party that receives a favorable Advisory Opinion is protected from OIG administrative sanctions, as long as the arrangement at issue is conducted in accordance with the facts submitted to the OIG.

No person or entity can rely on an Advisory Opinion issued to someone else. Because each opinion will apply legal standards to a set of facts involving certain known persons who provide specific statements about key factual issues, no third parties are bound, nor may they legally rely on these Advisory Opinions. As a practical matter, however, it would be hard for the OIG to reach a different interpretation in a nearly identical situation involving another individual or organization.

The OIG has the authority to issue such opinions when its receives a specific request from an individual or entity that is planning or currently involved in an arrangement that may be subject to the AKS, any of its Safe Harbors, the OIG Exclusion Authority, or the Civil Monetary Penalties Law. Opinions will not be issued on:

- Hypothetical situations
- General questions of interpretation
- Activities in which the party requesting the Advisory Opinion is not, and does not plan to be, involved
- The FMV of goods, services, or property
- Whether an individual is a bona fide employee
- The application of the Stark Physician Self-Referral Law

The OIG offers the following as examples of topics of the advisory opinions it has issued.

- A proposal by a radiology group to offer free insurance preauthorization services to physicians and patients.
- A proposal for an independent diagnostic testing facility to hire a doctor to read and interpret test results when that doctor is closely related to the owners of the independent diagnostic testing facility and is employed by a company that also employs other potential referral sources.
- A rewards program under which consumers would earn gasoline discounts based on the amount spent on purchases in retail stores and pharmacies, including cost-sharing amounts paid in connection with items covered by federal healthcare programs.
- Concerning certain aspects of an exclusive contract for emergency transport services between a municipality and an ambulance company that reimburses the municipality for dispatch services and for certain costs incurred when municipal firefighters drive transports.
- A nonprofit, tax-exempt, charitable organization's proposed arrangement to provide counseling from a law firm regarding financially needy patients' eligibility for federal- and state-funded benefits programs and assistance from the law firm in applying for benefits.
- A proposal to operate a website that would display coupons and advertising from healthcare providers, suppliers, and other entities.
- A proposal to establish a GPO that would be wholly owned by an entity that also wholly owns many of the potential participants in the GPO, and to pass through to participants in the GPO a portion of the payments received by the GPO from vendors.
- An online service that would facilitate the exchange of information between healthcare practitioners, providers, and suppliers.
- A proposed arrangement under which an entity would furnish allergy testing and immunotherapy laboratory services within various primary care physicians' medical offices.
- A hospital's domiciliary services program that provides transportation, lodging, and meal assistance to certain patients and their family members.
- An online referral service whereby postacute care providers would pay a fee to electronically receive and respond to referral requests from hospitals for postdischarge care.
- A nonprofit, tax-exempt, charitable organization's proposal to provide assistance with cost-sharing obligations to financially needy individuals, including Medicare and Medicaid beneficiaries, diagnosed with certain specified diseases.

- An arrangement in which a hospital pays a cardiology group compensation that includes a performance bonus based on implementing certain patient service, quality, and cost savings measures.

A request for an Advisory Opinion must be based on actual current facts or a proposed transaction or arrangement that is very likely to be implemented if the opinion is favorable. The OIG does not want to waste its time or resources. The OIG is required to collect a fee for preparing an Advisory Opinion; the rate in 2012 was $86 per hour. The formal request should include the following:

- The identity of the individual or entity making the request.
- A complete, detailed description of all the facts surrounding the proposed arrangement, including the background of the parties and their negotiations, as well as key terms and copies of the pertinent documents.
- Signed certification from the requesting parties that the information is complete and accurate.
- A commitment to implement the arrangement in good faith if a favorable opinion is issued.

To guide healthcare individuals and organizations in making requests for Advisory Opinions, the OIG has offered these materials.

Preliminary Checklist for Advisory Opinion Requests (a list of technical requirements; information that describes the issues and arrangements; and required certification): https://oig.hhs.gov/fraud/docs/advisoryopinions/precheck.htm

Recommended Preliminary Questions and Supplementary Information for Addressing Requests for OIG Advisory Opinions: https://oig.hhs.gov/fraud/docs/advisoryopinions/prequestions.htm

From the first Advisory Opinions in 1997 through the end of 2011, the OIG issued 256 of the opinions. The full text of all of them is available on the OIG's website: https://oig.hhs.gov/compliance/advisory-opinions/index.asp. The OIG usually redacts specific information regarding the requestor and certain privileged, confidential, or financial information associated with the individual or entity.

Every Advisory Opinion follows approximately the same format. It begins by reciting the Factual Background for the request, typically a description of the Proposed Arrangement. Next is a statement of the relevant Law and its Analysis as applied to that arrangement. The OIG then reaches its Conclusion about the legality of the arrangement. A typical concluding sentence reads

> Based on the facts certified in your request for an Advisory Opinion and supplemental submissions, we conclude that . . . although the Proposed Arrangement could potentially generate prohibited remuneration under the anti-kickback statute if the requisite intent to induce or reward referrals of Federal health care program business were present, the OIG would not impose administrative sanctions . . . in connection with the Proposed Arrangement.

The last section of the opinion expresses some Limitations issued only to the requestor of the opinion; they will not bind any other agency than DHHS, and they apply only to the specific arrangement.

STUDY QUESTIONS

1. How could a hospital, physician, or pharmacy get into trouble under the AKS by offering discounts for its services or products? Read the actual language of the appropriate Safe Harbor if necessary to understand where the risks lie.
2. What are the possible outcomes if a healthcare organization implements a transaction or arrangement that does not satisfy any Safe Harbors?
3. What is the purpose of a Special Fraud Alert? Who is likely to receive copies of the alerts and what will they do with them?

Learning Exercises

1. Sit down with a friend or classmate who is unfamiliar with the subject of healthcare compliance and explain the substance and purpose of Safe Harbors, Special Fraud Alerts, and Advisory Opinions. Continue discussion until they understand the differences.
2. You are the head of Medical Staff Relations for a 220-bed teaching hospital in a large midwestern city. The CEO of the hospital has asked you to design a program for the hospital to make available to its staff physicians the equipment and services necessary for them to connect to the hospital's electronic health record and pharmaceutical prescribing systems. Briefly describe the key features of such a program that will enable it to avoid liability under the AKS.
3. Pick a hypothetical topic affecting a hospital, drug company, DME supplier, or other healthcare entity. It involves its plan to enter into an arrangement with a large physician group that will be mutually beneficial

for both parties. There is some uncertainty about the legality of the arrangement under the AKS. Draft a request for an Advisory Opinion from the OIG. The exact facts of the arrangement are less important than the form of the request. Be sure to check the OIG's Compliance Program Guidance on preparing such requests.

4. Call the phone number for the OIG regional office responsible for receiving fraud and abuse reports for the state in which you are located. (It is listed at the end of the example Special Fraud Alert given previously.) Explain that you are studying OIG's enforcement of the healthcare fraud law. Ask how they would respond to a person who was attempting to report a suspected incident of fraud or abuse. What information would they seek from that person? What would their next steps be?

Reference

1. Solicitation of New Safe Harbors and Special Fraud Alerts, 42 CFR Part 1001.

Chapter 7

Corporate Integrity Agreements

Learning Objectives

After completing class sessions based on this chapter, a student will:

- Know how government authorities learn about the failure of healthcare organizations to comply with laws.
- Understand the function of a Corporate Integrity Agreement (CIA) both as an enforcement tool and a guide to effective compliance practices.
- See how the Office of the Inspector General (OIG) decides whether to offer a CIA to a provider charged with fraud and abuse.
- Discover how an organization can commit fraud or abuse and still avoid program exclusion or submission to a CIA.
- Become familiar with the basic structure and key provisions of most CIAs.
- Recognize the recommended ingredients of an organizational Code of Conduct.
- Be prepared to design the content of a training session on compliance for all covered persons.
- Learn how an organization must deal with Ineligible Persons.
- Recognize a Reportable Event and how it should be handled.
- Understand the several reports that an organization must submit during the term of a CIA.
- Realize the penalties an organization may suffer if it fails to perform its CIA obligations.
- Comprehend the role of an Independent Review Organization (IRO) and how to maintain its independence and objectivity.

INTRODUCTION

When a healthcare organization fails to comply with one of the several federal fraud and abuse laws (False Claims Act, Anti-Kickback Statute, Stark Physician Self-Referral Law, Civil Monetary Penalties Law), a few different things can happen. A reckless, unscrupulous organization might try to hide or ignore the incident. Eventually, the violation will be discovered with far more disastrous consequences for the organization—legal, financial, and reputational.

Government authorities learn about failures to comply through several routes.

- Disgruntled current or former employees report violations, anonymously or in connection with a workplace grievance or a wrongful discharge lawsuit.
- Relatives or friends of employees may get involved.
- Medical staff physicians and other professionals unhappy with organization policies complain.
- Reports or complaints are submitted by contractors, vendors, or competitors.
- Reports are made by patients about fraud and abuse by their providers; such reports are actively encouraged by Medicare.
- False Claims Act qui tam suits are brought by any of these people, who are further protected by whistle-blower protection laws in some states.
- Medicare fiscal intermediaries and carriers make reports, relying on their auditors and fraud and abuse specialists.
- Medicare Strike Forces (multiagency units of federal and state investigators, prosecutors, and analysts) work together to identify, investigate, and prosecute Medicare fraud.
- The Administration on Aging of the Department of Health and Human Services (DHHS) funds Senior Medicare Patrols that recruit and train retired professionals and other senior citizens to recognize and report instances or patterns of healthcare fraud.
- Recovery Audit Contractors—specialized auditors paid by Medicare on a contingency fee basis to review payments made to providers and suppliers that bill Medicare—identify and correct improper payments, both over and under.
- The healthcare organizations themselves self-report their violations to the government, using protocols specifically designed for them.

The penalties for proven violations are diverse and severe: criminal fines, civil monetary penalties, damages (often tripled), imprisonment, and exclusion from participation in federal healthcare programs.

A CIA is a tool used by the OIG in the DHHS, the federal agency responsible for the Medicare and Medicaid programs, to enforce fraud and abuse laws. When it applies to smaller healthcare organizations like physician practices, it is simply called an Integrity Agreement.

The CIA is negotiated between the OIG and a healthcare provider that has been under investigation for False Claims Act violations or found guilty of fraudulent acts involving Medicare or Medicaid. It is incorporated into a civil settlement between the OIG and the provider. In return, the OIG agrees "not to seek an exclusion of that health care provider or entity from participation in Medicare, Medicaid and other Federal health care programs." A CIA is employed when the OIG feels that the provider can be redeemed under the prodding of a CIA. If the provider organization then breaches terms of the CIA, the OIG is likely to impose stipulated penalties and proceed to exclude the organization from federal healthcare programs.

The OIG has stated the criteria that it uses in deciding whether to propose and negotiate a CIA: (1) whether the provider self-disclosed the alleged misconduct; (2) the monetary damage to the federal healthcare programs; (3) whether the case involves successor liability; (4) whether the provider is still participating in the federal healthcare programs or in the line of business that gave rise to the fraudulent conduct; (5) whether the alleged conduct is capable of repetition; (6) the age of the conduct; (7) whether the provider has an effective compliance program and would agree to limited compliance or integrity measures and would annually certify such compliance to the OIG; and (8) other circumstances, as appropriate.

The term of a CIA is typically 5 years. The OIG negotiates the agreement and monitors its implementation. All the CIAs are based on the principles of the Federal Sentencing Guidelines of 1995. Then they are adapted to the scope and resources of the organization and the specific violations that were the source of the CIA. While the CIAs are primarily enforcement tools, the OIG also uses them as "a mechanism to advise [healthcare providers] concerning what [the OIG] feels are acceptable practices to ensure compliance with applicable Federal and State statues, regulations and program requirements."

In some cases, it is possible for a provider to commit a fraud and abuse violation yet avoid being subject to a CIA. To do so, it must self-report any federal healthcare-related violations and demonstrate that it is establishing a robust, effective compliance program.

In 2006, the OIG refined the use of CIAs by reducing the obligations of organizations that already maintained "robust and effective compliance programs which include internal auditing mechanisms." This refers to entities that currently are making a strong, good faith effort to comply. For them, the OIG proposes Compliance Certification Agreements (CCA) that have less demanding requirements. Essentially, they ask organizations to certify that they will continue to maintain their existing compliance programs for a shorter period than a full CIA and comply with fewer reporting obligations.

Almost all CIAs include the traditional seven elements of an effective compliance program as described in all of the OIG's 14 Compliance Program Guidances. The specific terms of a particular CIA depend on the facts and circumstances surrounding the organization and its practices. In shaping the CIA, the OIG takes into account factors like the severity and extent of the underlying misconduct, the nature and resources of the provider, the provider's existing compliance capabilities, and whether the case resulted from a self-disclosure.

REVIEW OF THE TEXT OF A TYPICAL CIA

A good way to understand the requirements of a CIA and its impact on the affected organization is to read through a typical CIA. At this location, https://oig.hhs.gov/fraud/cia/agreements/BHC_Sierra_Vista_Hospital,_Inc_04232012.pdf, you will find the CIA imposed upon BHC Sierra Vista Hospital (BHC) effective April 23, 2012. There is great similarity among the CIAs negotiated by the OIG; nearly identical language is used in all of them. The following are the primary sections of the BHC agreement and their meaning for the organization.

Preamble

Here, the agreement states its purpose to promote compliance with all relevant laws and program directives. Simultaneously with signing this agreement, BHC is entering into a Settlement Agreement with the OIG. That settlement resolves claims against BHC brought under the False Claims Act without further prosecution or penalty, on the condition that BHC meets its obligations under the CIA.

Term and Scope of the CIA

The time period during which BHC must meet those obligations is 5 years. That is the standard term for a CIA. In other cases, it has been as low as 2 years and as high as 8 years.

This provision makes clear that the CIA applies to a wide range of people associated with BHC. The owners, officers, directors, trustees, and employees are naturally covered. The physicians and other clinicians who are members of the hospital's active medical staff are not direct employees, but independent contractors. They are included. Finally, all contractors, subcontractors, agents, and other persons who provide patient care items or services or who perform billing or coding functions on behalf of BHC come within the purview of the CIA.

The hospital has control over its employees and can manage their activities rather closely. Its relationship with the medical staff is looser, defined through the medical staff bylaws and the agreements physicians make when they join. If necessary, the bylaws can be amended to require specific compliance-specific behaviors of the physicians. The hospital can influence the actions of its contractors through the language in those agreements.

Corporate Integrity Obligations

Compliance Officer and Committee

The hospital is required to appoint a Compliance Officer within 90 days of the effective date of the CIA. In itself, that provision is a bad sign, indicating that BHC did not already have a designated Compliance Officer. Such a position is essential, even mandatory, in an organization of significant size. In negotiating CIAs, the OIG does take into account the size and resources of the affected organization. In the case of modest-size physician practices, it requires that the practice "designate a person to be responsible for compliance activities (Compliance Contact)." This is a little less than the appointment of a full-blown, full-time Compliance Officer.

In BHC's case, the Compliance Officer must be a member of senior management (a member of the C-suite), report directly to the CEO, and have the authority to communicate directly with the governing board whenever he or she deems it necessary. This gives the Compliance Officer very high status and influence in the organization, on the level with Chief Financial Officers and Chief Medical Officers. It makes it easier for them to enforce compliance behavior throughout the organization. The CIA also states that the Compliance Officer must not be subordinate to either the General Counsel (legal) or Chief Financial Officer. These are two positions that might be involved in noncompliant activities or at least be willing to hide them. They should not be able to manipulate the compliance work of the Compliance Officer.

The Compliance Officer's job should be as full time as possible. Non compliance work responsibilities should be limited and not interfere with compliance duties. Once a Compliance Officer is appointed, BHC must notify the OIG promptly if a new person takes the job.

The second key component in an organization's compliance infrastructure is a Compliance Committee. One must be appointed within 90 days of the execution of the CIA. The Compliance Officer heads the Committee. Other members include senior managers of compliance-related departments like billing, clinical, human resources, audit, and operations.

The CIA discusses the compliance obligations of the governing board. It must meet at least quarterly to review the performance of BHC's compliance program. Every year that the hospital is operating under the CIA, the board must issue a resolution stating that:

> The Board of Trustees has made a reasonable inquiry into the operations of Sierra Vista's Compliance Program including the performance of the Compliance Officer and the Compliance Committee. Based on its inquiry and review, the Board has concluded that, to the best of its knowledge, Sierra Vista has implemented an effective Compliance Program to meet Federal health care program requirements and the obligations of the CIA.

Naturally, the board must believe that the statement is true and accurate.

Written Standards

Within 90 days of the CIA's effective date, BHC must distribute and implement a written Code of Conduct applying to all the persons and entities covered by the agreement. Adherence to the Code must be a factor in every employee's performance evaluation. The Code must cover four things:

1. BHC's commitment to full compliance with federal healthcare program requirements
2. BHC's requirement that all persons covered by the CIA comply with federal healthcare program requirements and its own policies and procedures
3. BHC's requirement that all covered persons report to the Compliance Officer suspected violations of federal healthcare program requirements
4. The right of anybody to use the BHC Disclosure Program, without fear of retaliation and with an expectation of confidentiality and anonymity

These are the basic elements of a good compliance code of employee behavior; they cover all the bases. A rather demanding provision of the CIA says that, also within 90 days of the CIA taking effect, all the individuals to whom it applies must certify in writing that they have received, understood, and will follow the Code of Conduct. That is a tight time frame. Within those first 90 days, BHC must draft and implement the Code, distribute it to all the affected parties, and obtain back from them a written certification of acceptance.

The hospital must periodically review the Code to determine if revisions are necessary. If changes are made, the same written certification from each covered person must be collected.

Again within the same 90 days, the CIA asks BHC to develop and put into force Policies and Procedures that will carry out its compliance program—including the requirements outlined in the CIA as well as normal federal healthcare program requirements. The CIA places special emphasis on issues of documentation and medical necessity. If an organization does not already have in place a simple compliance structure, 90 days is not a lot of time to prepare the Policies and Procedures needed to create one. Within 120 days of the effective date, copies of the Policies and Procedures must be made available to all covered persons.

Training and Education

As Training and Education is one of the seven OIG-recommended components of a good compliance program, it is not surprising that it also is a requirement of every CIA. Both general and specific trainings on compliance must be provided. Within 90 days, BHC must give each covered person at least 2 hours of General Training, and then another 1 hour each year after that. Newly hired or contracted persons must receive the training within 30 days.

Within 120 days, each person covered by the CIA must also (in addition to the General Training) receive at least 4 hours of Specific Training, plus another 2 hours each year thereafter. Newly hired or contracted persons must receive their Specific Training within 30 days. This training should include discussion of these topics:

- Federal healthcare program requirements regarding the accurate coding and submission of claims
- Policies, procedures, and other requirements applicable to the documentation of medical records
- Personal obligation of each individual involved in the claims submission process to ensure that such claims are accurate
- Applicable reimbursement statutes, regulations, and program requirements and directives
- Legal sanctions for violations of the federal healthcare program requirements
- Examples of proper and improper claims submission practices
- Examples of proper and improper medical necessity documentation

The members of the hospital's governing board must receive the same General Training as other covered persons. In addition, they must be given training that deals with the responsibilities of corporate governance.

All these people receiving these various forms of training must certify in writing that they did so. The content of the training sessions must be reviewed annually and updated to take into account changes in federal healthcare program requirements as well as issues that have arisen during the hospital's internal audits and CIA-mandated Claims Review.

The CIA makes an interesting exception for active members of the medical staff, primarily physicians. The hospital is required only to "use its best efforts to encourage such active medical staff members to complete the training." This seems to acknowledge that BHC, like many hospitals, has less leverage over the physicians on its medical staff.

Review Procedures

The OIG does not simply trust that these measures, appointment of a Compliance Officer and Compliance Committee, preparation of a Code of Conduct and Policies and Procedures, and presentation of Training Sessions, will produce a compliant working environment in the hospital. It requires an independent review of BHC's operations to determine what actually is taking place.

First, the hospital must contract with an independent outside organization (such as an accounting, auditing, or consulting firm) to perform two defined reviews. The entity is referred to as an Independent Review Organization, or IRO.

Claims Review

The IRO shall review BHC's coding, billing, and claims submission to Federal healthcare programs and the reimbursement received. It shall prepare a Claims Review Report on its findings.

Unallowable Cost Review

For the first year of the CIA, the IRO will conduct a review of BHC's compliance with its obligation not to charge federal or state payors for unallowable costs (as defined in the Settlement Agreement of which the CIA is a condition) and its obligation to identify to those payors any unallowable costs included in previous charges to them. The unallowable cost analysis must include charges made in any cost reports, cost statements, information reports, or payment requests already submitted by BHC or any affiliates. In conducting this review, the IRO may need to review cost reports or financial statements from previous years. It shall prepare an Unallowable Cost Review Report on its findings, including its opinion on whether BHC is charging for unallowable costs.

If the OIG believes that either the Claims or Unallowable Costs Review fails to conform to the CIA, or the ensuing reports are inaccurate, it may carry out its own Validation Review of the reviews and the reports. Before the Validation Review begins, BHC may request a meeting with the OIG to discuss the results and findings of its reviews, to present additional information, or to propose an alternative to the Validation Review. The OIG commits itself to a good faith effort to resolve any review issues with BHC before conducting a Validation Review.

In its reports to the OIG, the IRO must certify that it has evaluated its own independence and objectivity and found them to be acceptable. The question of an IRO's independence and objectivity is such a sensitive issue that the OIG issued a Guidance on the topic. This is discussed later in this chapter.

Disclosure Program

Within 90 days of the CIA effective date, BHC must establish a well-publicized Disclosure Program to enable employees and other covered persons to disclose, to the Compliance Officer or someone else who is not in their chain of command, "any identified issues or questions associated with [BHC's] policies, conduct, practices, or procedures with respect to a Federal health care program believed by the individual to be a potential violation of criminal, civil, or administrative law." The program must accept anonymous disclosures and ensure that there will be no retaliation.

Upon receiving a disclosure, the Compliance Officer must gather relevant information in the course of a preliminary, good faith inquiry into the allegations to decide whether a more in-depth investigation is necessary. A disclosure log should be maintained, summarizing each disclosure received, the status of the inquiry conducted, and any corrective action taken.

Ineligible Persons

The OIG does not want hospitals (or other healthcare providers) that it pays to employ or contract with so-called Ineligible Persons. These are individuals or entities that are currently excluded, debarred, suspended, or otherwise ineligible to participate in the federal healthcare programs, or that have been convicted for any of the criminal violations described in 42 U.S.C.§ 1320a-7(a).[1] The OIG here asks BHC to identify such people in two

[1] This example of federal criminal law dealing with healthcare fraud and abuse-type violations is worth reading. The language can be found here: http://www.law.cornell.edu/uscode/text/42/1320a-7. Most lawyers use an expensive legal research service like Westlaw or Lexis-Nexis to look up legal sources like this one. However, it is also possible simply to Google search the citation. You will usually end up at an excellent free website like this one maintained by the Cornell University Law School.

ways. One is by asking them, during the hiring or contracting process, to identify themselves as Ineligible Persons. The second is to check the names of current and prospective employees and contractors against the OIG List of Excluded Individuals/Entities and the General Services Administration's List of Parties Excluded from Federal Programs.

When the BHC discovers an Ineligible Person among its ranks, it does not have to fire the individual or entity. However, it must remove the person from responsibility for hospital operations related to federal healthcare programs, and ensure that the person's compensation as well as any products or services he prescribes are not paid for by such programs. In many cases, it might make more sense to end the hospital's relationship with the person.

Notification of Government Investigation or Legal Proceedings

If BHC learns that a government entity (federal, state, or local) has begun an investigation or legal proceeding alleging that BHC committed a crime or engaged in fraudulent activities, it must notify the OIG within 30 days. Another OIG notification must be given within 30 days of the resolution of the matter.

Repayment of Overpayments

It is not uncommon for healthcare providers to receive payments that are in excess of the amount they are owed from federal healthcare program payors. These overpayments usually are the result of miscoding, billing misunderstandings, or other clerical errors, but can be related to attempts at fraud and abuse. Under BHC's CIA, it must repay the amount within 30 days of discovering it and correct the problem that caused it within 60 days. Some hospitals have ponderous, slow-moving administrative bureaucracies, though not necessarily BHC. It may be a challenge for such hospitals to take the required action within the 30-, 60-, and 90-day deadlines stipulated in most CIAs.

Reportable Events

In a separate provision, the CIA summarizes the reports that it wants to receive from the hospital. It uses the term Reportable Events. It includes the following:

- A substantial overpayment
- A matter that a reasonable person would consider a probable violation of criminal, civil, or administrative laws applicable to any federal healthcare program for which penalties or exclusion may be authorized

- The employment of or contracting with a covered person who is an Ineligible Person
- The filing of a bankruptcy petition by BHC

When BHC has made a considered determination that a Reportable Event has occurred, it must notify the OIG within 30 days. The notification should include:

- A complete description of the Reportable Event, including the relevant facts, persons involved, and legal and federal healthcare program authorities implicated.
- A description of BHC's actions taken to correct the Reportable Event.
- Any further steps BHC plans to take to address the Reportable Event and prevent it from recurring.
- If the Reportable Event has resulted in an overpayment, a description of the steps taken by BHC to identify and quantify the overpayment.

If the Reportable Event seems to involve nothing more than a violation of the Stark Physician Self-Referral Law, the required report should be submitted through the Centers for Medicare and Medicaid's self-referral disclosure protocol (SRDP).

Changes to Business Units or Locations

Under the CIA, the hospital must tell the OIG whenever there is a change in any of its "business units or locations." This refers to departments, divisions, subsidiaries, joint ventures, and other organizational components of BHC, as well as individual offices and facilities. The OIG wants to know if a business unit or location that furnishes services reimbursed by a federal healthcare program is moved or closed. A report should be made within 30 days of the move or closure.

A similar report is required whenever BHC establishes or purchases a new unit or location that furnishes federally reimbursed healthcare services. The same thing is true if the hospital decides to sell a unit or location.

It is through a healthcare organization's business units and locations that fraud and abuse is committed, and through them that compliance with relevant federal laws must take place. The OIG naturally wishes to be kept informed of the existence of each organization's components and what is happening to them.

Implementation and Annual Reports

Besides reports about specific events that occur, the OIG wants to be kept up-to-date about the hospital's compliance and violation-prevention activities during the 5-year term of the CIA. To begin with, within 150 days after the effective date of the CIA, the BHC must submit to the OIG a written report summarizing the status of its implementation of the CIA's terms. This report must include:

- Name of the Compliance Officer and any non compliance duties he or she may have
- Names of the members of the Compliance Committee
- Copy of the Code of Conduct that has been prepared
- Numbers and percentage of people who have completed the Code of Conduct certification
- Summary of Policies and Procedures prepared under the CIA
- Description of trainings and numbers who have attended them, with special mention of medical staff participation
- Description of the CIA-mandated Disclosure Program
- Information on the hospital's IRO, particularly regarding its independence and objectivity
- Description of the process by which BHC deals with Ineligible Persons
- List of all BHC locations and their Medicare provider numbers
- Description of BHC's corporate structure, including parent and sister companies, and subsidiaries

After that initial comprehensive statement from the hospital, the OIG wishes to receive an annual report in each of the 5 years of the CIA's term. Those reports must contain:

- Changes in the Compliance Officer and Compliance Committee members
- Governing board's resolution that it has review BHC's compliance with the CIA and federal healthcare program requirements
- Summary of any changes to the Code of Conduct
- Number and percentage of people who have certified their adherence to the Code of Conduct
- Summary of any changes to the CIA-mandated Policies and Procedures
- Description of trainings and numbers who have attended them, with special mention of medical staff participation
- Copies of all Claims and Unallowable Cost Reviews

- Hospital's response to those reviews along with corrective actions for problems that were identified
- Certification from the IRO regarding its independence and objectivity
- Summary of Reportable Events during the year and corrective actions taken
- Detailed report of the aggregate overpayments that have been returned to federal healthcare programs
- Summary of the items in the Disclosure Log that relate to federal healthcare programs
- Summary description of any ongoing government investigation or legal proceeding alleging criminal or fraudulent activity
- Description of changes to the list of BHC's locations

In the initial and subsequent annual reports, the hospital Compliance Officer must certify that:

- The hospital is in compliance with all the CIA terms.
- The information in the report is accurate and truthful.
- The hospital has complied with its claims-related obligations under the Settlement Agreement associated with the CIA.

The OIG asks the hospital to identify any part of its reports or other submissions to the OIG that may constitute trade secrets, or information that is commercial or financial and privileged or confidential, and therefore potentially exempt from disclosure under the federal Freedom of Information Act (FOIA).

OIG Inspection, Audit, and Review Rights

In the CIA, the OIG asserts its right to examine or request copies of the BHC's books, records, and other documents and supporting materials, and to conduct on-site reviews of BHC's locations for the purpose of verifying and evaluating its compliance with the terms of the CIA and the federal healthcare programs in which it participates. The OIG also may interview the hospital's employees, contractors, or agents who consent to be interviewed. The employees may choose to be accompanied by a hospital representative during the interview.

Document and Record Retention

The CIA requires that BHC maintain for inspection all documents and records relating to its reimbursements from the federal healthcare programs and to its compliance with the CIA for 6 years from the effective date of the CIA.

Disclosures

The OIG promises to make a "reasonable effort" to notify BHC before it releases any of the information that BHC has submitted under the CIA and designated as trade secrets, or privileged or confidential. The hospital's rights are protected under the FOIA, 5 U.S.C.§ 552.[2]

Breach and Default Provisions

The CIA goes into considerable detail about how the OIG will respond if BHC breaches or defaults on the provisions in its CIA. This section makes very clear how seriously a healthcare organization must view a CIA.

The BHC agrees with the OIG that it will pay a Stipulated Penalty of $2,500 for each day that it fails to take CIA-required actions regarding:

- A Compliance Officer
- A Compliance Committee
- A written Code of Conduct
- Written Policies and Procedures
- The training of covered persons and board members
- A Disclosure Program
- Ineligible Persons screening and removal requirements
- Notification of government investigations or legal proceedings
- Reporting of Reportable Events
- Engagement and use of an IRO
- Submitting the Implementation Report or any Annual Reports
- Submitting any Claims Review Report or Unallowable Cost Review Report

The Stipulated Penalty is $1,500 for each day that BHC fails to grant access for OIG inspections, audits, and reviews. It is $5,000 for each false certification that BHC submits as part of its Implementation Report, any Annual Report, or as required by the OIG. For a failure to comply with any other obligation of the CIA not covered by these other penalties, the hospital will pay $1,000 per day. The hospital can suspend a monetary penalty by

[2] The FOIA governs the release of information that has come into the possession of the Federal government. The basic provisions of the law can be seen here, http://www.law.cornell.edu/uscode/text/5/552. A full explanation of the law and how to use it to request information from the Federal government is available here, http://www.foia.gov/

requesting, before the due date for an activity, an extension of time to perform any act or file any notification or report required by the CIA.

When the OIG determines that the BHC has failed to comply with any of its CIA obligations and that Stipulated Penalties are appropriate, it will send the hospital a Demand Letter seeking payment of the penalties. Within 10 days of receiving the letter, BHC must either cure the breach and pay the penalties, or request a hearing to dispute OIG's determination that it failed to comply.

Stipulated Penalties are not the worst punishment that the OIG can administer. In the case of a Material Breach by BHC of the CIA, it may be excluded from participation in federal healthcare programs. That means that it cannot submit claims for reimbursement under Medicare, Medicaid, or other federal programs. The result is often a dramatic decrease in an organization's revenues.

A Material Breach is defined as:

- A repeated or flagrant violation of the obligations under the CIA.
- A failure by BHC to report a Reportable Event, take corrective action, and make the appropriate refunds.
- A failure to respond to a Demand Letter concerning the payment of Stipulated Penalties.
- A failure to engage and use an IRO.

When such a breach has occurred, the OIG will send to the hospital a Notice of Material Breach and Intent to Exclude. The hospital then has 30 days to demonstrate to the OIG that it has brought itself into compliance with the CIA obligations that were the basis for the Material Breach, that it has cured the breach, or that it cannot be cured within the 30 days and the hospital is pursuing with due diligence action to cure the breach. If, at the conclusion of the 30-day period, BHC is unable to show the OIG one of those three proofs, the OIG may exclude the hospital from participation in the federal healthcare programs. The exclusion will have national effect and will also apply to all other federal procurement and nonprocurement programs.

The CIA defines in great detail the rights of the hospital to challenge the various determinations and decisions made by the OIG. This may be accomplished first by seeking a review by a DHHS administrative law judge (ALJ) and, if appropriate, appealing that decision to the DHHS Departmental Appeals Board (DAB). A decision by the DAB or a decision by an ALJ, if not appealed, are considered final. They may not be appealed to a court of law.

Effective and Binding Agreement

It is worth noting that the CIA is binding on the "successors, assigns, and transferees" of the BHC. If a unit or facility of the BHC is sold or transferred to another entity, it still must satisfy the requirements of the CIA.

Appendices

The CIAs for most large healthcare entities also contain two appendices, and this is the case for BHC. The first concerns the IRO mentioned previously in the agreement; the second expands upon the annual Claims Review that the IRO must perform.

The IRO tone appendix briefly discusses the topics of IRO Engagement, IRO Qualifications, IRO Responsibilities, IRO Independence and Objectivity, and IRO Removal or Termination. In the wake of numerous corporate financial scandals over the last decade, the independence and objectivity of an auditing body like the IRO has become more important. As a result of the Sarbanes-Oxley Act and an increased focus on issues relating to auditor independence, the OIG in 2004 issued a formal Guidance on IRO Independence and Objectivity that was revised in 2010.

The main message of the Guidance is that IROs have a continuing obligation to self-assess both their objectivity when performing IRO reviews as well as their independence. It defines objectivity as "being independent in fact and in appearance when providing audit and attestation engagements, maintaining an attitude of impartiality, having intellectual honesty, and being free of conflicts of interest." To be independent, both "the audit organization and individual auditor must be free from personal, external, and organizational impairments to independence and must avoid the appearance of such impairments of independence."

The OIG recommends two paths to achieving IRO objectivity and independence. First, the IRO must not perform non-audit activities involving management functions or decisions. Second, it must not review its own work. The Guidance gives examples of activities that would and would not impair the IRO's independence and objectivity.

These activities ARE NOT likely to impair the IRO's independence and objectivity:

- IRO personnel furnish general compliance training that addresses the requirements of the provider's CIA and introduces employees to the provider's overall compliance program.
- The IRO performs routine tasks relating to the provider's confidential Disclosure Program, such as answering the confidential hotline or transcribing the allegations received via the hotline.

- The IRO performs the Ineligible Persons screening by entering the employee names into the exclusion databases and providing the screening results to the provider.
- The IRO evaluates the provider's existing compliance program before the provider's CIA is executed, presents its conclusions regarding the strengths and weaknesses of the provider's existing compliance program, and makes recommendations regarding areas for improvement.
- The IRO provides personnel to perform work plan procedures that are developed by the provider's internal audit department and are not related to the subject matter of the CIA reviews.
- The IRO furnishes consulting services to the provider under an arrangement that is completed prior to the start of the CIA reviews, and the services (1) are not related to the subject matter of the CIA reviews and (2) do not involve the performance of management functions.
- The IRO performs an assessment of the strengths and weaknesses of the provider's internal controls, even if those controls relate to the subject matter of the CIA review, as long as the IRO is not responsible for designing or implementing corrective action based on its internal controls assessment, or otherwise performing management functions.

These activities ARE likely to impair the IRO's independence and objectivity:

- A provider uses a billing system or coding software that was developed or designed by the IRO and the IRO is hired to perform a Claims Review.
- IRO personnel furnish specific training that addresses the subject matter of the CIA review.
- The IRO develops the provider's policies, procedures, or internal controls.
- The IRO participates in decision-making related to the confidential Disclosure Program, such as determining which allegations warrant further investigation or the appropriate corrective action to take in response to compliance allegations.
- The IRO performs an assessment of the strengths and weaknesses of the provider's internal controls associated with the specific risk areas that are addressed in the CIA and is hired by the provider to design or implement new processes or internal controls that relate to the subject matter of the CIA reviews.
- The provider outsources its internal audit function to the IRO.

- The IRO is engaged to provide consulting services to the provider during the term of the CIA on a matter that is related to the subject matter of the CIA reviews.

The second appendix provides details on the annual Claims Review to be performed by the IRO. It describes a preliminary Discovery Sample of paid claims that must be taken and reviewed. Based on the error rate found, a Full Sample and Systems Review may be required. The appendix also explains the information that the IRO must include in the Claims Review Report it prepares for each sample it takes. In particular, the findings from the Claims Review must be expressed in both narrative (description of billing and coding system, reasons for errors found, patterns detected) and quantitative results (statistical representation of error rates).

This CIA is an excellent example of the remedial measures imposed upon a large hospital offering inpatient and outpatient psychiatric services for adolescents and adults, whose fraud and abuse problems were in the areas of billing and coding. This has been the focus of most CIAs for the last couple decades. In the last few years, however, many of them have been based on financial relationships with referral sources (involving settlements of Stark and Anti-Kickback Law charges) and drug manufacturer off-label marketing practice reviews. There is much more diversity in the character of currently negotiated CIAs.

STUDY QUESTIONS

1. What could a healthcare organization do to improve the chances that it would be offered a CIA and spared a Medicare program exclusion in the event that it was found to have committed a fraud and abuse violation?
2. Most CIAs include the recommended seven elements of an effective compliance program among their provisions. What are those seven elements? Find that information in other chapters of this text or on the Internet.
3. The CIA applies to a wide range of "covered persons" with some connection to the affected organization, including contractors, subcontractors, vendors, and other third parties. How does the organization persuade them to cooperate with its CIA-mandated initiatives—training, Code of Conduct, reviews conducted by the IRO, Disclosure Program, Ineligible Persons, and so forth?
4. What is an Ineligible Person?
5. What are some examples of Reportable Events?

6. Describe how you would set up a Disclosure Program that does the best possible job of encouraging covered persons to report suspected violations or noncompliance.
7. What is OIG's policy regarding the reporting of federal healthcare program overpayments by providers under CIAs?
8. What is the purpose of a Discovery Sample conducted by an IRO for a CIA Claims Review?

Learning Exercises

1. Go to this page on the OIG website for a list of currently active CIAs: https://oig.hhs.gov/compliance/corporate-integrity-agreements/cia-documents.asp. Open and read the CIAs for several types of healthcare organizations that are different from the BHC Sierra Vista psychiatric hospital whose CIA is discussed in this chapter. Try a pharmaceutical company, a testing laboratory, a physician practice, an academic medical center, and an ambulance service. Find the language and provisions in those documents that are different from the CIA in the BHC case. What do you think is the reason for the unique terms in those agreements?
2. You work for a healthcare organization that has just entered into a CIA. You have been asked to identify and contract with an appropriate IRO to perform the reviews required by the CIA. Explain where you will look to find an entity capable of serving as an IRO, the criteria you will use in choosing the best one for your organization, and what terms you will include in the contract with the IRO in order to elicit the desired performance from them.

References

1. Medicare Program Integrity Manual, Chapter 4—Benefit Integrity, http://www.cms.gov/Regulations-and-Guidance/Guidance/Manuals/Internet-Only-Manuals-IOMs-Items/CMS019033.html
2. OIG Guidance on IRO Independence and Objectivity, https://oig.hhs.gov/fraud/cia/docs/oig_guidance_on_iro_independence_2010.pdf
3. Section of the OIG website dealing with CIAs, https://oig.hhs.gov/compliance/corporate-integrity-agreements/index.asp

Section II

Elements of a Good Compliance Program

This section describes the structure and inner workings of what has come to be accepted as the model for healthcare compliance programs. Chapter 8 provides an overview of all the seven basic components of a compliance program. The other chapters explain individually six of those components.

The seventh component is concerned with policies and procedures, which typically focus on risk areas that are unique to each type of healthcare organization. They are discussed in Section III.

Chapter 8

Compliance Programs in General

Learning Objectives

After completing class sessions based on this chapter, a student will:

- Recognize the benefits of a comprehensive compliance program.
- See the connection between the Federal Sentencing Guidelines and the compliance programs required by the Office of the Inspector General (OIG).
- Be familiar with the seven standard components of a mandatory compliance program.
- Know the role of a Compliance Officer (CO) and her preferred position within the organization.
- Also know the supporting role played by the Compliance Committee (CC).
- Understand the purpose of the policies and procedures element of a compliance program, especially their application to risk areas.
- Be able to outline a compliance training initiative, including curriculum, schedule, and participants.
- Appreciate the value of open communication channels for transmitting questions and complaints.
- Learn the purposes and methods of auditing and monitoring compliance activities.
- Know how to describe a responsible disciplinary program for dealing with employee misconduct and noncompliance.
- Receive an introduction to the kind of investigation necessary when non-compliance is suspected.
- Discover what some healthcare organizations are doing with their compliance programs.

INTRODUCTION

Any healthcare organization seriously interested in conducting business in a legal and ethical manner must have a compliance program. The provision of healthcare services and products is too complex an undertaking and subject to too many laws to assume that lawful work conduct will happen by itself. Whether by accident or intention, things will go wrong. Laws will be violated. A compliance program is a multi-faceted infrastructure of rules, trainings, penalties, and response protocols that will reduce the incidence of noncompliance, detect it faster when it happens, and prevent its recurrence. Over the last two decades, there has developed a proven format for a good program. It is described best in the OIG Compliance Program Guidances.

COMPLIANCE PROGRAMS ARE REQUIRED

Since 1998, the OIG in the Department of Health and Human Services (DHHS) has been encouraging healthcare organizations participating in federal healthcare programs to adopt voluntary compliance programs. Toward that end, it issued Compliance Program Guidances tailored to 12 different types of healthcare organizations. The Guidances provide details on the content of the compliance programs that the OIG recommended.

In 2010, the Patient Protection and Affordable Care Act (PPACA) was enacted with the intent to reform many aspects of healthcare financing and delivery in the United States. One of its provisions requires that healthcare organizations participating in Medicare or Medicaid implement a compliance program that incorporates core elements defined by the DHHS Secretary. The Secretary has proposed adopting the existing requirements of the Federal Sentencing Guidelines.

It is unlikely that the DHHS will make significant changes in the seven program elements that it has emphasized and repeated in Program Guidance over the last decade and a half. There are subtle differences in the Guidances for each type of healthcare organization, primarily with regard to the areas of highest compliance risk. It is possible to discuss the components of a good generic compliance program, starting with the benefits to the organization of adopting such a program.

BENEFITS OF A COMPLIANCE PROGRAM

There is no denying that, to most healthcare organizations, a comprehensive compliance program looks like just another expense on top of so many other cost pressures that they are facing. Therefore, it is worth noting the very clear benefits produced by compliance activities.

- First and foremost, now that the programs are mandatory, their implementation allows an organization to participate in Medicare and Medicaid, major sources of revenue for most healthcare entities.
- The existence of a compliance program demonstrates an organization's commitment to good corporate citizenship. This carries weight with customers, regulators, and members of the public.
- It enables the organization systematically to root out, correct, and prevent misconduct and illegal behavior.
- The program infrastructure becomes a central clearinghouse for information on legal and payor requirements that apply to the organization.
- A key feature of a compliance program is a methodology that encourages employees to report suspected misconduct or noncompliance.
- The program also compels the organization to develop a rigorous protocol for investigating and resolving incidents of misconduct or noncompliance. This includes a variety of corrective actions.
- By following the precepts of its compliance program, the organization reduces its exposure to civil damages, monetary penalties, criminal sanctions, administrative remedies, program exclusions, qui tam law suits, and the imposition of Corporate Integrity Agreements (CIAs).
- The existence and operation of a compliance program enhances the organization's public image and reputation.
- To be effective, a compliance program will require the organization to improve many aspects of its operations, such as medical records documentation and the process for preparing and submitting claims.
- The program will provide valuable information on employee understanding of good compliance practices and their propensity toward misconduct.
- It gives the organization an ability to react more quickly and effectively to employees' reports of misconduct and noncompliance.
- A well-conceived program improves communication and cooperation among healthcare entities that may share in the responsibility for noncompliant acts.
- One of the results of a compliance program is the opening of communication channels that empower employees to ask questions and report misconduct.

INFLUENCE OF THE FEDERAL SENTENCING GUIDELINES

Medicare and Medicaid are federal healthcare programs, governed by federal criminal laws. Frequently, fraud and abuse by healthcare individuals and organizations has led to criminal charges and convictions. Fines and jail sentences have been imposed on individuals for their fraudulent actions. The presence of a compliance program may affect the amount of the fine and duration of the sentence. The Federal Sentencing Guidelines explain precisely how a program will reduce an organization's "culpability score."

The introductory commentary to the Guidelines explains the relevance of compliance programs to the federal sentencing process.

> These guidelines offer incentives to organizations to reduce and ultimately eliminate criminal conduct by providing a structural foundation from which an organization may self-police its own conduct through an effective compliance and ethics program. The prevention and detection of criminal conduct, as facilitated by an effective compliance and ethics program, will assist an organization in encouraging ethical conduct and in complying fully with all applicable laws.

The Guidelines list the seven minimum requirements of an "effective compliance and ethics program."

1. The organization shall establish standards and procedures to prevent and detect criminal conduct.
2. The organization's governing authority shall be knowledgeable about the content and operation of the compliance and ethics program and shall exercise reasonable oversight with respect to the implementation and effectiveness of the compliance and ethics program.
3. The organization shall use reasonable efforts not to include within the substantial authority personnel of the organization any individual whom the organization knows, or should have known through the exercise of due diligence, has engaged in illegal activities or other conduct inconsistent with an effective compliance and ethics program.
4. The organization shall take reasonable steps to communicate periodically and in a practical manner its standards and procedures, and other aspects of the compliance and ethics program, by conducting effective training programs and otherwise disseminating information appropriate to such individuals' respective roles and responsibilities.

5. The organization shall take reasonable steps (a) to ensure that the organization's compliance and ethics program is followed, including monitoring and auditing to detect criminal conduct; (b) to evaluate periodically the effectiveness of the organization's compliance and ethics program; and (c) to have and publicize a system, which may include mechanisms that allow for anonymity or confidentiality, whereby the organization's employees and agents may report or seek guidance regarding potential or actual criminal conduct without fear of retaliation.
6. The organization's compliance and ethics program shall be promoted and enforced consistently throughout the organization through (a) appropriate incentives to perform in accordance with the compliance and ethics program; and (b) appropriate disciplinary measures for engaging in criminal conduct and for failing to take reasonable steps to prevent or detect criminal conduct.
7. After criminal conduct has been detected, the organization shall take reasonable steps to respond appropriately to the criminal conduct and to prevent further similar criminal conduct, including making any necessary modifications to the organization's compliance and ethics program.

The OIG clearly had these guidelines in mind when it began drawing up its Compliance Program Guidances for numerous types of healthcare organizations. All the Guidances propose the same seven basic components of a good compliance program. They apply only to healthcare organizations, and each Guidance focuses on one particular type of organization. The Guidances provide much greater detail about the content of each component, and about the unique compliance risk areas present in each organizational type.

SEVEN BASIC COMPONENTS OF A RECOMMENDED COMPLIANCE PROGRAM

The actions described in the OIG Program Guidances do not, by themselves, constitute a compliance program. They are guidelines that healthcare organizations should refer to when designing their own programs. The numerous differences among organizations require that they establish different compliance programs. They operate in different parts of the healthcare industry; they sell their products or services to different customers; they deal with different vendors, suppliers, and independent contractors; they face different kinds of legal risk; and they have different amounts of resources to devote to a compliance program. The OIG acknowledges these differences. As a result, it has different compliance expectations for organizations.

Nonetheless, the Program Guidances reveal some general principles of which all healthcare entities and their officials should be aware. To begin with, at a minimum, a comprehensive compliance program should include the following seven elements:

1. The development and distribution of written standards of conduct, policies, and procedures governing employee behavior in operational areas at high risk of noncompliance.
2. The designation of a CO and a CC to develop and manage the organization's compliance activities.
3. The development and implementation of regular training and education programs on compliance issues for employees.
4. The establishment of several channels of communication between employees and the CO for the purpose of receiving reports of suspected noncompliance and questions about the organization's compliance program.
5. The conduct of regular audits and ongoing monitoring to assess the effectiveness of compliance activities and identify emerging compliance problems.
6. The application of disciplinary action against employees and agents who have violated the organization's compliance rules and contributed to noncompliance events.
7. The investigation of suspected noncompliance followed by appropriate corrective action.

Following is a more detailed discussion of each of these elements.

Organizational Infrastructure of a Compliance Program: Compliance Officer (CO) and Compliance Committee (CC)

This element establishes the personnel infrastructure on which the following six elements are built. As a practical matter, the CO is likely to be the first person in the organization focusing all of his or her energies on implementing a compliance program and preventing violations.

The organization designates a single person to serve as CO. In large organizations, this should be a full-time job responsibility. In smaller entities, with fewer employees and other resources, it may be necessary for the designated individual to share compliance duties with other existing work responsibilities.

The status of the CO within the organization is critical. It determines the authority he or she will have to carry out compliance functions. The best practice is for the CO to be a member of the C-suite, on the same level with the Chief Financial Officer (CFO) or the Chief Medical Officer. His or her title might even be Chief Compliance Officer. Like those other executives, the CO would report directly to the Chief Executive Officer (CEO) or President of the organization.

In addition, the CO must have direct access to the governing board. The CEO should not have the authority to deny or restrict that access. The CO also should be able to count on the full cooperation of other senior executives. Among the resources available to the CO must be advice from a legal counsel expert in health law. At the same time, the OIG prefers not to see the CO subordinate to either the organization's General Counsel or CFO. In a case of misconduct or suspected fraud, both those officials might have an interest in pressuring the CO to relax his or her compliance efforts.

The reason for the CO's high position in the organization is to prevent interference by other officials in his or her efforts to prevent fraud, abuse, and other forms of noncompliance in the organization.

The compliance function in any modern healthcare organization entails a wide range of activities, for which the CO is ultimately responsible.

- Overseeing and monitoring the implementation of the compliance program.
- Reporting on a regular basis to the organization's governing board, CEO, and CC on the progress of implementation.
- Assisting individuals and units in establishing methods to improve the organization's efficiency and quality of services and to reduce its vulnerability to fraud, abuse, and waste.
- Periodically revising the compliance program in light of changes in the organization's needs, and in the laws and requirements of public and private payor health plans.
- Developing, coordinating, and participating in a multifaceted educational and training effort that focuses on the elements of the compliance program, and seeks to ensure that all appropriate employees are familiar and compliant with federal and state standards.
- Ensuring that independent contractors and agents who furnish products and services to the organization are aware of the requirements of its compliance program regarding coding, billing, and marketing, among other things.
- Coordinating personnel issues with the organization's Human Resources or Personnel Department to ensure that the National

Practitioner Data Bank and the OIG's List of Excluded Individuals and Entities have been checked with respect to all employees, medical staff, and independent contractors.
- Assisting the organization's financial management in coordinating internal compliance review and monitoring activities, including annual or periodic reviews of departments.
- Independently investigating and acting on compliance-related matters, including the design and coordination of the investigations and resulting corrective action.
- Developing policies and programs that encourage managers and employees to report suspected fraud and other improprieties without fear of retaliation.
- Collaborating with the organization's legal counsel in the appropriate reporting of any self-discovered violations of federal healthcare program requirements.
- Reviewing documents and other evidence related to compliance incidents and activities.
- Reviewing the organization's interactions with federal healthcare programs and healthcare professionals to look for potential legal or program violations.

In performing these duties, the CO must communicate and coordinate effectively with individuals and departments throughout the organization.

The CO is ultimately accountable to the governing board for the organization's compliance with all relevant laws and program requirements. This person may be in the position of having to tell other high company officers to stop what they are doing in order to avoid a violation. This may take considerable courage and stamina. The CO may be the public face of the organization on compliance issues, dealing with strategic partners, stakeholders, the media, and even customers/patients. If the organization is formally charged with violations, the CO will likely have to play a leading role, with legal counsel, in preparing the organization's defense, perhaps even serving as a witness.

The importance of the CO's authority cannot be overemphasized. In conscientiously carrying out his or her duties, the CO may appear to stand in the way of an organization's market, financial, and strategic goals. He or she may be viewed as an irritant by the rest of the executive team. When legal crises, ethical dilemmas, and allegations against successful managers arise, the CO will have to make unpopular decisions.

This person's authority can be strengthened in several ways. The CO can be appointed by a vote of the governing board. The CEO can give the CO regular recognition and active support. The compliance head can be seen to have unrestricted access to the CEO and the governing body, whenever the need is felt. The CO may be invited to provide input to the job evaluations of executives and managers.

The CO's partner in planning and administering the compliance program is the CC. This group typically is composed of representatives from pertinent areas of the organization: legal, internal auditing, human resources, security, risk management, clinical staff, and key operating units. The individual members should have the time to take from their normal duties to spend on compliance tasks.

There are two possible visions of the CC's mandate. One is that they function as advisors to the CO, to be called on in the most challenging situations. The Committee might also hear appeals from the CO's decisions. In the other vision, the Committee members perform more substantive work, helping the CO design, implement, and maintain the compliance program. The choice between these two visions may depend upon the size of the organization's resources and staff. The OIG acknowledges that very small entities, like some physician practices, may not be able to set up a CC at all. In such cases, a task force should be created to address problems when they arise.

Written Standards, Policies, and Procedures to Guide Work Behavior

If a healthcare organization wants its employees to follow certain rules in carrying out their jobs, the first step is to put those rules in writing. The Program Guidances for all 12 types of healthcare entities include an element for written standards, policies, and procedures. This is an example of the language used.

> Every compliance program should develop and distribute written compliance standards, procedures, and practices that guide the [organization] and the conduct of its employees throughout day-to-day operations. These policies and procedures should be developed under the direction and supervision of the compliance officer, the compliance committee, and operational managers. At a minimum, they should be provided to all employees who are affected by these policies, as well as physicians, suppliers, [third party] agents, and contractors, as applicable to those entities. In addition to general corporate policies and procedures, an effective compliance program should include specific policies and procedures for the different clinical, financial, and administrative functions of [the organization].

In practice, these words call for three categories of directives. The first is a broad Code or Standards of Conduct. The second is policies and procedures that prescribe general principles of employee behavior that comply with the various laws that impact healthcare organizations. The third is policies and procedures that describe, in detail, how employees should perform their jobs in the functional areas at highest risk of misconduct and violation (e.g., billing and collection, marketing, relationships with referral sources). There may even be a fourth group of policies and procedures that explain how the elements of the program will be administered.

Code of Conduct. The OIG recommends that the first step in an organization's documentation of its compliance rules be a Code of Conduct, a sort of "constitution" setting out the basic values and principles that employees are expected to follow in the everyday performance of their jobs. Unlike more detailed operating policies and procedures, the Code of Conduct should be brief, quickly understood, memorable, and applicable to all employees and agents. It should articulate the organization's philosophy, summarize basic legal principles, and inform employees how to respond to practices that may violate the philosophy or principles.[1] It is possible to prepare a focused Code of Conduct that takes no more than a page or two.

The organization's leadership will view the Code of Conduct as a reflection of the character of the entity and, indirectly, its own character. The organization's employees will look at the Code as one of the primary terms and conditions of their employment. The Code of Conduct will impress the public in general as evidence of the organization's good citizenship and worthiness as a source of healthcare good or services. The Code tells suppliers, vendors, third-party agents, and strategic partners that the organization is a high-integrity, trustworthy business partner.

General policies and procedures. The next level of compliance documents outlines the organization's commitment to abide by the wide variety of external requirements and constraints imposed on it. Generally, these include the laws related specifically to the healthcare industry that are the focus of this text, the whole range of other laws (e.g., environmental protection, employment discrimination) that apply to all businesses, and the requirements for participation in federal healthcare programs like Medicare and Medicaid. Many employees will not encounter these laws in their day-to-day work, but it still is a good idea for them to be aware of them.

Specific policies and procedures. The rules that are written and enforced at this level dictate, in very practical terms, how employees working in areas

---

[1] These are the Codes of Conduct of two large teaching hospitals: Stanford Hospital and Clinics, http://stanfordhospital.org/overview/conduct.html, and University Hospitals (Cleveland, OH), http://www.uhhospitals.org/about/mission-and-vision/code-of-conduct

at high-risk of noncompliance are to perform their jobs. The OIG Program Guidances are especially useful in drawing up these documents. The bulk of the Guidance for each type of healthcare organization is devoted to a description of the risk areas that the OIG has identified for that organization type, along with specific suggestions for policies and procedures to address the risk.

For instance, the Program Guidance for physician practices draws attention to the importance of accurate medical record documentation, and then suggests that each practice implement guidelines to ensure the following:

- The medical record is complete and legible.
- The documentation of each patient encounter includes the reason for the encounter; any relevant history; physical examination findings; prior diagnostic test results; assessment, clinical impression, or diagnosis; plan of care; and date and legible identity of the observer.
- Codes used for claims submission are supported by documentation and the medical record.
- Appropriate health risk factors are identified. The patient's progress, his or her response to, and any changes in, treatment, and any revision in diagnosis is documented.

In another example, concerning hospitals, the Program Guidance discusses the need to scrutinize hospital relationships with physicians for possible violations of the Stark Physician Self-Referral Law. It then recommends that the hospital ask these questions:

- Is there a referral from a physician for a designated health service? If not, then there is no Stark Law issue (although other fraud and abuse authorities, such as the Anti-Kickback Statute, may be implicated). If the answer is "yes," the next inquiry is:
- Does the physician (or an immediate family member) have a financial relationship with the entity furnishing the designated health services (DHS) (e.g., the hospital)? Again, if the answer is "no," the Stark Law is not implicated. However, if the answer is "yes," the third inquiry is:
- Does the financial relationship fit in an exception? If not, the statute has been violated.

The particular standards, policies, and procedures developed will be unique to each healthcare organization and will be based on its existing written rules, the results of an internal compliance risk assessment, an expert legal analysis, the organization's prior compliance experiences, best practices of similar organizations, requirements for participation in both federal and private healthcare programs, and the OIG's official publications

(Program Guidances, Special Fraud Alerts, Advisory Opinions, Annual Work Plans) and enforcement activities. These are the most practical, detailed, and critical of all an organization's directions to employees.

Administrative Policies and Procedures. These are the organization's written directives on how to implement the other six elements of its compliance program. They will address issues like:

- Delegating compliance responsibility from the CO and the CC to unit managers throughout the organization, particularly those overseeing high-risk areas.
- Taking compliance behaviors into account during the performance evaluations of managers and other employees.
- Communicating the policies and procedures to the employees who need to see them.
- Requiring employee participation in compliance training programs.
- Installing auditing and monitoring systems to detect misconduct and noncompliance.
- Establishing several alternative channels of communication to receive employee reports.
- Incorporating compliance standards into contracts with employees, contractors, suppliers, and vendors.
- Defining the steps to be followed in response to detected incidents of noncompliance.

It is not enough simply to write down the standards, policies, and procedures. They also must be communicated to, and understood by, the people who will put them into practice. These materials must be presented to employees and others in formats that take into account their languages, education levels, and backgrounds. Innovative communication methods should be used to keep the message of these documents constantly in the forefront of employees' minds. They should know the basic principles of compliance by heart, while having quick access to the finer details that tell them how to perform their jobs. Employees should be asked to acknowledge in writing that they have received copies of the relevant rules, they understand them, and they agree to follow them.

Education and Training Programs on Compliant Work Behavior

Once an organization has prepared good compliance-related standards, policies, and procedures and made them easily available to employees, it must give those employees forceful, persistent training in applying the rules to their own work. The OIG Program Guidances provide brief but useful direction on how that training should be carried out.

Every healthcare organization should provide appropriate training to employees when they first are hired and then again, at regular intervals, as they continue in their jobs. New employees should receive an initial training within 30–60 days of their initial employment. The best practice is to incorporate the training into the new employee's orientation, which typically takes place within a week or two of the hire date. The periodic trainings should occur at least annually, as a matter of principle. More frequent training sessions should be scheduled when there have been significant updates or changes in the compliance rules or the organization's compliance program.

The curriculum of a basic compliance training program will include these topics:

- Overview of federal and state laws, regulations, and administrative guidelines
- Summary of healthcare laws specific to the organization (e.g., False Claims Act, Anti-Kickback Statute, Stark Physician Self-Referral Law)
- Coding requirements for billing and claims
- Principles of a compliant claim development and submission process
- Program requirements and conditions of participation for public and private healthcare plans
- Organization's code of ethical behavior
- Marketing practices that comply with applicable laws
- Referral source relationships that comply with applicable laws
- Statement of the organization's commitment to abide by all legal requirements
- Key features of the organization's compliance program
- Mechanisms for raising compliance questions and reporting compliance problems

These subjects might be covered in a more sophisticated or ambitious program.

- Case studies of ethical dilemmas that employees might encounter
- A decision-making protocol for complex ethical situations
- Compliance resources and how to use or access them
- Expectations of managers and supervisors for overseeing their subordinates' compliance behavior
- Regular updates on recent changes in legal and program requirements

Organizations should require that employees attend a minimum number of hours of training sessions each year. Their attendance and active participation should be a condition of their continued employment, and a failure to satisfy that condition should lead to disciplinary action, including possible termination. The adherence to the compliance principles taught in the training sessions should be a factor in the annual evaluation of each employee's performance. To demonstrate that all this has happened, the organization should keep records of its training activities, in the form of attendance logs and copies of teaching materials used and distributed.

Compliance training sessions should be directed at all levels of the healthcare organization: members of the governing body, the CEO, other top executives, managers and supervisors, other employees, and nonemployee clinicians. To the fullest extent possible, it is also a good idea to require, or at least strongly urge, independent contractors, vendors, and suppliers to attend some of the training sessions.

A variety of teaching methods can be used: in-person classes with internal or third-party instructors, interactive computer programs, interactive CD/DVDs, streaming video courses, self-study, group study, and printed materials, among others. The tone and format of all teaching should be tailored to the characteristics of the participants, taking into account their education and reading levels, language preferences, and ethnicities.

Open Communication Channels for Questions and Reports

There are two good reasons why an employee might want to speak with a company compliance official. The employee may wish clarification of one of the organization's standards, policies, or procedures as it applies to the performance of his/her job. An employee may have discovered evidence of possible misconduct or noncompliance by another employee and want to report it to someone in authority. A responsible organization wants to encourage these types of communication. It especially wants to hear about potential compliance violations. This is accomplished by establishing clear channels of communication between employees and the organization's compliance officials.

The more willing that employees are to speak up about suspected misconduct, the sooner that the organization will learn about serious violations, initiate investigations, determine the gravity of the misconduct, and take corrective actions. Employees will feel more confident expressing their concerns if they believe that they will be taken seriously, that they will not suffer retaliation, and that identified problems will be handled appropriately.

The first step for an organization is to create a work environment, an organizational culture, in which employees feel comfortable talking about problems they have observed, compliance related and otherwise. Reliable, confidential mechanisms must be put in place to receive reports from employees reluctant to speak openly to a manager or supervisor. The organization should systematically follow up on and document all reports received to ensure that they were investigated and resolved promptly and appropriately. The documentation should be summarized and passed on to higher management and the governing board.

The best course for a healthcare organization that can afford it is to establish more than one communication channel for compliance reporting. Because some employees will prefer one channel over another, this strategy maximizes the likelihood that problems will be brought to the attention of the management. The traditional mechanisms are to speak directly to one's supervisor, to a higher level manager, or to someone in the Human Resources Department. These approaches do not allow for much anonymity. A popular alternative is a telephone hotline, administered internally or outsourced, through which anonymous reports can be made. Other options are a dedicated email address, a question/complain box, an independent intermediary, and employee exit interviews. Whichever options are chosen, they should be convenient for employees and one or another should be accessible at all times.

To be most effective, the communication channels must be supported by a handful of essential policies. There must be assurance that the identity of employees who use the channels and the information that they report will be kept confidential. It will need to be explained, however, that at a certain point in the ensuing investigation, it may be necessary to reveal the employee's identity. Employees must also feel confident that they will suffer no retaliatory disciplinary actions. On the other hand, it should be made clear that an employee will not absolve him or herself of responsibility for a violation by being the person who reports it to the organization.

The organization should inform its employees of the standard investigatory process that will be followed whenever a report of suspected misconduct or noncompliance is received. Predictability and uniformity in this process will inspire employee confidence, making them more will willing to use it.

Once the communication channels have been opened, the organization should publicize their existence frequently and in as many ways as possible. Initially, the CEO might issue an announcement, followed by posters, newsletter articles, and periodic notices. An employee wishing to file a report should not have to think hard about where and how to do it.

Ongoing Monitoring and Auditing of Compliance Activities

After all its effort in constructing a compliance program (designating a CO and CC, writing standards, policies and procedures, conducting training and education, and opening channels of communication), an organization needs to constantly evaluate how well that program is performing. It accomplishes this through regular monitoring and auditing.

Monitoring is the persistent review of activities in the course of normal day-to-day operations by an organization. The best monitoring is embedded in those operations and is conducted automatically. Auditing is a more formal, discrete review of an organization's compliance with a select set of criteria, such as laws and payor program requirements, or the organization's own compliance program standards. Organizations with sufficient resources will conduct a combination of monitoring and auditing activities.

Monitoring may be performed simply to ensure that a compliance program is working as intended. It also may follow up on a corrective action plan to ensure that the desired improvements are taking effect. A monitoring function can be carried out by review staff independent of the organization or by employees who work in the area under study.

Choices must be made about what activities to monitor or audit; an organization cannot afford to watch everything. As a group, the OIG Program Guidances describe a few generic areas that deserve scrutiny in nearly all types of healthcare organizations. They are the laws governing kickback arrangements, physician self-referrals, CPT/HCPCS ICD-9 and 10 coding, claims development and submission, payor reimbursement, cost reporting, and marketing practices. The organization also should be paying attention to rules and policies that have been the focus of attention by Medicare, Medicaid, and private payors, as evidenced by OIG Annual Work Plans, Special Fraud Alerts, Advisory Opinions, audits and evaluations, and the initiatives of law enforcement agencies. Finally, the monitoring process will look at the compliance risk areas that are unique to each particular organization—as indicated by the Program Guidance for its organization type, its prior compliance problems and experience, the results of its own past audits, and patient satisfaction surveys and complaint records.

An audit is a highly structured examination of an organization's most critical compliance activities. It typically is conducted once every year, in exactly the same fashion, using the same methods, in order to permit comparisons from year to year. This tracking over time can show the positive effects of a corrective action previously taken, a steady improvement (or deterioration) in the functioning of the compliance program, or the existence of new problems or risk areas. If the goal is to identify trends, the first audit has to be especially thorough in order to establish a baseline for all subsequent reviews.

The audit is performed by different people than those who conduct the ongoing monitoring. They usually are outside experts, often from a professional audit firm. An objective independent viewpoint is a valuable feature of these audits. Auditors must have adequate authority to obtain relevant information like documents and records. They need to be able to interview personnel who can comment on the documents and compliance events.

The scope and frequency of both audits and monitoring will vary according to the budget and staff available for compliance matters. Other factors that enter into the design of the monitoring and auditing functions are the organizational structure of the entity, its corporate mission, its overall risk profile, the lines of business it conducts, and the makeup of its workforce.

Both monitoring and annual audits follow a basic multistep process. First, a choice is made about the information to be gathered and studied. For high volume data like claims or medical records, a methodology for taking a sample must be selected. The data are gathered, tabulated, and reviewed. They then are analyzed and conclusions reached. Those conclusions, accompanied by recommendations for changes, improvements, or corrective actions are reported to the appropriate decision makers (typically, the CO, the CEO, and the governing board).

There is a variety of methods for gathering representative samples of operational data. The following are the most common:

- Interviews of staff working in the relevant areas (coding, billing and claims, marketing, and patient care)
- Survey questionnaires administered to those same employees
- Observational site visits to departments and facilities
- Reviews of records and source documents (medical and financial) that back up claims and reports submitted to Medicare
- Trend analyses that reveal deviations from norms

Audits and monitoring are useful compliance tools only if they lead to action when called for. They may reveal actual misconduct or violations of law, flaws in the way the compliance program is working, or general opportunities for improvement in the program or other operational areas (e.g., billing, medical records, physician relations, and marketing). The urgency of the response to problems identified will depend on their severity. If there appears to be a violation of criminal, civil, or administrative law, the organization should immediately consult a healthcare-experienced attorney. It is possible that it will be necessary to notify certain government agencies within a matter of days. In many cases, the CO will launch an investigation to determine the facts behind the reports that have been received. When those facts warrant it, corrective action will be taken. This may involve dealing with a negligent or misbehaving employee, reengineering a malfunctioning system, renegotiating the relationship with a vendor or independent contractor, or reallocating resources to high-risk areas of operations.

The CEO and the governing board should receive regular reports on the results of the ongoing audits and monitoring, along with special reports on significant incidents of noncompliance.

Disciplinary Action Against Noncompliant Employees and Contractors

Sometimes, noncompliance and outright violations of law are the result of poorly designed systems operated by otherwise conscientious employees. In some cases, however, it is the people themselves who are the source of the problems. Their culpability can range from simple negligence to gross negligence or recklessness, and even deliberate intent. The organization must be prepared to respond proportionately and constructively to these behaviors. If not, they are likely to be repeated.

When an organization becomes aware of possible noncompliance, a sequence of four steps should be implemented. Investigate the report to determine what occurred, whether misconduct or noncompliance was involved, its seriousness, and the apparent causes. If there is even a hint of noncompliance, put a stop to the problematic activity in order to mitigate any damages. Identify individuals with any culpability for the incident. Take appropriate disciplinary action regarding those individuals.

There are a few characteristics of a good disciplinary action process. First, there must be a formal system for administering discipline. It must encompass discipline for employees who engage in misconduct or noncompliance and for employees who fail to detect misconduct by others. The disciplinary penalties must be consistent and proportional to the severity of the misconduct.

The official description of the disciplinary procedure should list the levels of disciplinary action that may be imposed. The traditional measures are an informal conversation with the employee's supervisor, a verbal warning to the employee, a written warning, and, finally, dismissal from the organization. Some organizations use suspensions without pay and demotions. These do not work well in practice and are not advised.

It must be clear that the disciplinary measures will be applied equally and consistently throughout the workforce, extending to executives, managers, and supervisors, as well as employees in general. Punishment should also be dispensed to managers who should have known of the misconduct but failed to detect it. When an employee's misconduct has been found without dismissal being necessary, the aberrant behavior should be taken into account in the employee's performance appraisal.

Healthcare organizations are responsible not only for the actions of their employees but also for those of their agents. An agent performs services on behalf of an organization without being employed by the organization. The relationship between the two is often defined in a legally binding contract. The category of agents includes independent contractors, locum tenens physicians, temporary employees, and those permitted to work on the organization's premises (i.e., medical staff members). Agents are in a position to cause compliance problems almost as readily as employees, yet the organization lacks the same direct control over them.

Organizations must take steps to ensure the compliant behavior of their agents. It starts by giving them a copy of the organization's compliance program and, simultaneously, requesting a copy of the agents' programs. Though they are likely to differ in many respects, significant conflicts between them should be removed. It should be ascertained that the agents' compliance programs are being fully implemented. The contract with an agent should stipulate that it will conform to the organization's compliance program as fully as possible. That conformity should be made a condition of the contract. The agent should understand that noncompliant actions on its part may lead to termination of the contract with the organization.

Investigation of Noncompliance Followed by Corrective Action

Most revelations of possible misconduct or noncompliance require further investigation to bring out all the facts. When the original suspicions are borne out, decisive actions must be taken to correct the problem. Failure to do this can cause serious harm to an organization's mission, workforce morale, public reputation, and legal status.

Simple, inadvertent errors resulting in receipt of overpayments can be handled through normal repayment channels. When it looks like fraud is involved, an internal investigation should be conducted. Depending on the seriousness, this may involve outside legal counsel, financial auditors, or other healthcare experts. It is usually a good idea to prepare in advance a protocol for carrying out an investigation, rather than making up a methodology on the spot and under pressure. It will cover these points:

- The person in the organization who will decide when an investigation is necessary, the structure of the investigation, and those who will lead and conduct it

- The criteria for deciding when an attorney or other experts should be brought into the investigation
- A mechanism for evaluating the progress of the investigation and deciding when to conclude it
- Policies for protecting the security of information gathered and the anonymity of individuals who testify during the investigation

A completed investigation will contain several elements: documentation of the alleged violation, a description of the investigative process that was followed, copies of interview notes and key documents, a log of witnesses interviewed and documents reviewed, results of the investigation, disciplinary actions taken, and corrective actions implemented.

If the investigation exposes noncompliance, a variety of actions may be appropriate.

- Discipline or dismissal of employees who recklessly or deliberately committed the misconduct and termination of contracts with agents who engaged in noncompliant acts
- Repayment of overpayments received
- Reporting of the noncompliance to government agencies under the OIG Self-Disclosure Protocol
- Reporting of specific incidents to criminal or civil law enforcement authorities
- Revision or reengineering of internal systems that contributed to the noncompliance
- Changes to the compliance training and education curriculum
- Retraining of relevant personnel or hiring of new personnel with different qualifications
- Modification of existing policies or procedures that contributed to the noncompliance, or development of entirely new policies and procedures

COMPLIANCE PRACTICES IN THE HEALTHCARE INDUSTRY

The Health Care Compliance Association (HCCA) is a membership organization representing compliance and ethics professionals in the healthcare industry. The Association conducts regular surveys of its members about the compliance activities of the entities where they work. In 2008, on the basis of nearly 700 responses from COs, the HCCA reported the following information on compliance training, budget, staff, staff education, and compensation.

It should be kept in mind that two-thirds of the respondents worked in a health system, hospital, or health plan. Six percent of the replies were from physician practices and another 3% originated in nursing facilities.

Compliance training was mandatory in almost all the responding organizations. On average, half the employees spent 1–3 hours each year in compliance training. Ten percent spent 3–6 hours, and a third of the total devoted less than an hour. In three-quarters of the cases, the training was offered once a year. The most common training methods were computer-based/web-based training (72%), instructor-led classroom training (65%), self-study module (31%), and video training (30%). In 41% of the organizations, compliance training was mandatory for nonemployees and optional in another 20% of the cases. Two-fifths of the entities provided no training for nonemployees.

Almost 60% of the surveyed organizations attempted to measure the effectiveness of their compliance programs using methods such as:

- Self assessments within each business unit
- Surveys of employee awareness and training effectiveness
- Scorecard measuring overall compliance effectiveness
- Evaluating trends within the organization
- Comparing to industry benchmarks
- Testing awareness and tracking results after training occurs

When the surveyed COs were asked what goals they aimed to achieve with their compliance programs in the next 3 years, their answers were:

- Monitoring/auditing (82%)
- Education/training (75%)
- Evaluate program effectiveness (69%)
- New/revised policies and procedures (64%)
- Employee awareness (62%)
- Risk assessment (57%)
- Conduct benchmarking exercises (37%)
- Health Insurance Portability and Accountability Act of 1996 (HIPAA) regulation compliance (34%)
- Privacy (29%)
- Security (28%)
- Reporting mechanisms (27%)
- Transition to electronic health records (26%)

These were the substantive areas that they covered in their compliance programs:

- Privacy, information security (85%)
- Conflict of interest (85%)
- Coding and billing (84%)
- Stark, Anti-Kickback (77%)
- Program-excluded persons (60%)
- Contract management (56%)
- Emergency Medical Treatment and Labor Act (EMTALA) (53%)
- Quality of care (52%)
- Employment issues (49%)
- Cost reporting (42%)
- Clinical research (39%)
- Antitrust (36%)
- Sarbanes-Oxley Act (31%)
- Joint Commission on Accreditation of Healthcare Organizations (JCAHO) (27%)
- Transition to electronic health records (27%)
- Environmental issues (24%)
- Tax issues (22%)

The location of the CO's position in the organizational hierarchy was described as officer of the company (29%), senior management (57%), and middle management (10%). The number of women filling CO positions has grown steadily, from 48% of the total in 1999 to 72% in 2008. These are the company officials to whom the CO directly reports.

- CEO/President (46%)
- Chief Compliance Officer (32%)
- Governing board (29%)
- Other C-suite executive (12%)
- Compliance Committee (11%)
- Legal counsel (7%)
- CFO/finance (7%)
- Audit Committee (6%)

Nearly every one of the responding entities said that it had a CC, most of the time chaired by the CO. The Committee's primary responsibilities were:

- Planning (70%)
- Management of audits (66%)

- Management of investigations (63%)
- Report to the governing board (59%)
- Self-disclosures (45%)
- Enforcement authority (45%)

These figures only represent the practices of the organizations and types of organizations that responded to the HCCA survey. The field of healthcare compliance is constantly changing. Every year, there are new laws, regulations, and court decisions; government agencies launch new enforcement initiatives; and the affected organizations reassess the priority that they place on rigorous compliance.

STUDY QUESTIONS

1. What is the connection between the OIG Program Guidances and the Federal Sentencing Guidelines?
2. Where is the position of CO located in the organizational hierarchy? Why is that location so important to the CO's work?
3. What is the relationship between the CO and the CC?
4. What should a healthcare organization do if it cannot afford a full-time CO and if it does not have enough personnel to staff a CC?
5. An organization could write hundreds of policies and procedures about every task performed by its employees. How does it decide which activities to focus its compliance efforts on?
6. What is a Code of Conduct? What topics does it cover and what is its purpose? Do you have personal Code of Conduct?
7. As an employee of a pharmaceutical manufacturer, by what method would you prefer to receive compliance training?
8. As an employee of a modest-size third party billing company, by what means would you prefer to report your suspicions about noncompliant behavior you have observed?
9. Explain the difference between a compliance audit and ongoing monitoring of compliant work behavior.
10. Describe three characteristics of a good disciplinary process.
11. From the viewpoint of a healthcare organization (e.g., hospital or health system), what is the difference between an employee and an agent?
12. Explain what leverage an organization has in persuading an agent (e.g., vendor, contractor, consultant) to adopt its own compliance

program, to follow the rules of the organization's compliance program, and to attend compliance training sessions.

13. What determines how much effort and resources an organization should invest in an investigation of suspected employee misconduct or noncompliance?
14. Describe at least six responses an organization could take upon discovering that one of its employees has committed acts of healthcare fraud.

Learning Exercises

1. In the process of making compliance programs mandatory, the PPACA drew special attention to the compliance programs of nursing facilities, specifying eight (not seven) required elements of the programs. Do a little Internet research to find out what that new eighth element is. It is found in Section 6102 of the PPACA.
2. Review the Code of Ethical Business Conduct, Policies and Guidelines for the Apria Healthcare organization, a provider of integrated home healthcare products and services, found here: http://www.apria.com/wps/portal/apria/home/about-us/corporate-compliance-program. It is not the equivalent of a full corporate compliance program, though it does cover a lot of related issues. Read the document and notice which parts of it seem to address some of the basic elements in a required compliance program. How effectively does it deal with those issues? To perform this kind of review for another organization, look for the "Compliance Handbook" of "Banner Health," a nonprofit, multistate system of hospitals.
3. Without rereading this chapter, describe briefly the seven basic elements of a mandatory compliance. If you cannot do it easily, go over the elements repeatedly until you have them memorized.
4. You are the designated CO for a group practice of 15 physicians. Describe the steps that you would take to identify the "risk areas" for which you would like to write compliance policies and procedures.
5. A longstanding employee tells you, the CO, that she does not want to attend this year's compliance training session because she attended the session last year and she knows that there have been no changes in the laws or the compliance program rules since then. Describe a nuanced response that you will give to her.

References

1. Evaluating and Improving a Compliance Program, A Resource for Health Care Board Members, Health Care Executives, and Compliance Officers, HCCA 2003.
2. 2012 Guidelines Manual, United States Sentencing Commission, November 2012.
3. 10th Annual Survey—2008 Profile of Health Care Compliance Officers, HCCA 2008.
4. This is the section of the OIG website dealing with Compliance Programs. It includes links to all 12 of the OIG Compliance Program Guidances for specific types of health care organizations. https://oig.hhs.gov/compliance/compliance-guidance/index.asp. These are those links.
   Nursing Facilities (Original 2000 and Supplemental 2008)
   https://www.oig.hhs.gov/authorities/docs/cpgnf.pdf
   https://oig.hhs.gov/compliance/compliance-guidance/docs/complianceguidance/nhg_fr.pdf
   Recipients of PHS Research Awards (2005)
   https://oig.hhs.gov/fraud/docs/complianceguidance/PHS%20Research%20Awards%20Draft%20CPG.pdf
   Hospitals (Original 1998 and Supplemental 2005)
   https://oig.hhs.gov/authorities/docs/cpghosp.pdf
   https://oig.hhs.gov/fraud/docs/complianceguidance/012705HospSupplementalGuidance.pdf
   Pharmaceutical Manufacturers (2003)
   https://oig.hhs.gov/authorities/docs/03/050503FRCPGPharmac.pdf
   Ambulance Suppliers (2003)
   https://oig.hhs.gov/fraud/docs/complianceguidance/032403ambulancecpgfr.pdf
   Individual and Small Group Physician Practices (2000)
   https://oig.hhs.gov/authorities/docs/physician.pdf
   Medicare + Choice Organizations (now Medicare Advantage) (1999)
   https://oig.hhs.gov/fraud/docs/complianceguidance/111599.pdf
   Hospices (1999)
   https://oig.hhs.gov/authorities/docs/hospicx.pdf
   Durable Medical Equipment, Prosthetics, Orthotics, and Supply Industry (1999)
   https://oig.hhs.gov/authorities/docs/frdme.pdf
   Third-Party Medical Billing Companies (1998)
   https://oig.hhs.gov/fraud/docs/complianceguidance/thirdparty.pdf
   Clinical Laboratories (1998)
   https://oig.hhs.gov/authorities/docs/cpglab.pdf
   Home Health Agencies (1998)
   https://oig.hhs.gov/authorities/docs/cpghome.pdf

Chapter 9

Role of Compliance Officer

In the Fall of 2011, the American Health Lawyers Association asked its members in which law-related fields they expected to see growth in the near future. A total of 56% expected growth in in-house counsel at healthcare organizations, and 69% thought that the number of consultants to the healthcare industry would increase. However, the largest share, 76%, believe that the profession of "Compliance Officers" will grow.[1]

On February 27, 2012, US News and World Report released its latest Best Jobs of 2012 Report, based on the Labor Department's employment projections. In an overview, the report details 50 jobs that were selected from five "quick-to-hire" industries: business, creative services, health care, science and technology, and social services. The job of Compliance Officer ranked 13 on the list of best business jobs.[2]

"The Bureau of Labor Statistics projects compliance officer employment growth of 15 percent between 2010 and 2020. That's 32,400 new jobs and 26,200 replacement jobs. There were 216,600 compliance officers in 2010."

Learning Objectives

After completing class sessions based on this chapter, students will learn:

- The status that a Compliance Officer should hold in an organization.
- The best location for the Compliance Officer position in the organizational hierarchy.
- The relationship between the Compliance Officer and the Board of Directors/Trustees.
- How the Compliance Officer's role may differ between a large organization (health plan, hospital) and a small organization (modest-size physician practice).
- The strong legal requirements for the existence of a Compliance Officer.
- The strong business arguments for the existence of a Compliance Officer.

[1] AHLA Connections, February 2012, p. 48.
[2] http://money.usnews.com/money/careers/articles/2012/02/27/best-jobs-2012-compliance-officer

- The value that a Compliance Officer brings to an organization.
- The functions that a Compliance Officer performs for an organization.
- Typical qualifications for an applicant for a position as Compliance Officer.

INTRODUCTION

The compliance activities of a healthcare organization are arranged into a program that requires close and careful management. This is best done by a single individual with overall responsibility for compliance, in the same way that one person oversees finance or marketing. That person is the organization's Compliance Officer (CO).

It is virtually a legal requirement that healthcare organizations appoint someone to take the lead on compliance issues. There is also a persuasive business argument for appointing such an individual.

Important questions must be answered about the placement of that person within the organization. What is the role of a designated CO, and what kind of authority should he or she be given? Who is the best possible CO in an organization—the Chief Executive Officer (CEO), General Counsel, or some other designee? Or should it be an entirely new position dedicated to compliance?

Will compliance be a full-time job or just one of the duties of an employee concerned with other matters? Are the expectations of the CO less in an organization with fewer resources—such as a small physician group practice? How many and what kinds of resources are adequate to support the CO in her work? What might be the official title of this person?

Where would he or she be located in the organizational hierarchy, on the organization chart? To whom does the CO report and who reports to the CO? What is the relationship of the CO with the board of directors or trustees? With whom in the organization will the CO typically interact?

What is the full range of the CO's duties? What specific authorities does he or she have for carrying them out? What skills and qualifications are needed to competently perform the job of a CO? How should the performance of the CO be measured?

This chapter provides some general responses to those questions, but each healthcare organization will have to find the best answers for its unique situation. A compliance program tailored to a particular organization will also take into account:

- Organization's strategic vision, mission, and objectives
- Organization's values and Code of Ethics

- Organization's existing culture
- Organization size and resources
- Management style prevalent in the organization
- Priority of ethics among organization board members and executives
- Industry mood for ethical, compliant behavior
- Organization's record of violations and ethical misconduct

LEGAL RATIONALE FOR THE COMPLIANCE OFFICER POSITION

There are strong legal arguments for an organization to appoint a single person to oversee its compliance activities. There are no laws making such an appointment mandatory, but the benefits of doing so are inescapable.

The Compliance Guidelines[3] (for different types of healthcare organizations) issued by the Office of the Inspector General (OIG) in the federal Department of Health and Human Services (DHHS) state that a CO should be designated to serve as the focal point for compliance activities. The CO's duties go beyond being a simple "focal point." He or she is the overseer of all the organization's compliance activities.

The Federal Sentencing Guidelines for Organizations (FSGO) issued by the U.S. Sentencing Commission provide that organizations convicted of most federal crimes deserve a reduction in the fines assessed "if the offense occurred even though the organization had in place at the time of the offense an effective compliance and ethics program."[4] Two of the elements of such a program concern the compliance officials in the organization.

> Specific individual(s) within high-level personnel shall be assigned overall responsibility for the compliance and ethics program.[5]

This language refers directly to a person serving as CO.

> Specific individual(s) within the organization shall be delegated day-to-day operational responsibility for the compliance and ethics program. Individual(s) with operational responsibility shall report periodically to high-level personnel and, as appropriate, to the governing authority, or an appropriate subgroup of the governing authority, on the effectiveness of the compliance and ethics program. To carry out such operational responsibility, such individual(s) shall be given adequate resources, appropriate authority, and direct access to

---

[3] http://oig.hhs.gov/compliance/compliance-guidance/index.asp
[4] http://www.ussc.gov/Guidelines/2011_Guidelines/Manual_PDF/index.cfm
[5] §8B2.1(b)(2)(B) of the FSGO.

> the governing authority or an appropriate subgroup of the governing authority.[6]

In an organization large enough to require and to afford assigning several people to compliance duties, other employees may assist the CO in carrying out the day-to-day operational tasks of the compliance program. This language seems to describe those people. In most organizations, they would be subordinate to the CO, who would report to higher-level executives and the governing board.

The presence of an authoritative CO managing an effective compliance program may also be a factor in the decision of federal law enforcement authorities to bring charges for criminal misconduct by an organization's officers, directors, employees, or agents.[7]

VALUE PROPOSITION FOR THE CO POSITION

The legal incentives of the FSGO and the OIG provide the bare minimum reasons for designating a CO. Beyond that, the expense of a CO and the compliance program that she implements might seem to contribute little to the organization's overall performance and mission. In fact, the money is well spent on achieving several important goals.

The CO is the one person in the organization tasked with maintaining a persistent, system-wide view of its legal and ethical conduct. He or she protects the organization from the most severe penalties when violations do occur. This person urges other organizational leaders aggressively to prevent misconduct and tackle it when it happens. He or she constantly reminds all employees of the organization's commitment to compliant ethical business behavior.

The CO helps establish and maintain operating standards that boost the organization's reputation and brand name, which in turn makes it easier to attract customers, employees, partners, and investors. He or she contributes to the creation of a positive, high-integrity organizational culture that raises employee morale and loyalty. Public opinion and political support tends to favor such organizations.

There may even be a correlation between the ethical behavior instilled by a CO and the stock price of a publicly traded healthcare organization. In its 2010 list of the World's Most Ethical Companies, the research-based Ethisphere Institute found that the top 100 companies on the list had

---

[6] §8B2.1(b)(2)(C) of the FSGO.

[7] Principles of Federal Prosecution of Business Organizations, Title 9, Chapter 9-28.00.

outperformed both the S&P 500[8] and the FTSE 100[9] since 2005.[10] On that list, there are five healthcare organizations (Cleveland Clinic, Hospital Corporation of America, J M Smith Corporation, Johns Hopkins, and Premier) and two medical device companies (Becton, Dickinson and Company, and Royal Phillips).

LOCATION AND TITLE OF THE CO

In some organizations, the CO is referred to as the Chief Ethics and Compliance Officer. Not only is ethical behavior closely intertwined with actions that comply strictly with the law, but a workforce that is focused on doing more than the letter of the law requires, that is predisposed to doing the right thing whether the law requires it or not, is more likely to observe legal mandates as a matter of course.

The responsibilities of a CO and his or her impact on the welfare of the organization require that the position be located among the top executives of the organization. In a large entity like a teaching hospital, health system, or pharmaceutical company, this person will have the title of CO and sit in the executive suite just below the CEO. The CO will have the same rank and status as the Chief Financial Officer (CFO), Chief Medical Officer (CMO), or Chief Information Officer (CIO).[11]

It is key that the CO have enough status and authority to carry out his or her duties. A CO's line of reporting is perhaps the single biggest influence on his or her credibility within the organization. This includes having direct, immediate access to the governing board, the CEO, and other senior managers. When viewed on an organizational chart, the CO should report directly to a member of the C-suite[12] or actually be a member herself. Under the optimal arrangement, the CO is hired by the board of directors, his or her performance is evaluated by the board and the CEO, and termination decisions are made only by the board.

The OIG Compliance Guidances recommend that the CO not serve simultaneously as CFO or General Counsel. The CO should not have to

---

[8] US stock index of 500 large publicly traded corporations.

[9] UK stock index of 100 large publicly traded corporations.

[10] http://ethisphere.com/past-wme-honorees/wme2010/

[11] Some of the other titles given to this person might be Compliance Officer, Director of Business Ethics and Compliance, Government Regulatory Manager, and Risk Assessment Manager. The responsibilities are sometimes assigned to these officials: CFO or VP of Finance, Controller, internal official in charge of Audits or of Accounting, and General Counsel. As a general rule, if the organization can afford it, compliance and ethics should be the full-time responsibility of a single individual carrying a title that indicates that status.

[12] An organization's most important senior executives, most of whose titles begin with "Chief."

go through the CEO to communicate with the governing board; he should have direct access. When interacting with the board, the CO may talk to the entire board, the audit committee, a compliance subcommittee, or a designated member knowledgeable about business ethics and compliance.

The title, position, and reporting relationships of the CO will vary depending on the nature, size, and resources of the organization. The optimal model works fine for a large, well-managed entity like a hospital system, a managed care organization, or a pharmaceutical company.

The OIG understands that smaller organizations, like physician practices, small diagnostic labs, or medical transcription services, cannot afford to assign one full-time person to handle compliance duties. There compliance duties will be assigned to a current employee with other responsibilities, perhaps the business/office manager or the person in charge of claims filing. Her compliance work will take up only a part of her work time. On compliance matters, she will report to the physician partners or other business owners. The organization may allocate a few hundred dollars a year for this person to purchase compliance materials and attend compliance education seminars and conferences.

Where resources and personnel permit, the CO will create and head up a department, office, or committee that advises him, helps implement the compliance program, and adds expertise that the CO may lack.

It is just as important that the CO have an unrestricted channel of communication to employees throughout the organization, as well as patients served, providers serving the patients, and vendors trading with the organization. He must be able to interact, without anyone else's approval, through email, letter, phone, and face-to-face meetings, at times and on issues of his choosing.

At the same time, all these people must feel free to communicate with the CO about compliance matters, particularly the possible occurrence of illegal acts. They must be able to send messages in confidence without fear of retaliation. These assurances should be put into written policy.

SCOPE OF RESPONSIBILITY OF THE CO

An organization's CO, whether he bears the title of Chief Ethics and Compliance Officer or simultaneously serves as Legal Counsel, Claims Manager, or Audit Officer, will perform a handful of broad responsibilities. He is the single high-level official responsible for defining and enforcing the organization's behavioral standards. He will be held accountable for the performance of the compliance program, whether success or failure. He is recognized as performing a function critical enough to justify his presence on the executive team. He will participate in major organization decisions that bear on compliance and ethics. He will focus fixatedly on compliance and ethics.

CO JOB DESCRIPTION

The overriding function of the CO is to ensure that the organization is in full compliance with all relevant laws in all of its activities and it responds aggressively to any incidents of noncompliance. Toward that goal, the CO will perform several activities.

The broad duties of the CO are clear-cut, though the details will vary from one organization to another. The specific tasks will be written into the individual's job description. It should be prepared before efforts are made to recruit a person for the position. As the duties of a CO are likely to be evolving for some time, his or her job description should be reviewed and revised regularly.

Lead the Organization's Entire Compliance and Ethics Program

The CO has ultimate authority over all the organization's efforts to comply with laws and operate an ethical business. This person must do more than merely administer a program and its policies and procedures. She must lead the entire workforce to embrace the cause of compliance and ethical behavior to the point that it becomes instinctive. She will accomplish this by defining a vision of organizational compliance, then laying out the path by which it can be achieved. Employees should turn to the CO for insight and inspiration about compliance matters.

Personally Acquire and Maintain Up-to-Date Knowledge on Legal Compliance Requirements and Ethical Standards Affecting the Organization

The body of law with which healthcare organizations must comply is constantly changing and evolving. New laws are enacted and old laws may be revoked—at both the federal and state levels. New regulations are regularly issued under existing laws as the enforcement agencies attempt to improve quality and efficiency in government programs, and reduce fraud and abuse in their financing. Both the government agencies and affected healthcare organizations regularly bring lawsuits to challenge the laws and regulations, resulting in court decisions that often reinterpret them. Over time, even ethical standards may change as community or society values change.

The CO must do her best to stay informed about these changes to the extent that they may impact the compliance obligations of the organization. Profession and industry-sponsored publications, websites, and listservs are good, low-intensity sources of this information. An experienced health law attorney either employed or retained by the organization will be able to provide updates that are both more comprehensive and relevant. The new legal requirements may explain exactly what organizations must do in order to comply; private associations (e.g., American Medical Association, Medical Group Management Association, American Heart Association, Pharmaceutical Research and Manufacturers of America) quickly offer additional practical guidance.

Evaluate Organization Operations to Identify Areas at Risk of Noncompliance and Misconduct

One of the CO's early steps in formulating a compliance program will be to conduct a risk assessment to determine where the organization is particularly vulnerable to problems. Two obvious examples are the department that files claims and the sharing of patient personal health information (PHI) between a hospital and physicians in their private practices. Once the risk areas are identified, the CO will ensure that the compliance program is configured to address them. New risk assessments should be carried out at regular intervals thereafter.

Delegate Responsibility for Implementation of the Compliance Program in Each Risk Area

In large organizations, it is necessary to identify one or more individuals in each area of heightened risk to supervise compliance activities performed there. These are not necessarily full-time positions. The people must interpret and transmit the CO's directives on compliance, see that they are followed, and report back to the CO on problems and incidents.

Keep the CEO, Governing Board, and Owners of the Organization Fully Informed of the Organization's Legal Risks, the Compliance Activities Designed to Minimize Them, Any Compliance Incidents That Occur, and the Organization's Response to Them

In performing his duties, the CO works on behalf of the entire organization (particularly its owners, if it is a private entity) to protect it from legal hazard. If the CO uses poor judgment or makes a mistake, the unpleasant results can occur suddenly, without warning. A poorly designed compliance program is exposed when the OIG brings a legal action for false or inaccurate claims going back several years. The top executives and governing board want to know how well the organization is anticipating and preventing such problems.

The CO normally will not communicate directly with the shareholder-owners of a large publicly held healthcare organization. Instead, he will talk with the governing board that represents those shareholders. In smaller, closely held entities like physician practice partnerships or privately held close corporations, the governing board frequently is composed of the owners.

These communications should not be one-way; the governing board and the owners should be encouraged to ask questions and offer suggestions.

To satisfy their information needs, the CO must keep these parties informed of his work and its effectiveness. This means explaining the structure and operation of the compliance program until they fully understand it. Once the program is established, he will report periodically on how well it performs its designed activities (e.g., reducing coding errors, preventing PHI leaks) and how effective it is in avoiding compliance incidents. If and when major incidents occur, the CO immediately will inform these key individuals. He will explain how the organization has responded and the final resolution reached with the regulatory agency.

Freedom to Address Compliance Matters Without Fear of Reprisal from Management

A conscientious CO will have to make unpopular decisions that may inhibit some business functions, perhaps antagonizing other managers. As a general rule, no one else in the organization should have the authority to countermand the CO's directives and decisions.

Ensure That All Departments Concerned with Compliance Issues (e.g., Legal, Security, Finance, Auditing, Security, Government Affairs, IT, and Human Resources) Are Working in Unison to Protect the Organization

While the formal Compliance Committee may lead the organization's efforts at law observance, there often are other departments that play important roles in the process. Some examples are the Legal/General Counsel, the office that handles various forms of security, the IT Department responsible for the systems through which errors may occur, the Human Resources Department concerned with the employees who may commit the errors or abuse, and Government Affairs/Relations. One of the CO's duties is to make sure that all these organizational units are in synch with the compliance program and with each other.

Supervise the Members of the Compliance Office, as Well as People Monitoring Compliance Issues in High-Risk Areas and Departments Throughout the Organization

The CO will function as the supervisor of the employees who are part of the Compliance Department, Office, or Committee, as well as a secondary or co-supervisor of individuals throughout the organization with special responsibilities for maintaining compliance. Proficient direction of those people can enhance the compliance performance of the entire organization.

Employ Appropriate Communication Media for Informing the Organization's Employees, Officers, Agents, Subcontractors, Vendors, and Customers of the Compliance Policies and Procedures They Are Expected to Follow

The success of a compliance program depends to a large degree on how effectively it communicates with the parties that have a stake in the organization's compliance. These stakeholders naturally include the organization's employees, executives, and board of directors. In addition, there are several other parties who may figure into compliance issues and who must be kept informed. Every healthcare organization relies on a large number of contractors, subcontractors, vendors, suppliers, and other third parties to produce its goods and services. Customers or patients play roles in many compliance complaints, often as pawns or victims.

The CO must ensure that the organization's message on compliance reaches all these stakeholders. This task is complicated by the fact that the message is different for each stakeholder group and the most effective communications media are different as well. It is important to say the right things to the right people in the right way.

Establish Working Links with External Third Parties That Have an Effect on the Organization's Compliance Activities

Effective communication is just one of the elements in the relationships that must be maintained with these third parties. The organization needs to work with its agents to ensure that they do not commit noncompliant acts that implicate the organization. The deeds of outsourced billing companies, medical transcription businesses, and contracted ancillary service providers can create vicarious liability for a hospital or physician practice.

From a different perspective, the CO should aim for positive working relationships with the regulatory agencies that have jurisdiction over the organization's operations. Whether responding to nonlegal agency requests or seeking informal opinions from an agency, it is important to be cordial and business-like, responsive, and cooperative. This pays off when an agency investigation is launched or a legal complaint is filed.

Engage with Individuals and Departments Throughout the Organization in Order to Influence Those Tasks That May Have Compliance Implications

There are few tasks performed by a healthcare organization that might not conceivably become involved in a noncompliance incident. The CO cannot be involved with all of them. However, it must be her goal at least to stay informed of how the tasks are being carried out and to have appropriate input on their performance. Some tasks and functions are more critical to compliance than others.

In 2007, the Open Compliance and Ethics Group (OCEG) conducted a "Governance, Risk & Compliance Strategy Study"[13] of about 250 organizations in a variety of industries, including but not restricted to health care. When asked in which business processes their compliance personnel were engaged, the respondents gave these answers.

Managing financial resources	69%
Developing vision and strategy	64%
Managing external relationships	55%
Managing information technology (IT)	54%
Developing and managing human capital	52%

All processes occur outside the direct authority of the Compliance Program and the CO. The Finance Department manages the organization's financial resources; strategic planning is the province of the governing board, the CEO, and C-suite executives. The CEO and the Office of Public Relations or Affairs, if one exists, handle external relationships. Most

[13] http://archive.oceg.org/view/obs-grcstrategy

organizations have an IT Department or designated IT person. Human capital or resources is managed by the Personnel or Human Resources Department. Because each can play a role in an incident of noncompliance or its resolution, the CO needs to have a good working relationship with all of them.

The engagement can take many forms: receiving regular reports about process activities, attending key meetings, being consulted about key decisions, and having direct access to the managers of the processes.

Work with the Marketing and Public Affairs Departments to Promote the Organization's Commitment to Compliance Behavior and High Ethical Standards to the Public

There is a lot of promotional value in projecting a public image of the organization as both ethical and legally compliant. Such a reputation may make it easier to recruit new executives and other employees; the best physicians are likely to be more willing to affiliate with a highly regarded hospital or physician group. Vendors and contractors may feel more comfortable doing business with an organization known for its integrity. Customers and patients may be instinctively drawn to an organization that appears to practice high levels of integrity. Political and community leaders are more likely to look favorably upon a well-behaved corporate citizen. Even enforcement officials may be predisposed toward leniency for an organization with an impeccable reputation.

It is not the job of the CO personally to broadcast this positive image of the organization. He will work with representatives of the Marketing and Public Affairs/Relations Departments to find tasteful ways to send the message. This is one of the ancillary benefits of running an ethical, compliant organization and it should not be missed.

Carry Out Regular Assessments of the Program's Performance

An organization can design a compliance program with many different features, and it can implement those features with varying degrees of success. Because the stakes of failure are so high (noncompliance and the resulting penalties), one of the CO's highest priorities is to ensure that the organization has the best program for its purposes and executes it flawlessly. This calls for continual reassessment of the program.

The competent CO will keep himself informed of "best practices" in compliance programs at other healthcare organizations. He then will make appropriate upgrades to his own program. He will set objectives for the performance of the program's functions. For instance, the percentage of claims that are reviewed for coding errors before filing, the number of hours of off-site compliance training received by employees, or the frequency of reviews of subcontractor operations for compliance. Actual performance of the activities will be measured against the objectives set for them. Over time, the CO should be able to steadily improve the design and operation of the program.

Carry Out Regular Measurements of the Program's Effectiveness

The success of a compliance program in carrying out its designed functions is different from the program's effectiveness in minimizing compliance issues. Normally, the former leads to the latter, but not necessarily. The ultimate test is whether the organization is keeping compliance problems at an acceptable level. This, too, requires setting objectives and constantly measuring progress toward their achievement.

The best way to drive performance of any project is to set measurable goals to be achieved. The CO makes sure this is done for the compliance program. A typical objective is reducing the number of claims that are denied or rejected by a payer and returned to the organization for correction. The number can be measured to determine whether it is declining. If the objectives are not being met, the CO needs to ask two questions: Is our compliance program designed to be the best suited to our organization? If it is optimally designed, are we carrying it out as well as we can?

Remember, the CO's ultimate responsibility is to make sure that the organization complies with all applicable laws as fully possible, not simply maintain a smooth-running compliance program.

Implement Initiatives to Foster an Ethical Culture Throughout the Organization

A compliance program will be much more effective if it is implemented within an organizational culture that is predisposed toward ethical, high-integrity behavior. The CO, along with other executives and managers, can foster such a mindset through their own role-modeling behavior, the employee behaviors that they reward and punish, and the policies that they enforce within the workforce. If the current culture does not encourage compliance, it can be modified. The effort can take several years, but the result can make a big difference in compliance.

Serve as Primary Organizational Resource for Reimbursement and Regulatory Information

Employees throughout the organization, particularly those concerned with coding, claims, and IT, have regular needs for up-to-date information on reimbursement, privacy, and other compliance issues. It is the job of the CO to operate a program that makes that information available to them. Sometimes, it is enough to simply pass on documentation issued by payers and regulators; other times, the CO will want to consult with employees on how best to avoid compliance problems in their departments.

QUALIFICATIONS FOR THE POSITION OF CO

After preparing a job description, the organization must decide what qualifications will lead to a candidate most capable of performing the job's tasks. A job description by itself is an insufficient basis for screening CO applicants. The particular qualifications that an organization can demand will depend on its size and the scope of the CO's responsibilities. These are some basic criteria.

Experience in Managing People

This will include not only the employees in the Compliance Office who report directly to the CO but also other employees in other departments whose work impacts compliance. A well-conceived compliance program is less effective if the people implementing it are not managed competently. People management is not always intuitive. Through training or experience, the CO candidate should be able to demonstrate a capacity for drawing the best out of people, motivating and inspiring them.

Ability to Work with High-Level Stakeholders

The CO in a larger organization must deal on a regular basis with people of high status and authority: members of the board of directors or trustees, the CEO, other chief executives, government regulators, and vendor officials. It is necessary that he have the confidence, poise, and social skills to do that work constructively.

Familiarity with Business Operations

Whether for-profit or nonprofit, an organization is engaged in a business composed of a multiplicity of interdependent functions: finance, billing and claims, marketing, human resources, production, clinical services, and the like. While the CO need not be competent in every one of them, he or she should understand the role each plays in achieving the organization's vision. This will lead to a comprehension of how the functions might stray into noncompliant behavior. Typically, this familiarity will be the result of at least 10 years of experience.

Familiarity with the Organization's Industry

The organizations in many industries are required to comply with numerous laws and regulations, some universal (e.g., antitrust and tax) and others industry specific. Only to a limited extent are the skills of a person experienced with compliance in one industry transferable to another industry. It is highly advantageous for the CO to have some education and work history in the healthcare industry generally and the organization's specific sector of it.

Detailed Knowledge of Compliance Issues and Programs

The CO must have a solid grounding in the laws and regulations that impact the particular healthcare organization she is joining, as well as the programs, policies, and procedures that will ensure compliance with them. The CO does not need to be a lawyer—though it would help—but he should be able to discuss compliance issues with the organization's internal or external legal counsel. Being sensitive to and knowledgeable about compliance and ethical issues cannot be learned on the job. A good CO candidate will have formal education in the subject—through a degree program or attendance at high-quality workshops.

Strong Personal Sense of Ethics

The CO is going to be much more effective in her work if she already possesses a strong sense of ethical and compliant behavior in business. It is not easy to acquire this trait; it normally is instilled in a person during childhood or young adulthood. The challenge is to evaluate a candidate's moral principles during the screening process. Attention to episodes in the applicant's work history and thoughtful questioning during the interview can usually bring out the necessary information.

Free from Conflicts of Interest

It is essential that the person in the position of CO be free of conflicts of interest that would compromise her believability and objectivity in combating noncompliance. This could include nonbusiness relationships with people or units within the organization whom the CO might have to report and discipline for violations, financial dealings with outside individuals or entities whose actions might threaten the organization's reputation, or any other connections that could lead the CO to make decisions that are contrary to the organization's interest.

Proven Communication Skills

The CO will transmit the message about compliant and ethical behavior through her communication skills. This includes confidence in speaking to groups and individuals, and a degree of eloquence in her written words. Powerful ideas carry less weight if they are not communicated persuasively.

These basic criteria will work for most healthcare organizations. Particular entities, in certain healthcare sectors/industries and healthcare markets, may seek other characteristics of their CO candidates.

STUDY QUESTIONS

1. Are compliance and ethics so important in modern healthcare organizations that the CO deserves a place in the executive suite along with the Chief Finance Officer, Chief Marketing Officer, Chief Medical Officer, and Chief Technology Officer?
2. After reading this chapter, are you willing to consider building a career as a CO? If so, what additional steps should you take to prepare yourself to satisfy the qualifications laid out in the chapter and the job description requirements in Learning Experiences #3?
3. Of the activities in the CO job description explained in the chapter, which ones will be most difficult for you to perform? Which activities will be the easiest?
4. You are the CO of a 230-bed teaching hospital. You have just read a newspaper article reporting that a physician on the hospital's medical staff has been charged with violations of the False Claims Act in his private practice. The charges include upcoding and billing for unnecessary services. Do you believe that there is any way that the hospital could be implicated in the physician's misdeeds? What is your first reaction to receiving this information? If it appears that the charges are legitimate and some disciplinary action is necessary, what are your options? When you suggest

suspending the physician from the medical staff for 6 months, the Chief Medical Officer reminds you that the physician refers a large number of patients to the hospital. Does this make a difference to you?

5. How would you describe your personal code of ethics? Under what circumstances would you be willing to overlook a minor inadvertent incident of noncompliance?

Learning Experiences

1. If you believe that someday you might like to work as a Compliance Officer, visit the website of the Ethics & Compliance Officer Association (ECOA): http://www.theecoa.org/iMIS15/ECOAPublic/. Browse the site, noticing the resources and services that it offers. Is this the sort of professional organization that you could rely upon for support in your job?
2. Contact a healthcare organization in your area. It could be a hospital, a health plan, or a physician practice. Explain that you are studying healthcare compliance and ethics, are considering a career as a compliance professional, and would like to interview their CO about the work that she does. On the basis of what you have read in this chapter, you might ask which of the CO duties she performs in her job, whether she has all the resources and authority she would like to carry out her job, who she reports to, what kinds of compliance issues she has had to deal with, and whether she addresses ethical questions as well.
3. Review the corporate CO job descriptions at the following website of the Health Care Compliance Association. What are the reasons for the differences among them? Can you imagine one day performing the jobs they cover? http://hcca-info.org/Content/NavigationMenu/ComplianceResources/SampleJobDescriptions/default.htm

References

1. Compliance-related associations and their websites:
Ethics and Compliance Officer Association
http://www.theecoa.org/iMIS15/ECOAPublic/
"a member-driven association exclusively for individuals responsible for their organization's ethics, compliance, and business conduct programs."

Ethics Resource Center
http://www.ethics.org/
"a nonprofit, nonpartisan research organization, dedicated to independent research that advances high ethical standards and practices in public and private institutions."

Society of Corporate Compliance and Ethics
http://www.corporatecompliance.org
"exists to champion ethical practice and compliance standards in all organizations and to provide the necessary resources for compliance professionals and others who share these principles."

Health Care Compliance Association
http://www.hcca-info.org
"The association for health care compliance professionals." Operates at the same location as the Society of Corporate Compliance and Ethics.

American College of Healthcare Executives
http://www.ache.org/aboutache.cfm
"an international professional society of more than 40,000 healthcare executives who lead hospitals, healthcare systems and other healthcare organizations."

2. Leading Corporate Integrity: Defining the Role of the Chief Ethics and Compliance Officer, Ethics Resource Center, 2007.
http://www.ethics.org/files/u5/CECO_Paper_UPDATED.pdf

Chapter 10

Directors and Trustees

Learning Objectives

After completing class sessions based on this chapter, students will learn:

- Place of boards of directors or trustees in the organizational hierarchy.
- Basic legal duties of all members of organizational governing boards.
- Corporate compliance duties unique to governing boards in health care.
- Specific involvement of governing board members in compliance programs.
- Legal penalties for inadequate compliance effort.
- Potential personal liability for individual board members.
- Criteria for assessing board effectiveness in overseeing compliance.

THE PLACE OF BOARDS OF DIRECTORS OR TRUSTEES IN THE ORGANIZATIONAL HIERARCHY

The highest authority in an incorporated organization is the governing board. In a for-profit corporation, the members of that board are usually called directors; not-for-profit corporations are typically governed by trustees.

In a for-profit corporation, the directors act as the representatives for the shareholders and are usually elected by them. Because nonprofit organizations are established to serve some public purpose, the board trustees represent the interests of the general public. They are not chosen directly by members of the public, but rather are selected and appointed by the organization itself. Frequently, it is a requirement of the organization's nonprofit charter that the composition of its board reflect the demographic makeup of the community it is serving.

The board members hire the CEO of an organization to carry out and manage its strategic and operational activities. They count on the CEO carrying out his or her duties within the limits of the law. There is a delicate balance that directors/trustees must find between giving the CEO and other top executives complete autonomy in running the organization and micromanaging every significant decision they make.

TRADITIONAL LEGAL DUTIES OF HEALTHCARE GOVERNING BOARDS

Governing board members of any healthcare organization have basic roles and responsibilities to perform.[1]

Setting and following strategic direction. The board has the final sign-off on the long-term direction of the organization and regularly ensures that the strategic objectives are being pursued.

Management oversight. One of the board's most essential responsibilities is monitoring and measuring the performance of management, particularly the CEO. It wishes to ensure alignment between performance and the organization's strategic direction and goals.

Financial oversight. They protect and build the organization's financial resources, making sure that they are spent for legal reasons related to its goals.

Care quality oversight. Starting with the *Darling v. Charleston Community Memorial Hospital* case in 1965, hospitals and their boards have been held legally liable for the quality of care delivered at their facilities. This includes preventing medical errors and protecting patient safety.

Board evaluation and growth. The board members continually evaluate how well they are carrying out their responsibilities. They also take active steps to develop their own competencies.

Public voice. Board members often must act as the public voice of the organization, particularly with not-for-profit entities. They advocate on behalf of the community they serve and for public health policies.

The law has established three fiduciary duties that define how board members must perform these responsibilities.

Duty of loyalty. Board members must always act in the interests of the organization, and never in their own interests. This duty also requires that they reveal any possible conflicts of interest with the organization's mission.

Duty of obedience. Board members shall ensure that their decisions and those of the organization adhere to the stated corporate mission. If it is a not-for-profit organization, the mission will be a charitable one.

---

[1] Based on "Board Roles and Responsibilities," The Governance Institute, 2005, www.governance-institute.com

Duty of care. Board members must stay informed, pay attention, show curiosity, and make the best decisions they can. They must acquire all reasonably available and pertinent information. They must act in good faith, with the level of care that a normally prudent person would show in the same circumstances, and in a manner they reasonably believe is in the best interests of the organization.

It is accepted that directors and trustees will not be infallible. They cannot know everything about a topic under consideration and are justified in relying on advice and information from management. Their decisions may not be perfect.

In performing their duties, governing boards carry out two types of actions. They make specific, actionable decisions, and they exercise oversight of the routine operations of the organization. The oversight function is best explained in a series of court decisions involving Caremark International,[2] a provider of patient care and managed care services. The board must make a good faith effort to establish an organizational information and reporting system that informs it when issues about compliance with applicable laws arise. When such issues come up, the board must take steps to prevent or remedy the situation. If it fails to do so and violations and losses result, individual board members may be held liable. This is the essence of the board's compliance responsibility.

The Caremark court cases provided further detail on the limits of the board's compliance obligations. The scope and structure of the required reporting system is a matter of business judgment. Even the best designed system may not identify activities that are potential violations of the law. Without some specific warning, board members need not take assertive steps to discover compliance problems. However, once they receive some evidence of wrongdoing, either through the reporting system or other means, they must investigate further until the matter has been resolved.

LEGAL RISKS OF INADEQUATE COMPLIANCE EFFORTS

The governing board's failure to ensure effective compliance protection presents serious legal risks to the organization as a whole and, in unusual cases, to individual board members.

The primary threat to healthcare organizations is enforcement activities by government agencies and private payers designed to prevent fraud, abuse, and waste. They increasingly are assisted by the efforts of private

[2] In re Caremark International Inc. Derivative Litigation, 698 A.2d 959 (Del. Ch. 1996).

whistle-blowers. When they are successful, several sanctions can be imposed on the noncompliant organizations.

- Court allows payers to recoup the improper payments.
- Criminal and civil monetary penalties are assessed against the organization.
- Both the organization and individual providers are excluded from participation in specified healthcare programs (e.g., Medicare, Medicaid).
- Both organizations and individuals are convicted of criminal fraud.
- The healthcare program, through the Office of the Inspector General (OIG) of the Centers for Medicare and Medicaid Services (CMS), requires the organization to enter into a Corporate Integrity Agreement (CIA) that mandates a comprehensive compliance program, independent audits, annual reporting, and OIG oversight.

Only in extreme circumstances do the courts hold individual board members personally liable for breaches of their duty of oversight for organizational compliance. Their accusers typically are—in for-profit entities—shareholders in a derivative suit[3] or a regulatory agency like the Securities and Exchange Commission. Trustees of not-for-profit organizations are most likely to be attacked by a state attorney general.

If the risks of personal liability become a reality, governing boards frequently have additional protection. Most organizations provide their board members with directors' and officers' (D&O) liability insurance that covers the cost of defense attorneys, settlements, awards, and judgments. Furthermore, the corporate bylaws of some organizations offer to indemnify board members for court judgments against them.

CRITERIA FOR ASSESSING BOARD OVERSIGHT OF ORGANIZATIONAL COMPLIANCE ACTIVITIES

In performing their compliance oversight duties, governing board members must make themselves familiar with many details of the compliance program. The OIG, in collaboration with the American Health Lawyers Association (AHLA), has developed a checklist of the most important program characteristics.[4] They offer a good guideline for board members. They are presented in the following sections in the form of questions and answers.

---

[3] This was the basis of the Caremark cases.

[4] "Corporate Responsibility and Corporate Compliance: A Resource for Health Care Boards of Directors," prepared by the OIG of the U.S. Department of Health and Human Services (DHHS) and the AHLA.

Compliance Program Structure

How is the compliance program structured and who are the key employees responsible for its implementation and operation? How is the Board structured to oversee compliance issues?

Board members should ensure that the program structure is logical and likely to achieve the goals set for it. They should be able to describe it articulately to another person.

How does the organization's compliance reporting system work? How frequently does the board receive reports about compliance issues?

The system needs to keep itself up to date, do its best to prevent violations, promptly discover violations when they occur, make it easy for persons to report violations, thoroughly investigate reported violations, and take aggressive steps to correct procedures that allow violations to occur. Board members should feel comfortable with the frequency and thoroughness of compliance reports they receive.

What are the goals of the organization's compliance program? What are the inherent limitations in the compliance program? How does the organization address these limitations?

Like any operational undertaking, the compliance program should have a few clear-cut goals. At the same time, to be realistic, it must acknowledge the limits on what it can accomplish. This should be followed by an explanation of how the organization will try to work around the limits. Here is a simple example of these basic principles of a compliance program.

Goal: Prevent all compliance violations.

Limitation: Still possible for a violation to occur.

Work around: Discover the violation ASAP, investigate it, and take all appropriate remedial action.

Does the compliance program address the significant risks of the organization? How were the risks determined and how are new compliance risks identified and incorporated into the program?

Different types of healthcare organizations face different kinds of legal risks. Physician practices in different specialties will be more prone to commit coding errors for the different kinds of services they deliver. An organization that is more geographically dispersed (e.g., a multistate nursing home or hospital chain) may offer more opportunities for unsupervised illegal employee behavior.

Well-run organizations recognize their risks and, where they cannot be eliminated entirely, take steps to minimize the damaging effects. As both laws and enforcement emphases change, the compliance program must adapt.

What will be the level of resources necessary to implement the compliance program as envisioned by the Board? How has management determined the adequacy of the resources dedicated to implementing and sustaining the compliance program?

The best-conceived compliance program will not achieve its intended purposes unless it is backed up by adequate resources, in terms of money, personnel, space, and management support. The OIG accepts that smaller organizations with fewer resources (e.g., a three-physician group practice) will not be able to support as elaborate a compliance program as a larger, better financed entity (e.g., a multispecialty group practice of 200 physicians).

Does the Compliance Officer have sufficient authority to implement the compliance program? Has management provided the Compliance Office with the autonomy and resources necessary to perform assessments and respond appropriately to misconduct?

One of the most important resources required by a compliance program is the support of top management. This manifests itself in the authority delegated to the head of the program, the Compliance Officer, and the decision-making freedom she needs to carry out the program's mandates.

Have compliance-related responsibilities been assigned across the appropriate levels of the organization? Are employees held accountable for meeting those compliance-related objectives during performance reviews?

Compliance with healthcare laws and regulations is not solely the responsibility of the Compliance Officer and the compliance program. They carry out their work primarily through tasks performed by employees throughout the organization. These will include coding and billing clerks, most financial managers, and others who work with or support them, including top executives. A factor in the performance reviews of these same people should be adherence to compliance policies and procedures.

Policies and Procedures

Has the organization implemented policies and procedures that address compliance risk areas and established internal controls to counter those vulnerabilities?

The compliance program guides the organization and its employees in appropriate behavior through policies and procedures. The Compliance Officer gives specific directions on how to handle the most common risk situations. To be effective, employees must be aware of the procedures and trained in their application.

How has the Code of Conduct or its equivalent been incorporated into corporate policies across the organization? How do we know that the Code is understood and accepted across the organization? Has management taken affirmative steps to publicize the importance of the Code to all employees?

Many organizations prepare and publicize a Code of Conduct for their employees. It makes sense to include basic compliance-related principles in that Code.

Preventing Violations

Once a sound compliance program structure is in place, attention turns to its two primary tasks: preventing violations and responding to violations.

What is the scope of compliance-related education and training across the organization? Has the effectiveness of such training been assessed? What policies/measures have been developed to enforce training requirements and to provide remedial training as required?

Everybody whose work touches on compliance issues must receive education and training on what to do to avoid violations. Conducting the training with the right employees in the room may not be enough. They should be tested periodically on their knowledge and actual work practices. When the program or its underlying laws change, another round of training may be necessary.

How is the board kept apprised of significant regulatory and industry developments affecting the organization's risk? How is the compliance program structured to address such risks?

The compliance landscape is changing constantly. New laws are enacted, new regulations are promulgated under existing laws, and new enforcement initiatives are launched under all laws. New vulnerabilities to violations may emerge in healthcare financing and delivery operations. These developments will have varying impacts on different types of organizations. The compliance programs need to be able to learn about these changes as soon as they occur, evaluate their effect on the organization, and take appropriate precautions against them. The board simultaneously must be kept apprised of all these activities.

How are "at risk" operations assessed from a compliance perspective? Is conformance with the organization's compliance program periodically evaluated? Does the organization periodically evaluate the effectiveness of the compliance program?

Regular evaluations should be performed on the operational areas that are most susceptible to violations to determine their adherence to compliance policies and procedures. They must be following the prescribed prevention protocols. In addition, there should be regular assessments of how well the compliance program is carrying out its mission.

What processes are in place to ensure that appropriate remedial measures are taken in response to identified weaknesses?

When weaknesses are discovered, either in the compliance procedures or in the program itself, there must be processes in place to make immediate corrections.

Responding to Violations

Even the best-intentioned organizations with the most thorough compliance programs still sometimes commit violations of applicable laws. They must be prepared for that possibility.

What is the process by which the organization evaluates and responds to suspected compliance violations? How are reporting systems, such as the compliance hotline, monitored to verify appropriate resolution of reported matters?

There must be in place a quick-reaction process that investigates and evaluates violation reports, immediately halts the violative behavior, takes steps to prevent its recurrence, and determines how to treat the violator and what to report to the government. Later, the event should be revisited to make sure that the correction has taken full effect.

Does the organization have policies that address the appropriate protection of whistle-blowers and those accused of misconduct?

There are two ways that employees become factors in failure to comply. They commit the acts, either intentionally or inadvertently, that result in a violation. Or they notice the violation and "blow the whistle" on the illegal activity. The organization must have clear procedures for handling both types of employees, particularly in protecting their legal rights.

What is the process by which the organization evaluates and responds to suspected compliance violations? What policies address the protection of employees and the preservation of relevant documents and information?

It is important to have a detailed protocol on the steps to be followed when a violation is discovered or suspected. It should be followed immediately and to the letter, with little room for improvisation. In addition to protecting employees, all relevant documents and information must be preserved.

What guidelines have been established for reporting compliance violations to the board?

Some if not all of the noncompliance events should be reported to the board, or the Compliance Committee. Board members must know how serious, or not, are the compliance problems the organization faces.

What policies govern the reporting to government authorities of probable violations of law?

Certain violations must be reported to the appropriate law enforcement authorities. Sometimes doing so minimizes possible penalties. There should be no uncertainty about when and how such reports need to be submitted.

STUDY QUESTIONS

1. If the trustees of a nonprofit organization represent the interests of the general public, how might members of that public attempt to influence those trustees and, through them, the organization?
2. What does the word "fiduciary" mean?
3. After reading this chapter, would you accept a request to serve on the governing board of a local hospital? Keep in mind your fiduciary responsibilities for compliance, the potential for personal liability, and balance these against the protection you would receive from D&O insurance.
4. If you were on the board of a healthcare organization, how much information would you want to receive about its compliance activities? How often would you want to hear about violation events? Would you want to hear about all of them, or just the most serious?

Learning Exercises

1. If you have access to legal resources, either through a nearby law school library or through the Internet, find and study the decisions in the Caremark International cases. The citation for the primary decision is In re Caremark International Inc. Derivative Litigation, 698 A.2d 959 (Del. Ch. 1996). There were several cases in the series. Look for them all. Pick out three statements by the court that you think have the strongest impact on how board members must carry out their duties.
2. Do a little Internet research into D&O liability insurance. Learn what sorts of events or behavior it covers and what it does not cover. What are the dollar limits on the coverage?

3. Try to discover a court decision that held the directors of a corporation personally liable for a breach of their fiduciary duties. For help, contact an attorney in the corporate law department of a local law firm. Tell her that you are doing research for a course and you would like to find a copy of a case decision like this one.
4. With your instructor's assistance, arrange with a local healthcare organization to interview the members of its governing board, using the questions from the OIG checklist. Assess the board's awareness of its compliance duties and recommend measures to improve the board's readiness. Prepare a confidential written report of the team's findings for submission to the organization.

References

1. Broader perspectives; higher performance. State of Compliance: 2011 Study, PWC and Compliance Week, http://www.pwc.com/us/en/risk-management/gc/compliance-survey.jhtml
2. Corporate Responsibility and Health Care Quality: A Resource for Health Care Boards of Directors, Office Of Inspector General of the U.S. Department of Health and Human Services and the American Health Lawyers Association, 2007, oig.hhs.gov
3. An Integrated Approach to Corporate Compliance: A Resource for Health Care Organization Boards of Directors, Office of Inspector General of the U.S. Department of Health and Human Services and the American Health Lawyers Association, 2004, oig.hhs.gov
4. Corporate Responsibility and Corporate Compliance: A Resource for Health Care Boards of Directors, Office Of Inspector General of the U.S. Department of Health and Human Services and the American Health Lawyers Association, 2003, oig.hhs.gov
5. The Health Care Director's Compliance Duties: A Continued Focus of Attention and Enforcement, Office of Inspector General of the U.S. Department of Health and Human Services and the American Health Lawyers Association, 2010 www.healthlawyers.org/complianceduties
6. A Guide to the Board's Compliance Oversight Duties, McDermott Will & Emery, BoardRoom Press, August 2011, governanceinstitute.com

Chapter 11

Internal Investigations

LEARNING OBJECTIVES

After completing class sessions based on this chapter, students will learn:

- Situations in which an organization will need to conduct an investigation or audit.
- Steps in conducting an organization's own internal investigation.
- When and how to interview employees and third parties in connection with a compliance investigation.
- When and how to review documents and records in connection with a compliance investigation.
- Contents of a well-prepared investigation report.
- Potential sources of an agency-driven investigation.
- Legal forms of inquiry initiating an agency investigation.
- Best responses to an agency-driven investigation.
- When an organization should conduct an internal compliance audit.
- Detailed guidelines for conducting a compliance audit.
- How to take advantage of attorney-related privileges and protections.

INTRODUCTION

An organization conducts an internal investigation in order to discover whether a violation of law has occurred or is likely to occur soon. There are three motivations for carrying out some sort of internal investigation.

1. There has been an internal clue or report that a violation has occurred. This could include a complaint by a whistle-blower. The report may or may not be accurate; it is the purpose of the investigation to determine that.
2. On its own initiative, a government agency has launched an investigation into some aspect of the organization's operations. The organization becomes aware of this through an informal agency

inquiry, a subpoena, a search warrant, or discovery or depositions associated with a lawsuit brought by the agency against the organization. It must respond.

3. As part of an ambitious compliance initiative, the organization wishes to conduct periodic audits of its compliance-sensitive activities to detect weaknesses, and assess the effectiveness of the compliance program itself.

HOW INTERNAL INVESTIGATIONS FIT INTO THE CONTEXT OF COMPLIANCE PROGRAMS

Internal investigations are an integral component of an effective compliance program.

When an organization receives a report or a complaint that a compliance violation has occurred or suspicious behavior has been observed, it is a sign that the program has not worked perfectly to prevent such incidents. At the same time, the problem has been discovered before a government agency has become aware of it. The organization has an opportunity to control the resolution of the problem. In addition, it has been alerted to possible deficiencies in its compliance program and can take action to correct them.

Regular audits of all or part of a compliance program are real-life tests of its effectiveness. They discover problems with the functioning of the program and the compliance performance of the organization, before a whistle-blower or a government agency has to bring it to its attention. This is an optimal situation in which the organization is in full control of its compliance activities.

Compliance matters have not gone well if a government agency has found it necessary to initiate some form of legal inquiry and conduct its own investigation into suspected violations of law. The organization has no choice but to respond to that inquiry and perhaps the legal action that follows it. If the inquiry shows that the organization has been negligent or reckless about compliance, the agency may compel it to accept and implement a Corporate Integrity Agreement[1] (CIA) designed to improve

---

[1] A comprehensive CIA typically lasts 5 years and includes requirements to:

- Hire a Compliance Officer/appoint a Compliance Committee
- Develop written standards and policies
- Implement a comprehensive employee training program
- Retain an independent review organization to conduct annual reviews
- Establish a confidential disclosure program
- Restrict employment of ineligible persons
- Report overpayments, reportable events, and ongoing investigations/legal proceedings
- Provide an implementation report and annual reports to the Office of the Inspector General (OIG) on the status of the entity's compliance activities

Additional information is available at: http://oig.hhs.gov/compliance/corporate-integrity-agreements/index.asp

its compliance performance. In any event, the organization will recognize its shortcomings and carry out its own changes in compliance activities.

ORGANIZATION-INITIATED INTERNAL INVESTIGATION

An employee, perhaps working in the claims department of a hospital, notices some irregular performance data (large number of claims in one CPT code, a sharp drop in claims denials) or observes another employee failing to follow prescribed work procedures. Unsure whether there is a good explanation for these events, but trained to report any anomalies with compliance implications, the employee follows a protocol for communicating the observations to a designated Compliance Officer.

The Compliance Officer then follows a multistep investigation procedure outlined in the organization's compliance plan. A good procedure takes into account these factors.

Use Trained, Trusted Employees to Carry Out the Investigation

The investigation starts with the Compliance Officer. In a small organization, such as a medium-size physician practice, she may be responsible for carrying out the entire investigation. Any others involved should be trusted employees trained in the techniques of investigation. They should be knowledgeable about the activity or department where a problem is suspected, and about the applicable legal requirements that must be satisfied. They will be people of good judgment and discretion. They are willing to make hard decisions and express unpopular opinions. They will not tailor their conclusions to satisfy or protect certain other employees. They can be trusted to maintain confidentiality throughout the investigation. Premature disclosure of the facts or the names of involved individuals can jeopardize the organization's legal defense of the matter, its reputation, and the legal rights of individual employees.

Because of potential conflicts of interest, the employees selected to carry out the investigation should not have any connection to the area where the suspected conduct happened. It also is preferable that they not be inclined to initiate a qui tam action.

Consider Using an Attorney

For all but the most trivial incidents, it is a good idea to at least consult with an attorney about the handling of the investigation. If the matter seems serious and the organization has the resources, conduct the investigation under the aegis of an experienced lawyer. This makes it much easier to take advantage of the attorney-client or work product privileges.

In the optimal scenario, the attorney has overall responsibility for directing the investigation. She communicates directly with top management; all reports are funneled through her. She controls the flow of information about the investigation.

Consider Using a Consultant

If the organization lacks the time, the experienced personnel, or the expertise to carry out the investigation, it might consider bringing in an outside consultant, a person who specializes in guiding these types of investigations. The consultant performs the bulk of the investigative work, but channels his findings through an attorney to maximize the protection of privileges.

A consultant does not have the same tight relationship with the organization as a trusted employee or an attorney. His duties should be carefully defined—what issues he will examine, what authority he will have, what document access he will have, and the dates of his involvement with the investigation.

Conduct an Investigation That Fits the Suspected Misconduct and Violations

On the basis of the suspicions or allegations, a step-by-step investigation plan is prepared. The direction of the investigation depends on the scope and nature of the potential problem. As the investigation proceeds and it seems more or less serious than originally thought, it may have to be expanded or contracted, or refocused. Additional resources may have to be committed.

The investigative techniques and methodology that will be used should be discussed with management and the organization's attorney. It is worth thinking about the impact on the organization when the investigation becomes apparent to the workforce. Anxiety levels may rise, workflows may be disrupted, and productivity may fall off. Some employees may be hesitant to cooperate in the investigation.

A good investigation will examine and document the following issues:

- Nature and scope of the problem incident (e.g., dollar amounts, time duration, programs, and payors affected)

- Applicable statutes, regulations, and rules concerning the possible violation, including regulatory guidances
- Clarity or ambiguity of the applicable rules and standards
- Knowledge and intent of the persons involved, including employees and third parties
- Prior incidents of misconduct or violation within the same department or among the same employees
- Exactly how the incident took place. Was it an isolated mistake or error of judgment, a system failure, a technical problem, a conscious attempt to defraud?
- Actions that might be taken to mitigate, correct, or prevent the problem

These are some of the techniques that the investigators will use in their work.

Personnel Interviews

People are almost always involved in an incident of noncompliance. They may have failed to follow a procedure, followed a poorly conceived procedure, accidentally or mistakenly committed a violative act, approached their work with a careless or reckless attitude, or deliberately set out to commit fraud. If they themselves did nothing, they may have witnessed someone else's questionable behavior. The investigators will seek relevant information from current employees (all levels, including managers), former employees, customers, patients, providers, vendors, payors, and other third parties who deal with the organization. They may even wish to speak with representatives of regulatory agencies.

In planning the interview phase, several questions must be answered. How many current and former employees will be interviewed? How many people outside the organization? Specifically who will be interviewed? In some cases, the investigators may want to talk with a representative of a third-party entity (e.g., a billing subcontractor), but not know the identity of that person. Where will the interviews be conducted? It is best to hold interviews away from the workplace. There will be no interruptions and the interviewees will feel less inhibited. Who will conduct the interviews?

Before beginning the interviews, the investigators should discuss with experienced attorneys how to conduct them safely and effectively, especially from a legal point of view. It should be made clear to the interviewees that it is the organization that is conducting the interview (not the government and not someone acting on the employees' behalf) and that the organization will decide how the results will be used. If there is a chance that an interviewee may be the target of a parallel government investigation into the same issues, she should be advised of her right to legal counsel before cooperating with the organization. If this is the case, will the organization provide and pay for an attorney to represent the interests of interviewed employees? At the same time, it should be made clear to each interviewee that if he or she does not cooperate with the organization's investigation, his or her employment may be terminated. The employer organization has a right to do this.

Begin each personal interview with a standard warning that the information gathered will be used to guide the organization in understanding its legal risks and planning its remedial moves. It will not result in a word-for-word transcription of the conversation. If the employee has already spoken with government investigators, it is fair to inquire what she was asked and what she disclosed. The government frequently asks employees not to reveal what was discussed in the government interview, but this request is not mandatory or legally binding.

The questioning of contractors, regulators, and others with no allegiance to the organization must be managed carefully. The information that is sought from them or disclosed to them during interviews could reveal violation problems that the organization is having. The regulators might decide to take enforcement action on the basis of what they hear. Contractors might decide to report their suspicions to the regulators. Some protection may be afforded by making anonymous inquiries through an attorney or a state-wide trade or professional association.

An investigative interview is more than a simple question and answer session. Certain interview styles are more effective than others at eliciting the desired information. Even cooperative employees must be questioned artfully to learn what they know. It also is essential to determine when someone is lying. Training in interview skills may be appropriate for the investigators. The process and results of each interview should be documented.

Records and Documents Review

After people, the next most crucial topic of investigation will be records and documents. This will include a large number and variety of sources.

- Bills, claims, cost reports, financial statements
- Clinical or medical records
- Internal policies and procedures
- Internal communications, like emails, memos, directives, performance assessments, audit results

- External communications with vendors, providers, patients, contractors, suppliers, regulators
- Compliance program rules, regulations, manuals, posters, fraud alerts, advisory opinions, agency guidances

At the very beginning of the investigation, before any interviews have been conducted, all employees should be instructed not to destroy, delete, or modify any records or documents that may be the subject of the investigation. The documents must be secured, organized, and classified for careful examination. The organization may have in place a formal policy for disposing of records after a specified period of time. That policy should be suspended until the matter under investigation has been resolved. Avoid any actions that might be interpreted as attempts to hide or destroy incriminating evidence.

A decision must be made about the persons who will review the documents. They should be familiar enough with the document matters to be able to understand them, but not so much that they might be biased about the direction of the investigation.

A unique form of documents will be the data stored on computers within the organization. This part of the investigation will take into account data distributed across a local area network (LAN) or a wide area network (WAN), on individual computers and laptops, as well as data saved on servers or third-party "clouds" outside the organization. Email messages will be a vital source of evidence: investigators must be aware of where and how they are saved and stored. It is helpful if all related computers (hardware, software, data) can be secured.

To maintain the security of relevant documents and computers, it may be necessary to limit access to particular offices before searching them. The investigators must determine how many such offices will be secured, which ones, and how the decision will be presented to their occupants.

As documents are collected, they should be stored in secure locations. They must be protected against attempts by employees (or others) with potential personal culpability or other motives, to confiscate, destroy, or alter documents that might implicate them. The organization must be as sensitive to this possibility as the government surely will be. With regard to any related documents, the organization cannot compel employees to release personal documents or nonemployees to release documents from third-party organizations.

Finally, there will be a decision about whether the results of the interviews and searches will be preserved orally or in writing. If the latter, will the investigative team hang on to their original notes or discard them when they have been translated into a final report. The best course usually is a write-up of the findings as part of an investigation that takes full advantage of several attorney-associated privileges.

Report Based on Investigation Findings

The results of the investigation, captured in investigator notes and written findings, will be translated into a report. Legal counsel normally will oversee the preparation of this report. It should be kept strictly confidential, with limited circulation within the organization. A comprehensive report will include these elements.

- Facts discovered by the investigators
- Facts sought or suspected but still unknown
- All the laws implicated or potentially implicated by the revealed facts
- Attorney's analysis of the facts in light of those laws
- Specific facts that point to potential causes of the compliance incident
- Detailed description of the incident that may have been noncompliant
- Statement of incident's impact on the health, safety, and quality of care
- Time period during which the incident occurred
- Identity of the individuals (employees and other) involved in the incident
- Identity of the individuals who should have detected/noticed/reported the noncompliance
- Estimate of the enormity of the issue, financially, legally, and otherwise

After the Report Is Completed

The tricky part of an organization-initiated investigation is deciding what to do with the results. At the very least, management must act to address the internal operational failings that it has discovered. It should do this whether or not there is external law enforcement pressure.

The first step will be to determine the corrective action needed to fix the problems. This may take the form of personnel changes, personnel retraining, reorganization of the affected departments or work flows, modification of policies and procedures, and reallocation of resources. It may be necessary to discipline employees, depending on their degree of intent or negligence. If third-party individuals or organizations (vendors, suppliers, subcontractors) were involved, the organization will wish to review those relationships. It may appear that the existing compliance program and policies failed to prevent or detect the problem. In that case, the organization's entire compliance program and policies should be reviewed closely.

The second step is the decision whether to disclose the results of the internal investigation to government authorities and to repay monies wrongly received from them. The problem may be a simple Medicare or Medicaid billing error that merely requires a repayment, or there may be signs of more serious wrongdoing. The decision should be made after close consultation with legal counsel experienced in such matters.

There are benefits to disclosure of the incident. As a result, the organization may avoid criminal liability or more serious criminal penalties. It is likely to reduce the liability for civil damages. The act of disclosure makes a whistle-blower lawsuit less justifiable.

On the other hand, government authorities are likely to want to look more closely at the verified facts in the disclosure, perhaps leading to the discovery of additional violations. Alerted by the disclosure, the authorities may launch their own investigation to search for more incriminating facts. In the end, the organization could be hit with penalties for conduct that might have otherwise remained undiscovered.

AGENCY-DRIVEN INVESTIGATION INQUIRY

This is the worst-case investigation scenario. An enforcement agency has found reason to suspect noncompliant behavior by an organization that violates laws and is costing the government money. The agency wants to learn more to determine the scope of the noncompliance. It approaches the organization in a variety of ways.

These initiatives must be taken very seriously and handled with great dispatch. They will be emotionally upsetting, and probably damaging to the organization's morale and reputation. Responding to them will consume time and money. The potential consequences are severe: multimillion dollar damage awards and settlements, civil and criminal penalties, exclusion from the Medicare and Medicaid programs, and criminal convictions.

Source of the Inquiry

Serious investigative inquiries can come from numerous government agencies with the authority to enforce healthcare laws and regulations.

The powers of the Centers for Medicare and Medicaid Services (CMS) (responsible for Medicare and Medicaid, and the Stark Act), the Solicitor's Office in the Department of Labor (responsible for Occupational and Safety Health Administration regulations), the Office of Civil Rights (responsible for the Health Insurance Portability and Accountability Act [HIPAA]) and the Office of the Inspector General (OIG; responsible for the Anti-Kickback Statute) in the Department of Health and Human Services (DHHS), the Department of Justice, as well as the 50 state attorneys general can be applied against healthcare organizations.

Legal Form of the Inquiry

The inquiry can come in several legal forms. Good attorneys will understand them immediately. However, nonlegal organizational staff are most likely to receive first notice of the agency's interest and must respond promptly. These legal forms are arranged in ascending order of severity.

Informal Inquiry

The least threatening form of official inquiry is an informal request for information about a specific issue of possible noncompliance. The request may come in the form of a letter, phone call, or personal visit from the investigating agency. It may concern the organization's own operations or those of another entity with which it has dealings or does business. For instance, a specialty group practice that receives referrals from a primary care clinic may be suspected of taking kickbacks. A diagnostic laboratory may have submitted miscoded claims for tests conducted at a hospital's request.

Because of the informal nature of the inquiry, the organization is not legally required to respond, but it is generally a good idea to show a willingness to cooperate. Otherwise, the agency's suspicions may be aroused even further. However, there is some flexibility in that response, and the organization will want to avoid unnecessarily disclosing any potentially harmful information.

Government agents may approach employees independently, without telling the organization. They may visit them at their homes. In the workplace, if an attorney is accompanying the employees, the agents may attempt to separate the two. Employees should be advised that they are not obliged to speak with the agents. On the other hand, the organization may not forbid employees talking with agents voluntarily. It may ask employees to report if they are contacted directly by a government agent. Employees have a right to be represented by a lawyer during an interview. The organization may provide a lawyer to assist the employee and may pay for a lawyer to represent the employee, but a lawyer who is representing the organization may not also represent an employee.

Subpoena *Duces Tecum* ("Bring with You")

This subpoena for the production of evidence is a court summons ordering a named party to appear before the court and produce documents or other tangible evidence for use at a hearing or trial. Some enforcement agencies inherently possess this authority, while others must request a subpoena from a court. A subpoena usually is presented personally to an organization staff member at the worksite.

All subpoenas have a few basic features:

- The specific work activities or processes about which documentary evidence is sought
- The specific types of documents sought (e.g., medical records, claims forms, emails)
- The number of years for which the documents are sought
- The time period within which the documents must be provided

When a subpoena is received, the organization should immediately contact legal counsel. A smaller organization—a 5-person physician practice, for instance—is not likely to have an attorney experienced in handling matters like this. It may be necessary very quickly to find a qualified lawyer to help in guiding the response. Any delay could lead to contempt charges or civil penalties.

A subpoena is usually an indication that the government agency is working on a more formal and invasive investigation of the organization. While a response is virtually mandatory, it should be carefully planned with an attorney to demonstrate an intention to cooperate and to satisfy the strict terms of the subpoena, but without disclosing unrequested or privileged information. The subpoena will include a future return date by which the documents must be offered up. The organization or its attorney should directly contact the investigators as soon as possible and stay in frequent contact with them.

Search Warrant

When an organization receives a subpoena, it will have days, if not weeks, to produce the requested documents. An investigating officer who shows up at an organization facility with a search warrant in hand is after documents immediately. No delays. No time to prepare a response.

A search warrant is a judicial document that authorizes enforcement officers to search a person or place for the purpose of discovering evidence of guilt for use in criminal prosecutions. Officers obtain search warrants by submitting affidavits and other evidence to a judge or magistrate to establish probable cause to believe that a search will yield evidence related to a crime. If satisfied that the officers have established probable cause, the judge or magistrate will issue the warrant. The warrant grants them the authority to enter the premises at a specified location, to search for specified documents, to take possession of the documents, and remove them from the location.

The unannounced appearance of a law officer with a search warrant can be a traumatic event. It is a good idea to have anticipated the possibility and prepared a response strategy or protocol.

Without a search warrant, the organization does not have to provide immediate access to documents. It must provide "reasonable" access. Without a search warrant, a government agency may not seize original documents. Nor may it take personal, nonorganizational documents.

When agents show up with a search warrant, ask for a copy of the warrant and the supporting affidavit, and get them to the organization's legal counsel as quickly as possible. Read the warrant immediately and carefully. The agents may only search areas described in the warrant and take document listed there. After sending all employees home, follow the agents during their search. Do not interfere, but make a list of the areas searched, the documents taken, and the questions asked. The questions do not need to be answered and can be declined with a referral to legal counsel. Obtain the names and contact information for the agents conducting the search and the agencies they represent.

Later, issue a statement to employees explaining the reasons for and circumstances of the search visit. During the visit and thereafter, do not allow any documents or other related evidence to be modified, removed, or destroyed.

Legal Action

When an agency wishes to bring a lawsuit or legal action against a healthcare organization for violation of a law, it prepares and files with the court a criminal complaint stating facts to support the allegation. A judge of the court determines whether there is "probable cause" for the charges and, if so, issues a summons. It states a date by which the defendant individual or organization must respond. A copy of the complaint and summons is then served physically on the defendant. At that point, the defendant is on notice that a legal action is underway.

A civil law complaint is slightly different. A showing of probable cause is not necessary. The complaint sets forth the agency's claim for relief from damages caused (e.g., overpayments to the organization) or wrongful conduct (e.g., miscoding of claims).

It is highly unlikely that a government agency would initiate legal proceedings without first gathering information by one of the three methods above. It is much more likely that a whistle-blower would file a qui tam action on behalf of the government on the basis of the whistle-blower's own knowledge. The organization could be served with a complaint without prior notice. In addition, if the government decides to take over prosecution of the case, the organization may first learn about when it receives discovery requests and depositions.

Responses to the Inquiry

The urgency and focus of the organization's response will depend substantially on the form and content of the inquiry instrument. It starts with strong efforts to protect the integrity of any evidence relevant to the inquiry. The organization should instruct its owners, directors, shareholders, executives, managers, providers, staff, independent contractors, subcontractors, and others with access to or in control of relevant information that none of that information may be destroyed. If the organization has an established document disposal policy (e.g., discarding claims submission records after 5 years), the implementation of that policy should be suspended until the concern of the investigating agency has been resolved.

The next move is to identify the parts of the organization that are the target of the inquiry. It might be a practice that is widespread throughout the organization. The government may be concerned only with the actions of a single department or a few related departments. The focus could be on a handful of employees or a single individual. The suspect behavior might also involve third parties (e.g., suppliers, vendors, contractors, consultants) with which the organization has business dealings.

With that information in hand, an appropriate person can be designated to manage the response. Part of the response entails protecting documents and organizational units that are not the subject of the investigation. For instance, if the problems seem to lie with the billing department, the medical records unit, or a particular physician's referrals, steps should be taken to "quarantine" the people involved in those areas from the rest of the organization. This could be accomplished by monitoring the contacts and communications with those areas. The purpose is to protect the independence and credibility of the unaffected parts of the organization. Implementing a virtual barrier like this also protects documents outside those areas from falling under the subpoena.

When a healthcare organization is faced with serious legal threats, it needs a competent attorney to guide it in its dealings with the investigating agency. It has three options.

Many organizations are large enough to employ their own in-house legal counsel. Such a person offers the advantages of a good understanding of the organization's business operations coupled perhaps with specific knowledge of the activity under investigation. Directly employing an attorney is frequently more cost-efficient than relying on outside counsel. The downside of relying on in-house counsel is that she may have advised the organization on the legality of the activity, making it hard for her to be objective about the investigation. If the investigating agency also is examining that legal advice, the attorney may have a conflict between her personal interests and those of the organization. Finally, the attorney's presence as a committed, salaried employee of the organization may give the impression that she was somehow complicit in the suspect activities.

In contrast to an in-house attorney, the organization can turn to an independent outside lawyer experienced in compliance investigations but whom the organization has never consulted before. This is the only option for an organization that currently lacks an in-house counsel or one with the requisite experience, or is not represented by an outside counsel or one with the requisite experience.

Using such an attorney avoids conflict of interest problems as well as claims that the attorney's prior advice contributed to the noncompliant events. The absence of prior history means, arguably, that the attorney's current advice will be more candid and objective.

On the other hand, an attorney new to the organization will have no knowledge of its business operations and the kinds of compliance challenges it faces. He or she will have to spend time and resources gaining the necessary familiarity. The organization also may be hesitant about fully trusting an attorney with whom it has not worked before on so sensitive a matter.

Perhaps the best solution, if it is available, is an outside counsel with whom the organization has worked closely in the past, and who has experience with compliance investigations. Such a person is likely to have advised the organization on structural and transactional business matters over a period of years. She may even have assisted the organization in conducting compliance audits. Again, this prior working relationship may appear to bias the counsel's objectivity.

An organization's choice among these three options will depend on the gravity and scope of the investigation, the amount of its own resources, its established relationships with attorneys, and the compliance expertise of those attorneys.

It is especially important for an organization confronted by government law enforcement investigators to leverage as fully as possible the document protections available through its attorney relationship.

ORGANIZATION-INITIATED INTERNAL AUDIT

Chapter 8 of the 2010 Federal Sentencing Guidelines Manual, dealing with the sentencing of organizations, specifies seven steps an organization must take to have an effective compliance and ethics program. The existence of such a program is used for determining the organization's "culpability score"[2] and its "recommended conditions of probation."[3] In other words, its level of culpability will be lower and, if probation is called for, the conditions will be less strict.

The fifth of those steps states the following:

> The organization shall take reasonable steps –
>
> (A) to ensure that the organization's compliance and ethics program is followed, including monitoring and auditing to detect criminal conduct;
>
> (B) to evaluate periodically the effectiveness of the organization's compliance and ethics program;[4]

Such audits, or investigations, are not taken in response to internal reports of possible compliance violations or to the initiation by government authorities of their own investigations. Instead, the audits are conducted to make sure an existing compliance program and policies are operating at peak effectiveness. For that reason, they have slightly less urgency than those other investigations. Incidentally, they may discover violations of which no one was previously aware.

The terms "monitoring" and "auditing" are sometimes used synonymously, but they have different meanings. To monitor a work process or procedures involves a routine spot check for any obvious compliance issues. An audit is a more formal, systematic investigation intended to assess compliance with legal standards and identify existing or potential compliance violations.

---

[2] U.S. Sentencing Commission Federal Sentencing Guidelines Manual, §8C2.5 (f): http://www.ussc.gov/guidelines/2010_guidelines/Manual_HTML/Chapter_8.htm

[3] U.S. Sentencing Commission Federal Sentencing Guidelines Manual, §8D1.4 (c)(1): http://www.ussc.gov/guidelines/2010_guidelines/Manual_HTML/Chapter_8.htm

[4] U.S. Sentencing Commission Federal Sentencing Guidelines Manual, §8B2.1 (5) (A) & (B): http://www.ussc.gov/guidelines/2010_guidelines/Manual_HTML/Chapter_8.htm

Baseline Versus Routine Audits

The first ever audit by an organization establishes a baseline of compliance effectiveness for future audits. Depending on what is discovered, subsequent audits will occur at 3-month to annual intervals.

With a baseline in hand, routine audits will be conducted on a regular schedule. Depending on the size and complexity of the organization, the availability of resources, the nature of its health-related work, its history of compliance problems, and changes in the laws, the schedule might be monthly, quarterly, semiannually, or annually. The schedule should be specified in the compliance plan itself.

Routine audits may target diverse areas of the organization, focusing on different sources of compliance risk. They may rotate among departments, and may or may not include a review of claims.

Scope of Audits

The scope of each audit must be defined clearly in advance. This should be guided by the latest information about legal developments and enforcement initiatives, as well as known organizational risk areas. Knowledge of high priority legal issues can be acquired from several sources.

The DHHS OIG regularly issues compliance guidance on common risk areas, as well as Fraud alerts and Advisory Opinions. It also issues an annual work plan that describes in considerable detail the issues and types of providers on which it will be concentrating its enforcement efforts in the next 12 months.[5] The CMS instructs Recovery Audit Contractors (RACs)[6] on the issues for which they may conduct audits. Those issues can be found on the websites of each RAC. The CMS Comprehensive Error Rate Testing (CERT) Program publishes reports describing the kinds of documentation, coding errors, and billing errors to which it will be paying attention. The OIG also has established a Health Care Fraud and Abuse Control Program[7] that issues annual reports of fraud recoveries and prosecutions.

Most organizations will be familiar with known risk areas and prior incidents of noncompliance. These should be evident from prior audit reports, public and private payor correspondence, claims denials, and data analysis.

With this foundation of knowledge, an organization can direct its audit to the points of highest legal risk and potential impact on its operations.

---

[5] The work plan for 2012 can be found at: http://oig.hhs.gov/reports-and-publications/workplan/index.asp

[6] http://www.cms.gov/rac

[7] http://oig.hhs.gov/reports-and-publications/hcfac/index.asp

Type of Audit

Audits can vary in the range of activities that they explore and the audit techniques employed. They can look at one small part of a large multistep process or the entire process from beginning to end. For instance, the point at which a clinician assigns a CPT code to the service provided versus the full chain of tasks that turn that code into a claim that is filed and eventually paid, perhaps after a denial by the payor.

The audit may examine a modest number of compliance-related events and reach informal rough conclusions, or it may consist of a more all-encompassing survey that produces statistically valid results.

An audit may consist of a review of medical records and claims documentation, or it may consist entirely of an analysis of data. Document and record reviews work best for checking issues like medical necessity, record cloning, and the existence and legibility of medical orders. Data analysis is the technique of choice for identifying billing unit or place of service errors.

When an organization wishes to study claims filings, it must decide whether to conduct the investigation before the claims are submitted or after they have been adjudicated.

Personnel Conducting the Audit

The same options for staffing an internal investigation are available to organizations for their internal audits, but the final choices are usually a little different. The core of the investigative team is composed of organization employees with appropriate expertise and training, with ancillary guidance roles for third-party consultants and experts. The advantages of this approach are lower cost, and the employees' history with the organization and loyalty to it, as well as their knowledge of its systems and work processes. The disadvantages are insufficient experienced internal staff, lack of resources to support the audit, hesitation of employee interviewees to talk with employee interviewers, and a perceived lack of objectivity. Frequently, the investigation is a result of the efforts of both internal staff and outside experts.

Audit Standards

To be useful, an audit must be based on recognized criteria, benchmarks, reference points, and standards. The organization's compliance performance must be compared to some kind of yardstick. These will be found in laws and regulations (e.g., False Claims Act, Stark Law, Anti-Kickback

Statute, HIPAA), OIG Compliance Program Guidances, CMS conditions of participation and coverage, payor (public and private, local and national) payment policies and determinations, payor correspondence, and organization-specific industry guidelines. Depending on the focus of the audit, different standards will be consulted.

Reporting Audit Results

There are two types of outcomes from a compliance audit. Deficiencies may be revealed in the organization's compliance efforts that need to be corrected or strengthened. In addition, major or minor violations may be discovered that require prompt remedial action.

At the conclusion of the audit, there should be a debriefing among the investigators to reach agreement on the findings, resolve disputes, and clarify uncertainties. Top management can be given a heads-up on the results they will see in the final report. That report should concentrate on operational shortcomings and avoid conclusions about compliance with or violations of laws or regulations. Afterward, legal counsel can review the findings to determine whether corrective actions like repayments or disclosures are called for.

Basic Audit Techniques

An audit uses the examination techniques of an internal investigation—personnel interviews and document reviews—along with the methodology of data sampling.

Personnel Interviews

Audits almost always involve employee interviews at some point. Careful preparations should be made for the interviews. The main thrust of the audit will dictate the types of information sought from the interviews. In turn, this will lead to the framing of specific questions for the interview subjects. It is a good idea to prepare a formal, standard questionnaire to ensure consistency across the interviews. The individual questions should encourage open-ended responses rather than yes or no answers.

To elicit their full cooperation, employees must feel assured that their responses will be kept confidential. The interviews should be conducted in an environment where the employee is relaxed and not intimidated. The best way to accomplish this is to hold the interviews away from the workplace and under the direction of outside consultants who are not part of the employee's work contacts.

Document Review

Most audits also will require a review of documents, the specific types depending on the chosen nature of the assessment. For instance, if the organization was reviewing its diagnosis-related group (DRG) validation procedure, it would look at the medical record for each admission, the related UB claim form (standard CMS reimbursement claim form, currently denominated UB-04), and the remittance advice or notice. Reviews of physician compensation or medical director relationships would include the underlying contracts as well as time sheets, payment records, tax filings, and schedules. An analysis of an aged credit balance report along with account notes and payor correspondence would be the basis of a credit balance audit. The goal is to review every document that is relevant to the subject of the audit and not a single document more. Document reviews can be expensive, disruptive, and time consuming.

Data Sampling

An area of great concern in healthcare organizations is the possibility of error or fraud in the submission of claims for reimbursement. Even modest-size healthcare organizations submit tens of thousands of claims a year; submissions from larger entities may run into the millions. It would consume too much time and money to audit all the claims filed by an organization over, say, the last 3 years. To evaluate a large population of items, the answer is to look at only a sample of the total number. Using sophisticated statistical methods, the results drawn from a carefully selected subset of the total data population are extrapolated to the whole. To be useful and acceptable, the methods must be reviewed, if not designed, by a statistics professional trained in probability sampling and estimation methods.[8]

Most sampling projects follow a few basic steps:

- The time period from which the items will be sampled (e.g., claims submissions during the last 2 years).
- The population of items that will be sampled (e.g., claims submissions for certain CPT codes). This is called the "sample frame."
- The sample plan by which the sample size will be chosen, the sample items to be selected, acquired, and reviewed.
- Execution of the sample plan, including review of each sample item.
- Determining the extent of noncompliance (e.g., coding errors, underpayments, overpayments).

Properly conceived, data sampling can produce results as accurate as an audit of an entire population.

[8] CMS Manual Publication 100-08, ¶3.10.1.5.

Evaluating the Results and Correcting the Problems

On the basis of the audit results, the organization will determine the location and nature of process defects in its existing operations. Thoughtful decisions must be made about what did not work well in the past and what improvements are necessary going forward. With the new knowledge from the audit, the organization can take several actions.

- If the audit reveals operational practices that are noncompliant without creating major law violations, the affected work process is immediately modified to bring it into compliance.
- If it turns out that there has been a significant violation with major repercussions (in terms of a large number of claims affected or a large overpayment by a payor), the organization will consult with its legal counsel in deciding about disclosure and repayment.
- In either of those cases, the intention, recklessness, or negligence of employees may have played a significant role in the noncompliant behaviors. The employees must be disciplined appropriately and the behaviors corrected.
- If the audit reveals deep-seated problems with the claims submission process, it may be necessary to withhold further submissions until corrections can be made.
- Policies and procedures will be changed or new ones issued to ensure compliant practices in the future.
- Education and training is provided to all affected employees regarding their use of the new policies and procedures.

ATTORNEY-RELATED PROTECTIONS

In conducting its own investigations and audits, and in responding to government-initiated investigations, an organization should take full advantage of several "privileges" available through its relationships with attorneys. The purpose of these privileges is to ensure that information and observations that the organization gathers are kept confidential to the fullest extent possible. They are not used to hide incriminating evidence previously discovered. There are four categories of attorney-related protection.

Attorney–Client Privilege

This privilege protects from discovery or mandatory disclosure communications between an attorney and his client for the purpose of giving legal advice. A client cannot be compelled to reveal verbal or written communications received from his or her attorney. Likewise, the attorney is not obliged to disclose communications from the client. When an organization receives a subpoena or other legal request for information, it does not have to turn over advice from an attorney about the events under investigation.

To take advantage of this privilege, the organization's attorney should directly carry out or at least manage the compliance investigation. All decisions and communications regarding the investigation should pass through the attorney. This privilege extends to interviews of the organization's employees, but not employees of other organizations. Third parties assisting in the investigation, such as consultants, should be employed or directed by the attorney. Even if executed properly, a privilege intended to further a crime or fraud will not be valid.

It is important to prevent accidental disclosure of protected communications. This would effectively waive the privilege. For instance, a physician under investigation for billing or coding errors consults an attorney who sends a letter explaining the physician's legal rights and options. The letter contents would be privileged. However, if the physician shares the letter with a colleague in a similar situation, the privilege would be waived.

Work Product Privilege

This privilege protects from disclosure documents or information prepared "in anticipation of litigation or for trial."[9] This includes actual or threatened litigation. Forms of protected work product are documents, notes, analyses, opinions, interview transcripts, facts and evidence uncovered by the attorney's review, and conclusions of the attorney. Work performed in response to a government compliance investigation will be covered; work that is part of a regular compliance audit is not.

Self-Evaluation Privilege[10]

A growing number of courts have recognized a privilege for information stemming from a healthcare organization's self-analysis and evaluation activities. A good example is the notes from a meeting of a medical staff's Medical Records Committee that found some questionable entry practices. The Committee then takes steps to correct and prevent such problems in

[9] Fed. R. Civ. P. 26(b)(3)

[10] The Embryonic Self-Evaluative Privilege: A Primer for Health Care Lawyers, O'Neil and Charnes, 5 Annals Health L. 33 (1993)

the future. By protecting those notes, the privilege encourages individuals and organizations to engage in self-evaluation without fear that their actions will be used against them.

Advice of Counsel

Some statutes require that the individual or organization "knowingly" violate the law in question. If the organization can show that it did not believe that its actions were in violation, it will be able to escape liability. One way of doing that is showing that the organization relied on an attorney's advice. This defense requires that the organization ...

> prior to taking the actions in question
> in good faith
> consult with an attorney
> whom it believes to be competent, and
> after disclosing all relevant facts to the attorney
> seek his advice on the legality of the proposed actions, and
> act in strict reliance on that advice.

In order to take advantage of this defense, the organization must reveal its communications with its attorney, thereby surrendering any attorney–client privilege it may have enjoyed. A decision is necessary about which course offers the greatest protection, attorney–client or advice of counsel. The organization cannot have both.

STUDY QUESTIONS

1. What is the difference between a search warrant and a subpoena *duces tecum*?
2. If an organization is conducting regular compliance audits, why should an internal investigation ever be necessary?
3. If you were the Compliance Officer for a small community hospital, where would you find an experienced attorney to advise the hospital on compliance matters?
4. Exactly what details should an internal investigation reveal about incidents of possible noncompliant behavior?
5. In interviewing an employee who may have been involved in some noncompliant practices, perhaps deliberately, perhaps unknowingly, what would you do to make him or her feel at ease and willing to cooperate?

6. A person identifying herself as an agent of the OIG has, at 9:30 on a Monday morning, shown up unannounced at the front desk of the medium-size physician group practice where you work. She says that she has a warrant to search for specific documents related to suspected fraudulent billing practices. Without looking back at that section of this chapter, what are the first five things that you will do?
7. You are the Compliance Officer of a medical diagnostic laboratory. One of your employees arrives at work in the morning and tells you that he was approached on the street in front of your facility by a person claiming to represent a Medicare RAC. He asked the employee questions about the lab's billing practices. The employee excused himself and wants to know how to handle these situations. What is a RAC? What advice will you give to the employee?
8. What is the difference between a civil lawsuit and a criminal lawsuit? A little Internet research might help with an answer.
9. The organization has had no reports of possible compliance violations. No enforcement agencies have been in touch about suspected fraudulent practices. Why would the organization want to conduct a compliance audit? Why do it more than once?
10. If the concept of data sampling interests you, do a little research to learn the basic principles of statistical analysis needed to make this a part of a compliance audit.
11. Explain the difference between "attorney–client privilege" and "work product privilege."
12. What is one good way of losing the protection of the attorney–client privilege?

Learning Experiences

1. With the support of your instructor, contact a local healthcare organization (hospital, small or large physician practice) and invite a representative to speak to the class about steps it takes to make sure that its compliance program is functioning effectively.
2. Conduct a role play of a government agent's visit to a healthcare facility. She has a search warrant and is looking for documents that she will seize. One student plays the government agent, another plays the organization employee who will interact with the agent. The classroom is the organization facility. The agent enters the classroom, interacts with the employer, and begins her search. The employee responds in the ways recommended in this chapter.

References

1. Investigations of Health Care Compliance, Townshend and Campbell, 2009 Emerging Issues 4783, LexisNexis, Matthew Bender & Co. (December 30, 2009).
2. Conducting Internal Investigations in Health Care Organizations, A Practical Guide on How to Resolve Allegations of Wrongdoing, Kusserow, AIS Health, 2011.

Chapter 12

Repayments and Disclosures

Learning Objectives

After completing class sessions based on this chapter, students will learn:

- The circumstances when a healthcare organization will consider disclosing a possible violation of law and reimbursing an overpayment to the government.
- The government agencies to whom the disclosures will be made, and how to choose among them.
- The legal bases for an organization's obligations to disclose and repay.
- The good reasons for an organization to self-disclose possible improper conduct and offer repayment.
- The disadvantages that can result from self-disclosure.
- The different ways to manage disclosure of merely negligent erroneous billing and activity involving legal wrongdoing.
- The importance of the advice of legal counsel in managing the disclosure process.
- The changes in self-disclosure requirements created by the Patient Protection and Affordable Care Act (PPACA) of 2010, the health reform law.
- The process by which a healthcare organization will conduct a self-disclosure.
- The differences between the Office of the Inspector General's (OIG's) Self-Disclosure Protocol (SDP) and the Stark Self-Referral Disclosure Protocol (SRDP).

INTRODUCTION

Either as a result of an internal investigation following a report of non-compliant practices, a routine compliance audit, or the discovery of a Medicare or Medicaid billing error in the normal course of business, a healthcare organization will be faced with difficult decisions about disclosing to government authorities what has happened and repaying amounts that it wrongfully received. At the very least, immediate steps must be taken to correct the error or faulty practices.

Providers who discover that they have submitted an erroneous bill to a federal healthcare program can disclose the deed in a number of different ways, depending on the nature and severity of the error. A provider may choose voluntarily to disclose to one or more of the following entities:

- The Centers for Medicare and Medicaid Services (CMS)
- An intermediary or carrier that handles reimbursements for the CMS
- The OIG of the Department of Health and Human Services (DHHS)
- The U.S. Department of Justice (DOJ) and its Federal Bureau of Investigation (FBI)
- A relevant state's Medicaid Fraud Control Unit
- A relevant state's agency responsible for licensing and regulating the provider's activities

As a practical matter, a provider should never think about *not* disclosing its errors at all. Its decisions should focus on when to make the disclosure and what information should be disclosed. Before making these decisions, the provider should speak with an attorney experienced in fraud and abuse matters.

LEGAL BASES FOR REPAYMENT AND DISCLOSURE

There are several federal laws that create an obligation to report and return Medicare and Medicaid overpayments.

Patient Protection and Affordable Care Act

The primary mandate for Medicare and Medicaid self-disclosure and repayment appears in Section 6402 of the PPACA of 2010, the so-called ObamaCare law. The section states that:

> If a person has received an overpayment, the person shall (A) report and return the overpayment to the Secretary, the State, an intermediary, a carrier, or a contractor, as appropriate, at the correct address; and (B) notify the State, an intermediary, a carrier, or a contractor to whom the overpayment was returned in writing of the reason for the overpayment.
>
> An overpayment must be reported and returned by the later of (A) the date which is 60 days after the date on which the overpayment

was identified, or (B) the date any corresponding cost report is due, if applicable.

The term "person" includes a provider of services, supplier, Medicaid managed care organization, Medicare Advantage organization, or Medicare Part D prescription drug plan sponsor.

While this basic requirement is fairly simple, there are a few possible complications. It may take considerably longer than 60 days from the time that a possible problem is "identified" for an organization to conduct a full internal investigation, determine whether a violation occurred, report it, and return the overpayment. In some cases, the process may take several months. This otherwise unambiguous rule is relatively new and the CMS is likely to issue a regulation clarifying the matter.

There is a good chance that the provider organization received copayments from patients as part of the transaction that caught the attention of the CMS. These will need to be refunded as well, along with any secondary payors that may have been involved. In addition, some states have laws comparable to the federal False Claims Act that call for disclosure and repayment. They need to be checked.

Disclosures and repayments typically are transmitted to the Affiliated Contractor (AC) to whom providers submit claims and from whom they receive payments. A Medicare insurance carrier is a good example of an AC.

The CMS has issued an Overpayment Refund Form that it recommends AC's use. It might also be used by providers, but at this time that is not required.

When an AC receives a voluntary repayment from a provider, it is required to gather information about the incident behind it. Organizations can expect to be asked about these issues.

- The amount of the repayment
- Why the voluntary refund is being made
- How the problem was identified
- What sampling techniques were used in the identification
- What steps were taken to ensure that the causes of the problem were corrected
- The dates by which the corrective actions were in place
- The time period for the events that led to the repayment
- The provider numbers of the individuals involved in the events
- Details of the claims that were the basis of the repayment
- How the amount of the repayment was calculated
- The assessment that determined the time frame for the problem incidents

The Overpayment Refund Form includes a check-off list of possible reasons for a repayment, like these.

- Incorrect service date
- Duplicate payment
- Incorrect CPT code
- Not our patient
- Modifier (of CPT code) added or removed
- Billed in error
- Service not rendered
- Medical necessity not met
- Patient enrolled in health maintenance organization (HMO)
- Secondary payer responsibility

False Claims Act

The federal False Claims Act (FCA) imposes treble damage awards and possible penalties of $5,500 to $11,000 in the case of anyone, in the healthcare field or otherwise, filing a false claim against the federal government. Most states have similar laws regarding state claims. The FCA is the most common tool used against healthcare fraud and abuse.

The law provides an opportunity for defendant organizations to reduce the damage level to double damages by disclosing an FCA violation within 30 days of becoming aware of it.

Under the "reverse false claims" language of the FCA, it is a violation for a person or organization to make a fraudulent statement in order to avoid or reduce an "obligation" to make a payment to the federal government. The funds that an organization receives falsely or undeservedly constitute such an obligation. By failing to disclose these funds and presumably trying to avoid its obligation, the organization commits a violation of the FCA.

Stark Physician Self-Referral Law

The Stark Law prohibits physicians from referring patients to receive certain "designated health services" payable by Medicare from a person or organization with which the physician has an impermissible financial relationship. Some referrals may be protected by narrowly defined exceptions to the Stark prohibition. If services are delivered on the basis of a prohibited referral, they may not be billed; if they are billed, they may not be paid; and if they are paid, the payment must be returned.

The effects of the Stark Law can be quite painful. For one thing, the circumstances in which a prohibited physician financial relationship exists, a prohibited referral has been made, a prohibited claim filed, and a prohibited payment made are sometimes subjective and obscure. It is not inconceivable that the Stark Law might be violated inadvertently. For instance, a diagnostic laboratory may be unaware that an immediate family member of a frequently referring physician owns some of its stock. As a result, the claims submitted for the tests requested by that physician violate the Stark Law and the payments must be returned. Depending on the size of the physician's practice and how long the prohibited referrals were accepted, there could be thousands of filed claims and millions of dollars in overpayments, leading to millions of dollars in required repayments.

As required by the PPACA, the Secretary of the DHHS issued a "protocol to enable healthcare providers ... to disclose an actual or potential violation"[1] of the Stark Law. To take advantage of the protocol, organizations or individuals must submit specific information about the incident and compliance program.

1. The name, address, national provider identification numbers (NPIs), CMS Certification Number(s) (CCN), and tax identification number(s) of the disclosing party.
2. A description of the nature of the matter being disclosed, including the type of financial relationship, the parties involved, the specific time periods the disclosing party may have been out of compliance, and the type of designated health service claims at issue. In addition, the description must include the type of transaction or other conduct giving rise to the matter, the names of entities and individuals believed to be implicated, and an explanation of their roles in the matter.
3. A statement from the disclosing party regarding why it believes a violation of the Physician Self-Referral Law may have occurred, including a complete legal analysis of the application of the Physician Self-Referral Law to the conduct and any physician self-referral exception that applies to the conduct and/or that the disclosing party attempted to use.
4. A description of the potential causes of the incident or practice (e.g., intentional conduct, lack of internal controls, circumvention of corporate procedures or government regulations).

[1] https://www.cms.gov/PhysicianSelfReferral/98_Self_Referral_Disclosure_Protocol.asp

5. The circumstances under which the disclosed matter was discovered and the measures taken upon discovery to address the actual or potential violation and prevent future instances of noncompliance.
6. A statement identifying whether the disclosing party has a history of similar conduct, or has any prior criminal, civil, and regulatory enforcement actions (including payment suspensions) against it.
7. A description of the existence and adequacy of a preexisting compliance program that the disclosing party had, and all efforts by the disclosing party to prevent a recurrence of the incident or practice in the affected division as well as in any related healthcare entities (e.g., new accounting or internal control procedures, new training programs, increased internal audit efforts, increased supervision by higher management).
8. A description of appropriate notices, if applicable, provided to other government agencies, (e.g., Securities and Exchange Commission, Internal Revenue Service) in connection with the disclosed matter.
9. An indication of whether the disclosing party has knowledge that the matter is under current inquiry by a government agency or contractor.

Once that information has been submitted, the organization must expect that the CMS will ask for additional "financial statements, notes, disclosures, and other supporting documents." In reviewing all this material, the CMS may discover additional Stark violations. If it does, they will be treated separately, outside the context of the initial disclosure. An organization contemplating a disclosure would do well first to conduct a thorough internal investigation to make sure that there are no other problems lurking.

The great benefit of using the protocol process is that the CMS is "authorized" to reduce any overpayments owed by the disclosing healthcare organization. It is not required to do so. There are several factors that it may take into account in determining the amount of reduction.

1. The nature and extent of the improper or illegal practice
2. The timeliness of the self-disclosure
3. The cooperation in providing additional information related to the disclosure
4. The litigation risk associated with the matter disclosed
5. The financial position of the disclosing party

This particular disclosure protocol applies only to suspected violations of the Stark Law. If an organization is concerned about incidents that may have violated the Anti-Kickback Statue (AKS) alone, or the AKS in conjunction with Stark, it must utilize another protocol first issued in 1998, the Provider SDP.[2] It is easy to confuse the two protocols.

Stark Law Self-Referral Disclosure Protocol ("SRDP")
- Created in 2010
- Applies to Stark Law only

OIG Self-Disclosure Protocol ("SDP")
- Created in 1998
- Applies to AKS, alone or with a Stark disclosure

The CMS emphasizes that the SDP is not to be employed if an organization simply wants a judgment from the CMS that an actual or potential Stark violation has occurred. A disclosure through the SDP is to be made solely "with the intention of resolving ... overpayment liability exposure for the conduct ... identified." Otherwise, an organization should use the CMS physician self-referral advisory opinion process.[3]

Anti-Kickback Statute

The AKS states that anyone who knowingly and willfully receives or pays anything of value (a "kickback") to influence the referral of federal healthcare program business, including Medicare and Medicaid, can be held accountable for a felony. Violations of the law are punishable by up to 5 years in prison, criminal fines up to $25,000, administrative civil monetary penalties up to $50,000, and exclusion from participation in federal healthcare programs.

Although the government does not pay a false claim as a direct result of a kickback, the PPACA made it clear that claims for services or products "resulting from" AKS violations are false or fraudulent for the purposes of the FCA.

Self-disclosure may make sense to provider organizations if it reduces the severe penalties associated with AKS violations. Criminal prosecutors have discretion in pursuing formal enforcement actions; a disclosure may persuade them to the side of leniency. The SDP is the accepted method for making disclosures of AKS violations.

---

[2] 63 Fed. Reg. 58,399 (October 30, 1998)
[3] 42 CFR §411.370 through § 411.389

Health Insurance Portability and Accountability Act (HIPAA)

There are not many situations involving HIPAA violations that seem to warrant disclosure and repayment. However, HIPAA was the underlying basis for a landmark court case against East Tennessee Health Consultants (ETHC),[4] in which the federal government for the first time brought criminal charges against a provider organization for failure to refund overpayments. The organization retained credit balances (overpayments) for private payors and patients until they specifically demanded them. In addition to the use of criminal sanctions, the government showed a willingness to go after overpayments involving not just the Medicare and Medicaid programs, but private payors and individual patients as well.

The liability for repayment to private payers under the ETHC case has not been firmly established in the law. Until that happens, any obligation an organization has to return payments to which it is not entitled will be found in the language of its contract with each private payer. There also may be applicable provisions in state insurance laws.

BENEFITS AND DISADVANTAGES OF SELF-DISCLOSURE

There are strong incentives for organizations to disclose voluntarily statutory violations they have discovered on their own initiative.

Benefits

- The healthcare organization will be able to develop a more congenial, less adversarial relationship with the enforcement officials.
- The organization may have more influence over the conduct of the government investigation and the issues that are emphasized.
- There may be a reduced likelihood of subpoenas or search warrants being issued to the organization.
- The penalties assessed for a violation of the FCA may be reduced.
- It is less likely that the government will bring a formal prosecution in the first place.
- If the OIG or DOJ chooses to negotiate a settlement of the matter, the terms may be less onerous.
- Besides any civil legal action, the government may decide not to pursue a criminal prosecution.

[4]United States ex rel. Kristi Moore and *Valarie Byrd v. East Tennessee Health Consultants, P.C. et al.,* No. 3:03-CV-577 (E.D. Tenn. Jan. 4 2007)

The U.S. Sentencing Guidelines[5] call for the calculation of a defendant's "culpability score," which is used to determine the fine that it will pay. The guidelines provide that the score will be significantly reduced if a defendant organization "reported the offense to appropriate governmental authorities, fully cooperated in the investigation, and clearly demonstrated recognition and affirmative acceptance of responsibility for its criminal conduct." This can lead to a major reduction in the fines levied—by as much as half.

The OIG has stated that it might be more flexible in deciding the terms of the Corporate Integrity Agreement (CIA) that it frequently requires of offending healthcare organizations. In some cases, it will not require a CIA at all. In making those decisions, the OIG looks at the following factors.

- The scope and seriousness of the misconduct
- The risk of recurrence, a function of the organization's preventive measures taken
- The effectiveness of the organization's compliance program in identifying and reporting the offensive activities
- The organization's cooperation in the disclosure verification process

If a whistle-blower decides to bring a qui tam lawsuit against the organization, the offensive matter is going to be disclosed in any event. By disclosing first or simultaneously, the organization gains several benefits. It has a chance to manage the case as it unfolds and work to reduce its negative impact. A self-disclosure allows the organization to frame the issues to its advantage, control the flow of information, interpret that information as it is made public, manage the publicity that develops, and do its best to maintain the organization's reputation. Self-disclosure will not prevent a whistle-blower lawsuit from proceeding.

The Medicare Prescription Drug, Improvement, and Modernization Act[6] (MMA) rewards self-disclosers by prohibiting the CMS from conducting nonrandom prepayment reviews based on a provider's disclosure of a billing problem unless it is an indication of a sustained or high error rate.

Disadvantages

There are a few reasons why self-disclosure may not seem like a good idea. They usually do not justify trying to keep an incident secret.

[5] Federal Sentencing Guidelines Manual, § 8C2.5(g): http://www.ussc.gov/guidelines/2011_Guidelines/Manual_PDF/index.cfm

[6] The Medicare Prescription Drug, Improvement, and Modernization Act of 2003, § 934, Pub. L. No. 108-173, 117 Stat. 2066 (2003)

- Without the self-disclosure, the enforcement authorities may never have discovered the incident, the organization's reputation would never have been damaged, and it would never have had to make repayments.
- There is no guarantee that a prosecutor will be persuaded by the self-disclosure to forego bringing a criminal action against the organization.
- If an action is brought, the self-disclosure may not negate or reduce the level of criminal intent behind the incident.
- Once an organization has made some disclosure, it may be expected to be more forthcoming about all matters.
- As a result, other issues may emerge and other offensive practices revealed.
- A relatively minor event may become much larger, serious, and more expensive.
- The enforcement authorities may view the incident more seriously and impose a much greater penalty than the organization expected.
- The authorities may conclude that the organization's compliance efforts were inadequate, despite the disclosure, and impose a burdensome CIA.

IMPORTANCE OF LEGAL COUNSEL

In making its decision about whether to disclose, as well as the practical steps in that disclosure, it is critical that an organization consult with a health law attorney. Disastrous consequences for the organization and its providers can result from an absence of competent legal input.

Well-experienced legal counsel can sort out the legal ambiguities that often exist in these cases as a result of poorly written Medicare regulations and inaccurate interpretations by private fiscal intermediaries.

CARRYING OUT A SELF-DISCLOSURE

Once a healthcare organization becomes aware of an error involving Medicare or Medicaid funds, it next must decide to which agency to make the disclosure. Trivial, infrequent, truly negligent billing errors usually are best reported to the relevant Medicare claims processing contractor. These will include carriers, Medicare Administrative Contractors (MACs), Fiscal Intermediaries (FIs), and Regional Home Health Intermediaries (RHHIs).

That decision should be based on a variety of factors. Did the erroneous billing incident involve actual illegal activity? If so, was the illegality civil or criminal in nature? How exposed to prosecution are members of the organization? How well do the facts of the matter fit within the terms of the two leading self-disclosure protocols (OIG and Stark)? Is there a risk that a third party involved with a particular enforcement authority will bring a qui tam action? How have each of the most relevant agencies handled similar self-disclosed incidents in the past? Are any of the agencies especially busy with more important cases? Occasionally, political motives may impact the decision if the prosecutor might use the case to build his own career.

The format for carrying out a self-disclosure is similar, but not identical, under the two available protocols.

When the organization has conducted its initial review and discovered activities that may have violated any federal law (civil, criminal, or administrative), it should turn to the OIG SDP. Normally, this will be based on a perceived violation of the AKS. It may be combined with misconduct under the Stark Law, but the SDP may not be used for Stark violations alone. The SDP also is not applicable to simple errors that do not reflect wrongdoing.

The disclosure must be physically mailed to the OIG and incorporate[7]:

1. A complete description of the conduct being disclosed
2. A description of the provider's internal investigation or a commitment regarding when it will be completed
3. An estimate of the damages to the federal healthcare programs and the methodology used to calculate that figure or a commitment regarding when the provider will complete such estimate
4. A statement of the laws potentially violated by the conduct

The internal investigation should produce a report that describes the nature and extent of the problematic incident, the discovery methodology employed, and the organization's response to its findings. The last component is a self-assessment estimating the financial impact on government programs.

The OIG will scrutinize the disclosure statements, assertions, and conclusions. It may then follow up with a review of documents and records, interviews of witnesses, and on-site visits and investigations.

The Stark SRDP is used when the organization's initial investigation reveals a potential violation of the Stark Law, without other laws implicated.

The disclosure must be submitted electronically to the CMS as well as by physical mail. It should include specific details about the possible violation.[8]

---

[7] OIG 2008 Open Letter: http://oig.hhs.gov/compliance/open-letters/index.asp
[8] https://www.cms.gov/PhysicianSelfReferral/98_Self_Referral_Disclosure_Protocol.asp

- The identity of the disclosing party and its affiliated entities, and a description or diagram that illustrates the entities involved in the actual or potential violation.
- A description of the transaction or arrangement, which should include details regarding the parties involved, the time periods in which the parties have been out of compliance, and the type of designated health service claims that are at issue.
- A description of why the disclosing party believes there is an actual or potential violation of the Stark Law. If a Stark Law exception was utilized in structuring the transaction or arrangement, such exception should be mentioned, as well as the elements of the exception that were met and those that were not met. In addition, a description of the potential causes of the incident or practice should be included.
- A description of how the violation was discovered and what specific measures were taken to address the violation and to prevent future abuse.
- A statement indicating whether the disclosing party has a history of similar problems, regardless of whether such conduct resulted in criminal, civil, and/or regulatory enforcement actions.
- A description of the disclosing party's preexisting compliance program and any actions or measures taken to restructure the arrangement.
- A statement indicating whether the disclosing party has knowledge of whether such transaction or arrangement is under investigation by a government agency or contractor, provided, however, that the SRDP specifies that a disclosing party is not precluded from self-disclosing merely because it is already subject to government inquiry.
- A financial analysis of the recoupment amount that is actually or potentially owed pursuant to the Stark Law, along with a description of the methodology utilized to arrive at this amount.
- A signed certification from the disclosing party or its authorized representative that the disclosure is truthful and based on a good faith effort to resolve any potential liability.

The CMS requires that the disclosing party "demonstrate that a full examination of the disclosed conduct has occurred." It also expects the organization to perform a financial analysis of the scope of the violation it is disclosing, including the amount of the overpayment (by year), the method of calculating the overpayment, and the auditing process underlying the analysis.

In response to the disclosure submission, the CMS will carry out its own process of verification of the information disclosed, while simultaneously coordinating its actions with the OIG and the DOJ. On the basis of what it sees in the disclosure, the CMS may determine that the matter should be referred to law enforcement authorities for civil or criminal violations. It may also choose to recommend that the OIG or DOJ prosecute the disclosing party for FCA liabilities, civil monetary penalties, and any other relevant legal responsibilities.

STUDY QUESTIONS

1. As Compliance Officer for a healthcare organization, in what circumstances would you choose NOT to disclose suspicious billing activity?
2. What actions should an organization take BEFORE it decides to disclose possibly illegal conduct?
3. What is the difference between the SDP and the SRDP, and in which circumstances should each be used?
4. What benefits might a healthcare organization gain by self-disclosing that it has violated a federal law?
5. When submitting a disclosure, what are at least 10 items of information that must be included?
6. What useful contributions does a healthcare lawyer make to the self-disclosure decisions and process?
7. To what government agencies is it possible to make a self-disclosure?

Learning Experience

1. Make a 10-minute presentation and argument to the rest of the class in support of an organization deciding not to self-disclose suspicious activity it has discovered.

References

1. CMS website on the Self-Referral Disclosure Protocol, with changes from the PPACA, https://www.cms.gov/PhysicianSelfReferral/98_Self_Referral_Disclosure_Protocol.asp
2. OIG website on the Self-Disclosure Protocol, https://oig.hhs.gov/compliance/self-disclosure-info/index.asp
3. Video of 2011 HEAT Provider Compliance Training–OIG Self Disclosure Protocol section begins at 6:15 point, http://www.youtube.com/watch?v=49oalycme_g

Chapter 13

Training and Education

Learning Objectives

After completing class sessions based on this chapter, a student will:

- Be able to designate which healthcare organization stakeholders must receive compliance training.
- Understand the difference between general and specialized compliance training.
- Discover the basic elements of an effective compliance training program.
- Know how to document an organization's compliance training activities.
- Learn how to acknowledge compliance training participation in carrying out an employee's performance appraisal.
- Be able to describe the content of both general and specialized compliance training sessions.
- Be familiar with the different instructional formats that may be used in compliance training.
- Know how often and for how long to schedule compliance training sessions.
- Have a good idea of what other healthcare organizations are doing in the area of compliance training.
- Be prepared to conduct an evaluation of an existing compliance training program.

INTRODUCTION

One of the seven basic elements of an effective compliance program as recommended and defined by the Office of the Inspector General (OIG) is training and education. In the standard OIG list of those elements, training and education come third. The first calls for "designating a compliance officer and compliance committee"; they serve as the catalysts for the entire compliance program. The second is "implementing written policies, procedures, and standards of conduct"; these are the rules of the program by which it minimizes compliance risks. In many healthcare organizations, the Compliance Officer serves as the instructor for training sessions that are designed to communicate the policies, procedures, and standards to the organization's employees. These are the people who, deliberately or inadvertently, can create noncompliance problems for the organization. It is through training and education that they learn how to perform their jobs in a compliant fashion.

WHO SHOULD RECEIVE THE TRAINING

New Employees

It is important to begin shaping the work performance of new employees as soon as possible after they are hired. People are most impressionable when they are new to an organization. At that early stage, focused training will improve the chances that an employee carries out his or her job in a compliant manner.

It is generally recommended that an employee receive compliance training within 30 to 60 days of commencing employment. The best organizations provide the training during the first couple weeks, often incorporating it into the employee's orientation.

All Employees and Agents—General Training

All employees should receive two types of compliance training. The organization should require employees at all levels to attend general training sessions. Their purpose is to "communicate effectively its standards and procedures to all employees and affected physicians, independent contractors, and other significant agents by requiring participation in training programs and disseminating publications that explain specific requirements in a practical manner."[1]

All employees should be included in the training sessions—whether or not they appear to perform compliance-related work activities. A heightened familiarity throughout the organization with laws, regulations, and program requirements helps create a culture of compliant behavior. It is not always predictable when an employee's work may have an impact on compliance. Finally, any employee may become aware of some noncompliant activity that needs to be reported.

[1] OIG Compliance Program Guidance for Third Party Billing Companies.

A large share of the work at one of the most common forms of healthcare organization–the hospital–is performed by physicians who are not employees of the organization. They, too, must be reached by the training. They make many of the decisions that can lead to compliance issues–determining medical necessity, categorizing a procedure for coding purposes, basing referrals on prohibited incentives, and investing in clinical laboratories. Hospital management has less control over them as members of the medical staff–they are independent contractors, not employees. Participation in compliance training can be written into their terms of membership on the medical staff. In most cases, the physicians need their relationship with the hospital as much as the hospital needs the patients that they admit. There is a trend of hospitals employing physicians, which will overcome the traditional lack of control over them.

Vendors, suppliers, consultants, and other independent contractors must be included in compliance training. They often perform tasks that can create fraud and abuse violations. In legal terms, they are "agents" of the healthcare organization. They do work that it might otherwise do itself. They represent the organization and act on its behalf. The organization can be held liable for the misdeeds of its agents. They must be educated about compliance-safe practices and procedures. Attendance at the trainings can be made a condition of the contracts between a healthcare organization and its agents. The agents can be brought into the organization's training sessions or compliance seminars can be conducted at the agents' worksites.

Select Employees and Agents—Specialized Training

Employees and agents who work in high-risk areas for compliance violations should receive training that is tailored to their specific job tasks. The positions that fit into these categories will vary somewhat from one type of healthcare organization to another, and will include the following:

Governing board members (directors, trustees)

Corporate officers (Chief Executive Officer [CEO] and other C-suite members)

Managers (mid-level and front-line supervisors)

Employees (claims preparation and submission)

Employees (who may affect accuracy of claims)

Sales and marketing

Medical records

Information technology

Financial management and accounting

Cost control and reporting

Because the work of these people is so closely tied to potential fraud and abuse violations, they deserve training that addresses the specific tasks that they perform. That training will explain the ways they might violate the law, and the detailed policies and procedures they should follow to remain compliant.

DOCUMENTATION OF TRAINING AND EDUCATION ACTIVITIES

The OIG expects healthcare organizations to maintain documents related to their training and education activities as evidence of their efforts to steer their employees away from noncompliant work behaviors. The following documentation recommendations are gleaned from the OIG's several Program Guidances.

- At the end of each training session, each attendee must sign a form certifying that he or she understands and is committed to the organization's Code of Conduct.
- The employer certifications become part of the employee's personnel file.
- The training and the certification should be repeated/updated annually.
- The instructors leading the trainings, whether in-house or third-party contractors, should sign similar certifications.
- The organization should keep full records of the trainings that it conducts, including the dates, hours spent, attendee list, and materials distributed.

COMPLIANCE IS A FACTOR IN PERFORMANCE EVALUATIONS

Compliance with laws and program requirements is a part of every employee's job in the healthcare industry. It is common sense that an employee's compliance behavior should be a factor in assessing his or her performance. The periodic performance appraisals should take into account employees' attendance at training sessions and their participation in these activities. Consistent failure to meet the training requirements should result in disciplinary action, including the possibility of dismissal from the organization.

The OIG makes further training demands of managers and supervisors. In addition to attending the training sessions themselves, they must instruct their subordinates to do the same thing. Managers also are in a position to carry out informal, day-to-day compliance training of their employees through mentoring, monitoring, reminders, and availability to answer questions.

CONTENT OF THE TRAINING SESSIONS

The OIG has made specific recommendations for the content of the general training sessions and the specialized training that addresses compliance risk in the coding and billing areas. There are other specialized risk areas that require their own specialized training, but coding and billing are the sources of the largest number of fraud and abuse violations.

General Compliance Training Curriculum

These are compliance topics with which every employee, contractor, and vendor should be familiar.

- Federal and state laws, regulations, and guidelines, with emphasis on fraud and abuse
- Federal, state, and private payor program requirements
- Corporate ethics and the organization's Code of Conduct
- Emphasis on the organization's commitment to comply with all legal and program requirements
- Overview of the organization's compliance program
- Requirements of acceptable coding practice
- Explanation of the claims development and submission process
- Acceptable marketing practices in light of current legal and program standards
- Mechanisms for reporting suspected violations, misconduct, and noncompliance
- Patient rights in matters with compliance implications
- Most common compliance problems

Specialized Coding and Billing Training Curriculum

These are examples of topics that might be covered in a specialized training session. The exact content depends on the work activities of the employees participating. For instance, IT personnel will be concerned with issues related to the Health Insurance Portability and Accountability Act (HIPAA), and pharmaceutical marketing representatives need to hear about off-label promotion, while billing and coding staff have traditional False Claims Act interests.

- Reimbursement terms and practices of public and private payors
- Prohibition against giving or receiving remuneration to induce referrals
- Proper selection, sequencing, and confirmation of diagnoses
- Improper alterations to clinical records and other documentation
- Submitting a claim for "physician services" actually delivered by a nonphysician
- Proper documentation or confirmation of services rendered
- Correct application of coding (ICD-9 and CPT codes) rules and guidelines
- Signing a form for a physician without his or her authorization
- Inadequate privacy and security protections in computer systems
- Employee's duty to report misconduct or noncompliance
- Routine waiver of copayments
- Unbundling of service normally billed in a bundle
- Inappropriate balance billing
- Inadequate resolution of overpayments
- Accurate billing for services ordered, performed, and reported
- Compliance with Medicare conditions of participation
- Prescribing procedures and medications without proper authorization
- Record retention requirements
- Legal penalties for deliberate or reckless false billing

RESOURCES DEVOTED TO COMPLIANCE TRAINING

There may be a temptation to skimp on money, people, and time devoted to compliance training, in the belief that "there probably will not be any problems anyway" and it makes no direct contribution to the organization's bottom line. That would be a serious mistake.

If a "problem" does occur, the monetary penalties, legal expenses, costs of responding to the accusations, distractions from management focus, damage to employee morale and public reputation will make compliance training seem like a bargain. A decent, effective compliance education effort can be put together with rather modest resources. The OIG itself recognizes that smaller healthcare organizations cannot support the same elaborate, and expensive, compliance program as much larger entities.

If the organization cannot develop in-house training expertise, it can contract with outside consultants as they are needed. National and local professional and industry associations often sponsor lower-cost training workshops. If the organization does not wish to prepare its own training materials, or purchase those available from private companies, it can turn to the free resources available from the OIG, like these: https://oig.hhs.gov/compliance/provider-compliance-training/index.asp.

The amount budgeted for mandatory employee compliance education varies depending on the media through which it is delivered. One of the simplest and most cost-effective methods is computer or web-based education, which cost approximately \$3.50 to \$7.00[2] per participant. It will cost over \$5,000 to produce live training sessions with an outside instructor serving several hundreds of attendees. The sessions can be videotaped and used later with other groups of employees.

Computer or web-based training can automatically record employees' attendance and their completion of the training material. It also can test their comprehension of the material. Employees can access this type of training at their leisure, as long as they do so by specified deadlines. It differs from live training in that space does not have to be found to assemble a group of employees at one time. Compliance staff are not required to be present to oversee the event. This training format is more easily communicated to persons outside an organization's facilities, like private practice physicians, consultants, and vendors. Automated training has one major shortcoming: No one is available to answer any questions the employees may have.

Whether live or automated, the training must be accessible to employees and others for whom English is not their first language. Training materials and presentations must be translated into appropriate languages.

INSTRUCTORS FOR THE COMPLIANCE TRAINING SESSIONS

There are several options for instructors to present the compliance training sessions. Quite often, when the organization can afford a full-time Compliance Officer, that person also will lead the training classes. If enough

[2] These data are from an article entitled "Budgeting for Compliance by Emily Rayman, Compliance Officer for Community Memorial Health System (Venture, CA) in the June 2011 issue of Compliance Today. This system is composed of 2 hospitals and 11 family practice health centers.

resources are available and large numbers of employees and others require regular training, it may be more cost-effective to develop in-house trainers. They offer the advantage of a specialized understanding of the organization's operations and compliance challenges. Smaller healthcare entities usually choose to outsource their training to companies or individuals who offer expertise in compliance instruction.

TIMES AND DURATION OF THE COMPLIANCE TRAINING

There are rules of thumb for the frequency and duration of compliance training sessions. A general, introductory training should be provided to new employees within 30 days of their hiring, if not literally as part of their orientation programs. Updated versions of the general training should be pushed out to all employees at least once a year, even if there have been no major changes in the content. Employees in high compliance risk areas should also receive their own annual specialized trainings. The typical training session lasts 2 to 3 hours. Any variations on these standards should be on the side of more frequent sessions of longer duration. Employees cannot be told often enough about safe compliance practices.

FORMAT OF THE COMPLIANCE TRAINING

Effective compliance training can employ a variety of media and formats. Any approach is fine as long as it serves to reduce the risk of non-compliance and law violations. That is a function of the content of the training, the design of the program elements and how they work together, and the ability of the trainers to present them.

The two basic delivery alternatives are live and electronic. In a live training, a group of employees (or physicians, vendors, contractors) is gathered in a space located within the organization or at an outside facility. There may be just a handful of participants or as many as one or two hundred. The training session can be designed and presented by the organization's own staff trainers. The entire process can be contracted out to a firm that specializes in compliance matters. Skilled third-party trainers can be hired solely to present content prepared by the organization. The employees could be sent as a group or individually to attend compliance training workshops offered by private consulting companies, trade or industry associations, or professional societies.

An electronic training program can be delivered to individual employee computers, across the organization's local network, or via the Internet. The organization can develop the program content or buy it from a third party. It can be designed to include tests that assess each participant's comprehension of the material. As long as they complete the program by a certain date, employees interact with the program when they can fit it into their schedules. They are paid for the time they spend in training.

In either format, many organizations have found it useful to include cases, either hypothetical or based on real compliance problems they have faced. This also is a suitable time to survey the participants on their own ethical values (in response to the case settings), their opinions of the values of the organization and its managers, and the effectiveness of the training.

TRAINING AND EDUCATION GUIDANCE FROM CORPORATE INTEGRITY AGREEMENTS

When the OIG concludes that a healthcare organization has committed serious violations of fraud and abuse laws and serious penalties are called for, the organization often can avoid program exclusion (from Medicare) by acceding to a Corporate Integrity Agreement (CIA). Those agreements mandate compliance practices that organizations should be carrying out anyway, including training and education. As such, they are a source of useful direction on that topic. This is what CIAs typically emphasize.

- At least 2 hours of general training each year for all compliance-related persons. This training should explain the organization's detailed obligations under the CIA, its compliance program, and its Code of Conduct.
- At least four additional hours of specific training for all relevant compliance-related persons, and then 2 hours each year thereafter. This training should cover:
  - Federal healthcare program requirements regarding the accurate coding and submission of claims.
  - Policies, procedures, and other requirements applicable to the documentation of medical records.
  - Personal obligation of each individual involved in the claims submission process to ensure that such claims are accurate.
  - Applicable reimbursement statutes, regulations, and program requirements and directives.

  - Legal sanctions for violations of the federal healthcare program requirements.
  - Examples of proper and improper claims submission practices.
  - Examples of proper and improper medical necessity documentation.
- Members of the board of trustees (or directors) must receive 2 hours of board-specific training that addresses the responsibilities of board members and corporate governance.
- Each person who was required to attend those trainings must certify, in writing, that he or she received the required training.
- Persons leading the training sessions must be knowledgeable about the subject matter.
- The organization must annually review and update the training to reflect changes in federal healthcare program requirements, any issues discovered during internal audits or the claims review required by the CIA, and any other relevant information.
- If the organization decides to provide computer-based training, it must make available qualified and knowledgeable staff or trainers to answer questions and provide additional information to the individuals receiving such training.
- The organization (in this case, a hospital) must make the general and specific training available to all of its active medical staff members and shall use its best efforts to encourage those members to complete the training. (This language seems to recognize that a hospital does not have enough leverage over its medical staff physicians to command their attendance at training sessions.)

COMPLIANCE TRAINING PRACTICES OF HEALTHCARE ORGANIZATIONS

Another source of information on best practices in compliance training and education comes from the latest survey of Compliance Officers conducted by the Health Care Compliance Association (HCCA). It was reported in 2009 and based on data collected in 2007. These were some of its findings.[3]

Of the 836 entities that returned their survey forms, 96% said that compliance training was mandatory for their employees. Nearly the same percentage (90%) provide training updates after the initial sessions. The time each employee spends on compliance training each year varies: 51% receive

[3] It may be worth reading the entire survey, found on the HCCAnet social network website (http://community.hcca-info.org/HCCA/Home/) under the title, 9th Annual Survey - 2007 Profile of Health Care Compliance Officers.

1–3 hours, 33% get 1 hour or less, 12% spend 3–6 hours, and 3% are trained for 6 hours or more. Periodic update training takes place once a year for two-thirds of employees. Ten percent are updated twice annually, 6% quarterly, and 3% every other year.

Compliance training for nonemployees is provided by 64% of healthcare organizations. Two-thirds of those made it mandatory; it was optional in the rest.

The surveyed companies employed the following training methods.

Live classroom training (Compliance Officer as instructor)	68%
Live classroom training (other instructors)	47%
Computer-based/web-based training	71%
Video training	32%
Self-study modules	34%

One-third of the organizations include a line item for training and education activities in their compliance budgets. The other two-thirds charge those training costs to individual departmental budgets. The total money spent each year on compliance training varies according to the total revenue and the number of employees of each healthcare organization. This is the distribution of the size of annual compliance training budgets among the healthcare organizations surveyed.

$0–$5,000	29%
$5,000–$15,000	14%
$15,000–$30,000	7%
$30,000–$55,000	5%
$55,000–$100,000	6%
$100,00–$200,000	5%
$200,000+	4%

The survey found that an average 7% of the compliance budgets of the responding organizations was allocated to training. Another 4% went toward compliance staff education.

A little over 16% of the companies surveyed said that they had full-time trainer or educator positions on their compliance staffs. This means that other compliance-savvy people designed and conducted the training sessions. In two-thirds of the cases, it was the Compliance Officer.

Sixty percent of the organizations surveyed measure the effectiveness of their overall compliance programs. Of those, one of the top five metrics that they follow is "Employee Awareness–Education and Training." Among the methods they use to make those measurements are surveys of employee awareness and training effectiveness, and tests of awareness and tracking of the results.

COMPLIANCE TRAINING PRACTICES OF THE MD ANDERSON CANCER CENTER

Another way of learning how best to structure a compliance training program is to look at what other highly regarded healthcare entities have done. The MD Anderson Cancer Center at the University of Texas is a very highly rated cancer treatment and research center comprising 600 inpatient beds, several research buildings and outpatient clinic buildings, two faculty office buildings, and a patient-family hotel in addition to other off-site facilities for clinical and research use. On its website, http://www.mdanderson.org/about-us/compliance-program/index.html, it shares many documents describing its compliance program. This is an excerpt from the section of its Hospital Compliance Plan explaining its education efforts.

> Compliance with all applicable laws and regulations is one of MD Anderson's priorities. Workforce Members at MD Anderson must be knowledgeable about MD Anderson's Institutional Code of Conduct and policies and plans regarding institutional compliance issues. Strict compliance with applicable laws, rules, guidelines, as well as institutional policies and plans is a condition of employment. Failure to comply may result in disciplinary action, including termination.

MD Anderson's initial orientation requirements for faculty, employees, trainees, volunteers, and certain contractors include a mandatory compliance education component with instruction regarding the Institutional Code of Conduct, the Institutional Compliance Program, MD Anderson's compliance plans, federal and state laws governing health care and research, and Workforce Members' responsibilities regarding compliance with, and reporting violations or potential violations of, institutional policies and applicable laws. Workforce Members who participate in the initial orientation process are given a copy of MD Anderson's Standards of Conduct: Do the Right Thing booklet. The booklet contains an acknowledgement card that Workforce Members are required to sign and return signifying that they have received, read, and agree to abide by the booklet. The acknowledgement card is retained in the individual's personnel file. The booklet also contains a compliance reminder card with the Institutional Code of Conduct and relevant Institutional Compliance Office contact information, which Workforce Members are instructed to keep in their badge holders.

Once a year each employee is required to complete the "Employee Education Event" (EEE). EEE involves reading information on policies and procedures and completing a quiz, which tests for comprehension of the information. Additionally, the Institutional Compliance Program trains workforce members throughout the year on general and specific compliance issues.

A variety of teaching materials, tools, methods, and languages are used, as necessary. In addition, messages stating MD Anderson's overall policies and procedures regarding institutional compliance and other significant governmental compliance information are posted in prominent areas of MD Anderson. Ongoing education is provided as appropriate to discuss new and emerging compliance issues and information. The Institutional Compliance Office maintains records, including attendance logs and presentation materials, related to its education and training sessions. Failure to comply with the education requirements may lead to disciplinary action.

In addition to general compliance education, it is imperative that all Workforce Members of MD Anderson receive specific and appropriate compliance education and training within his/her area of focus. When a specific training need has been identified, the Compliance Officer oversees such departmental compliance training and monitors the attendance and outcome of this training.

This is another real-world example: Boulder Community Hospital describes its compliance activities and the specific obligations of the Compliance Officer, managers, and employees on its website (http://www.bch.org/compliance-policies/education-and-training.aspx).

EVALUATING TRAINING AND EDUCATION PROGRAM

Organizations determined to keep their operating practices within the law and program requirements will regularly evaluate how well their training and education efforts are working. The OIG provides the following question guidelines for hospitals to consider when reviewing training programs. They can easily be applied to other types of healthcare organizations.

- Does the hospital provide qualified trainers to conduct annual compliance training for its staff, including both general and specific training pertinent to the staff's responsibilities?
- Has the hospital evaluated the content of its training and education program on an annual basis and determined that the subject content is appropriate and sufficient to cover the range of issues confronting its employees?
- Has the hospital kept up to date with any changes in federal health-care program requirements and adapted its education and training program accordingly?
- Has the hospital formulated the content of its education and training program to consider results from its audits and investigations; results from previous training and education programs; trends in hotline reports; and OIG, CMS, or other agency guidance or advisories?
- Has the hospital evaluated the appropriateness of its training format by reviewing the length of the training sessions; whether training is delivered via live instructors or via computer-based training programs; the frequency of training sessions; and the need for general and specific training sessions?
- Does the hospital seek feedback after each session to identify shortcomings in the training program, and does it administer post-training testing to ensure attendees understand and retain the subject matter delivered?
- Has the hospital's governing body been provided with appropriate training on fraud and abuse laws?
- Has the hospital documented who has completed the required training?
- Has the hospital assessed whether to impose sanctions for failing to attend training or to offer appropriate incentives for attending training?

This kind of regular review is necessary to ensure that the training does not become obsolete.

SUMMARY OF THE BASIC ELEMENTS OF AN EFFECTIVE COMPLIANCE TRAINING AND EDUCATION PROGRAM

It should be clear that many factors must be considered in designing and implementing a compliance training program that actually minimizes the risk of law violations and failure to observe payor program requirements.

In its Compliance Guidance for nursing facilities, the OIG summarizes the most important elements this way:

- Training should cover the provider's compliance program, fraud and abuse laws, federal healthcare program requirements, and other issues unique to an employee's job duties.
- Training should be tailored to an employee's job responsibilities.
- Training should be provided to employees and to physicians, independent contractors and other agents of the facility, and their participation should be a term of their employment or contractual arrangement with the facility.
- Training should be provided in a way most accessible to the participants. This may be live in-person training for some employees, video or computer-based instruction for others, and written materials for still others. The method used should always include an opportunity for the employee to ask follow-up questions.
- Training can be provided for the facility by company employees, consultants, attorneys, or outside experts such as billing consultants, as appropriate, based upon the topic being taught and the level of expertise needed.
- Training materials and methods should take into account the skills, experience, and knowledge of individual participants.
- The facility should document all compliance training provided, including the date of the training, a summary of the material covered, who attended, and the name and qualifications of the trainer.
- Training should include the various risk areas identified by the OIG in its Compliance Guidance tailored to the particular healthcare organization, as well as other risk areas identified through experience and internal audits and monitoring of operations.
- Participation in compliance training should be a condition of employment or a contractual relationship (for physicians, vendors, or other third parties) and failures to participate in such training should be disciplined by established methods (including termination of employment or of existing contracts where appropriate).

STUDY QUESTIONS

1. Why is it important to provide new employees with compliance training so soon after they are hired?
2. What are two or three reasons for providing compliance training to employees who do not work in areas at high risk of fraud and abuse violations?

3. How could an organization persuade its suppliers and vendors to attend compliance training sessions, or sponsor their own training programs?
4. How could a hospital persuade the doctors on its medical staff to attend compliance training sessions?
5. What sorts of compliance training should be provided to the board of trustees or directors of a healthcare organization?
6. What should be included in the documentation of an organization's compliance training activities?
7. As a manager of employees, explain precisely how you would take into account their participation in compliance training in evaluating their job performance. Do you care whether they understood the training material or is it sufficient that they attended the training sessions?
8. If you had a choice between video or computer-based training and live classes with in-person instructors in providing training to the 25 employees in your department at a pharmaceutical company, which would you choose and why?

Learning Exercises

1. In a planned presentation, try to persuade the other members of your class to adopt a compliance training program. They are all physicians in a large group practice. They are skeptical about the need to spend the time and money necessary to support such a program. They are under great stress in other parts of their practice (reduced reimbursements, patient engagement, quality outcomes) and see no need for this kind of training, at least for them personally.
2. Design the curriculum for a 2-hour compliance training for the employees of a local nursing home. Use the Program Guidance for Nursing Facilities mentioned in the References. List the topics that will be covered and the amount of time spent on each.

References

1. OIG Compliance Program Guidance for Third Party Medical Billing Companies, Federal Register, Vol. 63, No. 243, December 18, 1998, pp. 70147–70148.
2. OIG Supplemental Compliance Program Guidance for Hospitals, Federal Register, Vol. 70, No. 19, January 31, 2005, p. 4875.

3. OIG Original Compliance Program Guidance for Hospitals, Federal Register, Vol. 63, No. 35, February 23, 1998, pp. 8994–8995.
4. OIG Compliance Program Guidance for Nursing Facilities, Federal Register, Vol. 65, No. 52, March 16, 2000, pp. 14300–14301.
5. Health Care Fraud Prevention and Enforcement Action Team Provider Compliance Training, https://oig.hhs.gov/compliance/provider-compliance-training/index.asp#materials
6. Medicare Learning Network, Provider Compliance Products, http://www.cms.gov/Outreach-and-Education/Medicare-Learning-Network-MLN/MLNProducts/ProviderCompliance.html
7. 9th Annual Survey - 2007 Profile of Health Care Compliance Officers Health Care Compliance Association

Chapter 14

Auditing and Monitoring

Learning Objectives

After completing class sessions based on this chapter, a student will:

- See how the monitoring and audit functions fit into the overall compliance program.
- Know the purpose of a compliance risk assessment in preparing for the monitoring and audit functions.
- Become familiar with the most common risk areas requiring compliance attention.
- Receive an introduction to the concept of the revenue cycle.
- Understand the difference between monitoring and auditing.
- Discover several frequently used monitoring methods.
- Learn the basic elements of a good audit procedure.
- Appreciate the details of a typical audit procedure.

INTRODUCTION

Once a healthcare organization has established a compliance program, designated a Compliance Officer, written appropriate policies and procedures, and educated and trained all relevant employees, contractors, and suppliers, the work is not over. It cannot be assumed that the policies and procedures that were created are fully suited to the task, or that the employees are actually following them. The legal risks that compliance aims to prevent are so serious that the organization must closely observe how well it all is working, and be ready to step in and make adjustments. It accomplishes this through a three-step process.

It begins with a detailed assessment of the legal risks that the organization faces in its operations. On the basis of the assessment results, the organization initiates an ongoing program of monitoring the activities in all the high-risk areas. In addition, it periodically conducts more intensive audits of the effectiveness of its compliance efforts in units or departments that seem to be in greatest danger of law violations. Together, these steps should keep the compliance program functioning smoothly, minimizing the number and severity of compliance incidents.

Monitoring is an ongoing process that is carried out automatically every day. It usually is performed by independent audit personnel (if the organization can afford them) or by the operational staff who work in each particular risk area.

Auditing is a discrete, planned event that takes one to several days typically once a year, more often if the organization is under compliance enforcement scrutiny. Compliance audits are carried out by individuals who have expertise in the areas being audited, but do not actually work in the units being studied. If the resources are available, some organizations hire an independent audit firm to perform their audits.

This is an outline of a typical compliance program and where the assessment, monitoring, and audit activities fit into it.

1. Become familiar with relevant laws, regulations, and payor requirements.
2. Perform a risk *assessment* and identify high compliance risk areas.
3. Develop and disseminate policies for specific issues and risk areas.
4. Provide employee training on the laws, regulations, requirements, and policies.
5. Initiate ongoing *monitoring* of compliance with the laws, regulations, and policies.
6. Conduct periodic in-depth *audits* of especially problematic or high-risk operating areas.
7. Take appropriate corrective actions.

COMPLIANCE RISK ASSESSMENT

The purpose of a compliance risk assessment is to determine where an organization should focus its monitoring and auditing activities in its operations. Those activities cannot be applied universally throughout the organization. Every unit or department does not present the same level of compliance risk. The first step is to prepare a list of potential risks unique to the organization.

This list will vary according to the general type of organization (hospital vs. physician practice vs. pharmaceutical company), the nature of its operation (rural community hospital vs. academic medical center, primary care practice vs. specialty emphasis), and its compliance history (frequent billing violations, operating under a Corporate Integrity Agreement). This is a sampling of common risk areas or indicators of risk:

- Failure to comply with terms of existing Corporate Integrity Agreement.
- Employing or doing business with a physician, other clinician, external facility, supplier, or contractor on the Office of the Inspector General (OIG) List of Excluded Individuals and Entities.
- Submitting claims to Medicare for services that were not "medically unnecessary."
- Submitting claims to Medicare for services that were not performed.
- Submitting claims to Medicare based on inadequate or inaccurate documentation.
- Providing payments or compensation to physicians that are excessive, not fair market value, or intended to induce referrals.
- Failure to file reports required by Medicare, the OIG, the Department of Justice (DOJ), state Medicaid, or other government agencies.
- Failure to comply with privacy or security regulations of the Health Insurance Portability and Accountability Act of 1996 (HIPAA).
- Ignorance of target areas in annual OIG work plan.
- Failure to comply with human subjects protocols in clinical trials.
- Failure to identify, report, and resolve conflicts of interest.
- Increased frequency of reports and complaints of suspected noncompliance.

Each of the OIG Compliance Program Guidances for specific types of organizations describes the risk areas where those organizations are most vulnerable.

The next step is to categorize and assemble the data that the organization possesses about these risk areas. This requires a focus on individual operational tasks that may be performed in a noncompliant way.

Most compliance problems arise at some point in the revenue cycle of practitioners and organizations providing healthcare services. The revenue cycle involves the majority of people in these organizations. It is the core of the organization's value chain. It is where patient care and financial processes intersect. The cycle begins when a patient first attempts to contact the organization and use its services. It culminates when the organization finally receives payment for providing the services. There are many steps along the way and most of them pose potential compliance risks. Each of them generates documents and data that can be useful in the monitoring and auditing effort. They fall into several categories common to most healthcare organizations.

- Initial patient access to the organization
- Scheduling of the patient's visit
- Registration of the patient upon arrival
- Admission of the patient to the practice or the hospital
- Management of the patient's care
- Referral to other providers for additional care
- Management of the patient's overall case
- Capturing related charges and coding them
- Transcribing the medical chart
- Entering and documenting the charges
- Managing denials of coverage
- Billing and collections from government payors
- Billing and collections from private payors
- Billing and collections from patients
- Collection agency interactions
- Uncollectible debt adjustments and write-offs
- Subsequent patient complaints

There also are other more indirect sources of information on compliance risks.

- Surveys of employees, contractors, physicians, and patients
- Compliance-related incidents (patient safety, patient complaints, compliance complaints, hotline reports, staff turnover, sick time and absenteeism, overtime)
- Financial data and plans (budget variances, Sarbanes-Oxley compliance, organizational liquidity)
- Legal action against the organization (workers compensation, theft, qui tam lawsuits, medical malpractice)
- External reviews (Joint Commission, independent auditor, regulatory agency investigations and evaluations)
- Long-term organization strategies (joint ventures, mergers, or acquisitions)
- Industry and regional benchmarks
- OIG Annual Work Plans, Advisory Opinions, Office of Investigation Reports, and Office of Audit Services Reports
- Local medical review policies
- Local coverage decisions
- Medicare bulletins
- Centers for Medicare and Medicaid Services (CMS) updates

With these data on potential compliance risks, the organization can make decisions about where to allocate its monitoring and auditing resources. This involves analysis of the risks and discussions with senior executives and compliance managers about their tolerance for different types of risk so that priorities can be set among them. Each risk can be rated by its impact on the reputation, finances, and legal exposure of the organization.

At this point, two things happen. Immediate improvement or corrective action plans are implemented to deal with the most serious live risks that have been identified. This may require revising or introducing policies, instituting new controls, and providing additional education and training. The second action is to initiate an ongoing monitoring program and a schedule of periodic audits that will carefully observe operations in the high-risk areas.

COMPLIANCE MONITORING

Monitoring should be an inherent part of the day-to-day operations of any healthcare organization. It is critical to a successful compliance program. The OIG states that "an effective program should incorporate thorough monitoring of its implementation and regular reporting to senior hospital or corporate officers. Monitoring is generally thought of as the day-to-day reviews to ensure everything is in order, whereas auditing is a more comprehensive and often topic-specific evaluation." Monitoring may uncover the need for a more focused, in-depth audit.

Good monitoring will look at two facets of the organization: one is the operational activities that might violate fraud or other laws, and the other is the compliance processes intended to prevent those violations.

The extent and frequency of monitoring reviews will depend on the size of the organization, its organizational structure, strategic objectives, lines of business, workforce composition, available resources, any prior history of noncompliance, the number and complexity of the risk areas identified, and the organization's tolerance for risk in each area. As the monitoring proceeds, more problems may be found in certain areas, calling for more intensive monitoring to discover the causes.

The primary tool of the monitoring process is data gathering. Most of the events or transactions that are the subject of monitoring occur so often that it is not cost-effective to follow and analyze each and every one of them. Many hospitals file millions of reimbursement claims each year. Instead, an organization uses statistical techniques to collect a sample of the data that is representative of the entire population of data. The sample data are analyzed and conclusions are reached about error rates, noncompliant practices, ineffective procedures and systems, and failures in the compliance program itself.

The data can be used to create custom management reports to call managers' attention to exceptions from accepted practice. An example is the filing of reimbursement claims within a specified time deadline, or including certain documentation with each claim. With this information, the managers can take appropriate corrective action. Someone can conduct a spot check of critical tasks to see if they are being performed properly. This could determine whether the medical record matches the services that are billed. It can be helpful to hold competence interviews of employees to see if they understand the compliant way that their job duties are to be performed.

Other monitoring methods also are available. These are examples.

- On-site visits to separate facilities, announced and unannounced
- Surveys of employees, physicians, and contractors on compliance issues
- Reviews of written materials and other documents reflecting the practices, policies, and procedures of the organization
- Testing of risk area employees on their familiarity with compliance-related laws, regulations, and payor requirements
- Contracting with outside third parties to carry out reviews of systems and processes
- Background checks on employees to determine their prior compliance history as well as their appearance on the OIG Exclusion List
- Reports from the organization's compliance complaint hotline

The particular methods employed will vary according to the type of organization. For instance, a medical billing company might review samples of medical records for each physician practice it serves, or evaluate how well each practice complies with Medicare and private payor contract requirements.

When an organization begins to conduct monitoring, the first batches of data that it collects will constitute a baseline against which future activity will be measured—either a worsening of certain compliance problems or progress in bringing them under control. From that point forward, a part of monitoring is to notice and investigate trends in the data gathered.

Monitoring reports will be compiled weekly, even daily, and passed on to the Compliance Officer. More serious problems and disturbing trends will be communicated to the full Compliance Committee, top executives, and the governing board. Managers will hear about the issues that affect their units.

COMPLIANCE AUDITING

Auditing is a rigorous, focused, and structured process designed to evaluate the operational health of distinct parts of an organization, identify problem areas, and provide the basis for corrective steps. Most organizations employ an accounting firm to conduct an annual audit of their financial statements. A compliance audit serves a similar purpose in examining an organization's legal health.

The auditing function is governed by professional standards, and performed by specially trained and certified individuals who are independent of the process being audited and often the organization as well. It resembles monitoring but differs in that it is more independent, more objective, and carried out less often—typically once a year. The monitoring program will often identify areas or topics for more intensive study through an audit.

These are the basic elements of good audit procedure.

1. Define the overall *purpose* of the audit. What compliance issues, in what risk areas, will be examined? How do the issues involve the organization's operations? What compliance laws and OIG enforcement goals are implicated?
2. Explain how the *results* will be used?
3. With legal input, decide whether the audit will be implemented under the attorney-client *privilege*.
4. Define the *scope* of the audit: the units involved, the people to be questioned or surveyed, the documents to be reviewed, and the data to be gathered and analyzed. How much time will be dedicated to the audit?
5. Lay out an audit *work plan* step-by-step. What tasks will be performed in what order? What statistical and other methodologies will be used?
6. Carry out the audit.

In a model compliance plan, the OIG recommends audit procedures like these:

> Compliance audits should be conducted in accordance with pre-established comprehensive audit procedures and should include, at a

> minimum: (1) on-site visits; (2) interviews with personnel involved in management, operations, billing, sales, marketing, and other related activities; (3) reviews of written materials and documentation ....; and (4) trend analysis studies.
>
> We suggest that the audit or other analytical reports specifically identify areas where corrective actions are needed. In certain cases, subsequent audits or studies would be advisable to ensure that the recommended corrective actions have been implemented and are successful.

The focus of the audits may change from year to year. The idea is to concentrate attention on matters that have been causing the organization problems with its compliance (as indicated by the results of ongoing monitoring) or that have been identified by the OIG as the source of heightened enforcement concerns (as reflected in OIG Work Plans, Special Fraud Alerts, audits, and other law enforcement initiatives). A narrow focus for a compliance audit is better than a wider focus. This makes it easier to isolate issues, identify problems and their solutions, and apply very efficient action plans.

Examples of possible corrective action and follow-up steps are voluntary reporting of detected violations to enforcement agencies, return of funds to payors, expansion or redirection of the audit, training for certain physicians and staff, disciplinary action, and revision of existing policies and procedures.

EXAMPLE OF A TYPICAL AUDIT PROCEDURE

These are the procedures for an audit intended to determine whether the claims filed by a healthcare provider organization for reimbursement by Medicare satisfy the requirement that the services delivered were "medically necessary." They are based on materials prepared for a presentation to the Health Care Compliance Association.

Sample Selection

Select a time frame for which a sample of patient accounts will be extracted.

Define the population of patients who received diagnostic testing (the basis of the medical necessity determination) during the audit period.

Define key data points needed to conduct useful data extraction.

Determine the volume of diagnostic test activity by facility, department, or type of diagnostic test. Look at this from the viewpoint of the departments that both request and perform the tests.

Extract the patient account sample using an approved sampling methodology.

Supporting Documentation

These documents are collected for each patient in the audit sample.

- Copy of the order or requisition for the tests
- Authentication for any verbal test orders
- Any notations on the test order about the patient's signs or condition
- The diagnosis noted on the test order
- The results of the diagnostic test
- The emergency department (ED) record for patients coming through the ED
- Copy of the claim forms
- National coverage determinations (NCDs) and applicable local coverage determinations (LCDs)
- Copies of any Advance Beneficiary Notice (ABN)[1] or Notice of Exclusion from Medicare Benefits (NEMB) for the patient

Data Entry and Gap Reconciliation

- Create an audit framework into which the collected data (existence or absence, accuracy or inaccuracy of medical necessity documentation) will be poured.
- Find causes for missing documentation.
- Identify the billing code (ICD-9 or 10) for each test recorded.
- Note compliance of payment with NCDs or LCDs, or not.
- If no billing code noted, review test request and results to see if another diagnosis code is justified.
- If documentation (or lack thereof) suggests an absence of "medical necessity," talk with the treating physician.
- Investigate process failures and recommend corrective action.

---

[1] The ABN is a report given to Medicare beneficiaries to let them know that Medicare is not likely to pay for certain services.

Data Analysis and Problem Definition

Process errors may be the reason that claims are denied for lack of "medical necessity." These actions are taken to find those errors and correct them.

- Determine the rate of claims denied for "medical necessity" reasons by facility, department, physician, and service type, noting trends and exceptions.
- Where the rates are excessive, identify the root cause and whether the requirements for "medical necessity" are being met.
- Review the process by which "medical necessity" is determined and reeducate clinicians on how it works and the proper use of ABNs.
- Ensure that the process informs clinicians of likely denials and how to use ABNs.
- Regularly review irregularities in the "medical necessity" verification process that may lead to claims denials.

Several decisions will be based on the results of an audit. The organization will initiate corrective action plans that may alter work processes. Or it may conclude that there is not enough evidence to warrant significant changes. Detected violations will be self-disclosed to the OIG. Overpayments will be returned to Medicare or other payors. A lot depends on the accuracy and reliability of the audit. For this reason, it is important that the audit process be thoroughly documented. This will include the audit plan, survey results, interview notes, work flow charts and checklists, sampling methodology, relevant policies and procedures, immediate reaction plans, and follow-up monitoring plans. The documentation should be sufficient to permit an independent reviewer of the audit to reach the same conclusions.

To see what a hospital organization, the Boulder Community Hospital, has to say about its monitoring and auditing activities, review this webpage: http://www.bch.org/compliance-policies/monitoring-and-auditing.aspx.

STUDY QUESTIONS

1. What is the purpose of a compliance risk assessment? In what ways do monitoring and auditing depend on such assessments?
2. In the context of compliance, what does the term "risk area" mean?
3. What should a healthcare organization do with the information it gathers from its monitoring activities?

4. What information should be included in regular monitoring reports and who should receive them?
5. Use five words to describe the monitoring process. Use another five words to describe an audit.

Learning Exercises

1. Search on the Internet for information about *generally accepted auditing standards* for financial statement audits and the *standards for the professional practice of internal auditing* for internal audits. Which of the principles and practices displayed in those standards would be applicable to compliance audits?
2. One of the numerous focus areas in the OIG's Annual Work Plan for 2012 was described this way:

   > We will review the type of information that hospitals' internal incident-reporting systems capture about adverse events and determine the extent to which hospital systems captured adverse events and reported the information to external patient-safety oversight entities.

   You work for a hospital that is concerned that its internal incident-reporting system may not be functioning as effectively as it could be. It is worried that it might become the target of an OIG investigation. Your task is to propose a procedure for conducting an audit of that system. Use the typical audit procedure described in this chapter as a template. You probably should start by researching how an internal incident-reporting system works.
3. Do a little bit of research on the attorney–client privilege. How does it work and what would an organization have to do to take advantage of it? Why would an organization want to be able to rely on this privilege?
4. Computers are being used to manage both financial and clinical aspects of healthcare delivery operations. The federal government is offering financial incentives to providers who adopt "meaningfully useful" electronic health records systems. Speculate on how monitoring activities could be carried out electronically and automatically, without human intervention, by interfacing with the computer-based financial and clinical systems.

5. Visit the website of the professional association of professional auditors working in the healthcare field, the Association of Healthcare Internal Auditors, at www.ahia.org. Notice what kinds of issues they are interested in and the types of activities that they sponsor.

References

1. "Performing A Compliance Risk Assessment for Compliance Auditing & Monitoring In Healthcare Organizations," Mueller, Association of Healthcare Internal Auditors, Winter 2005, pp. 37–41.
2. OIG Compliance Program Guidance for Third-Party Medical Billing Companies.
3. OIG Compliance Program Guidance for Hospitals.
4. OIG Work Plan, Fiscal Year 2012.
5. "Using Computer Assisted Audit Techniques For More Effective Compliance Auditing and Monitoring in Healthcare Organizations," Mueller, Association of Healthcare Internal Auditors, Spring 2005, pp. 28–31.

Section III

Compliance in Specific Healthcare Organizations

Each chapter in Section III explains in some detail the content of compliance programs for 10 major types of healthcare organizations that receive reimbursement from federal healthcare programs like Medicare. Each of these types has been the subject of a federal Compliance Program Guidance.

Chapter 15

Hospitals

LEARNING OBJECTIVES

After completing class sessions based on this chapter, a student will:

- Be familiar with the basic elements of an excellent hospital compliance program.
- Know which hospital operational areas are at highest risk of compliance violations.
- Learn the importance of hospital-wide standards of conduct.
- Understand the typical responsibilities of a hospital Compliance Officer.
- Know the key steps in conducting compliance training and education.
- Appreciate the role of open lines of communication in minimizing compliance problems.
- Realize the need to monitor continuously the operation of the hospital compliance program.
- Discover the types of responses to possible compliance offenses.
- Have examined a good example of a real-life hospital compliance plan.

INTRODUCTION

The purpose of a compliance program and associated activities is to promote adherence to federal and state laws on fraud abuse and the program requirements of federal, state, and private health plans. They accomplish this by building a hospital organizational culture that encourages the prevention, detection, and correction of noncompliance events that violate federal and state law. The program itself demonstrates and defines the hospital's commitment to the compliance process. It is a powerful source of internal control in the areas of reimbursement, claims, and billing where a lot of fraud and abuse occurs and where government agencies have focused much of their regulatory and enforcement efforts.

The Office of the Inspector General (OIG) in the federal Department of Health and Human Services (DHHS) has supported the implementation of hospital compliance programs by issuing two detailed sets of recommendations on the structure of such programs and where their attention should be focused.[1]

COMPLIANCE RISKS UNIQUE TO HOSPITALS AND HOSPITAL SYSTEMS

Hospitals are subject to most of the same laws as other healthcare organizations and must develop programs to ensure compliance with them. These include the federal False Claims Act, the Anti-Kickback Statute, the Exclusion Authorities, and the Civil Monetary Penalties Law. However, there are aspects of these laws, as well as several other statutes, which create compliance obligations that are unique to hospitals and hospital systems.

Outpatient services rendered in connection with an inpatient stay. Certain such services may not be billed separately from the inpatient stay.

Submission of claims for laboratory services. Claims for such services should be submitted only after they are performed, when they are medically necessary, and when they are actually ordered by a physician and provided by the hospital laboratory.

Physicians at teaching hospitals. A hospital should submit claims on behalf of teaching physicians only for services actually provided, after appropriate documentation has been placed in the patient's medical record and signed by the treating physician, and after the physician has documented his/her presence during the service or procedure.

Cost reports. Medicare-certified hospitals are required to submit an annual cost report to a fiscal intermediary. The report contains information such as facility characteristics, utilization data, cost and charges by cost center, Medicare settlement data, and financial statement data. The report must not contain costs that are not based on appropriate and accurate documentation, costs must be allocated to cost centers accurately and on the basis of verifiable data, cost allocations to individual hospitals in a multihospital system must be accurate and based on verifiable data, and bad debt reporting must follow federal requirements.

[1] The original and supplemental Compliance Program Guidance for Hospitals:
http://oig.hhs.gov/authorities/docs/cpghosp.pdf
http://oig.hhs.gov/fraud/docs/complianceguidance/012705HospSupplementalGuidance.pdf

Recruitment of physicians to medical staff. Hospitals in physician shortage areas may have difficulty recruiting new doctors to join their medical staffs, particularly in certain specialties. The hospital may offer certain kinds of inducements to those physicians as long as they are based on fair market value and are not tied to the volume of patients that the physician brings to the hospital.

Attracting patient referrals to the hospital. Hospitals rely almost entirely on patients sent to them by physicians for admission. The hospital must not give and the physician must not accept anything of value in exchange for admitting a patient to the hospital.

Admission and discharge policies. The risks here concern failure to follow the "same-day rule," abuse of partial hospitalization payments, same-day discharges and readmissions, violation of Medicare's post-acute care transfer policy, and inappropriate churning of patients by long-term care hospitals sited on the same premises as acute care hospitals.

Supplemental payments. The OIG warns against improper reporting of the costs of "pass-through" items, abuse of diagnosis-related group (DRG) outlier payments, improper claims for clinical trials, improper claims for organ acquisition costs, and improper claims for cardiac rehab services.

Tax-exempt standards for nonprofit hospitals. A hospital must provide a minimum level of "community benefit" and pay its executives no more than "reasonable compensation" in order to qualify for section 501(c)(3) tax-exempt status.

Gain-sharing arrangements between a hospital and its physicians. Try to structure the arrangement to fit within the personal services safe harbor of the Anti-Kickback Statute. Where that is not possible, be prepared for legal challenges under that statute and the Stark Physician Self-Referral Law.

Antitrust implications of hospital decisions to merge with or acquire each other. In building ever larger multihospital systems or forming a strategic alliance with a local competitor, hospitals must respect the federal antitrust laws enforced by the Department of Justice.

Legal implications of trend for hospitals to purchase physician practices, align strategic hospital goals with those of physician practices, and enter into hospital-physician collaborations in support of an accountable care organization (ACO). The legal risks here are primarily antitrust, but fraud and abuse, and tax laws, also may be implicated.

Compliance with EMTALA in the operation of hospital emergency departments. Hospitals must provide emergency evaluation and treatment services within the full capabilities of their staff and facilities, in compliance with the Emergency Medical Treatment and Labor Act (EMTALA).

HIPAA Privacy and Security Rules. All hospitals that conduct electronic transactions must comply with the Privacy and Security Rules issued under the Health Insurance Portability and Accountability Act (HIPAA).

This multitude of legal threats and obligations makes a comprehensive compliance program mandatory for every hospital.

BENEFITS OF A HOSPITAL COMPLIANCE PROGRAM

In recommending the adoption of compliance programs, the OIG points to benefits in all areas of a hospital's operations. A well-conceived program will:

- Identify and prevent criminal and unethical behavior
- Ensure that the hospital is not submitting false and inaccurate claims to government and private payors
- Include a protocol that makes it easy for employees to report potential problems
- Facilitate prompt, thorough investigations of alleged misconduct by corporate officers, managers, employees, physicians, other healthcare professionals, independent contractors, and vendors
- Initiate prompt and appropriate corrective action
- Reduce the hospital's exposure to civil damages and penalties, criminal sanctions, program exclusion, and other administrative remedies
- Serve as a central source for hospital-wide distribution of information on laws, regulations, and other program directives regarding fraud and abuse
- Provide a more accurate view on the extent of employee and third-party behavior related to fraud and abuse
- Identify weaknesses in internal systems, controls, and management
- Improve the quality of care and the efficiency with which it is delivered
- Build the hospital's reputation with its workers, stakeholders, and the community for lawful and ethical provider and corporate conduct

For these reasons, a compliance program should be considered a worthwhile investment of the hospital's funds.

ELEMENTS OF AN OIG-RECOMMENDED HOSPITAL COMPLIANCE PROGRAM

The OIG believes that these elements can be tailored to fit the needs and resources of any type of hospital—large and small, teaching and community, urban and rural, and for-profit and not-for-profit, as well as multihospital systems. The OIG stresses the importance of incorporating all seven of the following elements in a hospital's compliance program.

1. The development and distribution of written standards of conduct as well as written policies and procedures that promote the hospital's commitment to compliance and that address specific areas of potential fraud, such as claims development and submission processes, code gaming, and financial relationships with physicians and other healthcare professionals.
2. The designation of a Chief Compliance Officer and a corporate Compliance Committee, charged with the responsibility of operating and monitoring the compliance program, and who report directly to the Chief Executive Officer (CEO) and the governing body.
3. The development and implementation of regular, effective education and training programs for all affected employees.
4. The maintenance of a process, such as a hotline, to receive complaints, and the adoption of procedures to protect the anonymity of complainants and to protect whistle-blowers from retaliation.
5. The development of a system to respond to allegations of improper/illegal activities and the enforcement of appropriate disciplinary action against employees who have violated internal compliance policies, applicable statutes, regulations, or federal healthcare program requirements.
6. The use of audits and other evaluation techniques to monitor compliance and assist in the reduction of identified problem area risks.
7. The investigation and remediation of identified systemic problems and the development of policies concerning the employment or retention of sanctioned individuals.

These are the recommended practical features of each of those elements.

Written Policies and Procedures

The framework of the compliance program consists of written policies and procedures that identify the most critical risk areas in the hospital and prescribe how people should act in those areas. They are prepared under the supervision of the Chief Compliance Officer and the Compliance Committee; they are distributed to every employee and third party whose work is affected by a policy. Risk areas are those functions or departments of the hospital that are especially susceptible to government regulation, noncompliance, and law enforcement. Through its investigation, audit, and enforcement activities, the OIG has determined the following activities and areas of hospital operation to be at high risk.

- Billing for items or services not actually rendered
- Providing medically unnecessary services
- Upcoding
- "DRG creep"
- Outpatient services rendered in connection with inpatient stays
- Teaching physician and resident requirements for teaching hospitals
- Duplicate billing
- False cost reports
- Unbundling
- Billing for discharge in lieu of transfer
- Patients' freedom of choice
- Credit balances—failure to refund
- Hospital incentives that violate the Anti-Kickback Statute or other similar federal or state statutes or regulations
- Joint ventures
- Financial arrangements between hospitals and hospital-based physicians
- Stark Physician Self-Referral Law
- Knowing failure to provide covered services or necessary care to members of a health maintenance organization
- Patient dumping

At the beginning of each year, the OIG prepares a Work Plan[2] that describes specific audits, evaluations, investigations, and other activities that it plans to initiate or continue with regard to programs like Medicare and Medicaid to protect their integrity. It is an indication of areas where it will focus its enforcement efforts. A hospital would be wise to review the Work Plan in structuring its compliance program. It also should pay special attention to vulnerable areas that are unique to its operations or have been the source of fraud and abuse problems in the past.

The policies and procedures should address several key issues.

[2] The current plan can be found here: http://www.oig.hhs.gov/reports-and-publications/workplan/index.asp#current

Standards of Conduct

These standards will define acceptable and unacceptable behaviors for all affected individuals in the performance of their jobs. They include the hospital's mission, goals, and ethical mandate and express its commitment to the principles of compliance.

The standards will apply to all of the hospital's governing board members, officers and executives, managers and supervisors, employees, physicians, other healthcare professionals, and, where appropriate, third-party contractors, vendors, and agents. They will apply as well to affiliated entities operating under the hospital's control (e.g., skilled nursing facilities, psychiatric units, home health agencies, rehabilitation units, outpatient clinics, dialysis facilities, and clinical laboratories), to hospital-based physicians, and to ancillary healthcare professionals (e.g., utilization review managers, nurse anesthetists, physician assistants, and physical therapists).

The standards should be published in the different languages and at the different reading levels appropriate to the audiences at which it is targeted. They should be updated whenever the relevant statutes, regulations, and program requirements are changed.

Claims Preparation and Submission Process

Several of the risk areas listed previously pertain to the process by which a hospital prepares and submits claims to payors for reimbursement of the services it has provided to Medicare and Medicaid beneficiaries. Hospital policies and procedures should reflect and reinforce the laws and regulations applying to claims submissions. They will accomplish this through specific provisions like these.

- A mechanism for maintaining effective, accurate communication channels between claims/billing staff and clinical staff.
- A requirement for timely, precise documentation of physician and other professional services delivered prior to billing.
- Submission of claims only when it is clear that appropriate documentation exists and is accessible for audit and review.
- Medical records used as the basis for submitted claims are organized and legible to facilitate their audit and review.
- The diagnosis and procedures reported on the reimbursement claim forms are based on the medical record.
- The documentation required for the accurate assignment of codes is readily available to the coding staff.
- The compensation given to the claims department, coding clerks, and claims consultants does not function in any way as an incentive to improperly code claims.

The OIG urges special attention to issues of medical necessity, DRG coding, individual Medicare Part B claims (i.e., evaluation and management codes), and patient discharge codes.

The claims policies and procedures should be developed in synchronization with private payor standards.

Medical Necessity

Policies and procedures should ensure that accurate, comprehensive definitions of the term "medical necessity" are provided to all individuals who must rely on and utilize them. The hospital should maintain documentation, like medical records and physician orders, to justify the medical necessity of the services delivered.

Anti-Kickback and Self-Referral Liability

The hospital's policies and procedures should control the activities that might create liability for it under the Anti-Kickback Statute and the Stark Law. They should:

- Ensure that contracts and arrangements with referral sources comply with these and other relevant laws and regulations.
- Prevent from being submitted for reimbursement any claims for patients who were referred to the hospital under contracts or financial arrangements that were intended to encourage such referrals in violation of the Anti-Kickback, Physician Self-Referral Law, and similar laws.
- Ensure that the hospital does not enter into financial arrangements intended to provide inappropriate reward to the hospital in return for a physician's ability to care for Medicare/Medicaid patients at the hospital.
- Favor payment practices that fall within the OIG Safe Harbor provisions of the Anti-Kickback Law.

Bad Debts

There should be policies and procedures governing the way the hospital's handles patients' bad debts. At least once a year, the hospital should review all Medicare bad debt expenses that it has claimed and whether it is properly reporting bad debts to the Centers for Medicare and Medicaid Services (CMS). It probably will want to consult with Medicare fiscal intermediaries about the reporting requirements. Beneficiary deductible and copayment collection efforts should be closely monitored. Routinely waived Medicare copayments and deductibles must not be claimed as bad debts.

Credit Balances

Written policy should dictate the timely and accurate reporting of Medicare and Medicaid credit balances. The hospital's IT system should be capable of tracking the credit balances on individual patient accounts. The tracking, recording, and reporting should be the responsibility of a single individual. As a check on that person, someone in the hospital's accounting department ought to review reports of credit balances, reimbursements, and adjustments on a monthly basis.

Record Retention

The hospital must implement a formal records system that encompasses the creation, distribution, retention, storage, retrieval, and destruction of documents. The relevant documents are those required by law for the hospital's participation in the Medicare and Medicaid programs and those essential to the integrity and effectiveness of its compliance program. The latter would include documentation of employee compliance training, compliance hotline logs, program modifications, and auditing and monitoring events.

Performance Management

As an incentive to compliant employee behavior, the terms of the hospital's performance management scheme should include adherence to the principles of the compliance program as a factor in evaluating the performance of all employees, particularly managers and supervisors. Periodic training should be provided to those employees in new compliance policies and procedures as they are written.

The OIG makes these specific recommendations for managers and supervisors responsible for coding, claims, and cost report preparation and submission.

- Discuss with all subordinates the compliance policies and procedures, and the legal requirements, applicable to their work activities.
- Inform all subordinates that compliance with those policies and requirements is a condition of their employment.
- Make clear that the hospital will discipline and dismiss, when appropriate, employees who violate its compliance policies and requirements.

In addition, the hospital should stress that managers and supervisors will be held accountable for a failure to instruct their subordinates about compliance or to detect noncompliant activity if reasonable diligence would have uncovered it.

Compliance Officer and Committee

To be effective, a compliance program must be accompanied by the designation of a Compliance Officer and a Compliance Committee.

Compliance Officer

The hospital designates a person to function as a Compliance Officer, the focal point for compliance activities throughout the organization. Depending on the size and resources of the hospital, compliance duties may occupy all or part of the person's work time.

While it is best if this person works full-time at his/her compliance duties, the size and resources of the hospital may dictate that they be assigned to someone with other work responsibilities. The hospital's Comptroller and General Counsel are two possibilities. However, the OIG warns against making the Compliance Officer subordinate to either of those two positions. The separation of their duties helps to ensure independent and objective legal reviews and financial analyses of the hospital's compliance activities. The Compliance Officer should have direct access to the hospital CEO and its governing board; the officer must have sufficient funding and staff to perform his/her compliance duties.

These are the typical responsibilities of a Compliance Officer:

- Managing and monitoring the operation of the compliance program.
- Regularly reporting to the hospital's governing board, CEO, and Compliance Committee on the operation and effectiveness of the compliance program.
- Modifying and updating the compliance program whenever government law, program requirements, and changed hospital circumstances demand.
- Creating education and training resources on all aspects of compliance and delivering them to appropriate employees.
- Ensuring that the hospital's independent contractors, vendors, agents, and other third parties are informed of the terms of its compliance program.
- Working with the hospital's Human Resources Department to compare all employees, medical staff, and independent contractors with names in the National Practitioner Data Bank and the Cumulative Sanction Report.
- Coordinating with the hospital's financial management office in reviewing and monitoring departmental compliance activities.

- Implementing policies and programs that encourage managers and employees to report, without fear of retaliation, suspected compliance problems or violations.
- Conducting independent investigations in response to reports of suspected compliance problems or violations, and launching appropriate corrective action.

The Compliance Officer must have the authority to carry out these responsibilities. This includes commanding the attention of executives, managers, and employees, and accessing documents and other information that relate to compliance activities.

Compliance Committee

The purpose of the Compliance Committee is to support the Compliance Officer and assist him/her in implementing the compliance program. Its duties include the following:

- Staying up to date on the hospital's market and industry environment, evolving legal requirements, and high-risk areas within its operations.
- Working with the relevant hospital departments to develop policies and procedures, including standards of conduct that promote employee compliance.
- Proposing and monitoring internal systems and controls designed to put into effect the policies, procedures, and standards.
- Preparing and executing a strategy to promote employee observance of the compliance program and detection of possible violations.
- Implementing a system that seeks out incidents of noncompliance, evaluates them, and takes appropriate action.

The OIG suggests that hospitals ask these kinds of questions to evaluate their compliance activities.

> Do the compliance program, committee, and officer have a useful, clearly defined mission?
>
> Do they have the necessary resources and independence to carry out that mission?
>
> Is there an appropriate relationship between the compliance function and the general counsel function—respectful, collegial, but not too friendly?
>
> Does the Compliance Committee include compliance savvy representatives from key hospital departments?

Is the Compliance Officer open to using ad hoc, short-term task forces to conduct special projects?

Does the Compliance Officer have direct access to the governing board, all members of top management, and experienced legal counsel?

Does the Compliance Officer have positive working relationships with key departments and operational areas?

Compliance Training and Education

A compliance program is carried out by a hospital's executives, managers, employees, physicians, and other healthcare professionals. To do this effectively, they must be trained initially in the principles of the legal requirements that impact the hospital and the internal compliance program that responds to those requirements. Then, they must be regularly retrained as the laws and the program change and evolve. New employees should receive training shortly after they begin work at the hospital.

The OIG suggests that employees receive a minimum number of hours of compliance education and training each year. They should be informed that their participation in the training programs is a condition of their employment and will be a factor in their performance appraisals. The Compliance Committee should document in detail all education and training activities, including attendance logs and copies of training material used.

The OIG recommends that the training programs emphasize federal and state laws, regulations, and guidelines (particularly those applying to fraud and abuse), private payor policies and requirements, coding requirements, claims preparation and submission procedures, and hospital marketing practices. It urges coverage of the following specific activities:

- Government and private payor reimbursement principles
- General prohibitions on paying or receiving remuneration to induce referrals
- Proper confirmation of diagnoses
- Submitting a claim for physician services when rendered by a nonphysician (i.e., the "incident to" rule and the physician physical presence requirement)
- Signing a form for a physician without the physician's authorization
- Alterations to medical records

- Prescribing medications and procedures without proper authorization
- Proper documentation of services rendered
- Duty to report misconduct

These are some standards for evaluating the effectiveness of a hospital's training and education efforts.

- Using qualified trainers to conduct the compliance training sessions.
- Annual evaluation of the content of training and education activities.
- Regular updating of training and education to reflect changes in federal healthcare program requirements.
- Regular review of the training configuration for length and frequency of sessions, live versus computer-based instruction, and the general versus specific focus of the training content.
- Gathering of participant feedback after each session.
- Testing of participants after each session to measure their learning.
- Delivering appropriate training even to the hospital's governing body.
- Disciplining employees for failure to attend training sessions.

Open Lines of Communication

Reporting of suspected incidents of noncompliance or violation requires that employees have open lines of communication to the Compliance Officer. It is a good idea to offer several independent reporting channels in the event of supervisors attempting to block the reports. Written policies protecting the confidentiality of employee communications and preventing retaliation are essential to encourage reporting.

The reporting may be permitted through a variety of means. The OIG encourages the use of hotlines, email messages, and written communications, by anonymous means if desired. Employees must be informed that, at some point in the investigation, it may become necessary to reveal their identities. Reports of suspected violations should be documented and investigated, scrupulously and immediately.

A hospital's communication environment might be measured by these factors.

- The hospital has cultivated an organizational culture that embraces open communication.

- It has implemented a mechanism, like an anonymous hotline, through which anybody (employees, contractors, patients, visitors, clinical staff) can report a suspected compliance issue.
- The hotline's existence is publicized, its calls are logged, and callers are informed of actions taken.
- All incidents of alleged fraud and abuse are investigated.
- Results of internal investigations are shared with management and directors.

Auditing and Monitoring

To maintain its functionality and effectiveness, the compliance program must be continuously watched. Under the direction of the Compliance Officer, there should be regular monitoring of program operations coupled with reports to the Compliance Committee and senior management.

A particularly effective form of monitoring are periodic audits carried out by internal or external auditors with knowledge of federal and state healthcare laws and regulations, and federal healthcare program requirements. The OIG encourages such audits and their emphasis on:

- Relationships with third-party contractors
- Potential kickback arrangements
- Potential physician self-referrals
- Current procedural terminology (CPT) and healthcare common procedure coding system (HCPCS) coding
- Claims preparation and submission
- Reimbursement procedures
- Cost reporting
- Marketing practices

The monitoring techniques might include a sampling protocol that begins with a baseline audit. That first audit is an initial "snapshot" of the compliance practices at the hospital. Subsequent audits identify and analyze variations from the baseline. When they reveal improper procedures, misunderstanding about the rules, and other systemic problems, prompt corrective action should be taken.

A technique similar to audits is an annual review of how well the activities of the compliance program are being performed. It determines whether program information is being disseminated, training sessions conducted, records kept, and disciplinary actions implemented. The review can employ methods like on-site visits, interviews with personnel in key departments, questionnaires, study of medical and financial records supporting submitted claims, and long-term trend analyses.

Responding to Detected Offenses with Corrective Actions

When behavior is detected that violates the hospital's compliance program policies, federal or state laws and regulations, or payor program requirements (Medicare, Medicaid, private), prompt and appropriate corrective action is essential to protect the hospital's reputation and legal status. There are many types of action that may be called for: return of overpayments to a payor, more rigorous enforcement of existing procedures, revision of existing procedures or creation of new ones, amendment/renegotiation of contracts with third-party agents, redirection of business to different third-party agents, new content for training and education initiatives, discipline or dismissal of employees, discipline or dismissal of physicians, referral to criminal or civil law enforcement authorities, preparation of a formal correction plan, and the filing of a voluntary self-disclosure to the OIG.

Where a violation of criminal, civil, or administrative law is detected, prompt reporting of the misconduct to the appropriate governmental authority will demonstrate the hospital's good faith and willingness to cooperate with the authority to correct the underlying problems. The OIG also will consider it a mitigating factor in determining penalties, assessments, and program exclusions.

In the course of uncovering potential violations, the Compliance Officer should take steps to secure and prevent the destruction of relevant documents and other evidence pertinent to the investigation.

These are some factors to consider in assessing how well a hospital deals with detected offenses.

Is there a response team (composed of personnel from compliance, audit, and other relevant functions) in place to investigate detected offenses immediately?

Are all incidents investigated promptly and thoroughly?

Are the corrective action plans based on root cause analyses of the alleged offenses?

Do subsequent reviews verify that the plans correct the underlying causes of the offenses?

Are identified overpayments promptly reported and repaid to the appropriate payor?

Are potential violations of law promptly reported to the appropriate law enforcement agency?

Disciplinary Action for Compliance Violations

There must be consequences for violations of both the laws and the compliance program policies and procedures. This will take the form of disciplinary actions of varying degrees of severity, ranging from verbal and written warnings to suspensions, revocation of staff privileges, dismissal, and financial penalties. The standards of conduct should describe how disciplinary incidents will be handled and the persons responsible for handling them. The consequences of noncompliant behavior should be administered fairly and equitably, appropriately and consistently. Disciplinary action should be meted out to not only the persons committing the violations but also to those managers and supervisors who oversee them.

The hospital should make every effort to avoid hiring persons who have already committed certain types of violations. Job or medical staff applicants should be required to disclose any criminal convictions as well as any program exclusions. On top of this, the hospital should conduct thorough background investigations that include reference checks. The information gathered in that way supports a hospital policy against employing anyone recently convicted of a healthcare-related criminal offense or who has been debarred, excluded, or otherwise denied participation in federal healthcare programs. If someone already employed is accused of such improprieties, the OIG recommends that they be temporarily removed from responsibility for or participation in such programs.

EXAMPLE OF A WELL-CONCEIVED HOSPITAL COMPLIANCE PLAN—MD ANDERSON CANCER CENTER

A good way to start designing a new hospital compliance plan or to assess an existing one is to study the best plans already implemented by other hospitals. One example is the compliance plan implemented by the MD Anderson Cancer Center at the University of Texas. A copy of the plan can be found at the MD Anderson website.[3] The site is a rich source of real-world compliance documents, including MD Anderson's Standards of Conduct; Fraud, Waste, and Abuse Policy; Non-Retaliation Policy, Conflict of Interest Policy, and Ethics Policy.

The plan opens with a brief letter from the hospital's president, strongly endorsing its aims and expressing his commitment to high standards of

[3] http://www.mdanderson.org/about-us/compliance-program/index.html

organizational behavior. It is followed by a succinct, yet comprehensive 10-point Code of Conduct. Some of the principles of that Code are:

- Avoid soliciting, accepting, or offering items of value in return for patient referrals.
- Provide, document, and bill for services with the greatest regard for law and ethics.
- Maintain a working knowledge of, and adhere to all local, state, and federal laws, rules, and guidelines.

The plan provides that Oversight of compliance activities will be the responsibility of a "multi-disciplinary Executive Institutional Compliance Committee, whose members are listed. Management of the compliance program is assigned to a Chief Compliance Officer, and his/her duties are listed."

The plan's section on Education describes the initial orientation requirements for employees, including their responsibility to report possible violations of law or hospital policies. The compliance program trains employees throughout the year on a variety of general and specific compliance issues. Thirteen specific issues are listed. Once each year, every employee is formally tested on his/her comprehension of compliance matters.

Under Ongoing Monitoring and Auditing, the plan states that the hospital conducts periodic audits of operations through on-site visits, interviews with personnel, and review of documentation, among other means. The Compliance Officer regularly reports audit findings and corrective action plans to the Compliance Committee, the hospital president, and the governing board.

Whenever a compliance issue is identified, the Compliance Officer promptly and fully investigates. Relevant documents and other evidence are protected against destruction. The investigation leads to a corrective action plan and disciplinary action, if it is warranted. Any misconduct that violates civil or criminal law is reported to the OIG.

The plan specifies the elements of the corrective action plan that is prepared: ceasing the problematic activity, repaying overpayments, reporting to governmental authorities, recommending and monitoring disciplinary action, instituting preventive measures, including remedial training and education, determining whether the problem is systemic, and monitoring of the corrective action. It also lays out the forms of disciplinary action that may be meted out to employees who commit compliance violations. They include mandatory remedial education, verbal warning, written warning, involuntary demotion, suspension without pay, and termination.

The plan emphasizes that promotion of the compliance program, and adherence to its requirements, is an essential element in evaluating job performance. Managers and supervisors are required to discuss all parts of the program with their subordinates and are held accountable for their compliance-related behaviors.

The hospital prohibits the employment of individuals with a criminal history related to health care or who have been excluded from program participation by several specific agencies: OIG, National Practitioner Data Bank, Federal Drug Administration, Office of Foreign Assets Control, Office of Research Integrity, and state agencies. Employees are screened four times a year for sanctions by those agencies.

A person may report his or her compliance concerns to a Fraud and Abuse Hotline, a Privacy Compliance Hotline, or directly to the Compliance Officer. A failure to report a potential violation may subject the person to disciplinary action. Calls to the hotlines are treated anonymously, if the caller prefers, and their confidentiality is protected to the extent possible.

The plan includes a section on record creation and retention that describes standards for creating, distributing, retaining, storing, retrieving, and destroying all documents required by federal or state law, or regulatory agencies.

A section on patient referrals restates the prohibitions of the federal laws against giving or accepting payments for referrals, routinely waiving insurance copayments or deductibles.

FURTHER SOURCES OF GUIDANCE ON HOSPITAL COMPLIANCE

1. https://oig.hhs.gov/compliance/compliance-guidance/index.asp

   This is the Compliance Guidance page of the OIG in the DHHS. It includes the Original Compliance Program Guidance for Hospitals (February 23, 1995) and the Supplemental Compliance Program Guidance for Hospitals (January 27, 2005).
2. http://www.omig.ny.gov/data/images/stories/compliance/compliance_program_guidance-general_hospitals.pdf

   This is the Compliance Program Guidance for General Hospitals issued on May 11, 2012 by the Office of the Medicaid Inspector General in the New York State Department of Health. New York requires specified Medicaid providers, including hospitals, to adopt and implement effective compliance programs and has provided these guidelines to hospitals for creating such programs. It is the only state to support its healthcare organizations in this way.

STUDY QUESTIONS

1. What are the seven OIG-recommended elements of a good hospital compliance program? Take the time right now to list them on a piece of paper, using four or five words to describe each one. If you are ambitious, memorize all seven.
2. What is the purpose of the OIG Work Plan and how does it help a hospital in designing and operating its compliance program? Review the latest Work Plan and identify those items that apply especially to hospitals.
3. What are a hospital's "standards of conduct"? Exactly what do they describe and what purpose do they serve? Distinguish standards of conduct from a code of ethics and from laws and regulations.
4. List five areas of hospital operation that are at high risk of compliance violations.
5. Who would be appropriate members of a hospital Compliance Committee?
6. What background and training should be expected of the person serving as Compliance Officer?
7. Briefly describe the curriculum of a compliance orientation session for a hospital's newly hired employees.
8. Imagine that you are the head of the hospital department responsible for preparing and submitting claims and bills for payment for services delivered to patients. What steps would you take to encourage your employees to report any suspicion of possible compliance violations?
9. What would you suggest as the key elements in a generic action plan to correct a pattern of errors in the claims submitted for payment by a hospital?
10. Briefly explain how a "root cause analysis" works.
11. Visit the website for the National Practitioner Data Bank.[4] Learn how it works and which practitioners are included.

---

[4] http://www.npdb-hipdb.hrsa.gov/

Learning Exercises

1. Think about the MD Anderson Cancer Center compliance plan in terms of the OIG recommendations described in this chapter. How well does the plan carry out those recommendations? What is your overall impression of the way that MD Anderson has described its compliance activities on its website? After reviewing those resources, are you more or less inclined to use the hospital as a patient? Does the website enhance the hospital's reputation?
2. After familiarizing yourself with the compliance program at MD Anderson, do some Google searching for compliance materials about other hospitals. Many hospitals have chosen to make at least some of their compliance resources public. These are a few to get you started.
   - The Hospital of Central Connecticut (THOCC)
     http://thocc.org/about/corporate_compliance.aspx
   - Onslow Memorial Hospital
     http://www.omhcompliance.org/
   - Nyack Hospital, New York-Presbyterian Healthcare System
     http://www.nyackhospital.org/Nyack-Hospital-About-Corporate-Compliance-Home.asp
   - Stanford Hospital & Clinics
     http://stanfordhospital.org/overview/conduct.html
   - Danbury Hospital
     http://www.danburyhospital.org/en/About-Us/Policies/Compliance.aspx

   Compare the compliance materials on those websites to those found on MD Anderson's website. For what reasons would a hospital want to make public information about its compliance activities? What features of each hospital's web presence seem particularly attractive or helpful? In what ways does the MD Anderson website seem superior? What impression are you left with after viewing each website? Is the hospital's reputation enhanced as a result of public access to its compliance information? Offer some specific recommendations on how each hospital could improve the presentation of its compliance materials—both in terms of substance and style.
3. Think about a modest-size hospital in a smaller city, a hospital with considerably fewer resources than a larger teaching hospital in a major city. How can it possibly implement a compliance program that meets the OIG recommendations, that gives it reasonable protection against compliance violations? Describe a compliance program that is slimmer,

consumes fewer resources, costs less money, and yet still does a good basic job of ensuring compliance with relevant laws and program requirements.

4. Perhaps with the support of your instructor, contact a local hospital and request an interview with the person responsible for its compliance activities. Learn from him or her the nature of those activities. Ask if he or she is satisfied with the effectiveness of the hospital's compliance efforts, as well as its actual compliance record. Compare what that hospital is doing to the OIG Guidance on Hospital Compliance.

References

1. OIG Original Guidance for Hospital Compliance Programs, https://oig.hhs.gov/authorities/docs/cpghosp.pdf
2. OIG Supplemental Guidance for Hospital Compliance Programs, https://oig.hhs.gov/fraud/docs/complianceguidance/012705HospSupplementalGuidance.pdf
3. OIG Guidance for Third Party Medical Billing Companies (provides good overview of billing issues for hospitals), https://oig.hhs.gov/fraud/docs/complianceguidance/thirdparty.pdf
4. OIG Annual Work Plans, https://oig.hhs.gov/reports-and-publications/archives/workplan/index.asp
5. Health Care Compliance Association (HCCA) is the primary association of healthcare compliance professionals, and a source of conferences, books, training videos, and networking, www.hcca-info.org
6. American Health Lawyers Association (AHLA) is the leading association of healthcare attorneys. It offers a variety of health legal resources (multiday conferences, webinars, forums, books and other printed materials, downloadable versions of those materials) addressing hospital concerns. Of particular interest is the 3rd edition of its Healthcare Compliance Legal Issues Manual, www.healthlawyers.org
7. Hospital Corporation of America (HCA) is the largest private operator of hospitals in the United States. This is its website dedicated to the management of Ethics & Compliance issues in a large sprawling for-profit hospital system, http://hcaethics.com/
8. This is the page of that website that explains its policies and procedures, http://hcaethics.com/policies/policies.dot

Chapter 16

Physician Practices

Learning Objectives

After completing class sessions based on this chapter, a student will:

- Be familiar with major healthcare-oriented fraud and abuse laws, their technical requirements, and the penalties that violators may expect.
- Discover the particular physician practice activities that are regulated by the fraud and abuse laws.
- Learn the content of the multistep voluntary compliance program recommended by the Office of the Inspector General (OIG) specifically for physician practices.
- Realize the concessions that the OIG compliance program requirements make for practices of limited resources.
- Know how to begin creating and implementing a compliance program for a physician practice that lacks one.
- Recognize the high-risk areas of practice operations on which the compliance program should concentrate.
- Appreciate the importance of appointing a practice-wide Compliance Officer, proper retention of records, and maintaining open lines of communication.

INTRODUCTION

Physician practices take a variety of forms. They range from the few remaining solo practice doctors (some still working out of home offices) to group practices with several hundred physicians. Modest-size practices may be composed of doctors from a single specialty. The larger groups are usually multispecialty with several locations. They have one thing in common with each other and with all other healthcare providers—the need to comply with the multitude of laws that govern their operations.

The number of laws, particularly at the federal level, dealing with fraud and abuse, and the pressure to know about them and obey them, has grown so great that a passive "hope for the best" attitude will not work. Responsible physician's practices have no choice but to implement aggressive, sophisticated programs to manage their compliance. Furthermore, after the enactment of the Patient Protection and Affordable Care Act (PPACA) of 2010, such programs are mandatory.

This chapter explains the primary legal obligations that apply to physician practices, the ways in which they may affect practice activities, and the terms of a compliance program that ensures the obligations will be met.

SOURCES OF COMPLIANCE OBLIGATION

Physician practices must comply with a variety of laws. Some examples are hour and wage laws, employment discrimination statutes, occupational and safety laws, financial reporting laws, and licensing and accreditation laws. The largest number of laws that have made compliance programs a necessity are federal statutes dealing with fraud and abuse and focusing on healthcare organizations. These are the most important such laws.

Fraud and Abuse Laws

There are five categories of federal laws governing potential fraud and abuse by physician practices: the False Claims Act, the Anti-Kickback Statute, the Physician Self-Referral Law, the Exclusion Authorities, and the Civil Monetary Penalties Law (CMPL). The laws are enforced by three federal government agencies: the Department of Justice (DOJ), the Centers for Medicare and Medicaid Services (CMS), and the OIG in the Department of Health and Human Services (DHHS).

False Claims Act (FCA)

The civil FCA makes it illegal for any person or organization (e.g., a physician practice), in health care or any other industry, to submit a claim for payment to the government (e.g., Medicare and Medicaid) that it knows or should know is false or fraudulent. Filing false claims may result in fines against the practice equal to as much as three times the loss suffered by the government plus $11,000 per false claim filed. Physician practices submit hundreds or thousands of claims annually, so the total fines can add up quickly.

Under the FCA, the practice does not need to *intend* to commit fraud. It is sufficient if the practice had actual *knowledge* of the fraud or acted in deliberate ignorance or reckless disregard of the truth or falsity of the relevant information. The civil FCA also allows private individuals (i.e., "whistle-blowers") to file a lawsuit on behalf of the federal government and receive a share of the money that is recovered. A whistle-blower could be a physician, a staff member, a vendor or contractor, a business partner, a competitor, or a patient—anybody who becomes aware of fraudulent behavior.

Anti-Kickback Statute (AKS)

The AKS is a criminal law that prohibits the knowing and willful payment of any form of "remuneration" to induce or reward patient referrals or other sources of revenue involving a service or item payable by a federal health program. This applies to medical services, drugs, equipment, and supplies that may be reimbursed under Medicare or Medicaid. The remuneration can take many forms besides cash: free rent on space in a medical office building, free meals and stays at expensive hotels, and excessive compensation for medical directorships or consultancies. The statute applies both to the parties offering or paying the kickbacks and to those soliciting or receiving the kickbacks.

There are both criminal and administrative penalties for violations of the AKS. Violators may receive monetary fines, jail terms, and exclusion from participation in federal healthcare programs like Medicare and Medicaid. In addition, under the CMPL, physicians, groups, or organizations that pay or accept kickbacks face penalties of up to $50,000 per kickback plus three times the amount of the remuneration involved.

Parties can avoid liability under the AKS by arranging their payment and business practices so that they come within one of several available Safe Harbors. These cover arrangements like personal service and management agreements, space rental agreements, investments in ambulatory service centers, payments to bona fide employees, and referral services. To receive full protection, an arrangement must satisfy all requirements of the particular Safe Harbor.

Although the AKS usually applies to providers and payors, it is also possible for patients to become implicated. For instance, there are Safe Harbors dealing with the waiver of copayments and the offering of free or discounted services.

Physician Self-Referral Law (Stark Law)

The law prohibits a physician from making referrals for certain "designated health services" payable by Medicare or Medicaid to an entity with which he or she (or an immediate family member) has a financial relationship (ownership, investment, or compensation), unless an exception applies. It prohibits the entity from presenting or causing to be presented claims to Medicare (or billing another individual, entity, or third-party payor) for those referred services. It establishes a number of specific exceptions and grants the Secretary of Health and Human Services the authority to create regulatory exceptions for financial relationships that do not pose a risk of program or patient abuse.

The "designated health services" include the following:

- Clinical laboratory services
- Physical therapy services
- Occupational therapy services
- Outpatient speech-language pathology services
- Radiology and certain other imaging services
- Radiation therapy services and supplies
- Durable medical equipment (DME) and supplies
- Parenteral and enteral nutrients, equipment, and supplies
- Prosthetics, orthotics, and prosthetic devices and supplies
- Home health services
- Outpatient prescription drugs
- Inpatient and outpatient hospital services

The law includes physician-related exceptions for:

- Physician services personally provided by another physician in the same group practice
- In-office ancillary services personally furnished by the referring physician
- Electronic prescribing
- Financial relationships based on ownership or investment interests in publicly traded securities and mutual funds
- Rental of office space or equipment through written leases that satisfy specified criteria
- Bona fide employment relationships
- Personal service arrangements
- Remuneration unrelated to the provision of designated health services
- Physician recruitment
- Isolated transactions such as the one-time sale of a practice or other property
- Certain group practice arrangements with a hospital
- Payments by a physician for items and services (e.g., clinical laboratory services)

The Stark Law is a strict liability statute; proof of specific intent to violate the law is not necessary. It is sufficient that the law was violated, even inadvertently or recklessly. As a practical matter, the law prohibits a person or entity from submitting or causing to be submitted any claim for payment that violates the restrictions on referrals.

The possible penalties for a violation include denial of payment for the provision of a designated health service under prohibited circumstances. If a person receives payment from an individual for services billed in violation of the law, he/she must refund the amount collected in a timely manner. A person who submits a bill or claim in violation of this law may be subject to a civil monetary penalty of not more than $15,000 for each service provided. In cases where hundreds or thousands of claims are involved, the total civil monetary penalties can be very high. A physician or other entity that enters into an arrangement (such as a cross-referral scheme) that has a principal purpose of ensuring referrals by the physician to the entity (in an attempt to circumvent the literal language of the Stark Law), a civil monetary penalty of not more than $100,000 may be assessed for each such arrangement.

Exclusion Statute

This law requires that the OIG exclude from participation in any federal healthcare programs individuals and entities convicted of the following types of criminal offense:

- Medicare or Medicaid fraud, including any other offenses related to the delivery of items or services under Medicare or Medicaid
- Patient abuse or neglect
- Felony convictions for other healthcare-related fraud, theft, or other financial misconduct
- Felony convictions for unlawful manufacture, distribution, prescription, or dispensing of controlled substances

The OIG also has the discretion to exclude individuals and organizations for other reasons, including:

- Misdemeanor convictions related to other forms of healthcare fraud
- Suspension, revocation, or surrender of a license to provide health care for reasons bearing on professional competence, professional performance, or financial integrity
- Provision of unnecessary or substandard services
- Submission of false or fraudulent claims to a federal health program
- Engaging in unlawful kickback arrangements
- Defaulting on health education loan or scholarship obligations

Of all possible penalties for fraud, exclusion may be the worst in the long term. It means that Medicare, Medicaid, and other federal healthcare programs, like TRICARE and the Veterans Health Administration (VHA), major sources of revenue for many practices, will not pay for items or services that a physician or a practice orders, prescribes, or provides. Individual excluded physicians may not bill directly for treating Medicare or Medicaid patients nor bill indirectly through a group practice or an employer. Furthermore, private-pay patients who receive an order or prescription from an excluded physician may not seek reimbursement from a federal healthcare program.

To protect fully against exclusion, a physician must avoid employing or contracting with excluded individuals or entities. This might occur in the context of a physician practice, a clinic, or any setting in which a federal healthcare program may reimburse for the items or services furnished by those excluded parties. To avoid potential liability, the physician or his/her practice need to check the OIG List of Excluded Individuals/Entities on the OIG website[1] prior to hiring or contracting with individuals or entities. After that, healthcare providers should periodically check that website to determine the participation/exclusion status of current employees and contractors. The website contains OIG program exclusion information and is maintained in both on-line searchable and downloadable formats. This information is updated on a regular basis. The website classifies excluded individuals and entities by: (1) the legal basis for the exclusion, (2) the types of individuals and entities that have been excluded, and (3) the state where the excluded individual resided at the time they were excluded or the state where the entity was doing business. The entire exclusion file may be downloaded for parties to set up their own databases of excluded parties.

Civil Monetary Penalties Law (CMPL)

Under this statute, the OIG is authorized to seek civil monetary penalties that vary according to the type of violation committed. The penalties range from $10,000 to $50,000 per violation. They may target violations like these:

- Presenting a claim that the person knows or should know is for an item or service that was not provided as claimed or is false or fraudulent
- Presenting a claim that the person knows or should know is for an item or service for which payment may not be made

[1] Available at http://oig.hhs.gov/

- Violating the AKS
- Violating Medicare assignment provisions
- Violating the Medicare physician agreement
- Providing false or misleading information expected to influence a decision to discharge
- Failing to provide an adequate medical screening examination for patients who present to a hospital emergency department with an emergency medical condition or in labor
- Making false statements or misrepresentations on applications or contracts to participate in the federal healthcare programs

Licensing, Certification, and Credentialing—Physicians and Other Clinical Staff

All physicians in active practice, as well as certain other clinicians, must be licensed in the states where they work. Physicians also have the option of earning certification by any of 26 boards representing specific medical specialties. While medical licensure indicates that a physician meets the minimum competency requirements to diagnosis and treats a wide range of basic medical problems, board certification is evidence that he/she has exceptional expertise in a specialty or subspecialty of medical practice. A state medical license is valid indefinitely—until it is suspended or revoked for some reason. Board certification needs to be renewed every 6–10 years to demonstrate that the physician's clinical knowledge and skills are up to date. States sometimes require that physicians who perform certain office-based procedures register their practice offices.

If a physician intends to admit patients to one or more hospitals and treat them there, he/she must be a member of the hospital's medical staff, must have admitting privileges, and must be permitted to perform a strictly defined range of clinical services. The process for obtaining these authorizations is called "credentialing" and must be done every 3 years.

Accreditation

Occasionally, a physician practice may operate a facility or service that qualifies for voluntary accreditation. For instance, the Joint Commission (the organization primarily responsible for accrediting hospitals) offers accreditation for ambulatory health care, surgery centers, office-based surgery, imaging centers, sleep centers, and urgent care centers. Such accreditations must be renewed at regular intervals.

SPECIFIC APPLICATION OF FEDERAL FRAUD AND ABUSE LAWS TO PHYSICIAN PRACTICES

The several federal fraud and abuse laws prohibit numerous physician activities that are problematic on their face. A few examples are:

- Accepting or soliciting monetary or nonmonetary remuneration in return for patient referrals or orders for goods or services
- Accepting money or gifts from drug companies, medical device manufacturers, or DME suppliers in return for use of their products
- Prescribing tests from a clinical laboratory in which the physician has an ownership interest, without satisfying the legal exception
- Dispensing controlled substances for which the patient has no medical necessity

Beyond those cases, the laws affect physician practice operations in three broad categories: the practice's dealings with other healthcare providers, external vendors, and payors.

Practice Relationships/Interactions/Dealings with Other Healthcare Providers

It is not uncommon for physicians to be invited to invest in healthcare-related businesses in the belief that they will have a special appreciation for the value of the services or products that they are selling. A hospital may be particularly anxious to persuade a physician to relocate to its service area and become a member of its medical staff—either because of the physician's reputation and patient-drawing power or a local shortage in the physician's specialty. To accomplish that goal, it may offer various forms of recruitment incentive to the physician. Problems may arise in both these areas.

Physician Investments in Healthcare-Related Businesses

In their practice of medicine, physicians interact with a wide variety of other healthcare providers, such as specialist physicians, radiologists, hospitals, nursing facilities, laboratory technicians, and physical therapists. All of those providers rely on referrals from physicians; some providers may attempt to offer incentives in return for the referrals. One form of such an incentive is the opportunity for the physician to invest in the organization to which he/she makes referrals. The best examples are imaging centers, diagnostic laboratories, equipment vendors, medical device companies, and physical therapy clinics. Research has shown that physicians make disproportionately more referrals to medical businesses in which they have an ownership interest than businesses that are totally independent.

The physician may make the referrals because he knows that he will share in the profits that the business earns from them. Or, it can be argued that, as an owner of the business, the physician sees more clearly the value of the services that it offers. In any event, such investments should be approached with caution. Every effort should be made to fit the investment agreement within one of the Stark Law exceptions or the AKS Safe Harbors. As a general rule, these exceptions/Safe Harbors require that all transactions be in writing, that prices be based on fair market value (FMV), that the physician's earnings from the business not reflect the volume of referrals that he has made, and that the parties sign the agreement.

These are some warnings that a proposed investment will not be acceptable.

- The physician makes no or little capital investment in return for the ownership interest.
- The business seems to offer very high rates of return for little or no financial risk by the physician.
- The business offers the physician a loan to permit him to make his capital investment.
- The physician is asked to assure that he will refer patients to, or order product or services from, the business.
- The physician expects that he will send more business to the entity without having a good clinical reason for doing so.

Physician Recruitment

Illegal inducements offered by hospitals to physicians who will join their medical staff and make referrals can create legal liability for both parties. It is possible for hospitals to provide legal relocation assistance and practice support for a few years through a carefully designed recruitment arrangement that falls within the specific parameters of the Stark Law and AKS. The simplest solution is to pay a physician employee a FMV salary, or pay FMV reimbursement to an independent contractor physician for specific services rendered to the hospital. The hospital–physician relationship should be structured in this way.

- The arrangement is set out in a signed written agreement.
- It includes no condition that the physician refer patients to the hospital.

- The remuneration paid to the physician is not based on the volume or value of any actual or anticipated referrals by the physician or other business generated between the parties.
- The physician is permitted to establish staff privileges at other hospitals and to refer business to any other entity. Referrals may, however, be restricted under an employment or services contract that complies with Stark's special rules on compensation applicable to bona fide employees or contractors.

There are additional requirements when the recruited physician is a member of a group practice.

- The agreement is in writing and signed by the hospital, the physician, and the group practice.
- The agreement between the physician and the group practice is in writing and signed by both parties.
- The remuneration is passed directly through to, or remains with the recruited physician, except for actual costs incurred by the physician practice in recruiting the new physician.
- Any costs allocated by the physician practice to the recruited physician do not exceed the actual additional incremental costs attributable to the recruited physician.
- The recruited physician establishes his/her practice in the hospital's service area and joins its medical staff.
- Records of the actual costs and the passed-through amounts are maintained for a period of at least 5 years and made available to the DHHS Secretary upon request.
- The physician is not required to refer patients to the hospital and is not prohibited from acquiring staff privileges at other hospitals.
- The remuneration is not determined in a manner that takes into account the volume or value of any actual or anticipated referrals by the recruited physician or the physician practice (or any physician affiliated with the physician practice) receiving the direct payments from the hospital.
- The physician practice does not impose on the recruited physician, practice restrictions that unreasonably restrict the recruited physician's ability to practice medicine in the geographic area served by the hospital. Noncompete and similar restrictions are permitted if they do not unreasonably restrict the recruited physician's ability to practice medicine in the geographic area serviced by the hospital. Some other practice restrictions are acceptable—on matters like moonlighting, solicitation of patients and employees, confidentiality

agreements, repayment obligations, and liquidated damages for breach of the recruitment agreement.
- The arrangement may not violate the AKS or any federal or state law or regulation governing billing or claims submission.

Physicians are sometimes asked to serve as the medical director of a hospital, hospital department, nursing home, or other facility. The purpose of such arrangements is not to steer payments to the physician in return for referring patients to the facility. The legitimate function of a medical director is to actively oversee clinical care in the facility; lead the medical staff to meet the standard of care; ensure proper training, education, and oversight for physicians, nurses, and other staff members; and identify and address quality problems. A medical directorship agreement should be a written, signed document that pays FMV for services actually rendered and without regard for the volume or value of referrals made.

Physician Relationships/Interactions/Dealings with External Vendors

Most external vendors in the healthcare industry are for-profit entities eager to persuade physicians to order their products or services for their patients. Some of the enticements they offer may be illegal.

Free Samples

Physicians are not required to welcome visits from pharmaceutical sales representatives. If they do, they can expect to be offered free product samples. It is legal for a physician to give these samples to patients free of charge, normally in cases where the patient otherwise could not afford them. It is illegal to sell the free samples to patients. If a physician practice chooses to accept free samples, it must have in place a facility for storing the samples in a way that segregates them from commercial drug inventory.

Physician–Industry Collaboration

Valuable medical advances can result when physicians share their expertise with pharmaceutical and medical device companies. However, those noble interests are not served when the companies use sham consulting agreements to buy physician loyalty for their products. Such perverse incentives distort the physicians' clinical decision-making and can lead to choices not in the best interests of patients. When a physician is offered the opportunity to work as a consultant or conference speaker for a drug or device sponsor, there should be rough equivalence between the compensation to be received and the services that will be provided. The compensation should represent FMV for the services, without regard for the physician's ability to refer patients. If the industry sponsor shows no interest in the physician's qualifications as a consultant and expects no advance preparation for a presentation, there is a strong likelihood that the offer violates the fraud and abuse laws.

Open Physician–Industry Relationships

Some drug, biologic, and device companies also will offer free lunches, other gifts, and subsidized trips to physicians in an effort to influence their prescribing practices. Accepting these offers constitutes a conflict of interest, whether or not the physician believes that they affect his/her judgment. There is pressure from several sources to reveal all industry payments and gifts to physicians, whether they are legal or not. Recent settlements by drug companies with the DOJ and the OIG have required that the companies provide those agencies with a list of the physicians they have paid or make ongoing public disclosure of all physician payments. The PPACA requires drug, device, and biologic companies to publicly report nearly all gifts or payments they make to physicians beginning in 2013. More and more academic research institutions are imposing restrictions on the dealings between their researchers, faculty members, and affiliated physicians and medical industry companies. These factors should be taken into account before a physician agrees to conduct industry-sponsored research, serve as a consultant for a drug, biologic, or device company, or apply for industry-sponsored research or education grants.

Conflict of Interest Disclosure

In addition to increased pressure on drug and other companies to reveal their payments to doctors, the physicians themselves are expected or required to disclose their conflicts of interest, whether legal or not. Conflict of interest policies are imposed by academic institutions, research facilities, state and federal grant sources (e.g., National Institutes of Health), and the Food and Drug Administration (FDA) in connection with applications for premarket approval of drugs or devices. Responsible physicians inform themselves about conflict of interest policies to which they are subject, honestly report any payments that fall under the policies, and manage their activities to minimize unethical influences. Err on the side of fuller disclosure.

Physician Relationships/Interactions/Dealings with Payors

One of the most problematic areas for fraud and abuse in a physician practice is its interactions with payors. The U.S. healthcare system relies extensively on third-party payors for the reimbursement of goods and services provided to patients. Patients themselves rarely pay the bills. Out-of-pocket payments by patients cover about 12% of all spending on health care.[2] Third-party payors are primarily private commercial insurers and public healthcare programs like Medicare and Medicaid. When the federal government pays for goods and services for Medicare and Medicaid beneficiaries, the federal fraud and abuse laws apply. Keep in mind that many states have adopted similar laws that cover state reimbursement programs and private payors. Physician practices should be concerned with potential payment fraud and abuse with all insured patients. Possible problems in this area include coding and billing, documentation of services provided, enrollment with CMS as a healthcare provider, authority to prescribe controlled substances, and acceptance of Medicare assignment.

Coding and Billing

Payments by Medicare or Medicaid for services provided to patients depend to a large degree on claims and documentation by the physicians who delivered the services. When a physician practice submits a claim for services it has performed for a Medicare or Medicaid beneficiary, it is sending a "payment due" bill to the federal government and certifying that it has earned the payment requested and complied with related billing requirements. Government payors have a wide variety of powerful criminal, civil, and administrative enforcement tools to use against physicians who violate that trust. If the practice knew or should have known that a claim it has submitted was false, it has committed a violation of federal law.

The government has the authority and means to audit claims and investigate providers when it suspects fraud. Suspicions of fraud and abuse may arise because of irregular billing patterns or complaints from "whistleblowers" (e.g., employees, patients, vendors, and competitors).

Fraud and abuse through coding and billing can take different forms. The specific service that a physician claims to have delivered is identified by an alphanumeric code.[3] A common basis for a false claim is "upcoding,"

[2] National Health Expenditure Projections 2010–2020: http://www.cms.gov/Research-Statistics-Data-and-Systems/Statistics-Trends-and-Reports/NationalHealthExpendData/NationalHealthAccountsProjected.html

[3] The current ICD-9 codes have been in effect for over 30 years. The services they describe have changed; the codes do not reflect the latest advances in medical technology and knowledge. In addition, the format limits the ability to expand the code set and add new codes. They are being replaced, by the year 2014, with the ICD-10 codes. For instance, ICD-10-CM codes are the ones designated for use in documenting diagnoses. They are three to seven characters in length and total 68,000, while ICD-9-CM diagnosis codes are three to five digits in length and number over 14,000. The ICD-10-PCS are the procedure codes and they are alphanumeric, seven characters in length, and total approximately 87,000, while ICD-9-CM procedure codes are only three to four numbers in length and total approximately 4,000 codes.

whereby a physician uses billing codes that indicate a more severe illness than actually existed or a more expensive treatment than was actually provided. Other examples of fraudulent coding are:

- Billing for services that the physician did not actually render
- Billing for services that were not medically necessary
- Billing for services that were performed by an improperly supervised or unqualified employee
- Billing for services that were performed by an employee who has been excluded from participation in the federal healthcare programs
- Billing for services of such low quality that they are virtually worthless
- Billing separately for services already included in a global fee, like billing for an evaluation and management (E&M) service the day after surgery

Documentation of Services Provided

A physician must be able to present accurate and complete medical records and other documentation to substantiate the services he/she has provided. If they have questions, the Medicare or Medicaid programs may review a practice's medical files. In addition to helping the physician respond to billing questions, good documentation practices[4] ensure that patients receive appropriate care from the physician and other providers, such as referral specialists, who rely on patients' medical histories.

Enrollment with CMS as a Healthcare Provider

In order to receive reimbursements from the federal government for services provided to Medicare and Medicaid patients, physicians must be enrolled in the Medicare and Medicaid programs. This is a three-step process.

1. Obtain a National Provider Identifier (NPI) number that uniquely identifies each healthcare provider.[5]
2. Complete the Medicare Enrollment Application.[6]
3. Complete the Medicaid Enrollment Application in each relevant state.

---

[4] See the CMS Documentation Guidelines for Evaluation and Management (E/M) Services at http://www.cms.gov/Outreach-and-Education/Medicare-Learning-Network-MLN/MLNEdWebGuide/EMDOC.html

[5] Available at https://nppes.cms.hhs.gov/NPPES/Welcome.do

[6] Available at http://www.cms.gov/Medicare/Provider-Enrollment-and-Certification/MedicareProviderSupEnroll/index.html

Once enrolled, the physician must ensure that every action taken in his name and under his provider number is legal, true, and accurate. In particular, only correct and honest claims must be filed under the number of the provider of the services underlying the claims.

Authority to Prescribe Controlled Substances

A physician in active practice must possess up-to-date credentials for writing drug prescriptions. This starts with obtaining from the Drug Enforcement Administration (DEA) a number that authorizes the physician to prescribe controlled substances. Individual states also require licensing and other credentials in order to write prescriptions. It is important to keep all these forms of authorization up to date.

Acceptance of Medicare Assignment

When a physician bills Medicare as an enrolled participating provider, he/she is "accepting assignment." By accepting assignment, the physician agrees that he/she will be satisfied with the Medicare payment he/she receives plus any copayment or deductible that Medicare requires the patient to pay. The physician may not seek any additional payments from the patient for services covered by Medicare. To do so is a violation of the physician's assignment agreement and may result in penalties.

Physicians who are not participating Medicare providers (do not have assignment agreements) do not receive payment directly from the Medicare program. Instead, they bill their patients who then must seek reimbursement from Medicare and those bill amounts may not be more than 15% higher than the Medicare fee schedule amount. To do otherwise is illegal.

These limits on physician billing of patients are also relevant to boutique or concierge practices that offer additional personalized services to patients in return for all-inclusive monthly or annual fees. The fees must not apply to services that are already covered by Medicare or they will be considered illegal double-billing.

COMPLIANCE PROGRAMS FOR INDIVIDUAL AND SMALL PHYSICIAN PRACTICES

A compliance program is a system of internal controls that enables a physician practice to more efficiently monitor its adherence to the numerous statutes, regulations, and administrative requirements that apply to them. Beginning over 10 years ago, the OIG has issued a series of guidelines for the creation of compliance programs by several major types of healthcare entities.[7] These guidelines are called Compliance Program Guidances. In 2000, the OIG released a Guidance for Individual and Small Group Physician Practices.

That Program Guidance describes seven components that the OIG considers a "solid basis" for building a voluntary compliance program.

- Conduct internal monitoring and auditing
- Implement compliance and practice standards
- Designate a compliance officer or contact
- Conduct appropriate training and education
- Respond appropriately to detected offenses and develop corrective action
- Develop open lines of communication with employees
- Enforce disciplinary standards through well-publicized guidelines

In recommending the implementation of a compliance program, the OIG acknowledges that most physician practices have more limited financial personnel resources than large entities like hospitals and nursing homes. For those practices, it lays out a phased step-by-step approach to developing a compliance infrastructure.

There is no single model for a physician practice compliance program. The scope and focus of the program will depend on the practice's resources, the compliance risk areas that exist in its operations, and its history of compliance problems. The compliance program that emerges should be tailored to the unique needs of the practice.

Compliance Programs Are Mandatory, Not Voluntary

For over a decade, the OIG had strongly urged healthcare providers, including physicians, to voluntarily adopt compliance programs. With the passage of the PPACA of 2010, physicians who treat Medicare and Medicaid beneficiaries are now required to establish a compliance program. Section 6401[8] of the PPACA specifically provides that healthcare providers must establish a compliance program that contains certain "core elements" as a condition of enrollment in government healthcare programs.

---

[7] Currently, the OIG has issued Compliance Program Guidances for the following eight industry sectors: hospitals, clinical laboratories, home health agencies, DME suppliers, third-party medical billing companies, hospices, Medicare + Choice organizations offering coordinated care plans, and nursing facilities. They are available at the OIG website: http://oig.hhs.gov/compliance/compliance-guidance

[8] 42 USCA §1395cc(j)(8)

Benefits of a Voluntary Compliance Program

There are tangible benefits from adopting a compliance program, some quite obvious, others not so apparent. The preparation and submission of claims will be sped up, resulting in faster reimbursements and improved cash flow. Greater accuracy in the coding of claims reduces the likelihood that payors will return claims for correction or clarification. The very existence of the compliance program demonstrates that the practice is making a good faith effort to submit claims according to CMS terms. That, plus the fewer noncompliance incidents that result, will reduce the chances that the CMS or OIG will want to audit the practice. The practice also is more likely to avoid conflicts with the Physician Self-Referral Law and AKS.

By maintaining maximum accuracy of clinical documentation, the program ensures that patients receive exactly the services they need and are prescribed. The visible operation of the program sends an important message to the practice's employees: that the practice takes very seriously the strict adherence to all government regulations and requirements and that the employees have an ethical duty to follow the program's conditions.

Innocent Errors Are Not Intentional Fraud

Some physicians are unclear whether the inadvertent, or even negligent, errors that they may make will be treated the same as intentional or recklessly fraudulent medical service claims. They are worried that innocent billing mistakes will subject them to criminal, civil, or administrative penalties. There is no reason for physicians to be concerned.

The FCA applies only to misdeeds that are committed with actual knowledge, reckless disregard, or deliberate ignorance of the falsity of the claim. It does not extend to mistakes, errors, or negligence. The CMPL, which offers administrative remedies, uses the same standard of proof as the FCA. Whenever a potential for criminal penalties exists, the standard is even higher—criminal intent to defraud proven beyond a reasonable doubt.

Without a provable violation of a criminal, civil, or administrative law, the only result of an erroneous claims filing is the return of any excess funds claimed and received in error.

MULTISTEP VOLUNTARY COMPLIANCE PROGRAM

A physician practice without substantial resources and previous compliance experience would be wise to develop a new compliance program through a series of graduated steps. The OIG suggests the following steps, designed to build a program composed of the seven recommended components. Initial development of the program might start with the risk areas that have posed the greatest problems in the past; frequently this is coding and billing. Within each area, the practice would review its claims denial, history, then identify and correct the most common sources of denials or overpayments.

Step One—Auditing and Monitoring

An ongoing evaluation process determines whether the practice's standards and procedures are accurate and up to date, and whether the overall program is proving effective. It discovers current problems and the risk areas associated with them. There are two types of reviews that might be part of this process.

> *Standards and procedures review.* This activity periodically examines existing standards and procedures to make sure that they are current and complete. Any gaps or obsolescence that is found should result in updates to reflect changes in government regulations or requirements, or other authoritative resources (e.g., coding guidelines).
>
> *Claims submission audit.* In this function, the practice person in charge of billing and a medically trained person collaborate to appraise bills and medical records for compliance with applicable coding, billing, and documentation requirements. The appraisal may be conducted on claims previously filed (retrospectively) or as they are being filed (concurrently).

The purpose of the initial claims audit is to establish a baseline or benchmark from which the practice can measure its progress toward improved compliance. The baseline audit examines the claim development and submission process, from patient intake through claim submission to final payment. It focuses on questions like these.

- Are bills accurately coded and do they accurately reflect the services provided?
- Is all relevant documentation being completed correctly?
- Are the services and items provided reasonable and necessary?
- Do any incentives exist to provide unnecessary services?

Once the baseline is established, periodic audits should be carried out at least once a year. An audit examines a randomly selected sample of medical records for coding accuracy. A typical sample is five or more medical records for each federal payor (Medicare or Medicaid) or 5–10 medical records per physician. If problems begin to emerge during the regular audits, more focused reviews on a larger sample should be conducted on a more frequent basis.

One of the key measures of success of a compliance audit is the response of a physician's practice when it reveals a problem. The specific action taken will depend on the circumstances and should occur immediately. Sometimes, the only necessary remedy is the repayment of monies received improperly with an explanation of the cause of the overpayment. If the matter seems more complex and serious, and the practice lacks the necessary in-house expertise, it probably is a good idea to consult with a coding/billing expert or a health law attorney. Create in advance a protocol for handling compliance issues as they arise.

Step Two—Establish Practice Standards and Procedures

Even better than responding well to compliance problems when they occur is preventing them from happening in the first place. This is accomplished by preparing written standards and procedures to govern the practice's operations. It begins by identifying high-risk areas within the practice and then setting up tight internal controls to counter the risks.

A physician practice creating its first compliance program may find it easier to get started by adopting the compliance standards and procedures of a third party with whom it has a relationship. Such parties could include an independent practice association (IPA), physician-hospital organization (PHO), accountable care organization (ACO), management services organization (MSO), third-party billing company, or a professional association like the Medical Group Management Association (MGMA). Another early initiative might be the assembly of a resource manual from publicly available information. As the practice gains experience, the manual grows to include the practice's own standards and procedures, relevant CMS directives, bulletins from private carriers and Medicare claims administrators, and OIG documents like Special Fraud Alerts, Advisory Opinions, Inspection and Audit Reports, and Annual Work Plans. This manual must be updated regularly and kept in an accessible form and place. Employees should be trained regularly in changes to the manual.

Because more modest-sized physician practices may lack the resources to establish a comprehensive, all-encompassing compliance program, the OIG recommends that they concentrate their initial efforts on risk areas where they may be most vulnerable. The agency points to four areas that particularly affect physician practices: coding and billing, reasonable and necessary services, documentation, and improper inducements, kickbacks, and self-referrals. After conducting an internal review, a practice should develop its own high-priority list.

Coding and Billing

In this area, frequent subjects of OIG investigations and audits are:

- Billing for items or services not rendered or not provided as claimed
- Submitting claims for equipment, medical supplies, and services that are not reasonable and necessary
- Double-billing resulting in duplicate payment
- Billing for noncovered services as if covered
- Knowing misuse of provider identification numbers, leading to improper billing
- Unbundling (billing for each component of a service rather than using the all-inclusive code that covers all its components)
- Improper use of coding modifiers
- Clustering (charging one or two average levels of service codes exclusively in the belief that some are actually higher or lower)
- Upcoding the level of service provided

The written standards and procedures should guard against all of these non compliant activities, whether intentional or accidental. Particular attention should be devoted to codes for diagnoses, and for E&M services.

Reasonable and Necessary Services

The practice's controls must ensure that claims are submitted only for services that its physicians find "reasonable and necessary" for the care of each particular patient. Medicare will only pay for services that meet its definition of that term—"for the diagnosis or treatment of illness or injury or to improve the functioning of a malformed body member."[9]

Documentation

Timely, accurate, and complete documentation verifies that a bill is correct as submitted. The documentation in this case takes the form of patient medical records and required payor forms like the CMS 1500 form.

Improper Inducements, Kickbacks, and Self-Referrals

All arrangements through which the practice refers patients to, or orders goods or services from, an external party, business, or vendor should be expressed in FMV terms. That means that the prices charged or paid for

[9] 42 USC. §1395y(a)(1)(A)

goods or services should be approximately those that would be charged or paid in the open market. Such arrangements are likely to exist with hospitals, hospices, nursing facilities, home health agencies, DME suppliers, and pharmaceutical manufacturers. Whenever the practice enters into such an arrangement, it should have the written contract reviewed by an experienced health lawyer.

The standards and procedures should address these kinds of arrangements:

- Financial relationships with outside entities to whom the practice may refer business that will be reimbursed by Medicare or Medicaid
- Joint ventures with entities supplying goods or services to the practice or its patients
- Consulting contracts or medical directorships
- Office and equipment leases with entities (e.g., hospitals) to which the physician refers

The standards and procedures also should prohibit the offering of inappropriate inducements to patients to win and retain their business. An example of unacceptable incentives is the routine waiver of coinsurance or deductibles without making sure that the patient is in financial need or trying to collect the cost-sharing amounts.

Retention of Records

It is important that the standards and procedures contain language on the retention of records, both clinical and business. This includes documents relating to patient care and to the practice's business activities, as well as internal audit results, internal investigations, and training/education efforts. The OIG recommends keeping them all in a binder.

Because there are legal implications to the way an organization manages its records, it is a good idea to institute a record management policy governing the creation, distribution, retention, and destruction of documents. The policy should take into account privacy concerns and federal and state laws on record retention. These are some typical document policy topics.

- The minimum length of time that different types of practice records must be retained
- The need to protect medical records against loss, destruction, unauthorized access, unauthorized reproduction, corruption, and damage
- The disposition of the medical records if the practice is closed or sold

Step Three—Designation of a Compliance Officer

After a baseline audit has been completed, high-risk areas have been identified, and an initial version of compliance standards and procedures have been developed, the natural next step is to select one member of the staff to oversee implementation of the compliance program. Depending on the size of the practice and the amount of its resources, the position may consume all or only part of the individual's time. For instance, the head of claims and billing may also take responsibility for compliance matters. Alternatively, the various compliance tasks could be allocated among several different staff members. At the very least, when a compliance issue arises, the OIG would like to be able to communicate with a single contact person within the practice.

The designated person or persons will handle the following tasks:

- Overseeing and monitoring the implementation of the compliance program.
- Establishing methods, such as periodic audits, to improve the practice's efficiency and quality of services and to reduce the practice's vulnerability to fraud and abuse.
- Periodically revising the compliance program in light of changes in the needs of the practice or changes in the law and the requirements of government and private payor health plans.
- Developing, coordinating, and participating in an employee training program that focuses on the components of the compliance program.
- Ensuring that the DHHS-OIG's List of Excluded Individuals and Entities, and the General Services Administration's (GSA's) List of Parties Debarred from Federal Programs have been checked with respect to all employees, medical staff, and independent contractors.
- Investigating any report or allegation concerning possible unethical or improper business practices and monitoring subsequent corrective action and/or compliance.

Step Four—Conducting Appropriate Training and Education

The practice now needs to provide education and training to its employees on the details of the compliance program that it has created, and how they must adapt their work behaviors to the requirements of the program. The training normally will focus on two areas—compliance and coding/billing, although the two can be combined. Begin by deciding which employees need training in each area. Then, determine the best format for the training:

in-person conducted in-house or by a third party (e.g., professional association, private payor/carrier, or community college), interactive web-based instruction, postings on physical or network bulletin boards, and various printed materials.

Compliance Training

Every employee should receive an initial training followed by update sessions at regular intervals. The training deals with both the underlying laws and regulations, and the terms of the practice's compliance program. The agenda should include a description of how the program operates, why it is important to the practice, the consequences of violating the program's standards and procedures, and the responsibilities of each employee in implementing the program.

Coding/Billing Training

This training ensures that staff who are responsible for coding, billing, and related functions understand the legal and compliance program standards they must satisfy. Among these standards are:

- Coding rules
- Claim preparation and submission procedures
- Proper signatures on physician authorization forms
- Proper documentation of services provided
- Submission of accurate bills for goods and services that meet billing standards and procedures

Step Five—Responding to Detected Offenses and Developing Corrective Action Plans

At this point, the practice should have a functional compliance program and employees who have been trained in its requirements. The real test of the program occurs when a noncompliance event is detected, triggering responses designed to correct it. Of course, an ideal program will prevent such events from happening at all.

The practice typically learns about such events through reports by individuals (e.g., employees, patients, and vendors), or unusual, extraordinary deviations from normal operations like dramatic changes in the number or types of claim denials, payor questions about the medical necessity or validity of claims, illogical patterns of code utilization, excessive coding errors, medical record inaccuracies, or evidence that services billed were not delivered. The practice may wish to consult with its health lawyer to ascertain the nature and gravity of the apparent violations.

Once noncompliance is detected, decisive action should be taken to correct it. The action could consist of a formal plan of changes in operating procedures, the return of overpayments to the payor, disclosure to a government agency, or referral to law enforcement authorities. It also may be appropriate to retrain, discipline, or dismiss the employees involved in the event.

In some cases, the practice may discover weeks or months later that a compliance violation occurred. This may be the result of a flaw in the program's detection methods; changes in those methods will be necessary.

Step Six—Developing Open Lines of Communication

The OIG values open communication so highly that it is one of the steps that it recommends for an effective compliance program. This refers to communications from employees, contractors, patients, or members of the public about suspected violations of law, failure to follow policies and procedures, or other forms of misconduct. Larger organizations can afford more elaborate, formal communication media. A physician practice of more modest size might start with a simple "open door" policy among compliance personnel, physicians, and other employees. This can be supplemented with notices posted in common areas, and on physical and electronic bulletin boards.

A good compliance communication system might include the following elements:

- A requirement that employees report conduct that they reasonably consider to be erroneous or fraudulent
- A statement that failure to report erroneous or fraudulent conduct is itself a violation of the compliance program standards and procedures
- An anonymous mechanism for reporting such conduct
- A simple, speedy procedure for processing the reports received
- Coordination with outside vendors, such as billing companies and medical transcription services, in managing compliance activities
- A method that protects the anonymity of the persons reporting suspicious conduct and the persons alleged to have engaged in such conduct
- Absolute assurance that a person reporting erroneous/fraudulent conduct will not suffer retaliation

At the very least, practice employees must know to whom they can turn for assistance in dealing with actual, suspected, or hypothetical compliance problems.

Step Seven—Enforcing Disciplinary Standards Through Well-Publicized Guidelines

Disciplinary measures are called for to ensure that employees fully appreciate the consequences of their noncompliant actions. Like all employee discipline, the sanctions against the employees must be appropriate to the infraction and consistent among all persons involved. The required measures should be flexible enough to take into account mitigating or aggravating circumstances. The practice may wish to apply discipline against both those who commit the violations and those who fail to report them.

The OIG suggests that the practice document any disciplinary actions that it takes in connection with incidents of noncompliance. This should include the date of the incidents, the name of the person who reported the incident, the name of the person who initiated the action, and the exact action taken. This information may prove useful if the OIG or another government agency subsequently becomes involved.

The OIG guidelines describe a compliance program that is well conceived and implemented as the equivalent of preventive medicine—actions taken today that reduce the likelihood of damaging effects in the future.

FURTHER SOURCES OF GUIDANCE ON PHYSICIAN COMPLIANCE

There are several other places that physician practices can look for further guidance on their legal obligations and compliance programs for addressing them.

- Experienced healthcare lawyers can analyze the issues and provide a legal evaluation and risk analysis of a proposed venture, relationship, or arrangement.
- The local state bar association may have a directory of attorneys in the area who practice in the healthcare field.
- A state or local medical society may be a good resource for issues affecting physicians and may have listings of healthcare lawyers in the immediate area.

- The physicians' specialty society may have information on additional risk areas specific to their type of practice.
- The local contractor medical directors for CMS are a valuable source of information on Medicare coverage policies and appropriate billing practices. The contact information for local contractors is available at http://www.cms.gov/MLNGenInfo/30_contactus.asp.
- The CMS's "Medicare Physician Guide: A Resource for Residents, Practicing Physicians, and Other Health Care Professionals" is available at http://www.cms.gov/MLNProducts/downloads/physicianguide.pdf. It provides an overview of the Medicare program and information on Medicare reimbursement and payment policies.
- The OIG's website[10] provides substantial fraud and abuse guidance.
- The OIG Compliance Program Guidance documents include compliance recommendations and discussions of fraud and abuse risk areas. These guidance documents are available at http://oig.hhs.gov/fraud/complianceguidance.asp.
- The OIG issues Advisory Opinions to parties who seek advice on the application of the AKS, CMPL, and Exclusion Authorities. Information on how to request an OIG Advisory Opinion and links to previously published OIG Advisory Opinions are available at http://oig.hhs.gov/fraud/advisoryopinions.asp.
- The CMS issues Advisory Opinions to parties who seek advice on the Stark Law. Information on how to request a CMS Advisory Opinion and links to previously published CMS Advisory Opinions are available at http://www.cms.gov/PhysicianSelfReferral/95_advisory_opinions.asp.

STUDY QUESTIONS

1. What is the difference between the Stark Law and the AKS?
2. For what kinds of violations could a physician or other practice employee be subject to criminal penalties?
3. What kinds of healthcare-related financial investments should a physician avoid?
4. In a few words, explain the terms "upcoding," "unbundling," "clustering," "program exclusion," and "whistle-blower."
5. What is the purpose of a "baseline" claims audit in establishing a compliance program?

---

[10] Available at http://oig.hhs.gov

6. List five things that might happen to a physician practice that chose NOT to implement a compliance program.
7. What is the difference between an honest mistake in filing a medical claim and the sort of misdeed that leads to liability under one of the fraud and abuse laws?

Learning Exercises

1. Both the pharmaceutical industry and the medical device industry have adopted codes of ethics governing their relationships with healthcare professionals. Visit these websites and note the types of unethical behavior that they prohibit. Do you think that they offer adequate protection and guidance for employees in those industries? Suggest three ways in which the codes could be improved.
   - PhRMA code of ethics—http://www.phrma.org/about/principles-guidelines/code-interactions-healthcare-professionals
   - AdvaMed code of ethics—http://advamed.org/issues/1/-span-class-highlightedwords-code-/span-of-ethics
2. With the help of an instructor, contact a local physician group practice, preferably one with five or more physicians. On the basis of your learning from this chapter, interview the person in the practice most responsible for compliance matters. The purpose of the interview is to acquire information about the structure of the practice's compliance program. Prepare your questions in advance of the interview.

   Ask to see a copy of the manual or standards and procedures dealing with compliance. How often do they update the standards and procedures? What steps do they take to encourage employees to report possible noncompliance incidents? Do not be surprised if the practice representative prefers not to discuss actual incidents of non compliance. However, it still might be worth asking.
3. Imagine that you are an entrepreneur with an idea for using the Internet to conduct remote monitoring of the medical conditions of patients with chronic diseases. Both Medicare and some private payors have agreed to reimburse for the monitoring service if a physician prescribes it for his/her patients. For startup funding, you would like to approach physicians who might see the clinical value of your new venture. Exactly how would you structure the financial relationship between the physician-investors and the venture? In what physician specialties would you seek investors?

References

1. U.S. Department of Health & Human Services, Office of Inspector General, "A Roadmap for New Physicians: Avoiding Medicare and Medicaid Fraud and Abuse," available at https://oig.hhs.gov/compliance/physician-education/index.asp
2. U.S. Department of Health & Human Services, Office of Inspector General, "OIG Compliance Program for Individual and Small Group Physician Practices" Federal Register, Vol. 65, No. 194, October 5, 2000, available at https://oig.hhs.gov/compliance/compliance-guidance/index.asp
3. Cynthia S. Marietta, J.D., LL.M., Health Law Perspectives (July 2011), Health Law & Policy Institute, University of Houston Law Center, "Small Group Physicians and Other HealthCare Providers: Now is the Time to Structure Your Mandatory Compliance Programs," available at http://www.law.uh.edu/healthlaw/perspectives/homepage.asp

Chapter 17

Nursing and Long-Term Care Facilities

Learning Objectives

After completing class sessions based on this chapter, a student will:

- Be familiar with different types of long-term care (LTC) facilities and the services that they provide to residents.
- Appreciate the scope of the nursing facilities industry.
- Be introduced to the compliance program mandate imposed on nursing facilities by the 2010 Patient Protection and Affordable Care Act.
- Recognize the benefits to a nursing facility of a compliance program.
- Understand how the basic elements of a recommended compliance program work in a nursing facility setting.
- Have received detailed knowledge about the primary compliance risk areas in nursing facilities.
- Realize the prevalence of healthcare fraud in the nursing facilities industry.

INTRODUCTION

The terms "nursing facility" and "LTC facility" encompass a wide range of institutions designed to meet different needs of elderly, disabled, and terminally ill people.

Nursing home. For its residents, a nursing home provides the highest level of care available outside of a hospital. This includes custodial care–help with feeding, bathing, dressing, and getting in and out of bed. Nursing homes differ from other senior housing facilities in that they also provide a high level of medical care. A licensed physician supervises each patient's care and a nurse or other medical professional is almost always on the premises. Skilled nursing care is available on site, usually 24 hours a day. Other medical professionals such as occupational or physical therapists may also be on staff.

The costs of nursing home care vary widely from state to state. They average around $80,000 a year. Insurance coverage for these costs is a patchwork. Medicare only covers limited stays in nursing homes. Skilled nursing or rehabilitation services are covered for a period of about 100 days after a hospitalization. Medicare does not cover custodial care if that is the only care needed. Residents with limited income and assets may qualify for Medicaid, which does cover most costs of nursing home care. However, all nursing homes do not necessarily accept Medicaid reimbursement.

There are two categories of nursing homes. Intermediate care facilities (ICFs) have certified nursing assistants (CNAs) on staff 24 hours a day rather than nurses and provide primarily assistance with the "activities of daily living," a common term that covers routine needs such as bathing, dressing, personal hygiene, toileting, and so forth. Skilled nursing facilities (SNFs) have either registered nurses (RNs) or licensed nurses on staff 24 hours a day and are intended for those patients who require ongoing medical care, such as physical therapy, wound care, respiratory therapy, pain management, a feeding tube, or dialysis in addition to assistance with activities of daily living.

In many cases, patients transition from a hospital stay to a SNF and then eventually to an ICF as their medical care needs diminish. A stay at a SNF can also be a temporary stop before the patient is able to return home or move to a less intensive type of care such as assisted living or in-home care.

Centers for Disease Control data show that, among residents over 45 years of age, 40% of males and 37% of females stayed less than 1 month in a nursing home, and another 20% of males and 19% of females stayed more than a month but less than 3 months. Only 4% of males and 7% of females had stays lasting longer than 5 years.

Independent living communities. In independent living retirement communities, the care recipient has full choice and control over all aspects of his or her life. He or she must be independent in all aspects of daily living such as bathing, dressing, mental alertness, and being able to walk. These communities come in many housing styles, including single-family dwellings, townhouses, duplexes, high-rise apartments, condominiums, and mobile homes, which are either rented or owned by the individual.

Assisted living facilities. Assisted living facilities are suitable for individuals who need little or no help. Each resident occupies his or her own apartment. All residents use shared spaces, which usually include living rooms, dining rooms, or laundry rooms. Minimal services, ranging from central dining programs to organized recreational activities, health, transportation, housekeeping, laundry, and security services, are usually available.

Residential care facilities. Residential care facilities offer housing for individuals who need assistance with personal care or medical needs. The facility is normally state licensed and must meet minimum staffing requirements. It is staffed 24 hours a day. To be eligible for residential care facilities, an individual usually must be fairly mentally alert; able to dress, feed, and take themselves to the toilet; able to eat meals in a central dining room; and need no more than moderate assistance with personal care or behavior supervision.

For compliance purposes, the key question is whether the facility provides care or other services for which it seeks reimbursement from the Medicare or Medicaid programs.

SIZE OF THE INDUSTRY AND TRENDS

In September 2012, there were 15,663 certified[1] nursing facilities in the United States down from 16,460 ten years earlier. About 68% of them were for profit, 25% nonprofit, and 6% government run. In those nursing facilities, there were 1,668,685 beds, little change from the 1,698,976 beds in 2002. There were 1,383,869 residents occupying those beds, representing a decline from 1,453,813 a decade before. This represents an occupancy rate of 86.3%. That rate peaked at 88.9% in 2006 and 2007.

The age of the nursing facility population (in 2009) breaks down this way:

Age	Percentage of Total
0–21	0.2
22–30	0.3
31–64	13.7
65–74	16.7
75–84	32.2
85–95	31.7
95+	5.2

COMPLIANCE PROGRAM MANDATE

Until 2010, it was optional, although highly recommended, for a nursing facility to establish a compliance program. The healthcare reform law enacted in that year, the Patient Protection and Affordable Care Act

[1] The appropriate state survey agency certifies that a nursing facility is in compliance with the federal requirements for participation in the Medicare and Medicaid programs.

(PPACA), stated that a nursing facility must have in operation a compliance and ethics program that is effective in preventing and detecting criminal, civil, and administrative violations under the Act and in promoting quality of care. It describes these eight components of such a program.

1. The organization must have established compliance standards and procedures to be followed by its employees and other agents that are reasonably capable of reducing the prospect of criminal, civil, and administrative violations under this Act.
2. Specific individuals among the high-level personnel of the organization must have been assigned overall responsibility to oversee compliance with such standards and procedures, and have sufficient resources and authority to ensure such compliance.
3. The organization must have used due care not to delegate substantial discretionary authority to individuals whom the organization knew, or should have known through the exercise of due diligence, had a propensity to engage in criminal, civil, and administrative violations under the Act.
4. The organization must have taken steps to communicate effectively its standards and procedures to all employees and other agents, such as by requiring participation in training programs or by disseminating publications that explain in a practical manner what is required.
5. The organization must have taken reasonable steps to achieve compliance with its standards, by implementing monitoring and auditing systems designed to detect criminal, civil, and administrative violations under the Act by its employees and other agents, and by having in place and publicizing a reporting system whereby employees and other agents can report violations by others within the organization without fear of retribution.
6. The standards must be consistently enforced through appropriate disciplinary mechanisms, including discipline of individuals responsible for the failure to detect an offense.
7. After an offense has been detected, the organization must take all reasonable steps to respond appropriately to the offense and to prevent further similar offenses, including necessary modification to its program to prevent and detect criminal, civil, and administrative violations under the Act.
8. The organization must periodically reassess its compliance program to identify changes necessary to reflect changes within the organization and its facilities.

This list is a restatement of the seven elements that the Office of the Inspector General (OIG) has been promoting for all healthcare organizations for the last 15 years.

1. Develop and distribute written standards of conduct, policies, procedures, and protocols that show the facility's commitment to compliance and to address specific risk areas for fraud and abuse.
2. Designate a Compliance Officer and a Compliance Committee with the mandate to develop, operate, and monitor the compliance program, and who report directly to the Chief Executive Officer (CEO), the governing body, and the organization's owners.
3. Develop and implement regular, effective education and training programs for all affected employees.
4. Open and maintain lines of communication between the Compliance Officer and all employees, including a channel for receiving complaints. The anonymity of whistle-blowers should be protected and they should not suffer retaliation.
5. Use audits to monitor compliance, identify problem areas, and help correct the problems.
6. Develop policies and procedures that apply appropriate disciplinary actions against employees and contractors who violate laws and regulations, payor program requirements, and organizational compliance rules.
7. Develop policies and procedures to enable investigation of detected problems, and respond to identified violations through corrective actions, repayments, and preventive measures.

Although the elements are listed by OIG in this order, it is not necessarily the sequence in which they need to be implemented. For instance, it may make more sense to appoint the Compliance Officer and Compliance Committee as a first step. Then, they can take the lead in carrying out the other pieces of the program.

In its 2012 Work Plan, the OIG stated that one of its priorities is to review Medicare- and Medicaid-certified nursing homes' implementation of compliance plans as part of their day-to-day operations and whether the plans contain elements identified in the OIG's Compliance Program Guidance. The OIG will assess whether the Centers for Medicare and Medicaid Services (CMS) has incorporated compliance requirements into the Medicare requirements of participation and whether CMS oversees provider implementation of plans. The PPACA requires nursing homes to operate a compliance and ethics program to prevent and detect criminal, civil, and administrative violations and promote quality of care. The Act required CMS to issue regulations by 2012 and SNFs to have plans that meet such requirements by 2013.

BENEFITS TO A NURSING FACILITY OF A COMPLIANCE PROGRAM

Although nursing facilities have a legal obligation to operate a compliance program, they also benefit in several distinct ways from compliance activities. They will be less likely to submit false or inaccurate claims or cost information to federal healthcare programs, a good idea in any event. In fact, they have a better chance of preventing any kind of illegal or unethical behavior, as well as noticing and correcting such behavior at an early stage. The existence of the compliance program encourages employees and other organization stakeholders to report potential problems, which in turn permits early investigation and corrective action, thereby reducing the risk of legal action under the False Claims Act (FCA) and administrative sanctions.

Speedy correction and fewer legal problems mean lower costs to the facility, not to mention the federal healthcare programs and the taxpayers who fund them. More effective compliance enhances resident satisfaction and safety through the delivery of higher quality health care. The compliance program demonstrates the organization's commitment to legal, responsible, high-integrity corporate behavior. It has the effect of improving the facility's reputation for reliability and quality and increasing its competitive strength in the marketplace and its standing in the community.

Through the compliance program, a nursing facility will be able to accurately evaluate the behavior of its employees and contractors. It will improve the quality, efficiency, and reliability of its service delivery systems. The program serves as a single dissemination point for information on relevant healthcare laws, regulations, and payor requirements.

BASIC ELEMENTS OF GOOD COMPLIANCE PROGRAMS

Written Standards, Policies, and Procedures

Professionally managed organizations prepare and distribute to their employees written rules to guide their conduct in day-to-day operations. These rules may take the form of policies, procedures, standards, and protocols. In this case, their purpose is to ensure that the employees follow not only the laws and regulations but also the principles of the compliance program itself. There will be general policies and procedures that apply to everyone who works in the organization. There also will be specific policies governing activities in particular clinical, financial, and administrative departments. The first set of standards is frequently a Code of Conduct.

Code of Conduct

The OIG compares an organization's Code of Conduct to a nation's constitution. It defines the fundamental principles and values that the organization wishes its employees to observe in their day-to-day work behavior. It should be brief, memorable, and apply to all employees. If necessary to be accessible to the employees, it should be adapted to different reading levels and translated into different languages. The OIG recommends that employees be required to state in writing that they have read and will follow the Code. That statement should be kept in each employee's personnel file.

Nursing facilities vary widely in the resources that they can commit to a compliance effort. However, a Code of Conduct is a simple, powerful document that can be prepared by any entity. These are a couple contrasting examples of Codes of Conduct. The first (Wissota Health) is succinct enough to take up just one webpage. The second (Golden Living) consumes 32 document pages. Which do you think is more effective in guiding the work behavior of employees?

> Wissota Health and Regional Vent Center, Chippewa Falls WI
> http://www.wissotahealth.com/about_us/code_of_conduct.phtml
>
> Golden Living family of healthcare companies
> http://www.goldenlivingcenters.com/sites/centers/uploads/file/CodeConduct-updated-8-9.pdf

The bulk of the policies and procedures that the OIG has in mind with its recommendations address the compliance risks in specific areas of operations unique to nursing facilities. These risk areas are explained in some detail after a discussion of the other six elements of a compliance program.

Compliance Officer and Compliance Committee

Another "bare minimum" compliance decision by even the smallest nursing facility is the appointment of one of its employees as Compliance Officer. It does not need to be a full-time responsibility; it can be combined with other work duties. It should be a high-level person with direct access to the CEO, governing body members, senior management, and legal counsel. The OIG advises against making the Compliance Officer subordinate to the organization's legal or financial officials. He or she may have to rely on the expertise of other employees in each relevant department or on outside consultants. When compliance issues arise, it is essential that the Compliance Officer have the authority to review relevant documents (e.g., medical and billing records, marketing materials, contracts and legal obligations).

These are the primary Compliance Officer responsibilities described by the OIG.

- Overseeing and monitoring implementation of the compliance program.
- Reporting on a regular basis to the nursing facility's governing body, CEO, and Compliance Committee on the progress of implementation, assisting in establishing methods to improve the efficiency and quality of services, and to reduce vulnerability to fraud, abuse, and waste.
- Periodically revising the program to reflect changes in the organization's needs, and in the law and policies of government agencies and private payors.
- Developing, coordinating, and participating in an educational and training program on the elements of compliance and ensuring that all employees and managers understand and comply with pertinent federal and state standards.
- Ensuring that independent contractors and agents who furnish physician, nursing, or other healthcare services to the residents of the nursing facility are aware of the residents' rights.
- Coordinating personnel issues with the nursing facility's human resources/personnel office to ensure that both the National Practitioner Data Bank and the OIG's List of Excluded Individuals/Entities has been checked with respect to all employees, medical staff, and independent contractors.
- Assisting the nursing facility's financial management in coordinating internal compliance review and monitoring activities, including annual or periodic reviews of departments.
- Independently investigating matters in response to reports of problems or suspected violations and initiating appropriate corrective action (e.g., improvements to nursing facility policies and practices, appropriate disciplinary action).
- Collaborating with the organization's legal counsel in reporting self-discovered violations of program requirements.

The purpose of the Compliance Committee is to advise the Compliance Officer and assist in the implementation of the compliance program. Small facilities may not be able to afford a permanent committee. Instead they can create ad hoc task forces whenever compliance problems come up. The OIG suggests these functions for the Compliance Committee.

- Analyzing the legal requirements with which the nursing facility must comply, and specific risk areas within the organization.
- Assessing existing policies and procedures in those risk areas for possible inclusion in the compliance program.
- Working with facility departments to develop policies and procedures that promote compliance with legal requirements.
- Developing and monitoring internal systems and controls to carry out the organization's policies.
- Determining strategies and approaches to promote compliance with program requirements and detection of any potential violations.
- Developing a system to solicit, evaluate, and respond to complaints and problems.
- Monitoring internal and external audits and investigations in order to identify deficiencies and correct them.

Training and Education

With a Compliance Officer in charge and policies and procedures ready to guide compliant employee behavior, the next step for the organization is to train the employees in the use of those policies and procedures. The training will be targeted not just at staff but also corporate officers, managers, healthcare professionals, and contractors. It should include both full- and part-time employees, as well as those hired temporarily.

Training should be offered to new employees shortly after being hired (usually within 30 days), to temporary employees before they are permitted to interact with residents, and regularly (at least once a year) to all current employees. Training instructors may come from within the organization or be engaged as outside consultants. Either way, they must be qualified to teach the subject matter and experienced in the ways of compliance.

Employees should be required to complete a minimum number of training hours each year. Update sessions should be offered as the facility's needs and the compliance laws change. Participation in the training sessions should be a condition of continued employment; failure to meet training requirements should result in disciplinary action. Adherence to the training lessons should be a consideration in each employee's performance evaluations.

The OIG describes two levels of training. Primary training is provided to everyone and covers these topics:

- Compliance with Medicare participation requirements relevant to employees' duties and responsibilities
- Prohibitions on paying or receiving remuneration to induce referrals
- Proper documentation in clinical or financial records
- Residents' rights
- The duty to report misconduct

Specialized training is for those staff members and contractors who deal with issues of claims development and submission processes, residents' rights, and marketing practices.

Lines of Communication

Once employees have been trained in the work requirements of the compliance program, they need to be able to ask questions about compliance and report suspected violations. To do this, they require open lines of communication with their immediate supervisors and, ultimately, the Compliance Officer. They also must feel confident that their communications will be kept confidential, and that they will not experience retaliation for speaking up.

The OIG suggests communication mechanisms like telephone hotlines, email forums, newsletters, suggestion boxes, and even employee exit interviews. The means of utilizing them should be widely publicized throughout the organization. Nursing facilities also are required to post the names, addresses, and telephone numbers of all pertinent state-level client advocacy groups such as the state survey and certification agency, state licensure office, state ombudsman program, the protection and advocacy network, and the state Medicaid Fraud Control Unit.

Compliance matters brought to the attention of the organization must be documented and investigated immediately to determine their veracity. Full information on reports and complaints should be included in regular reports to the Compliance Committee, the CEO, and the governing board.

Auditing and Monitoring

The organization will do its best to design and maintain a compliance program that guides its employees to perform their duties in full observance of laws, regulations, and program requirements. However, it cannot assume that the program will always work as well as intended. The program design may turn out to be less effective than hoped, or it may be implemented poorly, or the conditions (legal, political, market, operational) on which the design was based may change, or the employees may not respond to the dictates of the program as anticipated, or the compliance results being achieved may not be satisfactory. The organization determines whether these problems are occurring through auditing and monitoring.

The auditing and monitoring functions are focused on two groups of activities within the nursing facility: the provision of services to the residents and the operation of the compliance program itself. Are the services being provided in conformance with all relevant laws, regulations, and program requirements? Are all elements of the compliance program being carried out satisfactorily?

Auditing and monitoring are two different types of review. The *monitoring* function persistently observes the performance of specific routine activities within the nursing facility organization. On a regular basis (daily or weekly), it gathers data on the ways that those activities are carried out and the results that are achieved. It notices trends over time and looks for deviations from norms. For instance, the facility may track the number of claims that are denied by payors, both in absolute terms and as a percentage of all claims. It is almost inevitable, in any healthcare organization, that some claims will be denied because of innocent errors. However, if the number or percentage of denials is steadily increasing or the denial rate is above an acceptable level, it may indicate a problem in the facility's process for preparing and submitting reimbursement claims. The problem could lead to the filing of false claims and a violation of law. Immediate corrective action would be called for.

When a compliance program is first implemented, the OIG recommends that employees or hired consultants conduct a "snapshot" assessment of the organization's compliance performance to serve as a baseline or benchmark for future measurements. The monitoring efforts that follow will review the facility's day-to-day operations and their adherence to relevant laws and regulations, as well as the requirements of the Medicare program, Medicare fiscal intermediaries and carriers, and private payors, and how well they are satisfying the elements of the compliance program. They will particularly focus on the rules governing claims development, billing and cost reports, and the facility's relationships with third parties because these are where the greatest legal risks lie.

The monitoring techniques may include:

- On-site visits to all facilities owned or operated by the nursing home owner
- Quizzing the billing and claims reimbursement staff on its knowledge of applicable program requirements and claims and billing criteria

- Statistical sampling of high-volume activities like claims preparation and filing and completion of resident medical records
- Unannounced mock surveys and audits
- Examination of the organization's complaint logs and investigative files
- Legal assessment of all contractual relationships with contractors, consultants, and potential referral sources
- Reevaluation of deficiencies cited in past surveys for state licensing requirements and Medicare participation requirements
- Checking personnel records to determine whether individuals who previously have been reprimanded for compliance issues are now conforming to facility policies
- Survey of the nursing facility's employees and staff concerning adherence to the Code of Conduct and other policies and procedures, as well as their work loads and ability to address the residents' daily living needs
- Validation of qualifications of nursing facility physicians and other staff, including verification of applicable state license renewals
- Trend analysis, or longitudinal studies, that uncover deviations in specific areas over a period of time
- Analyzing past survey reports for patterns of deficiencies to determine if the proposed corrective plan of action identified and corrected the underlying problem

An *audit* is a discrete, in-depth review that is conducted at periodic intervals; focuses on particular departments, operations, or risk areas; and is designed to look for actual compliance problems and legal violations. It can use many of the same data gathering and analysis techniques as monitoring. The target of the audit often is determined by factors such as:

- The content of Corporate Integrity Agreements (CIAs) that the OIG has negotiated with similar healthcare organizations found in violation of the laws
- Operational risk areas specified in the Program Guidance for each type of organization
- Operational risk areas identified by the organization during monitoring efforts and previous audits
- Operational areas that have been the subject of OIG investigations and charges
- History of deficiencies and enforcement actions

The systematic conduct of monitoring and audits can persuade enforcement officials to give a facility more favorable treatment under the Federal Sentencing Guidelines.

Disciplinary Guidelines

When employees act in disobedience of the nursing facility's Code of Conduct, policies, and procedures, they should know that there will be consequences. The compliance program accomplishes this by drafting and disseminating throughout the workforce the procedures that will be followed for handling improper conduct and the penalties that may be imposed. The penalties could include oral warnings, written warnings, suspension, dismissal, or monetary fines depending on the seriousness of the misconduct.

The procedures should be administered in a fair and equitable manner, and they should be applied consistently to all employees, including corporate executives, managers, and supervisors. Everyone should feel that he or she will be subject to the same types of disciplinary action for the same categories of misconduct.

Responding to Misconduct

The nursing facility's Compliance Officer, in conjunction with other management officials, must be prepared to respond quickly and appropriately to any reports or signs of noncompliance or legal violations. In most cases, the first step will be an investigation, one that varies depending on the scope and severity of the misconduct. If the case appears to be quite serious, it may be advisable to contract with an outside attorney, auditor, or compliance expert to help with the investigation.

The investigation typically will involve personal interviews and a review of relevant documents. The dossier of the investigation should contain documentation of the alleged misconduct, a description of the investigative process (including the objectivity of the investigators and methodologies utilized), a log of the witnesses interviewed and the documents reviewed, copies of interview notes and key documents, the conclusions of the investigation, any disciplinary action taken, and corrective actions implemented.

Several different decisions might be made on the basis of an investigation. State laws frequently require immediate reporting of alleged incidents of mistreatment, neglect, abuse of residents, or misappropriation of resident property to facility management and other officials. An organization can avoid the costs and disruptions associated with a government-directed investigation and civil or administrative litigation by voluntarily disclosing evidence of possible fraud through the OIG's Provider Self-Disclosure Protocol (SDP). Where there appear to be violations of law, it will be necessary to refer the incident or person to criminal or civil law enforcement authorities.[2] The investigation may make clear that changes are necessary in the facility's operating practices or compliance procedures. If the misconduct or errors have resulted in overpayments by payors to the facility, repayments must be made promptly.

RISK AREAS UNIQUE TO NURSING FACILITIES

It helps to know what areas of a nursing facility's operations are most susceptible to fraud and other violations and are of current concern to the enforcement community. Facility management then can focus its compliance efforts in those areas. The OIG has described in considerable detail several such risk areas in the Program Guidances that it issued in 2000 and 2008.

Quality of Care

The quality of the care delivered in any health organization is important, but it takes on a new dimension in a nursing facility. The patients or residents are dependent on the facility for all their healthcare needs. They are at a stage of life that requires a more holistic view of a person's health status. The OIG recommends that nursing facilities make a commitment to provide the care and services necessary to attain or maintain each resident's "'highest practicable physical, mental and psychosocial well-being."

In pursuit of that commitment, facilities should measure their performance against Medicare participation requirements and their own internal quality of care protocols. The care outcomes for each resident should be measured and regularly reviewed and analyzed. When deemed necessary, the protocols should be modified.

---

[2] The most appropriate authorities are likely to be the OIG, the Criminal and Civil Divisions of the Department of Justice, the U.S. Attorney in relevant districts, the Federal Bureau of Investigation, and the other investigative arms for the agencies administering the affected federal or state healthcare programs, such as the State Survey Agency, the State Medicaid Fraud Control Unit, the Defense Criminal Investigative Service, the Department of Veterans Affairs, and the Office of Personnel Management.

A good way to pinpoint the areas of highest compliance risk and legal vulnerability is to review the deficiencies discovered during the variety of surveys to which nursing facilities are subject—annual state agency surveys, validation surveys, and complaint surveys.[3] Additional useful information can be found in the requirements for nursing facility participation in the Medicare and Medicaid programs. These are the special areas of concern for quality of care mentioned in the 2000 Program Guidance.

- Absence of a comprehensive, accurate assessment of each resident's functional capacity and a comprehensive care plan that includes measurable objectives and timetables to meet the resident's medical, nursing, and mental and psychosocial needs
- Inappropriate or insufficient treatment and services to address residents' clinical conditions, including pressure ulcers, dehydration, malnutrition, incontinence of the bladder, and mental or psychosocial problems
- Failure to accommodate individual resident needs and preferences
- Failure to properly prescribe, administer, and monitor prescription drug usage
- Inadequate staffing levels or insufficiently trained or supervised staff to provide medical, nursing, and related services
- Failure to provide appropriate therapy services
- Failure to provide appropriate services to assist residents with activities of daily living (e.g., feeding, dressing, and bathing)
- Failure to provide an ongoing activities program to meet the individual needs of all residents
- Failure to report incidents of mistreatment, neglect, or abuse to the administrator of the facility and other officials as required by law

The 2008 Program Guidance adds these issues that frequently arise in enforcement cases involving the quality of care provided to nursing facility residents.

Sufficient Staffing

Staffing has been a problem for many nursing facilities. They have failed to provide staff in sufficient numbers and with appropriate clinical expertise despite federal law requiring them to do so. The relationship between staff-to-resident ratios, staff competency, and quality of care is complex. Important factors in assessing a nursing facility's staffing arrangement are resident case-mix, staff skill levels, staff-to-resident ratios, staff turnover,

---

[3] These are explained at greater length in 42 CFR 488.

staffing schedules, disciplinary records, payroll records, timesheets, and adverse event reports (e.g., falls or adverse drug events), as well as interviews with staff, residents, and residents' family or legal guardians. To meet this legal requirement, facilities are strongly encouraged to assess their staffing patterns regularly to ensure that there are enough people with the skills necessary to meet the unique care needs of the residents.

Comprehensive Resident Care Plans

Medicare and Medicaid regulations require nursing facilities to develop a comprehensive care plan for each resident that addresses his or her medical, nursing, and mental and psychosocial needs and includes reasonable objectives and timetables. Team members from all the disciplines involved in each resident's care should contribute to the preparation of these plans. This may be facilitated by scheduling meetings to accommodate the full interdisciplinary team, completing all clinical assessments before the meeting is convened, opening lines of communication between direct care providers and interdisciplinary team members, involving the resident and the residents' family members or legal guardian, and documenting the length and content of each meeting.

A common point of contention in nursing facilities is the level of participation of attending physicians in resident care. It can be difficult to ensure that a physician supervises each resident's care when they often are not present at the facility on a daily basis. Fuller physician involvement can be encouraged by providing advance notice of care planning meetings, and deciding whether the involvement should occur through the use of consultation and postmeeting debriefings, telephone conferencing, or personal attendance.

Medication Management

The law requires nursing facilities to provide "pharmaceutical services (including procedures that assure accurate acquiring, receiving, dispensing, and administering of all drugs and biologicals) to meet the needs of each resident." Furthermore, poor management of medications can lead to resident injury and even death. Specific problems that may arise are threats to patient safety, adverse drug interactions, and irregularities in a resident's drug regimen. They can be addressed by implementing processes that maintain accurate drug records and track the location and use of medications, and by regularly training all staff in the principles of proper medication management. A leading role in a nursing facility's handling of drugs should be played by its consulting pharmacist. Medicare regulations require that the facilities employ or contract with a licensed pharmacist to advise on all aspects of pharmacy services for residents.

Psychotropic Medications

The OIG has found two problems with psychotropic drugs—their unnecessary use and their inappropriate use as a chemical restraint of residents. Federal law prohibits facilities from using any medication as a means of chemical restraint for "purposes of discipline or convenience, and not required to treat the resident's medical symptoms." In addition, resident drug regimens must be free from unnecessary drugs. Nursing facilities have a positive obligation to keep residents' medication usage to the lowest level allowed by their medical condition.

They can accomplish this by ensuring that there is sufficient evidence whenever medication is used, and by monitoring, documenting, and reviewing each resident's use of psychotropic drugs. The facility also should educate its care providers in appropriate monitoring and documentation practices, and audit the drug regimen reviews and care plans for every resident. The attending physicians, the medical director, the consultant pharmacist, and other care providers should work together in this effort.

Resident Safety

Nursing facility residents have a legal right to be free from abuse and neglect. Of particular concern is harm caused by staff and fellow residents. Facilities should take steps to ensure that they are protecting their residents from these risks. The OIG recommends these three strategies.

Promote Resident Safety

Federal regulations require that nursing facilities take steps to prohibit mistreatment, neglect, and abuse of residents. This may take the form of injuries resulting from staff-on-resident abuse and neglect, resident-on-resident abuse, or abuse from unknown causes. Nursing facilities need to develop and implement policies and procedures to prevent these types of behavior. They need also to create a mechanism for staff, contractors, residents, family members, visitors, and others to report threats, abuse, mistreatment, and other safety concerns confidentially to senior staff empowered to take immediate action.

Monitor Resident Interactions

A sometimes hidden problem in many nursing facilities is the abuse committed by one resident toward another resident. This usually is a result of the failure to properly screen and assess, or the failure of staff to monitor, residents at risk for aggressive behavior. The answer is heightened awareness and monitoring of inter-resident abuse. The techniques used are thorough incoming resident assessments, comprehensive resident care plans, periodic ongoing resident assessments, and proper staffing assignments.

Screen Facility Employees

Nursing facilities are prohibited from employing individuals found guilty of abusing, neglecting, or mistreating residents, or individuals with a finding entered into a state nurse aide registry concerning abuse, neglect, mistreatment of residents or misappropriation of their property. There are several places to turn for preemployment background screening. Potential employees should be checked against criminal record databases in all states where they have worked or resided. Each applicant's education, licensing, certifications, and training should be verified. Many states have requirements that nursing facilities conduct these checks for all professional care providers, such as therapists, medical directors, and nurses.

Residents' Rights

The rights of residents in nursing facilities have been established, at the federal level, by the Budget Reconciliation Act of 1987, and by laws in many states. Each facility has a legal obligation to recognize and protect residents' rights "to a dignified existence that promotes freedom of choice, self-determination, and reasonable accommodation of individual needs." The OIG defines these areas of particular risk for violation of those rights.

- Discriminatory admission or improper denial of access to care
- Verbal, mental, or physical abuse, corporal punishment, and involuntary seclusion
- Inappropriate use of physical or chemical restraints
- Failure to ensure that residents have personal privacy and access to their personal records upon request and that the privacy and confidentiality of those records are protected
- Denial of a resident's right to participate in care and treatment decisions
- Failure to safeguard residents' financial affairs

Submission of Accurate Claims

Submitting a false claim, or causing a false claim to be submitted, to a federal healthcare program may subject the individual, the entity, or both to criminal prosecution, civil liability (including treble damages and penalties) under the FCA and exclusion from participation in federal healthcare programs. Examples of false or fraudulent claims include claims for items not provided or not provided as claimed, claims for services that are not medically necessary, and claims when there has been a failure of care. The FCA also applies to duplicate billing, insufficient documentation for claims, and false or fraudulent cost reports.

The OIG has identified several types of fraudulent transactions unique to nursing facilities. Some facilities have improperly classified residents into a higher (and higher paying) resource utilization group (RUG). This leads to inaccurate reporting of resident case-mix data to Medicare. This problem can be resolved by better training of the people collecting the underlying data and those charged with analyzing and responding to the data. Periodic internal and external validation of the data also may prove useful.

The provision of physical, occupational, and speech therapy services has created legal problems for some nursing facilities. They improperly utilize therapy services to inflate a resident's RUG classification to obtain additional reimbursement. They over-utilize therapy services billed to Medicare Part B on a fee-for-service basis. They under-utilize therapy services billed to Part A on a prospective payment basis. These problems can be avoided by:

- Requiring that therapy contractors provide complete and contemporaneous documentation of each resident's services
- Regular and periodic reconciliation of the physician's orders and the services actually provided
- Interviews with the residents and family members to be sure services are delivered
- Assessments of the continued medical necessity for services during resident care planning meetings

Federal healthcare programs will not pay for goods or services furnished by an individual or entity that has been excluded from participation in those programs. To ensure that it does not submit claims for such items, a nursing facility must screen all prospective owners, officers, directors, employees, contractors, and agents prior to engaging their services against the OIG List of Excluded Individuals/Entities and the U.S. General Services Administration's excluded parties list. It also should remove any such persons from responsibility for the facility's operations related to federal healthcare programs if the facility receives notice that he or she is excluded.

Another requirement of nursing facilities is that they offer appropriate restorative and personal care services to residents to enable them to maintain the highest practical level of functioning. Those services include care to avoid pressure ulcers, active and passive range of motion, ambulation, fall prevention, incontinence management, bathing, dressing, and grooming activities. There have been problems when facilities billed for services not provided or so deficient that they constituted no care at all. That amounts to the filing of false claims. What they must do to ensure that these services are actually delivered and are of an acceptable level is conduct resident and staff interviews, medical record reviews, consultations with attending physicians, the medical director, the consultant pharmacists; executives must also make personal observations of care delivery.

In the 2000 Program Guidance, the OIG lists a number of more traditional reimbursement risk areas that may be present in nursing facilities.

- Billing for items or services not rendered or provided as claimed
- Submitting claims for equipment, medical supplies, and services that are medically unnecessary
- Submitting claims to Medicare Part A for residents who are not eligible for Part A coverage
- Duplicate billing
- Failing to identify and refund credit balances
- Submitting claims for items or services not ordered
- Knowingly billing for inadequate or substandard care
- Providing misleading information about a resident's medical condition on the minimum data set (MDS) or otherwise providing inaccurate information used to determine the RUG assigned to the resident
- Upcoding the level of service provided
- Billing for individual items or services when they either are included in the facility's per diem rate or are of a type that must be billed as a unit and may not be unbundled
- Billing residents for items or services that are included in the per diem rate or otherwise covered by the third-party payor
- Altering documentation or forging a physician signature on documents used to verify that services were ordered and/or provided
- Failing to maintain sufficient documentation to support the diagnosis, justify treatment, document the course of treatment and results, and promote continuity of care
- Filing false cost reports

Nearly every type of organization delivering health care to Medicare or Medicaid patients is likely to commit one or more of these violations, deliberately, recklessly, or inadvertently, at one time or another.

Federal Anti-Kickback Statute (AKS)

The operation of a nursing facility depends almost exclusively on referrals, both incoming and outgoing. Patients are referred to such facilities by physicians and other healthcare professionals, hospitals and hospital discharge planners, hospices, home health agencies, and other nursing facilities. In the course of treating those patients/residents, the facilities may make referrals to hospices; durable medical equipment (DME) companies; laboratories; diagnostic testing facilities; LTC pharmacies; hospitals; physicians; other nursing facilities; and physical, occupational, and speech therapists. The AKS prohibits any kind of remuneration to induce or reward a referral.

The OIG suggests a series of questions that a nursing facility ask to determine if it is at risk of an AKS violation.

- Does the nursing facility provide anything of value to persons or entities in a position to influence or generate federal healthcare program business for the nursing facility?
- Does the nursing facility receive anything of value from persons or entities for which the nursing facility generates federal healthcare program business?
- Could one purpose of an arrangement be to induce or reward the generation of business payable in whole or in part by a federal healthcare program?
- Does the arrangement or practice have a potential to interfere with, or skew, clinical decision-making?
- Does the arrangement or practice have a potential to increase costs to federal healthcare programs or beneficiaries?
- Does the arrangement or practice have a potential to increase the risk of overutilization or inappropriate utilization?
- Does the arrangement or practice raise patient safety or quality of care concerns?

If a nursing facility finds that it is involved in a legally risky arrangement, its first step should be to try to fit the arrangement into one of the AKS Safe Harbors.[4] These are the ones most suited to nursing facilities.

- Investment interests
- Space rental
- Equipment rental
- Personal services and management contracts

[4] A Safe Harbor is a set of conditions within which there is complete protection from AKS liability.

- Discount
- Employee
- Electronic health records items and services
- Managed care and risk-sharing arrangements

When a suitable Safe Harbor is not available, a nursing facility should carry out a general evaluation of the proposed arrangement, looking at the following factors: nature of the relationship between the parties, manner in which the participants were selected, manner in which the remuneration was determined, value of the remuneration, nature of items and services provided, potential federal program impact, potential conflicts of interest, and manner in which the arrangement is documented.

In its 2008 Program Guidance, the OIG describes several practices that present a heightened risk of fraud or abuse in nursing facilities. It urges close scrutiny of them. Among them are:

- Provision of free goods or services to an existing or potential referral source
- Provision or receipt of goods or services at non-fair market value rates
- Arrangements with physicians to provide medical director, quality assurance, and other services
- Discounts offered to customers who submit claims to federal healthcare programs
- Hospice offer of free nursing services for nonhospice patients to induce referrals of hospice patients
- Hospital payments to reserve beds in nursing facilities to induce referrals of patients from the nursing facilities to the hospital

Stark Physician Self-Referral Law

The Stark Law prohibits a physician from referring Medicare or Medicaid patients for certain "designated health services" (DHS) to an entity with which the physician or an immediate family member has a "financial relationship." Nursing facility services are not DHS for purposes of the Stark Law. However, nursing facilities do use laboratory, physical therapy, and occupational therapy services, which are covered by the Stark Law. The facilities should review all financial relationships with physicians who refer or order DHS to ensure compliance with the Stark Law. They should pay particular attention to relationships with attending physicians and physicians who are owners, investors, medical directors, or consultants to the facility.

Supplemental Payments

As a condition of participating in the Medicare program, nursing facilities may not charge a resident/beneficiary for covered services in excess of the amount paid by Medicare. Facilities must ensure that residents and their families are not billed for such charges.

Medicare Part D Enrollment

Medicare beneficiaries may choose to buy Part D coverage for their pharmaceutical needs. They also may choose the plan from which they will obtain that coverage. The Medicare program states that "under no circumstances should a nursing home require, request, coach or steer any resident to select or change a plan for any reason."

HIPAA Privacy and Security

The Privacy Rule under the Health Insurance Portability and Accountability Act (HIPAA) of 1996 protects against the disclosure of patient protected health information (PHI). The Security Rule describes the administrative, technical, and physical safeguards that facilities must have in place to ensure the confidentiality of PHI. Under both rules, nursing facilities have some flexibility in designing their own privacy policies and procedures. The OIG urges facilities to verify compliance with all applicable Privacy and Security Rule provisions, including standards for use and disclosure of PHI, both with and without patient authorization, as well as the provisions pertaining to permitted and required disclosures.

PREVALENCE OF FRAUD IN NURSING FACILITIES

If there seem to be a lot of potential risk areas in nursing facility operations, it is because there are. U.S. society as a whole does not pay a lot of attention to its infirm elderly members, being content to "warehouse" them in nursing facilities. The residents in nursing facilities often are not in a physical or mental condition to notice fraud and abuse going on around them, or to speak up about it. This creates an environment where fraud can be committed without being readily noticed.

In 2012, the OIG issued a report finding that SNFs improperly billed Medicare in one-quarter of all claims submitted in 2009, costing Medicare \$1.5 billion in inappropriate payments. This represented 5.6% of the

$26.9 billion paid to SNFs in that year. After reviewing the medical records supporting 499 claims submitted to Medicare in 2009, OIG found that a large percentage of the inappropriate charges resulted from upcoding attributable to claims for "ultrahigh" therapy in SNFs. OIG's review also determined that SNFs: (1) billed inaccurate RUGs in 23% of claims, 57% of which was attributable to unnecessary therapy; and (2) misreported information on the MDS for at least one item in 47% of all claims, 30% of which was attributable to misreporting the amount of therapy the beneficiary needed or received.

Another OIG report in 2012 revealed that nearly all (99%) of nursing facility records for elderly residents receiving atypical antipsychotic drugs failed to meet one or more federal requirements for resident assessments and/or care plans. Provider records did not contain evidence of compliance with federal requirements for care plan development. One-third did not contain evidence of compliance regarding resident assessments. Eighteen percent of records did not contain evidence to indicate that planned interventions for antipsychotic drug use occurred.

The *Baypointe Rehabilitation and Skilled Care Center*, a nursing home, agreed to pay $351,255 to resolve its liability under the Civil Monetary Penalties Law (CMPL). Baypointe employed an excluded nurse as its assistant director of nursing from January 2006 to July 2009. OIG excluded the nurse after the Mississippi Board of Nursing revoked her license following a positive preemployment drug test. The government contended that Baypointe should have known that the nurse was excluded.

In January 2011, *Senior Care Group, Inc.*, of Tampa, FL, agreed to pay the United States $953,375 to settle allegations that the nursing home company, which operated two SNFs in the western mountains of North Carolina, defrauded the Medicare Part A program. Senior Care's rehabilitation contractor placed intense management pressure on employees to maximize billings, billed for services that were unnecessary and then forwarded the billings for those unnecessary services to Senior Care for submission to Medicare. As an example of the unnecessary services performed, occupational therapy to elderly Alzheimer's syndrome patients who could never expect to return to the workforce was regularly provided. As a condition of settlement, Senior Care was required to enter into a CIA with DHHS/OIG under which the company will be monitored for a period of 5 years to ensure that the company does not commit fraud against government healthcare programs in the future.

Vanguard Health Care Services (and other related entities) agreed to pay $2 million as part of a settlement agreement to resolve allegations of false claims and illegal kickbacks. Between 1998 and 2008, Vanguard allegedly submitted claims to Medicare for enteral (nutrition) therapy goods and services that were also billed to the Tennessee and Mississippi Medicaid programs. Vanguard allegedly failed to disclose the relationship between its LTC facilities (which billed Tennessee and Mississippi Medicaid for the enteral therapy goods and services) and Vanguard Healthcare Ancillary Services (which billed Medicare Part B for the same enteral therapy goods and services). Vanguard also allegedly submitted claims to Medicare for certain free items, namely pumps used to deliver nutritional products and intravenous poles used in the administration of enteral therapy that Vanguard had received at no cost from a third-party supplier in order to induce referrals.

A report in September 2012 by the Government Accountability Office found that nursing homes were the subject of 253 criminal healthcare fraud investigations in 2010. This represented 3.2% of all such investigations for all types of providers. During 2010, 14 nursing homes were found guilty or pled guilty or no contest. In that same year, 100 nursing homes were the subject of civil healthcare fraud investigations—4.3% of the total. Seventy-five nursing homes were excluded from Medicare program participation.

STUDY QUESTIONS

1. What are the unique features of a SNF that distinguish it from other types of LTC facilities?
2. What are the eight compliance program elements mandated by the 2010 PPACA, and what are their similarities to the elements promoted by the OIG for all healthcare organizations?
3. Describe the recommended location of the Compliance Officer within the organizational structure of a nursing facility. To whom should the Officer report and not report? Why?
4. Briefly explain the difference between the monitoring and auditing functions. Exactly what activities do these two functions look at?
5. How can the quality of care provided to nursing facility residents be affected by fraudulent actions of the facility's employees?
6. In what ways could a nursing facility violate the AKS?
7. List three kinds of inaccurate claims that a nursing facility could submit for reimbursement.
8. List five basic rights of nursing facility residents.

Learning Exercises

1. Get a copy of the OIG Work Plan for 2012 (or a more current year) here: https://www.oig.hhs.gov/reports-and-publications/archives/workplan/2012/Work-Plan-2012.pdf and review the OIG's enforcement intentions for "nursing homes" on pages 10–12. If you were working as a Compliance Officer for a nursing facility or chain of nursing facilities, how could you use this information from the Work Plan?
2. Write a Code of Conduct for the employees of a nursing facility, using no more than 250 words.
3. You are unlikely to be able to get the staff at a nursing facility to talk about their compliance practices. If you can, it would be very useful. It might be worth a try. If you have any thoughts of someday doing compliance work in a nursing facility, it would be worthwhile to spend at least a few hours in one. There often are opportunities to do short-term volunteer work at these facilities, sometimes just providing companionship to the residents. Consider it.

References

1. "OIG Compliance Program Guidance for Nursing Facilities," Federal Register, Vol. 65, No. 52, March 16, 2000.
2. "OIG Supplemental Compliance Program Guidance for Nursing Facilities," Federal Register, Vol. 73, No. 190, September 30, 2008.
3. "Fraud and Abuse in the Provision of Services in Nursing Facilities," Special Fraud Alert, OIG, May 1996.
4. "OIG Work Plan 2012".
5. "Semiannual Report to Congress, April 1, 2012–September 30," 2012, OIG.
6. "Health Care Fraud Types of Providers Involved in Medicare, Medicaid, and the Children's Health Insurance Program Cases," Report to Congressional Requesters, Government Accountability Office, September 2012.
7. "The Department of Health and Human Services and The Department of Justice Health Care Fraud and Abuse Control Program Annual Report for Fiscal Year 2011," February 2012.

Chapter 18

Hospices and Home Health Agencies

Learning Objectives

After completing class sessions based on this chapter, a student will:

- Comprehend the differences and similarities between hospices and home health agencies (HHAs) in the services they offer, the markets they serve, and the needs they meet.
- Be familiar with the most common types of fraud in these two types of institutions.
- Learn how to design and implement a recommended seven-element compliance program tailored to the specific needs of a hospice or a HHA.
- Appreciate the benefits afforded by the operation of an effective compliance program.
- Realize the purpose and value of a well-drafted Code of Conduct.
- Know all the compliance risk areas unique to hospices.
- Know all the compliance risk areas unique to HHAs.
- Be able to draw up policies and procedures that address each of those risk areas, particularly the ones dealing with claim development and submission, and Medicare eligibility requirements.
- Be introduced to the potential for fraud in the relationships between hospices and nursing homes.
- Understand how to select a good Compliance Officer and Compliance Committee.
- Learn how to undertake a useful compliance auditing and monitoring program.
- Be exposed to some of the worst examples of fraud committed by hospices and HHAs.

INTRODUCTION

"Home care organizations" include home healthcare agencies, home care aide organizations, and hospices. Some of these organizations are Medicare certified, which allows providers to bill Medicare for reimbursement. Agencies that are not Medicare certified cannot be reimbursed through Medicare. The two types of entities that have received the most attention from the Office of the Inspector General (OIG) of the Department of Health and Human Services (DHHS) are hospices and home healthcare agencies. Each has been the subject of their own OIG Compliance Program Guidance.

The Hospice Care Industry

Hospices provide expert medical care, pain management, and emotional and spiritual support tailored to the needs of patients terminally ill with any disease. A hospice focuses on caring, not curing. In most cases, care is provided in the patient's home but may also be provided in freestanding hospice centers, hospitals, nursing homes, and other long-term care facilities.

A family member usually serves as the primary caregiver and helps make decisions for the terminally ill individual. Members of the hospice staff make regular visits to assess the patient and provide additional care or other services. Hospice staff are on-call 24 hours a day, 7 days a week.

The hospice team typically is composed of the patient's personal physician, a hospice physician or medical director, nurses, home health aides, social workers, bereavement counselors, clergy or other spiritual counselors, trained volunteers, and speech, physical, and occupational therapists. Working together, the team develops a care plan that meets each patient's individual needs for pain management and symptom control.

In 2011, approximately 1.65 million patients received services from a hospice. Of this number, about 1.05 million patients died under hospice care, 300,000 were discharged alive, and another 300,000 remained under hospice care. The use of hospice services increased dramatically between 2001 and 2007, from 19% of all Medicare decedents to 30%. The average length of time for which they received hospice services in 2011 was 69 days. In 40% of the cases, the services are provided in the patient's private residence, 18% of the time in a nursing home, 26% in an inpatient hospice facility, and 7% each in an acute care hospital and a residential facility.

The first hospice program opened in 1974. There were 3,533 Medicare-certified hospices in April 2011. In that same year, 60% of the hospices treating Medicare patients were for-profit, 34% were not-for-profit, and the rest were government owned. During the first decade of the 21st century, there has been a marked shift from nonprofit to for-profit ownership, one-fifth of Medicare-certified hospices closed or left Medicare, and 40% experienced changes in ownership.

In 2010, Medicare expenditures on hospice care totaled about $13 billion. The Medicare Hospice Benefit is the predominate (84%) source of payment for hospice care. There are four general levels of hospice care:

Home-based Care

- *Level 1.* Routine home care: Patient receives hospice care at the place he/she resides. (In 2011, routine home care comprised 97% of hospice patient care days.)
- *Level 2.* Continuous home care: Patient receives hospice care consisting predominantly of licensed nursing care on a continuous basis at home. Continuous home care is only furnished during brief periods of crisis and only as necessary to maintain the terminally ill patient at home.

Inpatient Care

- *Level 3.* General inpatient care: Patient receives general inpatient care in an inpatient facility for pain control or acute or complex symptom management that cannot be handled in other settings.
- *Level 4.* Inpatient respite care: Patient receives care in an approved facility on a short-term basis in order to provide respite for the caregiver.

The Home Healthcare Industry

Home health care allows individuals with limited independence to remain in their homes by providing medical equipment and services to the beneficiary in the home. Acute illness, long-term health conditions, permanent disability, or terminal illness are some of the reasons a person might require home health care. Home health services and supplies typically are provided by nurses and aides under a physician-certified plan of care.

To qualify for Medicare coverage of home health services, a person must be confined to his or her home, except for short trips for medical care, and require a skilled service like physical therapy, speech-language pathology, or intermittent skilled nursing. A physician must certify to these facts and prescribe the home health services.

To be covered by Medicare, home health services must be provided by a Medicare-certified HHA. Payment will be made for skilled nursing services, home health aide services, physical and occupational therapy, speech-language pathology, medical social services, medical supplies other than drugs and biologicals, and durable medical equipment.

In 2011, about 3.4 million Medicare beneficiaries received home health services from almost 11,633 HHAs. Preliminary data for 2010 indicated that Medicare spent about $19.4 billion on home health services.

OIG GUIDANCE FOR COMPLIANCE PROGRAMS

When the OIG of the DHHS embarked upon its fight against healthcare fraud and abuse over 20 years ago, it wished to offer instructions on how to avoid statutory violations and the resulting legal liability. It began issuing detailed "Guidances" on how to create an organization-wide program to ensure compliance with relevant laws and regulations. Each Program Guidance was targeted at a particular type of healthcare entity. The OIG has issued Guidances for 12 types of organizations.

The second Guidance that came out, in August 1998, described a compliance program for HHAs. About 1 year later, hospices were the subject of their own Program Guidance. The terms of these Guidances are very similar. The most significant area of difference is in the "risk areas" that the OIG wishes to see addressed through each organization's written policies and procedures. This chapter discusses those risk areas separately for HHAs and hospices. It treats the other sections of a compliance program in a generic fashion.

The OIG has established a standard structure for a compliance program, composed of seven elements covering these topics:

1. Standards, Policies, and Procedures
2. Compliance Officer and Committee
3. Training and Education
4. Reporting and Investigating
5. Enforcement and Discipline
6. Monitoring and Auditing
7. Response and Prevention

The organization-specific risk areas are addressed in the first element.

BENEFITS OF AN EFFECTIVE COMPLIANCE PROGRAM

The OIG believes that there are nationwide positive outcomes from the implementation of compliance programs by hospices and home healthcare agencies. They are a reduction in healthcare fraud and abuse, strengthening of the operational effectiveness of the healthcare system,

improvement in the quality of care delivered, and reduction in the costs incurred. In addition, the OIG cites numerous benefits to individual organizations.

To start with, a good program helps a home care organization fulfill its legal duty to ensure that it is not submitting false or inaccurate claims. The program enables it to carry out its fundamental care-giving mission. It assists in identifying any weaknesses in internal systems and management.

Implementation of a comprehensive compliance program enables an entity to take these beneficial steps.

- Concretely demonstrate to employees and the community the organization's commitment to honest and responsible provider and corporate conduct.
- Provide a more accurate view of employee and contractor behavior relating to fraud and abuse.
- Identify and prevent illegal and unethical conduct.
- Tailor compliance activities to the organization's specific needs.
- Improve the quality, efficiency, and consistency of patient care.
- Create a central distribution point for information on compliance-related laws, regulations, and program requirements.
- Establish a mechanism that enables employees to report potential problems.
- Develop procedures that facilitate the prompt, thorough investigation of alleged misconduct by corporate officers, managers, employees, independent contractors, consultants, and healthcare professionals.
- Initiate immediate, appropriate, and decisive corrective action.
- Through early detection and reporting, minimize the organization's exposure to civil damages and penalties, criminal sanctions, and administrative remedies, like program exclusion.

What follows is a review of the seven elements of the kind of compliance programs required of HHAs and hospices.

STANDARDS, POLICIES, AND PROCEDURES

Violations of fraud and abuse laws are invariably the result of misconduct by employees or third parties. The shaping of employee actions begins with general principles embodied in a Code of Conduct. The standards in such a code should guide employees in performing their jobs professionally and legally. After reciting the organization's mission, values, and goals, the Code should express the organization's behavioral expectations for all its members—directors, executives, managers, supervisors, clinicians, contractors, and vendors. It should be comprehensible to all these people, translated into other languages as necessary. Each of those persons should be required to sign a statement certifying that he or she has received, read, and understood the Code.

With a Code of Conduct in place, the next step is the development of a body of written policies and procedures that prescribe, in some detail, how certain compliance-sensitive tasks should be performed. They will focus on tasks in those areas of organization operations that have been identified as presenting a heightened risk of misconduct or violation. The risk areas described next were highlighted in the original OIG Guidance. They are based on the problems discovered through the OIG's audit, investigative, and enforcement activities. When an organization designs its own compliance program, it also will pay special attention to those parts of its operations that have been the source of compliance difficulties in the past. The policies and procedures written for those risk areas need to be integrated into the other elements of the compliance program, particularly the training and education, and the auditing and monitoring.

COMPLIANCE RISK AREAS UNIQUE TO HHAS

The Program Guidance for HHAs included a list of 31 risk areas that might conceivably be present in such organizations. It is unlikely that one organization would be vulnerable in all these areas. In any event, it is not possible to "concentrate" on so many areas. The Guidance followed this list with a more detailed and helpful discussion of several select risk areas.

- Billing for items or services not actually rendered
- Billing for medically unnecessary services
- Duplicate billing
- False cost reports
- Credit balances—failure to refund
- Incentives paid to actual or potential referral sources (e.g., physicians, hospitals, patients, etc.) that may violate the Anti-Kickback Statute
- Joint ventures between parties, one of whom can refer Medicare business to the other
- Stark Physician Self-Referral Law
- Billing for services provided to patients who are not truly "homebound"

- Billing for visits to patients who do not require a qualifying service
- Overutilization and underutilization
- Knowing billing for inadequate or substandard care
- Insufficient documentation to show that services were performed and to support reimbursement
- Billing for unallowable costs of home health coordination
- Billing for services provided by unqualified or unlicensed clinical personnel
- False dating of amendments to nursing notes
- Falsified plans of care
- Untimely and/or forged physician certifications on plans of care
- Forged beneficiary signatures on visit slips/logs that verify services were performed
- Improper patient solicitation activities and high-pressure marketing of uncovered or unnecessary services
- Inadequate management and oversight of subcontracted services, resulting in improper billing
- Discriminatory admission and discharge of patients
- Billing for unallowable costs associated with the acquisition and sale of HHAs
- Compensation programs that offer incentives for number of visits performed and revenue generated
- Improper influence over referrals by hospitals that own HHAs
- Patient abandonment in violation of statutory and federal healthcare program requirements
- Knowing misuse of provider certification numbers
- Duplication of services provided by assisted living facilities, hospitals, clinics, physicians, and other HHAs
- Knowing or reckless disregard of willing and able caregivers when providing home health services
- Failure to adhere to HHA licensing requirements and Medicare conditions of participation
- Knowing failure to return overpayments made by federal healthcare programs

Claim Development and Submission

In most healthcare entities, the process by which they prepare and submit claims for reimbursement to payors is an area particularly vulnerable to fraud and abuse, both deliberate and inadvertent. It is the point at which money can be drawn illegally out of the system. To prevent this, the OIG recommends that HHAs take several steps.

- Provide for sufficient and timely documentation of all home health services prior to billing to ensure that only properly documented services are billed.
- Make sure that claims are submitted only when appropriate documentation supports the claims and the documentation is maintained, organized in a legible form, and available for audit and review. The documentation should record the activity leading to the record entry, the identity of the individual providing the service, and information supporting medical necessity and other reimbursement coverage criteria.
- Ensure that the diagnosis and procedure codes for home health services reported on the reimbursement claim are based on the patient's medical record and other documentation, and comply with all official coding rules and guidelines. The codes used by the billing staff should accurately describe the service that was ordered by the physician and performed by the HHA.
- Ensure that the compensation for billing personnel does not offer any financial incentive to submit claims regardless of whether they meet applicable coverage criteria or accurately represent the services rendered.
- Conduct regular pre-and post-submission review of claims to ensure that they accurately represent the medically necessary services actually provided, are supported by documentation, and conform with applicable coverage criteria.

Among those measures, particular attention is directed to four narrower issues.

Medical necessity. Claims should only be submitted for services that the HHA has good reason to believe were medically necessary and ordered by a physician. This can be achieved by pre- and post-billing clinical reviews designed to verify that patients have received the appropriate level and number of services billed, and that the services were medically necessary.

Homebound beneficiaries. Home health services may be reimbursed under Medicare Parts A and B only if the beneficiary is "confined to the home." The HHAs providing those services must verify and document the specific factors that qualify a patient as homebound.

Physician certification of the plan of care. By enacting the following policies and procedures, an HHA can ensure that its claims for home health services are ordered and authorized by a physician.

- Before an HHA submits bills for reimbursement, a plan of care must be established and signed by a qualified physician.
- The plan must be periodically reviewed by a physician for the beneficiary to continue to qualify for Medicare coverage of home health benefits.
- Home health services are only billed if a physician has certified that the services provided to a patient are medically necessary and meet the requirements for coverage by Medicare.
- The HHA willingly assists physicians in determining the medical necessity of home health services and formulating an appropriate plan of care.
- The HHA documents any assessment it has made of a beneficiary's home health needs, which are used by the physician in developing a plan of care.
- The HHA educates physicians about their duty to certify patients for Medicare reimbursement of their home health services.

Cost reports. HHAs must submit annual cost reports to Medicare for reimbursement of administrative overhead and other general costs. The OIG makes numerous suggestions to the HHAs for preparing those reports. These are some of them:

- Costs are not claimed unless they are reimbursable, reasonable, and are based on appropriate and accurate documentation.
- Allocations of costs to various cost centers are accurately made and supportable by verifiable and auditable data.
- Unallowable costs are not claimed for reimbursement.
- Costs are properly classified.
- Management fees are reasonable and necessary, and do not include unallowable costs, such as certain acquisition costs associated with the purchase of a HHA.
- Any return of overpayments, including those resulting from an internal review or audit, is appropriately reflected in cost reports.
- The Medicare fiscal intermediary is notified promptly in writing of errors discovered after the submission of the HHA cost report.

Anti-Kickback and Physician Self-Referral Laws

Because HHAs rely so heavily on referrals from individuals and other entities, there is concern about their susceptibility to anti-kickback and self-referral violations. They are urged to take several steps to prevent this happening: all relationships with potential referral sources should be reviewed by expert counsel, no claims should be submitted for patients referred under questionable relationships, and the HHA should not offer incentives of any sort to anyone to induce referrals.

COMPLIANCE RISK AREAS UNIQUE TO HOSPICES

The Program Guidance for Hospices includes a list of risk areas only slightly shorter than the one for HHAs (28 vs. 31). There is some overlap between the two lists. The problems described here are unique to hospices.

- Uninformed consent to elect the Medicare Hospice Benefit.
- Admitting patients to hospice care who are not terminally ill.
- Arrangement with another healthcare provider who a hospice knows is submitting claims for services already covered by the Medicare Hospice Benefit.
- Falsified medical records or plans of care.
- Untimely and/or forged physician certifications on plans of care.
- Inadequate or incomplete services rendered by the Interdisciplinary Group.
- Insufficient oversight of patients, in particular, those patients receiving more than 6 consecutive months of hospice care.
- Hospice incentives to referral sources (e.g., physicians, nursing homes, hospitals, patients, etc.) that may violate the Anti-Kickback Statute, including improper arrangements with nursing homes.
- Overlap in the services that a nursing home provides, which results in insufficient care provided by a hospice to a nursing home resident.
- Improper relinquishment of core services and professional management responsibilities to nursing homes, volunteers, and privately paid professionals.
- Providing hospice services in a nursing home before a written agreement has been finalized, if required.
- Billing for a higher level of care than was necessary.
- Pressure on a patient to revoke the Medicare Hospice Benefit when the patient is still eligible for and desires care, but the care has become too expensive for the hospice to deliver.
- Billing for hospice care provided by unqualified or unlicensed clinical personnel.
- False dating of amendments to medical records.
- High-pressure marketing of hospice care to ineligible beneficiaries.

- Improper patient solicitation activities, such as "patient charting."
- Inadequate management and oversight of subcontracted services, which results in improper billing.
- Sales commissions based upon length of stay in hospice.
- Deficient coordination of volunteers.
- Improper indication of the location where hospice services were delivered.
- Failure to comply with applicable requirements for verbal orders for hospice services.
- Nonresponse to late hospice referrals by physicians.

The same advice was given to review the hospice's prior history of noncompliance to discover problem areas on which heightened attention should be focused. The OIG added its own collection of risk areas that have caused it the greatest concern. They relate primarily to the eligibility of patients for Medicare reimbursement.

Eligibility Requirements

At the time the hospice Compliance Program Guidance was issued, the eligibility of hospice patients for Medicare coverage had been the frequent subject of OIG audits and investigations. To minimize this problem, the agency made several policy and procedure recommendations to hospice management.

- Provide for complete and timely documentation of the specific clinical factors that qualify a patient for the Medicare Hospice Benefit.
- Delineate who has authority to make entries in the patient record.
- Emphasize that patients should be admitted to hospice care only when appropriate documentation supports their reimbursement eligibility criteria and only when such documentation is maintained, appropriately organized in a legible form, and available for audit and review.
- Indicate that the diagnosis and procedure codes for hospice services reported on the reimbursement claim should be based on the patient's clinical condition as reflected in the medical record and other documentation, and should comply with all applicable official coding rules and guidelines.
- Provide that the compensation for hospice admission personnel, billing department personnel, and billing consultants should not offer any financial incentive to bill for hospice care regardless of whether applicable eligibility criteria for reimbursement is met.

Hospices are directed to pay particular attention to three related issues.

Terminal illness as an eligibility requirement. It may seem obvious. For a hospice patient to receive reimbursement for hospice services under Medicare, the patient must be "terminally ill." To ensure that this always is the case, every hospice should take steps to verify that each patient is in the terminal stages of a disease and document the specific criteria for terminal illness. This can be accomplished if:

- Before a patient is admitted for hospice services, the hospice physician and attending physician review and certify the admitting diagnosis and prognosis.
- The patient's medical record contains complete documentation to support the certification made by the hospice physician or attending physician.
- The patient or lawful representative is informed of the determination of the patient's life-limiting condition.
- The patient or lawful representative is aware that the goal of the hospice is directed toward relief of symptoms rather than the cure of the underlying disease.
- A patient's medical condition and status is sufficiently reviewed during Interdisciplinary Group meetings.
- The clinical progression/status of a patient's disease and medical condition are properly documented.

It should be noted that sometimes patients are admitted to hospices for other than medical reasons (alleviate nonterminal suffering, only viable treatment for long-term decline in health status). Unfortunately, patients can be certified for the Medicare Hospice Benefit only when the patient's life expectancy is 6 months or less.

Plan of care. It is common sense that a hospice should establish and maintain a plan of care for each of its patients. It should have policies and procedures that make this possible. These are what the OIG suggests.

- Before a hospice bills for hospice care provided to a patient, it must establish a plan of care.
- The plan should include: (i) an assessment of the hospice patient's needs and (ii) identification of the scope and frequency of services needed to meet those needs.
- The plan of care must be reviewed and updated, at intervals specified in the plan, by the attending physician, hospice physician, and the Interdisciplinary Group.[1]

[1] The Interdisciplinary Group is the team responsible for the holistic care of the hospice beneficiary. It is this team that is responsible for development and review of the beneficiary's plan of care.

- The hospice should document any review or update of a hospice patient's plan of care.
- The hospice should regularly review the appropriateness of the services and level of services being provided, the patient's admission to hospice, and specific treatment modalities.

Levels of hospice care. The hospice must make clear to its physicians that Medicare will pay only for services that are reasonable and necessary for the palliation or management of terminal illness and were ordered by a physician or other appropriately licensed individual. Because the actual payment amount is based upon the level of care provided, the hospice must be able to supply documentation, such as physician orders and other patient medical records, to support the level of services provided. The medical condition of hospice patients is likely to change dramatically. For that reason, periodic clinical reviews should be conducted to determine the level, frequency, and duration of the services and whether they are justified by each patient's condition.

Hospice Arrangements with Nursing Homes

In the past, the OIG has found that hospices that enroll nursing home patients are especially vulnerable to fraud and abuse. To prevent problems, several deterrent steps should be taken.

Most importantly, the hospice and the nursing home should jointly establish a coordinated plan of care that is based on an assessment of the individual's needs and unique living situation in the nursing home. Beyond that, the hospice must maintain an independent role in treating the conditions of a nursing home patient.

- The hospice makes all covered services available to meet the needs of a patient and does not routinely discharge patients in need of costly inpatient care.
- The hospice retains professional responsibility for services (e.g., personal care, nursing, medication for relieving pain control) furnished by nursing home staff.
- All the care furnished by a nursing home related to the terminal illness or related conditions is in accordance with the hospice plan of care.
- The hospice and the nursing home communicate with each other when any changes are indicated to the plan of care.
- Evidence of the coordinated plan of care is present in the clinical records of both providers.
- Substantially all the core services are routinely provided directly by hospice employees and the hospice does not rely on employees of

the inpatient facility to furnish needed nursing, physician, counseling, or medical social services.
- The hospice keeps its forms and documentation of services separate from the nursing home's forms and documentation.

There is another danger in arrangements with nursing homes. Nursing home operators determine which hospices will be allowed to provide hospice services to their residents. It is in the hospices' interest to curry favor with those operators. If they go too far, they can violate the Anti-Kickback Statute. These are the practices that the hospices must avoid.

- Offering free or below fair market value goods to induce a nursing home to refer patients to the hospice.
- Making "room and board" payments to the nursing home in amounts in excess of what the nursing home would otherwise have received directly from Medicaid.
- Paying above fair market value for "additional" non-core services that are not included in Medicaid "room and board" payments to the nursing home.
- Referring hospice patients to a nursing home to induce the nursing home to refer its patients to the hospice.
- Providing staff at its expense to the nursing home to perform duties that otherwise would be performed by the nursing home.

COMPLIANCE AS A FACTOR IN PERFORMANCE APPRAISALS

Compliance occurs when employees perform their jobs within laws and regulations. To guide their employees' job performance, employers conduct performance appraisals. If employers wish to steer those employees toward compliance, they must include it as a factor or criterion in the appraisal process. The OIG urges that hospices owners do exactly this, through these policies and procedures.

- Discuss with all supervised employees and independent contractors the compliance policies and legal requirements pertinent to their function.
- Inform all supervised personnel that strict compliance with these policies and requirements is a condition of employment.
- Disclose to all supervised personnel that the hospice will take disciplinary action up to and including termination for violation of these policies or requirements.

- Sanction managers and supervisors who fail to adequately instruct their subordinates or fail to detect noncompliance with policies and legal requirements.

ESTABLISHMENT OF A COMPLIANCE INFRASTRUCTURE: COMPLIANCE OFFICER AND COMPLIANCE COMMITTEE

The second of the seven standard compliance program elements concerns the establishment of the infrastructure within each organization that is responsible for implementing the other elements of the program. It starts with a Compliance Officer and a Compliance Committee.

Compliance Officer

The entity, home care agency or hospice, must designate one of its employees as Compliance Officer. Small organizations may not be able to make this a full-time job. In that case, compliance duties can be added to a person's other responsibilities. Either way, this person must have the authority to carry out those duties, including the ability to review all documents and other evidence related to compliance. He or she must be a high-level person in the organizational hierarchy, with direct access to the governing board, the Cheif Executive Officer (CEO) or president, other top executives, and legal counsel. The Compliance Officer must have sufficient staff and resources to perform his job fully. That job entails these specific responsibilities.

- Overseeing and monitoring the implementation of the compliance program.
- Reporting on a regular basis to the governing body, CEO, and Compliance Committee on the progress of implementation, and to reduce the hospice's vulnerability to fraud, abuse, and waste.
- Periodically revising the program in light of changes in the organization's needs and in the law and policies and procedures of public and private payor health plans.
- Developing, coordinating, and participating in an educational and training program that focuses on the elements of the compliance program, and ensures that all employees are knowledgeable of, and comply with, federal and state standards.
- Ensuring that independent contractors, who furnish physician, nursing, or other healthcare services to the clients, or billing services

to the organization, are aware of the requirements of the hospice's compliance program.
- Coordinating personnel issues to ensure that the National Practitioner Data Bank and the List of Excluded Individuals/Entities have been checked with regard to all employees, medical staff, and independent contractors.
- Assisting financial management in coordinating internal compliance review and monitoring activities.
- Independently investigating and acting on matters related to compliance, including the design and coordination of internal investigations and any resulting corrective action.
- Maintaining the momentum of the compliance program and the accomplishment of its objectives long after the initial years of implementation.

Compliance Committee

An organization needs also to designate a Compliance Committee to advise the Compliance Officer and assist in the implementation of the compliance program. The committee should be composed of persons with a variety of skills, work expertise, and personality traits. It serves as an extension of the Compliance Officer. Some entities may lack sufficient resources to support a full-time Compliance Committee. The alternative for them is to assemble a "task force" when serious compliance problems arise.

The OIG suggests the following functions for this committee.

- Analyzing the legal requirements with which it must comply and the risk areas they imply.
- Reviewing current policies and procedures in these risk areas for possible inclusion in the compliance program.
- Working with individual departments to create standards of conduct and policies and procedures to promote compliance among employees.
- Recommending and monitoring the development of internal systems and controls to implement the organization's standards, policies, and procedures as part of its daily operations.
- Determining a strategy to promote compliance with the program and detection of any potential violations (e.g., reporting mechanisms, employee training, discipline of employee misconduct).
- Developing a system to solicit, evaluate, and respond to complaints and problems.

- Monitoring internal and external audits and investigations for the purpose of identifying troublesome issues and deficient areas, and implementing corrective and preventive actions.

COMPLIANCE TRAINING AND EDUCATION

Once compliance-focused policies and procedures have been written, the employees must be trained to follow them. The organization must make a systematic effort to communicate its standards and policies to all affected employees, physicians, managers, and independent contractors. For some employees, the training will be in general in scope, explaining the federal and state laws and regulations, and public and private program requirements that apply to the organization. For employees working in the areas of highest compliance risk—billing and collections, and marketing—the training must be more specific.

New employees should receive training as soon as possible after they are hired. Regular employees should be required to participate in a minimum number of training hours each year. Participation should be a condition of their continued employment, and failure to comply with training requirements should be grounds for disciplinary action. In addition, adherence to the principles of the compliance program should be a factor in each employee's performance appraisal.

LINES OF COMMUNICATION FOR COMPLIANCE COMPLAINTS/REPORTS

If employees do not understand the compliance policies and procedures, the Compliance Officer needs to hear about it. If someone discovers or suspects misconduct, violations, or other forms of noncompliant behavior, the Compliance Officer should know about it. For this to happen, there need to be open channels of communication between the Compliance Officer and all relevant parties (employees, managers, contractors, vendors, patients, the public). These can take the form of hotlines, websites, forums, e-mails, written memos, newsletters, bulletin boards, suggestion boxes, or any other medium that is convenient for potential users.

The communications options should be promoted to all employees. Employees should understand that they can ask questions or file reports anonymously. Reports of possible substantial violations should be documented, investigated, and dealt with promptly. A log should be kept of all activity through the compliance lines of communication, with regular reports to the governing board, top management, and the full Compliance Committee.

DISCIPLINARY ACTION FOR NONCOMPLIANCE

Sometimes, despite published compliance policies and procedures, and training programs, employees and others will still fail to comply with laws, regulations, or Program Guidelines. To combat this, the organization—hospice or HHA—must be prepared to take disciplinary action against them. The affected employees must be aware that they may be subject to such discipline.

Every organization must have a written policy that does several things:

- It describes the types or behaviors that may trigger disciplinary action.
- It defines the levels of disciplinary action that may be imposed.
- It makes clear that the sanctions will vary according to severity of the misconduct.
- It explains the procedures that will be used for handling disciplinary issues, and the persons who will be responsible for carrying them out.
- It states that the policy applies to all levels of employees from top to bottom.

It is essential that the policy be applied fairly, equitably, and consistently. Every manager or supervisor should understand his or her responsibility to enforce the policy. When there is a compliance failure and an employee requires discipline, his or her supervisor should be held accountable.

To minimize the need for disciplinary action, before new employees are hired, they should be subjected to a thorough background investigation, including a check of references and criminal record. In a point unique to healthcare provider entities, the OIG List of Excluded Individuals/Entities (that is, excluded from participation in federal healthcare programs) should also be consulted.

When a complaint against an employee or independent contractor is resolved with a conviction or exclusion, the organization should be prepared to terminate the employment or the contract of that individual.

AUDITING AND MONITORING COMPLIANCE EFFORTS

There is no guarantee that a compliance program, once conceived and implemented, will function at optimal effectiveness, either immediately or in the future under changing conditions. The organization needs constantly to audit and monitor the program's performance. The "performance" includes whether people follow the rules of the program itself; whether they adhere to the laws, regulations, and other requirements that are the focus of the program; and whether the incidence of errors, misconduct, and violations are reduced as a result.

The OIG suggests several monitoring techniques, but anything can be used that gets the job done. It offers these examples:

- Regular, periodic compliance audits by internal or external auditors.
- Visits with and interviews of patients.
- Analysis of utilization patterns.
- Testing clinical and billing staff on their knowledge of reimbursement coverage criteria and official coding guidelines.
- Assessment of relationships with physicians, hospitals, and other potential referral sources.
- Unannounced mock surveys, audits, and investigations.
- Reevaluation of deficiencies cited in past surveys for Medicare conditions of participation.
- Examination of complaint logs.
- Checking personnel records to determine whether any individuals who have been reprimanded for compliance issues in the past are among those currently engaged in improper conduct.
- Interviews with personnel involved in management, operations, claim development and submission, and patient care.
- Questionnaires to solicit the opinions of a sample of the organization's employees.
- Interviews with physicians who order services provided to the organization's patients.
- Reviews of clinical documentation, financial records, and other documents that support claims for reimbursement and Medicare cost reports.
- Validation of qualifications of physicians who order services for patients.
- Evaluation of the organization's written policies and procedures.
- Trend analyses that may reveal deviations, positive or negative, from an established baseline.

Sampling is a popular and inexpensive technique for showing changes in key parameters over time.

The results of the monitoring undertaken should be analyzed, distinct problems should be identified, conclusions should be reached, and recommendations for corrective action should be made. All these need to be reported to the governing board, top executives, the Compliance Committee, and probably legal counsel. Appropriate corrective action then needs to be taken. The auditing and monitoring process, and the changes that it leads to, should be documented.

RESPONDING TO AND CORRECTING NONCOMPLIANCE

The final component of a good compliance program explains how an organization will deal with violations of its own program rules, failures to comply with federal and state laws, and other types of misconduct. This section should state that, upon receiving reports or reasonable indications of suspected noncompliance, the organization will begin an immediate investigation to determine its severity. Based on its findings, it will take decisive steps to correct any problems that it has identified. These steps may include immediate referral to criminal and/or civil law enforcement authorities, a corrective action plan, a report to a relevant government agency, and the return of any overpayments.

The internal investigation typically consists of interviews with affected or involved individuals and reviews of relevant documents. Depending on the seriousness of what emerges, it may be a good idea to bring in outside legal counsel, professional auditors, or healthcare experts to aid in the investigation.

The OIG emphasizes two kinds of remedies: repayments and disclosures. It is not uncommon, in the course of processing and paying large volumes of claims, for payors to make inadvertent overpayments. (They also make underpayments, but that does not involve fraud and abuse.) There are established channels between payors and providers for the repayment of these amounts. These are used in the vast majority of cases. Where the overpayment appears to be the result of fraudulent behavior by the provider, not only must the amount be promptly repaid, there has to be a disclosure of the incident.

The OIG maintains a voluntary self-disclosure program that is based on four prerequisites: (1) the disclosure must be on behalf of an entity and not an individual; (2) the disclosure must be truly voluntary (i.e., no pending proceeding or investigation); (3) the entity must disclose the nature of the wrongdoing and the harm it causes to a federal healthcare program; and (4) the entity must not be the subject of a bankruptcy proceeding before or after the self-disclosure. The disclosure must be made within 60 days of discovering the possible violation.

The OIG likes to receive such reports or disclosures. In return, it will recognize them as a demonstration of the entity's good faith and willingness to cooperate with government officials to correct the problems identified. As a more practical matter, the OIG will consider any voluntary disclosure as a mitigating factor in setting administrative sanctions, like monetary penalties and program exclusions.

EXAMPLES OF HOSPICE VIOLATIONS OF LAW

On January 2, 2013, the DHHS announced that it had entered into a settlement agreement with an Idaho hospice provider to resolve alleged violations of the Health Insurance Portability and Accountability Act of 1996 (HIPAA) Security Rule. Following the theft of an unencrypted laptop computer containing electronic protected health information (E-PHI) of 441 patients, the provider notified the DHHS Office for Civil Rights (OCR) as required. The OCR conducted an investigation of the incident and found that the hospice had failed to conduct a risk analysis to safeguard E-PHI and did not have in place policies or procedures to address mobile device security as required under the HIPAA Security Rule. The settlement agreement requires the entity to pay DHHS $50,000 and enter into a corrective action plan.

In 2009, *Southern Care, Inc.*, a hospice company, paid $24.7 million to settle a False Claims Act (FCA) case brought against it. The company operated hospices in 15 states. The alleged fraud involved patients that were not eligible for hospice care (they were not terminally ill), lack of documentation of terminal illness, and marketing to potential patients with the promise of free medications, supplies, and the provision of home health aides. Southern Care also entered into a 5-year Corporate Integrity Agreement with the OIG as part of the settlement. The whistle-blowers who initiated the action received almost $5 million.

In 2009, *Kaiser Foundation Hospitals* settled an FCA lawsuit by paying $1.8 million to the federal government. The Hospitals allegedly failed to obtain written certifications of terminal illness for a number of its patients.

In 2006, *Odyssey Healthcare*, a national hospice provider, paid $12.9 million to settle a whistle-blower lawsuit for submitting false claims. The allegations were that Odyssey billed Medicare for providing hospice care to patients when they were not terminally ill and therefore ineligible for Medicare Hospice Benefits. A Corporate Integrity Agreement was a part of the settlement. The whistle-blower received $2.3 million.

In 2005, *Faith Hospice, Inc.*, settled FCA claims for $600,000. It was alleged that Faith Hospice billed Medicare for providing hospice care to patients, more than half of whom were not terminally ill.

In 2005, *Home Hospice of North Texas* settled an FCA charge for $500,000 regarding allegations of fraudulently billing Medicare for ineligible hospice patients.

In 2000, a Michigan osteopath, *Donald Dreyfuss*, settled an FCA suit for $2 million related to his recommending a particular hospice to the staff of his nursing home in return for payments from the hospice. He also pleaded guilty to criminal fraud charges that included a violation of the Anti-Kickback Statute.

EXAMPLES OF HHA VIOLATIONS OF LAW

In December 2012, *Rose Ray-Vasser*, the owner of a St. Louis home healthcare agency, was sentenced to 30 months in prison and ordered to pay $398,000 in restitution for false Medicare billing. Vasser owned Blessed Hands Home Health Services, which provided in-home nursing and personal care to elderly and disabled individuals. From 2006 to 2011, she and her company billed Medicare for services that had not actually been provided, also paying patients for the use of their names on the false claims. Blessed Hands also pleaded guilty to one felony count of healthcare fraud and was placed on probation for 3 years in addition to repaying the money.

In October 2012, the Medicare Fraud Strike Force arrested 91 individuals—among them doctors, nurses, and other licensed medical professionals—for their alleged participation in Medicare fraud schemes involving approximately $429.2 million in false billing. About $230 million of the fraudulent billing was for home healthcare fraud, with more than $100 million in mental healthcare fraud, another $49 million in ambulance transportation fraud, and millions more in other forms of fraud. The various charges against the defendants include conspiracy to commit healthcare fraud, healthcare fraud, violations of the Anti-Kickback Statute, and money laundering. The defendants participated in schemes to submit Medicare claims for treatments that were either medically unnecessary or were never provided. In some cases, patient recruiters, Medicare beneficiaries, and other coconspirators were paid cash kickbacks in return for supplying beneficiary information to providers, allowing the providers to submit fraudulent reimbursement claims to Medicare for services that were not necessary or were never provided.

In August 2012, *Jawad Ahmed* pleaded guilty in federal court to one count of conspiracy to commit healthcare fraud after managing a $13.8 million Medicare fraud scheme, according to the Federal Bureau of Investigation. Ahmed managed the HHA Physicians Choice Home Health Care, LLC (Physicians Choice) and used the company to deliver kickbacks to recruiters who supplied him with billing information for Medicare beneficiaries. He then billed Medicare for home health services that were never needed or performed. Ahmed also gave kickbacks to Medicare beneficiaries who pre-signed forms and visit sheets saying they received health services that were never actually performed. Ahmed also managed Phoenix Visiting Physicians, LLC from May 2010 to September 2011, where coconspirator Dwight Smith signed home care referrals for Medicare beneficiaries he had not seen or treated, and the company employed non-licensed doctors who performed unnecessary home care evaluations to non-homebound patients. Ahmed faced a maximum potential penalty of 10 years in prison and $250,000 in fines.

STUDY QUESTIONS

1. For what reasons would a patient seek admission to a hospice?
2. For what reasons would a patient require the services of a HHA?
3. List five benefits to an organization from creating an effective compliance program.
4. What features of an existing compliance program might render it ineffective?
5. List five risk areas unique to a hospice.
6. List five risk areas unique to a HHA.
7. In the context of HHAs, what do the terms "medically necessary" and "homebound" mean?
8. How could a supervisor take compliance behavior into account in evaluating the job performance of her subordinates?
9. If a small organization (a 10-bed hospice) has designated a strong Compliance Officer, why should it also appoint a Compliance Committee?
10. Give three examples of communication channels a HHA could open in order to encourage the reporting of compliance problems.

Learning Exercises

1. Most people know the names and locations of area hospitals, physician groups, and sometimes even nursing homes. Do a little research to identify the hospices and HHAs operating in your area. Use the Internet or telephone, and talk to hospitals or nursing homes to get names. Try contacting a hospice; explain that you are considering a career that may involve hospices and would like to make a site visit.
2. Amedisys, LHC Group, Gentiva, and Almost Family are the four largest publicly traded home health companies. They all have websites. They also all have appeared in the news for a variety of reasons for the last several years. Do some Internet research to learn more about them. Can you find any information on their compliance record? Are they the sort of organizations for which you might like to work someday?
   - Amedisys, http://www.amedisys.com/
   - LHC Group, http://lhcgroup.com/
   - Gentiva, http://www.gentiva.com/
   - Almost Family, http://www.almostfamily.com/
3. Either independently or, if you are studying this text as part of a course, with the support of your instructor, contact a local hospice or HHA. Explain your career ambitions, the course you are taking, and this textbook that you are reading. Ask if a representative from the organization would come to one of the class sessions to speak about its compliance efforts. This could be an opportunity to get some real-life, first-hand information about such issues in these kinds of organizations.

References

1. "OIG Compliance Program Guidance for Hospices," Federal Register, Vol. 64, No. 192, October 5, 1999.
2. "OIG Compliance Program Guidance for Home Health Agencies," Federal Register, Vol. 63, No. 152, August 7, 1998.
3. "Hospice Services," Chapter 11, Report to the Congress: Medicare Payment Policy, MEDPAC, March 2012.
4. "Hospice Care in Medicare: Recent Trends and a Review of the Issues," Chapter 6, Report to the Congress: Medicare Payment Policy, MEDPAC, March 2012.
5. "Home Health Care Services," Chapter 8, Report to the Congress: Medicare Payment Policy, MEDPAC, March 2012.
6. An informal yet revealing description of the numerous pressures that hospices and home health agencies are under to commit fraud. "Home Health and Hospice Fraud Update: Free Staff to Referral Sources, Billing Medicaid

During a Medicare Episode, and Health Fairs," Home Care & The Law, Vermont Assembly of Home Health Agencies, October 2010, www.vnavt.com/HCATL_10_09_24_oct_referrals_color.pdf
7. National Association for Home Care & Hospice, http://www.nahc.org/
8. National Home and Hospice Care Survey, http://www.cdc.gov/nchs/nhhcs.htm
9. Staff Report On Home Health and the Medicare Therapy Threshold, Committee On Finance, United States Senate, September 2011.

Chapter 19

Clinical Laboratories

Learning Objectives

After completing class sessions based on this chapter, a student will:

- Be familiar with the areas of highest compliance risk in clinical laboratory operations.
- Be able to describe the seven key components of a recommended compliance program.
- Understand the multiple duties of the laboratory's Compliance Officer.
- Learn the importance of opening lines of communication with employees and how to accomplish this.
- Become familiar with the techniques of auditing and monitoring the operation of a compliance program.
- Discover the variety of ways that the laboratory should respond to suspected misconduct and legal violations, including employee discipline and corrective action plans.
- Realize the substantial benefits to a clinical laboratory of implementing an effective compliance program.

INTRODUCTION

A clinical laboratory performs tests on clinical specimens to gather information about the health of a specific patient regarding the diagnosis, treatment, and prevention of a disease he or she may have. A physician decides that such a test would be useful in his or her clinical decision-making for a patient, collects the specimen (blood, tissue, urine) from the patient, sends it to the laboratory, and interprets the results that the laboratory reports.

The clinical laboratory industry represents 2.3% of total national healthcare expenditures and is growing at an average annual rate of 6% to 7%. Total industry revenues in 2011 were roughly $62 billion out of total national healthcare spending of about $2.7 trillion.

Clinical laboratories are found in three general locations: within hospitals, within physician offices, and as independent for-profit entities. Eleven publicly held laboratories represent 72% of the independent laboratory market. Hospital and independent laboratories conduct a higher percentage of high-complexity/higher-reimbursed tests than physician office laboratories. Clinical laboratory revenues are divided among those three segments in this way:

Hospital laboratories	60%
Independent laboratories	35%
Physician office laboratories	4%

Clinical laboratory test volumes break down in this way:

Hospital laboratories	55%
Independent laboratories	33%
Physician office laboratories	10%

This is the payor mix for hospital laboratories:

Fee for service	26%
Medicare Part A	23%
Medicare Part B	22%
Medicaid	14%
Out of pocket	5%
Capitated	7%

The compliance programs in nearly all healthcare-related entities are based on the Office of Inspector General's (OIG's) Program Guidances. Although Guidances have been issued for several different types of healthcare organizations, they prescribe the same basic programmatic structure in terms of personnel, documents, policies, procedures, and practices. The Guidance for clinical laboratories was published in 1998.

It was the first Program Guidance to come out, in response to a wave of sensational legal cases involving most of the leading independent laboratories as well as many hospital laboratories. The cases concerned practices that had been tolerated without prosecution for years—like kickbacks between the laboratories and physicians, marketing strategies that encouraged physicians to order unnecessary tests, lack of medical necessity, improper orders for tests, and unbundling chemical panels and profiles. They resulted in settlements amounting to hundreds of millions of dollars and severe damage to the public reputation of the laboratories.

COMPLIANCE RISK AREAS

The OIG Compliance Guidance on clinical laboratories describes what it considers to be the areas of highest risk within a laboratory's operations. These are the areas on which the organization should focus its attention and compliance efforts.

Medical Necessity

A laboratory's compliance program should communicate to its physician clients that claims submitted for its services will be paid only if they are covered, reasonable, and necessary for the beneficiary, given his or her clinical condition. The laboratory should be able to produce or quickly obtain documentation to support the medical necessity of the service.

While the OIG recognizes that physicians can order any tests that they believe are appropriate for a patient, it would like physicians to be made aware by the laboratory that Medicare will pay only for tests that meet Medicare coverage criteria and are reasonable and necessary to treat or diagnose a specific patient.

To achieve these ends, the OIG recommends that laboratories take several steps.

Design test requisition forms (for use by physicians) to capture the required compliance information and to promote conscious ordering of tests by the physicians. The form should ensure that the physician has made an independent medical necessity decision with regard to each test. It would be a good idea if physicians were encouraged to submit diagnosis information for all tests ordered.

The laboratory should provide all physician clients with annual written notices describing the Medicare policy for medical review of laboratory tests, explaining that Medicaid reimbursements will never be more than the equivalent Medicare reimbursements, and that organ or disease-related panels (groups of tests) are reimbursed only when all components are medically necessary.

Require physicians to sign a form acknowledging that he or she understands the potential implications of ordering customized profiles (a physician-specific group of commonly ordered laboratory tests).

When there is a likelihood that an ordered test will not be covered, before the test is performed, the beneficiary should be given written notification that the payment for the test is likely to be denied.

Implement methods for determining excessive utilization of laboratory services by a physician. One way is to use an outside consultant to analyze the laboratory's patterns of utilization and investigate any apparent abnormalities. Another way is to analyze test utilization data by Current Procedural Terminology (CPT) or Healthcare Common Procedure Coding System (HCPCS) codes, for the top 30 tests performed each year.

Billing

All the claims for testing services submitted by a laboratory must correctly identify the services ordered by the physician and performed by the laboratory.

This begins by ensuring that the CPT or HCPCS codes on the claim accurately describe the service that was ordered and performed. This requires systematic review by the laboratory of the appropriateness of the codes before the claims are submitted.

The laboratory should be confident that it can support the tests that it bills to Medicare with documentation obtained from the physician ordering the tests. It should not try to fill documentation gaps by using information from earlier dates of service, entering diagnosis information that has justified reimbursement in the past, using computer programs that automatically insert diagnosis codes, or simply making up information for claim submission purposes. What the laboratory should do is contact the physician who placed the order for up-to-date supporting information.

If a laboratory receives a specimen without a valid test order or one that is ambiguous, it again should contact the physician to verify which tests he or she wants and then perform them before submitting a claim for reimbursement. Medicare makes payments only for tests that are ordered, needed, performed, and covered.

Some laboratory tests are performed to produce results used in clinical calculations, such as low-density lipoprotein (LDL), so-called "bad" cholesterol. The laboratory must make sure that it does not bill for both the tests and the calculations in which they are used.

Reliance on Standing Orders

Generally, standing orders for tests are acceptable only in connection with an extended course of treatment, perhaps for a chronic disease. Due to the too often abusive use of such orders, their use is discouraged. Medicare and its reimbursement contractors can and may ask for additional documentation to support the medical necessity of such tests. The OIG asks that laboratories periodically monitor standing orders. Standing orders should have a fixed term of validity and be renewed when the term expires.

Compliance with Applicable OIG Fraud Alerts

The OIG and Centers for Medicare and Medicaid Services (CMS) periodically issue fraud alerts describing activities that raise special legal and enforcement concerns. Laboratories are urged to bring these alerts to the attention of their compliance and legal staff, who in turn should make sure that any conduct described in the alerts is immediately stopped and corrected.

Marketing

Every laboratory must ensure that the means by which it markets its services to physicians and others is honest, clear, correct, nondeceptive, and fully informative. It is important that physicians and other persons authorized to order tests fully understand the services offered by the laboratory, as well as the specific services that will be provided when tests are ordered.

Prices Charged to Physicians

The prices that laboratories charge physicians should be written into policies that ensure that they do not constitute inducements to gain the physicians' business. One way that this can happen is when a laboratory charges physicians a price below fair market value for their non-federal healthcare program tests to persuade them to order their federal healthcare program tests from the laboratory. Such a strategy would be a violation of Anti-Kickback Statute and False Claim Act.

Retention of Records

Laboratory compliance programs should include a provision that all records required by federal or state laws, or by the programs themselves, will be created and maintained. They will be invaluable if the laboratory becomes the target of a government investigation.

Compliance as an Element of a Performance Plan

Compliance programs are implemented by and through an organization's employees. To maximize program effectiveness, promotion of and adherence to compliance policies and procedures should be a factor in evaluating the performance of managers, supervisors, and other employees. In addition, everybody should receive training and periodic retraining in the latest compliance laws, policies, and procedures. It is the responsibility of managers and supervisors to discuss with their subordinates the legal requirements and compliance policies applicable to their duties, to inform them that strict compliance with the requirements and policies is a condition of their employment, and to advise them that they may be subject to disciplinary action, including termination, for violation of the requirements and policies.

KEY ELEMENTS OF A CLINICAL LABORATORY'S COMPLIANCE PROGRAM

A clinical laboratory addresses these risk areas through a formal, rigorous compliance program. The recommended features of the program are similar to those for other types of healthcare organizations. However, some aspects are unique to the setting of a clinical laboratory. These are the elements of a good program.

Written Policies, Procedures, and Standards of Conduct

To make clear how it wants its employees to behave in each of the previously mentioned risk areas, a clinical laboratory will prepare in writing detailed policies and procedures. They will incorporate the practices described earlier. The laboratory will also develop standards of conduct for those employees. The standards will require that employees observe and follow the policies and procedures, along with the underlying laws, regulations, and program requirements regarding fraud, waste, and abuse.

These standards, translated and interpreted as necessary, should be made available to all employees. They should be regularly updated as the policies, procedures, laws, and regulations are modified. Each time an employee is presented with a new version of the conduct standards, he or she should be asked to sign a statement certifying that he or she has received, read, and understood them.

Designating a Compliance Officer (CO) and a Compliance Committee (CC)

To put the policies, procedures, and standards of conduct into practice, the laboratory must create an enforcement infrastructure. The keystones of this effort are the designation of a CO and a CC.

The CO serves as the catalyst and focal point for the laboratory's compliance activities. The ideal candidate for this position has a master's degree in a related field (health management, human resources, public health), a minimum of 10 years work experience in the healthcare sector, and a deep familiarity with the operations of clinical laboratories, and the laws and program requirements applying to them. There should be evidence of strong leadership skills.

This person may work full time at carrying out compliance duties or combine the job with other responsibilities—depending on the size and resources of the laboratory. To properly perform the job, the CO must have sufficient authority to gather relevant documents and other information (contracts, agreements, billing and claims information, marketing activities) and question employees on compliance matters. This includes sufficient funding and staff to perform his or her responsibilities fully. He or she also must have direct access to the organization's Chief Executive Officer (CEO) and board of directors. This means that the CO position should not be subordinated to, for instance, the Chief Financial Officer, the corporate Legal Counsel, or the Claims/Billing Manager.

At a minimum, the CO should be responsible for carrying out these functions:

- Overseeing and monitoring the implementation of the laboratory's compliance program.
- Reporting regularly to the CEO, the governing body, and the CC on the progress in implementing the compliance program, while reducing the laboratory's vulnerability to fraud, abuse, and waste.
- Developing and distributing to all affected employees policies and procedures on compliance.
- Periodically revising the program as the needs of the organization change, and the law, regulations, and requirements of public and private payors evolve.
- Developing, coordinating, and leading an educational and training program that aims to make all managers and employees knowledgeable about pertinent payor standards and requirements, as well as the laboratory's compliance program, and ensuring their compliance with them.
- Ensuring that physicians who order services from the clinical laboratory are informed of the laboratory's compliance program standards with respect to coding, billing, and marketing, among other things.
- Assisting the clinical laboratory's financial management in coordinating internal compliance review and monitoring activities, including annual or periodic reviews of policies.
- Responding to reports of problems or suspected violations through independent investigations and corrective actions.
- Developing policies and programs that encourage managers and employees to report suspected fraud and other improprieties without fear of retaliation.

Other duties will become obvious if the laboratory deals with a unique mix of physician clients or has had a history of compliance problems and statutory violations.

In most organizations, the CO needs to be assisted and advised by a CC. Its functions will include the following:

- Analyzing the laboratory's regulatory environment, the legal requirements with which it must comply, and the specific risk areas that they create within the organization.
- Evaluating existing policies and procedures that address these areas for possible incorporation into the compliance program.
- Working within the clinical laboratory to develop standards of conduct and policies and procedures to promote compliance.
- Recommending and monitoring the development of internal systems and controls to implement the clinical laboratory's standards, policies, and procedures as part of its daily operations.
- Determining the best strategies for promoting observance of the compliance program and detection of any potential violations.
- Developing a system to solicit, evaluate, and respond to problems and complaints.

Like the CO, the CC's mandate may expand as the laboratory's business grows and diversifies.

Conducting Effective Training and Education

To be useful, the laboratory's policies, procedures, and standards of conduct need to be communicated to employees through a training and education program. All affected employees should be required to attend specific compliance-related training when they are first hired and on a regular basis after that. The curriculum of the training sessions should cover these topics:

- Federal and state statutes, regulations, and program requirements
- Public and private payor reimbursement principles
- General prohibition on paying or receiving remuneration to induce referrals
- Corporate ethics
- The organization's commitment to compliance
- The organization's compliance program
- Proper translation of narrative diagnoses
- Billing only for services ordered, performed, and reported
- Physician-approved amendments to requisition forms

- Proper documentation or confirmation of services rendered
- Duty to report misconduct
- Coding requirements, claim development, and claim submission processes
- Marketing practices

There may be basic training sessions for all employees that provide a general introduction to compliance issues and responsibilities, combined with specialized instruction for those working in coding, billing, and marketing.

New employees should be targeted for training early in their employment. Further instruction should follow on a regular basis, as a refresher, or whenever significant changes in compliance policies and procedures occur. The OIG recommends that employees be required to participate in a minimum number of educational hours each year. Records should be kept of the attendees at each training session, the topics covered, and the material distributed.

Attendance and participation in the training programs should be made a condition of continued employment; failure to comply with training requirements should result in disciplinary action; and adherence to compliance program requirements should be a factor in the performance appraisal of every employee.

Developing Effective Lines of Communication

Open lines of communication between a laboratory's employees and its CO facilitate the reporting of suspected incidents of fraud, abuse, and waste. If the organization does not make it easy for employees to complain, they have the option of expressing their frustration by suing the laboratory under the qui tam provisions of the False Claims Act. This includes the opportunity to seek clarification of any confusion or doubt they may have about a laboratory policy or procedure.

Several independent communication channels should be implemented to prevent reports from being diverted by supervisors or other employees. They may take the form of hotlines, suggestion boxes, emails, written memoranda, and newsletters. Reports indicating substantial violations of law should be documented and investigated promptly to determine their veracity. Logs should be kept of communications received and included in the regular reports to the CC, the CEO, and the governing body.

If employees are to trust and use the communication channels, confidentiality and nonretaliation policies must be prepared and publicized. It should be possible for employees to submit complaints or reports anonymously. They should also be informed that, at some point, as the investigation proceeds and government authorities become involved, their identities may have to be revealed. The cases of employees who may have participated in illegal conduct or other forms of malfeasance will raise complex legal and management issues. They should be handled in close consultation with a lawyer.

Enforcing Standards Through Well-Publicized Disciplinary Guidelines

A good compliance program provides guidance on how to handle executives, managers, supervisors, and employees who fail to comply with the laboratory's policies and procedures, standards of conduct, and laws and regulations. The guidelines will set forth the levels of disciplinary action that may be imposed on those employees. They will range from verbal warnings through written warnings and individual counseling to dismissal. The OIG urges that intentional or reckless failure to comply should warrant more severe sanctions. The procedure for evaluating these types of misconduct and determining the appropriate discipline should be explained in the standards of conduct.

Every effort should be made to apply the disciplinary guidelines fairly and consistently to all employees, regardless of their positions or status within the organization. Executives or managers should not be treated more favorably than lower-level employees. In addition, managers or supervisors of employees should be held accountable for their failures to adhere to policies, procedures, laws, and standards.

When hiring new employees who will have discretionary authority regarding compliance with laws or regulations, it is a good idea to conduct a balanced, prudent background investigation, including a reference check. The application should require the applicant to disclose any previous criminal convictions. In particular, a laboratory policy should prohibit the employment of persons recently convicted of a criminal offense related to health care, or who are listed as debarred, excluded, or otherwise ineligible for participation in any federal healthcare programs. It also should terminate the employment or other contract arrangement with any current employee or contractor who is convicted, excluded, or debarred.

Auditing and Monitoring

It is not sufficient for a laboratory to develop good compliance guidelines for its employees, train them to apply them in their work, and trust that this will avoid compliance problems. It must take the proactive step of monitoring and reporting on the laboratory's compliance performance on a regular basis. An effective monitoring technique recommended by the OIG is periodic compliance audits conducted by internal or external auditors. At a minimum, these should look at the laboratory's compliance with laws governing kickback arrangements, the physician self-referral prohibition, CPT/HCPCS coding and billing, ICD-9 and 10 coding, claim development and submission, reimbursement, marketing, reporting, and record keeping. The audits should pay attention to issues that Medicare has indicated are a high priority through OIG Special Fraud Alerts, OIG's own audits and evaluations, the annual OIG Work Plan, and other publicly announced law enforcement initiatives.

Another recommended monitoring technique uses sampling protocols to measure significant variations from a baseline picture of the laboratory's compliance practices. Outside consultants, lawyers, or accountants, or in-house staff with expert knowledge of compliance requirements, help the laboratory take an initial snapshot of the organization. Significant deviations from that baseline should trigger appropriate investigations to determine their causes. This should be followed by corrective actions that fit the problem or error. If the deviation resulted from a system fault or innocent mistake, no discipline is necessary. On the other hand, if it was caused by improper procedures, negligence or recklessness, misunderstanding of rules, including fraud and systemic problems, the laboratory should take prompt steps to correct the problem. If deliberate fraud or violations of the False Claims Act appear to be involved, the matter should be reported to the OIG or the Department of Justice (DOJ).

In addition to persistently checking for compliance failures, at least once a year the laboratory should review how well the compliance program is carrying out its primary functions (e.g., up-to-date policies and procedures, training, disciplinary steps, and other corrective action). This typically will involve measures like these:

- On-site visits
- Interviews with personnel involved in management, marketing/sales, operations, coding/billing, claim development and submission, and other related activities
- Questionnaires developed to solicit impressions of a broad cross-section of the clinical laboratory's employees and referring clients
- Review of requisition forms and other documents that support claims for reimbursement
- Review of written materials and documentation produced by the laboratory and used by physicians and other individuals authorized to order tests
- Trend analyses, or longitudinal studies, that seek deviations in billing or ordering patterns over a given period

When problems are identified, steps are immediately taken to correct them, and the laboratory documents its efforts.

Responding to Detected Offenses and Developing Corrective Action Initiatives

In even the best-run clinical laboratories, conscientious employees and ongoing monitoring will reveal some shortcomings in a laboratory's compliance practices. What is critical is how the laboratory's CO and other management officials respond. Failure to immediately address such problems can cause long-term damage to an organization's public reputation, credibility with payors, and legal status.

Depending on the nature and severity of the suspected violations, corrective steps could include an immediate referral to criminal or civil law enforcement authorities, implementation of a corrective action plan, a report under the OIG's Self-Disclosure Protocol, and the submission of any overpayments. These decisions will be based on an internal investigation consisting of interviews and review of relevant documents. A record should be kept of all actions taken, including documentation of the alleged violation, a description of the investigative process, copies of interview notes and key documents, a log of the witnesses interviewed and the documents reviewed, the results of the investigation (e.g., disciplinary action taken), and the corrective action implemented.

The laboratory's compliance efforts must become particularly intense when there is credible evidence of a criminal, civil, or administrative law violation. The matter should be reported to the appropriate governmental authority, typically the OIG or the DOJ, within a minimum of 60 days. Prompt reporting will demonstrate the clinical laboratory's good faith and willingness to work with governmental authorities to correct and remedy the problem. Also, the OIG has stated that it will consider such responsive behavior in determining administrative sanctions such as penalties, assessments, and exclusions.

BENEFITS OF AN EFFECTIVE COMPLIANCE PROGRAM

Even though a compliance program is now mandatory for a clinical laboratory, there are so many benefits that it would be a serious misjudgment to forego one. The primary advantage of such a program is that it dramatically reduces the likelihood that the laboratory will submit false or incorrect claims to federal or state government health programs, or to private payors. In addition, the rigor and scrutiny of a compliance program:

- Enhances the ability of the laboratory to provide high-quality services.
- Identifies weaknesses in its internal systems and management ranks.
- Demonstrates the laboratory's commitment to honest and responsible corporate conduct.
- Provides a more accurate insight into employee behavior regarding fraud and abuse.
- Identifies and prevents criminal and unethical conduct.
- Improves the efficiency and consistency of all organizational services.
- Establishes a single central source for information on statutes, regulations, and program directives related to healthcare fraud and abuse.
- Includes the development of mechanisms that facilitate employee reporting of potential problems.
- Incorporates procedures that enable the prompt, thorough investigation of alleged misconduct by corporate officers, managers, and other employees.
- Demands immediate, appropriate, and decisive corrective action.
- Reduces the laboratory's exposure to civil damages and penalties, criminal sanctions, and administrative remedies like program exclusion.

An effective compliance program is a sound investment.

STUDY QUESTIONS

1. What steps could a clinical laboratory take to encourage physicians to make testing referrals to it without violating the Anti-Kickback Statute?
2. What is the clinical laboratory's responsibility for ascertaining whether there is a "medical necessity" for the tests that physicians request from it?
3. List at least three pieces of information that a clinical laboratory must receive from a physician requesting a test so that it can submit a proper claim for reimbursement.
4. What is a "standing order" for laboratory tests and how can they create compliance problems for a clinical laboratory?
5. Explain the role of the CC, how it supports the CO, and the ideal relationship between the two of them.
6. Describe a curriculum for an introductory training session on compliance for new employees of a clinical laboratory.

Learning Exercises

1. Look up two or three examples of OIG Special Fraud Alerts (https://oig.hhs.gov/compliance/alerts/index.asp), particularly the one dealing with "Arrangements for the Provision of Clinical Lab Service." Get a sense of the kind of issues they address and imagine how an affected organization or individual would adapt to comply with them.
2. Seek out an interview with a primary care physician and ask how he or she decides when to request a laboratory test and from which laboratory.
3. Sketch out a performance appraisal system that takes into account an employee's adherence to compliance-related policies and procedures.

References

1. OIG Compliance Program Guidance for Clinical Laboratories, Federal Register, Vol. 63, No. 163, August 24, 1998.
2. American Association for Clinical Chemistry, http://www.aacc.org/Pages/default.aspx. An international scientific/medical society of individuals who work in the clinical laboratory industry.
3. American Clinical Laboratory Association, http://www.acla.com/. A trade association representing 42 of the largest clinical laboratories.
4. Dark Daily, http://www.darkdaily.com/#axzz23FZO0yk3. A website providing e-news, management briefings, and other resources on topics affecting the clinical laboratory industry.
5. G2 Intelligence Reports, http://www.g2reports.com/Home. A website providing analysis and advice on the business performance of diagnostic testing laboratories and related medical services providers. Sponsored by Bloomberg BNA.

Chapter 20

Ambulance Providers and Suppliers

LEARNING OBJECTIVES

After completing class sessions based on this chapter, a student will:

- Understand the basic services provided by an ambulance supplier.
- Know the primary types of fraud and abuse committed by ambulance suppliers.
- See the traditional components of a compliance program applied to the unique setting of an ambulance supplier.
- Be familiar with the primary compliance risk areas facing ambulance suppliers.
- Learn about the anti-kickback risks with a variety of referral sources.
- Have a list of compliance policies and forms for use by ambulance suppliers.
- Be introduced to an outline for a model ambulance supplier compliance program.

INTRODUCTION

An ambulance is a vehicle designed and equipped to respond to medical emergencies and, in nonemergency situations, be capable of transporting beneficiaries with acute medical conditions. The vehicle must comply with state or local laws governing the licensing and certification of an emergency medical transportation vehicle. At a minimum, the ambulance must contain a stretcher, linens, emergency medical supplies, oxygen equipment, and other lifesaving emergency medical equipment and be equipped with emergency warning lights, sirens, and telecommunications equipment as required by state or local law.

For reimbursement purposes, Medicare classifies seven levels of ambulance service: Basic Life Support (BLS); Advanced Life Support, Level 1

(ALS1); Advanced Life Support, Level 2 (ALS2); Specialty Care Transport; Paramedic ALS Intercept; Fixed Wing Air Ambulance; and Rotary Wing Air Ambulance. Medicare Part B pays for ambulance transport if vehicle and staff requirements, medical necessity requirements, billing and reporting requirements, and origin and destination requirements are satisfied. Medicare Part B will not pay for ambulance services if Part A has paid directly or indirectly for the same services—which occasionally happens.

The companies that provide ambulance services are diverse. Some are large, many are small; some are for-profit, many are not-for-profit; some are affiliated with hospitals, many are independent; and some are operated by municipalities or counties, while others are commercially owned.

The Office of the Inspector General (OIG) has encountered numerous cases of fraud and abuse committed by ambulance companies. These are the leading examples.

- Improper transport of individuals with other acceptable means of transportation
- Medically unnecessary trips
- Trips claimed but not rendered
- Misrepresentation of the transport destination to make it appear as if the transport was covered
- False documentation
- Billing for each patient transported in a group as if he or she was transported separately
- Upcoding from BLS to ALS services
- Payment of kickbacks

In the interest of preventing these misdeeds, every ambulance company must implement a compliance program. It is mandatory after the enactment of the Patient Protection and Affordable Care Act. Otherwise, a healthcare organization may not participate in any federal healthcare program. The OIG's Compliance Program Guidance for Ambulance Suppliers specifies the same seven core elements applicable to other healthcare entities. However, there are some facets that are unique to the ambulance services industry.

ELEMENTS OF AN OIG-RECOMMENDED COMPLIANCE PROGRAM FOR AMBULANCE SUPPLIERS

The basic elements of a good compliance program for any healthcare organization are the following:

- Development of compliance policies and procedures
- Designation of a Compliance Officer
- Education and training programs
- Internal monitoring and reviews
- Responding appropriately to detected misconduct
- Developing open lines of communication
- Enforcing disciplinary standards through well-publicized guidelines

Once a program has been established, the ambulance company should review it periodically to take into account changes in the healthcare industry, its own operations and market, federal and state healthcare laws and regulations, and payor policies and requirements.

Policies and Procedures

These documents represent the written standards of conduct for daily operations of the ambulance company. They should be reviewed periodically, at least annually, and updated as needed. The reviews should compare the standards with the actual practices within the organization. For instance, if a policy states that the company will review 100% of all ambulance call reports (ACRs), that is what should be happening. Otherwise, it has immediately violated its own policy.

Training and Education

In its Guidance, the OIG emphasizes the value of cross-training of employees as a means of raising their overall awareness of compliance across job functions. It also recommends interactive training to enhance employee learning by allowing them to ask questions and receive feedback. Whenever possible, the OIG suggests the use of real life examples of compliance problems presented by personnel who have experienced them—emergency medical technicians (EMTs) and paramedics.

Review of the Claims Submission Process

Savvy ambulance suppliers conduct periodic reviews of the process by which they prepare reimbursement claims for submission. They aim to make sure that the claim contains the required, accurate, and truthful information sought by the payor. The review focuses on the information and documentation present in the ACR, the medical necessity for the transport based on the payor requirements, the coding of the claim, the copayment collection process, and the adequacy of the subsequent payor reimbursement.

The reviews will identify compliance errors. This knowledge should be taken to the next step by also evaluating the source and causes of the error. In determining acceptable error levels, the ambulance supplier can start with a baseline audit from which it measures progress or decline. Other useful benchmarks are available from other ambulance suppliers, industry associations, or payors.

The OIG makes some other suggestions about this review process:

- Review claims for errors before they are submitted.
- Review of paid claims will help determine error rates and possible over- or underpayments.
- Review claims denials for patterns that point to the source.

Review of the Coding and Billing Systems

The ambulance supplier periodically should analyze in detail the entire process by which it generates a claim for reimbursement, from beginning to end. Those details will include:

- How a transport is documented and by whom.
- How that information is entered into the supplier's automated system (if any).
- Coding and medical necessity determination protocols.
- Billing system processes and controls, including any edits or data entry limitations.
- Claims generation, submission, and subsequent payment tracking processes.

It is especially important to conduct a review when payor documentation or billing requirements are modified or when an ambulance supplier changes its billing software or claims vendors.

Avoiding Sanctioned Employees or Contractors

Federal law prohibits Medicare payments for services by a sanctioned employee or contractor, that is, a person or organization that has been excluded from participation in the Medicare program. To comply with this restriction, ambulance suppliers are urged to query the OIG and General Services Administration (GSA) exclusion and debarments lists before they employ or contract with new employees or new contractors. Furthermore, it is a good idea to check those lists at least annually to make sure that the company is not employing or contracting with individuals or entities that have been recently convicted of a criminal offense related to health care, or who are listed as debarred, suspended, excluded, or otherwise ineligible for participation in federal healthcare programs.

Identification of Risks Unique to Ambulance Suppliers

The OIG Compliance Guidance for ambulance suppliers identifies the most common and generic risks faced by those companies. Each organization also must pay attention to other risk areas that are unique to the ambulance services industry, to its particular market, or to its specific type of operation. For example, a small, rural not-for-profit ambulance supplier may present risk areas different from those of a large, for-profit ambulance chain that serves a primarily urban area.

To stay up to date with the risks affecting the ambulance services industry, the OIG recommends that ambulance suppliers review its pertinent publications like Advisory Opinions, Fraud Alerts, and Bulletins; Office of Evaluation and Inspections (OEI) reports, and Office of Audit Services reports. The starting point for finding all these documents is the OIG's home website: https://oig.hhs.gov.

SPECIFIC MEDICARE RISK AREAS FACING AMBULANCE SUPPLIERS

The OIG outlined these specific risk areas for ambulance suppliers in its Compliance Program Guidance.

Medical Necessity

A number of Medicare and Medicaid fraud cases concerned the use of ambulance transport that was medically unnecessary. Medicare Part B will pay for ambulance services only if the patient's medical condition makes another form of transport unadvisable. Once medical necessity has been established, Medicare will cover a beneficiary's transport:

- To a hospital, a critical access hospital (CAH), or a skilled nursing facility (SNF), from anywhere, including another acute care facility, or SNF.
- To his or her home from a hospital, CAH, or SNF.

- Round trip from a hospital, CAH, or SNF to an outside supplier to receive medically necessary therapeutic or diagnostic services.
- To the nearest appropriate renal dialysis facility from his or her home.

Upcoding

Another problem to be avoided is billing for a higher level of services when in fact a lower level was provided. For instance, in one case, an ambulance supplier submitted bills for ALS services when only BLS services were provided. In addition, the company did not even employ a person qualified to deliver ALS services. As a result, it wound up paying civil penalties and submitting to a 5-year Corporate Integrity Agreement (CIA).

Documentation

Faulty or incomplete documentation is a common risk area for ambulance suppliers. It must be stressed that the gathering of accurate and complete documentation is the responsibility of several ambulance personnel, including the dispatcher who received the request for transport, the ambulance personnel who conducted the transport, and the coders and billers who prepared and submitted the claims for reimbursement. The collected documentation should at least display the following information:

- Dispatch instructions
- Reasons why transportation by other means was inadvisable
- Reasons for selecting the particular level of service
- Information on the status of the individual being transported
- Identity of person ordering the trip
- Duration in time spent on the trip
- Dispatch, arrival at scene, and destination times
- Distance in miles traveled
- Pickup and destination codes
- Related zip codes
- Services provided, including drugs or supplies

Restocking

When treating emergency patients, both in the field and during transport, ambulance EMS personnel consume supplies and drugs that must be restocked before the next call for their services. The destination facility, typically a hospital, frequently restocks the ambulance. This normally does not cause any problems under the Anti-Kickback Statute (AKS). To be safe, the ambulance company can meet the requirements of the Safe Harbor designed for ambulance restocking.

The Safe Harbor authorizes restocking only of ambulances that are used for emergency transport. The ambulance supplier and the hospital may not both seek reimbursement for the items restocked. Either or both of them must keep records of the items. The restocking arrangement must not take into account the volume or value of patient referrals.

SPECIFIC MEDICAID RISK AREA FACING AMBULANCE SUPPLIERS

All states that receive federal Medicaid funds are required to make arrangements for transporting Medicaid recipients to and from medical appointments. This results in the use and coverage of some transport methods not covered by Medicare, such as wheelchair vans, taxi cabs, and ambulettes. Care must be taken to ensure that Medicare is not also billed for such transport services already covered by Medicaid.

KICKBACKS TO INDUCE REFERRALS FOR AMBULANCE SERVICE REQUESTS

The AKS prohibits the intentional payment of anything of value to induce or reward referrals for ambulance services that will be reimbursed by Medicare or Medicaid. The ambulance services industry is rife with opportunities and incitements to pay for referrals. Under the AKS, there are regulations that describe several Safe Harbors—acceptable pay practices that avoid liability under the law. The OIG urges ambulance suppliers to structure their arrangements with referral sources to take advantage of the protection offered by the Safe Harbors whenever possible.

The Safe Harbors most suitable for ambulance suppliers are for space rentals, equipment rentals, personal services and management contracts, discounts, employees, price reductions offered to health plans, shared risk arrangements, and ambulance restocking arrangements. The potential referral sources that might be covered by these Safe Harbors are public emergency medical dispatch systems ("911"), private dispatch systems, first responders, hospitals, nursing facilities, assisted living facilities, home health agencies, physician offices, staff of those entities, and patients themselves.

In configuring its relationships with those referral sources, the ambulance company should aim to set the prices for its services at fair market value in an arms-length transaction not taking into account the volume or value of existing or potential referrals. In addition, it should not offer or provide gifts, free items or services, or other incentives of greater than nominal value to those sources, and should not accept such gifts and benefits from parties soliciting referrals from the ambulance supplier.

HIGH-RISK REFERRAL ARRANGEMENTS FOR AMBULANCE SUPPLIERS

The OIG recommends that ambulance suppliers pay particular attention to their arrangements with certain types of referral sources: public EMS sponsors, paramedic intercepts and other first responders, hospitals and nursing facilities, and patients themselves.

Public EMS Sponsors

In keeping with the restrictions of the AKS, ambulance suppliers must not offer anything of value to cities, counties, or other public EMS sponsors in order to secure a contract. It is acceptable to provide those sponsors with free or reduced cost EMS for uninsured, indigent patients.

First Responders

In many situations, it is common practice for a paramedic intercept or other first responder to treat a patient in the field, with a second responder, an ambulance supplier, transporting the patient to the hospital. The ambulance company may end up reimbursing the first responder for its services. That first responder may, in turn, be in a position to influence the selection of the transporting entity. The OIG emphasizes that the ambulance supplier must avoid inflated payments intended to win referrals from the first responder.

Hospitals and Nursing Facilities

Hospitals and nursing facilities are major sources of nonemergency ambulance business. All the traditional cautions mentioned previously should be observed strictly when dealing with them.

Patients

In working with patients who request their own medical transport, ambulance suppliers must comply with not only the AKS, but also the Civil Monetary Penalties (CMP) law. The CMP prohibits anyone giving anything of value to Medicare or Medicaid beneficiaries to induce them to choose a particular practitioner, provider, or supplier of goods or services that will be paid for by Medicare or Medicaid. The usual examples of such inducements are providing some of the goods or services without charge, or waiving the copayments associated with them. Exceptions are permitted for financial hardship copayment waivers, goods or services of nominal value (less than $10 per item), and any payments that fit into one of the AKS Safe Harbors.

COMPLIANCE POLICIES AND FORMS

A full compliance initiative by an ambulance supplier will be composed of a number of policies and forms. Each facilitates one or more of the compliance activities described earlier. This is an example list of such policies and forms.[1]

- Compliance Checklist
- Policy Statement on Compliance
- Corporate Resolution Adopting Compliance Program
- Code of Conduct
- Policy on Staff Member Rights and Obligations in a Government Investigation
- Compliance Officer Job Description
- Record Retention Schedule
- Background Screening Policy
- Background and Reference Check Authorization Form
- Policy on Review of Patient Care Reports
- Policy on Amendment of Patient Care Reports
- Conflict of Interest Policy
- Policy on Complaint and Concern Reporting
- Compliance Complaint/Concern Reporting Form
- Policy on Contracting with Third-Party Billing Agencies
- Policy on Confidentiality of Patient Information
- Policy on Credit Balances/Overpayments

---
[1] From the law firm of Page, Wolfberg & Wirth, found at this location: http://www.pwwemslaw.com/default.aspx

- Overpayment Form
- Compliance Training Record Form
- Compliance Program Training Post-Test
- Sample Notice of Ambulance Restocking Program
- Notice of Exclusion from Medicare Benefits
- Physician Certification Statement
- Nonemergency Intake Form
- Financial Hardship Determination Policy
- Patient Questionnaire for Financial Hardship Determinations
- Patient Notice for Financial Hardship Determinations

SAMPLE AMBULANCE SUPPLIER COMPLIANCE PLAN

The compliance plan for the ambulance supplier, PHI Air Medical, can be reviewed at their website: http://www.phiairmedical.com/. Click on the link in lower left corner of their website: PHI Air Medical is an air ambulance provider that offers air medical services throughout the United States.

Notice several points as you look over the plan. It opens with an unequivocal statement of the plan's goal to ensure that all its employees "adhere to all applicable Medicare, Medicaid, and any other federally funded health care .... laws, rules and policies relating to the submission of claims for ambulance services, and the general operation of an air ambulance service." It emphasizes that the best way to avoid charges of fraud and abuse is to *prevent* them. The plan spends a full page explaining how important it is that every employee follow the plan, adding that the company intends to enforce all related policies and procedures.

Before discussing the details of the plan, employees are told to contact the company's Compliance Officer "when questions on compliance arise or to report potential violations or any concerns regarding compliance." There is a reference to a Compliance Hotline that can be used anonymously. Employees who report their compliance concerns will not be subject to adverse action or retaliation. This language effectively defines an open channel of communication for compliance matters and encourages its use.

The substance of the plan is organized around the OIG's seven recommended compliance program components. These are the headings and subheadings for the plan description.

1. Development of Compliance Standards, Policies, and Procedures
    a) Documentation
    b) Guiding Principles
    c) Compliance Standards and Procedures

   d) New Standards and Procedures
   e) Documentation Practices

2. Designation of the Compliance Officer and Other Oversight Responsibilities
   a) Compliance Officer
   b) Compliance Oversight Committee

3. Development of Education and Training Programs
   a) Overview of Compliance Training Programs
   b) Core Content of Our Compliance Training Program
   c) Compliance Officer's Role in Training

4. Development of Internal Monitoring and Reviews
   a) Coding and Billing Decisions
   b) Illegal Remuneration and Prohibited Referrals
   c) Billing and Claims Submission
   d) Assessment of the Claims Submission Process
   e) Integrity of Electronic or Computer Billing Systems
   f) Auditing and Monitoring
      - Who Should Conduct Audits and Reviews
      - Periodic Review of Claims Denials
      - System Reviews and Safeguards
   g) Disclosure of Review Results
      - Internal Disclosure
      - External Disclosure
   h) Overpayments

5. Responding Appropriately to Detected Misconduct
   a) Government Investigation
   b) Reporting Intentional Wrong-Doing to Authorities

6. Developing Open Lines of Communication
   a) Hotline and Other Mechanisms for Reporting Violations
   b) Protection of Staff Members
   c) Departing Staff Members—Exit Interview

7. Enforcing Disciplinary Standards
   a) Compliance as an Element of Performance Evaluation
   b) Disciplinary Procedures
   c) Record Retention

d) Relationship with Competitors/Vendors
e) Screening Staff Members and Contractors
f) Plan Modifications
g) Emergency Changes to the Plan

This is an excellent template for a compliance program for an ambulance supplier or for many other types of healthcare providers.

STUDY QUESTIONS

1. What is the difference between an emergency and a nonemergency transport? Can you think of situations where the distinction may not be clear or there is some overlap between the two characterizations?
2. Who decides that there is another form of transport available that makes an ambulance unnecessary?
3. What is the difference between the OIG's List of Excluded Individuals/Entities and the GSA's Excluded Parties List System? Start here, https://oig.hhs.gov/faqs/exclusions-faq.asp, to figure it out.
4. What is the difference between a hospital and a CAH? What are the unique features of a SNF, and how does it differ from a "nursing home"? Under what circumstances would a patient request his or her own ambulance transport? What are the reasons that a person would need to be transported to or from one of these facilities?
5. What does "ambulance restocking" mean and who pays for it? How can fraud and abuse problems result? Learn about the Ambulance Replenishing Safe Harbor under the Anti-Kickback Statute at Federal Register, Vol. 66, No. 233, December 4, 2001 p. 62979.

Learning Exercises

1. When you are out in public, begin to notice when an ambulance goes by. What are the signs of the kind of mission it is on? How fast is it moving? Is the siren being used? What route does it appear to be following? Where does it appear to be headed? Which of the Medicare levels of ambulance service does it seem to represent? Imagine who might have requested the ambulance service—hospital, physician, nursing facility, first responder, or patient.
2. Contact a local ambulance company, explain that you are considering working in healthcare compliance and are taking a course on the topic.

Ask if the company has a compliance plan or program that you can review. If the company is willing, set up an interview with its Compliance Officer or the person responsible for compliance. Try to learn which of the recommended elements of a good program the company is implementing. Ask which compliance risk areas present the greatest challenge for it.

3. Contact the local police department or 911 emergency response center. If there are several ambulance companies in the area, ask how they decide which one to call when there is an emergency.
4. For an organization preparing its own compliance program, there are three good sources of assistance. One is the OIG's Compliance Program Guidance for Ambulance Suppliers. Another is the actual programs or plans of real-world providers of ambulance services. One example from PHI Air Medical is mentioned in the text. The third source is the CIAs to which fraud and abuse offenders submit in order to avoid criminal prosecution. Go to this link, https://oig.hhs.gov/fraud/cia/agreements/ambulance_service_inc_11232009.pdf, to see an example concerning Ambulance Service, Inc. Review the agreement there and notice what compliance efforts it requires from the ambulance company. Look particularly at the sections on Policies and Procedures, Training and Education, Engagement of Independent Review Organization, Disclosure Program, OIG Inspection, Audit, and Review Rights, Breach and Default Provisions, Appendix A—Independent Review Organization, and Appendix B—Claims Review.

References

1. OIG Compliance Program Guidance for Ambulance Suppliers, Federal Register, Vol. 68, No. 56, March 24, 2003, p. 14245.
2. Medicare Benefit Policy Manual, Chapter 10—Ambulance Services.

Chapter 21

Third-Party Billing Companies

Learning Objectives

After completing class sessions based on this chapter, a student will:

- See how medical billing companies fit into the process through which providers seek reimbursement from federal healthcare programs.
- Appreciate the benefits that medical billing companies enjoy when they implement effective compliance programs.
- Gain detailed knowledge of the seven basic elements of a compliance program tailored to the needs of a medical billing company.
- Become familiar with the highest risk areas of operation unique to medical billing companies.
- Discover the primary responsibilities of a Compliance Officer and the members of a Compliance Committee.
- Be able to design the curriculum for a compliance training course for employees.
- Realize the value of open lines of communication between a Compliance Officer and a company's employees.
- Understand how best to administer disciplinary action against noncompliant employees.
- Know the importance of well-conceived compliance monitoring and specific techniques for carrying it out.
- Be aware of a company's options in responding to detected incidents of misconduct and noncompliance.

INTRODUCTION

The medical billing process is an ongoing transaction between a direct provider of healthcare services and the entity that pays for those services. The best example of a provider is a physician practice. The paying entities are either government healthcare programs, primarily Medicare and Medicaid, or private insurance companies and health plans. For each service or item that it provides to a patient, a claim or bill for reimbursement is submitted to the payor that covers that patient. The claim may be submitted electronically by the provider, in paper form by the provider, or in paper form by the beneficiary patient. The trend is toward electronic submission.

The preparation and filing of those claims is time and resource consuming. Each piece of information on the claim form must be accurate. If the patient data or the code assigned to the service or item are not correct, the claim will be denied, have to be corrected, and then resubmitted. The combined costs of administration (including documentation, coding, and billing) exceed 31% of United States healthcare expenditures, up from 22% in 1983. From 1969 to 1999, the personnel devoted to administrative grew from 18% to 27% of the healthcare labor force.

Many physician practices and other healthcare providers have chosen to outsource their tedious, complex billing procedures to third-party firms that specialize in preparing accurate claims, submitting them, and following through to final payment. Because of their specialization, billing companies are able to perform the same services at lower cost. Their improved accuracy rates frequently result in a higher percentage of claims being paid and higher total revenues for the provider. The typical services provided by a third-party billing company are insurance claim submission, insurance follow-up, reporting and analysis, patient invoicing and support, medical coding, transcription, and credentialing. In 2012, there were 9,227 billing companies serving healthcare clients. They employed 26,391 people and brought in $3.3 billion in revenues.

The largest volume of healthcare fraud and abuse complaints, violations, and convictions stem from the filing of claims for reimbursement. An entire federal statute, the False Claims Act, addresses these kinds of misconduct. The problems, deliberate or inadvertent, can arise whether the billing activities are performed in-house by the provider or outsourced to a third party. The provider is liable for the actions of its owns employees and its agents and contractors. Therefore, the compliance concerns of the billing companies are intertwined with those of its providers clients.

BENEFITS OF A COMPLIANCE PROGRAM

In 1998, the Office of the Inspector General (OIG) of the federal Department of Health and Human Services issued a Compliance Program Guidance for Third-Party Medical Billing Companies. It has provided structure and direction for the compliance programs adopted by medical billing companies since that time.

The over 9,000 third-party billing companies vary in size and available resources, but none are very large. The OIG acknowledges that not all of them will be able to implement the most comprehensive compliance program. It believes, however, that every company should make a good faith effort to carry out the objectives and principles described in the Guidance. Superficial and hastily constructed programs lacking ongoing monitoring will expose both the billing company and its clients to liability.

In light of the billing companies' intimate interaction with the operations of provider clients, the OIG encourages the companies to maintain open and frequent communications with those providers. It specifically recommends that the company and its clients coordinate the planning of their compliance programs. This includes agreeing on the division of compliance responsibilities. The terms of the arrangement between the company and the client should be written into their contract for billing services. It should make clear which functions are shared and which are the sole responsibility of each party.

The Guidance lists a number of benefits that come from establishing a compliance program.

- A good program incorporates internal controls that make more likely compliance with federal regulations, private payor policies, and internal guidelines.
- The program will compel better medical record documentation.
- It inevitably results in improved collaboration, communication, and cooperation among healthcare providers and those processing and using health information.
- A good program enables the company to react more quickly and accurately to employees' compliance concerns and to focus resources to address those concerns.
- The program will include an efficient communications structure and process that facilitates rapid response to identified compliance problems.
- It will serve as a concrete demonstration to employees and the community at large of the company's strong commitment to ethical, responsible corporate conduct.
- The program's mechanisms allow the development of an accurate assessment of employee and contractor behavior relating to fraud and abuse.

- It increases the likelihood of identification and prevention of criminal and unethical conduct.
- The program is a centralized source for distributing information on healthcare statutes, regulations, and other program directives related to fraud and abuse.
- It creates a methodology that encourages employees to report potential problems.
- Its procedures allow the prompt, thorough investigation of possible misconduct by corporate officers, managers, employees, and independent contractors.
- The existence of an effective compliance program will improve the company's relationship with its Medicare contractor.
- The program's early detection and reporting minimizes the loss to the government from false claims, which in turn reduces the company's exposure to civil damages and penalties, criminal sanctions, and administrative remedies, such as program exclusion.

INTRODUCTION TO BASIC COMPLIANCE PROGRAM ELEMENTS

The Compliance Guidance for third-party medical billing companies uses the same seven program elements that have been part of every other Guidance for other types of healthcare organizations before and since.

1. The development and distribution of written *standards of conduct*, as well as *written policies and procedures* that express the billing company's commitment to compliance and that address specific areas of potential fraud.
2. The designation of a *Compliance Officer* and a *Compliance Committee*, who are responsible for creating, maintaining, and overseeing the compliance program and who report directly to the Chief Executive Officer (CEO) and the governing body.
3. The development and implementation of regular, effective *education and training* programs for all affected employees and agents.
4. The creation and maintenance of a *process to receive complaints*, and the adoption of procedures to protect the anonymity of complainants and to protect them from retaliation.
5. The development of a system to *respond to allegations* of improper or illegal activities and the enforcement of appropriate *disciplinary action against employees* who have violated internal compliance

policies, applicable statutes, regulations, or federal, state, or private payor healthcare program requirements.
6. The use of audits and other risk evaluation techniques to *monitor compliance* and assist in the reduction of identified problem areas.
7. The investigation and *correction of identified compliance problems* and the development of policies addressing the nonemployment of sanctioned individuals

The OIG encourages companies to require that promotion of, and adherence to, these elements be a factor in evaluating the performance of all employees. Supervisors should discuss with their subordinates, and with relevant contractors, the compliance policies and legal requirements that apply to their work. Employees should be informed that strict compliance with the elements is a condition of their employment, and that violations will lead to disciplinary action up to and including termination. Managers and supervisors themselves may be disciplined for failure to properly instruct their subordinates or detect their noncompliance.

Written Policies and Procedures

In most well-run organizations, a majority of activities are described in written policies and procedures. They instruct members of the organization, employees and agents, on how to perform their jobs. Such documents can be an effective vehicle for defining compliant employee behavior. If an organization has not already created the appropriate policies and procedures, it must do so in the process of establishing its compliance program.

At the most general level are organizational standards of conduct. The OIG refers to them as a kind of "constitution." They are a set of fundamental principles, values, and framework that guides employees in conducting business professionally, competently, and ethically. They set forth the company's expectations for its governing body, officers, managers, employees, contractors, and other agents.

The other policies and procedures most relevant to a company's compliance efforts are those that apply to what are called "risk areas." These are the facets of operations that are most vulnerable to misconduct leading to fraud and abuse. This is where the company needs to focus its attention. The OIG suggests that each company start with the areas of special concern that it has identified through its investigative and audit functions.

This is a list of those areas.

- Billing for items or services not actually documented
- Unbundling

- Upcoding (e.g., diagnosis-related groups [DRG] creep)
- Inappropriate balance billing
- Inadequate resolution of overpayments
- Lack of integrity in computer systems
- Computer software programs that encourage billing personnel to enter data in fields indicating services were rendered though not actually performed or documented
- Failure to maintain the confidentiality of information/records
- Knowing misuse of provider identification numbers, which results in improper billing
- Outpatient services rendered in connection with inpatient stays
- Duplicate billing in an attempt to gain duplicate payment
- Billing for discharge in lieu of transfer
- Failure to properly use modifiers
- Billing company incentives that violate the Anti-Kickback Statute or similar federal or state statute or regulation
- Joint ventures
- Routine waiver of copayments and billing third-party insurance only
- Discounts and professional courtesy

In addition, the company is encouraged to conduct a comprehensive self-administered risk analysis or contract with independent risk professionals to do the same thing. The purpose of the analysis is to identify and rank the various compliance and business risks the company faces in its daily operations. It also should review its prior history of noncompliance for other problem areas.

There are additional risk areas for billing companies that also provide coding services to their clients.

- Internal coding practices
- "Assumption" coding[1]
- Alteration of the documentation
- Coding without proper documentation of all physician and other professional services
- Billing for services provided by unqualified or unlicensed clinical personnel
- Availability of all necessary documentation at the time of coding
- Employment of sanctioned individuals

To minimize the risk in these areas, the OIG urges companies to take steps to ensure that all coding and billing is based on full medical record

[1] The coding of a diagnosis or procedure without supporting clinical documentation.

documentation. In addition, the companies should maintain an up-to-date user-friendly index for coding policies and procedures to make sure that essential coding materials are readily accessible to all coding staff. There should be an emphasis on safeguarding the confidentiality of medical, financial, and other personal information that is part of the billing and coding process.

In its Compliance Program Guidance for billing companies, the OIG made detailed recommendations for billing company activities in four areas: the claims submission process, credit balances, the integrity of data systems, and a system for records retention.

Claims submission process. The written policies and procedures should define a mechanism for the billing and reimbursement staff to communicate effectively and accurately with provider-clients. They also should serve the following purposes.

- Proper and timely documentation of all physician and other professional services should be obtained prior to billing to ensure that only accurate and properly documented services are billed.
- Claims should be submitted only when appropriate documentation supports the claims and only when such documentation is maintained, appropriately organized in legible form, and available for audit and review. The documentation, which may include patient records, should record the time spent in conducting the activity leading to the record entry and the identity of the individual providing the service.
- The diagnosis and procedures reported on the reimbursement claim should be based on the medical record and other documentation, and the documentation necessary for accurate code assignment should be available to coding staff at the time of coding.
- The CPT, ICD, and other codes used by the coding staff should accurately describe the service that was ordered by the physician.
- The compensation for billing department coders and billing consultants should not provide any financial incentive to improperly upcode claims.
- There should be established a process for pre- and post-submission review of claims to ensure that claims submitted for reimbursement accurately represent the services provided, are supported by sufficient documentation, and are in conformity with applicable coverage criteria for reimbursement.
- Obtain clarification from the provider when documentation is confusing or lacking adequate justification.

The billing company should be willing to contract with physicians or other medical experts for advice on clinical issues to the coding staff.

Credit balances. Credit balances occur when payments, allowances, or charge reversals posted to an account exceed the charges to the account. The company should have a procedure in place that identifies and resolves such overpayments with the payor in a timely manner. Such accounts should be segregated from the active accounts until a repayment has been secured.

Data systems integrity. Billing companies deal with large volumes of sensitive personal data. They must back up those data regularly and securely. A complete and accurate audit trail for every piece of data should be maintained. A system should be implemented to prevent the contamination of the data by outside parties. They also should be protected against unauthorized access or disclosure.

Records retention system. In the course of their business, billing companies work with a large number of records and other documents. This includes records required by federal and state laws, and by public and private healthcare programs, and documents relating to the functioning and effectiveness of their compliance programs. They all must be maintained for different periods of time as required by law or in anticipation of future investigations. Each company must have a formal system for creating, distributing, retaining, storing, retrieving, and destroying these materials.

Compliance Officer and Compliance Committee

The second element of a recommended compliance program is the appointment of a Compliance Officer and formation of a Compliance Committee. Larger organizations may make the Compliance Officer position a full-time job; in smaller entities with fewer resources, one person may have to add compliance to his or her other duties. One of the necessary features of this job is the authority to speak directly to the company's governing board, its CEO, top executives, and legal counsel; to conduct inquiries and investigations into incidents of suspected violation; and to review all documents and other evidence related to compliance activities. The OIG recommends that Compliance Officer perform these functions:

- Overseeing and monitoring the implementation of the compliance program
- Reporting regularly to the governing body, CEO, and Compliance Committee on the progress of implementation and the ongoing effectiveness of the program
- Periodically revising the program in light of changes in the organization's needs and in the law and requirements of public and private payor health plans

- Reviewing employees' certifications that they have received, read, and understood the standards of conduct
- Developing, coordinating, and participating in educational and training activities on the elements of the compliance program
- Coordinating with the human resources or personnel office to ensure that providers, employees, or contractors have not been excluded from participation in federal healthcare programs
- Assisting financial management staff in conducting internal compliance review and monitoring activities, including annual or periodic reviews of individual departments
- Independently investigating and acting on matters related to compliance, including designing and coordinating the investigations and taking appropriate corrective actions
- Developing policies and programs that encourage managers and employees to report suspected fraud and other improprieties without fear of retaliation

In performing these tasks, the Compliance Officer is strongly encouraged to coordinate compliance functions with the Compliance Officers of the company's provider-clients.

The Compliance Committee should be composed of representatives from operations, finance, audit, human resources, utilization review, medicine, coding, and legal, as well as employees and managers of key operating units. One of the duties of the Compliance Officer is to train the committee members on the compliance policies and procedures and manage them in the carrying out the following responsibilities:

- Analyzing the organization's regulatory environment, the legal requirements with which it must comply, and identified risk areas
- Working with specific departments and with provider-clients to develop standards of conduct and policies and procedures that promote compliance
- Recommending and monitoring the development of internal systems and controls to implement the standards, policies, and procedures as part of its daily operations
- Determining other initiatives to promote compliance with the program and detection of potential violations
- Developing a system to solicit, evaluate, and respond to complaints and problems
- Monitoring internal and external audits and investigations in order to identify troublesome issues and deficient areas, and implement corrective and preventive action

Compliance Training

Once the standards of conduct, policies, and procedures have been created, it is necessary to train employees to follow them in their work. Newly hired employees should receive training shortly after they start work, perhaps as part of their orientation, certainly within the first 30 days. Thereafter, there should be training sessions at least annually, to remind employees of existing standards and introduce new standards. Special trainings should be scheduled when there is a significant change in the law or program requirements.

There should be general training sessions for the entire workforce (including governing board members, the CEO, senior executives, managers, and supervisors) and focused sessions for employees working in the highest risk areas like coding, billing, and marketing.

The OIG suggests this curriculum for the general training.

- Public and private payor reimbursement principles
- Prohibitions against paying or receiving remuneration to induce referrals
- Proper selection and sequencing of diagnoses
- Improper alterations to documentation
- Submitting a claim for physician services when rendered by a non-physician
- Proper documentation of services rendered, including the correct application of official coding rules and guidelines
- Signing a form for a physician without the physician's authorization
- Duty to report misconduct

In planning compliance training, it is a good idea to consult with the company's provider-clients to ensure that a consistent message is being delivered and avoid any potential conflicts in the implementation of policies and procedures. If appropriate, employees from the billing company and client organizations might attend the same training sessions.

It is particularly important to drive home the compliance message to marketing and financial personnel, who may feel compelled by the pressure to meet business goals to engage in prohibited practices.

All affected personnel should be required to participate in each training as a condition of their continued employment. Their comprehension of the training material can be checked through testing. The participants should be asked to sign a statement acknowledging their understanding of compliance principles and their commitment to carrying them out.

A variety of teaching methods can be employed, such as interactive training, teleconferencing, web-based text and video classes, live classroom sessions, and written materials. The training should be offered in several different languages when the billing company has a culturally diverse staff. Training instructors may come from outside or inside the organization. The billing company should retain records of its compliance training activities, including attendance logs and material distributed to participants.

Open Lines of Communication

For a company's compliance effort to succeed, there must be an open line of communication between the Compliance Officer and the employees who may cause or come in contact with compliance problems. This usually means several independent paths that an employee can use to report suspicions of fraud, waste, or abuse without worrying that a supervisor or other person will sidetrack the report. Examples of these paths are hotlines, suggestion boxes, email, electronic forums or bulletin boards, and written memoranda. Written policies must assure employees that they can make reports anonymously and that they will not be exposed to retaliation.

There also should be a less complicated procedure for people who simply want an explanation of a compliance policy or issue. Questions received and answers given should be shared with other staff. Another good idea is to hold exit interviews with departing employees who may be more willing to speak candidly about compliance problems. It may be helpful to get employee input as the company is developing these communication and reporting systems.

When the information received through these communication channels suggests that substantial violations have occurred, it should be documented and an investigation begun promptly. All such reports should be recorded, including the substance of the investigation, its findings, and any actions taken as a result.

Disciplinary Action to Enforce Compliance

Even after thorough training and education, some employees will fail to comply with the billing company's standards of conduct; policies and procedures; federal, state, or private payor healthcare program requirements; or federal and state laws. It may be deliberate or the result of gross negligence. The company must have in place a mechanism for taking appropriate disciplinary action against such behavior.

The discipline must be imposed on any persons who fail to comply, whether corporate officers, managers, supervisors, or employees. There should be a detailed procedure for handling disciplinary problems that identifies who will be responsible for making the decisions. Different degrees of disciplinary action should be imposed, depending on the culpability of the individual, and the consequences of his or her misconduct. The actions may range from oral warnings to written warnings, suspension, financial penalties, and termination.

The disciplinary actions must be carried out on a fair and equitable basis, and in an appropriate and predictable manner. Such action needs to be consistently applied and enforced for the disciplinary policy to have the required deterrent effect. All levels of employees should be subject to the same disciplinary action for the commission of similar offenses.

All new employees who have discretionary authority to make decisions that may involve compliance should be subject to a reasonable and prudent background investigation, including a reference check. Every job applicant should be required to disclose any prior criminal convictions. The OIG strongly recommends that the billing company prohibit the employment of individuals who have been recently convicted of a criminal offense related to health care or who are listed as debarred, excluded, or otherwise ineligible for participation in federal healthcare programs. If such a condition is discovered in existing employees, they should be removed from direct responsibility for or involvement with all federal healthcare programs.

Third parties with whom the company does business present a special challenge. A decision may have to be made to terminate contracts with vendors or outside contractors who will not or cannot comply with laws, regulations, payor requirements, and the company's compliance program.

Monitoring Compliance Performance

It is important for the billing company regularly to confirm that its compliance efforts are working as intended. This is accomplished by monitoring and auditing those activities.

The subjects of the monitoring are both how well employees follow the policies and procedures laid down by the compliance program, and how well, as a result, the company operates within federal and state laws, and the requirements of public and private healthcare program requirements. In the case of billing companies, this means specifically compliance with laws governing kickback arrangements, coding practices, claim submission, reimbursement, and marketing, as well as compliance with specific rules and policies that have been the focus of attention by Medicare fiscal intermediaries or carriers, and law enforcement, as evidenced by OIG Special Fraud Alerts, OIG audits and evaluations, and other law enforcement initiatives. The company also will want to look closely at high risk areas identified by its own analyses.

The extent and frequency of the monitoring will depend on the company's size, available resources, and prior history of noncompliance. The OIG recognizes that smaller entities cannot implement compliance programs as comprehensive as those of much larger organizations.

The monitoring function involves the continuous gathering of information about these compliance issues. It becomes an embedded part of an organization's routine operations. It may be supplemented by discrete audits conducted at regular intervals by internal or external auditors with compliance experience, focusing on areas of interest or concern.

The OIG suggest these data-gathering techniques for use in the monitoring process.

- On-site visits
- Testing billing and coding staff on their knowledge of reimbursement and coverage criteria (by presenting hypothetical scenarios of situations experienced in daily practice and assessing responses)
- Unannounced mock surveys, audits, and investigations
- Examination of the billing company's complaint logs
- Checking personnel records to determine whether any individuals who have been reprimanded for compliance issues in the past are among those currently engaged in improper conduct
- Interviews with personnel involved in management, operations, coding, claim development and submission, and other related activities
- Questionnaires developed to solicit impressions of a broad cross-section of the billing company's employees and staff
- Reviews of written materials and documentation prepared by the different divisions of a billing company
- Trend analyses, or longitudinal studies, that look for deviations, positive or negative, in specific areas over a given period

As the monitoring proceeds, or as audits are conducted, and results analyzed, reports should be made to the full Compliance Committee, members of the governing body, and senior management. When monitoring detects significant variation from established policies and procedures, there should be an immediate investigation to determine the cause. When specific problems or misconduct are discovered, corrective steps should be taken. If the cause seems to have been improper procedures, a misunderstanding of rules, or systemic flaws, the response probably will be a revision of existing policies and procedures.

There is a chance that the violations that are revealed will involve or have been committed by the billing company's provider-clients. In those cases, a serious and immediate dialogue must be opened with them. The commercial relationship with those clients must not prevent the company from reporting them to law enforcement officials when appropriate. If a provider demonstrates a pattern of misconduct and noncompliance, the company may wish to reassess and perhaps terminate its relationship with that provider.

In any event, evidence of more serious wrongdoing will require a more substantial response.

Responding to Violations and Taking Corrective Action

Despite its best efforts, a billing company may still encounter violations of its compliance program; failures to comply with applicable federal or state law, rules, and program instructions; and other types of misconduct. If they are not addressed aggressively and responsibly, they will damage the company's reputation, expose it to major legal liability, and incur costs that can quickly amount to millions of dollars.

Upon reports or reasonable indications of noncompliance, the first step is a prompt and thorough investigation to determine their seriousness. This is followed by some form of corrective action, which may include referral to criminal or civil law enforcement authorities, a plan to modify in-house operations, a report to certain government agencies, refunds to payors of overpayment amounts, and notification to provider-clients when they are implicated in the matter. If the same issues keep occurring—overpayments, coding errors, and insufficient documentation—they may be a sign of a systemic problem, requiring some structural changes.

The investigation that is conducted will consist primarily of personal interviews with employees and review and analysis of documents, leading to conclusions and recommendations. It may be advisable to bring in outside attorneys, auditors, or healthcare experts to assist. A full investigatory record should be compiled, consisting of documentation of the alleged violation, a description of the investigative process (techniques and methodologies used), copies of interview notes and key documents, a log of the witnesses interviewed and the documents reviewed, and the outcome of the investigation (disciplinary action taken and corrective action implemented). It is essential that all relevant documents and other evidence be protected against destruction or alteration.

Government authorities want to hear about incidents of serious misconduct that involve violations of criminal, civil, or administrative law. The billing company must report them to the appropriate authority. Among others, these are the OIG of the Department of Health and

Human Services, the Criminal and Civil Divisions of the Department of Justice, the U.S. Attorneys in the relevant districts, and the other investigative arms for agencies administering the affected federal or state healthcare programs.

The OIG urges billing companies to report their own illegal misconduct within 60 days. It points out that not only is this a demonstration of its willingness to cooperate with the government in resolving the underlying problems, but also will be considered a mitigating factor in determining any administrative sanctions.

Billing companies are in a unique position to discover errors and violations by their provider-clients. The OIG acknowledges that, "This unique access to information may place the billing company in a precarious position." It notes the importance of a positive and interactive relationship between the two parties. With this in mind, the OIG suggests that, when a billing company makes such a discovery, it refrain from submitting questionable claims and notify the provider in writing within 30 days.

If the provider continues with the misconduct or flagrant fraudulent or abusive conduct, the OIG recommendations are more severe. Specifically, avoid submitting false or inappropriate claims, terminate its contract with the provider, and report the misconduct to the authorities within 60 days.

The billing company's reports to government authorities should be accompanied by all the evidence that it has gathered in its investigation. It is not unusual for the authorities to ask the company to continue its investigation and notify them of the results.

The OIG has a particular interest in overpayments by federal or state healthcare programs to providers. This is understandable as it involves spending of public funds that is not warranted by the services provided. The agency wants to see prompt identification of any overpayments to both the providers and the payors involved. The company then should encourage the providers promptly to return the overpayments to the programs.

CRIMINAL LIABILITY FOR FALSE CLAIMS SUBMITTED BY MEDICAL BILLING COMPANIES

It is not easy for a medical billing company to commit healthcare fraud on its own. Because its business involves filing claims for services delivered by providers, any fraud normally requires the connivance of providers. Although they do not occur often, these are two examples of billing company personnel being found criminally liable for false claims violations.

Diana Sotto and All Medical Billing Solutions

Diana Sotto owned and ran All Medical Billing Solutions (All Medical), a company that provided billing services to medical providers for Medicare and other health insurances. Sotto also was involved in the purchase and management of Project New Hope (PNH), a medical clinic.

PNH's business changed substantially following the purchase, both with regard to Medicare billings and the patients' medical conditions. Prior to the purchase, PNH had billed Medicare less than $26,000 and received slightly more than $10,000 in payment, while in the 2 weeks or so following the purchase, PNH billed Medicare more than $262,000 and received approximately $125,000. Prior to the purchase, none of PNH's patients had AIDS, while after the purchase all of PNH's patients were treated exclusively for AIDS.

Patients were given cash payments of $200 each time they went to the clinic, regardless of whether they received treatment. PNH billed Medicare for treatment of 45 individuals, all of whom had AIDS. In several instances, the quantities of prescription drugs for AIDS infusion therapy in PNH's bills far exceeded the quantities PNH actually purchased. For example, PNH billed for 1,183 vials of the drug Procrit but only purchased 74 vials. In many instances, claims that Sotto submitted to Medicare were for quantities much higher than what was shown on the treatment sheets and far in excess of the amount that could possibly be administered to an individual.

Sotto received 5% of all Medicare receipts as payment for her billing services, but in addition, she received substantial amounts from PNH in the form of checks made payable to sham corporations that Sotto owned or helped to form.

Sotto and six other codefendants were charged in a six-count indictment with various healthcare fraud and money laundering offenses. Soto was charged with: (1) conspiracy to defraud the United States and to pay and receive healthcare kickbacks, (2) conspiracy to commit healthcare fraud, and (3) conspiracy to launder money. In 2010, Sotto was found guilty and sentenced to 121 months in prison.

Rhonda Fleming and Advanced Medical Billing Specialists

Rhonda Fleming formed a medical billing company, Advanced Medical Billing Specialists (AMBS), to submit fraudulent claims for durable medical equipment (DME) to Medicare. To qualify for Medicare reimbursement, each claim submitted must include the DME company's supplier number, as well as specific physician, patient, prescription, and cost information. AMBS initially used the supplier number from a related DME company Fleming had formed, but that supplier number was revoked shortly after Fleming formed AMBS. Accordingly, Fleming purchased a supplier number from King Arthur, the owner of Hi-Tech Medical Supply (Hi-Tech), in exchange for a promised monthly salary of $13,000.

Fleming also purchased stolen patient information from former employees to facilitate fraudulent billing on the supplier numbers. Fleming, moreover, was intimately involved in minute details of the fraud, requiring her employees to submit frequent status reports and giving detailed instructions on how to submit claims.

Along with two co-conspirators, Fleming was convicted of violating and conspiring to violate statutes on healthcare fraud, wire fraud, and money laundering. She was sentenced to 360 months of imprisonment.

STUDY QUESTIONS

1. What are the advantages to a provider, a physician practice for instance, of using a third-party billing company to prepare and file its reimbursement claims rather than doing this in-house?
2. If you have already covered one or more other chapters in Sections 2 or 3 of this text, try to write down the seven recommended elements of a good compliance program, without looking back at the text in this chapter. By now, you should know them all by memory.
3. Go through the list of risk areas suggested by the OIG and make sure that you understand exactly what the potential problem is. How could it happen? Deliberately or inadvertently? If necessary, talk to classmates or do a little Internet research.
4. In what ways could computers and the Internet be used to facilitate communications between employees and the Compliance Officer? Think about the different topics that employees might wish to communicate.
5. How often should a billing company perform monitoring? Audits? Exactly what kinds of information and data should it gather through those activities?
6. If a billing company hears about what might be a serious violation of the law regarding false claims, describe the first three steps it should take.

Learning Exercises

1. It would be useful if an interview with the Compliance Officer or a compliance-aware manager at a local medical billing company could be arranged. There are obvious questions about the structure of its compliance program, the risk areas that concern it most, and the effectiveness of its compliance efforts. It would be especially interesting to learn how the company would react, even hypothetically, if it discovered serious misconduct or violations by one of its provider clients.
2. Read the article entitled "How to Start My Own Medical Billing & Coding Company."[2]

   In light of what you have learned about the process of preparing and submitting medical reimbursement claims, do you think that the steps outlined in the article would be sufficient to start a successful medical billing company? What problems do you think might arise?

References

1. "OIG Compliance Program Guidance for Third-Party Medical Billing Companies," Federal Register, Vol. 63, No. 243, December 18, 1998.
2. "Health Claims Processing in the US," TM Floyd & Company, 2006.
3. "Medical Insurance: An Integrated Claims Process Approach, Fourth Edition," Valerius, Bayes, Newby & Seggern, McGraw-Hill Higher Education, 2010.
4. "Healthcare Trends: Everything You Wanted to Know, The Year in Review—And Outlook for 2010," Healthcare Billing & Management Association, 2010.

[2] http://smallbusiness.chron.com/start-own-medical-billing-coding-company-2258.html

Chapter 22

Medicare Advantage

Learning Objectives

After completing class sessions based on this chapter, a student will:

- Understand how Medicare Advantage Organizations (MAOs) work and the opportunities they present for noncompliance, fraud, and abuse.
- Discover the concept of FDR entities and the responsibility of MAOs for their compliance activities.
- See how an MAO can ensure that its FDRs are aware of its compliance policies and procedures.
- Become aware of the more detailed guidelines that the Center for Medicare and Medicaid Services (CMS) provides for the mandatory compliance programs of MAOs.
- Learn the numerous specific responsibilities of the Compliance Officer (CO) and the Compliance Committee (CC) in a MAO.
- Be able to plan the agenda of a good general compliance training initiative.
- Appreciate the importance of open lines of communication between an organization's compliance officials and its employees.
- Recognize the characteristics of effective disciplinary standards.
- Find out how to use audits and monitoring to evaluate compliance and detect fraud and abuse.
- Learn about program exclusions, special investigation units (SIU), and self-reporting.
- Be familiar with methods for responding to compliance issues that occur.

INTRODUCTION

Under traditional Medicare coverage, individual beneficiaries obtain medical services from providers who then bill and are reimbursed by Medicare, a federal healthcare program administered by the CMS. Under Medicare Advantage

(MA), a private third-party entity–a MAO–comes between the beneficiaries and CMS. The individual enrolls with a MA plan. The plan contracts with a select group of providers (physicians and hospitals, among others). The individual visits the providers for his/her medical care. The providers are compensated by the MA plan. The MA plan is compensated by CMS.

The Balanced Budget Act of 1997 (BBA) established a new Part C of the Medicare program, known then as the Medicare+Choice (M+C) program, effective January 1999. As part of the M+C program, the BBA authorized CMS to contract with public or private organizations to offer a variety of health plan options for beneficiaries, including coordinated care plans, like health maintenance organizations (HMOs), provider sponsored associations (PSOs), and preferred provider organizations (PPOs). These health plans provide all Medicare Parts A and B benefits, plus additional benefits not covered under the traditional Medicare program.

The M+C program was renamed the MA program under the Medicare Prescription Drug, Improvement, and Modernization Act of 2003 (MMA). The MMA established the Medicare Prescription Drug Benefit (Part D) and amended the Part C program to allow MA plans to offer prescription drug coverage. Most MA plans now package together the benefits of Medicare Part A, Medicare Part B, Medicare Supplemental Insurance (Medigap), and Medicare Part D (Prescription Drug Coverage)–all in one convenient plan. Part C and Part D often are discussed together because medications are a large part of the treatment plans for many Medicare beneficiaries.

For people who choose to enroll in a MA health plan, Medicare pays the private health plan a fixed amount every month. Members typically also pay a monthly premium in addition to the regular Medicare Part B premium to cover items not covered by traditional Medicare, such as prescription drugs, dental care, vision care, and gym or health club memberships. In exchange for these extra benefits, enrollees may be required to see only the providers in the network of providers with whom the plan has contracts. To see a provider outside that network may require permission or extra fees.

In 2011, the MA program included over 3,400 individual plans, serving more than 12 million beneficiaries and paid those plans $124 billion. Those 12.1 million enrollees represent one-quarter of all Medicare beneficiaries and a 6% increase from 11.4 million beneficiaries in 2010. Eight million of those beneficiaries were enrolled in HMOs. Three and a half million were members of PPOs, which saw much more rapid growth than the HMO plans.

CMS sets the rules for MA plans and regulates the private companies who operate them. Some examples of private companies that offer MA plans are Aetna, Cigna, Coventry, Health Net, Humana, and United HealthCare.

In 2010, the compliance environment for healthcare organizations was altered dramatically by the Patient Protection and Affordable Care Act (PPACA). The "Obamacare" health reform law ratcheted up the requirements for the compliance programs that these entities must implement. For over a decade, the Office of the Inspector General (OIG) of the Department of Health and Human Services (DHHS) had encouraged hospitals, physician practices, nursing facilities, and other healthcare organizations voluntarily to adopt such programs. The PPACA made those programs mandatory.

From the beginning, MA plans were required to implement compliance programs as a condition of participation in Medicare. That mandate was enforced by the CMS rather than the OIG. Although the OIG issued the Compliance Program Guidance for Medicare + Choice Organizations Offering Coordinated Care Plans in 1999, the primary authority on MA compliance is the Medicare Managed Care Manual (Chapter 21 of the Compliance Program Guidelines). Under the authority of PPACA, the CMS significantly strengthened the terms of Chapter 21 in an update issued in July 2012.

SEVEN BASIC ELEMENTS OF A MANDATORY COMPLIANCE PROGRAM FOR MA PLANS

There are three major sources of federal government direction on the content of compliance programs: the Federal Sentencing Guidelines, the OIG Compliance Program Guidances, and the CMS Compliance Program Guidance for Medicare Contractors. They all incorporate the same seven basic program elements.

1. Written Policies, Procedures, and Standards of Conducts
2. CO, CC, and High-Level Oversight
3. Effective Training and Education
4. Effective Lines of Communication
5. Well-Publicized Disciplinary Standards
6. Effective System for Routine Monitoring and Auditing
7. Prompt Response to Compliance Issues

Because the CMS guidelines expressed in the Medicare Managed Care Manual are mandatory, they are the basis for this description of a recommended MA compliance program. One of the keys to understanding these guidelines is noticing their use of three essential terms: "must" (required by statute or regulation), "should" (expected by the CMS), and "best practices" (recommended by the CMS). They define the urgency of implementing specific guidelines.

FDR ENTITIES

With the introduction of MAOs, new levels were added to the payment and regulatory pathway between the CMS and Medicare beneficiaries. The CMS has special names for them.

A MAO that has a contract with CMS to offer one or more MA plans is called a "plan sponsor." The sponsor may have a contract with another party to provide administrative or healthcare services to Medicare beneficiaries. That party is called a "first tier entity." The first tier entity may also have contracts with other parties in a chain that continues down to the level of the provider who delivers services to a beneficiary. Those other parties are called "downstream entities." There may be still other entities that are related to the MAO by common ownership or control, and perform some of the MAO's management functions, furnish services to Medicare beneficiaries, or lease real property/sell goods to the MAO. The CMS calls them "related entities." As a group, these are referred to as "FDR entities", as in first, downstream, and related.

For example, a single MAO may offer several types of MA plans—HMO and PPO, individual and employer, "standard" and "value." In order to deliver services through those plans, it contracts with first tier entities like large physician group practices, primary care clinics, independent practice associations (IPAs), hospitals, allied service providers, laboratories, and pharmacy benefit managers. These entities then contract with downstream entities like individual physicians, small physician group practices, pharmacies, quality assurance firms, claims processing firms, billing agencies, and marketing firms. Those entities may contract even further downstream: a pharmacy contracts with an individual pharmacist, a marketing firm contracts with an individual marketing consultant. Eventually, at the end of this chain are people who interact directly with Medicare patients—physicians, pharmacists, and ancillary care providers.

Being familiar with these levels is important because they can be the source of compliance problems for a MAO. Not only that, but the MAO must work with its FDR entities to prevent and resolve the problems. It has no choice. The CMS guidelines require that each MAO assert a substantial degree of control over the compliance efforts of its FDR entities.

BROAD CMS REQUIREMENTS FOR MA COMPLIANCE PROGRAMS

The CMS requires that all sponsors adopt and implement an effective compliance program. To be effective, the program should be tailored to each sponsor's unique organization, operations, and circumstances, and must receive adequate resources to carry out its activities.

It is clear that sponsors may enter into contracts with FDRs to provide administrative or healthcare services to their enrollees. However, they may not delegate compliance program administrative functions (e.g., CO, CC, compliance reporting to senior management) to entities other than its parent organization or corporate affiliate. Sponsors are permitted to use FDRs for compliance activities like monitoring, auditing, and training.

The bottom line is that the sponsor is ultimately responsible for fulfilling the terms of its contract with CMS, and for meeting Medicare program requirements. This means that CMS can hold the sponsor accountable for the failure of its FDRs to comply with Medicare program requirements. These are the sorts of activities that a sponsor might delegate to a FDR entity, but for which the sponsor is still responsible.

- Sales and marketing
- Utilization management
- Quality improvement
- Applications processing
- Enrollment, disenrollment, membership functions
- Claims administration, processing, and coverage adjudication
- Appeals and grievances
- Licensing and credentialing
- Pharmacy benefit management
- Hotline operations
- Customer service
- Bid preparation
- Outbound enrollment verification
- Provider network management
- Processing of pharmacy claims at the point of sale
- Negotiation with prescription drug manufacturers for rebates, discounts, or other price concessions on prescription drugs
- Administration and tracking of enrollees' drug benefits
- Coordination with other benefit programs like Medicaid, state pharmaceutical assistance, or other insurance programs
- Healthcare services

Because of this overriding responsibility, the sponsor must correctly identify which of its contracted partners qualify as FDRs. Sponsors should have processes in place to evaluate and classify all third parties with which they contract. The CMS recommends that the sponsor take these factors into account.

- The function to be performed by the third party.
- Whether the function is something the sponsor is required to do under its contract with CMS, federal laws and regulations, or CMS guidelines.
- The extent to which the function impacts enrollees.
- The extent to which the third-party interacts with enrollees, either orally or in writing.
- Whether the third party has access to beneficiary personal health or other information.
- Whether the third party has independent decision-making authority or simply takes directions from the sponsor.
- The extent to which the third party is in a position to commit healthcare fraud, waste or abuse (FWA), and harm enrollees in the process.

WRITTEN POLICIES, PROCEDURES, AND STANDARDS OF CONDUCTS

The foundational document in shaping ethical, compliant behavior by employees and FDRs is a Code of Conduct, a set of overarching values and principles that provide a context for the more specific policies and procedures. To maximize its impact, the Code of Conduct should be enacted by a resolution of the governing board. This communicates to employees, FDRs, regulatory agencies, and the community at large that ethics and compliance are valued at the highest level of the sponsor organization.

Policies and procedures are the written documents that describe two things: the features of the compliance program itself (e.g., communication channels, training requirements, and disciplinary action) and the performance of the operational functions where the organization is at greatest risk of noncompliance. The documents tell employees and FDRs exactly how to carry out their normal work tasks in conformity with the laws, regulations, and payor requirements that apply to those risk areas. The organization identifies its highest risk areas by conducting internal risk assessments, reviewing its prior history of compliance and enforcement problems, and heeding OIG and CMS communications on their greatest compliance concerns (e.g., Special Fraud Alerts, Advisory Opinions, and

Annual Work Plans). As those concerns evolve, the organization must continually update its policies and procedures.

If they are to be useful, the policies, procedures, and standards of conduct must be distributed to the employees of the sponsor and its FDRs. Distribution must occur within 90 days of a new employee being hired or any of the documents being updated. After that, the documents must be distributed annually.

In dealing with FDRs, the sponsor may distribute its own policies, procedures, and standards to them. Alternatively, it may evaluate and then recognize the FDRs' policies, procedures, and standards as equivalent to its own. It is a good idea to include in FDR contracts a provision requiring that they distribute these documents to their employees and then to periodically check up to make sure they have done so.

COMPLIANCE OFFICER, COMPLIANCE COMMITTEE, AND HIGH-LEVEL OVERSIGHT

A sponsor organization must designate a CO and a CC, both of which must report directly and be accountable to the Chief Executive Officer (CEO) of the organization.

The CO position should be full-time. It should be filled by an employee of the sponsor. This is a responsibility that cannot be delegated to a FDR entity. The CO implements the compliance program and leads its day-to-day operations. He or she defines the program structure, training requirements, reporting and complaint mechanisms, response and correction procedures, and compliance expectations of all personnel and FDRs. These are the specific duties mentioned in the CMS guidelines:

- Ensure that Medicare compliance reports are provided regularly to the governing body, CEO, and CC. Reports should include the status of the compliance program's implementation, the identification and resolution of suspected, detected or reported instances of noncompliance, and other compliance oversight and audit activities
- Remain aware of daily business activity by interacting regularly with the organization's operational units
- Create and coordinate training programs to ensure that the sponsor's officers, governing body, managers, employees, FDRs, and other individuals working in Medicare activities are knowledgeable about the sponsor's compliance program, its written standards of conduct, compliance policies and procedures, and all applicable statutory and regulatory requirements

- Develop and implement methods that encourage managers and employees to report Medicare program noncompliance and potential FWA without fear of retaliation
- Maintain a compliance reporting mechanism that is coordinated with the internal audit department and the SIU,[1] if one exists
- Respond to reports of potential FWA, coordinate internal investigations with the SIU or internal audit department, and take appropriate corrective or disciplinary actions
- Ensure that the OIG and Government Services Administration (GSA) exclusion lists are checked monthly with respect to all employees, governing body members, and FDRs
- Maintain documentation on each report of potential non-compliance or FWA received from any source
- Oversee the development and monitoring of the implementation of corrective action plans
- Coordinate fraud investigations with the SIU and the appropriate NBI MEDIC[2]

In one of its most far-reaching provisions, the CMS manual states that "The compliance officer, in his/her discretion, need not await approval of the sponsor's governing body to implement needed compliance actions and activities." Taken literally, this means that, in compliance matters, the CO's authority is superior to that of the governing body.

The CO should have the authority to:

- Interview the sponsor's employees and other relevant individuals regarding compliance issues
- Review company contracts and other documents pertinent to the Medicare program
- Review the submission of data to CMS to ensure that it is accurate and in compliance with CMS reporting requirements
- Independently seek advice from legal counsel
- Report potential FWA to CMS, its designee or law enforcement
- Conduct or direct audits and investigations of any FDRs

[1] An SIU is an internal investigation unit responsible for surveillance, interviews, and other investigation methods relating to potential FWA. Depending on its size and available resources, a sponsor must either establish a specific SIU or ensure that comparable investigative duties are conducted by the compliance department.

[2] Medicare Drug Integrity Contractors (MEDIC) are organizations that CMS contracts with to perform specific program integrity functions for Parts C and D under the Medicare Integrity Program. The MEDIC's primary role is to identify potential fraud and abuse in Medicare Part C and Part D. There is currently one National Benefit Integrity (NBI) MEDIC.

- Conduct or direct audits of any area or function involved with Medicare Parts C or D plans
- Recommend policy, procedure, and process changes

The CO should be independent of influence from the operational areas that he/she must police. This means that the CO may not have work responsibilities in those areas. He/she must work solely on compliance matters. The CO must have the authority to speak candidly to both the CEO and the governing body. The CO must be free to raise compliance issues without fear of retaliation. To accomplish this, the CMS recommends that this person may be dismissed from the CO job only if the governing body gives its approval.

The second key element of the compliance infrastructure is a CC. The CMS recommends that the CC members come from a variety of backgrounds, including senior executives (Chief Financial Officer, Chief Operating Officer), auditors, pharmacists, registered nurses, certified pharmacy technicians, in-house legal experts, statistical analysts, and managers from various departments at high risk of noncompliance. The Committee should be accountable to the organization's CEO and governing board.

The CC usually is chaired by the CO and, together, they oversee the operation of the compliance program. The CMS suggests the following list of possible responsibilities for the CC.

- Meet every 3 months or more frequently as necessary to provide oversight of the compliance program
- Develop strategies to promote compliance and the detection of any potential violations
- Review and approve the compliance training and ensure that it is effective and appropriately conducted
- Assist with the creation and implementation of the compliance risk assessment, and a compliance monitoring and auditing work plan
- Assist in the design, implementation, and monitoring of effective corrective actions
- Develop innovative ways to implement appropriate corrective and preventive action
- Review the effectiveness of the internal controls intended to ensure compliance with Medicare regulations in daily operations
- Support the CO's quest for staff and resources necessary to carry out his/her duties
- Ensure that the sponsor has appropriate, up-to-date compliance policies and procedures

- Ensure that the sponsor has a method for employees and FDRs to ask compliance questions and report potential noncompliance and FWA confidentially without fear of retaliation
- Ensure that the sponsor has a method for enrollees to report potential FWA
- Review and address reports of monitoring and auditing in high-risk areas and ensure that corrective action plans are implemented and monitored for effectiveness
- Provide regular and ad hoc reports on the status of compliance, with recommendations to the sponsor's governing board

The organization's governing body has an important role to play in an effective compliance program. The CMS requires that it exercise "reasonable oversight" of the compliance program, its implementation, and its effectiveness. This makes sense as a governing board has the ultimate authority and liability in any corporation. (The term "governing body" may apply to a Board of Directors, Board of Trustees, or any comparable body.)

The governing body should be knowledgeable about compliance risks and strategies and capable of evaluating the effectiveness of the compliance program. Toward that end, it should receive training regarding the structure and operation of such programs.

"Reasonable oversight" is defined in this way.

- Approving the standards of conduct
- Understanding the compliance program structure
- Remaining informed about the compliance program results
- Remaining informed about governmental compliance enforcement activity
- Receiving periodic updates from the CO and CC
- Reviewing the performance and effectiveness assessments of the compliance program

Beyond this, the governing body must ensure that certain critical compliance decisions are made—either by it, senior executives, or the CC. Compliance policies and procedures must be prepared, implemented, approved, and annually reviewed. There must be a review and approval of the compliance training program, a compliance risk assessment, the internal and external audit work plans as well as the audit results, corrective action plans proposed, appointment of the CO, and performance goals for the CO. The governing body also will want to evaluate the commitment of the senior management team to the organization's ethics and compliance objectives.

Some compliance programs work very well; others are less effective. The guidelines state that the governing body should collect measurable evidence of how well its compliance program is detecting and correcting compliance problems. They offer a number of good indicators of program effectiveness.

- Use of quantitative measurement tools (e.g., scorecards, dashboard reports, and key performance indicators) to report, and track and compare over time, compliance in key Medicare activities such as enrollment, appeals and grievances, and prescription drug benefit administration
- Use of monitoring to track and review open/closed corrective action plans, FDR compliance, notices of noncompliance, warning letters, CMS sanctions, marketing material approval rates, and training completion/pass rates
- Implementation of new or updated Medicare requirements, including monitoring or auditing, and quality control measures to confirm appropriate and timely implementation
- Detection of noncompliance and FWA issues through monitoring and auditing
- Increase or decrease in number and/or severity of complaints from employees, FDRs, providers, and beneficiaries
- Timely response to reported noncompliance and potential FWA, and effective resolution
- Consistent, timely, and appropriate disciplinary action

The sponsor should ensure that CMS is able to validate, through a review of governing body meeting minutes or other documents, the active engagement of the body in the oversight of the compliance program.

Another cog in the compliance machinery is the CEO and the other members of the executive suite. One of their jobs is to make sure that the CO is integrated into the organization and given the credibility, authority, and resources necessary to operate a robust and effective compliance program. The CEO must receive periodic reports from the CO about the high-risk areas within the organization, the strategies being implemented to address them, and the results of those strategies. The CEO also must hear about any governmental compliance enforcement activity involving the organization.

EFFECTIVE TRAINING AND EDUCATION

The sponsor must provide effective training and education for its employees, including the governing board, the CEO, and senior executives, along with FDR personnel. It must occur at least annually and be made a part of the orientation for new employees. Interestingly, the CMS guidelines state that the sponsor's compliance with "all Medicare program requirements" will be sufficient evidence that its training, education, compliance policies and procedures, and standards of conduct are effective. At the same time, the CMS provides a thorough 26-page self-assessment questionnaire[3] that a sponsor can use to "evaluate the effectiveness of [its] Medicare Compliance Program."

The guidelines describe two types of mandatory training–general and FWA. The agenda of the general compliance training should look something like this.

- A description of the compliance program, including policies and procedures, the standards of conduct, and the sponsor's commitment to business ethics and compliance with all Medicare program requirements.
- An overview of how to ask compliance questions, request compliance clarification, or report suspected or detected noncompliance. Emphasis should be on confidentiality, anonymity, and non-retaliation.
- The requirement to report any actual or suspected incidents of Medicare program noncompliance or potential FWA.
- Examples of reportable noncompliance that an employee might observe.
- A review of the disciplinary guidelines for noncompliant or fraudulent behavior.
- Attendance and participation in compliance and FWA training programs is a condition of continued employment and a factor in employee evaluations.
- A review of policies related to contracting with the government, such as the laws addressing gifts and gratuities to government employees.
- A review of potential conflicts of interest and the policy on their disclosure.
- An overview of the Health Insurance Portability and Accountability Act (HIPAA) and the Health Information Technology for Economic and Clinical Health (HITECH) Act and the importance of maintaining confidentiality of personal health information.
- An overview of the monitoring and auditing process.
- A review of the laws governing employee conduct in the Medicare program.

[3] A copy of the Medicare Advantage and Prescription Drug Compliance Program Effectiveness Self-Assessment Questionnaire can be found here: http://www.hcca-info.org/Content/NavigationMenu/ComplianceResources/ComplianceBasics/CompEvalCheckList.pdf

The sponsor may satisfy these training requirements through classroom training, online training modules, or attestation by employees that they have read and understood copies of the standards of conduct, policies, and procedures. However, it must be able to prove that the training was delivered. It can do this with training logs, employee attestations, and electronic certifications on completion of online trainings.

Just as important as training its own employees, the sponsor must connect with its FDRs. The minimum way of accomplishing this is to distribute its standards of conduct, policies, and procedures to the employees of the FDRs.

The CMS guidelines describe the mandatory training on FWA in a separate section and with greater emphasis. At a minimum, the training should cover the following topics.

- Laws and regulations related to Medicare Advantage FWA (i.e., False Claims Act, Anti-Kickback Statute, HIPAA/HITECH).
- Obligations of FDRs to have appropriate policies and procedures to address FWA.
- Processes for sponsor and FDR employees to report suspected FWA.
- Protections for sponsor and FDR employees who report suspected FWA.
- Types of FWA that can occur in the settings in which sponsor and FDR employees work.

Like the general training, it should be provided to the sponsor's and FDRs' employees. But the guidelines go further in requiring training for temporary workers and volunteers. They also ask the sponsor to provide FWA training directly to its FDRs or at least give them appropriate training materials. To facilitate the training of FDR employees, the CMS has created a standardized FWA training module. It can be found within the CMS Medicare Learning Network.[4] This module satisfies the CMS' FWA training requirement.

The training should be provided within 90 days of initial hiring and annually thereafter. More specialized training "may" be given to individuals whose work activities pose a high risk of FWA.

EFFECTIVE LINES OF COMMUNICATION

A sponsor must set up effective and confidential lines of communication between its CO and CC, on one hand, and its employees, managers, governing board, and FDRs, on the other hand. The lines must allow the anonymous and confidential reporting of potential compliances issues as soon as they arise.

---

[4] A selection of Medicare training materials can be found at the CMS Medicare Learning Network, including a number of web-based training courses lasting an average of 1 hour each: www.cms.gov/Outreach-and-Education/Medicare-Learning-Network-MLN/MLNProducts/Catalog.html

The flow of information will move in two directions. For instance, the sponsor will want to communicate to employees the CO's name, office location, and contact information; laws, regulations, and guidance for FDRs; and changes to policies and procedures and standards of conduct. In turn, the employees may want to seek clarification from the sponsor on compliance issues or report suspected noncompliance or FWA to the sponsor.

The CMS wants to see that the lines of communication are used. It insists that, in their policies and procedures, sponsors require all their own employees and FDR employees to report compliance concerns and suspected or actual violations related to the Medicare program to the sponsor. They also must educate their enrollees about the importance of identifying and reporting any FWA they may observe. The lines of communication must be part of a system that receives, records, responds to, and tracks questions about compliance and reports of suspected/detected noncompliance or FWA received from those employees. The system must maintain confidentiality, allow anonymity if desired, and emphasize the policy of non-intimidation and non-retaliation for good faith reporting of compliance concerns and participation in the compliance program.

The methods available for reporting compliance or FWA concerns and the confidentiality, non-retaliation policy must be publicized throughout the sponsor's and FDRs' facilities. Sponsors must make the reporting mechanisms user-friendly, easy to access and navigate, and available 24 hours a day for employees and FDRs. It is a best practice for sponsors to establish more than one type of reporting mechanism to accommodate the different ways in which people prefer to communicate.

WELL-PUBLICIZED DISCIPLINARY STANDARDS

Every sponsor must develop disciplinary standards, codified in policies and procedures, to be applied in cases of misconduct, noncompliance, or FWA by employees.

Those policies must:

- Require that employees participate in scheduled compliance training.
- Describe the sponsor's expectations for reporting of compliance issues.
- Explain the expectations for employee cooperation in the resolution of compliance issues.

- Define noncompliant, unethical, or illegal behavior through examples of problematic activities that employees might observe in their jobs.
- Deliver timely, consistent, and effective enforcement of the standards when noncompliant or unethical behavior is found.
- Ensure that any disciplinary action is proportional to the seriousness of the offense.

To encourage good faith participation in the compliance program, sponsors must publicize the standards to employees and FDRs through means such as newsletters, presentations at staff meetings, general compliance trainings, an intranet site, posters around the facility, and communications with the FDRs.

Sponsors must be able to demonstrate to the CMS that their disciplinary standards are enforced in a timely, consistent, and effective manner. To accomplish this, the sponsors must maintain their records on compliance disciplinary actions for 10 years. The records must include the date a compliance violation was reported, a description of the violation, the date of investigation, a summary of findings, the disciplinary action taken, and the date it was taken. Sponsors should periodically review these records of discipline to ensure that disciplinary actions are appropriate to the seriousness of the violation, fairly and consistently administered, and imposed within a reasonable timeframe.

As an incentive to behave compliantly, sponsors are encouraged, although not required, to include compliance as a factor in employee performance appraisals. The guidelines also recommend, as a best practice, that sponsors publicize the disciplinary actions that they take against employee violations. This can be done by including de-identified case histories in company newsletters.

EFFECTIVE SYSTEM FOR ROUTINE MONITORING, AUDITING, AND IDENTIFICATION OF COMPLIANCE RISKS

The CMS guidelines devote 10 of their 54 pages to a statement of the need for sponsors to maintain a system for identifying and regularly monitoring compliance risks. The system should include internal audits and monitoring and, when appropriate, external audits. Their purpose is to evaluate the sponsor's compliance with CMS program requirements and the effectiveness of its compliance program. The scope of the monitoring extends to the FDRs.

To be more specific, these review efforts must look at the entity's compliance with Medicare regulations, sub-regulatory guidances, contractual agreements, and all applicable federal and state laws, as well as its internal policies and procedures aimed at Medicare program noncompliance and potential FWA.

Monitoring and audits have slightly different meanings, even if their end results are the same. Monitoring activities are regular reviews performed as a part of normal operations to confirm ongoing compliance and to ensure that corrective actions are undertaken and effective. An audit is a formal review of compliance based on a particular set of standards or benchmarks—typically a particular law, regulation, or payor program requirement. The standard states that business activities should (or should not) be performed in a certain way; the audit determines whether the activities actually satisfy the standard.

Together, the audit and monitoring functions should be part of a systematic work plan. All plans are not the same—they will reflect the size, structure, and resources of each organization and the unique compliance risks that it faces. Normally, the CO is the person who coordinates and oversees the execution of the plan. He or she also must receive regular reports on the results of the auditing and monitoring, and the status of any corrective actions taken. In turn, the CO should pass on a summary of that information to the CC, the CEO, senior management, and the governing board.

Rather than launching an auditing/monitoring initiative without any foundation, the CMS requires a sponsor to conduct a baseline assessment of its major compliance and FWA risk areas. The assessment will look at all the business operational areas that have something to do with Medicare. It will be concerned with risks in each area to both the sponsor and the Medicare program. The guidelines provide a list of topics of particular concern for sponsor organizations: marketing and enrollment violations, agent/broker misrepresentation, selective marketing, enrollment/disenrollment noncompliance, credentialing, quality assessment, appeals and grievance procedures, benefit/formulary administration, transition policy, protected classes policy, utilization management, accuracy of claims processing, detection of potentially fraudulent claims, and FDR oversight and monitoring.

The next step for the sponsor is to prioritize the risk areas identified by the assessment according to their impact on the sponsor. The auditing/monitoring work plan should match those priorities. Because the organization's risk profile, as well as legal and Medicare requirements, change over time, the plan must be reviewed regularly and revised to take into account new priority risks.

The risk assessment serves as the baseline or starting point for designing the auditing/monitoring work plan. A typical plan will include these features.

- The audits to be performed
- Schedule of all monitoring and auditing activities for the calendar year
- Announced or unannounced audits
- Internal or external audits
- Types of audit and methodology
- Resources needed to conduct the audits
- Individuals responsible for supervising and conducting the audits
- Date by which final report submitted to CO
- Operational activities subject to regular monitoring
- Frequency of reports on monitoring results
- Process for responding to audit and monitoring results
- Follow-up review of corrective actions taken

In determining the types of audits to include in the work plan, sponsors must determine which risk areas will most likely affect the sponsor and prioritize the monitoring and audit strategy accordingly. The auditing or monitoring methodology will involve:

- Selecting sponsor facilities, pharmacies, providers, claims, and other areas for review
- Determining appropriate sample size for the data to be collected
- Extrapolating the audit findings to the full universe

Subsequently, the sponsor must conduct a follow-up review by auditing or monitoring areas previously found noncompliant to determine if the corrective actions taken have fully addressed the underlying problem.

The CMS guidelines are specific about a sponsor's oversight responsibilities for its FDRs. Sponsors are fully responsible for the lawful and compliant administration of the Medicare Parts C and D benefits under their contracts with CMS, even if the sponsor has delegated some of that responsibility to FDRs. The sponsor must monitor and audit its first tier entities to ensure that they are in compliance with all applicable laws and regulations, and to ensure that the first tier entities are monitoring the compliance of the entities with which they contract (the sponsors' "downstream" entities). Sponsors must also monitor any related entities to ensure they are in compliance.

Sponsors must include in their work plan the number of first tier entities that will be audited each year and how the entities will be identified for auditing. Remember, these entities often will be hospitals and physician groups—in significant numbers. The sponsor must audit them even when they also are performing their own audits. When corrective action by a first tier entity is called for, the sponsor must make sure that it happens.

The CMS also recommends, as a best practice, that sponsors regularly track and document compliance using dashboards, scorecards, self-assessment tools, and other mechanisms that show the extent to which operational areas and FDRs are meeting compliance goals. Levels of compliance and noncompliance should be publicized to employees and shared with senior management.

OIG AND GSA PROGRAM EXCLUSIONS

The OIG and the GSA maintain lists of people and organizations that are excluded from participation in federal healthcare programs. This typically is a result of fraudulent or other criminal acts they have committed. The official names of these lists are the OIG List of Excluded Individuals and Entities (LEIE) and the GSA Excluded Parties Lists System (EPLS). Medicare will not pay for goods or services furnished or prescribed by anyone on these lists. Furthermore, sponsors may not use federal funds to pay for services, equipment, or drugs prescribed or provided by an employee, provider, supplier, or FDR excluded by the OIG or the GSA.

Sponsors are required to review the LEIE and the EPLS prior to the hiring or contracting of any new employee, temporary employee, volunteer, consultant, governing body member, or FDR, and monthly thereafter, to ensure that none of these persons or entities are excluded or become excluded from participation in federal programs.

The CMS Guidelines for MAOs specify the use of two additional tools for combating FWA—data analysis and SIUs.

Data analysis may be used to carry out a sponsor's duty to monitor operations in order to detect and prevent FWA. It functions by comparing claim information against other data (e.g., provider, drug or medical service provided, diagnoses or beneficiaries) to identify unusual patterns suggesting potential errors or potential fraud and abuse. Effective data analysis should:

- Establish baseline data to enable the sponsor to recognize unusual trends, changes in drug utilization over time, physician referral or prescription patterns, and plan formulary composition over time.
- Analyze claims data to identify potential errors and provider billing practices and services that pose the greatest risk for potential FWA.
- Identify items or services that are being overutilized.
- Identify other problem areas within the plan such as enrollment, finance, or data submission.
- Identify problem areas within the FDR entities (e.g., pharmacy benefit management, pharmacies, pharmacists, physicians, other healthcare providers and suppliers).
- Use findings to determine where there is a need for a change in policy.

The CMS defines a SIU as "an internal investigation unit, often separate from the compliance department, responsible for conducting surveillance, interviews, and other methods of investigation relating to potential FWA." The guidelines require that each sponsor establish its own SIU or ensure that similar investigative responsibilities are conducted by its compliance department. SIUs must be accessible through multiple channels such as via phone, email, Internet website, and mail. Sponsors must ensure that suspicions of FWA can be reported anonymously to the SIU.

Under certain circumstances, the CMS may wish to perform its own audits of a sponsor's or FDR's activities pertaining to any aspect of the services provided or amounts payable under its Medicare contract. It has the right to do this, and the sponsor must allow access to any auditor acting on behalf of the CMS or other federal government agency to conduct an on-site audit. Failure to do so may result in a referral of the sponsor or FDR to law enforcement authorities and the implementation of corrective actions, including "intermediate sanctions." Such sanctions may include

- Civil monetary penalties ranging from $10,000 to $100,000 depending on the violation
- Suspension of enrollment of Medicare beneficiaries
- Suspension of payment to the sponsor organization
- Suspension of marketing activities to Medicare beneficiaries

A typical audit will cover financial records, invoices, legal contracts, medical records, other patient care documentation, copies of prescriptions, provider and pharmacy licenses, claims records, signature logs, documentation of medication delivery, purchase records, and rebate and discount agreements, as well as interviews of the staff. In most cases, the CMS will provide reasonable notice to the sponsor of the time and content of the audit.

The OIG has independent authority to conduct audits and evaluations necessary to ensure accurate and correct payment and to otherwise oversee Medicare reimbursement.

PROCEDURES AND SYSTEM FOR PROMPT RESPONSE TO COMPLIANCE ISSUES

The final component of a compliance program is the process by which an organization responds to compliance issues that emerge. The CMS requires that sponsors implement procedures for:

- Responding promptly to issues as they are raised
- Investigating potential compliance problems as they are identified by audits and monitoring
- Correcting the problems so that they do not recur
- Voluntarily self-reporting potential Medicare fraud or misconduct
- Ensuring ongoing compliance with CMS requirements

Program noncompliance and FWA may occur at the level of the sponsor or its FDRs. It may be discovered through a hotline, a website, an enrollee complaint, during routine monitoring or an audit, or by regulatory authorities. Regardless of how the incidents are identified, sponsors must begin an inquiry as quickly as possible, but not later than 2 weeks after the date they were noticed.

A reasonable inquiry includes a preliminary investigation of the matter by the CO, or a member of the compliance staff, or the sponsor's SIU. If the issue appears to involve potential fraud or abuse and the sponsor does not have the time or resources to investigate it promptly, it should refer the matter to the NBI MEDIC[5] within 30 days of when the issue was discovered.

The guidelines distinguish between which entity should hear about which kinds of incidents. When serious noncompliance or waste occurs, CMS wants sponsors to refer the matter to CMS. When potential fraudulent or abusive activity is identified, CMS strongly encourages sponsors to refer the matter to the NBI MEDIC.

The corrective action that a sponsor takes in response to an incident of noncompliance or FWA must serve two purposes—correct the underlying

[5] The National Benefit Integrity (NBI) Medicare Drug Integrity Contractor (MEDIC) is a private organization that the CMS contracts with for a variety of Parts C and D program integrity services, including the detection and prevention of FWA. This is the website for that organization: www.healthintegrity.org/contracts/nbi-medic.

problem and make sure that it does not happen again. For these purposes, the CMS specifically mentions "root cause analysis," a powerful tool for determining what factors are actually causing or allowing a problem to occur. The sponsor must use this and other means to devise a corrective action that is tailored to the particular behavior, problem, or deficiency that was identified. The planned action must include "timeframes for specific achievements."

The sponsor also has responsibility for correcting deficiencies with its FDRs. It should develop detailed corrective action plans for noncompliance or FWA committed by the FDRs. The plans should explain the consequences if the FDRs fails to carry out the corrective actions satisfactorily. A sponsor also should include language in its FDR contracts that states what will happen if the FDR commits FWA or noncompliant acts. In many cases, this will mean termination of the contract.

As usual, the sponsor must thoroughly document all the deficiencies that it has identified, in both its organization and those of its FDRs, and the corrective actions that have been taken by all the parties concerned.

SELF-REPORTING POTENTIAL FWA AND SIGNIFICANT NONCOMPLIANCE

It is voluntary for a sponsor to "self-report" to a government agency when it has discovered FWA within one of its health plans, potential fraud, and abuse committed by one of its FDRs, significant incidents of Medicare program noncompliance, or significant waste of resources. If, after conducting an investigation, the sponsor determines that potential Medicare FWA has occurred, it should promptly report the matter to the NBI MEDIC. The sponsor also should consider reporting potentially fraudulent conduct to the OIG (using the OIG Provider Self-Disclosure Protocol) or the Department of Justice. When a sponsor discovers an incident of significant Medicare program noncompliance, it should report the incident to the CMS as soon as possible. Note that all these reporting options are expressed as "should," not "must." Self-reporting offers sponsors the opportunity to minimize the potential cost and disruption of a full scale audit and investigation, to negotiate a fair monetary settlement, and to potentially avoid an OIG permissive exclusion preventing the entity from doing business with federal healthcare programs.

ENFORCEMENT ACTIVITIES INVOLVING MAOs

Common types of Part C fraud are misrepresenting enrollment or encounter data to increase payments, receiving duplicative copayments or premiums from beneficiaries and submitting claims for services not provided.[6] Part D fraud includes billing for drugs not provided, altering prescriptions to obtain higher payment amounts, and using another person's Medicare card to obtain prescriptions.

As a contractor of the CMS, the NBI MEDIC is responsible for identifying and investigating potential Part C and Part D fraud and abuse, referring cases and making immediate advisements to the OIG, and fulfilling requests for information from law enforcement agencies. Less than 10% of MEDIC investigations and law enforcement referrals involve Part C.[7]

The MEDIC learns about possible fraud and abuse from a variety of sources—beneficiaries, law enforcement agencies, Part D plan sponsors, MA plan sponsors, and CMS. The CMS requires that MAO compliance plans include measures to detect, correct, and prevent FWA. However, CMS does not require MAOs to report the results of their compliance efforts.

The OIG has some concern that MA sponsors are not carrying out their fraud detection responsibilities as fully as they should. A recent OIG study[8] found that 19% of MAOs identified no fraud and abuse incidents at all. Just three of the 170 MAOs surveyed were responsible for 95% of the total 1.4 million incidents actually reported. The OIG concluded that MAOs "lack a common understanding of key fraud and abuse program terms and raise questions about whether all MA organizations are implementing their programs to detect and address potential fraud and abuse effectively." It recommended that the CMS take several steps to enhance its oversight of MAO efforts to deal with fraud and abuse. This rather poor performance will result in closer scrutiny of MAOs and many of them will not look good under that scrutiny.

[6] Other types of fraud investigated by MEDIC are suspect billing, billing for services never rendered, attempts to steal a beneficiary's identity or money, improper coding, marketing schemes, billing for ineligible consumers, inducements, bribes or kickbacks, double billing, overcharging the beneficiary, falsification of records or other data, false-front provider, and telemarketing schemes.

[7] This may change as the OIG has recommended that structural reforms in the MEDIC program are necessary to pursue what it believes are unearthed instances of fraud and abuse by MA plans.

[8] MAOs' Identification of Potential Fraud and Abuse, Office of Inspector General, DHHS, February 2012.

A good indication of the OIG's compliance concerns about MAOs can be found in its annual work plans. The following are examples from the plan for 2013:

- Evaluate MAOs' oversight of FDR contractors that provide enrollee benefits.
- Determine the extent to which MAOs oversee and monitor their contractors' compliance with regulations and examine the processes they use to ensure that contractors fulfill their obligations.
- Review notices of denied requests for services or payments that MA organizations sent to beneficiaries to determine whether the notices clearly explained beneficiaries' right to request reconsiderations and to appeal the ensuing determinations.
- Determine whether the diagnoses that MAOs submit to CMS for use in CMS's risk-score calculations comply with federal requirements, including review of medical record documentation to ensure that it supports the diagnoses submitted to CMS.

The CMS has the authority to take an enforcement action when it determines that a MAO-sponsored health plan is substantially failing to comply with program or contract requirements, is carrying out its CMS contract in a manner inconsistent with program requirements, or no longer substantially meets the conditions of the Medicare Parts C and D programs. The CMS has the following enforcement options: civil monetary penalties (CMP), intermediate sanctions, and contract terminations. A full list of the organizations receiving Part C or D enforcement actions is available on the CMS website.[9]

STUDY QUESTIONS

1. What is the difference between Medicare Part C and Part D?
2. How is a Medicare managed care organization different from the traditional way that beneficiaries receive Medicare benefits?
3. Define the three levels of FDR entities and give an example of each one.
4. What compliance responsibilities does an MA sponsor have for its FDRs?
5. How would you describe an organizational Code of Conduct?

---

[9] The webpage for Part C and Part D Enforcement Actions is here: http://www.cms.gov/Medicare/Compliance-and-Audits/Part-C-and-Part-D-Compliance-and-Audits/Part-C-and-Part-667D-Enforcement-Actions-.html

6. What is the purpose of the policies and procedures created under a compliance program?
7. How should a CO and a CC interact with each other to fulfill an organization's compliance goals?
8. What is the role of a governing body (Board of Directors or Trustees) in ensuring that a MAO's operations are fully compliant?
9. How do the curriculums of general compliance training and FWA training differ from each other?
10. Describe at least three alternative channels of communication through which compliance officials might receive clarification questions and misconduct reports.
11. Under what circumstances do you believe that an organization should dismiss an employee who committed a noncompliant or fraudulent act?
12. List five elements or features of a compliance auditing and monitoring work plan.
13. Why should an MAO be concerned with the OIG LEIE?
14. Under what circumstances should an MAO self-report an incident of noncompliance or FWA, and to whom should it make the report?

Learning Exercises

1. Determine if there are any MA plans operating in your area. Do some Internet research on them. Look for compliance-related information or materials on their websites. Does it seem adequate and useful? What impression of the organization does it give you? Look also for any noncompliance or fraud issues involving the plans. Search for relevant news items or a listing on the OIG website.
2. Using your answers to Study Question #3 about FDRs, draw a diagram showing their relationships to each other and to the sponsor. If possible, identify the FDRs at each of the three levels for one of the MA plans in your area.
3. Visit the CMS Medicare Learning Network on the Internet. (The link is given in the section on Effective Training and Education.) Go to the page on Web-Based Training Courses and watch some of the courses that interest you.
4. Find the OIG list of excluded individuals and entities on the Internet and download the list database. Observe the variety of individuals and

organizations that have been excluded from participation in federal healthcare programs.

5. Look up the term "root cause analysis" and learn how it works. Speculate on the other areas of human endeavor to which this tool could be applied. Are there ways that you might use it in your own life?

References

1. *Medicare Managed Care Manual*, Chapter 21, *Compliance Program Guidelines*, July 20, 2012.
2. *Medicare Managed Care Manual*, Chapter 15, *Intermediate Sanctions*, September 30, 2005.
3. *The Medicare Advantage Program: Status Report*, Chapter 12, Report to the Congress: Medicare Payment Policy, Medicare Payment Advisory Commission, March 2012.
4. *MEDIC Benefit Integrity Activities in Medicare Parts C and D*, Office of Inspector General, Department of Health and Human Services, January 2013.
5. *OIG 2013 Work Plan: Compliance Priorities for Sponsors of Part C and Part D Plans*, Payors, Plans, and Managed Care Practice Group, American Health Lawyers Association, January 2013.
6. DHHS website for all issues concerning the National Practitioner Data Bank and the Healthcare Integrity and Protection Data Bank http://www.npdb-hipdb.hrsa.gov/
7. *Healthcare Integrity and Protection Data Bank Guidebook*, Health Resources and Services Administration (HRSA), February 2000. http://www.npdb-hipdb.hrsa.gov/resources/HIPDBGuidebook.pdf
8. *National Practitioner Data Bank Guidebook*, Health Resources and Services Administration (HRSA), September 2001 http://www.npdb-hipdb.hrsa.gov/resources/NPDBGuidebook.pdf

Chapter 23

Pharmaceutical Manufacturers

Learning Objectives

After completing class sessions based on this chapter, a student will:

- Be familiar with the largest pharmaceutical manufacturers in the world and their track records for fraud violations.
- Understand the seven elements of the compliance program that the Office of the Inspector General (OIG) recommends for pharmaceutical manufacturers.
- Be able to describe the role of a drug company Compliance Officer (CO), her reporting relationships, and her responsibilities.
- Recognize the purpose of written corporate policies and procedures on compliance.
- Know the areas of greatest fraud violation risk within drug company operations.
- Be introduced to the compliance programs of the largest pharmaceutical manufacturers.
- Develop the ability to analyze drug company compliance programs for their effectiveness.
- Review a good example of a compliance program from the largest drug manufacturer in the world.
- Be aware of the several channels that a pharmaceutical company can offer to its employees for asking questions about compliance and reporting possible misconduct.

INTRODUCTION

Pharmaceutical manufacturers develop, manufacture, market, and sell the drugs that constituted 10% of the $2.6 trillion spent on health care in 2010. Their products have transformed the treatment of disease over the last several decades. Today, many health problems are prevented, cured, or managed effectively for years through the use of prescription drugs.

Spending on prescription drugs is a leading contributor to increases in total healthcare spending, though the rate of growth has slowed recently. The pharmaceutical share of the healthcare budget continues to cause concern, for multiple reasons:

- Increased utilization of prescription drugs
- Newer, high-demand drugs are more expensive
- Average drug prices have increased faster than inflation
- Costs of more expensive, less successful research and development must be covered
- Pharmaceutical manufacturers continue to invest large sums in marketing to doctors and patients

Countering those factors are the slowing in enrollment in the Medicare Part D prescription drug program, the rapidly increasing use of generic drugs (from 63% in 2006 to 80% in 2011), and the continuing loss of patent protection for many high-volume branded drugs.

LEADING PHARMACEUTICAL MANUFACTURERS AND THEIR FRAUD VIOLATION RECORDS

The pharmaceutical industry is composed of several very large companies engaged in intense competition. That compensation has been heightened over the last decade as the patents on many of their highest revenue-producing drugs have expired and the companies have struggled to find replacements. Under such market conditions, there may be a temptation to take legal and ethical risks.

The global market for pharmaceuticals reached $839 billion in 2011; the United States accounted for $320 billion of that amount. **Table 23-1** lists the top 10 pharmaceutical companies based on their revenues (in millions of dollars) for the years 2011 and 2010.

These are large corporations with substantial resources. What is the likelihood that they would allow activities that violate healthcare fraud laws? Public records show what companies are the targets of government prosecutions and the final outcomes (see **Table 23-2**). In such cases, when a finding of liability seems imminent, defendants frequently reach monetary settlements with the prosecution rather than go to trial. In addition, the companies involved also submit to Corporate Integrity Agreements (usually lasting 5 years) to avoid being excluded from participation in federal healthcare

Table 23-1 Top 10 Pharmaceutical Companies Based on 2011 and 2010 Revenue (in millions)

	2011	2010
1 Pfizer	$57,747	$58,523
2 Novartis	$47,935	$44,420
3 Sanofi-Aventis	$42,779	$37,403
4 Merck & Co.	$41,289	$39,811
5 GlaxoSmithKline	$35,594	$36,156
6 AstraZeneca	$32,981	$32,515
7 Johnson & Johnson	$24,368	$22,396
8 Eli Lilly & Co.	$22,608	$21,685
9 Abbott Laboratories	$22,435	$19,894
10 Bristol-Myers Squibb	$21,244	$19,484

Adapted from "Top 20 Pharma Report, Our annual look at the 20 biggest players in the Pharmaceutical marketplace", http://www.contractpharma.com/issues/2012-07/view_features/top-20-pharma-report/; http://www.contractpharma.com/issues/2011-07/view_features/the-top-20-pharmaceutical-companies/.

programs. **Table 23-3** shows the recent record of pharmaceutical manufacturers regarding fraud and abuse liability.

To prevent these kinds of legal scandal, the OIG offers a Compliance Program Guidance for Pharmaceutical Manufacturers. It is organized around the standard seven fundamental elements that it recommends for an effective compliance program. The purpose of these elements is to guide pharmaceutical manufacturers in controlling their internal operations in order to minimize the chances that violations of law and federal healthcare program requirements will occur. The discussion that follows applies those seven elements to the unique context of the pharmaceutical industry.

SEVEN ELEMENTS OF EFFECTIVE COMPLIANCE

All of the OIG's Compliance Guidances are based on the Federal Sentencing Guidelines and include seven elements. With one exception, they seem to follow a logical progression of implementation–from preparing the policies that employees should follow, to educating them in those policies, setting up mechanisms for them to ask questions or report misconduct, monitoring to make sure the policies are followed, disciplining failures to follow the policies, and investigating when the failures create serious problems. As a practical matter, it probably makes more sense to start this process with the designation of the CO and perhaps also the Compliance

Table 23-2 Largest Federal Fraud Settlements with Pharmaceutical Companies in Last 5 Years

$3.00 billion	GlaxoSmithKline (2012)	Off-label promotion, failure to disclose safety data, false and misleading promotion
$2.30 billion	Pfizer (2009)	Off-label promotion, kickbacks, promotion designed to defraud or mislead
$1.50 billion	Abbott Labs (2012)	Off-label promotion and marketing despite inadequate evidence of effectiveness
$1.40 billion	Eli Lilly (2009)	Off-label promotion and failure to provide information on side effects
$750 million	GlaxoSmithKline (2010)	Manufacture and distribution of adulterated drugs
$650 million	Merck (2008)	Fraudulent price reporting and kickbacks
$600 million	Allergan (2010)	Promotion of drugs for off-label uses
$520 million	AstraZeneca (2010)	Promotion of drugs for off-label uses
$425 million	Cephalon (2008)	Promotion of drugs for off-label uses
$423 million	Novartis (2010)	Promotion of drugs for off-label uses and kickbacks
$313 million	Forest Laboratories (2010)	Obstruction of justice, distributing an unapproved drug in interstate commerce, distributing a misbranded drug in interstate commerce, promoted drugs for unapproved uses, kickbacks, failure to inform CMS of drug non-coverage.

Adapted from Ten Largest Settlements and Judgment, Nov. 2, 2010 Ð July 18, 2010, Table 6 and Twenty Largest Settlements and Judgments, 1991 Ð July 18, 2012, Table 7, Pharmaceutical Industry Criminal and Civil Penalties: An Update, Almashat and Wolfe, Public Citizen, September 27, 2012, and from Justice News, Office of Public Affairs, U.S. Department of Justice, http://www.justice.gov/opa/pr/2012/July/12-civ-842.html; http://www.justice.gov/opa/pr/2009/September/09-civ-900.html; http://www.justice.gov/opa/pr/2012/May/12-civ-585.html.

Committee (CC). They are the ones who will implement the following steps leading to an effective compliance program:

- Implementing written policies and procedures
- Designating a CO and CC
- Conducting effective training and education
- Developing effective lines of communication
- Conducting internal monitoring and auditing

Table 23-3 Active Corporate Integrity Agreements with Pharmaceutical Companies in Mid-2012

Company	Years Covered
Abbott Laboratories	2012–2017
AstraZeneca	2010–2015
Sanofi-Aventis	2007–2012
Bayer HealthCare	2008–2013
Bristol-Myers Squibb	2007–2012
Eli Lilly	2009–2014
GlaxoSmithKline	2012–2017
Merck	2011–2016
Novartis Pharmaceuticals	2010–2015
Pfizer	2009–2014

Corporate Integrity Agreement Documents, OIG, DHHS, https://oig.hhs.gov/compliance/corporate-integrity-agreements/cia-documents.asp#cia_list, accessed March 12, 2013.

- Enforcing standards through well-publicized disciplinary guidelines
- Responding promptly to detected problems and undertaking corrective action

BEGINNING WITH COMMITMENT

The process of creating a compliance program is set in motion by a formal expression of commitment from the pharmaceutical company's board of directors or other governing body. In businesses pursuing multiple objectives, major new initiatives like a comprehensive compliance program require clear, unequivocal support from top management to be believable by the workforce. Management expresses that support through verbal and written communications. Beyond that, it allocates adequate resources (financial, personnel) to the effort, sets a hard timetable for implementation, and, ultimately, designates a person as CO to take responsibility for carrying out the timetable.

DESIGNATING A CO AND CC

The CO is designated to be the catalyst and focal point for the company's compliance activities. Ideally, compliance management is his or her only work responsibility. Only in the smallest companies might this be only a part-time duty. The CO must have sufficient authority to push the compliance agenda throughout the organization. During an investigation of suspected misconduct, he or she must be able to gather all relevant documents and other information. The CO often will have to ask probing questions and make some unpopular decisions. To accomplish this, the OIG recommends that the CO have direct access to the company's Chief Executive Officer (CEO)/president, the board of directors, other top executives, and corporate legal counsel. Normally the best way to achieve this is to make the CO a member of the C-suite, reporting to the CEO and on a level with the Chief Financial, Marketing, and Medical Officers. The CO position should receive the funding, staff, and other resources required to create change in the organization and to function independently.

The OIG describes the CO's responsibilities this way:

- Overseeing and monitoring implementation of the compliance program.
- Reporting on a regular basis to the company's board of directors, CEO or president, and CC on compliance matters and suggesting ways to reduce the company's vulnerability to fraud and abuse.
- Periodically revising the compliance program to respond to changes in the company's needs and applicable federal healthcare program requirements, identified weaknesses in the compliance program, or revealed systemic patterns of noncompliance.
- Developing, coordinating, and participating in an educational and training program that focuses on the elements of the compliance program, and ensures that all affected employees and management understand and comply with pertinent federal and state standards.
- Ensuring that independent contractors and agents are aware of the requirements of the company's compliance program with respect to sales and marketing activities, among other things.
- Coordinating personnel issues with the company's human resources/personnel office to ensure that the List of Excluded Individuals/Entities[1] has been checked with respect to all employees and independent contractors.
- Assisting the company's internal auditors in coordinating internal compliance review and monitoring activities.
- Reviewing and acting in response to reports of noncompliance received through the hotline (or other established reporting mechanism) or otherwise brought to his or her attention (e.g., as a result of an internal audit or by corporate counsel who may have been notified of a potential instance of noncompliance).

---

[1] One of the penalties that the OIG may assess against an individual or entity that violates one of the fraud and abuse laws is exclusion from participation in federal healthcare programs (Medicare, Medicaid). It generally is a good idea for law-abiding organizations to avoid doing business with excluded individuals or entities. It is easy to find the names of the people and organizations on the OIG List of Excluded Individuals/Entities here: http://oig.hhs.gov/exclusions/exclusions_list.asp

- Independently investigating and acting on matters related to compliance. To that end, the CO should have the flexibility to design and coordinate internal investigations (e.g., responding to reports of problems or suspected violations) and any resulting corrective action (e.g., making necessary improvements to policies and practices, and taking appropriate disciplinary action) with various company divisions or departments.
- Participating with the company's legal counsel in reporting any self-discovered violations of federal healthcare program requirements.
- Continuing the momentum and revision or expansion of the compliance program after the initial years of implementation.

The mandate of the CC is to advise the CO and assist in the implementation of the compliance program. The members of the Committee should possess certain technical skills and personality traits. To begin with, they must understand intimately the operations of the company, particularly in those areas at highest risk of noncompliance. This means knowing how and why decisions are made all along the organizational value chain. Building on this knowledge, the company trains the CC members in relevant federal fraud and abuse laws, federal healthcare program requirements, and the policies and procedures of its compliance program. Just as important are personal qualities like high integrity, good judgment, assertiveness, and accessibility, all of which serve to earn the trust and respect of the organization's employees.

WRITTEN POLICIES AND PROCEDURES

Every well-run organization uses written policies and procedures to guide its employees in how to perform their jobs. Pharmaceutical manufacturers must develop policies and procedures that describe methods that are compliant with the law. The CO and the CC work with the managers and supervisors in each operational area to prepare these performance guides.

The first document to be produced is a Code of Conduct—a body of fundamental principles and values to provide overall direction to employee work behavior. They state broad ethical and legal principles that pertain to every aspect of every employee's work. The best Code is succinct, easily readable, and universally applicable.

The greatest effort goes into the writing of the policies and procedures governing employee actions in the areas of operations where there is the greatest likelihood of potential liability under several key federal fraud and abuse laws and regulations. The highest risk areas vary over time. When the OIG first began encouraging the establishment of organizational compliance programs in the 1990s, its primary purpose was to rein in the fraud and abuse that contributes so much to the persistent increases in healthcare spending. That is still a major concern, but it has been joined by a desire to protect patient data security and the quality of care that is provided.

The original Compliance Program Guidance for Pharmaceutical Manufacturers issued in 2003 emphasized three areas of compliance risk for pharmaceutical companies. They are still valid subjects for concern.

1. Integrity of data used to establish or determine government reimbursement
2. Kickbacks and other illegal remuneration
3. Compliance with laws regulating drug samples

Integrity of Data Used to Establish or Determine Government Reimbursement

Many federal and state healthcare programs base their reimbursement rates for drugs on price and sales data submitted by pharmaceutical manufacturers. For this arrangement to work, those data must be accurate and complete. If a manufacturer knowingly fails to calculate or submit high-integrity data, it exposes itself to liability under the False Claims Act, the Civil Monetary Penalties Statute, and the Anti-Kickback Statute (AKS).

To satisfy this requirement, the prices reported by the manufacturers must accurately take into account price reductions, cash discounts, free goods contingent on a purchase agreement, rebates, up-front payments, coupons, goods in kind, free or reduced-price services, grants, or other price concessions or similar benefits offered to some or all purchasers. Any discount, price concession, or similar benefit offered on purchases of multiple products should be fairly apportioned among the products.

The methods that a drug company uses to determine the prices that it reports should be rational, consistent, and documented. Records of those methods should be retained for later scrutiny by the government if necessary.

Kickbacks and Other Illegal Remuneration

The federal AKS places limits on the sales, marketing, promotion, discounting, and purchaser relations activities of pharmaceutical companies. The part of the AKS that applies to these manufacturers prohibits offering or paying anything of value in return for purchasing, leasing, ordering, or arranging for or recommending the purchase, lease, or ordering of any item or service that may be reimbursed by a federal healthcare program. In other words, pharmaceutical companies or their representatives may not pay potential customers to buy their drug products. That would be a classic example of "kicking back" part of the purchase price to the buyer.

The penalties for violation of the AKS are criminal. In addition, violators may be subject to civil monetary penalties, exclusion from participation in federal healthcare programs, and possible liability under the False Claims Act.

There are steps that a pharmaceutical manufacturer can take to avoid these kinds of compliance problems. It starts by identifying the paying relationships that it has with individuals or entities that are in a position to generate federal healthcare revenues for it, either directly or indirectly. These typically will include purchasers, benefits managers, formulary committee members, group purchasing organizations (GPOs), physicians and certain allied healthcare professionals, and pharmacists.

The next step is to examine, candidly, the company's reasons for entering into each of these relationships. Is even *one* of the reasons to induce or reward the referral or recommendation of business that might be paid, totally or partially, by a federal healthcare program? That is all it will take to violate the AKS. Several other, lawful purposes will not offset a single unlawful purpose.

It is possible for a pharmaceutical manufacturer to examine its external relationships and take corrective action to make them safe. The OIG suggests criteria for judging the legal risk presented by a relationship.

- Does the arrangement or practice have a potential to interfere with, or skew, clinical decision-making?
- Does it have a potential to undermine the clinical integrity of a formulary process?
- If the arrangement or practice involves providing information to decision-makers, prescribers, or patients, is the information complete, accurate, and not misleading?
- Does the arrangement or practice have a potential to increase costs to the federal healthcare programs, beneficiaries, or enrollees?
- Does the arrangement or practice have the potential to be a disguised discount to circumvent the Medicaid Rebate Program[2] "best price" calculation?
- Does the arrangement or practice have a potential to increase the risk of overutilization or inappropriate utilization?
- Does the arrangement or practice raise patient safety or quality of care concerns?

[2] This is a program whereby drug manufacturers pay a rebate to state Medicaid programs whenever their products are dispensed to Medicaid patients in return for the opportunity to offer those products through Medicaid. The amount of the rebate is based on the "best price" charged by the manufacturer to other purchasers. That best price information is reported by the manufacturers, who have an interest in hiding price concessions they give to other buyers to avoid passing them on to Medicaid. http://www.medicaid.gov/Medicaid-CHIP-Program-Information/By-Topics/Benefits/Prescription-Drugs/Medicaid-Drug-Rebate-Program.html

In addition, the manufacturer can consult other sources like OIG Fraud Alerts and Advisory Bulletins discussing general types of prohibited practices, and OIG Advisory Opinions that assess situations facing specific organizations. It may request an Advisory Opinion about its own arrangements and relationships.

There are several options to correct a problematic paying relationship. The arrangement can be modified to remove the risky elements. The most secure solution is to restructure it so that it fits into one of the Safe Harbor exceptions under the AKS. The most relevant of those deal with personal services and management contracts, warranties, discounts, employees, GPOs, price reductions offered to health plans, price reductions offered to eligible managed care organizations, and price reductions offered by contractors with substantial financial risk to managed care organizations.[3] If no other strategy seems satisfactory, the arrangement can be terminated.

The OIG regulations point to several areas of specific risk for pharmaceutical manufacturers. A risky arrangement has the potential for abuse and should receive close scrutiny. It can be made safe through Safe Harbor structuring and will not necessarily lead to legal liability. These areas of risk involve relationships with three groups that are part of a drug company's distribution chain:

1. Purchasers and their agents
2. Persons and entities able to make or influence referrals (e.g., physicians)
3. Sales agents

RELATIONSHIPS WITH PURCHASERS AND THEIR AGENTS

> *Discounts and other remuneration to purchasers.* Discounting arrangements are common in the pharmaceutical industry. Because of the potential for deception in connection with the Medicaid Rebate Program, they must be reviewed carefully.
>
> The best way to handle discounts is to fit them into the discounts Safe Harbor under the AKS, or possibly the three Safe Harbors for price reductions to managed care organizations. To qualify for these exceptions, the discount must be in the form of a reduction in the price of the pharmaceutical arrived at through an arms-length transaction and issued at the time of the sale. If the

[3] The details of all these exceptions can be found at 42 C.F.R. § 1001.952.

Safe Harbor is to be effective, the company's sales and marketing personnel must be well-instructed in its conditions and follow them rigorously.

Product support services. Drug companies sometimes provide support services to their customers in connection with the sale of their products. Examples of these services are billing assistance tailored to the purchased products and reimbursement consultation. These services present no problem if they have "no substantial independent value." Difficulties arise when they are paired with services that do provide a benefit—such as a reimbursement guarantee (e.g., the purchaser needs to pay for the product only if it is reimbursed by a federal healthcare program).

Educational grants. Drug companies occasionally provide grant funding to their customers for a variety of educational activities. Such grants are problematic if they are conditioned in some way on the purchase of products or if the company has any influence over the content of the education or its presenter. This risk is most easily avoided by keeping separate the grant making and sales/marketing functions, and by using objective criteria for making the grants that do not take into product purchases.

Research funding. Drug manufacturers often contract with some of their healthcare customers to perform research for the manufacturers on a fee-for-service basis. To avoid anti-kickback problems, these arrangements should be structured to fall within the AKS personal services Safe Harbor. The payments to customers should be for legitimate, reasonable, and necessary services at fair market value levels. Within the drug company organization, the awarding of research contracts should be kept separate from the marketing activities.

RELATIONSHIPS WITH PERSONS AND ENTITIES ABLE TO MAKE OR INFLUENCE REFERRALS (E.G., PHYSICIANS)

Drug companies have financial relationships with a variety of people and organizations that do not themselves purchase drugs, but are in a position to influence the referral, ordering, or prescribing of the drugs. Physicians are the best example. Those relationships must be managed very closely to prevent anti-kickback violations. Anything of value given with the intention of generating such referrals is prohibited.

In an effort to cultivate positive relationships with physicians, pharmaceutical manufacturers give gifts, provide entertainment, and compensate them for a variety of personal services. Goods or services provided by the manufacturer are suspect if they eliminate an expense the physician would otherwise have incurred, or if they are sold to the physician at less than their fair market value. Even if a transaction is at fair market value or has a legitimate purpose, such as physician education, the law still will be violated if there also is an illegal purpose.

As usual, the best protection against legal exposure is placement within an AKS Safe Harbor, in this case either professional services and management contracts or employees. When Safe Harbor security is not available, the following factors should be examined:

- The degree of influence the physician has on the generation of business for the manufacturer.
- The extent to which the level of remuneration reflects the volume or value of business generated.
- Whether the remuneration is more than trivial in value; does it exceed the fair market value of the legitimate, reasonable, and necessary services rendered by the physician to the manufacturer?
- The potential of the remuneration to affect costs to federal healthcare programs or their beneficiaries, or to lead to overutilization.
- Whether acceptance of the remuneration diminishes the objectivity of the physician's professional judgment.
- Possible effects on patient safety or quality of care.

Most of these concerns are addressed by the Pharmaceutical Research and Manufacturers of America (PhRMA) Code on Interactions with Healthcare Professionals,[4] which provides useful and practical advice for reviewing and structuring drug company relationships with physicians.

In its Guidance to pharmaceutical manufacturers, the OIG goes on to discuss several high-risk relationships between manufacturers and physicians, and how to minimize that risk.

- "Switching" arrangements
- Consulting and advisory payments
- Payments for detailing
- Business courtesies and other gratuities
- Educational and research funding

---

[4] Find a copy of the Code here: http://www.phrma.org/about/principles-guidelines/code-interactions-healthcare-professionals

The most effective way to minimize the legal risk is to avoid these arrangements entirely. If the manufacturer wishes to pursue them, it should do its best to fit them into one AKS Safe Harbor or another. Compliance with the PhRMA Code will prevent a lot of problems. In general:

- The arrangement should be put in writing.
- The services involved should be legitimate, reasonable, and necessary.
- There should be bona fide purposes for the arrangement.
- The services must be actually delivered.
- The compensation should be at fair market value levels.
- Everything should be documented.
- The decision-making on the arrangements should be separate from the sales, marketing, or promotion of products.
- The arrangement must not be based in any way on physician referral of the manufacturer's products.

RELATIONSHIPS WITH SALES AGENTS

The bulk of pharmaceutical industry compliance problems start with sales and marketing personnel, both employees and independent contractors. Drug companies must engage aggressively with them on these issues. This requires implementing a regular, comprehensive compliance training program for the marketing people, educating them about the minimum PhRMA Code standards, applying corrective action and disciplinary policies to misbehaving sales agents, using the OIG's Advisory Opinion process when there are questions about the practices of sales agents, and monitoring sales force activities.

Special attention should be given to the compensation arrangements with sales agents. If possible, they should be structured to fit into one of the AKS Safe Harbors, most likely personal service or employment. When a Safe Harbor exception is not available, the following characteristics of the arrangement should be reviewed and appropriately adjusted:

- The amount of the agent's compensation
- The identity of the sales agent and his/her degree of influence over the target audience
- The nature of the marketing or promotional activity
- The item or service being promoted or marketed
- The composition of the target audience

Extremely large incentive bonuses or expense accounts are compensation features that will attract a lot of OIG attention. They suggest that the drug company intends to motivate the sales agents to take risks in generating sales revenue.

CONDUCTING EFFECTIVE TRAINING AND EDUCATION

The company next must teach its employees to follow these compliance-friendly policies and procedures in performing their jobs. It will accomplish this by requiring that employees and contractors who perform sales functions participate in appropriate training programs. The programs should include both general curricula and specific sessions that cover the AKS and how it applies to pharmaceutical sales and marketing practices, the calculation and reporting of pricing information, and the payment of rebates in connection with federal healthcare programs. Additional topics for training can be identified by managers of specific functions and departments within the organization, and by reviewing results of internal audits and monitoring, past compliance problems, and changes in federal healthcare program requirements.

The instructors for the training sessions may be company employees or outside consultants as long as they are qualified and experienced in presenting and discussing compliance-related issues. The trainings should be designed to allow participants to ask clarifying questions.

Participation in appropriate training sessions should be mandatory for relevant employees and independent contractors. New employees should receive training within 30 days of their hiring, preferably sooner, perhaps as part of their orientation. Thereafter, the trainings should be updated and repeated at least once a year. The employee training requirement should be expressed in terms of a minimum number of hours per year; tests should be used to measure the participants' comprehension of the subject matter. It should be made clear to employees that active participation is a condition of their continued employment, it will be a factor in their performance evaluations, and failure to satisfy the training requirements may subject them to disciplinary action.

The company should document all its training activities, including attendance lists, content descriptions, and materials distributed.

DEVELOPING EFFECTIVE LINES OF COMMUNICATION

A responsible pharmaceutical manufacturer expects more of its employees than attendance at training sessions and a good faith effort to apply what they learn there. These are important practices, perhaps the cornerstones of a robust compliance effort. However, they are incomplete without two additional compliance program features. Employees must have effective ways of asking questions about compliance that may come up during their work, and of reporting incidents that appear to violate compliance procedures and fraud and abuse laws.

Normally, the first option for an employee is to speak with his or her immediate supervisor. Some organizations find it helpful to adopt so-called "open-door policies" that permit individuals to approach their superior at almost any time. When it comes to reporting suspected violations, an alternative must be available in case the supervisor is the source of the problem. The designated CO can serve that purpose.

The person to whom an employee turns for clarification of company policies must be fully informed about them and the underlying laws and program requirements. Questions raised and answers given should be documented and, if useful, disseminated to other members of the workforce.

Reports of suspected compliance violations are a more sensitive matter. To encourage such reports, it is essential to establish communication channels that offer anonymity and confidentiality to employees who have something to say. They must also feel free from retaliation for their statements. Such channels typically consist hotlines, email forums, suggestion boxes, or any other methods that employees will use with confidence. Once the lines of communication are established, information on how to access them should be publicized to all employees and independent contractors.

A pharmaceutical manufacturer also may use more proactive means to identify areas of risk and concern. It can conduct periodic surveys of employees and sales representatives, and even customers, to obtain feedback on possible misconduct. It definitely should interview departing employees for their opinions on the compliance climate within the organization as well as specific problems of which they are aware.

The output of these various information-gathering mechanisms should be summarized, with personal identifiers removed, and passed on to the board of directors, the CEO, and the CC.

AUDITING AND MONITORING

One of the duties of the CO is to watch over the functioning of the company's compliance program, evaluate its effectiveness, and make recommendations for its improvement. This will occur through regular monitoring of program operations, coupled with periodic audits of its activities and the results they produce.

The audits may consist of prospective system reviews of the manufacturer's processes, protocols, and practices or retrospective reviews of actual practices in a particular area. The reviews can be conducted by internal or external auditors with relevant experience in compliance. They should focus on:

- The company's departments and units that are most directly involved with federal healthcare programs
- Risk areas identified by the OIG in its Guidance and Special Fraud Alerts
- Areas that have been a source of compliance problems for the company in the past

The primary thrust of the reviews is to determine whether policies are in place in the identified risk areas, they are being implemented, and they are being followed.

ENFORCING STANDARDS THROUGH WELL-PUBLICIZED DISCIPLINARY GUIDELINES

Most employees will put their compliance training into practice in their jobs. Disciplinary measures must be applied to those who fail do so, and they should be informed in advance of that possibility. The misconduct may include violations of the law, negligent failure to detect violations, and general noncompliance with the PhRMA Code or the manufacturer's own policies and procedures. The level of discipline will depend on the severity of the employee's misconduct and could range from oral or written warnings, through suspension, up to dismissal.

RESPONDING TO DETECTED PROBLEMS AND DEVELOPING CORRECTIVE ACTION INITIATIVES

Once the company, normally through its CO, receives information about a possible compliance violation, a couple things must happen. First, an immediate investigation should be launched to determine whether a substantial violation of the applicable law or requirements of the compliance program has occurred and, if so, to take decisive steps to correct the problem. If nothing else, the investigation should reveal the root causes of the identified problem.

When the investigation shows that there was more than a failure to comply with a company policy or a payor program requirement, but rather a violation of criminal, civil, or administrative law, a prompt report must be made to the appropriate federal and state authorities. Such reports demonstrate the pharmaceutical manufacturer's good faith and willingness to cooperate with governmental authorities to correct and remedy the problem. If the OIG decides to pursue the matter and eventually finds the company culpable, this will be considered a mitigating factor in determining any administrative sanctions.

REVIEW OF THE CONTENT OF A TYPICAL PHARMACEUTICAL MANUFACTURER COMPLIANCE PROGRAM

The OIG Compliance Program Guidance for Pharmaceutical Manufacturers describes an excellent model for any drug company. It is worthwhile to review what companies in the pharmaceutical industry actually have done in setting up their own compliance programs. On their websites, most of them have made some effort to explain their compliance activities. The breadth and detail varies considerably. Links to the compliance pages on the websites of 9 of the 10 largest pharmaceutical manufacturers are provided in one of the Learning Experience topics at the end of the chapter. The tenth of those companies is Pfizer; this is the link to the compliance information it publishes on the Internet: http://www.pfizer.com/about/corporate_compliance/corporate_compliance.jsp.

Following is a brief review of the content of Pfizer's description of its compliance activities. It is structured around the seven elements of an OIG-recommended compliance program.

Written Policies and Procedures

Rather than trying to summarize its relevant policies and procedures, Pfizer refers to three substantial documents on compliance. All three can be downloaded from the website.

Blue Book. This is Pfizer's name for its Code of Conduct, 53 pages that explain how the company expects its employees to conduct themselves with integrity. It touches on numerous areas like Healthcare Laws, Anti-Bribery and Anti-Corruption, Monitoring Product Safety, Social Media, Privacy of Personal Information, Equal Employment Opportunity, Alcohol and Drug Abuse, Human Subject Protection in Clinical Research, and Animal Welfare. The Code is not restricted to fraud and abuse matters.

White Guide. This 312-page document is intended to be the main compliance resource for U.S.-based non-sales colleagues supporting Pfizer's biopharmaceutical business. It covers topics like Advertising and Promotional Materials, Promotional Interactions with Health Care Providers, Patient Assistance Programs, and Clinical Research. The company commends the White Guide to its employees as a single resource on compliance rules relating to their day-to-day activities.

Orange Guide. This 321-page document is the companion to the White Guide. It is meant to be the main compliance resource for U.S.-based sales colleagues supporting Pfizer's biopharmaceutical business. It addresses subjects like Detailing to Health Care Providers, Interactions with Health Systems and Medical Groups, Speaker Programs for Health Care Providers, and Health Care Provider Payment Disclosure.

Compliance Officer and Compliance Committee

This section identifies the CO by name, specifies to whom he reports, and summarizes his responsibilities. Pfizer calls its CC the Compliance Division. Its responsibilities are also described here.

Training and Education

Pfizer uses online compliance education, which probably makes sense for an international organization with 110,000 employees. It also mentions the online access to the Blue Book, the Orange Guide, and the White Guide.

Lines of Communication

Several channels for reporting general issues and raising compliance concerns are listed. There is an "open door policy" that encourages all employees to contact their immediate supervisors regarding any compliance matters. They are assured that the communication will be kept as confidential as possible and there will be no retaliation.

The website lists four specific means for contacting the Pfizer Compliance Division: an email address, a postal mail address, a phone number, and a secure fax number. There is a phone number for a Compliance Hotline that is available around the clock all year long and in 70 languages (Pfizer has a diverse international presence). A web-based helpline also is available.

It is made clear that the Board of Directors and its relevant committees are accessible, but only to management and the Compliance Division.

Internal Monitoring and Auditing

This vital compliance function is briefly described, and reference is made to the Corporate Internal Audit Team. This appears to be a formal, full-time group carrying out monitoring and auditing. Only very large organizations could afford such a luxury.

Enforcement Through Discipline Pursuant to Published Guidelines

It is stated here that all employees and management are on notice that their failure to adhere to the company's compliance standards set out in the Blue Book, Orange Guide, and White Guide could have disciplinary consequences, including termination of employment.

Prompt Response and Corrective Action for Detected Problems

Pfizer succinctly expresses its support for prompt response and corrective action for detected problems.

Over a third of Pfizer's webpage on compliance activities deals with a California state law (SB 1765) that requires pharmaceutical companies to adopt a compliance program that, among other things, sets limits on gifts and incentives to medical or health professionals. The California law is representative of a small but growing number of states that are showing an interest in restricting interactions between drug sales representatives and healthcare providers. Pfizer maintains another webpage[5] dealing exclusively with Sales and Marketing Compliance.

There, it addresses the issues of Global Policy on Interactions with Healthcare Professionals, Ensuring Ethical Business Behavior Worldwide,

[5] http://www.pfizer.com/about/corporate_compliance/ethical_sales_and_marketing.jsp.

Direct-to-Consumer Advertising, and Disclosing Payments to Healthcare Professionals.

On the basis of its statements about compliance on its website, Pfizer might appear to be running a model compliance program. It covers all the elements of a good program. The three voluminous documents on compliance policies and procedures could not be more thorough and easy to understand. Of course, those words on a website must be translated into effective action in the workplace. In the end, the only question is whether all of Pfizer's compliance efforts actually prevent employee misconduct, noncompliance, and fraud violations.

STUDY QUESTIONS

1. What is an "open door policy" and when might it not be a good alternative for employees reporting misconduct?
2. Without reading the chapter again, briefly describe the seven elements of a recommended compliance program.
3. Who or what is likely to show up on the List of Excluded Individuals/Entities?
4. If an organization has a good, competent CO, what function does a CC perform?
5. How would you describe an organizational Code of Conduct to a person who had never seen one? Do individuals ever have personal Code of Conduct?
6. How does a drug company that pays its sales representatives on a commission basis and pressures them to increase their sales also persuade them to avoid giving kickbacks to their customers?
7. How would you explain a Safe Harbor under the AKS?
8. List at least three different categories of people who may have influence over the ordering or referral of healthcare goods or services, and explain how they exercise that influence.
9. Review the PhRMA Code on Interactions with Healthcare Professionals at the link given in the text. Does it do an adequate job of controlling the ways that drug sales representatives interact with physicians?
10. What would you do with an employee who attends compliance training sessions but does not participate in the exercises and discussions, and does poorly on the comprehension tests given afterward?
11. On what occasions should an employer report an employee's compliance misconduct to an appropriate federal or state enforcement agency?

Learning Exercises

1. These are links to the webpages describing the compliance programs for 9 of the 10 largest pharmaceutical manufacturers. The tenth manufacturer, Pfizer, is discussed in the text. Rather than enter the links manually, just Google the name of the manufacturer plus "compliance program." The desired website will be among the top listings.

   Review the program description for each manufacturer. Compare it to what you have learned in this chapter about the characteristics of a good program; also compare it to what the other manufacturers say about their compliance programs. On the basis of what you see on the website, what conclusions do you reach about the manufacturer's compliance efforts?

   Of course, an inadequate description on a website does not mean that there is not an excellent compliance program behind it. What is the importance of the impression created by each of these websites?
   - Novartis
     - http://www.pharma.us.novartis.com/info/corporate-responsibility/business-conduct/compliance.jsp
   - Sanofi
     - http://www.sanofi.us/l/us/en/layout.jsp?scat=9FB6A7F2-C558-4BD5-9D4C-05FF9ABB9A5C
   - Merck & Co.
     - http://www.merck.com/about/how-we-operate/compliance/home.html
   - GlaxoSmithKline
     - http://www.gsk.com/about/corp-gov-ethics.htm
   - AstraZeneca
     - http://www.astrazeneca-us.com/responsibility/corporate-transparency/us-compliance-program
   - Johnson & Johnson
     - http://www.jnj.com/responsibility/ESG/Governance/Codes_of_Conduct/Healthcare_Compliance
   - Eli Lilly & Co.
     - http://www.lilly.com/about/business-practices/ethics-compliance/Pages/ethics-compliance.aspx
   - Abbott Laboratories
     - https://www.abbott.com/citizenship/culture/ethics-compliance.htm
   - Bristol-Myers Squibb
     - http://www.bms.com/ourcompany/compliance_ethics/Pages/default.aspx

2. Despite the compliance efforts of the Pfizer drug company described in this chapter, in the last 10 years, it has settled two government cases (charging off-label promotion of drugs and kickbacks) for monetary payments of $2.3 billion and $430 million. Do a little Internet research to discover exactly what Pfizer actions were behind these charges. Then speculate on how they could have occurred despite the company's substantial, large-scale, well-publicized commitment to compliance. In what ways do you think failings in Pfizer's compliance program could have allowed these problems to occur? If Pfizer asked you, what recommendations would you make for enhancing its compliance program to prevent further incidents like these?
3. The term "off-label promotion" is not explained in this chapter. Do a little research and find out what it means.

References

1. OIG Compliance Program Guidance for Pharmaceutical Manufacturers, Federal Register, Vol. 68, No. 86, Monday, May 5, 2003, pp. 23731-23743.
2. Pharmaceutical Industry Criminal and Civil Penalties: An Update, Public Citizen website, http://www.citizen.org/hrg2073, September 27, 2012.
3. Pharmaceuticals & Biotech Industry Global Report–2011, an IMAP Health Care Report, http://www.imap.com/imap/media/resources/IMAP_PharmaReport_8_272B8752E0FB3.pdf
4. Report from February 23, 2012, Pharmaceutical Compliance Roundtable, Office of the Inspector General, Department of Health and Human Services, http://www.pharmacomplianceforum.org/docs/1202OIGPharma.pdf
5. Pharma Compliance Resources Guide, The Pharmaceutical Compliance Forum, http://www.pharmacomplianceforum.org/resources.html
6. "Punishing Health Care Fraud–Is the GSK Settlement Sufficient?" The New England Journal of Medicine, September 12, 2012, http://www.nejm.org/doi/full/10.1056/NEJMp1209249

Chapter 24

Durable Medical Equipment, Prosthetics, Orthotics, and Supplies

Learning Objectives

After completing class sessions based on this chapter, a student will:

- Be familiar with the medical products sold by durable medical equipment, prosthetics, orthotics, and supply (DMEPOS) manufacturers.
- Know the benefits of an effective compliance program for a DMEPOS supplier.
- Have a quick introduction to multiple risk areas that exist in DMEPOS supplier organizations.
- Understand the job prerequisites and responsibilities of a Compliance Officer and the members of a Compliance Committee.
- Be able to explain the different types of compliance training and their curriculums.
- See the value of open, multiple lines of communication between the Compliance Officer and the workforce.
- Learn a variety of techniques for auditing and monitoring an organization's compliance activities.
- Appreciate the need for compliance-related disciplinary action guidelines.
- Discover the basic types of corrective action a DMEPOS supplier might take in response to detected offenses.

INTRODUCTION

A variety of products are manufactured by the DMEPOS industry. The term durable medical equipment (DME) covers items that are:

- Able to withstand repeated use.
- Primarily and customarily used to serve a medical purpose.
- Generally not useful to a person in the absence of an illness or injury.
- Appropriate for use in the home.
- Likely to last for 3 years or more.
- Provided by specific suppliers that are approved by Medicare.
- Medically necessary for the beneficiary.

Some examples of this equipment are walkers, crutches, wheelchairs, power scooters, hospital beds, home oxygen equipment, diabetes self-testing equipment, parenteral/enteral supplies, breathing machines, and certain nebulizers.

Prosthetic devices include artificial limbs, terminal devices (e.g., hand or hook) and artificial eyes, parenteral and enteral (PEN) nutrition, cardiac pacemakers, prosthetic lenses, breast prostheses for post-mastectomy patients, maxillofacial devices, and devices that replace all or part of the ear or nose. Orthotics are rigid or semi-rigid devices, often called braces, which are applied to the outside of the body as a means either to support a weak or deformed body part or to restrict or eliminate motion in a diseased or injured part of the body.

The DMEPOS industry is highly fragmented with estimates of as many as 100,000 competitors offering a variety of different product lines. Some of them are providers of home care services and products, while others solely manufacture the products. Among the largest providers are Apria, Lincare, Rotech, Praxair, and American Homepatient. The largest manufacturers are Medtronic, Baxter, Johnson & Johnson, Invacare, and Agilent. At one extreme, there are at least a dozen corporations with annual sales exceeding $1 billion. At the other end of the spectrum are numerous smaller local companies operated by sole proprietors or families, some with less than $1 million in annual revenues. There are an increasing number of suppliers selling through mail order and the Internet.

The Centers for Medicare and Medicaid Services (CMS) reports that DME sales in 2013 were approximately $30 billion, representing 1.2% of total national healthcare expenditures. The sales are growing at a rate of 5% to 6% a year.

Two recent developments have increased the pressure on DMEPOS suppliers (providers and manufacturers) to compete even more aggressively for business.

The Medicare Modernization Act of 2003 established a new competitive bidding program for DMEPOS suppliers. Under the program, they compete to become Medicare contract suppliers by submitting bids to furnish certain items in defined competitive bidding areas, and the CMS awards contracts to enough suppliers to meet beneficiary demand for those items. Winners earn the right to solicit referral sources for Medicare patients and bill Medicare for their products and services. Winning the bid does not guarantee patient volume.

Beginning in 2013, the manufacturers or importers of certain DME products must pay an annual 2.3% sales or excise tax on their sales of those products.

OFFICE OF THE INSPECTOR GENERAL PROMOTION OF COMPLIANCE PROGRAM ADOPTION

Since 1998, the Office of the Inspector General (OIG) has aggressively promoted the adoption of comprehensive compliance programs by all entities participating in federal healthcare programs such as Medicare and Medicaid. The OIG Compliance Program Guidance for the Durable Medical Equipment, Prosthetics, Orthotics, and Supply (DMEPOS) Industry was the fifth such guidance issued, in 1999. The Patient Protection and Affordable Care Act (PPACA) of 2010 made such programs mandatory. To facilitate the adoption of these programs, the OIG has issued detailed Compliance Program Guidances for 12 different types of healthcare organizations.

The OIG acknowledges that healthcare entities come in many different sizes, with a wide range of staff and financial resources available to them. This is particularly true in the DMEPOS supplier industry. Therefore, the agency does not expect every supplier to implement compliance programs of the same scope and thoroughness. Abbreviated versions of the model programs are accepted. What the OIG is looking for is a commitment to the objectives and principles underlying the elements described in the Program Guidances.

All of the OIG Compliance Program Guidances are structured around the same seven basic program elements. They are based directly on the similar minimally required elements of an "effective compliance and ethics program" recommended in the Federal Sentencing Guidelines (FSG). Under the FSG, the potential fines and other punishment can be significantly reduced if an entity can show that it has such a program in place and that the criminal violation represented an anomaly in an otherwise law-abiding organization. The same thing is true of compliance programs that conform to the OIG Guidances.

These are the elements of a compliance program now mandatory for healthcare organizations.

1. Written policies and procedures
2. Designation of a Compliance Officer and a Compliance Committee
3. Conducting effective training and education
4. Developing effective lines of communication
5. Auditing and monitoring
6. Enforcing standards through well-publicized disciplinary guidelines
7. Responding to detected offenses and developing corrective action initiatives

BENEFITS FOR A DMEPOS SUPPLIER OF AN EFFECTIVE COMPLIANCE PROGRAM

Compliance programs that work well serve the interests of federal healthcare programs by minimizing waste and excessive spending, ensuring the optimal allocation of resources within the healthcare system, and helping patients obtain exactly the medical care that they need. There is a multitude of benefits that flow to individual DMEPOS suppliers as well. The most obvious is the assistance with fulfillment of their societal duty to obey all laws. The OIG suggests several others.

- The development of internal controls that assure compliance with federal and state laws and regulations, public and private payor healthcare program requirements, and internal guidelines.
- A concrete demonstration to employees and the community of the DMEPOS supplier's commitment to honest and responsible corporate conduct.
- The ability to obtain an accurate assessment of employee and contractor behavior relating to fraud and abuse.
- An increased likelihood of identifying and preventing criminal and unethical conduct.
- The ability to quickly and accurately react to employees' compliance concerns and effectively target resources to address those concerns.
- Improvement of the quality, efficiency, and consistency of providing services.
- Increased efficiency on the part of employees.

- A centralized source for distributing information regarding fraud and abuse and related issues.
- Improved internal communication.
- A methodology that encourages employees to report potential problems.
- Procedures that allow the prompt, thorough investigation of alleged misconduct by corporate officers, managers, sales representatives, employees, independent contractors, consultants, clinicians, and other healthcare professionals.
- Initiation of immediate, appropriate, and decisive corrective action.
- Early detection and reporting of false claims, thereby reducing the DMEPOS supplier's exposure to civil damages and penalties, criminal sanctions, and administrative remedies.

Resources spent on a compliance infrastructure should be viewed as a sound investment in the organization's ongoing success.

Written Policies and Procedures

Every professionally run business of any size already has policies and procedures that explain exactly how the organization's managers want the employees to carry out their work tasks. What the OIG is asking for are policies and procedures that also reflect the statutes, regulations, and other requirements that apply to business. The policies and procedures can do more than simply explain how to perform a job efficiently and competently, with high-quality results. They also should give direction on work practices that are in compliance with all applicable laws.

When they have been completed, copies of the policies and procedures should be distributed to all individuals affected by them and expected to follow them.

There are two categories of written compliance instructions. One is a set of broad conduct standards, often called a Code of Conduct. The other is more specific, detailed policies and procedures that guide employees working in functional areas where there is a high risk of compliance violations.

Standards of Conduct

These are fundamental principles, values, and a framework for all activities within the DMEPOS supplier organization. They serve as a sort of "constitution" for the whole organization and its workforce. The standards should include a basic commitment to compliance; a statement of the organization's mission, goals, and ethical principles; and its expectations for everybody associated with its operations (owners, governing board, senior executives, managers, marketing personnel, employees, vendors, contractors, and agents).

When employees receive their copies of the standards of conduct, they should be asked to sign a statement certifying that they read, understood, and will follow them.

Policies and Procedures for Specific Risk Areas

The OIG Compliance Program Guidance for DMEPOS entities lists 47 areas of special concern to the OIG. These are far more compliance risk areas than appear in the Program Guidances for any other type of healthcare entity. It is a reflection of the rather large number of fraud and abuse cases that have involved the DMEPOS industry for over 20 years. Many of the risk areas on the list also may exist in other types of healthcare organizations. For that reason alone, it is worth reviewing them.

> *Billing for items or services not provided.* The DMEPOS organization submits a bill for payment for goods or services that were never actually delivered to a beneficiary.
>
> *Billing for services that the DMEPOS supplier believes may be denied.* A DMEPOS supplier submits a bill or claim for services that are not covered by Medicare or that it knows or should have known were not medically necessary for the beneficiary. For those reasons the claim will be denied.
>
> *Billing patients for denied charges without a signed written notice.* No provider (including DMEPOS suppliers) may bill patients directly for services that will not be paid for by Medicare without first (before providing the service) obtaining an Advance Beneficiary Notice of Noncoverage signed by the patient.
>
> *Duplicate billing.* Duplicate billing occurs when the same or two different DMEPOS suppliers submit more than one claim for payment for the same patient, for the same service, for the same date of service, or to more than one payor. Although duplicate billing can result from simple error, fraudulent duplicate billing is often evidenced by systematic or repeated double billing and creates legal liability, particularly if any overpayment is not promptly refunded.
>
> *Billing for items or services not ordered.* In this case, the DMEPOS supplier bills for goods or services that were not ordered by a physician.
>
> *Using a billing agent whose compensation arrangement violates the reassignment rule.* As a general rule, Medicare will not pay an amount due to

a provider to another person to whom the provider has legally reassigned the right to receive the payment. There is an exception to this rule for reassignments to an agent who furnishes the provider with billing and collection services. However, the agent's compensation may not be tied to the amounts billed or collected.

Upcoding. The DMEPOS supplier submits a claim for reimbursement with a higher billing code for a more costly good or service than the one actually provided. For instance, billing for a more expensive piece of equipment when a less expensive piece of equipment is provided.

Unbundling items or supplies. A supplier submits claims for the individual components of a good or service when there is a billing code for the entire good or service as a unit or bundle. The components normally cost less when bundled together.

Billing for new equipment and providing used equipment. The DMEPOS supplier must indicate on the Medicare claim form whether the item provided is new or used. The reimbursement for a new item is higher than it is for a used item.

Continuing to bill for rental items after they are no longer medically necessary. Some DMEPOS products are provided on a rental rather than a purchase basis. At some point, a product may no longer be medically necessary. If the supplier is not aware of the change in the patient's needs, it may continue to bill Medicare for it. To avoid that, the OIG recommends that the supplier periodically contact the treating physician to ensure that the rental item still is medically necessary. When it is no longer necessary, the supplier should promptly pick up the item from the patient.

Resubmission of denied claims with different information in an attempt to be improperly reimbursed. This problem occurs when a DMEPOS supplier improperly alters the information on a previously denied claim and resubmits it in an attempt to obtain payment. For instance, if a claim with an accurate billing code is denied, the supplier might change the code to one that it believes is more likely to be reimbursable.

Refusing to submit a claim to Medicare for which payment is made on a reasonable charge or fee schedule basis. A DMEPOS supplier must submit a claim on behalf of a beneficiary for items that are Medicare benefits and reimbursable under the Medicare program. If a supplier refuses to file the claim, perhaps in the misguided belief that the item is not covered by Medicare, the beneficiary usually will be asked to pay.

Inadequate management and oversight of contracted services, which results in improper billing. An organization like a DMEPOS supplier may choose to subcontract its billing function to a third party. Inevitably, the supplier will have less direct control over that party than it would over an employee. The OIG recommends that the DMEPOS supplier closely supervise the subcontractor to prevent improper billing practices.

Charge limitations. Medicare providers and suppliers may not submit bills for items or services substantially in excess of their usual charges. The DMEPOS supplier's billing personnel should be aware that violation of this rule may lead to exclusion from the Medicare program.

Providing and/or billing for substantially excessive amounts of DMEPOS items or supplies. The term "overutilization" refers to the provision of or billing for substantially more items or supplies than are reasonable and necessary for the needs of a particular patient. While the medical need for an item must be determined by the treating physician, the DMEPOS supplier must ensure that the patient's condition meets the coverage, payment, and utilization criteria stated in the payor's requirements. The OIG recommends that if a supplier notices that it is providing and billing for an unusually large number of items for the same patient, it periodically contact the treating physician to confirm the medical need for the items. Those contacts should be documented.

Providing and/or billing for an item or service that does not meet the quality and standard of the DMEPOS item claimed. This practice involves providing or billing for an item that does not meet the requirement of the item ordered by the treating physician. Often, the item is simply of poor quality, perhaps even lacking Food and Drug Administration approval. It is essential that every DMEPOS supplier ensure that the items it furnishes to patients meet professionally recognized quality standards.

Capped rentals. Both public and private payors have requirements for DMEPOS suppliers providing rental equipment to beneficiaries. Such suppliers must give beneficiaries the option to purchase an item during the 10th continuous month of rental. After the 15th continuous month of rental, if the item is still medically necessary, the DMEPOS supplier must continue to provide the item without charge to Medicare or the beneficiary. The supplier also should ensure that it is performing basic safety and operational function checks after an item's use by each patient, as well as routine and preventative maintenance on its equipment. The DMEPOS supplier must ensure it has qualified staff or contractors to service, set up, and instruct the patient on the proper use of the equipment.

Failure to monitor medical necessity on an ongoing basis. If a DMEPOS supplier is providing the same items to a patient on a regular basis, it should periodically contact the treating physician to confirm that the items continue to be medically necessary. In addition, the item should be replaced or adjusted, in a timely manner, to reflect changes in the patient's condition.

Delivering or billing for certain items or supplies prior to receiving a physician's order and/or appropriate certificate of medical necessity (CMN). A DMEPOS supplier may not deliver an item to a patient or bill Medicare for the item unless it has received an order and a CMN from a treating physician.

Falsifying information on the claim form, CMN, and/or accompanying documentation. This practice involves supplying false information to be included on the claim form, the CMN, or other supporting documentation, usually with the intention of obtaining otherwise unavailable reimbursement. There are criminal penalties for doing this.

Completing portions of CMNs reserved for completion only by the treating physician or other authorized person. A CMN has four sections: Sections A and C are meant to be completed by the supplier and Sections B and D by the physician. In order to speed up the claims process, a supplier might be tempted to fill in the physician's sections. That is prohibited.

Altering medical records. Sometimes, a medical record could be altered or falsified in order to justify reimbursement for an item that is not medically necessary. It is a violation of civil and criminal laws to do so.

Manipulating the patient's diagnosis in an attempt to receive improper payment. In this case, the DMEPOS supplier alters the treating physician's diagnosis so that it can claim the patient has a medical condition that requires a reimbursable item, when the patient does not otherwise need that item.

Failing to maintain medical necessity documentation. The DMEPOS supplier bills for an item without the documentation for its medical necessity, such as the physician orders or CMNs.

Inappropriate use of place of service codes. For the purpose of obtaining reimbursement, the supplier uses a billing code to indicate an inaccurate location for the patient's use of an item. For instance, certain items are covered by Medicare if the beneficiary resides in his or her home, but not if he or she is a resident of a skilled nursing facility.

Cover letters that encourage physicians to order medically unnecessary items or services. DMEPOS suppliers have the option of attaching a cover letter to the CMN forms sent to treating physicians. It is acceptable for the letter to describe what is being ordered and how it is to be administered to the patient. The OIG becomes concerned when the letter tells the physician what to include in the CMN or otherwise tries to influence him or her to order medically unnecessary equipment.

Routine waiver of deductibles and coinsurance. DMEPOS suppliers are permitted to waive the Medicare deductible and coinsurance amounts only in cases of patient financial hardship. When they routinely forgive financial obligations, they may be inducing patients to use items or services that are unnecessary, simply because they are free. Suppliers must make a good faith effort to collect deductibles and coinsurance.

Providing incentives to actual or potential referral sources (e.g., physicians, hospitals, patients, skilled nursing facilities, home health agencies, or others) that may violate the Anti-Kickback Statute or other similar federal or state statutes or regulations. Examples of these prohibited practices are paying a fee to a physician for each CMN he or she signs, providing free gifts to physicians for signing CMNs, providing inducements to beneficiaries, and providing items or services for free or below fair market value to providers or beneficiaries.

Compensation programs that offer incentives for items or services ordered and revenue generated. Compensation programs with these kinds of incentives lead to the ordering of medically unnecessary items or supplies, and the "dumping" of such items or supplies in a facility or in a beneficiary's home.

Joint ventures between parties, one of whom can refer Medicare or Medicaid business to the other. The OIG is bothered by joint ventures between parties that supply goods or services paid for by Medicare and other parties in a position to order or refer such goods or services. For instance, several physicians may become investors in a DMEPOS business from which they might order products for their patients. The profits from the business are an incentive for them to order more products, perhaps unnecessarily. This is a violation of the Anti-Kickback Statute.

Billing for items or services furnished pursuant to a prohibited referral under the Stark Physician Self-Referral Law. This is similar to the joint venture problem. The Stark Physician Self-Referral Law prohibits physicians from making referrals for certain designated services (which include DMEPOS) payable by Medicare to an entity with which he or she has a financial relationship (ownership, investment, or compensation). In such an arrangement, the physician may not make a referral to the DMEPOS supplier and the supplier may not bill Medicare for furnishing the items.

Improper telemarketing practices. The OIG is concerned enough about this practice to have issued Special Fraud Alerts about it. DMEPOS suppliers are prohibited from making unsolicited telephone calls to Medicare beneficiaries regarding the furnishing of a covered item unless (a) the beneficiary has given written permission for the supplier to make contact by telephone; (b) the contact concerns a covered item that the supplier has already furnished the beneficiary; or (c) the supplier has furnished at least one covered item to the beneficiary during the preceding 15 months. Accordingly, the supplier may not submit a claim based on a prohibited phone solicitation. A DMEPOS supplier cannot avoid this prohibition by using an independent marketing firm.

Improper patient solicitation activities and high-pressure marketing of uncovered or unnecessary services. The DMEPOS supplier should create policies and procedures that prevent its sales staff from offering physicians, patients, or other potential referral sources incentives for their business, telling Medicare beneficiaries that they do not have to pay coinsurance amounts or can receive "free" services, and promoting items or services to patients that are unnecessary for their treatment.

Co-location of DMEPOS items and supplies with the referral source. In these cases, a physician allows a DMEPOS supplier to store inventory in his or her office. When the inventory items are dispensed to a patient, the supplier bills Medicare. The OIG is worried about Anti-Kickback Statute and Physician Self-Referral Law issues: The nearby availability of the items may encourage the physician to order them. The supplier may pay the physician an above-fair-market-value rent for use of the space.

Noncompliance with the federal, state, and private payor supplier standards. In order to be eligible to receive payment for a Medicare-covered item, a DMEPOS supplier must meet a total of 31 conditions and standards specified by the CMS. Private payors often impose their own additional prerequisites. Every supplier must institute mechanisms for constantly ensuring that it is complying with these standards.

Providing false information on the Medicare DMEPOS supplier enrollment form. Providing false information, or making false statements of material fact in an application for a benefit or payment under a federal healthcare program may subject a DMEPOS supplier to criminal penalties.

Not notifying the National Supplier Clearinghouse (NSC) in a timely manner of changes to the information previously provided on the DMEPOS supplier enrollment form. In order to be eligible to receive Medicare payment for covered items or services provided to Medicare beneficiaries, DMEPOS suppliers must formally enroll in the Medicare program by submitting an application to the NSC. The NSC processes the application and verifies the information it contains. DMEPOS suppliers must notify the NSC within 30 days of changes in their enrollment information.

Misrepresenting a person's status as an agent or representative of Medicare. It is unlawful for a DMEPOS supplier to represent itself as a Medicare representative. It might do this to persuade a patient or the patient's doctor that an item is necessary.

Knowing misuse of a supplier number, which results in improper billing. One DMEPOS supplier might use another supplier's billing number, because its number is no longer valid or it has not yet received a number. This misuse always is prohibited.

Failing to meet individual payor requirements. A DMEPOS supplier may need to submit claims to a variety of payors–Medicare, Medicaid, other federal programs, state programs, and private payors. In some cases, there may be a primary and a secondary payor. The supplier must be aware of the requirements of each payor and comply with them appropriately.

Performing tests on a beneficiary to establish medical necessity. Among the information required to support the billing for home use of oxygen is a medical documentation form and the results of certain simple laboratory tests. The DMEPOS supplier may be tempted to enter the information on the form or perform the tests. This is prohibited.

Failing to refund overpayments to a healthcare program. Due to innocent mistakes or simple negligence by the supplier or the payor, the supplier may receive a payment amount in excess of what it is due under the Medicare program. The OIG strongly recommends that every DMEPOS supplier maintain procedures for detecting such overpayments and then promptly repaying the amounts to Medicare.

Failing to refund overpayments to patients. Similar mechanisms should be in place to identify overpayments by patients. Those amounts should be promptly refunded to the patient.

Improper billing resulting from a lack of communication between the DMEPOS supplier, the physician, and the patient. Poor communications among a

DMEPOS supplier, treating physicians, and patients can result in the supplier inappropriately billing for items or supplies. To prevent this, the OIG recommends that the supplier periodically call the patient to ensure the item is still being used and operating properly, and periodically call the physician to ensure that the item is still medically necessary for the patient.

Improper billing resulting from a lack of communication between different departments within the DMEPOS supplier. Poor communication between the different departments (e.g., sales and billing) of a DMEPOS supplier may result in the filing of incorrect claims or equipment delivery problems. What the supplier needs to do is create mechanisms that facilitate and smooth communication among its departments.

Employing persons excluded from participation in federal healthcare programs. This problem arises when a DMEPOS supplier hires or contracts with individuals or entities who have been excluded from participation in federal healthcare or other programs. To avoid this problem, a DMEPOS supplier must check the OIG List of Excluded Individuals and Entities (LEIE) and the General Services Administration (GSA) Excluded Parties Lists System (EPLS) prior to hiring a new employee or contracting with a new outside party for the first time.

Many of the risk areas described in this list are present in other healthcare organizations. The length of the list is an indication of the extent of the compliance threat that faces these organizations. It also is an argument for committing substantial resources to a compliance program.

Designation of a Compliance Officer and a Compliance Committee

One of the first steps in the creation of an effective compliance program is the designation of a Compliance Officer to serve as the focal point for the organization's compliance activities. In a larger organization, this will be a full-time job; in a smaller entity, the assigned person may have other management responsibilities.

The position needs to have appropriate authority and the freedom to make decisions without fear of reprisal. Accordingly, this should be a high-level person within the organization. He or she should have direct access to the owners, governing board, president or Chief Executive Officer (CEO), senior management, and legal counsel. It should not be someone working in sales or marketing, who may face a conflict between his or her compliance goals and sales goals. The position also should not be subordinate to the general counsel, comptroller, or other financial officer.

The Compliance Officer's authority must extend to review all documents and other compliance-related information, such as patient records, billing records, records of its marketing activities, and evidence of the supplier's arrangements with other parties. He or she also should be able temporarily to halt the processing of claims if a problem is discovered in the procedure.

To succeed in the job, the Compliance Officer must have sufficient funding and staff. There is wide variation in the size of DMEPOS supplier entities. Some are so small that they cannot afford to devote the same financial or staff resources to compliance as much larger organizations. The OIG understands and accepts this, asking that they do the best they can with their limitations.

These are among the primary responsibilities of a Compliance Officer.

- Overseeing and monitoring the implementation of the compliance program.
- Reporting regularly to the owners, governing body, CEO, president, and Compliance Committee on the progress of implementation.
- Periodically revising the program in light of changes in the organization's needs, and in the statutes, rules, regulations, and requirements of federal, state, and private payor healthcare plans.
- Reviewing employees' certifications that they have received, read, understood, and will abide by the standards of conduct.
- Developing, coordinating, and participating in an educational and training program that focuses on the elements of the compliance program.
- Ensuring that independent contractors and agents who provide services (e.g., billing companies, delivery services, referral sources) to the DMEPOS supplier are aware of the requirements of the compliance program.
- Coordinating personnel issues (background checks, disciplinary actions) with the personnel department.
- Assisting the financial management department in coordinating internal compliance review and monitoring activities.
- Independently investigating and acting on matters related to compliance, including internal investigations and any resulting corrective action with internal departments, independent contractors, and healthcare professionals.
- Developing policies and programs that encourage managers and employees to report suspected fraud and other misconduct without fear of retaliation.
- Continuing the momentum of the compliance program and the accomplishment of its objectives after the initial implementation.

Where organization size and resources permit, a Compliance Committee should be established to support the Compliance Officer, who will manage the Committee. Because the Committee members are likely to be new to compliance, they will require training on the policies and procedures of the supplier's compliance program.

The OIG suggests that a Compliance Committee take on responsibilities like these.

- Analyzing the organization's regulatory environment, the legal requirements with which it must comply, and specific risk areas.
- Assessing how well existing policies and procedures address these risk areas.
- Working with individual departments to develop standards of conduct, policies, and procedures that promote allegiance to the principles of compliance.
- Recommending and monitoring the development of departmental systems and controls to carry out the organization's compliance principles as part of its daily operations.
- Determining the appropriate strategies to promote compliance with the program and detection of potential violations.
- Developing a system to solicit, evaluate, and respond to complaints and problems.
- Overseeing internal/external audits and investigations for the purpose of identifying problematic and poorly functioning areas, and implementing corrective actions.

Small DMEPOS suppliers may not be able to maintain a full-time Compliance Committee. In those cases, the OIG recommends that the entity create an ad hoc taskforce whenever compliance problems arise.

Conducting Effective Training and Education

To make sure that a DMEPOS supplier's employees understand and follow the compliance program rules, the Compliance Officer must conduct appropriate training and education, not once but repeatedly for as long as compliance is an issue. There should be two types of training. One is a general purpose introduction to the laws and payor requirements that must be observed, and to the elements of the supplier's compliance program. More specific, tailored training should be provided to employees who work in high-risk areas of the organization, like billing and claims submission, and sales and marketing.

The OIG recommends the following curriculum for the training targeted at claims development and billing staff.

- Public and private payor reimbursement principles related to their jobs
- Providing and billing for DMEPOS items without proper authorization
- Proper documentation of items and services provided, including the correct application of coding rules and guidelines
- Improper alterations to documentation like CMN and patient records
- Compliance with the federal, state, and private payor supplier standards
- Duty to report misconduct

This is the recommended curriculum for sales and marketing personnel.

- General prohibition on paying or receiving remuneration to induce referrals
- Offering free items or services to induce referrals
- Routine waiver of deductibles and/or coinsurance
- Disguising referral fees as salaries
- High-pressure marketing of noncovered or unnecessary services
- Improper patient solicitation
- Duty to report misconduct

It also is advisable for a DMEPOS supplier to inform its physicians, independent contractors, and other agents that it has implemented a compliance program.

All trainings should be provided on an annual basis or more frequently if there have been changes or updates to the compliance rules. Employees should be required to participate in a minimum number of training hours per year. Two to four hours is a common range. It should be made clear that training attendance is a condition of continued employment, and that failure to comply with training requirements may result in disciplinary action.

After the compliance program is up and running, and outside of the scheduled trainings, an effort should be made to keep compliance issues in the forefront of employees' minds. Posters, occasional memoranda, and newsletter articles can contribute to maintaining awareness. Some small suppliers have their employees meet on a regular basis to discuss recent Medicare and OIG announcements.

Developing Effective Lines of Communication

The effectiveness of a compliance program is greatly enhanced by open lines of communication between DMEPOS suppliers and their employees that facilitate the reporting of complaints, questions, misconduct, and suspected violations. It is a good idea to set up several independent reporting paths in case an employee feels more comfortable using one rather than another. Some examples are hotlines, emails, written memoranda, newsletters, suggestion boxes, websites, or intranet forums. Details on using the communication channels should be widely publicized, along with assurances of confidentiality and non-retaliation.

All matters reported should be documented and investigated to determine their veracity.

Auditing and Monitoring

To be sure that it is constantly serving its designed purpose, the compliance program must be backed up by an ongoing auditing and monitoring process. Such a process will evaluate two things: whether the program's requirements are being followed by employees, and whether the organization as a whole is complying with all relevant laws, regulations, and payor requirements.

The DMEPOS supplier should use internal or external auditors to conduct regular audits of operations within its departments and its external relationships with third-party contractors. The audits should emphasize the supplier's compliance with laws governing kickback arrangements, the physician self-referral prohibition, pricing, contracts, claim development and submission, reimbursement, and sales/marketing. In addition, they should examine the supplier's compliance with the federal, state, and private payor supplier standards, and the issues that have been the focus of particular attention by CMS, OIG, and law enforcement authorities.

The OIG Program Guidance offers a number of techniques for compliance auditing and monitoring. In fact, these techniques would be useful to almost any type of healthcare organization.

- Testing billing staff on their knowledge of reimbursement coverage criteria and official coding guidelines (e.g., present hypothetical scenarios of situations experienced in daily practice and assess responses)
- On-site visits to all facilities and locations
- Ongoing risk analysis and vulnerability assessments of supplier operations
- Assessment of existing relationships with physicians, and other potential referral sources
- Unannounced audits, mock surveys, and investigations
- Examination of complaint logs

- Checking personnel records to determine whether any individuals who have been reprimanded for compliance issues in the past are currently engaged in improper conduct
- Interviews with personnel involved in management, operations, sales and marketing, claim development and submission, and other related activities
- Questionnaires developed to solicit employee attitudes toward compliance
- Interviews with physicians or other authorized persons who order the supplier's items
- Interviews with independent contractors who provide services to the supplier
- Reviews of medical necessity documentation (e.g., physicians orders, CMNs), and other documents that support claims for reimbursement
- Validation of qualifications of physicians who order items provided by the supplier
- Evaluation of written materials describing the supplier's policies and procedures
- Utilization/trend analyses that uncover deviations, positive or negative, for specific billing codes or types of items over a given period

The results of these audits and monitoring should be summarized in reports that are submitted to the Compliance Officer, the Compliance Committee, senior management, and the governing body. The details of the audit and monitoring process should be documented as evidence of the organization's compliance efforts.

Small DMEPOS suppliers with limited resources will be at a disadvantage in conducting extensive compliance assessments. The OIG recommends that, at a minimum, these organizations survey a random sample of claims for the risk areas that they previously have identified. After carrying out an initial baseline audit, they can follow up with periodic audits that highlight deviations, positive and negative, from that starting point.

Enforcing Standards Through Well-Publicized Disciplinary Guidelines

Despite attendance at regular training sessions, some employees may still fail to comply with the DMEPOS supplier's standards of conduct, policies, and procedures; with federal and state statutes and regulations; or with public or private payor healthcare program requirements; The action may be inadvertent, negligent, or intentional, but it must be dealt with if the standards are to be upheld. This is done through a system of disciplinary actions that may be taken against misbehaving employees.

The possible actions should vary in their severity depending on the nature of the employee's offense. They typically include verbal and written warnings, probation, suspension, and dismissal. The system should describe the procedures that will be followed in handling disciplinary problems and the individuals responsible for making the decisions. The procedures should be consistently applied and enforced. All levels of employees should be subject to the same types of discipline for the commission of similar offenses. This includes executives, managers, employees, contractors, vendors, and other agents. In the case of non-employees engaged in misconduct, the primary disciplinary action can only be termination of contract.

Before new employees are hired or contracts executed with new external parties, whose work may involve compliance matters, the supplier should investigate their backgrounds, criminal records, and references. As a general rule, the supplier should not employ or deal with individuals or organizations that have been recently convicted of a criminal offense related to health care or that are listed as debarred, excluded, or otherwise ineligible for participation in federal healthcare programs.

Responding to Detected Offenses and Developing Corrective Action Initiatives

The DMEPOS supplier must immediately investigate any reported incidents of noncompliance or violation. The goal is to determine whether a material violation has occurred and, if so, take decisive steps to correct the problem and prevent its recurrence. The internal investigation typically involves interviews of employees and agents, coupled with a review of relevant documents like submitted claims, medical records, and CMNs. If the matter appears serious or the supplier lacks the necessary internal resources, it ought to consider engaging outside auditors, attorneys, or healthcare experts to assist in the investigation.

The corrective actions that the supplier might take include an internal corrective action plan (employee discipline, policy and procedure modifications, systems reengineering), a report to government program authorities (OIG, CMS), notification of civil law enforcement agencies, and the return of overpayments. If the misconduct appears to violate criminal law, the supplier must report the facts to the appropriate federal and state authorities within 60 days of discovering them.

The promptness with which the supplier reports possible violations and returns overpayments will be considered a mitigating factor by the OIG in determining administrative sanctions.

COMPLIANCE ENFORCEMENT ACTIVITIES/ INITIATIVES IN THE DMEPOS INDUSTRY

In 2010, the Inspector General of the Department of Health and Human Services (DHHS), testified before the House Subcommittee on Health about the OIG's efforts to combat healthcare fraud, waste, and abuse, as it relates to the DMEPOS industry. He stated that "Over the past three decades, OIG has identified significant levels of fraud and abuse related to this important Medicare benefit." These problems have led to steadily increasing OIG oversight of these entities. This included the enactment of several new statutes and regulations, including the PPACA. That act expanded CMS authority to regulate DMEPOS suppliers.

In 2011, the OIG reported the results of a survey of DMEPOS suppliers newly enrolled in the Medicare program. During their first year in Medicare, 26% of high- and medium-risk suppliers and 2% of low- and limited-risk suppliers had their billing privileges revoked or were placed on prepayment claims review. Thirteen percent of high- and medium-risk suppliers and 4% of low- and limited-risk suppliers omitted ownership or management information from their Medicare enrollment applications. Four percent of high- and medium-risk suppliers omitted information regarding criminal histories or adverse legal actions from their applications.

Each year, the OIG submits two semiannual reports to Congress on its legal and investigative activities related to Medicare and Medicaid. These are three cases from the report for Fall 2012.

As part of an organized crime ring takedown, *Arthur Manasarian and Sahak Tumanyan* were sentenced in a Medicare fraud scheme. Manasarian opened a DME company, Brunswick Medical Supply (BMS), in Brunswick, Georgia. Once BMS was operational, Manasarian stole the identities of hundreds of Medicare beneficiaries and physicians from multiple states and submitted claims to Medicare for medical equipment that was never provided. Manasarian was sentenced to 12 years of incarceration and ordered to pay over $1.8 million in restitution for conspiracy to commit healthcare fraud and aggravated identity theft. Tumanyan was sentenced to 5 years of incarceration and ordered to pay $308,963 in restitution, jointly and severally, on charges of money laundering conspiracy. Tumanyan, an Armenian national, will be deported after his incarceration. Additionally, Manasarian and Tumanyan were each excluded by OIG for 20 years and 15 years, respectively. This case was jointly investigated with U.S. Immigration and Customs Enforcement, the Federal Bureau of Investigation (FBI), and the Los Angeles County Sheriff's Office. The investigation of this scheme has led to more than 35 arrests.

AmMed Direct agreed to pay $18 million to resolve allegations that it violated the False Claims Act. From September 2008 to January 2010, AmMed, a supplier of diabetic testing supplies and other DME, allegedly billed Medicare and Tennessee Medicaid for diabetic testing supplies sold to beneficiaries through telephone cold calls, in violation of the prohibition against unsolicited telephone contact by suppliers. AmMed advertised and offered free cookbooks without any mention of diabetic testing supplies or without stating that AmMed was a DME supplier. When beneficiaries called to claim the cookbook, AmMed allegedly sold them diabetic testing supplies and submitted claims to Medicare and Tennessee Medicaid.

Sonja Ascoli was sentenced to 3 years' probation and ordered to pay $70,358 in restitution after pleading guilty to healthcare fraud. Ascoli worked as a sales representative for Planned Eldercare, Inc., a nationwide supplier of DME. To induce beneficiaries to attend her sales presentations, Ascoli advertised "no cost" custom fit shoes for diabetics and medical equipment for individuals suffering from arthritis. Ascoli obtained beneficiaries' Medicare and physician information and then suggested products that could help with their ailments. Ascoli then ordered as many DME products as possible for those beneficiaries without regard to whether they requested the products or had a medical need for the equipment. When beneficiaries complained about receiving items that they did not order, Ascoli allegedly told them to keep the products in the closet until they need them. Gary Winner, president of Planned Eldercare, was previously sentenced to 3 years and 1 month of incarceration and ordered to pay more than $2.2 million in restitution after pleading guilty to healthcare fraud, money laundering, and introduction of an adulterated and misbranded medical device into interstate commerce.

STUDY QUESTIONS

1. What is the OIG's attitude about smaller DMEPOS suppliers that cannot afford to implement the full array of recommendations described in the Compliance Program Guidance?
2. Quickly, without thinking, what are the seven basic elements of a good compliance program?
3. On the basis of your reading of the risk area descriptions, what are some acceptable ways for DMEPOS suppliers to promote their products to referral sources like physicians? Directly to patients?
4. What is the problem with billing that "unbundles" several items provided to a patient? In the billing context, what does "upcoding" mean?

5. Why do you think that a DMEPOS supplier must provide an item to patient for free after renting it to him or her for 15 months?
6. What is wrong with a DMEPOS supplier telling a beneficiary that he or she does not have to pay a deductible or coinsurance amount?
7. What options does a Compliance Officer have if he or she wishes to take disciplinary action against an employee for compliance misconduct, and the employee's manager does not agree with the action?
8. In what ways could employees working in sales and marketing create compliance problems for a DMEPOS supplier?
9. Imagine a supplier with a workforce of five employees selling a handful of DME products to a local market,. Describe two or more lines of communication that the supplier could open for the confidential reporting of suspected violations.
10. What are the features of the DMEPOS industry that make it so susceptible to fraud and abuse?

Learning Exercises

1. Pick three of the risk areas described in this chapter and propose a couple policies or procedures that a DMEPOS supplier could adopt to minimize each of the risks.
2. Do a little Internet research into CMNs. What kinds of information must be inserted into each of the four sections—A, B, C, and D? Do you remember which sections must be completed by the treating physician and which by the DMEPOS supplier?
3. How does program exclusion by the OIG work? What are the effects of exclusion from the Medicare program? How long does the exclusion last? What are some common reasons that healthcare workers and organizations are excluded from participation in federal healthcare programs? What does an individual or organization do until its exclusion has expired?
4. As the Compliance Officer of a DMEPOS manufacturer with annual sales of $75 million, after a thorough investigation, you have discovered that most of the 10-person staff of the claims preparation department have been filling in missing information on the CMN forms submitted by treating physicians. Their reason for this is that the physicians are sloppy in completing the forms and the submission of the claims can

be delayed by several days or weeks while the physicians are contacted. What disciplinary action, if any, do you propose to impose on these employees? What corrective actions would you like to take to prevent this practice from continuing?

References

1. *OIG Compliance Program Guidance for the Durable Medical Equipment, Prosthetics, Orthotics and Supply Industry*, OIG, DHHS, Federal Register, Vol. 64, No. 128, July 6, 1999.
2. *Durable Medical Equipment, Prosthetics, Orthotics, and Supplies (DMEPOS) Quality Standards*, CMS, DHHS, February 2012.
3. *The Basics of Durable Medical Equipment, Prosthetics, Orthotics, and Supplies (DMEPOS) Accreditation*, Fact Sheet, CMS, DHHS, February 2012.
4. *Durable Medical Equipment, Prosthetics, Orthotics, and Supplies (DMEPOS)*, Chapter 20, Medicare Claims Processing Manual. This chapter provides general instructions on billing and claims processing for DME, prosthetics and orthotics (P&O), PEN, and supplies.
5. *Program Integrity Problems With Newly Enrolled Medicare Equipment Suppliers*, OIG, DHHS, December 2011.

Chapter 25

Research Facilities

Learning Objectives

After completing class sessions based on this chapter, a student will:

- Have an appreciation for the scope and diversity of the biomedical research complex.
- Be introduced to four areas of high legal compliance risk facing biomedical research institutions.
- Understand what constitutes a "significant financial interest" and what will make it a "conflict of interest."
- Review a comprehensive list of responsibilities that institutions have for maintaining research objectivity.
- Know the available institutional options for managing conflicts of interest and biased research.
- Learn the three research-related risk areas with which the Office of the Inspector General (OIG) is most concerned.
- Discover the problems to avoid in financial management of research grants.
- Recognize the names of some major universities that have been caught in grant mismanagement.
- Find out the forms that research misconduct can take and what the "Final Rule" has to say about them.
- See the purpose of a "written assurance."
- Be able to list the actions that the Department of Health and Human Services (DHHS) can take in response to an incident of research misconduct.
- Be familiar with the required composition of an Institutional Review Board (IRB) and its duties to protect the human subjects of research.

INTRODUCTION

When people talk about the world class features of the United States healthcare system, they usually mention its biomedical research infrastructure. The combination of public and private funding sources (federal government agencies and pharmaceutical companies) and research institutions (government laboratories, academic medical centers, private foundations, and drug research facilities) is responsible for the development of drugs, treatments, and devices that have increased the life expectancy and improved the life quality of millions of people across the United States and around the world.

The United States spends approximately $110 billion a year on biomedical research. Private industry (pharmaceutical and medical device companies) accounts for about two-thirds of that amount. Government funding (primarily the National Institutes of Health or NIH) is responsible for 30%, and the remainder comes from charities, foundations, and individual donors. For the last two decades, the United States has been spending roughly 4.5% of its national healthcare budget on biomedical research.

From 1998 to 2003, a commitment was made to double the budget of the NIH from $13.6 billion to $27.3 billion. Since then, it has leveled off and, in inflation-adjusted terms, has declined slightly. These limits on funding alone put pressure on researchers and their institutions. In addition, the federal agencies connected with the NIH have expanded their regulation of all aspects of the research projects supported by this funding.

The number of research project grants funded by NIH has declined every year since 2004. In fiscal year (FY) 2012, the NIH made 44,500 research awards for a total of $21,461,283,355. The percentage of grant applications that are approved is 18%. The average award is $414,000 per year for 4.3 years. Approximately 50 institutions get 70% of the funds; approximately 20% of the individual investigators receive 50% of the funds.

More than 80% of the NIH's funding is awarded through almost 50,000 competitive grants to more than 300,000 researchers at over 3,000 universities, medical schools, and other research institutions around the United States and throughout the world.

In FY 2012, approximately three-quarters of NIH research awards and funding went to institutions of higher education. Those are generally academic medical centers. Nine percent of the dollars and 7% of the awards went to private research institutes. Independent hospitals claimed 8% of both awards and funding. Domestic for-profit corporations received 4%, and the remainder went to other domestic nonprofit entities and all types of foreign organizations.

Although they do not directly provide healthcare services or manufacture healthcare products, the organizations receiving NIH research funding make significant contributions to the effectiveness of the healthcare system in treating patients. There are several reasons why the federal government sees a need to regulate research institutions. They consume a modest but significant portion of federal budget spending. The results they achieve can dramatically affect the health and welfare of U.S. citizens. If research activities are poorly managed or conducted, those effects can be reduced. When humans are subjects of the research, they are in danger of injury or death. All these inherent risks can be moderated by well-conceived and implemented compliance programs on the part of research institutions. Several federal government agencies either mandate or recommend the features of those programs. The research institutions cannot ignore them.

AREAS OF HIGH COMPLIANCE RISK IN BIOMEDICAL RESEARCH

NIH-funded research institutions must comply with many of the same laws as other private non-profit and for-profit entities—environmental, occupational hazards, employee rights, wages and hours, and taxes. They also face legal obligations that are unique to the work that they do. Four of the most important are:

1. Conflicts of interest and objectivity in research
2. Cost allocation and reporting under NIH research awards
3. Clinical research misconduct
4. Protection of human research subjects

They are discussed in some detail in this chapter.

Conflicts of Interest and Objectivity in Research

The NIH has published mandatory standards designed to ensure that the design, conduct, and reporting of research funded by it will be free from bias resulting from investigator financial conflicts of interest. The standards apply to both the institution receiving the funding and the investigators participating in the research.

The definitions of a few key terms must be understood. An "institution" is any domestic or foreign, public or private, entity or organization that applies for or receives NIH research funding. An "investigator" includes the research project director, principal investigator, and any other person, regardless of title or position, who is responsible for the design, conduct, or reporting of research funded by the NIH. The term "financial conflict of interest" (FCOI) refers to a significant financial interest that could directly and significantly affect the design, conduct, or reporting of NIH-funded research.

A "significant financial interest" exists if an investigator has equity interests in, or receives remuneration from, a publicly traded entity during the preceding 12 months that exceeds a total of $5,000. "Remuneration" includes salary, consulting fees, honoraria, and writing fees; an "equity interest" includes stock, stock options, or other ownership interests. The term also comprises income from patents and copyrights. The entity or the patents and copyrights must relate to the investigator's institutional responsibilities.

Responsibilities of Institutions

In the interests of research objectivity, each institution must carry out these responsibilities.

- Maintain an up-to-date, written, enforced policy on financial conflicts of interest and make it available on a publicly accessible website.
- Inform each investigator of the institution's policy on financial conflicts of interest, the NIH regulations, and the investigator's responsibilities regarding disclosure of significant financial interests.
- Require each investigator to complete training on these matters before engaging in NIH-funded research and at least every 4 years.
- If the institution carries out NIH-funded research through a subrecipient (e.g., subcontractor), it must take reasonable steps to ensure that such subrecipient investigator complies with its policy and with NIH regulations.
- Designate an institutional official to solicit and review disclosures of significant financial interests from each investigator who is participating or planning to participate in NIH-funded research.
- Require that each investigator planning to participate in NIH-funded research disclose to the institution's designated official the investigator's significant financial interests prior to applying for the research.
- Require each investigator participating in NIH-funded research to submit an updated disclosure of significant financial interests at least annually during the period of the award.
- Require each investigator participating in NIH-funded research to submit an updated disclosure of significant financial interests

within 30 days of acquiring a new significant financial interest (through purchase, marriage, or inheritance).
- Provide guidelines for the designated institutional official to determine whether an investigator's significant financial interest is related to NIH-funded research and, if so, whether it is an FCOI.

An investigator's significant financial interest is related to NIH-funded research when the institution determines that the interest could be affected by the NIH-funded research; or is in an entity whose financial interest could be affected by the research.

An FCOI exists when the institution determines that the significant financial interest could directly and significantly affect the design, conduct, or reporting of the NIH-funded research.

- Take such actions as are necessary to manage financial conflicts of interest. This requires development and implementation of a management plan and, if necessary, a retrospective review and a mitigation report.
- Provide initial and ongoing FCOI reports to the NIH.
- Maintain records (for at least 3 years) relating to all investigator disclosures of financial interests and the institution's review of, and response to, such disclosures.
- Establish adequate enforcement mechanisms and employee sanctions to ensure investigator compliance.
- Certify in each funding application that the institution has in effect an up-to-date, written, and enforced administrative process to identify and manage financial conflicts of interest with respect to all NIH-funded research projects; will promote and enforce investigator compliance; and will manage financial conflicts of interest and provide initial and ongoing FCOI reports to the NIH.

The institution also has duties to review investigator financial interests and disclosures of those interests in several specific situations.

- Prior to actually spending funds under an NIH-funded research project.
- Whenever a new investigator joins a research project.
- Whenever the institution learns of a financial interest that an investigator has not disclosed.

In each of these cases, if the institution determines that there is a conflict of interest, it is obligated to implement a plan to manage the conflict. The management plan might include actions like these:

- Public disclosure of financial conflicts of interest (e.g., when presenting or publishing the research).
- For research projects involving human subjects research, disclosure of financial conflicts of interest directly to participants.
- Appointment of an independent monitor capable of taking measures to protect the design, conduct, and reporting of the research against bias from the FCOI.
- Modification of the research plan.
- Change of personnel or personnel responsibilities, or disqualification of personnel from participation in all or a portion of the research.
- Reduction or elimination of the financial interest (e.g., sale of an equity interest).
- Severance of relationships that create financial conflicts.

Whenever an institution implements a management plan it must monitor investigator compliance with the plan on an ongoing basis until the research project is completed.

In another interesting requirement, before it begins to spend any money under an NIH-funded project, an institution must post on a publicly accessible website complete details about any financial conflicts of interest of the investigators on the project. This presumably gives members of the public an opportunity to comment on the conflict circumstances. Also prior to expending NIH funds, the institution must submit a report to the NIH about any FCOIs it has found and its management plan for dealing with them.

All these efforts are intended to prevent an investigator's FCOI from compromising the objectivity of research funded by the NIH. Occasionally, they do not succeed. In the event that an investigator fails to comply with an institution's policy or management plan on FCOIs, resulting in bias in NIH-funded research, the institution must report the fact to the NIH. It also must describe the corrective action that it is taking. The NIH may respond with directions to the institution on how better to maintain objectivity in the project.

If a clinical research project to evaluate the safety or effectiveness of a drug, medical device, or treatment employs an investigator with an FCOI that has not been managed or reported by the institution, that investigator must be required to disclose the FCOI in each public presentation of the results of the research and to request an amendment to previously published presentations. This applies to both written and oral presentations.

If the NIH decides that a particular FCOI will bias the objectivity of research, NIH may impose special award conditions, suspend funding, or impose other enforcement mechanisms until the matter is resolved.

Cost Allocation and Reporting Under NIH Research Awards

A large number of research fraud incidents appeared in the media in 2005. Perhaps due to those reports, some members of Congress requested that the OIG look at how honestly and accurately NIH research dollars were being used. In November 2005, the OIG issued a Draft Compliance Program Guidance for Recipients of PHS Research Awards, its first Compliance Guidance that did not deal with entities participating in federal healthcare programs (Medicare and Medicaid). Six months later, the OIG withdrew the draft in favor of "an inter-agency initiative to develop voluntary compliance guidelines for recipients of Federal research funding from all agencies across the Federal Government." Those guidelines have not yet emerged. However, in the interim, agencies concerned with biomedical research have issued several more narrowly focused rules.

If and when a true interagency Compliance Guidance is produced, it may expand upon the draft version but is not likely to rescind any of its provisions. For the present, they serve as a sound basis for the design of a compliance program by the recipients of NIH research awards.

Most of the Draft Compliance Program Guidance (CPG) is a restatement of the principles laid down in the 11 previous CPGs for various types of healthcare organizations. After describing the benefits of adopting a compliance program, the Guidance goes through the traditional seven basic elements of such a program, as follows.

1. The development and distribution of written standards of conduct, policies, and procedures that reflect the institution's commitment to compliance.
2. The designation of a Compliance Officer and a Compliance Committee charged with the responsibility for developing, operating, and monitoring the compliance program, and with authority to report directly to the head of the organization, such as the president or the board of regents in the case of a university.
3. The development and implementation of regular, effective education and training programs for all affected employees.

4. The creation of effective lines of communication between the Compliance Officer and all employees, including a process to receive complaints or questions, and policies to protect the anonymity of complainants and to protect whistle-blowers from retaliation.
5. The use of audits and/or other risk evaluation techniques to monitor compliance and identify problem areas.
6. The enforcement of appropriate disciplinary action against employees or contractors who have violated institutional policies, procedures, or federal requirements for the use of federal research dollars.
7. The development of policies and procedures for the investigation of identified instances of noncompliance or misconduct. These should include directions regarding the prompt and proper response to detected offenses, such as the initiation of appropriate corrective action and preventive measures.

The Draft CPG goes on to add four provisions unique to the compliance setting for research award recipients. It defines an eighth program element with this wording:

> The clear definition of roles and responsibilities within the institution's organization and ensuring the effective assignment of oversight responsibilities.

There is a good reason for this. In all the healthcare entities covered by the other CPGs, there is a clear line of authority from the governing body through the Chief Executive Officer (CEO), senior management, mid-level managers, and supervisors to the employees who may commit the misconduct or violations. In the academic medical centers that receive the bulk of NIH funding, individual laboratories and principal investigators operate with more autonomy and less supervision. The opportunities to engage in noncompliant behavior are greater and less likely to be noticed. At least they were in the past. That must change and it is changing.

All previous CPGs included substantial lists of compliance "risk areas" existing within each type of healthcare organization. Some of the risk areas were unique to a particular organization type, but many were common to all types of organization. The Draft CPG describes three risk areas that are likely to occur only in academic medical centers receiving NIH research grants. The risk areas are so few in number because the OIG's original assignment was solely to address possible misuse of NIH funds. There are numerous other compliance hazards facing these institutions.

The first risk area concerns *time and effort reporting*. This refers to the institution's obligation to properly allocate costs between NIH-funded projects and non-NIH project activity.

The compensation for the personal services of researchers—both direct salary and fringe benefits—is typically a major cost of a research project. It must be reported correctly. Those researchers, particularly the principal investigators, often have responsibilities in addition to their research activities—teaching, clinical practice, and administrative duties. Segregating their time and effort among these responsibilities is not always easy. The failure to report this accurately could result in overcharges to funding sources like the NIH. Where the failure is intentional, the sponsoring institution could be subject to a civil or criminal fraud investigation.

The problem can take two forms. A researcher falsely reports the time he or she intends to devote to a particular project. The OIG offers the example of a researcher claiming that he or she will spend 50% of his or her time on each of three NIH-funded projects. In another case, a project might not account properly for the clinical practice time of its researchers, asserting that they will devote 70% of their time on a project when 50% of their time already is committed to clinical responsibilities.

The second risk area is about *properly allocating charges to award projects*. Research institutions commonly receive separate NIH awards for several projects in a single research area. Once costs have been properly apportioned between NIH-funded projects and other non-NIH activities costs, the NIH project costs then must be properly allocated among the several NIH-funded projects. It is essential that accounting systems be able to properly separate the amount of funding from each funding source. This becomes a fraud issue when principal investigators on different projects trade award funds among themselves. In one real-life civil fraud case, a research institution transferred costs from an overspent federally funded project to an underspent project in order to avoid refunding unused NIH funds.

The third risk area has to do with accurately *reporting financial support from other sources* for the same project. The OIG wishes to prevent NIH funding for a project that duplicates funding from another source. Institutions are required to disclose other funding sources when they first apply for NIH funding for a project. The availability of other funding affects the amount that the NIH will award to the project. In addition, human research subjects often are receiving medical care while they are participating in the research project. The cost of that care cannot be charged to both the research project and to Medicare or another health insurer. It is essential that the sponsoring institution be able to distinguish between costs and activities solely for research purposes and those that can be billed to an insurer.

Research institutions should not assume that the OIG's interest in the financial aspects of their research will stop with the three initial risk areas. On its own initiative or in response to a whistle-blower's complaint, the OIG will look for any instances of fraud or waste in the use of federal research funds. For one thing, faculty members at academic medical centers historically have had some freedom in how they applied for research grants and managed the funded projects. In light of the OIG's willingness to hold the institutions accountable for the deeds of their faculty, most of them now are monitoring faculty grant activity much more closely.

Enforcement Cases Involving Cost Allocation and Reporting

Some well-known academic institutions have reached settlements with enforcement authorities to resolve allegations of cost mismanagement of research grants. These are examples in the three leading risk areas.

Improperly Allocating Costs and Charges to Award Projects

Institute for Cancer Prevention

Drew down federal grant money to pay bills ineligible for reimbursement under grants. Settled for $2.3 million. Former Chief Financial Officer pled guilty to obstruction of justice for lying to federal agents concerning false statements used by the Institute in obtaining research grants from the federal government.

Mayo Foundation

Improperly transferred costs from overspent grants and internal cost centers to underspent grants, and inappropriately charged grant for costs unrelated to research sponsored by the grant. Mayo's accounting system was unable to monitor and manage charges made to federal grant awards in the manner required by federal law. Settled for $6.5 million. Whistle-blower in the case was a former accounting associate.

Harvard/Beth Israel Deaconess Medical Center

Improperly billed four NIH grants for $1.9 million over a 5-year period.

Examples of alleged inappropriate activity: Inappropriately paid salaries for researchers who did not work on the grants, principal investigator's salary charged to grants in excess of budgeted amounts, supply and equipment expenses incurred for projects unrelated to the grants, and expenses incurred by researchers who did not work on the grant. Settled for $2.4 million.

Yale University

Researchers "spent down" remaining grant funds near expiration dates via improper cost transfers. The university submitted time and effort reports that charged 100% to federal grants when researchers were actually engaged in unrelated work. Settled for $7.6 million.

Time and Effort Reporting Cases

Johns Hopkins University

Overstated the percentage of effort; falsely reported time and effort of employees who did not work on grants; and failed to maintain adequate compliance mechanisms to reconcile proposed effort with actual effort. Settled for $2.6 million. Whistle-blower in the case was an office supervisor.

Weill Medical College of Cornell University

Submitted false information in an annual progress report, billed costs that were unrelated to the studies being funded, and paid salary to employees who did not work on the grant. Settled for $4.3 million.

Reporting Financial Support from Other Sources

Rush University Medical Center

Improperly billed sponsor and Medicare for $670,000 in physician and hospital cancer research services that were not reimbursable. Violations attributed to poor synchronization of the Medicare rules, the compensation arrangements with the sponsors, and the financial statement in the informed consent form. Settled for $1.0 million. First settlement related solely to Medicare coverage of care provided to clinical trial subjects.

University of Alabama at Birmingham

Falsely billed Medicare for clinical research trials that were also billed to the sponsor of the research grants, and for a researcher's time spent on patient care when no patients had been seen. Settled for $3.4 million. Whistle-blowers in the case were a compliance officer and an academic physician.

Clinical Research Misconduct

In 2012, there were over seven million researchers worldwide with over two million articles published in over 25,000 journals. The competition for funding to support the research on which the articles are based is intense. In FY 2011, only 18% of NIH grant applicants were successful.

This sometimes leads researchers to behave in unethical ways—to engage in research misconduct.

Research misconduct is defined as fabrication, falsification, or plagiarism in proposing, performing, or reviewing research, or in reporting research results.[1] The term excludes honest error or differences of opinion. It is governed by the Public Health Service (PHS) Policies on Research Misconduct (referred to as the "Final Rule") issued in 2005 by the Office of Research Integrity (ORI) located within the DHHS.

The journal *Nature* published a study in 2005 that found roughly one-third of biomedical scientists in the United States committed some form of research misconduct. Another study commissioned by ORI in 2008 concluded that researchers were not properly reporting misconduct to their institutions, the institutions were not adequately investigating the reports they did receive, and the institutions were not fully reporting misconduct incidents to the federal government.

There are three elements to a valid claim of research misconduct: The activity must be a significant departure from accepted practices of the relevant research community; the misconduct must be committed intentionally, knowingly, or recklessly; and the claim must be proven by a preponderance of the evidence. The burden of proving that misconduct occurred is on the ORI or the researcher's institution.

The Final Rule imposes several duties upon institutions engaged in federally funded research.

- Have written policies and procedures for addressing allegations of research misconduct.
- Respond to each allegation of research misconduct in a thorough, competent, objective, and fair manner, ensuring that individuals responsible for carrying out the research misconduct proceeding do not have unresolved personal, professional, or financial conflicts of interest with the complainant, respondent, or witnesses.
- Foster a research environment that promotes the responsible conduct of research, research training, and activities related to that research or research training; discourages research misconduct; and deals promptly with allegations or evidence of possible research misconduct.
- Take all reasonable and practical steps to protect the positions and reputations of good faith complainants, witnesses, and committee

[1] Read about this interesting case of research misconduct at Harvard University before the controls described here were in place: http://en.wikipedia.org/wiki/John_Darsee.

members, and protect them from retaliation by respondents and other institutional members.

- Provide confidentiality to the extent possible to all respondents, complainants, and identifiable research subjects.
- Take steps to ensure the cooperation of respondents and other institutional members with research misconduct proceedings, including providing information, research records, and evidence.
- Cooperate with DHHS during any research misconduct proceeding or compliance review.
- Assist in administering and enforcing any DHHS administrative actions imposed on its institutional members.
- Have an active assurance of compliance on file with the ORI.

The last duty on the list requires some explanation. The institution must provide ORI with an assurance of compliance with the provisions of the Final Rule that includes establishing policies and procedures that implement those provisions, taking all reasonable and practical steps to foster research integrity, and informing research personnel of its policies and procedures for responding to allegations of research misconduct.

The policies and procedures must cover the following points.

- Protection of the confidentiality of respondents (those accused of misconduct), complainants, and identifiable research subjects.
- A thorough, competent, objective, and fair response to allegations of research misconduct within prescribed time limits, also ensuring that individuals responsible for carrying out the research misconduct proceeding do not have unresolved personal, professional, or financial conflicts of interest with the complainant, respondent, or witnesses.
- Notice to the respondents.
- Written notice to ORI of any decision to open an investigation.
- Opportunity for the respondents to provide written comments on the institution's inquiry report.
- Opportunity for the respondents to provide written comments on the draft report of the investigation, and for the investigation committee to consider the comments before issuing the final report.
- Protocols for handling the research record and evidence.
- Appropriate interim institutional actions to protect public health, federal funds and equipment, and the integrity of the NIH supported research process.

- Notice to ORI of any facts that may be relevant to protect public health, federal funds and equipment, and the integrity of the NIH supported research process.
- Institutional actions in response to final findings of research misconduct.
- All reasonable and practical efforts to protect the reputation of persons alleged to have committed research misconduct but who were not found culpable.
- All reasonable and practical efforts to protect the position and reputation of any complainant, witness, or committee member and to counter retaliation against them.
- Full and continuing cooperation with ORI during its oversight review or any subsequent administrative hearings or appeals. This includes providing all research records and evidence under the institution's control, custody, or possession and access to all persons within its authority necessary to develop a complete record of relevant evidence.

The Final Rule also imposes on research institutions responsibilities for maintaining custody of research records and evidence, conducting inquiries into allegations of research misconduct, on the basis of the inquiry deciding if an investigation is warranted, notifying ORI of a decision to initiate an investigation, conducting investigations according to prescribed guidelines, and upon completion of an investigation, submitting the following to ORI:

- A copy of the investigation report, with any appeals
- Whether the institution found that research misconduct occurred and who committed it
- Whether the institution accepts the conclusions of the investigation
- Any pending or completed administrative actions taken against the wrongdoer

Under the Final Rule, the ORI has the power to review allegations of research misconduct before, during, or after an institution has begun its inquiry. The ORI also has the authority to carry out its own separate investigation, or simply to review the institution's proceedings. After completing its review the ORI has two choices. It can close the matter without a finding of research misconduct, or it can recommend that DHHS take administrative action or pursue a settlement. These are some of the possible actions that DHHS might take.

- Clarify, correct, or retract the research record.
- Issue letters of reprimand to the institution.

- Impose special certification or assurance requirements to ensure compliance with the terms of NIH grants.
- Suspend or terminate an NIH grant.
- Restrict specific activities or expenditures under an active NIH grant.
- Review all requests for NIH funding from an institution.
- Impose supervision requirements on an NIH grant.
- Require certification of attribution or authenticity in all requests for support and reports to the NIH.
- Prohibit participation by the institution in any advisory capacity to the NIH.
- Recommend adverse personnel action if the respondent is a federal employee.
- Suspend or debar the institution or individual from receiving NIH grants.
- Seek to recover NIH funds spent in support of the activities that involved research misconduct.

Individuals and institutions may contest ORI findings of research misconduct and DHHS imposition of administrative actions by requesting a hearing before an administrative law judge.

Protection of Human Research Subjects

Because most biomedical research is designed eventually to create products or services that benefit human beings, it is unavoidable that, at some point in the research and development process, the products or services must be tested for their effectiveness and safety with human subjects. These tests are called "clinical trials" and they involve some degree of risk to the subjects (negative side effects or even death) against which they need some protection.

There is a host of legal requirements that apply to the conduct of clinical trials involving human subjects. If the research is federally funded but will not be used to support a submission for approval by the Food and Drug Administration (FDA), it will be governed by the regulations on protection of human subjects, and on promoting objectivity in research, as well as any additional requirements of the grant agency (i.e., NIH). If the research is not federally funded and will be used to support an FDA submission, it must satisfy a series of FDA-specific regulations.

The regulation entitled "Protection of Human Subjects" is composed of five subparts. The most important is Subpart A, the Basic DHHS Policy for Protection of Human Research Subjects, also known as the Common

Rule.[2] It lays out the basic principles of human subject protection. Subparts B, C, and D provide special protection for certain vulnerable groups (pregnant women, human fetuses and neonates, prisoners, and children). Subpart E deals with the registration of IRBs.

The Common Rule applies to all research involving human subjects conducted or supported by a federal agency such as the NIH. All such research must comply with the provisions of the Rule. There are limited exemptions for research conducted in educational settings, involving educational tests, and a few special situations.

A "human subject" covered by the Rule is a living individual about whom a research investigator wishes to obtain identifiable private information, or other data through intervention or interaction with the individual.

Written Assurance of IRB Functions

Every institution engaged in covered research must provide a written assurance to the NIH that it will comply with the provisions of the Common Rule. That assurance must contain the following items.

1. A statement of institution principles on how it will protect the rights and welfare of the human subjects of research that it conducts or sponsors.
2. Designation of one or more IRBs with sufficient staff and meeting space to support the IRBs' review and recordkeeping duties.
3. A list of IRB members identified by name; earned degrees; and other qualifications indicative of their anticipated contributions to IRB deliberations; and their employment relationship with the institution.
4. Written procedures that the IRB will follow:
    - For conducting its initial and continuing review of research
    - For reporting its findings and actions to the investigator and the institution
    - For determining which projects require more frequent review
    - For determining which projects need verification that no material changes have occurred since the previous IRB review
    - For ensuring prompt reporting to the IRB of proposed changes in a research activity
    - For ensuring that such changes in approved research may not be initiated without IRB review and approval

[2] The language of the Common Rule has been adopted by 15 other federal departments and agencies that fund research involving human subjects.

5. Written procedures for ensuring prompt reporting to the IRB, institutional officials, and the NIH of (a) any unanticipated problems involving risks to subjects or others, or any serious or continuing noncompliance with the Common Rule or the requirements of the IRB; and (b) any suspension or termination of IRB approval.

The assurance must be executed by a person acting for the institution and submitted to the NIH, which will evaluate it on the basis of the adequacy of the proposed IRB in light of the anticipated scope of the institution's research activities and the types of subject populations likely to be involved, the appropriateness of the proposed review procedures in light of the probable risks, and the size and complexity of the institution. On the basis of the evaluation, the NIH will approve or disapprove the assurance, or enter into negotiations to develop an approvable one.

Once the IRB has been established and approved, the institution must certify that every application for research funding that it submits to the NIH has been reviewed and approved by the IRB.

IRB Membership

The Common Rule gives very detailed specifications for the composition of the IRB. It must have a minimum of five members of varied backgrounds. As a group, they must possess sufficient experience and expertise; diversity of race, gender, and cultural background; and sensitivity to community attitudes to promote respect for the rights of human subjects. In addition to reviewing specific research activities, the IRB must be able to ascertain the acceptability of proposed research in terms of institutional commitments and regulations, applicable law, and standards of professional conduct and practice. To accomplish that, the IRB must include members knowledgeable in all those areas. If the research will involve a vulnerable category of human subjects, the Board also should include people familiar with and experienced in working with such people.

The IRB should not be composed exclusively of men or of women. It may not be composed entirely of the members of one profession. It must include at least one member whose primary concerns are in scientific areas, and one who is focused in nonscientific areas. There must be at least one member not affiliated with the institution. When appropriate, the IRB may invite the ad hoc participation of persons with special competence to assist in reviewing issues beyond the Board's regular expertise. No IRB member may participate in the review of a project in which he or she has a conflicting interest.

Research proposals must be approved by a majority of the IRB members present at a meeting attended by a majority of all the IRB members.

IRB Duties

An IRB has specific review responsibilities. It must review and have the authority to approve, to require modifications in, or to disapprove all research activities that come before it. It must require documentation of the informed consent obtained from research subjects. It must notify investigators and the institution in writing of its decision to approve or disapprove a proposed research project, or of modifications required to secure IRB approval of the project. An IRB must conduct continuing reviews of research it has approved at intervals appropriate to the degree of risk, but not less than once per year,

Criteria for IRB Approval of Research

The Common Rule specifies the criteria that an IRB must use in reviewing and then approving or disapproving a research proposal. The proposal must satisfy all of these requirements.

- Risks to the subjects are minimized.
- Risks to the subjects are reasonable in relation to anticipated benefits to subjects, and the importance of the knowledge that is expected to result.
- Selection of the subjects is equitable.
- Informed consent will be sought from each prospective subject.
- Informed consent will be appropriately documented.
- The research plan provides for monitoring the data collected to ensure the safety of subjects.
- There are provisions to protect the privacy of subjects and maintain the confidentiality of data.

Each IRB must have authority to suspend or terminate its approval of research that is not being conducted in accordance with the IRB's requirements or that has been associated with unexpected serious harm to subjects.

IRB Records

An IRB must maintain the following documentation of its activities.

- Copies of all research proposals reviewed
- Minutes of IRB meetings
- Records of continuing review activities
- Copies of all correspondence between the IRB and the investigators
- A list of IRB members and their qualifications
- Written procedures for the IRB as required by the Common Rule
- Statements of significant new findings provided to subjects

The records must be retained for at least 3 years.

Informed Consent

An investigator may not involve a human being as a subject in an NIH research project unless he or she has obtained the subject's informed consent. "Informed consent" is a legal term meaning, in this case, that a person has given his or her consent to play a role in a research project *after* being fully informed of what the role will entail. It is essential that a human subject understand what he or she will be doing, what will be done to him or her, and what possible negative effects might occur. The Common Rule provides great detail on the necessary elements of an effective informed consent. There are eight "basic" elements, followed by six "additional" elements. A written consent form must be used, approved by the IRB and signed by the human subject.

The Common Rule makes clear that the NIH may suspend or terminate its support for a research project if it concludes that an institution has materially failed to comply with the Rule's requirements.

Office of Human Research Protections (OHRP)

The OHRP within the DHHS is the agency responsible for ensuring compliance with the regulations governing the protection of human research subjects. It has the authority to conduct both for-cause and not-for-cause compliance oversight evaluations.

For-cause evaluations may occur in response to allegations from research subjects and their family members, individuals involved in the conduct of research such as investigators and study coordinators, institutional officials, and research publications. An institution may be selected for a not-for-cause evaluation due to: (a) the volume of research in which it is engaged; (b) whether it has a history of a low level of required reporting to OHRP; (c) the need to evaluate implementation of corrective actions following a previous for-cause compliance oversight evaluation; (d) geographic location; (e) status of accreditation by professionally recognized human subject protection program accreditation groups; and (f) status of recent human subject protection evaluations or audits by other regulatory agencies (FDA).

As a result of its compliance oversight evaluations, the OHRP may take or recommend one or more of the following actions.

- OHRP does not identify any areas of noncompliance.
- OHRP recommends voluntary improvements to the institution's human subject protection policies and procedures.
- OHRP determines that the institution's policies and procedures for protecting human subjects, the IRB review of research projects, or the conduct of those projects are not in compliance. It requires the implementation of corrective actions.
- OHRP determines that there is noncompliance and attaches conditions to its approval of the institution's written assurance.
- OHRP determines that there is noncompliance and suspends its approval of the institution's written assurance. This means all related research activities must be suspended.
- OHRP determines that there is noncompliance and recommends that an institution or an investigator be temporarily suspended or permanently removed from participation in specific projects, or that NIH scientific peer review groups be notified of an institution's or an investigator's past noncompliance prior to review of new projects.
- OHRP determines that there is noncompliance and recommends that institutions or investigators be debarred.
- OHRP refers the matter to another federal department or agency for further review and action.

STUDY QUESTIONS

1. Why do you think that NIH research funding was doubled over just a few years and then allowed to stagnate for most of the last decade?
2. What is wrong with a conflict of interest? Can the researcher simply ignore the influence of the significant financial interest?
3. What should an institution (an academic medical center associated with a well-known university) do if a popular, long-standing

professor-researcher refuses to cooperate with its policy on financial conflicts of interest, claiming that his financial interests are none of its business?

4. Give one example of how an institution or its researchers might commit a violation in each of the three risk areas dealing with cost allocation and reporting.
5. How can an institution keep track of the time that investigators actually spend on individual activities, including research projects? University professors do not fill out timecards.
6. Have you ever been engaged in fabrication, falsification, or plagiarism in writing a paper? How do you use information from a research source without copying most of it?
7. One of the institutional duties under the Final Rule is to "foster a research environment that promotes the responsible conduct of research." What actions could an institution take to accomplish that?
8. List three federal government agencies that are interested in compliance by research institutions.
9. Describe at least three steps an institution must take when it hears about an incident of possible research misconduct.
10. What responsibilities does one researcher have for checking on the trustworthiness of the work of other researchers?
11. What should a researcher do if he or she thinks that another researcher has fabricated data?
12. Have you ever been the subject in a clinical research study? If not, ask your friends. It is common for people, particularly students, to participate in such studies for the small sums of money they are paid. What was the experience like? What kinds of warnings did you receive before you signed a consent form? Were you at all concerned about your health or welfare as a result of the study?
13. What is the difference between the Common Rule and the Final Rule?
14. For what reasons is an IRB likely to disapprove a proposed research project?

Learning Exercises

1. Do a little research to find out the kinds of research projects that the NIH funds and the kinds of discoveries that they make.
2. The NIH maintains a Research Portfolio Online Reporting Tool (RePORT) where it is possible to search, using multiple variables, among the research projects that it has funded. The tool is found

at this website: http://projectreporter.nih.gov/. Use the tool to find projects at a particular educational institution or other organization, in a certain geographic area, or researching a specific disease or other condition. Contact the lead investigator for one of the nearby projects and interview him or her about his or her experiences in complying with the issues discussed in this chapter. Also, consider talking with the head of the IRB at your school or another nearby research institution.

3. The principal investigator on a research project studying hypertension needs a piece of specialized scientific equipment to continue the research. When preparing the purchase request, the investigator realizes that there is not enough money in the project budget. However, there are excess funds in another project on arteriosclerosis that the investigator leads. Both projects are funded by the NIH. The investigator wants to buy the equipment out of the second project budget. Is there a problem?

References

1. *Funding of US Biomedical Research*, 2003–2008, Dorsey et al, JAMA, Vol. 303, No. 2, January 13, 2010.
2. *Biomedical Research and Health Advances*, Hamilton Moses III, M.D., and Joseph B. Martin, M.D., Ph.D., NEJM, Vol. 364, No. 6, February 10, 2011.
3. *Subpart F - Promoting Objectivity in Research, Responsibility of Applicants for Promoting Objectivity in Research for which Public Health Service Funding is Sought and Responsible Prospective Contractors*, Federal Register, Vol. 76, No. 165, August 25, 2011.
4. NIH webpage on Financial Conflict of Interest, http://grants.nih.gov/grants/policy/coi/
5. NIH Slide Tutorial on Financial Conflict of Interest, http://grants.nih.gov/grants/policy/coi/tutorial2011/fcoi.htm
6. *Conflict of Interest in Medical Research, Education, and Practice*, Bernard Lo and Marilyn J. Field, Editors, Institute of Medicine, The National Academies Press, 2009. A PDF version of this book is available without cost from The National Academies Press at http://www.nap.edu/catalog.php?record_id=12598
7. *Draft OIG Compliance Program Guidance for Recipients of PHS Research Awards*, Federal Register, Vol. 70, No. 227, November 28, 2005.
8. *Public Health Service Policies on Research Misconduct*, Federal Register, Vol. 70, No. 94, May 17, 2005.
9. *Research Misconduct – Institutional Responsibility and an Invisible Crisis*, Goldstein, Journal of Health & Life Sciences Law, AHLA, December 2008.
10. *Research Misconduct: A New Area of Focus for Government Enforcement*, Carder-Thompson et al., Health Lawyers News, AHLA, February 2006.

11. *Basic HHS Policy for Protection of Human Research Subjects*, DHHS, 45 CFR 46 56 FR 28012, 28022, June 18, 1991.
12. *Financial Relationships and Interests in Research Involving Human Subjects: Guidance for Human Subject Protection*, Final Guidance Document, DHHS, May 5, 2004.
13. *OHRP's Compliance Oversight Procedures for Evaluating Institutions*, October 14, 2009.
14. *Guidance on Reporting Incidents to OHRP*, June 20, 2011.
15. Office for Human Research Protections (OHRP), http://www.hhs.gov/ohrp/
16. OHRP Determination Letters, http://www.hhs.gov/ohrp/compliance/letters/index.html

Compliance-Related Websites

These are links to websites for some of the most important information and documents concerning legal compliance by healthcare organizations. Most are sponsored by federal government agencies, particularly the Office of the Inspector General (OIG). There are a few good ones from non-governmental sources as well. There is a large volume of useful compliance-related material on the Internet, in the form of newsletters, open-access journal articles, blogs, and professional association resources. Creative Google searching will find them.

OIG RESOURCES

OIG homepage https://oig.hhs.gov/

OIG Fraud Prevention & Detection https://oig.hhs.gov/fraud.asp

OIG's Compliance Program Guidances https://oig.hhs.gov/fraud/complianceguidance.asp
Includes compliance program guidance materials for various industry sectors

Compliance Program Guidance for Medicare+Choice Organizations
https://oig.hhs.gov/fraud/docs/complianceguidance/111599.pdf

Compliance Program Guidance for Pharmaceutical Manufacturers
https://oig.hhs.gov/authorities/docs/03/050503FRCPGPharmac.pdf

Original Compliance Program Guidance for Hospitals
https://oig.hhs.gov/authorities/docs/cpghosp.pdf

Supplemental Compliance Program Guidance for Hospitals
https://oig.hhs.gov/fraud/docs/complianceguidance/012705HospSupplementalGuidance.pdf

Compliance Program Guidance for Ambulance Suppliers
https://oig.hhs.gov/fraud/docs/complianceguidance/032403ambulancecpgfr.pdf

Original Compliance Program Guidance for Nursing Facilities
http://www.oig.hhs.gov/authorities/docs/cpgnf.pdf
Supplemental Compliance Program Guidance for Nursing Facilities
https://oig.hhs.gov/compliance/compliance-guidance/docs/complianceguidance/nhg_fr.pdf

Draft Compliance Guidance for Recipients of PHS Research Awards
https://oig.hhs.gov/fraud/docs/complianceguidance/PHS%20Research%20Awards%20Draft%20CPG.pdf

Compliance Program Guidance for Individual and Small Group Physician Practices
https://oig.hhs.gov/authorities/docs/physician.pdf

Compliance Program Guidance for Hospices
https://oig.hhs.gov/authorities/docs/hospicx.pdf

Compliance Program Guidance for the Durable Medical Equipment, Prosthetics, Orthotics, and Supply Industry
https://oig.hhs.gov/authorities/docs/frdme.pdf

Compliance Program Guidance for Third-Party Medical Billing Companies
https://oig.hhs.gov/fraud/docs/complianceguidance/thirdparty.pdf

Compliance Program Guidance for Clinical Laboratories
https://oig.hhs.gov/authorities/docs/cpglab.pdf

Compliance Program Guidance for Home Health Agencies
https://oig.hhs.gov/authorities/docs/cpghome.pdf

Corporate Responsibility and Corporate Compliance Guide
https://oig.hhs.gov/fraud/docs/complianceguidance/040203CorpRespRsceGuide.pdf

OIG Advisory Opinions https://oig.hhs.gov/fraud/advisoryopinions.asp

Frequently Asked Questions about the Advisory Opinion Process https://oig.hhs.gov/faqs/advisory-opinions-faq.asp

OIG's Self-Disclosure Protocol https://oig.hhs.gov/fraud/selfdisclosure.asp

OIG Exclusions Program https://oig.hhs.gov/fraud/exclusions.asp

OIG's database of excluded individuals/entities https://oig.hhs.gov/exclusions/exclusions_list.asp

Anti-Kickback Safe Harbor Regulations https://oig.hhs.gov/compliance/safe-harbor-regulations/index.asp Provides the regulatory history of the Safe Harbors The current text of all the regulatory Safe Harbors is available at: http://edocket.access.gpo.gov/cfr_2010/octqtr/pdf/42cfr1001.952.pdf

Fraud Alerts, Bulletins, and Other Guidance from the OIG https://oig.hhs.gov/compliance/alerts/index.asp

Civil Monetary Penalties and Affirmative Exclusions https://oig.hhs.gov/fraud/enforcement/cmp/index.asp

OIG Fraud Hotline https://oig.hhs.gov/fraud/report-fraud/index.asp or 1-800-HHS-TIPS

OIG Most Wanted Fugitives https://oig.hhs.gov/fraud/fugitives/index.asp

Health Care Fraud Prevention and Enforcement Action Team Provider Compliance Training https://oig.hhs.gov/compliance/provider-compliance-training/index.asp

OIG Brochure "A Roadmap for New Physicians: Avoiding Medicare and Medicaid Fraud and Abuse" https://oig.hhs.gov/fraud/PhysicianEducation

Medical Identity Theft & Medicare Fraud https://oig.hhs.gov/fraud/IDTheft/

CMS AND OTHER GOVERNMENT RESOURCES

CMS homepage http://www.cms.gov/

CMS Contacts Information Page http://www.cms.gov/ContactCMS/
Lists public contact lines for CMS offices and provides a portal for accessing information about CMS national and local operations and key CMS programs

CMS Contacts Database http://www.cms.gov/apps/contacts/
Provides access to searchable directories of contacts on national and local levels for the Department of Health and Human Services, CMS offices, Fiscal Intermediaries, and Carriers

CMS Regional Office Overview http://www.cms.gov/RegionalOffices/

False Claims Act
http://www.justice.gov/jmd/ls/legislative_histories/pl99-562/pl99-562.html

Anti-Kickback Statute (see section 1128B(b) of the following)
Criminal Penalties for Acts Involving Federal Health Care Program
http://www.ssa.gov/OP_Home/ssact/title11/1128B.htm#f

- CMS Physician Self-Referral Law (Stark Law) Information
  - http://www.cms.gov/PhysicianSelfReferral/
- CMS Physician Self-Referral Law Advisory Opinions Library
  - http://www.cms.gov/Medicare/Fraud-and-Abuse/PhysicianSelfReferral/advisory_opinions.html
- Health Insurance Portability and Accountability Act (HIPAA)
  - http://aspe.hhs.gov/admnsimp/pl104191.htm
- HIPAA Privacy and Security Rules
  - http://www.hhs.gov/ocr/privacy/index.html
  - http://www.cms.gov/HIPAAGenInfo/
- Summary of the HIPAA Privacy Rule
  - http://www.hhs.gov/ocr/privacy/hipaa/understanding/summary/index.html
- Summary of the HIPAA Security Rule
  - http://www.hhs.gov/ocr/privacy/hipaa/understanding/srsummary.html
- Breach Notification Rule
  - http://www.hhs.gov/ocr/privacy/hipaa/administrative/breachnotificationrule/

- HIPAA Enforcement
  - http://www.hhs.gov/ocr/privacy/hipaa/enforcement/index.html
- Understanding Health Information Privacy
  - http://www.hhs.gov/ocr/privacy/hipaa/understanding/
- Departments of Health & Human Services and Justice Joint Campaign against Health Care Fraud
  - http://www.stopmedicarefraud.gov/
- The Patient Protection and Affordable Care Act
  - http://www.healthcare.gov/law/full/
- Federal Sentencing Guidelines
  - http://www.ussc.gov/Guidelines
- 2010 Federal Sentencing Guidelines Manual, Chapter 8, Sentencing of Organizations
  - http://www.ussc.gov/Guidelines/2010_guidelines/Manual_HTML/Chapter_8.htm
- TRICARE Fraud & Abuse
  - http://www.tricare.osd.mil/fraud
- National Practitioner Data Bank (NPDB) Healthcare Integrity and Protection Data Bank (HIPDB)
  - http://www.npdb-hipdb.hrsa.gov/
- Freedom of Information Act (FOIA)
  - http://www.foia.gov
  - http://www.justice.gov/oip/04_1_1.html
- Medicare Parts C and D Fraud, Waste and Abuse Training
  - http://cms.meridianksi.com/kc/ilc/course_info_enroll_lnkfrm_f1.asp?lgnfrm=wbt&table=crs&function=course_info_enroll&strBuildingID=5&strFunctionID=37&strFunctionPath=37&strFrom=Search&topic=All&keywords=
- New York State Office of Medicaid Inspector General (OMIG) http://omig.ny.gov

OTHER NON-GOVERNMENT RESOURCES

Code of Ethics for Pharmacists
http://www.pharmacist.com/code-ethics

Medicare Prescription Drug Benefit Model Guidelines: Drug Categories and Classes in Part D
http://www.usp.org/hqi/mmg/

Health Care Administrators Association (HCAA)
http://www.hcaa.org/

Heath Care Compliance Association (HCCA)
http://www.hcca-info.org

Society of Corporate Compliance and Ethics (SCCE)
http://www.corporatecompliance.org

American Health Lawyers Association (AHLA)
http://www.healthlawyers.org

Institute for Health Care Improvement (IHI)
http://ihi.org

National Health Care Anti-Fraud Association (NHCAA)
http://www.nhcaa.org

Corporate Responsibility and Health Care Quality—A Resource for Health Care Boards of Directors, U.S. Department of Health and Human Services Office of the Inspector General and the American Health Lawyers Association
http://oig.hhs.gov/fraud/docs/complianceguidance/CorporateResponsibilityFinal%209-4-07.pdf

Ethics Resource Center
http://www.ethics.org/

Glossary

accepting assignment When a physician fills out the basic CMS 1500 claim form requesting reimbursement under Medicare, he or she has the option of checking a box labeled "Accept Assignment?". By checking the box, the physician indicates that he or she will accept reimbursement from Medicare, at rates determined by Medicare, in full payment for the services delivered under Medicare Part B. The physician agrees that he or she will not attempt to collect additional payment from the beneficiary except for any applicable deductible or coinsurance amounts.

accountable care organization (ACO) An ACO is a carefully assembled group of healthcare providers (physicians, hospitals, laboratories, pharmacies) capable of meeting all the healthcare needs of the designated population of people at least 5,000) for whom they have assumed responsibility. The group commits itself not only to treat immediate medical problems but also to maintain health over the long term. The group is rewarded for improving quality and reducing overall costs. It shares in whatever savings it is able to achieve.

administrative law judge (ALJ) These are federal officials who preside at trial-like hearings to resolve administrative disputes between a government agency and a person or organization affected by a decision of that agency. They take sworn testimony, rule on questions of evidence, and make determinations of law and fact. They do not assess penalties or punishments. They are considered members of the executive branch of government, not the judiciary branch. There are 1,600 ALJ's working in over 30 federal agencies; 85% of them are employed by the Social Security Administration.

advance beneficiary notice of noncoverage (ABN) When a physician decides to provide an item or service to a Medicare beneficiary that he believes Medicare will not pay for, he may (and sometimes, must) give the beneficiary a written notice called an "Advance Beneficiary Notice of Noncoverage." The ABN lists the items or services that Medicare is not expected to pay for, an estimate of the costs for the items and services, and the reasons why Medicare may not pay. The beneficiary then may choose whether or not to accept the items or services, knowing that he or she may have to pay for them out-of-pocket.

advisory opinion, OIG An individual or organization in the healthcare industry may request from the Office of the Inspector General (OIG) an advisory opinion about the application of the OIG's fraud and abuse laws and regulations to the requester's existing or proposed business arrangement. The opinion is legally binding on the Department of Health & Human Services and the requesting party, but not on any other government agency. A party that receives a favorable advisory opinion is protected from OIG administrative sanctions, so long as the arrangement at issue is conducted in accordance with the facts submitted to the OIG.

affiliated contractor (AC) Affiliated contractors are private insurance companies under contract with Medicare to process claims submitted by physicians, hospitals, and other healthcare providers or suppliers, and submit payment to those providers in accordance with Medicare rules and regulations. Their responsibilities include determining whether a service claim is covered by Medicare and whether it will be paid. A fiscal intermediary is a type of AC.

ambulance call reports (ACR) These are records prepared by ambulance technicians responding to a call. They usually are found among the emergency room chart documents. The report form consists mainly of check-off boxes for "presenting problems" and treatments administered. It provides a chronology of the times when the call was received, the ambulance was dispatched, arrived at the scene, departed for the hospital, and arrived at the hospital. It will record the patient's vital signs, outward appearance, and mental state.

ambulance supplier Transport by ambulance is a service provided by two types of entities. An ambulance provider is a healthcare provider that owns and operates an ambulance service as an adjunct to its institutionally based operations. These include hospitals, critical access hospitals (CAH), skilled-nursing facilities (SNF), comprehensive outpatient rehabilitation facilities, home health agencies (HHA), and hospice programs. An ambulance supplier is not owned or operated by a provider and is enrolled in Medicare as an independent ambulance supplier. These include volunteer fire or ambulance companies, local government ambulance companies, privately owned and operated ambulance service companies, and independently owned and operated ambulance service companies. The OIG Compliance Program Guidance applies to both ambulance suppliers and providers.

annual work plans, OIG The annual work plans of the Office of the Inspector General (OIG) provides brief descriptions of new and ongoing reviews and activities that it plans to pursue with respect to DHHS programs and operations during the next fiscal year. It sets out OIG focus areas, very specific projects within those areas, and the primary objectives of each project. One example: "We will analyze claims data to determine how much CMS could save if it bundled outpatient services delivered up to 14 days prior to an inpatient hospital admission into the diagnosis related group (DRG) payment."

anti kickback statute Originally enacted in 1972 and subsequently expanded in 1977 and 1987. The statute prohibits anyone from offering a kickback, paying a kickback, or receiving a kickback in return for the delivery of healthcare services. Violation may result in civil monetary penalties, felony criminal conviction, program exclusion, and False Claims Act liability. The safest method of avoiding liability under the statute is to structure business arrangements to fall within the exceptions defined in the statute or the Safe Harbors defined in regulations.

antitrust The term refers to a small group of federal laws that prohibit a variety of business practices that restrain trade and competition. The term comes from the fact that, in the early part of the 20th century, businessmen like Carnegie, Rockefeller, Vanderbilt, Astor, and Mellon used a legal instrument called a "trust" to dominate the steel, oil, railroad, real estate, and finance industries. These laws prohibit practices such as cartels and collusions that restrain trade, price fixing, group boycotts, mergers, and acquisitions that tend to create monopolies, predatory practices designed to create monopolies, market allocation agreements, price discrimination, and tying arrangements.

attorney-client privilege In a criminal legal proceeding, an attorney may refuse to disclose confidential communications between the attorney and a client that are related to furnishing or obtaining professional legal advice. The privilege does not apply to communications made in furtherance of a fraud or other crime. The purpose of the privilege is to encourage clients to disclose to their attorneys all information pertinent to their legal matters. Frequently, the attorney and the client will structure their interactions to ensure that they will be covered by this privilege.

auditing This is a systematic, independent, unbiased examination of data, statements, records, operations, decisions, and activities of an organization, department, facility, system, process, or project for a stated purpose. It may be conducted by auditors internal or external to an organization. In the case of healthcare compliance, an audit determines how well an organization's compliance program is functioning and how effectively it is preventing and detecting incidents of legal violation.

baseline audit Each audit of an organization's compliance program measures changes in its operations and effectiveness in preventing fraud and abuse since the previous audit. The first audit conducted establishes a starting point or baseline against which all subsequent audits are compared.

beneficiary A beneficiary is a person who is entitled to receive benefits under a Medicare, Medicaid, or private health insurance plan.

beyond a reasonable doubt This term describes the standard of proof that the prosecution must meet in a criminal trial to achieve conviction. It is not 100% proof; it means that the only doubts about the defendant's guilt are unreasonable. No other logical conclusion can be reached from the facts except that the defendant committed the crime. It is the highest standard of proof in the legal system. In civil litigation, the standard is either "preponderance of the evidence" or "clear and convincing evidence." The first means that the prosecution has more evidence in its favor than the defense, even if it is just a little bit more. The second means that there is a high probability that the claimed facts are true.

bona fide Bona fide is Latin for "good faith." In the law, it refers to the state of mind and knowledge of the person committing an act. The individual acted without fraud or deceit; he lacked knowledge that the act might be dishonest or illegal; he genuinely believed that his actions were legitimate.

boycott A boycott is a voluntary collective action by a group of people to refrain from dealing with a person or organization. They typically refuse to buy or use the organization's products or services, or to do business with it in any way. The usual purpose of the boycott is to express disapproval of the organization's actions or to force it to accept certain conditions. In health care, the classic example is a group of independent physician practices refusing to sign contracts with a health plan because they disapprove of the contract terms.

breach notification rule This is a requirement under HIPAA that covered entities and their business associates provide notification following a breach of unsecured protected health information (PHI). A breach is an impermissible use or disclosure that compromises the security or privacy of the PHI enough to pose a significant risk of financial, reputational, or other harm to the affected individual. Under different circumstances, the notification must go to the affected individual, the DHHS, and media outlets.

business associates Under HIPAA, every healthcare provider that electronically transmits health information in connection with claims-related transactions, is a covered entity. A business associate is a person or organization that does work or provides services for a covered entity that involve the use or disclosure of individually identifiable health information. Examples of business associate services are claims processing, data analysis, utilization review, and billing. Business associates are as fully covered by HIPAA as the covered entity.

capitation This is a method by which many health plans and managed care organizations compensate the providers who deliver healthcare services to their members/beneficiaries. The physician or hospital agrees to provide a defined package of benefits to each member. In return, the health plan pays the provider a fixed dollar amount each month for each member. This often is referred to as a "per member per month" (PMPM) payment. The provider must use the capitation payments to meet all the healthcare needs of the member, regardless of how sick or well he or she might be. Capitation is an incentive for providers to manage the health of these members, and the care they receive, so that in the long run the treatment costs do not exceed the capitation payments.

Centers for Medicare and Medicaid Services (CMS) The federal agency within the Department of Health and Human Services (DHHS) that administers the Medicare, Medicaid, and the Children's Health Insurance Program. The reimbursements that pass though the CMS account for nearly 40% of national health expenditures. By 2021, federal, state, and local government healthcare spending is projected to be nearly 50 percent of national health expenditures, up from 46 percent in 2011, with federal spending accounting for about two-thirds of the total government share.

certificate of medical necessity (CMN) This is a document that Medicare requires before it will reimburse the cost of an expensive piece of durable medical equipment (DME). Examples are fully automatic hospital beds, special mattresses for the treatment of pressure sores, oxygen, certain wheelchairs, and seat lift mechanisms. There must be clinical information in the patient's medical record to support the need for each piece of equipment ordered.

Certification of Compliance Agreements (CCA) The OIG negotiates a CCA with a healthcare organization as part of a settlement of accusations that it has violated the False Claims Act. It is similar to a Corporate Integrity Agreement (CIA), except that the CCA requires the organization to maintain an existing compliance program. The program must contain the elements in the appropriate OIG Program Guidance, accompanied by other compliance obligations typically found in a CIA.

charitable organization This is a nonprofit organization that is set up for certain purposes, including charity, religion, education, science, literary, public safety, and athletics. The provision of healthcare services is accepted as a charitable purpose. These organizations qualify for 501(c)(3) tax-exempt status under the regulations of the Internal Revenue Service (IRS). As a result, they do not need to pay federal income taxes and persons who make donations to these organizations may deduct the amounts from their own income tax payments. Approximately 60% of the 6,000 or so hospitals in the United States are nonprofit charitable entities, while 25% are government-owned. The rest are for-profit.

civil lawsuit or action In the U.S. legal system, there are two broad categories of law—civil law and criminal law. The civil law deals with disputes between private parties, both individuals and organizations. A successful civil lawsuit usually results in compensation to the victim.

civil monetary penalties law (CMPL) The federal Civil Monetary Penalties Law gives the OIG the authority to impose substantial monetary penalties on healthcare organizations for filing false claims, soliciting payment for referrals of a Medicare beneficiary, and engaging in several other types of fraudulent activity. This state also authorizes the OIG to exclude individuals and entities from participation in federal healthcare programs. In a case of false claims, the penalties may be up to $10,000 for each item improperly claimed, and an assessment of up to three times the amount improperly claimed.

claims submission Healthcare providers must submit claims to payors in order to be reimbursed for the products and services they deliver to patients. If the claims are submitted inaccurately or improperly, the payor can deny them, delaying payment to the provider. The volume of claims that are submitted by all providers and the difficulty for payors to make sure they are accurate offers many opportunities for fraud and abuse.

Clayton Act, Section 7 Section 7 of the federal Clayton Act is an antitrust law that is concerned exclusively with mergers, acquisitions, joint ventures, and other arrangements among two or more entities. It prohibits one organization from acquiring the stock or assets of another organization if it will lessen competition or tend to create a monopoly in a defined market. This law is especially relevant to the current trend of healthcare organizations to consolidate through merger and acquisition.

clinical laboratory A clinical laboratory is a laboratory that performs tests on clinical specimens in order to gather information about the health of a specific patient regarding the diagnosis, treatment, and prevention of a disease he or she may have. A physician decides that such a test would be useful in his or her clinical decision making for a patient, collects the specimen (blood, tissue, urine) from the patient, sends it to the laboratory, and interprets the results that the lab reports.

CMS 1500 form The Form CMS-1500 is the standard paper claim form used by healthcare providers and suppliers to bill Medicare carriers, or Part A and B and durable medical equipment Medicare administrative contractors.

CMS Medicare Learning Network (MLN) Through the MLN, the CMS offers a wide variety of education products designed to help physicians and other healthcare professionals understand and comply with the business requirements of CMS programs.

Code of Federal Regulations (CFR) When a statute is enacted, a government agency is designated to enforce it. That requires the agency to issue detailed, sometimes voluminous rules and regulations that expand upon the language of the statute. The regulations may not create new law that goes beyond the terms of the statute. The regulations are published in the Federal Register and then are codified in the Code of Federal Regulations. To understand the full impact of a statute, it is essential also read the related regulations.

code (or standards) of conduct This is an organization's statement of the basic principles and values that will guide its employees in carrying out their work responsibilities. The OIG recommends that the code of conduct include a commitment to legal compliance. It also suggests that the organization's board of directors, senior management, medical and clinical staff representatives, and other personnel participate in developing the code of conduct. This document should be succinct, readable, and memorable.

coding and billing In order to receive revenues from public or private payors, a healthcare provider must tell them exactly what service it has provided to which patient. There are thousands of different services and each one has been assigned a 9- or 10-digit code. The correct code must be listed for the service provided. It is then submitted as a claim or bill to the payor. In addition, providers increasingly are having to bill the patients themselves for the amount of their co-payments. Providers and the entire healthcare system devote immense resources to the process of coding and filing claims.

coinsurance Coinsurance is a term that appears in many health insurance policies. It is the percentage of the cost of a covered service that is paid for by the beneficiary, after the deductible amount has been satisfied. For instance, if the insurance policy included a $1,000 deductible and a 20% coinsurance feature, and the patient received a service costing $1,500, her would owe $1,100. (The $1,000 deductible plus 20% of the remaining $500.)

community benefit One of the prerequisites for the tax-exempt status of a hospital, or other healthcare organization, is that it serves a charitable purpose. That purpose includes providing a benefit to the organization's surrounding community. The elements of the community benefit offered by a hospital include a community-oriented governing board, open staff privileges, emergency medical care, free or income-adjusted care, and health promotion.

community health needs assessment Under the Patient Protection and Affordable Care Act (PPACA) enacted in 2010, every tax-exempt hospital must conduct a community health needs assessment every three years to determine how well it is meeting the health needs of its immediate community. This community benefit is a prerequisite of its tax-exempt status.

compliance There is a large and growing number of federal laws that apply to healthcare organizations. The penalties for violating them include massive fines, jail terms, and exclusion from the Medicare program. To avoid such penalties, organizations must make diligent efforts to "comply" with the laws. The accepted way of doing this is to create and maintain a formal, rigorous compliance program.

compliance committee The mandatory compliance program includes a Compliance Committee. This group typically is composed of representatives from pertinent areas of the organization: legal, internal auditing, human resources, security, risk management, clinical staff, and key operating units. At the least, they advise the Compliance Officer. They also may help in the design, implementation, and maintenance of the compliance program.

compliance officer One of the seven elements of the compliance program required of all healthcare organizations calls for the appointment of a Compliance Officer. This person is responsible for creating and managing the compliance program. He is a member of senior management team with direct unimpeded access to the CEO and the governing board. He has the final word on compliance matters. The Compliance Officer is held accountable for the effectiveness of the compliance program in detecting and preventing legal violations.

compliance program A compliance program is a structured set of policies, procedures, and actions implemented by organizations to ensure that they prevent, detect, and deal with possible violations of law. Since the late 1990s, the OIG has issued several "compliance program guidances" that describe in detail model compliance programs for 10 different types of healthcare organizations. Since the 2010 enactment of the Patient Protection and Affordable Care Act, every organization is required to maintain such a program.

compliance program guidance, OIG The OIG has issued several detailed descriptions of the compliance programs that healthcare organizations must implement if they wish to be reimbursed under the Medicare and Medicaid programs. There are guidances for 10 types of healthcare organizations. Each one defines 7 elements of a good program: 1) policies and procedures, 2) Compliance Officer and Committee, 3) training and education, 4) open channels of communication, 5) auditing and monitoring, 6) employee disciplinary procedure, and 7) investigation of suspected noncompliance.

conflict of interest A conflict of interest exists when a person or an organization is interested in the outcomes of two or more different activities, and the appeal of one of the activities could prejudice the person's motivation to properly perform another activity. For instance, a practicing physician who also owns a laboratory that performs diagnostic tests has an interest in maximizing the profits of the laboratory. He also has an interest in prescribing only those tests for his patients that are clinically indicated. A desire for greater profits might lead the physician to order more tests than the patients truly need. It does not matter whether the desire for profits actually resulted in more tests. The conflict lies in the potential for distorted decision making.

conspiracy or to conspire It is a conspiracy for two or more persons to agree, usually secretly, to commit a criminal or other illegal act. In most cases, the commission of an illegal act by the parties and their conspiracy to commit the act are separate crimes. Section One of the Sherman Antitrust Act prohibits any "conspiracy in restraint of trade or commerce." Two or more persons or entities must act together to violate this law. A single person acting alone cannot violate Section One.

conviction A successful criminal prosecution results in a "guilty" finding and the conviction of the defendant.

cooperative hospital service organizations These entities are formed on a cooperative basis by two or more hospitals to provide a variety of administrative support services to the participants. Even though the individual hospitals may have 501(c)(3) tax-exempt status, the cooperative must qualify under section 501(e) of the federal tax code to enjoy the same tax-exempt benefits.

copayment Health insurance policies frequently require beneficiaries to pay part of the cost of a service they have received. It is usually expressed as a fixed amount. For instance, a $15 copayment may be required for each physician visit. The purpose of copayments is to encourage people to be more thoughtful before seeking medical care.

Corporate Integrity Agreement (CIA) In order to resolve a case against a healthcare organization brought under the False Claims Act or other civil fraud statutes, the OIG may negotiate a CIA. A typical CIA runs for five years and requires the organization to implement strict, detailed compliance policies and procedures. If the organizations fulfills the terms of the CIA, the OIG agrees not to seek its exclusion from Medicare, Medicaid, and other federal healthcare programs.

cost-sharing The purpose of most health insurance policies is to pay for any unexpected medical expenses incurred by the policyholder/beneficiary. The beneficiary frequently is required to share in some of those costs through deductibles, coinsurance, copayments, and similar charges. Cost-sharing does not include partial payment of premiums, balance billing for use of non-network providers, and the cost of non-covered services. The purpose of cost-sharing is to allow lower premiums for the policy and to encourage the beneficiary to use healthcare services more wisely.

covered entities The Privacy and Security Rules of the Health Insurance Portability and Accountability Act (HIPAA) apply to "covered entities." These include three types of organizations—healthcare providers (e.g., physician practices, hospitals), health plans, and healthcare clearinghouses.

CPT Current procedural terminology (CPT) codes are five-digit numbers assigned to the services and activities that a physician, or other clinical care practitioner, provides to a patient. They include diagnostic, medical, and surgical services. The codes are used on the claims that physicians file with payors for reimbursement of those services. The CPT codes are similar to the ICD-9 and ICD-10 code sets that are used primarily for identifying diagnoses rather than services. The CPT system is maintained by the American Medical Association (AMA).

criminal prosecution This is the criminal counterpart of a civil lawsuit. It is concerned with offenses against society's sense of right and wrong. It is initiated by a prosecution of a defendant and may result in his imprisonment.

critical access hospital (CAH) Critical access hospitals are rural community hospitals that receive special cost-based Medicare reimbursement. To be certified by Medicare as a CAH, a hospital must already be a Medicare participant and meet several criteria:

- located in a state with a State Medicare Rural Hospital Flexibility Program
- designated by the state as a CAH
- located in a rural area
- located more than 35 miles from the nearest hospital or more than 15 miles in areas with mountainous terrain or secondary roads
- no more than 25 inpatient beds
- annual average length of stay of 96 hours or less per patient for acute inpatient care
- 24-hour emergency care services 7 days a week

culpability score Under the Federal Sentencing Guidelines, the culpability score is a "measure of how culpable the organization was in committing and responding to the occurrence of the offense." All organizations begin with a culpability score of five. This number is then increased or decreased by these factors: organization size and its involvement in or tolerance of criminal activity, its prior history of similar offenses, violation of a judicial order was involved, obstruction of justice was involved, existence of an effective compliance and ethics program, and self-reporting, cooperation, and acceptance of responsibility. The score is used in calculating any fines levied against the organization.

damages In civil law cases, the court may award damages as a form of monetary compensation to a person (the plaintiff) who has suffered injury as a result of the wrongful conduct, deliberate or negligent, of another person (the defendant). There are two types of damages. Compensatory damages are designed to repay the plaintiff for actual losses he or she has incurred as a result of the misconduct. Punitive damages are levied against the defendant as a form of punishment for especially egregious actions. Sometimes a statute, such as the False Claims Act, may set a specific damage amount for the incident of misconduct.

deductible A deductible is a feature of most insurance policies, particularly health insurance. It is the amount the policyholder must pay out-of-pocket for healthcare services before the insurance company starts to make any payments. For instance, if a policy has a deductible of $1,000 and the policyholder receives medical care costing $1,500, the policyholder would pay the first $1,000 and the insurer would pay the remaining $500. Normally, the deductible is on an annual basis. Once the policyholder makes payments equaling the deductible, the insurer covers all costs for the rest of the year. The deductible starts again at the beginning of the next year.

The purpose of a deductible is to encourage policyholders not to use healthcare services unnecessarily.

defraud To defraud is to use deceit, deception, falsehoods, or misrepresentation to obtain money or anything of value from another person or organization. The purpose of healthcare compliance programs is to prevent, detect, and address violations of several federal laws aimed at attempts by healthcare organizations to defraud the federal government. Foremost among those laws is the False Claims Act. Violations may involve claiming reimbursement for services that were not medically necessary, that were never provided, or were not provided to Medicare beneficiaries. The false claims may be backed up by altered medical records or other forms of false documentation.

de-identified information Under the Health Insurance Portability and Accountability Act (HIPAA), the Privacy Rule protects individually identifiable health information. The Rule places no restrictions on the use or disclosure of de-identified information, that is, information (1) that does not identify the individual and (2) for which there is no reasonable basis to believe the individual can be identified from it. De-identification can be accomplished by either determining that the information could not, in its present form, be used to identify a specific person or by removing or encrypting the identifying information.

Department of Health and Human Services (DHHS) The DHHS is the executive branch department composed of numerous health-related agencies and programs. Among these are the Centers for Medicare and Medicaid Services (CMS), the National Institutes of Health (NIH), the Food and Drug Administration (FDA), and the Office of the Inspector General (OIG). The DHHS is responsible for spending one quarter of the federal government budget.

Department of Justice (DOJ) The DOJ is a federal executive branch agency responsible for prosecuting violations of federal criminal laws, as well as enforcing the civil provisions of other laws. Of particular concern to healthcare organizations is the enforcement of antitrust laws (e.g., Sherman Act, Clayton Act) by the Antitrust Division of the DOJ.

designated health services The Stark Physician Self-Referral Law prohibits physicians from making referrals for "designated health services" to entities with they have a financial relationship (stock, debt, employment compensation). Those services are clinical laboratory, physical therapy, occupational therapy, outpatient speech-language pathology, radiology and other imaging, radiation therapy, durable medical equipment, parenteral and enteral supplies, prosthetics, orthotics, and prosthetic devices, home health, outpatient prescription drugs, and inpatient and outpatient hospital services.

diagnosis-related group (DRG) Diagnosis-related groups are a system of classifying acute care hospital inpatients into approximately 500 groups based on the diagnoses that brought them to the hospital. The hospitals are reimbursed by Medicare and many private payors in fixed amounts for each DRG. The determination of those amounts takes into account the patient's diagnosis, the severity of the patient's condition, and the resources the hospital must use to treat the patient. The DRG payments are made prospectively and are intended to cover all the services the hospital may provide in treating the patient.

diagnostic tests Before a physician begins treating a patient, he or she must prepare a diagnosis of the patient's problem. To assist in this, the physician frequently prescribes one or more diagnostic tests to be performed at a clinical laboratory. He or she collects a specimen (blood, tissue, urine) from the patient, sends it to the laboratory, and interprets the results reported by the lab. The physician then is better able to make a clinical decision about treating the patient.

Directors' and Officers' (D&O) liability insurance In the course of their work for an organization, the governing body members and the senior executives make many decisions that may result in lawsuits against them. It is common for the organizations to purchase "D&O liability insurance" to protect these officials against personal liability and financial loss, including their attorney's fees, from wrongful acts committed—or allegedly committed—in their capacity as corporate officers. The liabilities may be based on civil, criminal, or regulatory investigations or trials. These officials' responsibility for violations of healthcare fraud and abuse laws would be covered by D&O insurance.

disciplinary action When, in the course of their work, employees behave in ways that violate organization policies and procedures, violate laws, disobey supervisory directives, or are otherwise contrary to the interests of the organization, they typically are subject to a range of disciplinary actions by a manager. Traditional disciplinary actions are informal cautions, verbal warnings, written warnings, suspensions, and dismissals. One of the seven elements of a mandatory compliance program is a mechanism for administering such actions to employees who have violated the organization's compliance rules and contributed to noncompliance events.

disqualified person If a nonprofit healthcare organization, such as a hospital, provides an economic benefit to a "disqualified person" without receiving something of fair market value in return (such as goods or services), it is engaging in an "excess benefit transaction" and risks compromising its tax-exempt status. Disqualified persons include the organization's president, CEO, COO, or CFO, major donors, family members of those individuals, plus anyone with more than a 35% ownership interest in an entity sponsored by the exempt organization. Others with substantial influence over the organization may also be considered part of this group—department or facility managers, major sources of revenue (high-referring doctors), those with the authority to hire and fire staff, supervisors of employees, and physicians with exclusive hospital contracts.

documentation The term "documentation" applies to the records, both hard copy and electronic, that are prepared in the course of many business activities. Some examples are medical records; financial records; information on claims filed, denied, and paid; lists of training programs conducted, materials distributed, and persons attending; records of compliance investigations conducted; and descriptions of employee disciplinary actions taken. Appropriate documentation is evidence of how well an organization's compliance program is functioning.

Drug Enforcement Administration (DEA) number The DEA number is assigned to individual healthcare providers like physicians by the Drug Enforcement Administration allowing them to write prescriptions for controlled substances.

electronic health record (EHR) This term is used to describe a longitudinal (ongoing over time) collection of personal health information concerning a single individual, entered and managed by healthcare providers, and stored electronically. It contains historical information on a person's health status and past interventions, their current health status and active interventions, and projected future status and activities. Specific data might include daily charting, physical assessment, admission notes, nursing care plan, referrals, present complaints (e.g., symptoms), past medical history, life style, physical examination, diagnoses, tests, procedures, treatment, medication, discharge, history, diaries, and immunizations. The EHR usually is part of a system tied in to practice management, billing and collection, electronic prescribing, population management, and quality management functions. A key feature is its ability to be transmitted back and forth to other providers. The term personal health record (PHR) usually describes similar documentation that is managed and controlled by the affected individual.

electronic protected health information (E-PHI) Electronic protected health information is a critical term under the Health Insurance Portability and Accountability Act (HIPAA). Health information concerns an individual's past, present, or future physical or mental health or condition, the provision of healthcare services to the individual, and the past, present, or future payment for those services–and that indentifies the individual. The use and disclosure of that information is protected by the HIPAA Privacy Rule, whether the information is in electronic, paper, or oral form. The protection of the HIPAA Security Rule applies only to E-PHI, health information that is transmitted electronically.

emergency medical services (EMS) These are medical services provided, typically by EMT's, to patients with emergency illnesses and injuries. The services are delivered at the site of the injury or illness prior to transporting the patient to a hospital for more comprehensive acute medical care.

emergency medical technicians (EMTs) These are specially trained and licensed healthcare providers who deliver medical care in emergency circumstances. They typically respond to emergency calls, perform a limited set of medical procedures on the spot, and transport patients to a hospital according to established guidelines and protocols. They may work in an ambulance service (paid or voluntary), as a member of a technical rescue team/squad, or as part of a fire or police department. EMTs are trained to assess a patient's condition and perform emergency medical procedures needed to stabilize the patient until he/she can be transferred to an appropriate facility for advanced medical care.

Emergency Medical Treatment and Active Labor Act (EMTALA) This statute governs when and how a patient may be refused treatment or transferred from one hospital to another when he is in an unstable medical condition. Hospitals that participate in Medicare and offer emergency services are required to provide a medical screening exam for every person who arrive in an emergency medical condition, including active labor, regardless of his/her ability to pay. The hospital then must stabilize the individual's emergency condition. If it does not have the capability to provide stabilizing treatment, it must transfer the person to a facility that can stabilize and treat.

e-prescribing E-prescribing refers to a provider's ability to electronically transmit an accurate, error-free, comprehensible directly to a pharmacy from the point of care. This function can be integrated with an EHR and practice management system.

ethics There are numerous definitions of this term. This is one of the best—a set of values and principles that guide individuals and organizations in the rightness and wrongness of their behaviors, above and beyond whatever the law may require. Many organizations promote a written Code of Ethics for the work-related actions of their employees. Most individuals follow a personal Code of Ethics, though they may not be conscious of it.

Ethics in Patient Referral Act of 1989 (Stark I) This was the first of three laws prohibiting physician self-referrals. This initial law dealt only with referrals to clinical laboratories. The second Stark Law, enacted in 1993, expanded the prohibition to a total of 12 designated health services (DSHs).

exceptions In the context of healthcare compliance, the term "exceptions" applies to the Physician Self-Referral (Stark) Law and the Anti-Kickback Statute (AKS). The Stark Law prohibits a physician from making referrals to an entity with which he has a financial relationship. The law and its related regulations define approximately 35 exceptions to this prohibition. If a physician referral arrangement fits squarely within one of the exceptions, it is not subject to the Stark Law. If it does not fit, it is prohibited. The AKS prohibits anyone from giving or receiving anything of value in return for a referral. The statute itself creates several exceptions that work like those under the Stark Law. In addition, regulations have been issued to establish a number of "Safe Harbors."

excess benefit transaction (EBT) This is a transaction by a tax-exempt organization that provides an economic benefit to a "disqualified person" that exceeds the value of the goods or services received from that person. Such transactions are prohibited and threaten the tax-exempt status of the organization.

exclusion authority, OIG For 23 different reasons, the OIG has the authority to exclude healthcare organizations and individuals from participation in federal healthcare programs like Medicare and Medicaid. Because so many healthcare entities rely on these programs for a major share of their revenues, exclusion can put them out of business. Among the reasons for exclusion are conviction of program-related crimes; fraud, kickbacks, and other prohibited activities; failure to take corrective action; and a misdemeanor conviction relating to healthcare fraud.

fair market value (FMV) This is a key term in determining the legality of many transactions among healthcare individuals and organizations. For instance, a common feature of the "Safe Harbors" under the Anti-Kickback Statute is that goods or services must be provided to referring physicians at FMV prices. If provided at less than FMV prices, the implication is that the discount was intended to buy the physician's referrals. Fair market value is the price at which a product or service would be exchanged in the open market between an independent, informed, unhurried buyer and a similar seller in an arm's length transaction.

false claim In this case, a "claim" is a sort of bill or invoice submitted to a federal program requesting reimbursement for a good or service provided under the terms of the program. The best example is a physician's claim for a service he or she has provided to a patient covered by Medicare. When there is no basis for the claim, it is "false." For instance, the service was never provided, it was provided but not necessary, or it was provided to a person not covered by Medicare.

False Claims Act This law prohibits the submission of false claims for payment, the use of false documents to support such claims, the retention of money owed to the federal government, or conspiring with others to commit any of those acts. It is the most common legal tool of the federal government in fighting healthcare fraud and abuse.

FDR entities This is the terminology that the OIG uses to describe the different types of individuals and organizations for whose compliance Medicare Advantage Organizations (MAOs) are responsible. Medicare Advantage is the managed care version of Medicare. The MAOs function like most managed care organizations. They usually offer several types of Medicare Advantage plans in which Medicare beneficiaries may enroll. In order to provide medical services to those beneficiaries, the MAO's contract with First Tier Entities like hospitals and large physician groups. Those entities then contract with Downstream Entities like pharmacies, small physician practices, and medical billing companies. These entities in turn may contract with a third level of Related Entities, consisting of organizations that perform management functions for the MAO and individual practitioners who directly serve the Medicare beneficiaries. First Tier, Downstream, and Related is abbreviated to FDR.

Federal Bureau of Investigation (FBI) The FBI is a governmental agency within the Department of Justice (DOJ) that performs two functions: investigating and enforcing federal criminal law and gathering domestic intelligence. Most of its activities do not directly concern the healthcare industry (violent crime, international criminal organizations, cyber-based attacks). The FBI shares responsibility with the Drug Enforcement Administration for enforcing the Controlled Substances Act of 1970. Its work in combating white collar crime and public corruption sometimes reveals information on possible healthcare fraud cases, which usually are referred to the DOJ.

Federal Drug Administration The Food and Drug Administration (FDA) is an agency within the Department of Health and Human Services. It is responsible for protecting and promoting public health through the regulation and supervision of food safety, tobacco products, dietary supplements, prescription and over-the-counter pharmaceutical drugs, vaccines, biopharmaceuticals, blood transfusions, medical devices, electromagnetic radiation emitting devices (ERED), and veterinary products.

federal healthcare program Several federal laws refer to "federal healthcare programs." For instance, the OIG has the legal authority to exclude certain noncompliant healthcare individuals and organizations from participation in federal healthcare programs. This includes these programs, Medicare, Medicaid, Children's Health Insurance Program, TRICARE (civilian health benefits for military personnel, military retirees, and their dependents), and the veterans' programs.

Federal Sentencing Guidelines The Federal Sentencing Guidelines are rules that set out a uniform sentencing policy for individuals and organizations convicted of felonies and serious (Class A) misdemeanors in the federal courts system. They do not apply to less serious misdemeanors. The Guidelines are discretionary, meaning that judges may consider them but are not required to follow them strictly in their sentencing decisions. The Guidelines use a points system that assigns points according to type of offense, how it was committed, and an offender's background.

Federal Trade Commission (FTC) Act This federal statute creates a Federal Trade Commission with the authority to prevent individuals and organizations from using unfair methods of competition and unfair or deceptive acts or practices that involve or affect commerce. It applies only to for-profit entities. The Act does cover the competitive behavior of commercial healthcare organizations. In carrying out its mandate, the Commission may seek monetary relief for conduct that injures consumers, issue regulations defining unfair or deceptive practices, and conduct investigations into the management and operation of entities engaged in commerce.

fee-for-service (FFS) The traditional method of reimbursing healthcare providers, particularly physicians, for the services they deliver to patients is called "fee-for-service." A separate fee is paid for each service, like an office visit, a test, or a procedure. There are two problems with this method. One is the huge administrative cost associated with coding, billing, and processing claims for millions of units of service delivered throughout the healthcare system. Second is the incentive that FFS offers to providers to deliver more services. As the volume of services increases so does the provider's revenue.

fiduciary duty (loyalty, obedience, care) The members of an organization's governing board have a fiduciary duty to the shareholders (for-profit) or to the general public (nonprofit). This would include the directors or trustees of a hospital, a health plan, or a pharmaceutical company. There are three fiduciary duties. The duty of Care requires that directors stay informed, pay attention, show curiosity, and make the best decisions they can. Under the duty of Loyalty, they must always act in the interests of the organization, and never in their own interests. Where both types of interest exist simultaneously, there may be a "conflict of interest." The duty of Obedience demands that the directors' decisions adhere to the organization's stated mission.

financial conflict of interest (FCOI) The National Institutes of Health (NIH) that funds a large share of medical research in the United States has issued mandatory standards designed to ensure that the research will be free from bias resulting from financial conflicts of interest on the part of the research investigators. That term is defined as a significant financial interest that could directly and significantly affect the design, conduct, or reporting of NIH-funded research.

financial relationship This term relates to the Physician Self-Referral Law which prohibits physicians from making referrals to entities with which they have a financial relationship. The relationship may take two forms. It could involve direct or indirect ownership of the entity, through holding stock, bonds, or debt of the entity. Alternatively, the relationship might be based on direct or indirect compensation from the entity, as when a physician is employed by a hospital.

first responders These are people, typically EMTs, firefighters, or police officers, whose job is to go immediately to the scene of an accident, a disaster, or other emergency to provide trained assistance.

fiscal year (FY) A fiscal year is a 12-month period used for defining and calculating annual financial statements in businesses and other organizations. It may run from January 1 to December 31, in which case it may be referred to as a "calendar year." The organization can choose whatever 12-month period it wishes for its FY.

fraud and abuse The CMS defines "fraud" as a person or organization making false statements or representations of material facts to obtain a benefit or payment to which it is not entitled. In other words, fraud includes the obtaining of something of value through misrepresentation or concealment of material facts. Examples are billing for services that were not furnished, or altering claims forms to received higher payments. It defines "abuse" as practices that result in unnecessary costs to the Medicare program. Abuse includes any practice that is inconsistent with the goals of providing patients with services that are medically necessary, meet professionally recognized standards, and are fairly priced. There have been rough estimates that fraud and abuse accounts for 10% of healthcare spending in the United States.

Fraud Enforcement and Recovery Act (FERA) This 2009 law was aimed primarily at the financial and other corporate fraud that was being reported regularly during the last decade. One of the ways that it accomplished this was to expand the grounds for liability under the False Claims Act, one of the most popular tools for combating fraud in the healthcare industry. In particular, the FERA expands the definition of a prohibited "claim" as well as the concept of a "reverse false claim."

Freedom of Information Act (FOIA) The Freedom of Information Act provides public access to federal government records created by executive branch agencies. Any person, including U.S. citizens, foreign nationals, organizations, associations, and universities, may submit a FOIA request asking for records held by the government. The presumption is that a record must be disclosed unless the government can show that it is covered by one of nine specific FOIA exemptions. The right of access is enforceable in federal court.

gain-sharing This is a bonus-based methodology for improving productivity, enhancing quality, and cutting costs. An organization begins by measuring the metric that it wants to work on, trains employees in how their work affects the metric, sets goals for improving the metric, calculates any monetary gains that result from the improvement, and shares them with the employees responsible. Hospitals frequently negotiate gain-sharing arrangements with their physicians in order to drive quality and efficiency improvements. In the past, the OIG has ruled that gain-sharing violates the Physician Self-Referral and Anti-Kickback laws. However, it also has granted waivers to allow such arrangements in several cases.

General Services Administration (GSA) The GSA is an independent federal agency responsible for managing and supporting the basic operations of most other federal agencies. It does not involve itself in policy matters. It procures products and communications systems for government offices; constructs, leases, and maintains public buildings; and provides transportation and office space among other functions.

general training One of the seven basic elements of an effective compliance program as recommended and defined by the OIG is Training and Education. Two types of training should be provided—General and Specialized. Employees at all levels should be required to attend General training sessions that cover the laws and regulations with which the organization must comply, and the basic principles of the program designed to ensure that compliance. Employees who work in areas at high risk for compliance violations (billing and collections, marketing, physician relationships) should receive specialized training in their particular job tasks.

governing board There is a hierarchy in almost every organization. At the highest level are the "owners." In a for-profit corporation, these are the shareholders. In a nonprofit charitable organization, these are the general public, the members of the community served by the organization. In both cases, the owners delegate responsibility for overseeing the entity's operations to a governing board. In a for-profit corporation, they usually are referred to as the Board of Directors. The comparable body in a nonprofit entity is the Board of Trustees. These boards hire the CEO, president, or other top executive of the organization, define the strategic direction for the organization, and monitor how well it is being achieved. The governing board also is ultimately responsible for the performance of the compliance program.

group purchasing organization (GPO) In the healthcare industry, groups of provider entities, such as hospitals, form GPOs to leverage their collective buying power to obtain price discounts on a variety of goods and services used in hospital operations. It is optional for the participating hospitals to purchase through the GPO. The typical items covered by a GPO are medical supplies, nutrition, pharmacy products, laboratory services, office supplies, and nonmedical related services. The GPO covers its operating expenses from the fees that vendors pay (up to 3.0% of total sales to the GPO members). Some vendors also provide clinical support, benchmarking data, supply chain support, and comprehensive catalogues of products and services.

Guidance on IRO Independence and Objectivity When the OIG enters into a Corporate Integrity Agreement (CIA) with an organization charged with violations of law, it requires that the organization, among its other obligations under the CIA, contract with an outside entity (typically an accounting, audit, or consulting firm) to perform certain reviews. The entity is called an Independent Review Organization (IRO), and it is essential that it be both independent and objective. The four-page Guidance on IRO Independence and Objectivity was issued by the OIG to explain how those qualities may be achieved.

Healthcare Common Procedure Coding System (HCPCS) Health plans and insurers process over 5 billion claims for payment each year. Standardized coding systems are used to ensure that these claims are handled in an orderly and consistent manner. The HCPCS is a standard code set used for this purpose, comprised of two subsystems. Level I is the Current Procedural Terminology (CPT), numeric codes used to identify medical services and procedures furnished by physicians and other healthcare professionals. Level II applies to products, supplies, and services not included in the CPT codes, such as ambulance services and durable medical equipment, prosthetics, orthotics, and supplies (DMEPOS) when used outside a physician's office.

health care fraud and abuse control office, OIG The Health Insurance Portability and Accountability Act (HIPAA) established a national Health Care Fraud and Abuse Control Program under the joint direction of the U.S. Attorney General and the Secretary of the Department of Health and Human Services acting through the latter's Office of the Inspector General (OIG). The program was designed to coordinate federal, state, and local law enforcement activities to combat fraud committed against all health plans, both public and private. The tools with which it carries on this fight are the Health Care Fraud Prevention and Enforcement Action Team (HEAT), and the Fraud Strike Force (a multi-agency team of federal, state, and local investigators designed to fight Medicare fraud). They use advanced data analysis techniques to identify high billing levels in healthcare fraud hot spots.

Health Care Fraud Prevention and Enforcement Action Team (HEAT) The HEAT is a joint effort of the Department of Health and Human Services (DHHS) and Department of Justice (DOJ). It focuses on geographic areas where healthcare fraud is most intense, uses real-time claims data to detect patterns of fraud, and leverages information sharing among agencies. Its most aggressive enforcement work is undertaken by its Medicare Fraud Strike Force, a multi-agency group of investigators operating in nine cities.

Health Care Quality Improvement Act (HCQIA) The HCQIA was enacted in 1986 to address the problem of incompetent physicians losing their licenses and practice privileges in one state, and moving to another state without any disclosure or discovery of their past history. The Act established the National Practitioner Data Bank to accumulate reports of physicians' prior adverse actions (loss of clinical privileges, licenses, and professional society memberships, as well as malpractice lawsuits) which in turn may be accessed by hospitals, state licensure boards, some professional societies, and other healthcare entities. In addition, the HCQIA provided immunity from civil money damages to encourage the participation of hospital staff physicians in peer review activities that frequently reveal physician incompetence.

Health Information Technology for Economic and Clinical Health (HITECH) Act of 2009 The HITECH Act created Medicare and Medicaid Electronic Health Record (EHR) Incentive programs that offer incentive payments to eligible professionals and hospitals that adopt, implement, upgrade or demonstrate meaningful use of certified EHR technology. The incentives continue until 2015, after which time penalties will be assessed for failing to demonstrate such use. The HITECH Act also established the Breach Notification Rule under HIPAA, required DHHS to conduct periodic audits to ensure covered entities are complying with the HIPAA rules, and strengthened civil and criminal enforcement of those rules.

Health Insurance Portability and Accountability Act of 1996 (HIPAA) This Act was enacted to protect against the privacy and security threats presented against the widespread and growing use of sensitive personal healthcare information throughout the healthcare industry. The Office for Civil Rights within the DHHS implements the Act through four rules. The Privacy Rule sets standards for individual privacy rights, and the use and disclosure of their health information by healthcare providers and plans. The Security Rule sets national standards for the security of electronic protected health information. The Breach Notification Rule requires covered entities and business associates to provide notification following a breach of unsecured protected health information. The confidentiality provisions of the Patient Safety Rule protect identifiable information being used to analyze patient safety events and improve patient safety.

Health Professional Shortage Area (HPSA) These areas are designated by the Health Resources and Services Administration (HRSA) as having shortages of primary medical care, dental or mental health providers. They may be defined in terms of geography (based on census tracts, counties, or townships), demography (low-income population), or institution (comprehensive health center, federally qualified health center, other public facility). The Centers for Medicare & Medicaid Services (CMS) provides a 10 percent bonus payment to physicians who furnish Medicare-covered services to beneficiaries in a geographic HPSA. Other federal programs may use HPSA status or data to determine eligibility.

home health agency This is a public or private entity that provides short-term (typically 60 days) skilled nursing or rehabilitative services to homebound persons following a decline in function or an acute illness. Home health agencies typically do not provide long-term care in the home. Medicare will pay the cost of the services when a physician orders skilled nursing care plus at least one other therapeutic service, usually physical or occupational therapy.

hospice A hospice provides expert medical care, pain management, and emotional and spiritual support tailored to the needs of patients with a terminal illness. A hospice focuses on caring, not curing. In most cases, care is provided in the patient's home but may also be provided in freestanding hospice centers, hospitals, nursing homes, and other long-term care facilities.

hospital medical director A medical director is a physician who serves as the leader of clinical activities at a hospital or other medical facility. This person guides and represents the medical staff. He or she develops and implements policies and procedures to ensure high quality and best practices in care delivery, supervises training and continuing education for the staff, and cooperates with the compliance officer to maximize compliance with all federal, state, and local laws. The medical director reports directly to the CEO or president of the hospital.

human subject In the context of health care, a human subject is a living individual about whom an investigator is conducting systematic research or a clinically oriented study. Systematic investigation involves the collection and analysis of data in order to answer a specific question. Examples of a research-oriented investigation include surveys, questionnaires, interviews, and focus groups. Examples of a clinically oriented investigation include analysis of biological specimens, epidemiological and behavioral studies, and medical chart review studies. Human subject research is carried out in fields like basic biology, clinical medicine, nursing, psychology, and pharmaceutical development.

ICD-9 and ICD-10 The Health Insurance Portability and Accountability Act (HIPAA) requires health plans and healthcare providers to use standard code sets to indicate diagnoses and procedures in their transactions concerning the treatment of patients. For instance, every claim for reimbursement by Medicare, Medicaid, or private payors has a code attached to it. The ICD-9 codes will be replaced by the ICD-10 codes for services delivered after October 1, 2014. The ICD-10-CM codes will be used for diagnoses; ICD-10-PCS codes apply to inpatient hospital procedures. All other procedures are covered by the already-existing Current Procedural Terminology (CPT) or Healthcare Common Procedure Coding System (HCPCS) codes. The transition to ICD-10 is occurring because ICD-9 produces limited data about patients' medical conditions and hospital inpatient procedures. ICD-9 is 30 years old, has outdated terms, and is inconsistent with current medical practice. The ICD-10 codes must be used by every provider and payor covered by HIPAA, not just those that submit Medicare claims.

illegal kickbacks The basic idea of a "kickback" is that the seller of a product or service gives (or kicks) back to the buyer a share of the price he has been paid as an incentive for the buyer to do business with him. There is nothing inherently wrong or illegal with this practice. In some industries, it may be common practice. However, there are numerous federal, state, and local laws that prohibit kickbacks involving government agencies and programs. In health care, the primary example is the Anti-Kickback Statute that prohibits anyone from offering a kickback, paying a kickback, or receiving a kickback in return for the delivery of healthcare services.

independent contractor Individuals who perform work for organizations fall into two legal categories—employee and independent contractor. The distinction is important to the organization because it determines whether it must withhold or pay taxes regarding the worker, or must provide employee benefits to him or her. Most of the requirements of a mandatory compliance program extend to independent contractors, as well as employees.

indepenent practice association (IPA) An IPA is a network of independent physician practices that contracts jointly with health plans and insurers at a negotiated per capita rate, for a flat retainer fee, or on a negotiated fee-for-service basis. To avoid liability for antitrust price-fixing, the practices in the IPA must share financial or clinical risk. The simplest way to do this is negotiate for capitation payments. Many IPAs also have found it advantageous to begin clinically integrating their practices. The IPA structure makes it easy to implement administrative cost sharing, coordinated care, case management, population management, and communications links among the practices. These are all features of the accountable care organization (ACO) format toward which the healthcare industry is moving.

indepentent review organization (IRO) When the OIG enters into a Corporate Integrity Agreement (CIA) with a healthcare entity charged with violations of law, it requires that the entity, among its other obligations under the CIA, contract with an IRO. This usually is an accounting, audit, or consulting firm that provides independent and objective reviews of the entity's systems and transactions. From the OIG's perspective, the IRO serves as an extension of the OIGs own auditing and monitoring activities. To qualify for the work, the IRO must possess expertise in relevant substantive matters, expertise federal healthcare program requirements, appropriate credentials/certifications, knowledge of statistical sampling, and sufficient staff and resources to perform the work on a timely basis.

ineligible person An ineligible person is a person or organization that is currently excluded, suspended, debarred, or otherwise ineligible to participate in federal healthcare programs; or has been convicted of a criminal offense related to the provision of healthcare items or services but has not yet been excluded, debarred, or otherwise declared ineligible. Organizations must be aware of which of its employees or independent contractors are ineligible persons so that it does not try to seek Medicare or Medicaid reimbursement for their goods or services. The names of ineligible persons appear on the OIG List of Excluded Individuals/Entities and the General Services Administration's List of Parties Excluded from Federal Programs.

in-office ancillary services The Physician Self-Referral (Stark) Law prohibits physicians from making referrals for "designated health services" (DHS) to organizations with which they have financial relationships, unless an exception under the law applies. The prohibition includes referrals to a physician's own practice. The two exceptions that may allow such referrals are for "physician services" and "in-office ancillary services." The latter exception allows medical practices to provide laboratory, radiology, outpatient prescription drugs, and other DHS without violating the law.

institutional review board Every research project that receives support, directly or indirectly, from the DHHS must form and use an IRB before interaction with human subjects can begin. An IRB is a formally designated committee within a research institution that approves, monitors, and reviews biomedical and behavioral research involving human subjects. The purpose of an IRB's work is to ensure, both in advance and by periodic review, that appropriate steps are taken to protect the rights and welfare of humans participating as subjects in the research. It has the authority to approve, modify, or disapprove research.

intermediate care facilities (ICF) These facilities are designed to provide custodial care for individuals unable to care for themselves as a result of physical or mental developmental disabilities. They need more supervision than in-home services offer but do not need the level of care provided by skilled nursing facilities. Federal regulations require that an ICF have a registered nurse as director of nursing and a licensed nurse on duty at least 8 hours a day. These facilities receive the bulk of their funding from Medicaid rather than Medicare.

internal investigation Model healthcare compliance programs encourage employees, third-party agents, and others to report suspicions or allegations of wrongdoing. The organization's immediate reaction must be to launch an internal investigation to determine the veracity of the claims. It should follow a strict multi-step procedure described in its compliance program. The investigation should use trained, trustworthy employees, perhaps with the help of an attorney or consultant, to conduct reviews of personnel and documents. A report should be prepared on the investigation findings. Decisions must be made about corrective actions to fix the problems identified, and whether to report the findings to government authorities.

Internal Revenue Service (IRS) The IRS is the federal government agency responsible for tax collection and tax law enforcement. It issues and enforces the regulations that determine what a healthcare organization, like a hospital, must do to qualify and maintain tax-exempt status.

Joint Commission (JC) This independent, nonprofit organization evaluates and accredits over 20,000 healthcare organizations, including general, psychiatric, children's and rehabilitation hospitals; critical access hospitals; home care organizations, including medical equipment services and hospice services; nursing homes, rehabilitation centers, and other long-term care facilities; behavioral healthcare organizations, addiction services; ambulatory care providers, including group practices and office-based surgery practices; and independent or freestanding clinical laboratories. It was previously known as the Joint Commission for Accreditation of Health Organizations (JCAHO). To earn and maintain JC accreditation, an organization must undergo an intensive multi-day on-site survey by a JC team three years. (Laboratories must be surveyed every two years.) Joint Commission standards address the organization's level of performance in key functional areas, such as patient rights, patient treatment, medication safety and infection control. JC accreditation is a prerequisite to reimbursement by Medicare, Medicaid, and most private health insurers.

joint venture This is a business arrangement in which two or more parties (individuals or organizations) pool their resources in order to accomplish a defined task. That task may be as broad or narrow as the parties choose. The joint venture may be a separate legal entity (corporation) distinct from parties' other business interests, or it may be the product of a contract between the parties. The terms of the arrangement indicate the parties' rights and responsibilities, their shares of ownership, degrees of control, and the division of profits. The life of the joint venture may be relatively brief–months or a few years, or it may continue to operate indefinitely.

knowing or knowingly This term is critical in a legal context because it frequently determines an individual's culpability for his or her actions. It means that the action was performed with full knowledge and understanding of the relevant facts, that the individual realized what he was doing and did not act through ignorance, mistake, or accident. As a practical matter, the individual acted intentionally.

legal judgment A legal judgment is a formal decision by a court that resolves all the contested issues between a plaintiff and a defendant, determines the rights and obligations of the parties, and brings an end to their lawsuit. A judgment normally is in writing. It makes a pronouncement about the law in the case. It states which party is the winner, and the remedies that it will receive. This may include money damages, injunctive relief, or both.

legal settlement A legal settlement is a negotiated resolution between the opposing parties of the issues in dispute in a court action. It is an alternative to going to trial over the issues. Settlements occur before or during the early stages of a trial. A settlement usually results when the defendant agrees with some or all of the plaintiff's claims and decides not to fight the matter in court. The defendant realizes that he or she is likely to lose in a trial proceeding and chooses to avoid the costs of further litigation. The terms of the settlement may require the defendant to pay money or change some of his policies or behaviors. When a settlement is concluded, the litigation is over.

liability The interpretation and application of this term in specific legal cases can mean that a party may have to pay monetary damages, pay a fine, cease certain activities or behaviors, perform other activities or behavior, or go to prison. Liability means legal responsibility for one's acts or omissions. It normally results when there is evidence that one party had a duty to act (or to not act), failed to fulfill that duty, and that failure was the proximate cause of injury to another party. Legal liability can be based upon contracts, common law torts, civil laws and regulations, and criminal statutes. The existence of liability can only be determined by a court.

list of excluded individuals and entities, OIG The OIG has the authority to exclude individuals and organizations from participation in federal healthcare programs. They must be excluded for patient abuse crimes, healthcare fraud felonies, and crimes involving controlled substances. The OIG has the option of excluding those who commit healthcare fraud misdemeanors, controlled substance misdemeanors, and prohibited kickbacks. Federal healthcare programs will not pay for anything furnished, ordered, or prescribed by an excluded person, by anyone who employs or contracts with an excluded person, or by a hospital for which the excluded person provides services.

list of parties debarred from federal programs, GSA The General Services Administration (GSA) is the federal government's landlord, providing office and work space services for most of its agencies. In addition, it is the central procurement agency, offering 18 million products and services from over 17,000 vendors to those agencies. When an agency encounters vendors who demonstrate a lack of "present responsibility," which may involve contractual or statutory misconduct, it places them on the GSA Excluded Parties List System (EPLS). The similar OIG list includes only those parties excluded by federal health agencies or programs. Healthcare entities that receive funds from federal government programs must not hire, enter into contracts with, or make purchases from persons or individuals who appear on this list.

managed care organization (MCO) These are integrated groups of doctors, hospitals, clinics, pharmacies, and other providers who consciously coordinate their treatment of their member's healthcare needs. A typical MCO combines the functions of health insurance and care delivery. They may also be called health plans or health maintenance organizations (HMOs). Managed care members initially choose a primary care physician (PCP), who sees them first when they have a healthcare issue. When it is appropriate, the PCP will refer a member to a specialist physician.

medical coding For the purpose of keeping track of the myriad services and products provided to patients within the healthcare system, and particularly to enable the filing of claims for reimbursement for those services and products, a medical code must be assigned to each item. The process of medical coding translates the narrative description of diagnoses, diseases, injuries, and treatments into numeric or alphanumeric designations. There are several code set standards in use.

- International Classification of Diseases, 9th revision, Clinical Modification (ICD-9-CM) Volumes 1 & 2, applies to diagnoses.
- ICD-9-CM Volume 3, applies to procedures.
- Current Procedure Terminology (CPT), applies to outpatient procedures.
- Health Care Common Procedure Coding System (HCPCS), applies to items and supplies and non physician services not covered by CPT codes.
- ICD-10-CM, applies to diagnoses, replaces ICD-9CM. (effective October 1, 2014)
- ICD-10-PCS, applies to inpatient hospital procedures. (effective October 1, 2014)
- National Drug Code (NDC), identifies the manufacturer, product, and package size of all medications recognized by the FDA.

"Medically necessay" and "medical necessity" A common form of healthcare fraud is the filing of a claim for medical services that were provided but were not medically necessary for the patient in question. These terms refer to healthcare services that a physician, exercising prudent clinical judgment, would provide to a patient for the purpose of evaluating, diagnosing, or treating an illness, injury, disease, or its symptoms. The services are consistent with generally accepted standards of medical practice, are clinically appropriate, are not primarily for the convenience of the patient or the physician, and are not more costly than an equally effective alternative.

Medicaid Medicaid is a health insurance program for low-income individuals and families. It is administered by individual states which must include a few very basic benefits and then can add other benefits of their choosing. Some optional benefits are prescription drugs, preventive care, case management, and physical therapy. The program costs are split roughly 50-50 between the federal government and the individual states.

Medicaid Drug Rebate Program The Medicaid Drug Rebate Program is a partnership between the CMS, state Medicaid agencies, and participating drug manufacturers that is intended to offset the federal and state costs of most outpatient prescription drugs dispensed to Medicaid patients. Approximately 600 drug manufacturers currently participate in this program. All fifty states and the District of Columbia cover prescription drugs under the Medicaid Drug Rebate Program. The program requires a drug manufacturer to enter into a national rebate agreement with the DHHS in exchange for state Medicaid coverage of most of the manufacturer's drugs. The manufacturer is then responsible for paying a rebate on those drugs each time they are dispensed to Medicaid patients. These rebates are paid by drug manufacturers on a quarterly basis and are shared between the states and the federal government to offset the overall cost of prescription drugs under the Medicaid program. The amount of the rebate varies from 13% to 23% of the average manufacturer price, depending on the type of drug (i.e., innovator, non-innovator, line extension).

Medicare Medicare is a national federally funded health insurance program for people aged 65 and older, as well as those with disabilities. The Centers for Medicare and Medicaid Services (CMS) is the agency within the DHHS that manages the Medicare program. There are four parts to Medicare: Part A covers inpatient care in a hospital or skilled nursing facility; Part B covers doctors' services and other services and supplies not covered by Part A; Part C is a managed care variant that includes both Parts A and B; and Part D covers medications.

Medicare Advantage (MA) Under traditional Medicare coverage, individual beneficiaries obtain medical services from providers who then bill and are reimbursed by Medicare. A Medicare Advantage Plan is a type of health plan offered by a private company that contracts with Medicare to provide beneficiaries with all Part A and Part B benefits. These plans include health maintenance organizations (HMOs), preferred provider organizations (PPOs), provider-sponsored organizations (PSOs), and private FFS plans. Most Medicare Advantage Plans also offer Part D prescription drug coverage. The individual enrolls with a MA plan. The plan contracts with a select group of providers (physicians and hospitals, among others). The individual visits the providers for his or her medical care. The providers are compensated by the MA plan. The MA plan is compensated by CMS.

Medicare conditions of participation and coverage In order to receive payments from the federal government for treating Medicare or Medicaid patients, healthcare organizations must satisfy minimum health and safety standards required by the CMS. The standards are set forth in "conditions of participation" or "conditions for coverage"; the term varies depending on the type of organization. As an example, the conditions of participation for hospitals cover functions like quality assessment and performance improvement program, medical staff, nursing services, medical record services, pharmaceutical services, radiologic services, laboratory services, food and dietetic services, utilization review, physical environment, infection control, discharge planning, and organ, tissue, and eye procurement. These conditions cover much of the same ground as the Joint Commissions accreditation standards for hospitals. Both are necessary.

Medicare fiscal intermediaries and carriers These are private entities under contract with CMS to process the Medicare claims submitted by healthcare providers. Carriers determine and make payments for Part B benefits payable on a charge basis. Fiscal intermediaries determine and make Medicare payments for Part A or Part B benefits payable on a cost basis. As a result of the Medicare Prescription Drug, Improvement, and Modernization Act, they are being replaced by Medicare Administrative Contractors (MAC) who competitively bid for contracts to process claims in 15 geographic jurisdictions.

Medicare Fraud Strike Force This is a joint effort of the Departments of Justice and Health and Human Services that brings together investigators from several different federal, state, and local agencies to fight Medicare fraud. It is the primary investigation and enforcement arm of the Health Care Fraud Prevention and Enforcement Action Team (HEAT). It currently is operating in nine cities of heightened fraud activity—Baton Rouge, Brooklyn, Chicago, Dallas, Detroit, Houston, Los Angeles, Miami-Dade, and Tampa Bay. Two of its most effective tools are Medicare claims data analysis and community policing.

Medicare Managed Care Manual In its 26 chapters and subchapters, the Medicare Managed Care Manual defines the terms that managed care health plans must satisfy to receive reimbursement as Part D Medicare Advantage (MA) programs. The manual addresses issues like beneficiary protections, quality assessment, relationships with providers, risk adjustment, compliance with state law, payments to MA organizations, and compliance program guidelines.

Medicare-Medicaid Anti-Fraud and Abuse Amendments of 1977 This law was enacted in response to widespread reports of fraud committed by some nursing home owners and their affiliated physicians against the Medicaid program. It gave each state the opportunity and funding to create a Medicaid Fraud Control Unit (MFCU) to investigate and prosecute provider fraud and resident abuse. These units are now mandatory with the federal government covering 75% of their operating costs.

Medicare and Medicaid Patient and Program Protection Act of 1987 This is the long name for the Anti-Kickback Statute which makes it unlawful to knowingly offer, pay, solicit, or receive any remuneration in exchange for referral of a patient or other business for which payment may be made by a federal healthcare program, like Medicare and Medicaid.

Medicare Parts A, B, C, and D The Medicare program has four parts. In general, Part A covers hospital services, Part B covers physician services, Part D covers prescription medications, and Part C covers Medicare Advantage health plans that typically offer all three of the other parts.

Medicare Prescription Drug, Improvement, and Modernization Act (MMA) This 2003 law made several significant changes to the 40-year old Medicare program. It added prescription drug coverage through a new Part D. It changed the name of the Part C Medicare+Choice private health plan option that was already available to Medicare beneficiaries to Medicare Advantage, and authorized them to offer coverage for Parts A, B, and D. The MMA created a new Health Savings Account option that employers may offer as an employee health benefit. The act required the CMS to use a competitive bidding process to select 15 Medicare Administrative Contractors to process claims in designated jurisdictions.

Medicare Shared Savings Program The healthcare reform law of 2010 authorized the Centers for Medicare & Medicaid Services (CMS) to establish a Medicare Shared Savings Program with the mandate to promote accountability for an entire patient population, coordinate items and services under Medicare Parts A and B, and encourage investment in infrastructure and redesigned care processes. Under the program, groups of providers must form or join an accountable care organization (ACO) in order to receive shared savings. An ACO must accept accountability for the quality, cost, and overall care of the Medicare beneficiaries assigned to it; have at least 5,000 beneficiaries assigned to it; include enough primary care professionals to treat those beneficiaries; implement a leadership and management structure with clinical and administrative systems; develop processes to promote evidence-based medicine and patient engagement, to report on quality and cost measures, and to coordinate care (e.g., telehealth, remote patient monitoring); satisfy patient-centeredness criteria specified by CMS, and agree to participate in the program for a minimum of three years. A qualified ACO may receive a share of the difference between its average per capita Medicare expenditures and the benchmark set by CMS. Ambitious ACOs can choose an arrangement with the CMS that entitles them to a larger share of the savings they generate in return for accepting financial penalties if the savings are only mediocre.

merger and acquisitions These are two means by which two organizations become one. When one entity takes over another entity (by purchasing the entire business or just its assets) and continues to operate largely as it did before, there has been an acquisition. When two companies combine their assets and operations, resulting in the formation of a new company, the process is described as a merger. Sometimes, when a much larger company acquires a smaller company, it may be announced as a merger, when in fact the first entity has acquired the second. Frequently the parties can choose whether to characterize their coming together as either a merger or an acquisition.

minimum data set (MDS) The Minimum Data Set (MDS) is part of a federally mandated process for clinical assessment of all residents in Medicare or Medicaid-certified nursing facilities. The entire process, called the Resident Assessment Instrument (RAI), provides a comprehensive assessment of each resident's functional capabilities and helps nursing facility staff identify health problems. MDS assessments are required for residents when first admitted to a nursing facility and then at periodic intervals. Among the 15 data points in the MDS are cognitive patterns, communication and hearing patterns, physical functioning and structural problems, psychosocial well-being, disease diagnoses, medication use, and treatments and procedures. MDS information is transmitted electronically by nursing facilities to the MDS database in their respective states, and then is passed on to the national MDS database maintained by the CMS. The MDS information determines each patient's Resource Utilization Group (RUG) category, which in turn determines the per diem rate paid to the facility for that patient.

"Minimum necessary" principle of the privacy rule The HIPAA Privacy Rule sets standards for the use and disclosure of individuals' protected health information (PHI) by covered entities. A principal requirement of the Privacy Rule is that a covered entity make reasonable efforts to use, disclose, or request only the minimum amount of protected health information necessary to accomplish the intended purpose of the use, disclosure, or request. For instance, a hospital may not disclose an entire medical record if only a portion of the record will satisfy the purpose of the requestor.

monitoring A key requirement of a mandatory compliance program is the ongoing monitoring by a healthcare organization of the technical functioning of its compliance program and of its record in complying with applicable laws and regulations. Its purposes are to identify program defects before they become serious, detect compliance issues so that they can be corrected, and measure progress in improving the program and its performance.

monopolize, monopoly, monopoly power These are critical terms under Section 2 of the Sherman Antitrust Act. A monopoly exists when a single organization or several organizations have dominant control of the sales of a commodity or service in a defined market. The act of creating an illegal monopoly ("monopolization") is defined legally as (a) the possession of monopoly power in a relevant market, and (b) the willful acquisition or maintenance of that power rather than power that grew or evolved as a result of a superior product, more astute management, or historical accident (e.g., "in the right place at the right time"). Monopoly power is simply the power to set prices in the market. When two or more entities set out to create a monopoly, they are said to be conspiring to control the market. Whether a monopoly exists at all depends heavily on how narrowly or expansively the market is defined.

National Benefit Integrity Medicare Drug Integrity Contractor (NBI MEDIC) The MEDICs are private organizations that the CMS contracts with to perform specific program integrity functions for Parts C and D of the Medicare program. There is currently one National Benefit Integrity MEDIC. Its mandate is to detect and prevent fraud, waste, and abuse, which it accomplishes in several ways. It monitors and analyzes data to detect patterns of fraud, waste, and abuse and to identify for further investigation plans, providers, and beneficiaries possibly engaged in such activities. The MEDIC invites reports of suspected abuse from plan sponsors, providers, and beneficiaries. From those starting points, it will investigate to determine the nature and validity of the suspicions. In appropriate cases, the MEDIC refers the matter to law enforcement agencies or other outside entities. If the case involves noncompliance or simple error, rather than fraud and abuse, the matter is returned to the CMS or the sponsor for follow-up and disposal.

National Institutes of Health (NIH) The National Institutes of Health (NIH), within the DHHS, is a single large agency that conducts, funds, and oversees a large share of the nation's medical research. It operates through 27 institutes and centers, each with a separate research agenda, often focusing on particular diseases or body systems. The leadership of the central NIH office actively manages the planning, activities, and direction of research operations. In doing this, it must be responsive to changing research needs expressed through Congressional legislation and budget appropriations. The NIH is the largest source of funding for medical research in the world, supporting thousands of scientists in universities and research institutions in every state and many countries around the world. More than 80% of the NIH's budget goes to more than 300,000 research personnel at over 2,500 universities and research institutions. In addition, about 6,000 scientists work in NIH's own Intramural Research laboratories, most of which are on the NIH main campus in Bethesda, Maryland. The main campus is also home to the NIH Clinical Center, the largest hospital in the world totally dedicated to clinical research.

National Practitioner Data Bank (NPDB) The NPDB is a federally maintained electronic database of actions that reflect on the professional competence or conduct of physicians. These types of information must be reported to the NPDB: medical malpractice insurance payments, adverse clinical privileging actions, negative action by the state licensing authority, adverse professional society membership actions, and Medicare or Medicaid program exclusions. The Data Bank may be accessed by hospitals, state licensure boards, some professional societies, plaintiffs' attorneys, federal/state healthcare agencies, law enforcement officials, and other healthcare entities with formal peer review. The information is considered confidential and is released only to the eligible entities or to physicians and other healthcare practitioners who wish to conduct a self-query.

National Provider Identifier (NPI) The NPI is a unique 10-digit number assigned by the CMS to every healthcare provider wishing to participate in federal healthcare programs. Once assigned, a provider's NPI is permanent and remains with him or her regardless of job or location changes. The Health Insurance Portability and Accountability Act (HIPAA) requires that the NPI be used in all electronic transactions covered by that act. One of the most important among those is the filing of claims for reimbursement.

National Supplier Clearinghouse (NSC) The NSC is a private entity that has a contract with the CMS to process applications from Durable Medical Equipment, Prosthetics, Orthotics, and Supplies (DMEPOS) suppliers for enrollment in the Medicare program. Enrollment is necessary for a supplier to be eligible to receive payment for covered services provided to Medicare beneficiaries. The NSC reviews the application information and conducts a site visit prior to ensure that each supplier satisfies the Medicare participation requirements. In appropriate cases, it also performs investigations into potential noncompliance and fraud by DMEPOS suppliers.

noncommercial activities The federal government's authority to enact antitrust laws affecting multi-state entities is based on the so-called Commerce Clause to the U.S. Constitution (Article I, Section 8, Clause 3) which gives it the power to "regulate commerce among the several states." Several federal courts have held that the laws do not apply to the activities of most nonprofit entities, like hospitals. It has not been fully resolved whether the laws do apply to the commercial activities carried on by some hospitals (e.g., gift shops, parking garages).

noncompliant Healthcare organizations are subject to a large number of laws, regulations, and program requirements. Their very existence depends on them obeying and complying with these constraints. The purpose of a compliance program is to minimize the number of organizational actions that do not follow the laws—that are noncompliant.

nonprofit This term is most relevant in identifying those organizations that may qualify for tax-exempt status under section 501(c)(3) of the federal tax code. That section requires that an entity be organized for other than for-profit purposes. These purposes are typically charitable, such as the promotion of health. The "non-profit" term means that the entity must not intend to maximize its profits. It does not mean that it cannot take in more money (revenues) than it spends (expenses). In fact, over time, a hospital must have net positive earnings to maintain its fiscal integrity and provide for growth and expansion. The earnings simply cannot be too large.

Non-Profit Institutions Act The 1936 Robinson-Patman Act made it illegal to discriminate in price between different purchasers of the same products or services. A violation will occur when an organization, perhaps a vendor of hospital supplies, sells the same product to two different hospitals at different prices and the price difference affects competition. To protect certain transactions, the Act was amended two years later by the Non-Profit Institutions Act so that it does not apply to hospitals and other charitable institutions not operated for profit that are purchasing supplies for their own use.

notice of material breach and intent to exclude This phrase relates to the Corporate Integrity Agreements (CIA) that the OIG enters into with some healthcare organizations as part of a settlement to resolve charges of healthcare fraud against them. The CIA imposes strict compliance-related conditions on the organizations for the next five years. If they fail to satisfy those conditions in some substantial way, the OIG may send them a Notice of Material Breach and Intent to Exclude. This means that, unless the organization can explain the breach or correct within 30 days, the OIG intends to exclude it from participation in all federal healthcare programs.

office of audit services, OIG This office carries out independent audits of federal healthcare programs and their contractors and grantees. The purpose is to reduce waste, abuse, and mismanagement and promote economy and efficiency throughout the DHHS. The office also assists the Office of Evaluation and Inspections and the Department of Justice in criminal, civil, and administrative investigations. It also oversees nonfederal audit activity and internal DHHS financial audits.

Office of Civil Rights This office within the DHHS is responsible for enforcing the Privacy and Security Rules under HIPAA, as well as the confidentiality provisions of the Patient Safety and Quality Improvement Act of 2005. It investigates civil rights, health information privacy, and patient safety confidentiality complaints to determine if there has been discrimination or a violation of the law and takes action to correct any problems found. The office also educates communities, and health and social service workers about these issues.

office of evaluation and inspections, OIG This OIG office conducts national evaluations of federal healthcare programs from a broad, issue-based perspective, followed by practical recommendations on improving their efficiency and effectiveness. It tracks legislative or regulatory changes, documented savings, improved coordination efforts and other benchmarks of its efforts. It works in concert with other components to identify vulnerabilities in the programs and recommend changes. The office also oversees the state Medicaid Fraud Control Units.

Office of Foreign Assets Control This office within the Department of the Treasury administers and enforces economic and trade sanctions based on foreign policy and national security goals against targeted foreign countries and regimes, international narcotics traffickers, those engaged in activities related to the proliferation of weapons of mass destruction, and other threats to the national security, foreign policy, or the economy.

Office of Human Research Protections (OHRP) The OHRP is the primary agency watching out for the rights, welfare, and wellbeing of human subjects involved in research conducted or supported by the DHHS. It does this through three divisions. The Division of Compliance Oversight looks for signs of noncompliance with DHHS regulations protecting human subjects, asks institutions to investigate any allegations, and prepares reports of its findings. It also conducts not-for-cause surveillance evaluations of institutions. The Division of Education and Development provides guidance to individuals and institutions conducting DHHS-supported human subject research. The Division of Policy and Assurances prepares policies and guidance on the requirements for human subject protections and distributes them to the research community.

Office of Inspector General (OIG) The OIG is the leading agency in fighting fraud, abuse, and waste in Medicare, Medicaid, and other federal healthcare programs. It is located within the DHHS and also includes the Office of Evaluation and Inspections, the Office of Audit Services, and the Office of Investigations. Among its duties, the OIG conducts audits, investigations, inspections, and evaluations concerning DHHS programs, identifies systemic weaknesses that might enable fraud and abuse, carries out activities to prevent and detect fraud and abuse, and detects offenders and abusers in DHHS programs so that corrective action can be taken. In collaboration with state and federal agencies, and with Medicaid Fraud Control Units, the OIG takes civil, criminal, and administrative action against providers who violate laws regulating federal healthcare programs. To facilitate legal compliance by healthcare organizations, the OIG issues Advisory Opinions, Special Fraud Alerts, and Compliance Program Guidances.

Office of Research Integrity (ORI) The sole function of this office is to maintain the integrity of the research carried on within several agencies of the Public Health Service, most notably the National Institutes of Health. Toward that end, it develops policies concerning the detection, investigation, and prevention of research misconduct, reviews and monitors misconduct investigations by institutions, researchers, and the DHHS, and recommends administrative actions to be taken as a result of those investigations.

off-label marketing The Food and Drug Administration approves drugs for a specific medical indication that will appear on the drug's label. Physicians are legally permitted, within their clinical judgment, to prescribe a drug for an unapproved, off-label indication. When they do that, they may ask the manufacturer for any data it may have on the proposed off-label use. The manufacturer may provide information in response to a request. It may not take any initiative in promoting any off-label use of the drug. Many drug manufacturers have marketed more aggressively than the law (Food, Drug and Cosmetic Act) allows and had to deal with the FDA's Office of Criminal Investigations.

Omnibus Budget Reconciliation Act of 1993 (Stark II) In the Omnibus Budget Reconciliation Act of 1989, among many other provisions, Congress prohibited physicians from making referrals to clinical laboratories in which they had a financial interest. That provision of the act is referred to as Stark I (after the Representative who sponsored it), the Physician Self-Referral Law. The Omnibus Budget Reconciliation Act of 1993 expanded the prohibition to several other healthcare services and applied it to both Medicare and Medicaid. This law is known as Stark II.

overpayment In the course of submitting, processing, and paying millions of claims for Medicare goods and services each year, it is inevitable that mistakes will happen, resulting in overpayments to providers from commercial and government payors. Sometimes, the payors or their fiscal intermediaries will demand repayment of such amounts, based on general, imprecise evidence. This places the onus on the provider to review its own records to verify that an overpayment occurred, determine the exact amount, and make appropriate restitution. Just as often, the provider itself discovers that it has been overpaid. It may be tempted to keep quiet about it, hoping that the payor will not figure it out. That would be a mistake. In fact, the Patient Protection and Affordable Care Act of 2010 requires providers to report and return any overpayments within 60 days of identifying them, or risk being held liable under the False Claims Act.

patient dumping The purpose of the Emergency Medical Treatment and Labor Act (EMTALA) is to ensure public access to emergency services regardless of ability to pay. To accomplish that, it requires that Medicare-participating hospitals that offer emergency services provide a medical screening examination when a person appears with an emergency medical condition, including active labor. It then must provide stabilizing treatment to the person. When a hospital fails to conduct the screening, provide stabilizing treatment, and often sends the person to another hospital, it is called "patient dumping."

Patient Protection and Affordable Care Act (PPACA) This 2010 law introduced a multitude of major reforms to the healthcare system that are being implemented over a five-year period. They serve the purposes of consumer protection, improving quality, lowering costs, increasing access to affordable care, and holding insurance companies accountable. The act is informally referred to as Obamacare. It requires most U.S. citizens and legal residents to have health insurance. It creates state-based Health Benefit Exchanges through which individuals can purchase coverage, with premium and cost-sharing credits available to individuals/families with low income and creates separate Exchanges through which small businesses can purchase coverage. Employers must provide insurance coverage to their employees or pay a penalty. The act imposes new regulations on health plans in the Exchanges and in the individual and small group markets. It also expands Medicaid to cover more people. From a compliance standpoint, the law's most significant provision is that it makes compliance programs mandatory for healthcare organizations.

penalties When an individual or organization commits some form of healthcare fraud or abuse, it can expect to be subjected to a variety of penalties—civil and criminal fines, prison sentences, and program exclusions. In a more technical legal sense, the term "penalties" refers to the civil monetary penalties and assessments that the OIG may seek for violations of the False Claims Act, the Anti-Kickback Statute, the Physician Self-Referral Law, and the Emergency Medical Treatment and Active Labor Act (EMTALA). The amount of the monetary penalty varies according to the type of violation committed. In the case of false or fraudulent claims, the OIG may seek a penalty of up to $10,000 for each item or service improperly claimed, and an assessment of up to three times the amount improperly claimed. In a kickback case, the OIG may ask for up to $50,000 for each improper act and damages of up to three times the amount of remuneration in question.

per se violation Violations of the Sherman Antitrust Act fall into two categories—"per se" and "rule of reason." Both categories require that the basic elements of a violation be present. For instance, under Section 1, there must be 1) an agreement, 2) which unreasonably restrains competition, and 3) affects interstate commerce. Those elements "in and of themselves" (Latin translation of the term "per se") constitute a per se violation. Examples are price fixing, bid rigging, market or customer allocations, and group boycotts. Under the rule of reason, there must be further inquiry into the practice's actual effect on market competition and the intentions of the individuals who engaged in the practice. Examples are exclusive dealing and supply chain restraints.

pharmacy benefits manager (PBM) Private sector entities that offer medical insurance, such as health plans, managed care organizations, and employers, often contract with pharmacy benefit managers (PBMs) to manage the prescription drug benefit that is usually part of the insurance coverage. The PBMs act as intermediaries between those entities and their beneficiaries, on one hand, and the drug manufacturers, on the other. They make money through service fees from the contracts for processing prescriptions, from operating mail-order pharmacies to serve the beneficiaries, and from negotiating discounted deals with pharmacies and drug makers. Their contracts can include incentives for cutting costs. The largest PBMs, Medco Health Solutions, Express Scripts, and Caremark Rx, manage over half the nearly four billion prescriptions dispensed in the United States each year.

Pharmaceutical Research and Manufacturers of America (PhRMA) PhRMA is a trade group representing the pharmaceutical and biopharmaceutical research companies in the United States. It's stated mission is to advocate for public policies that encourage the discovery of new medicines for patients by pharmaceutical and biopharmaceutical research companies.

PhRMA Code on Interactions with Healthcare Professionals This code is published by the PhRMA trade group for the pharmaceutical industry as a guide for its sales and marketing people on their interactions with the physicians who prescribe drugs. Its stated aim is to ensure that the interactions are "focused on informing healthcare professionals about products, providing scientific and educational information, and supporting medical education." The code has been felt to be necessary because of a history of drug company sales representatives offering a variety of gifts and incentives to physicians to influence their use of particular drugs. The incentives included free meals and transportation, free CME tuition, tickets to the theater or sporting events, vacation trips, scientific and educational conferences or professional meetings, consulting arrangements, and speaking opportunities.

physician group practice Physicians practice medicine in a variety of settings. In 2008, about one-third of the roughly 750,000 practicing physicians were in solo or two-physician practices. Another third were in group practices of 3 to 50 physicians, while 6% practiced in groups of more than 50 members. Thirteen percent were employed by hospitals, 7% were located in academic medical centers, 4% practiced for group or staff model HMOs, and 3% worked in community health centers. The definition of the term "group practice" is critical for groups wishing to take advantage of several of the exceptions under the Stark self-referral law. To qualify, two or more physicians must be "legally organized as a partnership, professional corporation, foundation, not-for-profit-corporation, faculty practice plan, or similar association." In addition, physician groups may share office space, expenses, equipment, employees, and increasingly, clinical information, income, and financial risk.

physician referral No single physician has the ability to treat all the ailments that a patient might have. The medical profession is divided into numerous specialties and subspecialties. When a physician encounters a condition or ailment that is beyond his or her ability, he or she refers the patient to another physician who specializes in understanding and treating that condition. Physicians also make referrals for a variety of other goods and services used in caring for their patients. Examples are lab tests, prescription drugs, dialysis services, wheelchairs, enteral/parenteral nutrition, and artificial limbs. The cost of all of these can be reimbursed by Medicare.

Physician Self-Referral Law (Stark Law) This is actually a series of three laws that prohibit physicians from making referrals for certain health services that will be reimbursed by Medicare to an entity with which the physician has a financial relationship. A typical example is a clinical laboratory partially owned by a physician who may be inclined to refer patients there for lab tests. The financial relationship may take the form of equity, debt, or compensation. The law and its regulations define over 30 exceptions for financial relationships that are considered acceptable.

plan of care In order to receive Medicare reimbursement for hospice or home health care, a plan of care must be established for each patient and signed by a qualified physician. The plan should include the services that the patient needs, how often the services are needed, which healthcare professionals will provide the services, the medical equipment that the patient needs, and the results that the physician expects from the care.

plan sponsor Medicare Part C allows public and private organizations to offer a variety of managed care plans to their beneficiaries, including HMOs, PPOs, and PSOs. The organizations and their plans are referred to as Medicare Advantage (MA). An MA organization that has a contract with CMS to offer one or more MA plans is called a "plan sponsor." It has special responsibilities for the compliance activities of the entities with which it subcontracts.

policies and procedures Policies and procedures are the rules that guide an organization's employees, all the way up to the CEO, in making their decisions and performing their tasks. A policy explains how the organization will act or react whenever a certain set of circumstances arises. For example, an organization has a maternity leave policy that grants a pregnant employee three months of paid leave followed by three months of unpaid leave. Or, it is a policy of a physician practice not to hire into its billing and claims department anyone who has been convicted of healthcare fraud within the last six years. A procedure describes the steps that should be followed in carrying out a particular task. For instance, the procedure for responding to an employee report of an incident of suspected noncompliance might look like this: 1) immediately notify the Compliance Officer, 2) assure the complainant of anonymity and nonretaliation, 3) begin an initial investigation, 4) gather and review relevant documents, 5) interview relevant employees, 6) reach tentative conclusion about the accuracy of the complaint and the gravity of the misconduct. A major purpose of policies and procedures is to ensure that similar situations are handled in a predictable, consistent, and systematic manner.

preponderance of the evidence This is the standard of proof in civil law suits, in contrast with the "beyond a reasonable doubt" standard that applies in criminal cases. In simple terms, it requires that there is more evidence in support of a party's position than there is against it. The standard is satisfied if the position is more likely to be true than not true.

price fixing This antitrust violation occurs when individuals or organizations, that otherwise are in competition with each other, agree on the prices that they will charge their customers. The result usually is to keep the prices at a higher level than competition would produce. On some occasions, physicians have tried to fix the prices that they will charge the managed care organizations with whom they must contract.

principal investigator (PI) There often are several researchers or investigators working on a particular research project. The principal investigator typically is the person who applies for the grant to fund the project, designs the research strategy, executes and manages it, is primarily responsible for completing it, and reports directly to the funding agency. Occasionally, the PI is chosen by the research team for his or her experience, leadership, and management skills.

program exclusion, suspension, debarment These terms refer to the formal methods by which individuals and organizations are prohibited from participating in or receiving funds from federal healthcare programs like Medicare and Medicaid. Furthermore, any entity that employs or contracts with an excluded, suspended, or debarred individual or organization to provide services reimbursed by Medicare risks serious civil and criminal penalties. The OIG is required to impose program exclusions on healthcare providers and suppliers who have been convicted of Medicare fraud; patient abuse or neglect; other healthcare-related fraud, theft, or other financial misconduct (felony); and the unlawful manufacture, distribution, prescription, or dispensing of controlled substances (felony). The OIG has the discretion to exclude an individual or entity for several other reasons, including a misdemeanor conviction relating to healthcare fraud; filing claims for excessive charges, unnecessary services, or poor quality services; failure to disclose required information, failure to grant immediate access, and failure to take corrective action; making false statements or misrepresentations of material fact; and a conviction relating to obstruction of an investigation.

promoting objectivity in research (regulations) These regulations are commonly referred to as the Financial Conflict of Interest (FCOI) regulation. Its purpose is to promote objectivity in research by establishing standards that ensure that the design, conduct, and reporting of NIH-funded research will be free from bias resulting from the investigators' financial conflicts of interest. It imposes substantial duties on the institutions conducting the research. In particular, they must maintain and enforce a FCOI policy, require investigators to complete FCOI training before beginning research, require investigators to disclose significant financial interests before applying for research funding, take appropriate action to manage FCOIs, and provide regular FCOI reports to the NIH.

prosthetics/orthotics Prosthetic devices (or prostheses) are artificial medical devices that are not surgically implanted and are used to replace a missing limb or appendage. Examples are artificial limbs, terminal devices (hand or hook) and artificial eyes, prosthetic lenses, breast prostheses for post-mastectomy patients, and maxillofacial devices. Orthotic devices (or orthoses) are rigid or semi-rigid devices, often called braces, which are applied to the outside of the body to support a weak or deformed body part or to restrict or eliminate motion in a diseased or injured part of the body. They usually are custom-fitted and custom-made.

protected health information (PHI) The HIPAA Privacy Rule protects all "individually identifiable health information" held or transmitted by a covered entity or its business associate, in any form or media, whether electronic, paper, or oral. This applies to information that relates to an individual's physical or mental health or condition, the provision of health care to the person, and the payment for that health care. It includes demographic data.

protection of human subjects (regulations) These are regulations issued by the DHHS to protect human subjects in research that is federally funded but will not be used in support of a submission for FDA approval. Part A of the regulations, also called the Common Rule, lays out the basic principles of human subject protection. It is concerned with the composition and operations of Institutional Review Boards and the acquisition of informed consent from human participants in a research project.

Public Health Service (PHS) The PHS and the Centers for Medicare and Medicaid Services (CMS) are the two largest components of the Department of Health and Human Services (DHHS). The primary agencies within the PHS are the Agency for Healthcare Research and Quality (AHRQ), Centers for Disease Control and Prevention (CDC), Food and Drug Administration (FDA), Health Resources and Services Administration (HRSA), Indian Health Service (IHS), National Institutes of Health (NIH), and Substance Abuse and Mental Health Services Administration (SAMHSA).

Public Health Service Policies on Research Misconduct (the Final Rule) The regulations that constitute the Final Rule are the federal government's attempt to prevent misconduct in the research that it funds. They were issued in 2005 by the Office of Research Integrity (ORI) located within the Department of Health and Human Services (DHHS). The rule requires that institutions engaged in federally funded research have policies and procedures on research misconduct, respond to misconduct allegations thoroughly and objectively, foster an environment that promotes responsible research, protect the positions and reputations of complainants, and assist in enforcing any DHHS administrative actions imposed on its institutional members.

publicly traded securities The term "securities" includes shares of stock, and bonds, in a for-profit corporation. They are "publicly traded" if they can be bought and sold on a stock exchange or in an over-the-counter market. Privately held securities are owned by a company's founders, management, or a group of private investors. Any sale of the shares takes place among those individuals, with strict limitations on their sale publicly.

***qui tam* lawsuits** One of the most powerful tools for combating healthcare fraud is the False Claims Act. The effectiveness of the act is greatly enhanced by a provision that allows private citizens to bring lawsuits against a person or organization who he or she believes is violating the act. The lawsuit is brought on behalf of the government. Often the government intervenes in the case and becomes a party to the suit in order to ensure its success and have a role in the conduct of the case and any negotiations. Private citizens who bring these lawsuits are called "whistleblowers"; they often are employees of the organization committing the fraud. As an incentive and reward the whistleblower in a *qui tam* case receives 15–25% of the recovery when the government intervenes and 25–30% if he or she must proceed on his or her own. The term "*qui tam*" is short for a Latin phrase that means "he who brings a case on behalf of our lord the King, as well as for himself."

recovery audit contractors The Recovery Audit Program is a CMS effort to detect and collect overpayments made on claims for services provided to Medicare beneficiaries. When underpayments are discovered, appropriate adjustments are made with the provider. The recovery audits and subsequent collection activities are carried out by four private contractors, each assigned to one of four geographic regions.

redlining This term describes a practice by which a healthcare provider or insurer discriminates against the residents of a defined ("outlined in red") geographic area, typically because they are low-income, less likely to have insurance, or at higher risk of medical problems. The discrimination takes the form of rejecting applications for insurance coverage, charging higher prices for goods and services, or denying access to services. Ultimately, this makes it difficult for an individual to obtain the health care he or she needs.

regulations The statutes that Congress enacts may seem comprehensive and voluminous, but they still cannot anticipate all the situations to which they will apply. For that reason, the government agency responsible for enforcing a statute is also given the authority to issue regulations that go into much more detail about the law's requirements. The agency proposes a set of regulations, conducts open hearings about them, allowing those affected by the regulations to offer their comments, and then publishes a final legally binding version of them. Regulations are published first in the Federal Register and then codified in the Code of Federal Regulations (CFR). Regulations are meant to interpret and expand upon the language of the statute. They absolutely may not create new law.

reimbursement The majority of health care delivered in the United States is paid for by a third party, typically a private or public insurer or payor. In order to receive payment, a healthcare provider must describe the service or product provided in a claim, which it then submits to the payor. If the claim meets all of its requirements, the payor "reimburses" the provider. The other type of payments are those made out-of-pocket directly by the patient receiving the services.

relator This is the technical legal term for the person or whistleblower who initiates a *qui tam* lawsuit under the False Claims Act.

repayment As the Medicare and Medicaid programs reimburse the millions of claims filed by healthcare providers, it is inevitable that errors occur, resulting in overpayments and, occasionally, underpayments. When a provider discovers an overpayment, the federal government insists that it take immediate steps to repay the amount. Frequently, the federal health programs will identify overpayments through its Recovery Auditors, for instance. Prompt repayment is expected in those cases as well.

reportable event A common provision of the Corporate Integrity Agreements (CIA) that the OIG negotiates with noncompliant healthcare organizations requires that the organization report certain events that may occur during the term of the agreement. These events are a substantial overpayment, a probable violation of criminal, civil, or administrative laws, the employment of or contracting with an "ineligible person," and a filing for bankruptcy. The first three of these events imply that the organization has violated the terms of its CIA. The OIG will want to hear about the corrective actions planned by the organization. If the events are serious and the organization's responses seem inadequate, the OIG may choose to take stronger enforcement action, including the program exclusion that the CIA was meant to forestall.

resource utilization group (RUG) The Medicare program uses RUGs to calculate its reimbursement rates for resident stays in long-term care facilities. The facilities use a Resident Assessment Instrument to evaluate residents' strengths, weaknesses, preferences, and needs in key areas of functioning. Part of the assessment is a "minimum data set" (MDS), a standardized set of essential clinical and functional status measures. The assessment data are used to prepare individualized care plans for each resident, and to assign the resident to one of 34 categories (44 categories if rehabilitation services are involved) representing the amount of resources the facility will utilize in caring for individuals within each category.

reverse false claim The False Claims Act normally is used to punish those who file a false claim seeking money from the government. When a person or organization makes a false statement or otherwise tries to hide an obligation owed to the government, it is called a "reverse false claim."

risk areas In healthcare organizations, there are certain areas of their operations that are at higher risk of violating one or another of the fraud and abuse laws. The best example is billing and claims. The areas of high risk vary from one organization to another, depending on the type of organization, the specific nature of its operations, and the market in which it competes. There are several ways to identify an organization's areas of high compliance risk. The Compliance Programs Guidances issued by the OIG for twelve types of organizations describe in detail the risk areas for each type. The OIG Special Fraud Alerts, Advisory Opinions, and Annual Work Plans draw attention to the areas where it has encountered problems with fraud and abuse. Actual legal cases, including settlements and the Corporate Integrity Agreements that often accompany them, are good indicators. The OIG encourages healthcare organizations to conduct periodic risk assessments. Each organization also can look at its own history of compliance difficulties. The risk areas are where an organization should concentrate its compliance efforts.

risk assessment In establishing a Compliance Program, one of the first steps recommended by the OIG is the performance of a Compliance Risk Assessment. Its purpose is to determine where in its operations an organization should focus its monitoring and auditing activities. Those activities cannot be applied everywhere throughout the organization. Every unit or department does not present the same level of compliance risk. The assessment also serves as a baseline against which future compliance effectiveness can be measured.

risk-sharing arrangements In health care, the term "risk-sharing" refers to the sharing of financial risk between providers and payors or among providers within the same entity (e.g., group practices or accountable care organizations). In other words, a provider will receive more or less compensation depending on his or her work behaviors. For instance, when a physician is paid on a capitated basis (fixed amount each month for each patient assigned to the physician), if he or she makes treatment decisions about a patient that cost more than the fixed amount, he or she will not receive any additional reimbursement. If the treatment costs are less than the fixed amount, the physician gets to keep the difference. Under a pay-for-performance arrangement, a physician receives a bonus or a withheld portion of his or her salary if he or she achieves clearly defined goals (e.g., quality of care, practice efficiency, patient satisfaction). Within the accountable care organizations that are being developed, groups of providers, including charged physicians and hospitals, are paid capitated amounts to manage all of the healthcare needs of a minimum of 5,000 Medicare beneficiaries for at least three years. Not only does the group have to manage those needs efficiently enough to keep the costs within the capitated amounts, it has to decide how to allocate the payments they receive among the group members. If a group of otherwise independent physicians agree to share financial risk, they usually will be treated as a single entity for antitrust purposes, allowing them to negotiate collectively with payors.

Robinson-Patman Act This is one of several federal antitrust laws, along with the Sherman Act, the Federal Trade Commission Act, and the Clayton Act. Under Robinson-Patman, an organization may not discriminate in the prices that it charges to different customers for goods or services of similar grade and quality. In some cases, a purchaser also may be held liable for encouraging or accepting goods at a price different from that offered to its competitors. In health care, these prohibitions could apply to the prices that providers charge to different patients or the prices charged by medical supply vendors to different hospitals.

rule of reason Violations of the Sherman Antitrust Act fall into two categories—"per se" and "rule of reason." Under the rule of reason, the first step is determining whether certain suspicious activity has occurred. Examples are acquisition or maintenance of a monopoly, non price vertical restraints, and resale price maintenance contracts. The second step is to evaluate the effect of the activity on competition in the relevant market. Does it constitute an unreasonable restraint on trade.

safe harbors The federal Anti-Kickback Statute prohibits anyone from offering a kickback, paying a kickback, or receiving a kickback in return for the delivery of healthcare services that will be reimbursed by a federal healthcare program. The statute is broadly written and covers arrangements that are not actually fraudulent. The OIG has adopted "safe harbors" to protect these accepted payment and business practices, as long as the practices fit exactly within the defined parameters. An arrangement that does not meet safe harbor criteria is not in automatic violation of the statute. Its legality is determined on a case-by-case basis. A few examples of safe harbors are investment interests, space rental, personal services contracts, referral services, and practitioner recruitment.

Sarbanes-Oxley Act (SOX) The SOX Act raised the financial reporting standards for all public company governing boards, top management, and public accounting firms. Individual top executives must certify the accuracy of their financial disclosures. Severe penalties may be imposed for fraudulent financial reporting and other activity. The law increases the independence of the outside auditors who must review the accuracy of corporate financial statements. The financial oversight responsibility of boards of directors also has been raised. This law was enacted in response to the flood of corporate financial scandals at the turn of the century involving companies like Enron, WorldCom, and Tyco.

search warrant This judicial document authorizes police officers to search a person or a physical place to obtain evidence of guilt to be used in a criminal prosecution. Police officers obtain search warrants by submitting affidavits and other evidence to a judge in an effort to establish "probable cause" to believe that a search will yield evidence related to a crime. If satisfied that the officers have established probable cause, the judge will issue the warrant.

security standards for the protection of electronic protected health information (the Security Rule) In conjunction with the Privacy Rule, the Security Rule makes up the bulk of the requirements imposed on healthcare providers, health plans, healthcare clearinghouses, and their business associates by the Health Insurance Portability and Accountability Act (HIPAA). Under this rule, covered entities must i) ensure the confidentiality, integrity, and availability of all electronic protected health information they create, receive, maintain, or transmit; ii) protect against threats or hazards to the security or integrity of the information; iii) protect against uses or disclosures of the information that are not permitted or required; and iv) ensure compliance with these terms by its workforce. To accomplish this, the rule describes a multitude of safeguards, standards, and specifications that must be implemented.

self-disclosure protocol (SDP), OIG This is a companion to the Self-Referral Disclosure Protocol (SRDP). While the SRDP applies exclusively to disclosures involving only the Physician Self-Referral law, this process can be used by healthcare providers to voluntarily identify, disclose, and resolve instances of potential fraud that might subject them to the OIG's civil monetary penalty (CMP) authorities. Under these authorities, the OIG may levy fines and assessments against, and exclude from participation in

Medicare and Medicaid, providers who commit a long list of fraudulent acts. These acts are described in 42 CFR Part 1003. They generally encompass the prohibitions found in the False Claims Act and the Anti-Kickback Statute. The SDP also should be used for violations involving both the Physician Self-Referral law and the Anti-Kickback Statute, but not for the Self-Referral law alone. In making a disclosure, the disclosing party must acknowledge that the conduct is a potential violation, and explicitly identify the laws that may have been violated. Prior to disclosure, the disclosing party should ensure that the conduct has ended. It is expected to conduct an internal investigation and report its findings to the OIG in its submission. It also should describe the corrective action it took upon discovering the conduct.

self-referral disclosure protocol (SRDP) The SRDP sets forth a process to enable providers of services and suppliers that are reimbursed by Medicare to voluntarily self-disclose actual or potential violations of the Physician Self-Referral (Stark) law. The provider or supplier must submit enough information to the CMS to allow it to analyze the nature and gravity of the violation. Since violations of the Stark Law often involve overpayments to the provider, the Secretary of DHHS is authorized to reduce the amount to be repaid by the provider in recognition of its voluntary disclosure. This SRDP is different from the OIG Self-Disclosure Protocol that applies to other federal criminal, civil, or administrative laws.

Senior Medicare Patrols (SMP) The SMPs constitute over 5,000 seniors and professionals like doctors, nurses, accountants, investigators, law enforcement personnel, attorneys, and teachers who volunteer their time and experience to show Medicare and Medicaid beneficiaries how to protect against, detect, and report fraud. They work one-on-one with the beneficiaries and give presentations to groups. They offer help in protecting individual identity, reading Medicare Summary Notices, and avoiding scams.

Sherman Act, Sections 1 and 2 The Sherman Act is the preeminent federal antitrust law. Section One of the Act prohibits "every contract, combination in the form of trust or otherwise, or conspiracy in restraint of trade or commerce among the several states." Two or more persons or entities must act together to violate this law. A single person acting alone cannot violate Section One. Section Two of the Sherman Act states that "every person who shall monopolize or attempt to monopolize, or combine or conspire with any other person or persons to monopolize any part of the trade or commerce among the several states or with foreign nations shall be deemed guilty of a felony." Despite the reference to felony guilt, most Section Two cases are prosecuted under civil complaints. This section can be violated by a single individual or organization.

skilled nursing facilities (SNFs) This is a type of nursing home recognized by the Medicare and Medicaid systems as meeting the long-term healthcare needs of individuals who have the potential to function independently after a limited period of care. A multidisciplinary team guides health care and rehabilitative services, including skilled nursing care.

Special Fraud Alert Since 1994, the OIG has issued 13 Special Fraud Alerts to call attention to particular fraudulent or abusive practices within the healthcare industry. They are disseminated to the healthcare provider community, as well as those charged with administering the Medicare and Medicaid programs. They identify activities of special concern to the OIG and that are likely to receive extra enforcement attention. Provider entities covered by an alert would be well advised to follow their warnings and requirements. These are some topics of Special Fraud Alerts: medical services to nursing homes, rental of space in physician offices by persons to whom the physicians refer, and telemarketing by durable medical equipment suppliers.

special investigation unit (SIU) The CMS requires that Medicare Advantage Organizations establish an SIU or, if it lacks the resources, ensure that typical SIU responsibilities are otherwise carried out by its Compliance Program. An SIU is an internal investigation unit responsible for conducting surveillance, interviews, and other methods of investigation designed to combat potential fraud, waste, and abuse. The SIU is not expected to perform law enforcement activities and should refer all fraud and abuse matters indicative of the NBI MEDIC or law enforcement agencies.

specific training One of the elements of a mandatory compliance program is education and training of employees and contractors. There are two broad categories of training–general and specific. The purpose of general training is to provide all employees and agents with a basic introduction to the law, regulations, and payor requirements that impact the organization, to the organization's policies and procedures that reflect those requirements, and to the components of the organization's compliance program that affect the employees. The specific training is targeted at those employees who work in the operational areas most vulnerable to fraud and abuse. These areas typically include claims submission, medical records, sales and marketing, and financial management. The training here focuses on the ways that fraud might occur in these areas, the work practices that must be avoided to prevent such fraud, and the sound, compliant policies and procedures that should be followed.

standard of proof In both criminal and civil court cases, there are two parties trying to persuade a judge or a jury that their version of events is the correct one and should be accepted. Each side is trying to prove or disprove key facts. The question is how strong does the proof have to be to show that a person is guilty or not guilty, liable or not liable. What standard of proof has to be met? In criminal cases, where the outcomes can be severe (e.g., imprisonment), the standard is "beyond a reasonable doubt." In civil cases, the standard usually is "a preponderance of the evidence."

Standards for Privacy of Individually Identifiable Health Information (the Privacy Rule) This is the title of a large body of regulations promulgated under the Health Insurance Portability and Accountability Act (HIPAA) of 1996. The fundamental purpose of the Privacy Rule is to define and limit the circumstances in which an individual's personal health information (PHI) may be used or disclosed by a covered entity or its business associates. A covered entity may use or disclose PHI only when the Privacy Rule requires or permits it, or when the affected individual has given his or her written authorization.

standing orders for tests In certain cases, a physician may issue an order that a particular diagnostic test for a specific patient should be repeated automatically until it is cancelled. Medicare will reimburse such "standing orders" only if certain conditions are met, including these: the test is appropriate for the known/suspected diagnosis, appropriate for the patient's clinical circumstances, and necessary for the patient's management. The order for the recurring test must be renewed at least annually. Documentation must show that all tests were reviewed and appropriate clinical action taken.

state-action doctrine Under this doctrine, state and municipal government entities are immune from federal antitrust lawsuits for actions that are based on a clearly enunciated state policy that has anticompetitive effects. When a state approves and regulates certain conduct, even if it is anticompetitive under federal standards, the federal government will the decision of the state. The same immunity extends to private entities that are acting under a specific anti-competitive state policy and are actively supervised by an agency of the state. This doctrine often is raised when physicians challenge the decisions of state boards of medicine on antitrust grounds. This doctrine was expressed in a landmark U.S. Supreme Court case, in *Parker v. Brown*, 317 U.S. 341 (1943).

statements of antitrust enforcement policy in health care The rapidly evolving healthcare industry, involving a variety of collaborative arrangements among provider entities, has presented new challenges for antitrust law enforcement officials. These statements were issued jointly by the Department of Justice (DOJ) and the Federal Trade Commission (FTC) to describe the arrangements that would not be subject to antitrust prosecution. These are some of the joint activities addressed in the statements: mergers among hospitals, hospital joint ventures involving high technology, joint purchasing arrangements among providers, and physician network joint ventures. In 2013, a statement was issued regarding accountable care organizations participating in the Medicare Shared Savings program.

statutes This is another name for a law. It should not be confused with a statue, which is a work of art. Statutes are written, debated, and enacted by the federal Congress or state legislatures. When they first are introduced into the Congress, they are referred to as "bills." When they are approved by the Congress, they are called "acts." When the President signs them, they become "statutes" or "laws."

subpoena *duces tecum* This is a court summons ordering the recipient to appear before the court and produce papers, documents, or other tangible evidence for use at a hearing or trial. The term "*duces tecum*" is Latin for "bring with thee."

tax-deductible donations Individuals may deduct the amount of the donations they make to tax-exempt organizations on their own income tax returns. This benefit is a strong incentive for people to make such charitable donations.

tax-exempt bond financing Tax-exempt bonds are debt obligations of state and local governments that are exempt from federal income tax and are issued in furtherance of governmental or other qualified purposes. Tax-exempt bonds are commonly issued to finance the long-term capital requirements of 501(c)(3) tax-exempt hospitals. The benefit to the hospitals is that the investors who buy the bonds are willing to accept lower interest rates because they do not have to pay taxes on the interest they earn. Lower bond interest payments are a saving to the hospitals.

tax-exempt status In order to encourage organizations engaged in certain types of charitable or other activities deemed beneficial to overall society, the Internal Revenue Service (IRS), the federal tax agency, grants tax-exempt status. As a result of this status, qualifying organizations do not have to pay federal income taxes. State tax authorities also exempt them from paying state income, sales, and property taxes. Furthermore, individuals may deduct the donations they make to such organizations from their own income tax payments. Most of these organizations receive their exempt status under section 501(c)(3) of the Internal Revenue Code.

unbundling Unbundling occurs when a provider submits separate claims with individual codes for a group of related services that are covered by a single comprehensive code. The total reimbursement for the services billed separately is higher than the reimbursement for the single bundled code. An example is the special reimbursement rates for a group of procedures commonly done together, such as the typical blood test panels performed by clinical laboratories. The "chemistry panel" checks total cholesterol, HDL (high-density lipoprotein), LDL (low-density lipo-protein), triglycerides, and the total cholesterol/HDL ratio (cardiovascular health), blood glucose (diabetes and coronary artery disease), and critical minerals such as calcium, potassium, and iron. Conceivably, separate blood tests could be performed for each of these characteristics.

unrelated business income Unrelated business income is the income from a trade or business regularly conducted by a tax-exempt organization and not substantially related to its exempt purpose or function, except that the organization uses the profits derived from this activity. The organization will have to pay taxes on such income. An example is the regular sale of pharmaceutical supplies to the general public by a hospital pharmacy, even though the pharmacy also furnishes supplies to the hospital and its patients in accord with its exempt purpose.

unsecured PHI Under the Health Insurance Portability and Accountability Act (HIPAA), a variety of healthcare entities are required to provide notification in the event of a breach of unsecured protected health information (PHI). Unsecured PHI is health information that has not been rendered unusable, unreadable, or indecipherable to unauthorized individuals through the use of a technology or methodology like encryption or destruction.

upcoding Providers must assign CPT codes to the services for which they submit claims to Medicare and other payors for reimbursement. When a code is assigned that indicates a different, and more expensive service than the one actually provided, it is called "upcoding" and it is illegal. For example, there are different codes for medical evaluation encounters lasting 10, 20, 30, 45, and 60 minutes, the longer the encounter, the higher the reimbursement. It is easy to assign a 45-minute code for an encounter that lasted only 30 minutes.

waiver A waiver is the voluntary relinquishment or surrender of a right or privilege that a person or organization possesses. For instance, healthcare providers generally may not waive their right to collect coinsurance or deductibles from a patient without ascertaining that he or she is in financial need. Such unauthorized waivers may be viewed as an incentive to the patient to use the provider's services.

whistleblower A whistleblower is a person who calls public attention to the misdeeds, misconduct, unethical or illegal behavior of an individual or organization that normally would have preferred to keep the matter quiet. The person "blows the whistle" on the organization, as a referee blows the whistle on an athlete committing a foul. Persons who file *qui tam* lawsuits under the False Claims Act are considered to be whistleblowers. These people are frequently employees of the organization with inside knowledge of its operations and who may already have complained to management without getting a response.

"willingly" A person acts willingly if he performs an action voluntarily, consciously, with free will, and without reluctance. This is an important term in defining the circumstances in which an individual or organization may be held liable for violation of a law. A violation may exist if certain actions were performed willingly, but not if they were the result of negligence or accident. Or, the penalties may be greater if the individual acted willingly.

work product privilege The written materials, exhibits, notes of conversations and interviews, reports of investigations, and other materials created by an attorney as he or she prepares to represent a client in litigation are the attorney's "work product." It is a rule of the procedures governing litigation that an opposing party may not gain access to that work product, nor can it be required to be introduced in court. It often is a good idea for an attorney and his or her clients to conduct their interactions in a way that they will be considered work product and protected from disclosure.

Index

Note: Page numbers followed by *f* or *t* indicate material in figures or tables, respectively.

D

E

G

Q

R

T

www.ingramcontent.com/pod-product-compliance
Ingram Content Group UK Ltd.
Pitfield, Milton Keynes, MK11 3LW, UK
UKHW020007180826
474417UK00001B/73

9 781284 244243